THE PELICAN HISTORY OF ART

EDITED BY NIKOLAUS PEVSNER

z 3

ARCHITECTURE IN BRITAIN 1530 TO 1830

JOHN SUMMERSON

JOHN · SUMMERSON

ARCHITECTURE IN BRITAIN
1530 TO 1830

PENGUIN BOOKS
MELBOURNE · LONDON · BALTIMORE

Penguin Books Ltd, Harmondsworth, Middlesex
Penguin Books Inc., Baltimore, Maryland, U.S.A.
Penguin Books Pty Ltd, Melbourne, Victoria, Australia

★

Text printed by R. & R. Clark Ltd, Edinburgh
Plates printed by Lund, Humphries & Co. Ltd, Bradford
Made and printed in Great Britain

★

Copyright 1953 Penguin Books Ltd
First published 1953

CONTENTS

Part One

The English Renaissance (1530–1610)

Part Two

Inigo Jones and His Times (1610–1660)

Part Three

Wren and the Baroque (1660–1710)

CONTENTS

Part Four

The Palladian Phase (1710–1750)

Part Five

Neo-classicism and the Picturesque (1750–1830)

The Plates

Notes will be found at the end of the chapter
to which they refer

viii

LIST OF FIGURES

The following are the abbreviations used in this and the List of Plates:

B.M.   British Museum
C.O.I.   Central Office of Information
L.C.C.   London County Council
M.o.W.   Ministry of Works
N.B.R.   National Buildings Record
R.I.B.A.   Royal Institute of British Architects
R.C.H.M.   Royal Commission on Historical Monuments

LIST OF PLATES

ACKNOWLEDGEMENTS

MY thanks are due, first and foremost, to those of my contemporaries from whose published works I have benefited. To name a few here would be invidious, to name all would be to infringe the function of the Bibliography which I hope I have so arranged as to make my indebtedness clear, chapter by chapter. Without the work of these writers, the making of this book would have been next to impossible. To Mr Howard Colvin, of St John's College, Oxford, I owe a rather special debt, not only for the generous purveyance, during the past ten years, of all sorts of discoveries, great and small, but for the privilege of reading in proof his *Biographical Dictionary of English Architects, 1660–1840*. Apart from the wealth of material contained in it, my fore-knowledge of this work has considerably modified the treatment of my middle and later chapters. As no future student will be able to work without Colvin at his elbow, I felt free to abandon with a clear conscience all pretence at providing dated lists of works and voluminous references: all are in Colvin, much fuller and more exact than I could have attempted. In addition, Mr Colvin has been good enough to read and comment on my own proofs.

Professor Henry-Russell Hitchcock was kind enough to read and criticize Appendix II, on American architecture; while to Miss Dorothy Stroud, Inspectress and Assistant in Sir John Soane's Museum, I owe a long-standing debt, not only for her precise and extensive knowledge of eighteenth-century matters but for much practical help in those of the twentieth.

The illustrations, drawn from over fifty different public and private collections, libraries, and photographic sources, have necessitated as many applications and consents, all of which are registered in the list of plates but to certain of which it is an obligation and a pleasure to make the special acknowledgements which follow.

The drawing by Thomas Sandby (Plate 59A) is reproduced by gracious permission of Her Majesty the Queen.

A number of photographs deriving from the inventories of the Royal Commission on Historical Monuments are reproduced here with the permission of the Controller of H.M. Stationery Office. These photographs (identified in the list of plates) are Crown Copyright. Certain plans published in the same inventories and one in the Edinburgh inventory of the Royal Commission on Historical Monuments (Scotland) have been either adapted or used to form the basis of plans in this book, again with the permission of the Controller of H.M. Stationery Office. Similarly Crown Copyright photographs have in four instances been used with the permission of the Ministry of Works.

A large proportion of the photographs are from the National Buildings Record and my thanks go to the Deputy Director, Mr Cecil Farthing, for his sympathetic assistance in gearing the active work of the Record, wherever possible, to suggestions made in connexion with this book. The second largest number of photographs from any one source is from the classic and indispensable collection of Country Life Ltd.

The following authorities and corporate bodies have allowed the reproduction of drawings, prints, and photographs in their possession and I hereby gratefully acknowledge their courtesy: The Dean and Chapter of St Paul's Cathedral; the London County Council; the Governors of the Bank of England; the Astronomer Royal; the Royal Academy of Arts; the Royal Institute of British Architects; the Architectural Association; the British Museum; the Bodleian Library, Oxford; the Trustees of Sir John Soane's Museum; the Winchester Museum; the Manchester Art Gallery; the Manchester Library Committee; the Leeds Art Gallery; All Souls College, Oxford; Worcester College, Oxford; Magdalene College, Cambridge; University College, London; the Committee of the Athenaeum; and the Trustees of the Chatsworth Settlement. In connexion with the illustrations for Appendix II, I would acknowledge the courtesy of the Maryland Historical Society, the Massachusetts Historical Society, and the Valentine Museum, Richmond, Va.

Among individuals who have helped me with the problem of finding illustrations, I would mention first Mr Talbot Hamlin, who most generously undertook to collect and transmit all but one of the illustrations for Appendix II. The exception is the drawing by Thomas Jefferson (Plate 191B), which is reproduced from Mr Fiske Kimball's magnificent monograph on the architect-President, with his kind permission. The Marquess of Salisbury has been good enough to allow the plan of Longleat (Fig. 3) to be based on a drawing in the Hatfield Collection. The Earl of Ilchester has permitted the reproduction from his book, *The Home of the Hollands* (published by John Murray), of the print of Holland House (Plate 30A) which hung in the house till the disaster of 1941. Mr Arthur F. E. Poley has allowed me to reproduce one of his incomparable drawings of St Paul's Cathedral (Plate 86). Mr A. E. Popham and Mr C. S. S. Higham kindly lent me photographic prints in their possession; and courtesy to reproduce has been extended by Messrs W. Simpson Bell of Edinburgh; Messrs Wilding of Shrewsbury; and Mr F. H. Crossley in respect of one of his own photographs. The Cambridge University Press has permitted the inclusion of the engraving (Plate 61B) from Willis and Clark's *Architectural History of the University of Cambridge*; and the University of North Carolina Press has granted the same privilege in respect of two plans (Figures 47 and 48) from the late T. T. Waterman's *Mansions of Virginia*.

Finally, to Mr Peter Darvall, A.R.I.B.A., I extend my thanks for his care with the plans.

J. S.

1 Eton Villas, London N.W.3

PART ONE

THE ENGLISH RENAISSANCE
⟨1530 – 1610⟩

CHAPTER I

ARCHITECTURE AT THE COURT OF HENRY VIII

THE thirty years preceding Queen Elizabeth's accession were, for architecture in Britain at large, fallow years. The people who were later to plant the counties so richly with halls, manor-houses, and mansions were either unborn or in their cradles. Their fathers, living in the strenuous course of a social revolution, bent themselves rather to the getting and keeping of land than to the raising of buildings on it. The landlords, for instance, who were enclosing commons, the new purchasers of monastic properties, had a more lively concern with husbandry and the law than with any of the arts; the land-surveyor and the lawyer were more vital to the Tudor revolution than the highly skilled artificer in wood, stone, or brick.

In the decades which are our concern in this chapter architectural interest converges emphatically on one point – the Court. Here, as in greater issues, Wolsey's fall marks a beginning. The Cardinal had been scarcely less than royal in his building works and Henry, then in his late thirties and turning from a life of civil pleasures and occasional generalship to one ruled by genuine monarchical ambition, took over from his minister not only estates and buildings themselves but the idea of rulership extravagantly housed. From 1529 till the end of his reign palace-building proceeded energetically, and here is the first and chief thread to be followed.

The Mid-Tudor Palace Style

In 1530 no royal palace was more recent than that which Henry's father, the first Tudor, had built at Sheen and called Richmond Palace on its completion in 1501. That building, one of the frugal King's few extravagances, was a great brick palace-castle on the French model, built round a courtyard and exhibiting exteriorly many tall, narrow towers, each with a lead crown flaring up from its summit; the walls were pierced liberally with un-fortresslike windows. Of the precise plan and architectural treatment we know nothing; but the tower at Windsor which bears the King's name and the glorious chapel he built at Westminster help us to understand something of its character. Richmond may well have been the fount of several important features which penetrate into the architecture of much later times.

I

Henry VIII was to emulate, if not to surpass, Richmond in his own palace of Nonsuch. But it was, fundamentally, a different kind of building. For Henry, as a builder, took his cue not from his father but from his chief minister, Wolsey. Wolsey had begun to build Hampton Court in 1515. In 1525, under the approaching shadows of disfavour, he had presented it, still incomplete, to the King. The gift accepted, Hampton Court became a Palace. As such it was completed. Four years later, upon Wolsey's final disgrace, Henry seized Wolsey's York Place ('Whitehall' from about 1530), although it belonged not to the Cardinal but to the see of York. There, again, he completed what Wolsey had begun. Thus, the impetus, in style and plan, passed from the Cardinal to the King, and in the Cardinal's buildings rather than in those of Henry VII is announced the style which Henry VIII was to promote throughout his reign.

*

Cardinal Wolsey's buildings were houses, not palaces; they were residences for a great churchman, not for a king, and they derive, therefore, not from previous palace architecture but from that type of domestic architecture which was common to colleges, monasteries, and the houses of bishops in the fifteenth century. This style of building had become greatly modified in an increasingly civilian atmosphere. It remained Gothic, but the Gothic was diluted, its character flattened. The taste apparent here is the same which dictated exaggerated breadth in men's clothes, which made women's head-dresses obtuse and low, and which blunted all the points in contemporary armour. In buildings, the pointed arch was reduced to the lowest curve compatible with security; roofs were depressed almost to dead flatness and concealed by parapets; mouldings were reduced to a few elementary formulas involving only the shallowest in-cutting. This extreme taste for the flat, the square, the shallow, which had been defining itself ever more clearly for over a century, represents the final withdrawal from the poetry of Gothic. It is a negative taste, an eliminating taste. It stylizes the past, reduces it to compact symbols – and dismisses it; it is the taste of the end of an epoch.

But it is also a taste peculiarly receptive to novelty. As the Gothic spirit is withdrawn, it leaves a void extremely attractive to alien ideas. The very negativeness of the Tudor style made it an appropriate matrix, a framework, for ornaments whose interest was intrinsic and not relative to their setting. Wolsey understood this when he enriched the towers of his gatehouse with terra-cotta medallions of Italian design, enclosing busts of Roman Emperors; and we shall find that this negativeness invited much else that was alien to English Gothic, until finally the fabric of the style itself became amenable to a wholly new discipline.

The plans of Henry VIII's palaces, in following Wolsey's pattern, followed the collegiate tradition and consisted principally of two courtyards, the first entered by a conspicuous gatehouse and surrounded by 'lodgings' for the habitation of court officials or guests; the second containing the hall, the chapel, and the lodgings of the King himself and his principal attendants.

The emphasis on the gatehouse is interesting. That feature had, from early medieval times, contained important rooms – the chamber of the abbot or the principal guest-chamber in a monastery; hence it became, in many cases, the nucleus of the 'private side' in a great complex of buildings, and, instead of being suppressed when the need for a heavily protected entrance was reduced, was, on the contrary, made yet more emphatic. At Hampton Court and elsewhere there are two gatehouses, one external, the other situated between the two courts and therefore redundant as a protected entrance and introduced merely as an architectural feature.

The gatehouse was the feature round which the new predilection for symmetry asserted itself. The building usually had octagonal turrets at the corners, the resulting plan – a square held by four octagons – being a shape which enjoyed great favour during the whole Tudor period. We meet it not only in these gatehouses but in fortifications on the one hand and such buildings as banqueting houses on the other. The theme is as old as the thirteenth century (St Augustine's, Canterbury, c. 1300) but took a new lease of life in the late fifteenth century and was one of the last Gothic ideas to be relinquished. The symmetry of the gatehouse itself was emphasized by its setting in the centre of an elevation, or still further, as in the great West Gatehouse at Hampton Court, by the addition of wings to itself, each terminating in an additional octagon turret.

The increased prominence of the gatehouse in no way diminished the importance of the Hall in the mid-Tudor palace. It remained what it had always been, the principal element in the layout, the centre of the life of the entire household, and the state dining-room and entertaining room of the King. There were, however, many more private apartments – solars, parlours, and chambers – and these tended to group themselves round the gatehouse. A particularly important addition to the domestic apartments was the Gallery, a long upper room appropriated to walking and conversation. This feature was not new in Henry VIII's time, even when Wolsey built galleries at Hampton Court and York Place. There was at least one gallery in Richmond Palace, supported on an open arcade,[1] and the idea probably derived from galleried cloisters built in France in the fifteenth century. The gallery was to become extremely important in English house design and was introduced in almost every considerable house up to the reign of Charles I.

The Chapel, in mid-Tudor palaces, did lose somewhat in architectural importance, though the loss is more apparent than real, being due largely to the new fashion in fenestration which deprived the chapel windows of their tracery and, on the other hand, enlarged the windows of ordinary domestic apartments. There was, however, a decided lapse of interest in the spiritual side of domestic planning and 'curious' carving found its way more readily to the great oriels of the hall or the lesser ones of the gatehouse than to the window over the private altar.

Henry VIII's Palaces

Of Henry VIII's palace architecture, the parts of Hampton Court which he added to Wolsey's buildings constitute the most important surviving example. It was Henry VIII who built the Hall (1531–6), a Gothic building with a hammer-beam roof (Plates 1B and 2). In spite of its soaring height, everything in the design is flattened, and even the roof, necessarily steep because of its construction, is so designed that it was possible to bring the gables to flat points at their summits. Henry also built the blocks flanking the main entrance and in doing so created an impressive symmetrical approach of a type which we shall find elsewhere about the same date. Of the interior, little that is original remains, but the watching-chamber has a plaster ceiling (1536) which is the prototype of much Elizabethan design. It is, in effect, a highly conventionalized imitation of a fan-vault – a flat surface with moulded ribs arranged in a geometrical pattern and brought down into decorative pendants at certain points; it is another good example of the Tudor tendency to reduce late Gothic features to compact, decorative formulas.

Of Whitehall Palace (1530–6) we know very little, because it was largely destroyed in the course of the seventeenth century. Here, Wolsey had already built a hall and much else, but Henry made great additions, especially on the west side of Whitehall, where he built, among other things, a gallery and an octagonal cock-pit. In the thoroughfare to Westminster he built the great brick gatehouse which was to become traditionally (and misleadingly) known as 'Holbein's Gate'. He built another gate, south of this, in a very different style, and to this we shall return.

At St James's Palace (1532–40), the gatehouse, the chapel, and some other parts survive. The gatehouse, with its octagonal turrets, is thoroughly characteristic of Henry's palace architecture. The chapel affects the fashion for flatness to an extreme degree. Not only is the principal window simply a large rectangle filled with two tiers of flat-arched lights, but the ceiling, like the one in the watching-chamber at Hampton Court, is quite flat and decorated with ribs in a geometrical pattern, each compartment filled with ornament.

Of Henry's building works at Bridewell, New Hall (or Beaulieu), Hunsdon, Greenwich, and elsewhere we know very little, but all evidence points to their having been very similar in style to the buildings we know. Only Nonsuch, the latest and greatest palace, has important differences, and before we come to that exceptional building we must look a little deeper into the organization and conduct of Henry VIII's royal works.

The Office of Works

No institution has been of more radical and lasting importance in English architecture than the department of State known as the King's Works or the Office of Works. The importance of the royal masons and carpenters in the development of English Gothic has long been realized, but the continuing significance of the organization to which they were attached, throughout the whole of the sixteenth and seventeenth centuries, has never been sufficiently appreciated. The Office of Works recruited the best abilities in all the trades and applied them to the architectural opportunities afforded by Crown expenditure. Those opportunities were often the greatest; but even when they were not, the royal Works continued as a nucleus of superior talent, its officers being employed by whichever patrons had the means to promote the most important buildings.

Unfortunately, no complete study has yet been undertaken of this important subject, and the constitution and character of the Office under Henry VIII is by no means clear. We can, however, gain a fairly good view of it by consulting the ampler documentation of later periods, and there is evidence that the department underwent little radical change during the second half of the sixteenth century. Indeed, a document[2] compiled in 1610, apparently from traditional sources, appears to bear a close relation to the Office as it was in 1538 or earlier, even the fees mentioned in it, which we can check against building accounts, being identical with those of the latter date. Following this document and various other sources, we may give a general account of the Office as it was when Henry was about to build Nonsuch, remembering only that an organization completely crystallized in 1610 was still very fluid at the earlier date.

The principal officer was the Surveyor or Surveyor-General. In Henry VIII's time the sphere of supremacy of this officer is doubtful; for there seem to have been separate surveyors, not necessarily under his authority, at the various palaces. Indeed, the surveyorship of Windsor Castle remained an independent office till Wren's time. By 1563, however, the Surveyor's full title, as rehearsed in his letters patent, indicates the measure of authority which he probably enjoyed nominally, if not in fact, at an earlier date. He is there described as 'Surveyor of (Queen Elizabeth's) Works in Her Highnes' Tower of London and in all and singular Her Majesty's Castles, Lordships and Manors usually reserved or which in time to come shall be appointed and ordained for Her Majesty's Repair and Abode'. This comprehensive style very likely derives from Wolsey's reorganization, from 1525 onwards, of the Royal Household, of which the office was, of course, in common with all the 'civil service', an integral part.

The Surveyors were mostly, though not always, artificers – either masons or carpenters. James Nedham, who held the office from 1532 to 1546, was a carpenter and is known to have designed (while he was Master Carpenter) the hall roof at Hampton Court. He was a nominee of Thomas Cromwell, and the office probably gathered administrative importance under his régime. Although styling himself 'accountant, surveyor-general and Clerk of the King's Works', there were other Surveyors in charge of specific buildings; Hampton Court, for instance, was under Richard Bennyce, Westminster under Thomas Canner.

Second to the Surveyor, though not subject to his authority, was the Comptroller. This office, like that of the Surveyor, had medieval antecedents, but appears to have lapsed and been reintroduced by Wolsey in 1528. His function was to insure the proper financial conduct of the Office and to act as a check on the Surveyors. He was, however, an artificer and a potential successor to the Surveyor in office.

Next to these two senior men came the Clerk Engrosser, the Purveyor, the Keeper of the Storehouse, the Clerk of the Check and the Clerk of the Comptrolment, and to these offices further clerkships of works were added from time to time, to look after works in hand. The Purveyor's task was the purely administrative one of buying the requisite stocks of materials and disposing annually of any surplus. The Clerks, however, were men of architectural experience, the Clerk Engrosser in particular being (at least from Elizabeth's time) something of a draughtsman.

As important as the Clerks and better paid than most of them were the Artificers. These included the Master Mason, Master Carpenter, three Master Joiners, the Serjeant Plumber, and the Master Glazier. The Master Mason and Master Carpenter enjoyed seniority over the others and were included, with the Surveyor and Comptroller, among the four principal officers of the Works, whose signatures (at least two) were required on all the pay-books presented for audit.

Finally, in the document of 1610 which we are following here, come two offices, obviously of prime importance, because their emoluments are equal to those of the Surveyor. They are the Surveyor of Mines and the Deviser of Buildings.

The last of these offices, that of Deviser of Buildings, is one of which we know extremely little, though its importance for our purpose might appear great. It seems to have had a medieval origin, but we never hear of it being filled after the time of Edward VI, and our information about it at any time is of the vaguest kind.[3] It is possible that, in 1539, a German, Stefan von Haschenperg, filled the office. He was suspended in 1543, and in the following year we first hear of a certain John of Padua,[4] who, Walpole tells us, occupied the position. Those are the only two names we can associate with the office of Deviser, and the fact that both are foreign suggests that it was reserved for specialists in some particular branch of building. Haschenperg, for instance, was employed as an expert on fortifications. John of Padua is mentioned in connexion with services both in architecture and music, though what precisely these services were no antiquary has yet succeeded in discovering.

One further office must be mentioned – that of the Serjeant Painter, who, though not strictly an officer of the Works (his fee being paid from another source), was closely associated with royal building operations and in charge of all paintwork, plain and decorative. From 1543 this office was held by Antonio Toto del Nunziata (1499–1556), an Italian who had come over here with Torrigiano to work on Henry VII's tomb and been granted letters patent of denization along with another Italian painter, Bartolommeo Penni (d. 1553) in 1537. Toto has been made into an important figure because of Vasari's statement that he built the principal palace of the King of England. He certainly did nothing of the kind, and the building accounts show his work to have been of that strictly specialized kind always expected from the Serjeant Painter.

A clear view of the Office of Works and its functions reduces some of the confusion which has hitherto attended the study of mid-Tudor Court architecture. The palaces were devised and built and largely adorned not by mysterious foreigners floating about Henry's Court, but by the officers whose business it was to do these things; and most of these officers were English. The precise form of each new building will, no doubt, have been settled by the senior officers in consultation. Their execution can often be assigned to individuals. Thus John Molton, Master Mason from 1528 till his death in 1547, built the hall at Hampton Court and the great gatehouse at St James's Palace. The carpentry at St James's will have been the work of his colleague John Russell (d. 1566), who advised on the design of the chapel roof at Trinity College, Cambridge. The royal building accounts are too fragmentary to enable us to make firm attributions in many cases, but the working principles are clear and enable us to examine, without prejudice, the important question of the infiltration of a foreign taste into this country.

Infiltration of the 'Antique' Taste

It is generally agreed that the first arrival of the Renaissance[5] into this country is represented by the work of that group of artists, headed by Torrigiano, which Henry VIII obtained from Italy to construct the tomb of his father at Westminster. That important episode in the history of English art is outside the limits of this book, nor did its effects endure for long after the date at which we begin. We have seen that one of this Italian group, Antonio Toto, remained to become Serjeant Painter, and it may be added that certain artists like Benedetto da Rovezzano (1474–after 1552) and Giovanni da Majano, who had worked for Wolsey, were in England at least till 1536.

But after Wolsey's fall the direct importation of Italian skill virtually ceased, and the influences which were to permeate English architecture for the next forty years came from another quarter altogether – from France.

In the ruins of the old parish church of Chelsea (destroyed 1941) still exist two remarkable capitals of a Renaissance type, one bearing a plaque carved in relief with the date 1528 (Plate 1A). In the Château de Chambord is a capital similar in nearly every respect and dated 1532. Obviously these two capitals come from one source; and obviously, in view of the known extent and character of the building operations of Louis XII and François I, that source is the Loire school of France.

The provenance of the Chelsea capitals is easily explained. For some years up to 1535, England and France were enjoying one of their periodic spells of peaceful existence and trading. One of England's principal imports from France was stone – chiefly from Rouen. That stone-carvers should follow the stone in which they were accustomed to work is not in the least surprising, and, in any case, the employment of foreigners for skilled work was a regular practice. That the Chelsea capitals should echo the Loire school so exactly is probably mere chance, and their design could, no doubt, with enough searching, be paralleled in Normandy at any date subsequent to 1520.

And Chelsea is not the only instance. Already in the 1520s, 'antick freezes' had appeared on monuments like that of the Countess of Salisbury at Christchurch, Hants. (1520); while the tomb of Lord Marney (d. 1523) at Layer Marney, Essex, is enriched with pilasters and baluster shafts instead of the usual tabernacle work of the Gothic tomb. The character of both these examples is decidedly French. At Brede in Sussex there is a monument dated 1537 made of Normandy stone and so obviously French in character that it may very well have been carved abroad and shipped to England whole.

Not only in masonry, but also in woodwork, the new taste crossed the Channel. There are some early specimens at Christchurch; but by far the most remarkable instance is the superb screen of King's College Chapel, Cambridge (Plate 3). This was erected, as the gift of Henry VIII, between 1533 and 1535, and is so mature and consistent in design that all authorities are disposed to call it the work of foreign artists. In design and detail it is closely related to the Rouen school of stone-carvers, and, although it is finer than anything to be found in Normandy, France must surely be the source of the work.

But if the earlier specimens of the new taste are sometimes attributable to foreigners (and it must be admitted that in very few instances is there documentary evidence of this), the new skill passed very soon into English hands. To prove this there is the documented case of the pendants to the hall roof at Hampton Court. This roof, as we have seen, was built under the direction of James Nedham. It is wholly English in design, except for certain carved details, including the spandrels and pendants of the hammer-beams; these have quite skilfully designed scrolls, balusters, and *putti*, and it appears from the building accounts that these were executed by Richard Rydge, who, it is fairly safe to assume, was an Englishman. At Weston Manor in Oxfordshire is another piece of Renaissance carving which is actually signed by Rydge. So there we have an English carver who, in 1533, or earlier, had already captured from some unknown source the technique of 'antick' carving in wood.

In stone-carving, there is the parallel case of John Chapman. His major activities, at Lacock and Longleat, belong to the next chapter, but it is important to note here that his name occurs among the King's masons at least as early as 1541.[6] Rydge and Chapman were probably outstanding artists of a rather rare type, and, very naturally, were employed on the royal Works. Their employment elsewhere was the equally natural result of the prestige which they earned in the King's business. Through such men as these the new taste spread about the country and varied versions of their Anglo-French ornamentalism are met with in various areas up to the time, in the late fifteen-sixties, when the style began to be superseded by a very different kind of classicism coming from Flanders in the hands of Protestant refugees.

All the earlier examples of the new taste are either monuments or fittings or carved details on structures of traditional English character. One of the first entire buildings to be brought completely under the sway of the new style was a gateway at Whitehall Palace, one of two gateways which, since they provide an instructive contrast, may be dealt with together.

The Whitehall Gatehouses

When Henry VIII took over York Place and built the multiple additions to it, westward of the thoroughfare now called Whitehall, he built across the part of that thoroughfare adjoining the Privy Garden two gatehouses. At the north end he built a typical Tudor structure, completed in 1532 (Plate 4A). It had the usual four corner-turrets and was constructed, apparently, of stone and flint arranged in a chequered pattern and adorned with glazed terra-cotta roundels containing busts, such as Wolsey had used long before at Hampton Court. For some curious reason this gateway was known to the eighteenth century as 'Holbein's Gate', though there was nothing about it that even remotely suggests his having designed it.[7] It was evidently a very handsome specimen of its English kind, for Vanbrugh pleaded against its demolition in 1719, and when at length it was taken down in 1759, an attempt, though unsuccessful, was made to re-erect it elsewhere.

At the southern end of the same street another gatehouse was built (Plate 4B), almost certainly by Henry VIII, although the date is uncertain. Here, a very different kind of design was adopted. All the main features – the central opening for horsemen and side openings for pedestrians, the corner-turrets – were traditional, but the detail throughout (except for the typically Tudor lights of the windows) was classical. The side openings were framed by Doric pilasters and surmounted by pediments. The main storey displayed two tall Ionic pilasters, while the openings here were adorned with a secondary Ionic order. A full entablature surmounted these and, above it, were round towers, with domical caps and, between them, a semicircular feature carved with the signs of the zodiac.

This singular building, whose destruction in 1723 nobody seems to have regretted, is as French in the character of its detail as much of the work of the period we have already described. As it is wholly English in general composition there is no reason to ascribe it to a foreign hand, and the ornament may well be the work of an Englishman of the John Chapman type employed in the royal Works. It is prophetic of much that we shall find, later on, in Elizabethan architecture and certainly one of the pioneer works of Henry's reign, though less important than the great palace whose building occupied the last nine years of it - the Palace of Nonsuch.

The Palace of Nonsuch

Henry VIII began to build Nonsuch in 1538, at a time when the revenues of suppressed monasteries were beginning to become available. He swept away the old village and church of Cuddington to provide himself with a perfect site. By 1545, £23,000 had been spent, but the Palace was incomplete in the year of the King's death. It passed into private hands under Mary and was completed, only to be demolished about 1670.

Nonsuch, like other great houses of the time, was built round two courts, an outer and an inner court, though the outer court was of later date and it is uncertain if Henry VIII intended it. The inner court, approached through a gatehouse and up a flight of steps, had a lower part of stone and an upper part of half-timber work, and this seems to have been enriched in a manner somewhat out of the ordinary. The really striking part of the building, however, was the block forming the far side of this inner court and facing outwards onto the gardens (Plate 5). This block consisted of a long range of building between two very large octagonal towers (not mere turrets) whose upper parts developed into many-windowed pavilions crowned by pointed lead roofs and a great many pinnacles.

This unusual composition may have been a deliberate attempt to emulate François I's great Château of Chambord, which had been in progress for twelve years when Nonsuch was begun and which, though still incomplete, will have been one of the architectural wonders of Europe. Henry was sensitive about the achievements of his French rival in every field, and some representation of Chambord may have induced him to order his artificers to introduce its main features at Nonsuch. They did so to the extent of building those great corner towers which, at least in Hoefnagel's famous drawing, are as fantastic in bulk and silhouette as those of the French château.

Even this work in its general architecture does not seem to have been beyond the powers of Henry's Office of Works. It was simply an unusually magniloquent expression of the favourite of all Tudor themes, the mass flanked by octagons; the summits of the towers were an elaboration of features conspicuous in the silhouette of Richmond. And so far as we know all the artificers employed on the *structure* were English.

In the decorative finishing, however, the furnishings and fountains, there is no question at all that Henry employed foreigners. In the inner court the native half-timber work was 'richly adorned and set forth and garnished with a variety of pictures and other antick forms of excellent art and workmanship'. So the survey of 1650 tells us. And John Evelyn, who visited Nonsuch in 1666, records more specifically that, in the spaces between the timbers, there were 'plaster statues and bass relievos', while the timbers themselves were covered in a revetement of slates, arranged in patterns. That Evelyn should have found that these plasters 'must needs have ben the work of some celebrated Italian' speaks highly for their quality. He adds that 'there are some mezzo-relievos as big as the life, the storie is of the Heathen Gods, emblems, compartments, etc.' This sounds rather like the kind of thing which had been proceeding at Fontainebleau since Rosso's arrival there in 1530. Rosso, as 'conductor of stuccoes and paintings', decorated the Galérie François Ier with frames and cartouches, introducing life-size figures in high relief and 'compartments' such as Evelyn's description of Nonsuch at once suggests.

Hardly any records of these adornments exist, but the connexion of Henry VIII's Court art with Fontainebleau is amply confirmed by a drawing (Plate 6A), formerly in the Louvre, for the decorations of a Throne Room or Presence Chamber, in which Henry's arms occur. This design, almost certainly connected with Nonsuch, is related to the style of Rosso. If we compare it with another surviving record, an engraving of a fireplace preserved at Reigate Priory, Surrey (Plate 6B), we get a good idea of the character of the interiors. Moreover, we see at once to what extent Elizabethan and Jacobean architecture were indebted to the Palace which, in those reigns, was still a cherished monument.

Near to Nonsuch Palace was a banquet-house, a half-timber building on a square plan with round corner turrets and rising to a lead-covered roof – a pleasure-castle on a theme which the Elizabethans, as we shall see, employed when it occurred to them to introduce a chivalresque reference to castellar architecture.

Henry VIII's Fortifications

We cannot leave our account of the building works of Henry VIII without making some mention of the fortresses he constructed on the south coast about 1539–40 as a precaution against the threatened combination of the two great European rivals, the Emperor Charles V and François I, to reclaim England for the Catholic Church. These fortresses include those of Sandgate, Deal, and Walmer, on the south-east coast and Pendennis and St Mawes in the west. There were others in the Thames estuary, at Dover, Southampton Water, and the Isle of Wight. Such castles were of a type new to England (where there had been no necessity for castle building for many years) and represent improvements adopted by French and subsequently by Italian and German builders. In plan many of them consist or consisted of low trefoil or multifoil citadels with provision for artillery and extensive outworks. Of their designers we know little beyond the fact that Stefan von Haschenperg was concerned, as Deviser,[8] with the Kentish castles; but Henry employed, in addition, an Italian painter, Girolamo da Trevigi, who was killed at the siege of Boulogne in 1544. Haschenperg left England under a cloud in the same year.

These castles, the first in England to be built by the Sovereign as head of the State and for its protection, are of no importance in the general development of English architecture, but represent an interesting by-way in the history of Renaissance fortification.

NOTES TO CHAPTER I

1. The remains of a gallery of this type are still clearly visible at Thornbury Castle, Glos., *c.* 1514, and Thornbury probably derived to some extent from Richmond. There is, for example, an oriel window there which links up with Henry's works at Windsor and Westminster. A drawing for a gallery, possibly at Whitehall, is in Cotton MSS., Aug. I.i.4.

2. 'A Survaye or Book of offices', Harl. 1857.

3. It is, of course, the equivalent of the French *deviseur*. Charles VIII's 'colony' at Amboise included two *deviseurs de bâtiments*, one of them being Fra Giocondo (1453–1515). In France as in England the office of Deviser was distinct from that of Surveyor. In Geoffrey Webb's view, the Deviser was usually an expert in the new learning, retained for consultation on matters of theory – fortification, iconography, etc. – rather than as an actual designer. This view fits satisfactorily the cases of Haschenperg and John of Padua in England.

4. John of Padua has been a famous will-o'-the-wisp ever since Horace Walpole assigned to him, on the strength of his Italian name and the style of his office, together with Holbein, the introduction into England of 'regular' architecture. There is, of course, no reason to regard him as any more important, in this respect, than Haschenperg. The 'office book' in which Walpole discovered a payment to him as Deviser is not now traceable, though the payment which Walpole quotes (£36 10s, the same as the Surveyor's) confirms the authenticity of his information. Nearly every classical work of the mid-Tudor period has, at some time, been assigned to John of Padua. W. Wilkins thought the name an *alias* of John Caius (p. 108) and other writers have identified him, fantastically enough, with John Thorpe (p. 27). Rymer's *Foedera* gives two extracts showing that John of Padua was receiving a fee or pension from 1544 and that it was confirmed to him by Edward VI in 1549; in those extracts he is not, rather strangely, described as Deviser. Miss E. Auerbach has kindly informed me that she has found a still later reference to John of Padua in 1555–6 at the Public Record Office (E 405/122 Tellers Roll 3 & 4 P. & M., f. 34).

5. I must enter a warning here against the too free use of this word in connexion with English architecture. The Renaissance was a movement originating in Italy in the fourteenth to the fifteenth century and having as its mainspring the recognition of the artistic values of classical antiquity. The Renaissance proper was over in Italy by 1520. In France and England during the sixteenth century the artistic products of the Renaissance *and its sequel* profoundly affected the arts, but the use and enjoyment of those products is not necessarily analogous to their use and enjoyment in Italy. This applies especially to the use in Elizabethan times of Flemish and German versions of Italian Mannerism, anti-Renaissance in origin and remote from the Renaissance spirit in their later development.

6. That appears to be the date of a fragment of the King's Works Accounts discovered in an Oxford binding and preserved at the Bodleian (MS. Eng. Hist., b. 192, f. I). In the same MS. a Thomas Chappman is mentioned as importing timber, and there is also an Edmond Chapman.

7. Holbein was in England from 1527 to 1528, and again in 1530, while from 1537 he was permanently in the pay of the King till his death in 1543. Tradition early associated his name with several English buildings, notably a porch (since rebuilt as a garden-house) at Wilton. Vertue and, after him, Walpole, were confident about this attribution, but as Sir William Herbert took full possession of Wilton only in 1544 and Holbein died in the previous year it can hardly be taken seriously. In any case, the porch has characteristically French details and is not remotely like any of Holbein's known architectural designs. The drawing by him for a fireplace (probably at Bridewell) in the British Museum is the only real evidence we have of architectural work by Holbein in England. The ceiling of St James's Palace Chapel is attributed to him in R.C.H.M., London (West), but no authority is given. The

general design derives from an engraving in Serlio first published in 1540, the date of the ceiling, and the attribution, though not impossible, is unlikely. The attribution of the Chelsea Church capitals (p. 7) to Holbein is a guess dating from 1898.

8. In the Declared Accounts of the exors. of Robert Lord (PRO. E 351/2199) he is referred to as 'Surveyor of the castles on the Downs, otherwise called Devisor'. For an account of Haschenperg's career see Mr O'Neil's paper in the Bibliography.

CHAPTER 2

MID-TUDOR PATRONAGE AND THE NEW FASHION
⟨1540–1570⟩

THE royal Works supplied the most conspicuous building schemes of the last seventeen years of Henry's reign. But not much less prominent was a considerable number of great country-houses built almost exclusively by men who had managed to extract from the casualties of the times great advantage to themselves. Such men were the lawyers who handled the transfer of monastic properties, and those who served Henry as diplomats or courtiers in the difficult episode of the divorce. They were the first and most able bidders for the monastic dividends.

Take, for example, two men who were successively Chancellors of the Court of Augmentation, the instrument created by Henry to deal with the confiscated estates. The first Chancellor was Richard Rich, an unattractive character, remembered for his base treatment of More and Fisher. The second was Edward North, who retained the office till the end of Henry's reign and added the London Charterhouse to his possessions. Both these lawyer-statesmen secured handsome shares of the property which passed through their hands, Rich housing himself lavishly at Little Leighs, Essex, and North at Kirtling Hall, Cambs. Similar in ownership and type, these two houses were similar in their fate, both being ruined except, in both cases, for the enormous turreted gatehouses which survive. Appropriately enough; for the gatehouse, placed about the middle of a more or less symmetrical range of buildings, was easily the greatest feature of these and many other houses of the time. While the hall and the chapel declined in majesty, the gatehouse retained the symbolic splendour it had reached in the previous century.

To these two houses one may add Titchfield, Hants. (Plate 7A), another case where everything is now in ruins except the vast gatehouse, which the mason Thomas Bartewe built out of the old nave for Sir Thomas Wriothesley, Lord Chancellor from 1544. The case of Titchfield reminds us not to think of the redistribution of the monastic properties as wholly abrupt and arbitrary. Wriothesley had been closely associated with Titchfield Abbey, perhaps as its steward. He moved into the monastic premises with remarkable promptitude in 1537, and the gateway with symmetrical wings which he built was exactly the kind of thing which a wealthy religious house might have desired to build had its life been prolonged. There is no fundamental architectural difference between the gatehouse at Titchfield and that built at the end of the fourteenth century by the canons of Thornton Abbey. Bartewe himself must have been one of many masons who had served the monks and lived to serve their successors in similar ways.

All these were courtyard houses, their architectural interest being focused within rather than without the courts. In this they were typical, and there are few exceptions among the greater houses. Barrington Court, Somerset, however, is an exception of some importance (Plate 7B; Figure 1). It was built, perhaps before 1530, by Henry Daubeny, a friend of the King, who attended him at the Field of the Cloth of Gold and eventually became Earl of Bridgewater. Barrington is purely Tudor-Gothic in style, but the plan is near symmetrical, with the hall block and two wings enclosing three sides of an *open* court and a projecting porch on the centre of the hall block. The angles between the hall block and the wings are filled by square projections, one constituting the hall oriel and the other a gratuitous feature introduced for the sake of symmetry. This plan, which fore-shadows a common Elizabethan type, is a summary in formal terms of the medieval

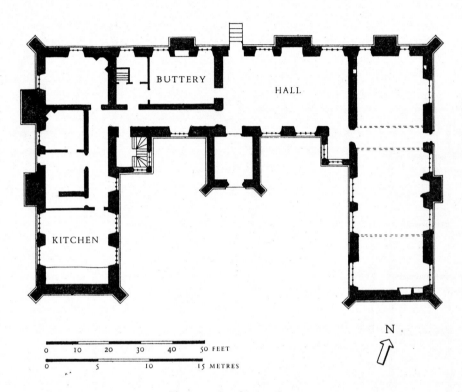

Figure 1. Barrington Court

house comprising a hall block with developments at either end along the sides of a fore-court. A plan of the sort had already emerged at The Vyne, Hants., built certainly before 1530; while the formalization of the square corner projections, which we shall hence-forward call the 'extruded corner', is already visible in the courtyard house of Sutton Place, Surrey (1523–5). Moreover, Henry VIII's extensions to Hampton Court gave the entrance front of that building, fortuitously perhaps, a shape rather similar to that which we see at Barrington.

Little Leighs, Kirtling, Titchfield, and Barrington are all Tudor-Gothic in style, seeking a new formality without the aid of foreign ideas or ornaments. Sutton Place, indeed, contains within its dry rectilinear pattern some trifling ornaments of a foreign kind, executed in terra-cotta, and there are several other examples of the same date and material. A house which summarizes very well the architectural situation in the 1530s is Hengrave

Hall, Suffolk (Plate 8; Figure 2). Begun about 1525, it is built round a square court. The entrance front has a prominent gateway and a roughly symmetrical arrangement of subsidiary towers. Over the main entrance is a triple bay-window, of a kind associated with Henry VII's building works, but decorated with fine and rich carving of a Renaissance kind – shields supported by pairs of *putti* in Roman armour. Dated 1538, this is the only hint of classicism in the building, the reason being that this window was the individual work of a mason not otherwise connected with the building.

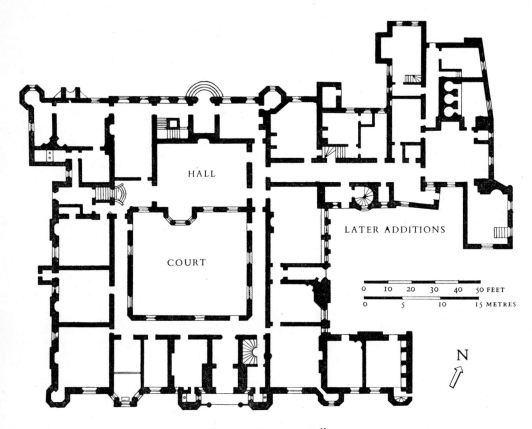

Figure 2. Hengrave Hall

The building accounts and inventories of Hengrave happen to survive,[1] and the picture they give of the way in which a great house was 'assembled' rather than 'designed' is valuable at this juncture in English architecture. Sir John Kytson, a wealthy merchant, contracted with John Eastawe to 'macke a house at Hengrave of all manor of mason's worck and bricklaying, as well as the labourers concerning the same, according to the frame which the said Jhon has seen'. This was a contract for the carcase of the house. A later contract was made with Thomas Neker for 'seelyng' the house, which would be carpenter's work and included panelling and fittings. But even the masonry was not wholly in Eastawe's hands, for the bay-window of the gatehouse, just mentioned, was the separate work of John Sparke; another bay-window, that of the hall, was also excluded from Eastawe's work. Who was responsible for the 'frame' (doubtless a diagram on paper or parchment) we do not know, unless it was Robert Watson, mentioned as the 'ruler' of the building in the second contract. The main artistic responsibility for the house is divisible between four people – Eastawe, Neker, Sparke, and the author of the 'frame', and of these the last was probably the least important, in the sense that the grouping and massing of the building shows little artistic ambition and small departure from established tradition.

Sparke's bay-window is typical of the kind of ornamentalism coming into Tudor architecture. Carving of this sort appears occasionally in most parts of the country. The panel on the porch at Cowdray, Sussex (1535–9), is a good example. At Montacute there is a superb heraldic panel (1546) moved, in the eighteenth century, with the front to which it belongs, from Clifton Maybank, Dorset; Binghams Melcombe in the same county has a panel perhaps from the same hand. Such features, nicely merged in their late Gothic frames, are pointers to the progress of the 'antick' taste. But how was this progress encouraged and maintained? What was its mainspring? There must have been some active element in society propagating the new cult, some group of well-informed patrons on whose encouragement craftsmen depended and to whom other men building great houses looked for example.

There was, of course, the Court, unquestionably the principal centre of artistic development. But in the later years of Henry VIII's reign and still more in that of his successor we can discern a group of personalities whose patronage extended both within and without the Court and who propagated the new fashion in several different parts of England.

Patronage of the Mid-Tudor Renaissance

We do not know enough about the men who composed this group to write of them with the confidence with which we write, for instance, about the patrons of Palladianism in the eighteenth century. But we can say that all were in one way or another connected with Edward Seymour, who, as Duke of Somerset, became Protector in 1547. They constituted, indeed, the lay intelligentsia of that particular moment in English history. We cannot put our finger on this man or that as being a leader, but it is chronologically convenient to begin with Sir William Sharington (? 1495–1553). Sharington was one of the lesser political adventurers of Henry VIII's reign, serving more eminent servants of the King, notably Sir Francis Bryan, who had been to Rome on the divorce business, and, later, Thomas Lord Seymour of Sudeley, the future Protector's brother. He acquired the monastic property of Lacock, Wilts., in 1540, and between that year and 1549, when he narrowly escaped the fate of his second master, carried out much rebuilding. Not all his work at Lacock survives, but there is a conspicuous octagonal tower (Plate 9A), and there are doorways, a fireplace, and the respond of an arcade, all of which show a knowledge of and a feeling for classical detail much in advance of their time. Sharington seems to have taken a keen personal interest in building; and in his portrait, which hangs at Lacock, we see him standing against a wall of antique masonry. But he also employed a clever mason called John Chapman, who, we know, had worked on the royal buildings in about 1541 (p. 8). If all the carved work at Lacock is Chapman's it includes the refined balustrade on the tower, and two stone pedestal tables (Plate 9B) in the top and second rooms of the tower respectively. These are richly carved with satyrs, terms, consoles, and fruit in a style very similar to that which we find in Normandy. A fireplace in the stone gallery has Doric pilasters and a correctly moulded entablature; while the respond of an unbuilt arcade in the stable court consists of a well-executed Ionic order on a pedestal. Especially French in character is a miniature vault with pendants, in a room in the tower.

Chapman's work is symptomatic of that new influence in decorative detail which was coming to England in increasing force from the Continent – almost always from France. That he had worked for the King tends to confirm one's impression that the Office of Works was the main receiving centre of the new influences. Chapman's reputation was considerable, but there were other masons doing the same kind of work. At Bristol, for instance, there survives a tiny fragment of a conduit-house, built about the middle of the century. The ornament on it is an exact repeat of that on a fireplace of similar date in Bisham Abbey, Berks., only twenty-seven miles from London. Do these two trivial fragments mark the trail of some mason, moving, as Chapman did, from patron to patron and carrying the new style from London to the West? Obviously we cannot know. But all the evidence points to diffusion from London, through the operations, both official and private, of artificers in the King's service.

The names of Sharington and Chapman are again associated in the reconstruction by the Duke of Northumberland of Dudley Castle, now in ruins but still exhibiting features reminiscent of the work at Lacock. But both this and Lacock are overshadowed by a much more important building, the design of which may confidently be associated with Sharington's friend and Wiltshire neighour, Sir John Thynne.

Old Somerset House

John Thynne (d. 1580), 'an ingenious man and a traveller' and Steward to Protector Somerset, was younger than Sharington and an active builder for some thirty years. His greatest achievement, Longleat House, belongs mostly to another chapter, but that, as we shall see, owed much to a previous essay, the palace he superintended[2] for his master, the Protector Somerset, soon after Henry VIII's death in 1547.

Somerset House (Plates 10 and 11), as built for the Protector between 1547 and 1552, was unquestionably one of the most influential buildings of the English Renaissance, and requires close analysis. There is a plan of it among the Thorpe drawings in the Soane Museum, which shows us a two-storey house built round a quadrangle which is entered, from the Strand, through a gateway in three storeys, adorned with superimposed orders. The whole of the Strand front (Plate 10), which follows, in a general way, the English collegiate formula, is in fine ashlar masonry, and to left and right are slightly projecting window-bays continuing through two storeys, adorned with columns at both levels and surmounted by ornamental parapets. Similar windows appear in the courtyard, at the further end of which is the hall block with a loggia. The Strand sky-line, balustraded, is perfectly flat, except where it is interrupted by pairs of ornamental chimneys and the extra height of the gateway and window-bays.

The entrance gateway is extremely interesting for, although its prominence and position is exactly what one would expect in a palace of this date, its character is wholly different. Moreover, it derives certainly from France, and is in some respects comparable to parts of the Château of Écouen, near Paris, as reconstructed in the 1550s for the Constable of France, Anne de Montmorency. There can be no question of derivation. Yet not only the 'triumphal arch' on the ground floor, but the curious combination of a projecting central pier between two windows, with pairs of columns to left and right, seen in the middle storey of the Somerset House gateway, are very close to the gateway and north pavilion of the Château. The loggia across the hall block, standing between extruded corners, may be an afterthought but is still probably the first of its kind in England.

Quite as important as the gateway and loggia of Somerset House, for the future of English architecture, were the two-storey window-units of the Strand front. These displayed a favourite French motif in the coupling of two windows, framed by side and centre columns, under a pediment. The theme recurs in Longleat and in a series of houses deriving from it. Above each window-unit was a pierced parapet introducing the 'cipher-and-square'. This motif, which was to become so common a feature of Elizabethan and Jacobean decoration, is not typically French. It did, however, occur in a fireplace and other decorations at Nonsuch which, as we have seen, are connected with the Fontaine-bleau school.

Somerset House was probably the first deliberate attempt to build in England a house composed altogether within the classical discipline. And the models for several parts of it were French. We need not hesitate to name Thynne as its principal creator; for, as we shall see, he had in his lifetime a reputation as a builder, and was able to draw. The final Longleat confirms the common authorship of the two buildings in several ways. Of the influence of Somerset House on the course of Elizabethan architecture we shall find plenty of evidence. It proceeded not only through Thynne himself but through another, younger, member of the group we are discussing, a man who was the Protector's private secretary during the building of Somerset House – no less a man and no less a builder of houses than William Cecil, the future Lord Burghley.

At the same time that Somerset House was building, Thynne was engaged on a house of his own on the site of the present Longleat. It was hardly more than a reconstruction of the old Priory buildings there and we know nothing of its architecture. During the years of political crisis preceding Mary's accession in 1553, Thynne was not architecturally active, but his obvious unacceptability at Court under the new régime no doubt sent him, as it sent others of his group, to the country and to house-building. In 1554 he was employing Chapman and in 1557 made the first of a series of contracts with a Somerset mason, William Spicer (see p. 26), to build important extensions to Longleat, extensions which were to become part of the present building. That house was partly burnt and entirely remodelled from 1567 onwards, so that we cannot know to what extent it approached the character of Somerset House. But the accounts do tell us not only of Chapman's presence but of a window to the gallery, 'of freestone with columpnes', of 'chimneys of columns 17 ft. high', of architraves, friezes, pilasters, capitals, and bases, and of staircase towers rising above the roof. In short, it looks as if most of the ideas contained in the final Longleat, which belong to Elizabeth's reign, were evolved during Mary's and we can hardly doubt a close association between them and the still recent masterpiece in the Strand, with which Thynne had been so closely associated.

If we join the names of Sharington and Thynne and young William Cecil with those of the men they served – the Protector Somerset, his brother, and his eventual arch-enemy the Duke of Northumberland – we find that we have a group of names representing a circle with a lively interest in the new style during the fifteen-forties and fifties. And the picture can be somewhat amplified. It is known, for instance, that in 1550 the Duke of Northumberland actually sent one of his household, John Shute (d. 1563), to Italy, 'to confer with the doings of the skilful masters in architecture, and also to view such ancient monuments thereof as are yet extant'. Although the results of Shute's visit did not appear in print till 1563, and were then not very informative about Rome or Roman architects, the fact of this energetic patronage is significant.

Shute went to Italy; Italy was on the lips of the connoisseurs. But the evidence of the buildings themselves goes to show that France was the actual source of most of the classical work of the 1550s and 60s. Some of this influence came through immigrant masons, some through Nonsuch, where the Fontainebleau school seems so richly to have penetrated, some, no doubt, through travelled virtuosi like Thynne or like his friend and Cecil's, Sir Thomas Smyth, a keen amateur of architecture who was also for some years ambassador at Paris.[3]

Before Elizabeth came to the throne the promising circle of patronage at the Protector's Court had been violently disrupted. The axe had accounted for the Lord Protector himself, his brother, and nearly for Sharington; it had accounted for the Duke of Northumberland. The younger men, however, including Sir John Thynne, Sir William Cecil, and Sir Thomas Smyth, survived in prosperity to prosecute the cause of classical architecture in England. All three were busy building for themselves during Mary's reign.

Of Thynne's first house at Longleat we have already spoken. Cecil's adventures at Burghley House started a little later.

William Cecil came into his family estate in 1552 and within four years had started to rebuild the house. The surviving correspondence relating to Burghley begins with a letter from Roger Warde, 'Mason to Sir W. Cecil', asking his master for certain details of dormer windows and gables. Five years earlier, Warde had supplied a 'platt' to Sir William Cavendish for Chatsworth, so he appears to have been a mason of some experience. Yet he asks Cecil for the most specific instructions, even requiring him to 'drawe a tryke of the upryght for youre lucan [lucarne or dormer] wyndowe and the gabylle end over hytt'. Cecil evidently had a really intimate knowledge of building and could put pencil to paper to express his meaning.

The existing hall at Burghley, with its lofty rectangular oriel and open timber roof, no doubt belongs to this collaboration between Warde and Cecil, and it is barely tinged with any feeling for the new style. When, ten years later, in 1566, another stage was reached in the rebuilding of Burghley, Sir Thomas Gresham's Royal Exchange, in London (p. 113), had just been begun; and Cecil took the opportunity of employing a Flemish mason called Henryk who was going backwards and forwards between London and Antwerp in connexion with Gresham's building. Henryk procured paving-stones for Cecil, and in 1567–8 was concerned with the construction of pillars for a gallery. These were to be made abroad, but the 'pattern' for them was given by Cecil himself. None of this work survives, and the one scrap of Henryk's work which we have is a drawing of a very ordinary four-light bay-window, endorsed in Cecil's hand 'Hendrik's plat of my bay windowe'.

Contemporary with this stage in the construction of Burghley was Cecil's erection of the first part of Theobalds, Herts., for his eldest son; but we know little about this building (demolished in 1670) apart from the plan, recorded by Thorpe. The building of Longleat, Burghley, and Theobalds bring us well into the reign of Elizabeth. We cannot place beside them at this date many houses of equal strategic importance in the history of English architecture. At Gorhambury, Herts. (1563–8), Sir Nicholas Bacon built a Tudor brick courtyard-house with tall octagonal towers at the outer corners of the main front, reminding one of Sharington's tower at Lacock, and with a highly ornate classical porch of two orders with inlaid marble (or 'touch') panels and Roman figures in niches, the detail having a close affinity with certain buildings in the Paris area.[4] A slightly later and more important house was Copped Hall, Essex, built by Sir Thomas Heneage between 1564 and 1567 (demolished in the eighteenth century). Here, if Thorpe's record is to be trusted, was a quite determined attempt to evolve a house which should have an effect both inwardly to its courtyard and outwardly to the gardens and park. The courtyard was not entirely closed but approached, on the entrance side, through a low fore-building, while at the rear was an open loggia. That is distinctly a French innovation; and drawings of the porch and two fireplaces show decided influence of the Fontainebleau school.

But the general picture of early Elizabethan architecture is not yet a very lively one. With the preceding decades, it belongs to the rather flat, indifferent mid-Tudor landscape in which we can trace only certain scattered developments towards a new manner of building. All these developments were to be eclipsed by the series of prodigy houses which reached completion from 1570 onwards. But before we come to these we must explore more fully the conditions of building in Elizabethan England.

NOTES TO CHAPTER 2

1. They are printed in L. F. Salzman, *Building in England down to 1540*, 1952, pp. 574 and 582.

2. There are three other claimants to the design. Richard Pallady was described as 'clerk of the works' to the Protector, when, with Somerset and others, he was sent to the Tower in 1549. He seems to have been of similar rank to Thynne, but there is no mention of his possessing artistic interests and his clerkship may have been purely administrative. Inevit-

ably, John of Padua (p. 6) has been mentioned as the architect of Somerset House, but the whole character of the design makes the employment of an Italian improbable. Lastly, Robert Lawes is mentioned in Wheatley and Cunningham, *London Past and Present*, III, 269, as Clerk of the Works. In Add. MS. 5755, f. 272, however, his position is clarified as household servant and store-keeper.

3. Sir Thomas Smyth (1513–77) may have been

an influence of considerable importance. He was Secretary of State in 1548 and went on several missions abroad during Somerset's Protectorate. He lived quietly during Mary's reign, building himself a house at Ankerwyke, near Eton, of which we know nothing. Under Elizabeth, he was ambassador in Paris, 1562–6, and built, from about 1564, Hill Hall, Essex. The house has been much altered, but it seems always to have had the giant Doric order which is its principal feature. A catalogue of Smyth's library in 1566 gives six editions of Vitruvius, and in 1568 Cecil was writing to Paris for a book on architecture which he had seen 'at Sir Thomas Smith's'. In his will Smyth makes it clear that he prepared the 'platt and deseigne' of Hill Hall himself, though with the advice of a London carpenter, Richard Kirby (d. 1600), whom he designates 'cheife architect overseer and master of my workes'.

4. Particularly striking are certain idiosyncrasies in the Ionic order found also at the church of Marines (Seine-et-Oise). Hautecœur, *L'Arch. classique en France*, 1943, i, p. 452.

CHAPTER 3

ELIZABETHAN ARCHITECTURE: INFLUENCES
AND METHODS

THERE is no 'Elizabethan Style'. Elizabethan architecture consists of the Tudor-Gothic tradition, ever more and more diluted and, in proportion to its weaknesses, capable of being made the medium of new arrangements of plan and new arrangements of detail – new detail. These new arrangements are crystallized first in a certain number of great Elizabethan houses, each of which is unique, a prodigy, an attempt to make and display, at one blow, a completely integrated style. It is true that certain characteristics, here and there, are shared by these houses and that such characteristics became the common property of English building; but that happened only at the end of the reign, so that it led to a vernacular manner which may more properly be called Jacobean than Elizabethan.

In building their great houses, the Elizabethans had an objective of innocent simplicity. It was, in a word, splendour. They had no outside criteria of excellence; there was no foreign manner which they envied and sought to emulate. For, although foreign fashions in ornament, and sometimes in plan, were excitedly adopted, they were adopted for the intrinsic pleasure they gave rather than from any sense of apprenticeship to foreign achievements greater than their own. If Ancient Rome and modern Italy received their homage, it was homage to a legend. Nor did they believe that they fell much short of this legend themselves. Thus, as early as 1577, Harrison[1] wrote: 'If ever curious building did flourish in England, it is in these our years wherein our workmen excel and are in manner comparable in skill with old Vitruvius and Serlo'. Longleat, Kirby, and Holdenby were then very new and seemed final and perfect of their kind. As indeed, in a sense, they were; for it is only by insisting falsely on the importance of accurate grammatical interpretation of classical elements that we are tempted to see them as groping preliminaries to the Italian classicism of Inigo Jones. We should not see them so. Their virtues emerge through their freedom – their original strokes of massing, recession, and silhouette. Their rather intemperate and careless use of classical detail is not always of primary relevance, and, although it is essential to follow this thread very closely because of its ultimate importance, we must see it, to begin with, as what it was – simply a decorative fashion which gave immediate pleasure.

The New Fashion

Classical architecture made its way in England not as a method of building but as a mode of decorative design. Although this mode of design was largely an affair of columns and entablatures, pediments and consoles and the enrichments commonly applicable to these things, it circulated independently of such concrete propositions. It had as great an appeal to the engraver, the jeweller, the worker in plaster or glass as it had to the mason. A pair of columns carrying entablature and pediment was a pretty conception for a porch; but it was likewise a pretty conception for an engraved title-page; and the engraver suffered far fewer restrictions in elaborating the theme. The 'new fashion' (as John Shute called it in the 1560s) was a form of applied design and was picked up by every sort of designer. In building it was still, precisely, a form of applied decoration: it was applied to the old stock of building tradition. Only to a limited extent did it get into the bones of that tradition and affect its gait and movement.

The 'new fashion' in design, acknowledged and cultivated rather sparsely under Mary and Edward VI, came flooding into England under Elizabeth. In the fifteen-sixties the English upper classes discovered Europe; and, conversely, Europe discovered the English. On the one hand, noblemen's sons passed regularly from Cambridge to France and Italy, bringing back every novelty of dress, manner, and speech which they could attach to their minds, their persons, or their baggage. On the other hand, adventuring foreigners crossed the Channel to hawk their wares or their skill in and around the Court of Elizabeth. The influx was a matter of remark at the time as much as it is in the perspective of history. The Italianate or Francophil Englishman was a stock figure in the theatre; his vices were the moralist's target. The old conventions of dress collapsed into a wonderful chaos of personal interpretation, with ruffs, steeple-crowned hats, battlemented hats, and every variety of doublet and hose competing in a bazaar of exotic novelty. The 'new fashion' in architecture was but one of many new fashions; and when John Shute published the first English engravings of the orders in 1563 he was feeding the same stream which brought us coaches and starch in 1564 and tobacco in 1565.

What Englishmen got from Italy and France was, in literature and the arts, considerable; but in the visual arts it was nothing compared with what flowed in upon them, uninvited, from the Low Countries and especially from Antwerp. Antwerp in 1560 was the supreme international commercial exchange of Europe and a cultural exchange of no less importance. Antwerp exported art. She had exported art for a hundred years and now continued to do so in great volume, although it was no longer altar-pieces and retables but books and engravings. These were manufactured in quantities and circulated all over northern Europe. Whereas the art of Italians and Frenchmen had to be fetched, the art of Antwerp flowed in of its own accord. And after the Duke of Alva's persecutions from 1566 onwards, protestant Flemings came in person bringing their arts and trades with them.

So, wherever we look in Elizabethan England, we may expect to find the influence of Flanders and especially of those Flemish illustrators who, for some eighty years from 1560, maintained a flow of miscellaneous material which found its way easily enough across the Channel. This material included Bible illustrations, illustrated books on topography and travel, records of pageants, books of decorative borders and cartouches and patterns for the carver, the joiner, the jeweller, and the architect. The name of one publisher in particular is important – Hieronymus Cock (1510–70); he employed Italians, Flemings, and Germans in his firm, and their interpretations of classical design exercised far more influence in England than anything coming directly from the Mediterranean.

The Antwerp school of design was, in relation to Italy, provincial and excessively mannered. The engravers worked in the tradition of Dürer, in a coarsened version of his style. Their conception of Italian design derived not from the High Renaissance of Raphael and Bramante but from Michelangelo and his successors, from the Mannerist designers of the first half of the sixteenth century, with their elaborate rhythms and perverse combinations of antique forms. This difficult and complex style the Flemings worked on in the light of their own northern Gothic experience, often seizing on minor details and giving them an affected and illogical importance.

Thus, from Antwerp came that strange decorative system, so important in Elizabethan architecture, which we call *strap-work*. The original hints for this system came from the shields, scrolls, and cartouches in early *cinquecento* decoration, while its development under Rosso at Fontainebleau, in particular, soon penetrated into Flanders. In the hands of the Flemish engravers, the idea of an architecture cut, as it were, out of parchment or leather, a light-as-air architecture writhing and curvetting in space, became something too delightful to be lost sight of for a moment. The architects took up the theme with enthusiasm, using it first in interiors or in festive buildings of a temporary kind, and then in brick and stone.

Besides strap-work, the Italian *grottesche* exercised an enormous appeal. These were the decorative fantasies which had been recaptured from ancient Roman house, tomb, and theatre decoration and used, pre-eminently, by Raphael in his decoration of the Vatican loggias. Grotesques of this kind were arranged in panels, often combined with strap-work cartouches and published as *compartimenta* for the use of decorative artists.

Strap-work and *compartimenta* proved at least as exciting to English taste as the five orders themselves. They seemed the very richest fruits of antiquity; for it had not yet occurred to the English mind to look for the original stem and the roots of the antique tree. Not yet did Englishmen begin to feel the fascination of re-discovering Rome; they were happy to receive, on trust, a 'new fashion' which they were able to believe belonged somehow to the world of Julius Caesar and Augustus, of Seneca, Virgil, and Pliny.

Behind the flummery of strap-work and grotesques there was, however, a rather more substantial influence. It was that of the north Italian architect Sebastiano Serlio (1475–1552) who, posthumously and at long range, influenced English architecture more than any other single man. Serlio, the professional legatee of Baldassare Peruzzi, spent a great part of his working life in compiling a treatise on architecture. The first two books (actually Books 4 and 3 in the complete works) were published in Venice in 1537 and 1540. In 1541 Serlio went to the French Court and there brought out two more books in 1545; a fifth book was added in 1547 and a sixth in 1551. Long after Serlio's death, a seventh volume based on his collected papers was published (1575) in Frankfort.

From the English point of view, the most important edition is probably the Venetian quarto of 1566, containing Books 1-6, but the Frankfort edition of 1575, with the posthumous material, also had its effect, as we shall see. But, quite apart from the direct influence of the work on major English buildings such as Longleat, Wollaton, and Hardwick, Serlio came to England in the works of others – notably in John Shute's book and in all the Flemish books which deal with the orders. Shute's book, *The First and Chief Groundes of Architecture*, came out in the year of its author's death, 1563. It is a thin folio, dedicated to the Queen, containing a general essay on architecture, and descriptions, with copper-plate engravings, of the five orders (Plate 12). Shute, as we have seen (p. 19), was in the service of the Duke of Northumberland who, in 1550, sent him to Italy. He describes himself as 'painter and architecte', was probably a member of the Painter Stainers' Company, and is known to have done miniatures. His engravings are very competent but his treatment of his subject is remarkable chiefly in that it shows not the slightest evidence of first-hand experience of Italy. Serlio, obviously, is his prime authority, and he has used Vitruvius and also Philander's commentary on that author. To consult these sources it was hardly necessary to go to Rome; Shute's book is essentially a home-made product.

Later editions of Shute are recorded as having appeared in 1579, 1584, and 1587, so he must have been widely used, but apart from a curious instance at Kirby (see p. 38), it is difficult to prove a connexion between Shute's book and contemporary buildings, since one can hardly differentiate between a free treatment of the Serlian orders and a free treatment of those of Shute. And Elizabethan treatments of the orders were mostly free.

Even greater in repute than Serlio was Vitruvius, the first-century Roman writer, editions of whose work in Latin, Italian, and French were available by the end of Henry VIII's reign.[2] But he was less immediately useful than certain books imported from Switzerland, Germany, and Flanders. Hans Blume's *Quinque Columnarum*, etc., first published in Zürich in 1550, was in use in England certainly by 1570. J. Vredeman de Vries's *Architectura* appeared in Antwerp first in 1563, and his *Compartimenta* in 1566. De Vries's lavish use of strap-work (Plate 13) was influential, though cases of direct derivation from the plates are rare. Much later came Wendel Dietterlin's book on the orders (1593) and his sensational *Architectura* (Nuremberg, 1594–8), a collection of extravaganzas of the most sinister character. Dietterlin's name became famous in England (as 'Ditterling'), but only one case of direct imitation – a pilaster at Charlton, Kent – is at present recorded.

This does not by any means exhaust the list of architectural books available to Englishmen at the time. Alberti was certainly known, probably in the French editions of 1512 and 1553; the treatises of Labacco (1552), Cataneo (1554), Vignola (1563), and Palladio (1570) may have found their way to England from time to time, though we do not hear of them, while Lomazzo's treatise (1584) was translated into English by Haydocke in 1598. Among French books, du Cerceau's *Architectura* (1559) and *Les Plus Excellents Bâtiments* (1576) and Philibert de l'Orme's *Nouvelles Inventions* (1561) and *Le Premier Tome d'architecture* (1568) were known and used; indeed, Lord Burghley sent to Paris for the *Nouvelles Inventions* when he was engaged on the last lap of Burghley House.

But whatever use may have been made of all these, Serlio was unquestionably the most widely recognized authority. For decorative inspiration, however, designers turned to the products of the Flemish and German printing-presses rather than to evidence from Italy or France.

Designers and Craftsmen

Ever since any considerable curiosity has existed about Elizabethan architecture, the question has been asked: who were the Elizabethan *architects*? It is an unreal question and has no answer, for to introduce the word 'architect' with all its later associations into the Elizabethan picture is to confuse the issue hopelessly. Nothing remotely like an 'architectural profession' existed. The word was rarely used in the sixteenth century and its connotation was in every sense ornamental. Shute described himself as an architect in 1563, though he was a painter-stainer by calling and may have built little or nothing. The title seems to have been adopted by or applied to craftsmen who knew how to handle the new architectural grammar in any material. The truth is, of course, that the craft of building was still conducted almost exactly as it had been for hundreds of years: that is to say, by master workmen who were apprenticed and trained in the quarry or the workshop. The central character in a building undertaking was usually the 'principal freemason'. His status was that of an artisan; his responsibility for the design of a building varied with the extent to which his employer thought fit to interfere. He might himself produce a 'platt' and 'uprights' and then proceed directly to execute them. Or he might be merely the agent of an employer who wished to mould his house to his own conception, using the mason as his executive. Or, again, there might be a third party, in the shape of an agent or surveyor, who settled matters of design in whole or in part.

We cannot, with absolute precision, say who designed any Elizabethan building, even the great and memorable masterpieces of the age, and to indulge in 'attributions' is to take more for granted than we ought. The plan of a house may have been conceived by one mind, its architectural treatment by another, and either of those minds, or some other, may have modified the original intentions while the building was going up. This fluidity is often apparent in Elizabethan architecture and sometimes results in those unexpected and original combinations in which much of its attraction lies.

There were, of course, eminent personalities in the building world. The obvious place to look for them is among the officers in the Queen's Works – the Surveyor, Comptroller, Master Mason, and Clerks especially. That the names of these men are not well known during the Elizabethan period is due partly to the fact that Elizabeth herself built so little, but partly also to simple lack of documentation. There is no doubt that many of them were distinguished and very able men and, moreover, were extensively engaged by private builders. The Surveyor appointed shortly after the Queen's accession was John Revell, but he was succeeded in 1563 by Lewis Stocket (d. 1578), who was responsible for a new Custom House and Exchequer buildings. Thomas Graves, who followed him, designed the first Banqueting House in Whitehall (1581–2), a building of timber with canvas walls, painted 'with a worke called rustike, much like to stone', a quaint anticipation of Inigo Jones's rusticated building on the same site. Thomas Blagrave succeeded Graves in 1587 and was, in 1594, followed by Robert Adams (d. 1595), whose main interest seems to have been fortification and some of whose beautiful drawings, entrusted to Lord Burghley after Adams' death, are at Hatfield. Adams was succeeded by William Spicer, probably the same Spicer, a mason from Nunney, who had worked for Sir John Thynne at Longleat in 1559 (see p. 18); his term of office lasted till the end of the reign, and he must have been a very old man when James I brought his own Master of the Works from Scotland and caused him to share Spicer's office till the latter's death. This Scottish intruder, Sir David Conyngham, we shall meet again. His Surveyorship was very brief. He was succeeded by Simon Basil who, dying in 1615, gave place to Inigo Jones.

It happens that, although the Surveyors were the leading people in the building world of Elizabeth's time, we know more about some of their junior officers. The name of Robert Stickelles (d. 1620), for instance, has various associations. He was one of the Clerks, but aspired to the Surveyorship at one time and wrote to Sir Robert Cecil inviting him to put him to the test 'in the mathematical sciences, or in the rules of architecture, of shipbuilding, or of fortifying, house-building or any such ingenious causes'. He designed, among other things, a demountable pinnace. We know from his will that he was a free-mason and possessed both 'books and working tools', and in the British Museum there is a slight memorandum on architecture from his hand.

Another Clerk was John Symandes (d. 1597), a pupil of Lewis Stocket. He was a joiner by trade but left, in his will, 'tools for working in free-stone and hard-stone', as well as instruments for measuring land and a really princely wardrobe. He was a fine draughtsman. At Hatfield there are designs by him for a small gateway and for remodelling Beaufort House, Chelsea.

But the most famous name among the officers of the works, in Elizabeth's reign, is undoubtedly that of John Thorpe (c. 1563–1655). It is famous solely because of the accident that a book of drawings by him, probably the most important document relating to Elizabethan architecture which we possess, survives at the Soane Museum in London. The book has made Thorpe famous, and a misunderstanding of its precise nature has made him into an impossible and totally unhistoric character, a leading 'architect' of this period. The facts are that Thorpe was the son of a Northamptonshire mason and entered the Office of Works, at an early age, about 1583. He was employed there for some eighteen years, was disappointed in his hope of promotion, and became a successful land-surveyor, a colleague of John Norden, with whom he was associated in the survey of Crown properties.

Thorpe's book is a record book in which we find drawings of well-known houses of his time and earlier, as well as a number of plans (Plate 30B, for example) evidently prepared by Thorpe himself for a variety of people, mostly small officials of James I's Court. Thorpe was, indeed, an architect in the sense that he made 'platts' (and sometimes, but rarely, 'uprights') for people who required his services. But this does not mean that he 'designed' the houses. The preparation of a 'platt' for a fee was a common practice among surveyors of the time and did not necessarily involve any further connexion with the building.

Notwithstanding innumerable printed assertions that Thorpe was the 'architect' of Longleat, Kirby, Wollaton, Audley End, and nearly every other great Elizabethan and Jacobean house, it is certain that he had nothing to do with most of these buildings. He was not a dominating figure; a less skilful draughtsman than, say, Adams or Symandes, he was typical, no doubt, of the Works officials and Surveyors of his time. His book is an immensely valuable document, but unique rather in its survival than in its nature, and perhaps a specimen of the sort of compilation which Surveyors made for their personal use and that of their successors. The rather later Smythson collection of drawings at the

Royal Institute of British Architects, which has features in common with that of Thorpe, and specimens of which are given on plates 17B, 34B, and 37B, tends to support this view.

Of Elizabethan drawings in general something must be said. The accurate scale plan (or 'platt') was in common use and hardly different from the plans of succeeding centuries up to our own. Elevations, however (or 'uprights'), were generally less accurate, the relation between main proportions and details being freely distorted. A conventional perspective element was frequently introduced, such as we find in medieval drawings going back to the thirteenth century. Clearly, the working out of a building depended largely on the mason's (or carpenter's) pre-vision and experience and the 'traceries' done on the site rather than on any documentary formulations.

A Documented Case

As a conclusion to this chapter we may usefully examine one of the few really well documented cases of the building of an Elizabethan house – not a house of special import-ance, but one which on that account may be taken as fairly typical of its time. That it no longer stands is unfortunate, and we are cheated of the pleasure of correlating the docu-ments with their subject. But, even so, the history of Kyre Park, Worcestershire, is of great illustrative value.

Sir Edward Pytts bought the manor and castle of Kyre in 1586, when he was forty-five. He immediately set about acquiring stone and brick for the building of a house, raising some of the stone in his own park with his own labour and a hired quarryman, but more from quarries in Shropshire, Gloucestershire, and near Bath, some of this stone being carried part of the way by water. In 1588 he began to keep a book in which he wrote up a record of his building works and the money spent. It was the year of the Armada, a fact which he notes at the beginning. In that year also he obtained his first plan, from John Symons (or Symandes, see p. 27) of London, to whom he paid 40s and, later on, £3 for a new plan, 'according to my newe purpose'. His chief mason at this time was John Chaunce, from Bromsgrove, who, with his workmen, had 7d a day each and boarded themselves.[3]

By 1592, the house was sufficiently advanced for chimney-pieces to be considered and Pytts bargained with 'Garrett Hollyman' (i.e. Gerard Holleman, who will have been one of the family of Flemish carvers of that name, who did many monuments in England) to make two chimney-pieces, 'the carving thereof being the storeyes of Susanna and Mars and Venus'. The Mars and Venus chimney-piece cost £15.

The timber for Kyre came from Dudley Park, but was sawn at Kyre. Thatched 'hovels' were erected for the masons to work in. By 1595 part of the house was complete and Pytts was thinking out 'titles' or texts with which to adorn it.

A second stage in the building operations at Kyre came sixteen years later, when Pytts had evidently determined to extend and complete his house. In 1611 he brought John Bentley, one of the freemasons working on Sir Thomas Bodley's buildings at Oxford (see p. 109) down to Kyre, 'to drawe me a newe platte'. Similarly, he brought 'S'gianson of Coventry' for the same purpose, 'though he did nothing'. Finally, he called a conference with his old mason, Chaunce, and three quarrymen, and engaged Chaunce as 'my cheiff mason, workman and survey'r of the work'. Chaunce was to have full board and lodging and £10 a year till the work was completed.

Even then, Pytts had not quite finished with professional advice, for in 1613 he paid 'Stickles of London' (see p. 27) a fee for 'drawing the platt of my house anewe'. This, however, may have been the London house for which he had previously paid 'Carter[4] of Giles Lane' 40s, 'for drawing the upright'. In any case, at Pytts's death in 1617, Kyre Park was left in the hands of John Chaunce, and £2000 of the estate was ear-marked for the finishing of it, 'according to the platte remayning in Chaunce's handes drawn by my dictation'. Pytts's will contains a memorandum that 'the said John Chaunce hath in his keeping one booke of Architecture of myne wch he hath promised to deliver unto me'.

As Kyre Park was wholly rebuilt in the eighteenth century, we cannot pursue Pytts's preparations to their solid outcome. But the record gives a vivid picture of an Elizabethan building adventure. Especially noteworthy is the fluidity of the proceedings. Materials are got together before a plan has been determined, and the plan is bought from a surveyor in London who is not called upon for any supervision or even to inspect the site. Fireplaces are obtained from foreign craftsmen when they are wanted. The real ruler of the building is the owner himself, who, in the last stages, made his chief workman his surveyor and lent him a book (Serlio, Shute, or de Vries, no doubt) to guide him in matters of decorative detail.

One effect of such a picture as that given by the Kyre records is to underline the impossibility of attributing any house of the period to any one person. These houses grew under the free dictation of their builders, suggestions and decisions coming from various quarters at various times. All the evidence we have points to the circumstances described at Kyre as being thoroughly typical, and it will be useful to bear them in mind when we come to examine, as we shall in the next chapter, the greater Elizabethan houses.

NOTES TO CHAPTER 3

1. William Harrison (1534–93), whose *Description of England* first appeared in that year. In the 1584–7 edition he added the name of Alberti.

2. Vitruvius was first printed in Rome, without illustrations, about 1486. The first illustrated edition was published at Venice in 1511, edited by Fra Giocondo. Both these editions were in Latin. Then, in 1521, came the Como edition, edited by Cesare Cesariano, with entirely new illustrations, and text in Italian. These two editions of 1511 and 1521, with their highly imaginative 'restorations' of buildings described by Vitruvius, supplied the material for

many others in several languages. Philander's edition of 1545 (dedicated to François I), with few but fine engravings, was much quoted, but all previous editions were eclipsed by that of Daniele Barbaro, Venice, 1556, whose engravings were, for the first time, both artistic and scholarly.

3. This compares unfavourably with the wages paid by the Queen's Works, where masons and carpenters received 12d a day, and labourers 8d.

4. Possibly Francis Carter (see p. 95 n.), father of Edward Carter, who worked under Inigo Jones.

CHAPTER 4

THE PRODIGY HOUSES OF QUEEN ELIZABETH'S REIGN

SUPREME among the buildings of Queen Elizabeth's reign are the great houses built by the ministers and courtiers, the civil and political servants who surrounded her. Elizabeth herself built nothing of great importance. Her improvements at Windsor and the few official buildings executed in her time, were inconsiderable in extent and in quality compared with such adventures as Longleat or Kirby or Wollaton – the adventures of private gentlemen living remote from the Court. To call Elizabethan architecture a Court art would be misleading; and yet no architectural effort has ever originated more decidedly in the prestige and personal influence of a sovereign. Much of Elizabethan architecture is the expression – conscious and deliberate – of a cult of sovereignty. Most of the greatest houses – Burghley, Theobalds, Holdenby, and many more – were built or enlarged specifically as places in which to receive the Queen, as tributes and as monuments of loyalty.

This cult of sovereignty was something very real to the Elizabethans, and it provided an opportunity and a text for less conscious or, at least, less easily specifiable desires. Under Elizabeth the country had found stability after four decades of continual turmoil. A generation grew up which did not remember the dissolution and hardly remembered the Protectorate. At the level of the nobility this generation found its honours mature and stable; most of the Earls and Barons were the second, third, or fourth in their successions. Confident and secure, the ambition they inherited from their lawyer and merchant ancestors sought outlets of a more fantastic and brilliant kind than the collection of land or the attainment of office.

And building was one of these outlets – building for the Queen, building in rivalry with others, building to the limit of their resources and beyond. It took about six years for the Elizabethan age to become really Elizabethan – for the Queen's Court to take on the romantic colour it did, to become the centre of the cult, the precinct of Oriana. By about 1564 the scene was complete, and in that year the Royal Progresses, which roused so much ambition to build and excitement in building among those who were qualified, by rank and wealth, to entertain the Queen, took on their almost fabulous character. A Royal Progress took place every summer, but some Progresses were more extensive and more splendid than others. The whole Court and its equipment would descend on the selected lords and gentlemen of the counties to be visited; and the Queen certainly did not expect that expense would be spared in receiving and entertaining her. It was not; and the mere anticipation of a visit to some remote part of England would set masons and carpenters feverishly working on a new or extended house which should not only be fit for the occasion but an imperishable memorial of it. It is not for nothing that guide-books still record among the scanty facts relating to a country-house that 'Queen Elizabeth slept here'.

Like so much great architecture, these country-houses were what an economist[1] has grossly called 'conspicuous waste'. Both Burghley and Hatton confessed to having spent more than even they could afford on houses which they did not need. Hatton paid but the most hasty visits to the vast fabric of Holdenby and yet did not hesitate to buy and complete the neighbouring Kirby when its owner and builder died. Sir Francis Willoughby built Wollaton purely and simply as an extravaganza. And country gentlemen, of little account outside their own counties, copied the spirit of their betters and built as arrogantly as they could.

If we look at the list of Elizabeth's ministers of State and Court officials we shall find the names of most of the great builders of the time. But to these we shall need to add the names of the high sheriffs of the counties and of a few men whose fortunes alone made them liable to the tax and privilege of a royal visit.

There was a great difference between a house designed simply as a family seat and one designed for the reception of the Court. The difference lay chiefly in the number of 'lodgings' required in a house of the latter kind – a 'lodging' being a suite of two or three rooms suitable for the residence of a person of quality. These 'lodgings' dictated, for a time, the continuation of the old courtyard plan, the two long sides of the courtyard being devoted to accommodation of this kind, while the side opposite the entrance comprised the hall and kitchens, with those ancillary rooms which had now become essential to any considerable house – the summer and winter parlours and perhaps, in addition, a withdrawing room. Upstairs a 'long gallery', stretching perhaps over a range of 'lodgings' and a 'great chamber' where the Queen herself would sleep and hold her Court, were essential. But all this accommodation could be, and eventually was, built into loftier and more compact forms than the old courtyard shape and in this, as we shall see, Elizabethan planners showed some ingenuity.

It is not easy to group the greater Elizabethan houses in an orderly and significant way, and any grouping is bound to ignore some cross-current or other which suggests another arrangement. But the following grouping is useful for the purpose of exposition:

i. Sir John Thynne's final rebuilding of Longleat; the work at Wardour Castle; Wollaton; Worksop; Hardwick. With all these, the name of Robert Smythson is associated.

ii. Kirby Hall; Holdenby; the final Burghley. A famous Northamptonshire group, sharing certain French influences.

iii. Wimbledon; Montacute; and some other houses on the H-plan, native in conception and exhibiting many features which became common in the subsequent reign.

Longleat, Wollaton, Worksop

Longleat, Wilts. (Plates 14 and 15; Figure 3), is the first great monument of Elizabethan architecture and perhaps, indeed, the greatest. As we have seen, Sir John Thynne had been an active builder, both for himself and others, during the Protectorate. The Longleat which developed from 1554 was certainly very advanced in style, but it was burnt when barely complete in 1567. In 1568 a new 'model' was prepared, so that the final structure must represent something more than a mere restoration of the damaged house. It was being slated in 1573 and Queen Elizabeth stayed there in 1575. It seems probable that the top storey was not added until after Thynne's death in 1580.

Thus, the Longleat we know to-day is the creation of a considerable period – perhaps as long as thirty years – and we cannot put a finger on the precise date at which the final

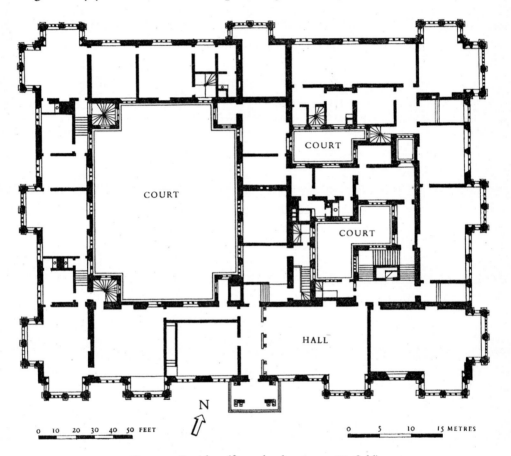

COURT

COURT

COURT

HALL

N

0 10 20 30 40 50 FEET

0   5   10   15 METRES

Figure 3. Longleat (from the drawing at Hatfield)

conception emerged. This long period of effort and revision may, indeed, account for the wonderful originality of Longleat. For it is not a French house or a Flemish house, any more than it is a traditionally English house. It stands alone in the European architecture of its time.

The first things to be observed about Longleat are its absolute symmetry on both axes and its complete extraversion. It is, without compromise, an *outward-looking* house. All chimney-stacks and staircase-towers rise from the two inner courts (where much of the older house is incorporated), so that the exterior presents a four-sided palace, nearly all window, glittering and resplendent.[2] It is true that a few French houses had sought and achieved this effect. The Château de Madrid, for instance, in progress throughout the middle decades of the century, had both the symmetry and the extraversion of Longleat; and St Germain-en-Laye (c. 1540) has the internal staircase-towers with domical summits. But Longleat is very far, in style, from either of these. It is really an inside-out version of the traditional English courtyard-house, organized symmetrically and handled in the light of what its builder had learned in the creation of old Somerset House.

Somerset House, indeed, is the immediate source for one of the main features of Long-leat – the bay-window unit. And here, as in the London building, these units *avoid the corners*, thus following English bay-window practice instead of capitulating to the French pavilion plan. The design of these units follows closely those of Somerset House and would confirm the suspicion that Thynne was the prime source of design in both cases, even if his active participation were not an established tradition and the subject of some lampooning during his lifetime.

Longleat surpasses Somerset House in coherence of design, just as it surpasses most later Elizabethan architecture in restraint and refinement of detail. It represents, indeed, as no other building does, the momentary 'High Renaissance' of our architecture.

If Thynne was, as we have supposed, the effective master of his own building works, he employed, for the last rebuilding, a mason of altogether exceptional parts. In the same year that the final 'model' was prepared, he procured, on the recommendation of the Queen's Master Mason, a certain Robert Smythson (? 1536–1614) to be his principal freemason. This man, who was to prove one of the great geniuses of English architecture, was then thirty-three and had been working for the Vice-Chamberlain, Sir Francis Knollys, probably at the (lost) house of Caversham, near Reading. How much he knew of the new style when he came to Thynne is doubtful, for all his later work grows, in one way or another, out of Longleat.

When Thynne died, in 1580, Robert Smythson seems already to have left Longleat for other sites. In 1578 Thynne's neighbour, Sir Matthew Arundell, refitted his old fortress-dwelling at Wardour, introducing a Serlian rusticated archway and some other openings in a style unmistakably associated with Longleat and therefore with Smythson, but still more obviously associated with Wollaton, the house which Arundell's brother-in-law started to build in Nottinghamshire in 1580.

Wollaton Hall, Notts. (Plate 16; Figure 4), was Smythson's next task. His new master, Sir Francis Willoughby, Sheriff of Nottinghamshire, had entertained the Queen in his old house but now, in anticipation of further visits, set about building, on a prominent site, a unique and exceedingly pretentious palace. This building is Robert Smythson's chief work. He settled in the district, acquired property and the style of 'gentleman' and, dying in 1614, was buried in Wollaton Church. His epitaph records that he was 'Archi-tecter and Survayor unto the most worthy house of Wollaton with divers others of great account'; so here we have as precise evidence concerning the authorship of a design as we can hope for – a case almost unique in Elizabethan architecture.

Like Longleat, Wollaton is 'outward-looking' – indeed extravagantly so, for there is no courtyard at all. The plan is, for England, revolutionary, and scarcely a vestige of tradition survives in it. It is nearly square, and symmetrical on both axes, making a pattern which may have been used before in pavilions and banqueting houses but had never been made the starting-point of a fabric of this scale. Where this pattern comes from is, on this occasion, pretty clear. Serlio, in his third book, describes the Poggio Reale built for King Alfonso V at Naples in the middle of the fifteenth century, and then gives a design of his own comprising the same elements, namely, a rectangle, with four squares attached to its corners. At the centre of the design is a great square, windowless hall. Now these are precisely the elements we find at Wollaton, but the planner has enlarged the design verti-cally and horizontally. To cover more ground he has made a second square grow out of the first at each corner; and to light the windowless hall he has thrust this feature upwards

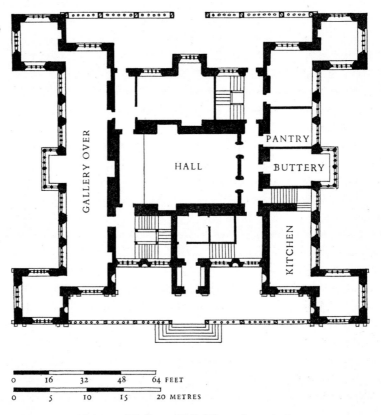

Figure 4. Wollaton Hall (Thorpe's version)

to allow for a clerestory; finally he has surmounted the whole with a 'great chamber' with turrets at the angles. The derivation from Serlio is obvious, but it is confirmed by the Serlian handling of the orders and by the introduction of a fireplace in the hall taken almost line for line from Serlio's fourth book.

Serlio, however, is not the only bookish influence at Wollaton. De Vries is strongly in evidence. The general treatment of the exterior, with the banded shafts (a feature already used at Wardour), the strap-work gables, the cartouches, the quasi-Gothic windows of the central block, and various whimsical additions to the pilasters and en-tablatures all derive directly from plates in the publications of de Vries. In short, Wollaton is a pastiche – a fitting together of ideas and features from several sources. The Serlian plan rises into a sort of fantastic castle, something Arthurian or like the symbolic castles of Spenser or the pasteboard castles which were besieged and captured, with their fair garrisons, at Court junketings. It is immensely to Smythson's credit that he was able to marshal all these themes into a design which, if a trifle top-heavy, does contain, as Hawksmore observed[3] in 1731, 'some true stroaks of architecture'.

Wollaton is unique not only in design but in the marvellous quality of its execution. So accomplished is this that it seems to endorse the traditional employment of foreigners (the tradition, inevitably, says 'Italians'); and although no foreign names occur in the building accounts[4] they leave us to guess how Smythson expended the fairly large sums entrusted to him for 'task-work', under which head it would be normal for the carving to be included.

Wollaton was finished in 1588, and thereafter we hear nothing of Robert Smythson, until we read his epitaph. However, there is convincing evidence, among the Smythson drawings at the Royal Institute of British Architects, that he was concerned with at least two more very large houses, and some lesser ones. One of these, Worksop Manor, was built for George Talbot, 6th Earl of Shrewsbury, and another, Hardwick Hall, for his widow who, indeed, was probably the prime mover in both cases. 'Bess of Hardwick's' passion for building is one of the curiosities of Midland history.

The exact date of Worksop Manor, Notts. (Plate 17A), is uncertain, but it must be between the Earl's marriage in 1568 and his death in 1590. It was burnt in 1761, and nothing of it remains.

Worksop may have been based on an existing but unfinished manor-house of the Talbots, and its plan was not quite so regular as Buck's view would have us believe. Nevertheless, the general bulk and pattern of it was dramatic; and owed, very evidently, much to Longleat. Roughly, it was as if Longleat had been compressed into one of its shorter sides and then built upwards half as high again. There were four narrow towers at the centres of the four elevations – none of them, rather strangely, being staircase-towers. Each was capped by a domed lantern. No orders seem to have been applied to the exterior, but the duality of the Longleat window-unit was retained.

The resulting plan is a long oblong with excrescences at the ends, at the centres of the sides and, of course, where the four wings project. It is quite different from either the whole or any part of Longleat or from Wollaton, and altogether a very surprising creation. Unlike Wollaton there is no obvious Serlian derivation, though there is a plan in the seventh book which may conceivably have suggested this shape. There is no question at all that Smythson was capable of very free design.[5]

The transition from Worksop to Hardwick Hall, Derbyshire (Plate 19B; Figure 5), built between 1590 and 1597, is simple, the general conception being very close. If the upper storey of Worksop is cut away, leaving only the projecting units rising above the parapet as towers, making the end towers conformable to them, and eliminating the other two, we have Hardwick precisely. It is a house of great and romantic beauty, such as Worksop must have been, and the emphasis on towers gives it something of the castellar silhouette of Wollaton. In detail Hardwick is, and Worksop may have been, less brilliant than

Wollaton, the carving being of quite a homely Anglo-Flemish kind; clearly, no 'Italians' were employed here.[6] The plan-shapes of the two houses are similar, but only at Hardwick was the hall placed on the axis of the main entrance. That innovation, with the *contraction* of the house into a single pile, of complex silhouette, was Robert Smythson's chief legacy to his successors.

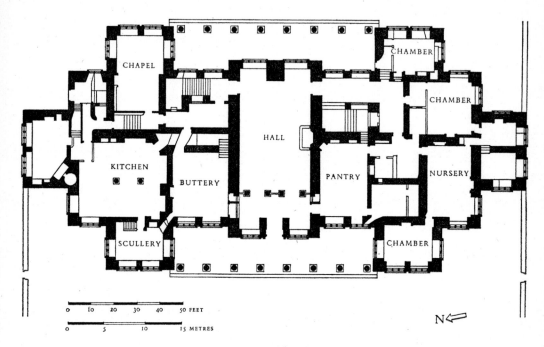

Figure 5. Hardwick Hall

In the Midlands, several important houses can claim relationship with Worksop and Hardwick. Barlborough Hall, Derbyshire (Plate 19A. Dated 1583; for Francis Rodes, Justice of the Common Pleas), and Heath Old Hall, near Wakefield, Yorks. (dated 1584; for John Kaye), are houses of nearly identical form which, while echoing Worksop, forecast the silhouette of Hardwick, so that a connexion with Smythson may be surmised. In Lincolnshire, Doddington Hall (Plate 23A), built by the Bishop of Lincoln's registrar, Thomas Taylor, about 1595, is a close imitation of Worksop and has details recalling Wollaton.

This group of Smythsonian houses, all developing in some way from Longleat and thus ultimately from Somerset House, form a great and splendid branch of the tree of English architecture. But the Elizabethan trunk put forth also some very different boughs.

Kirby, Holdenby, and the Completion of Burghley

Two years after Sir John Thynne had begun his final rebuilding of Longleat, a North-amptonshire knight, Sir Humphrey Stafford of Blatherwycke, began the construction of a most festive and extravagant house at Kirby, Northants (Plates 20A and 21A; Figure 6).

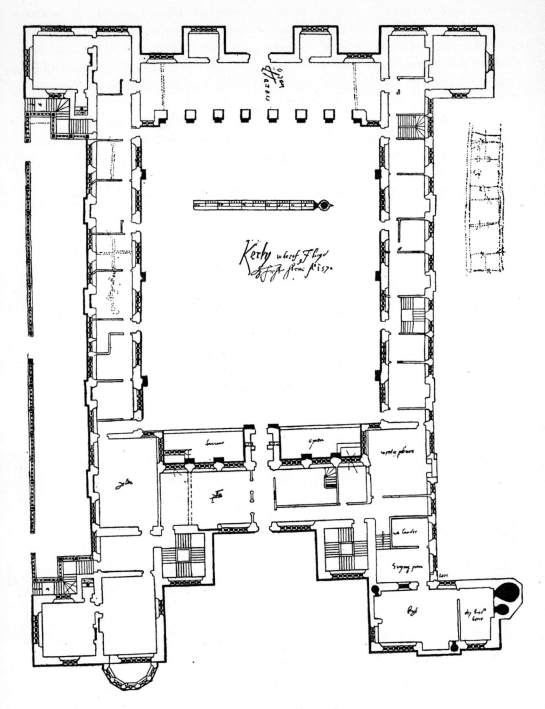

Figure 6. Kirby Hall (from Thorpe)

Kirby is a great curiosity. Thorpe gives a plan which differs considerably from the executed version but bears the inscription, *Kerby whereof I layd y^e first stone A^o 1570*. In that year John Thorpe was about seven, so that if he did lay the first stone (which is possible; there are sixteenth-century instances of children performing this ceremony) it would seem that his father Thomas Thorpe (d. 1596) will have been the principal mason of the building. Now there are earlier buildings in the district – notably the porch at Dingley, dated 1558 – like enough to Kirby to suggest that they are by the elder Thorpe. They are crude mixtures of Tudor and the French fashion and this blend is carried over into Kirby, where, however, there seems to be a new infusion of French influence. The plan of Kirby is the traditional plan brought up to date – a long rectangle with the hall block (on old foundations) at one end and a loggia at the other. Much of the masonry is simple Tudor stuff. In the courtyard, however, are buttress-pilasters of a type common around Paris[7] but unique, so far as we know, in England. There are also various crude quotations from Serlio and one from the Venetian-style title-page of Shute's *Chief Groundes*. The whole is an amazing mixture of sophistication and bucolic ignorance.

Kirby was incomplete at its builder's death in 1575,[8] by which time Holdenby, the enterprise of Sir Christopher Hatton, had been begun in the same county. It was almost totally destroyed in the Commonwealth but Thorpe, whose family was probably concerned in its erection, gives the plan. It had two great courtyards and Hatton told Burghley that it was modelled on Theobalds. It was probably also influenced by Heneage's Copped Hall, having, like that house, a low forebuilding to the entrance front, instead of the traditional gatehouse – an important innovation from France.

Like Copped Hall, Holdenby was both inward-looking and outward-looking, its great boast being the immense, symmetrical south front whose fenestration was all but continuous between the centre and end pavilions. 'As bright as Holdenby' was an expression which could have been coined ten years before the couplet about Hardwick Hall being 'more glass than wall'. Hatton was still building at Holdenby in 1583, the date on the two surviving gateways of the forecourt, bizarre structures which, however, prove to be improvisations on gateways given in Serlio's sixth book.

Hatton hardly used his new house, nor did he build it for use. The spirit in which he did build it is nicely reflected in a letter of Burghley's, written while staying at Holdenby in his host's absence:

SIR, I may not pass out of this good house without thanks on your behalf to God, and on mine to you, nor without memory of her Majesty, to whom it appeareth this goodly perfect ... work is consecrated.

And, after speaking of Theobalds and Holdenby together:

God send us both long to enjoy Her, for whom we both meant to exceed our purses in these.

Sir Thomas Heneage praised Holdenby to the skies, describing it as 'altogether even the best house that hath been built in this age'.

Lord Burghley's letter of thanks and praise to Hatton is dated 1579, a year in which Burghley himself was much occupied with building. For, more than four years previously, he had inaugurated the almost complete reconstruction of the house where he had already done so much. This reconstruction went on for twelve years or more, the last date on the complete Burghley being 1587. Burghley House (Plates 20B and 21B) will not have rivalled Holdenby, for it has but one courtyard and that a narrow one. Burghley tells us that he limited his work to the rebuilding of an existing house on existing foundations.

But if, in general plan, Burghley was not adventurous, its extraversion was as complete (on three sides) as Longleat's and, moreover, it contains some interesting and original features. Thus, in the courtyard are three towers, or pavilions. The two lateral towers are capped with pierced 'attics' exactly similar to those at old Somerset House. The clock tower, in its lower stages, seems to echo Philibert de l'Orme's work at Anet, while the spire, or, as Burghley will have thought of it, the obelisk, which surmounts the clock looks like an imitation of de l'Orme's chapel at the same château (finished in 1549). French influence is certainly paramount in the great stone-vaulted stair at Burghley, which is closely related to the Cathedral vault at Langres (Haute-Marne).

To whom may all this work, so fully informed with French influence, be attributed? There is no document to tell us whom the Lord Treasurer employed as his designer. The natural thing for so exalted a statesman would be to enlist the talent of the Queen's works. We know that he employed Hawthorne, the Surveyor at Windsor, for his new courtyard (1572) at Theobalds, and at Burghley the names of Stocket and Graves and those of their principal craftsmen should be borne in mind, always allowing for the intrusion of continental masons or carvers.

Wimbledon and the H-plan

In the year of the Armada, 1588, Thomas Cecil, Burghley's son, obtained a lease of the manor of Wimbledon and here began to build a house of the first importance. It was pulled down early in the eighteenth century, but is tolerably well recorded. Wimbledon House (Plate 22A; Figure 7) was built on a plan approximately resembling an H and was perhaps the first house of its size to use this plan in the form in which it was to become so general in the next three decades.[9] The H-plan was by this date frequent in the vernacular but here we find it given a monumental aspect, with the extruded corners brought up as handsome towers with pointed roofs. Here is something totally different either from the Smythson series, Theobalds, Copped Hall, or the Northamptonshire group. Very severe in treatment, it relies for its effect on *recession* through a series of planes from the stepped terraces inwards to the courtyard. On the entrance side the recession is quite shallow, so that the extruded corners (window-bays) only just fit in; the main effect is on the steeply sloping hill-side which may, indeed, have prompted the composition. No previous houses had shown quite this flair for recession (though Wollaton approaches it, in a wholly different way). From this time on, however, it was to be developed to a prodigious extent, as we shall see in the next chapter.

Edward Phelips, a successful lawyer, built his house at Montacute, Somerset (Plate 22B), some years later than Wimbledon: it was finished about 1599. It is the most splendid and complete example of its kind remaining to us. The plan is Wimbledon reversed, with the wings curtailed. The superstructure, of three storeys, rises to a balustrade except where

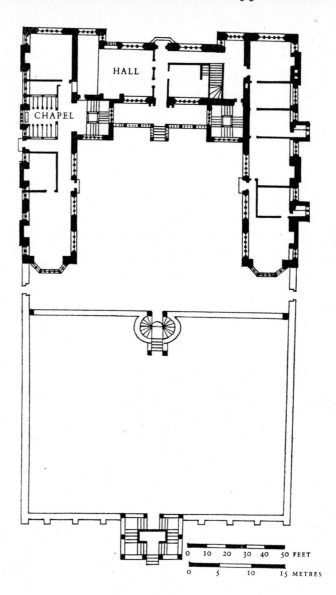

Figure 7. Wimbledon House

curved Flemish gables intervene. The string-courses are diminutive entablatures, but the orders are not expressed, the fenestration is rather casual, and the character of the whole is essentially native: far less advanced in style than Wimbledon or any of the Smythson houses.

In the fifteen-eighties and nineties several great houses followed this same H-plan. Condover Hall (Plate 23B), finished by Judge Thomas Owen in 1598, omits the extruded corners, so that its plan is simply a broad blunt H. It is the work of a local genius among masons, Walter Hancock (d. 1598), whose work may be seen at Shipton Court (*c.* 1589)

40

and Shrewsbury Market Hall (p. 114) in the same county. Hancock used his de Vries but remained solidly native in his compositions, and Condover is crowned by large plain gables: an unusual (though not unique) feature of the house is the introduction, in the centre block, of a low 'mezzanine' over an open loggia, these two features originally providing a closed and open 'long gallery' respectively.

Symbolic Houses

In several of the houses so far mentioned we have noticed a certain element of pure extravagance, bearing no relation whatever to the domestic functions of the building. Wollaton, in particular, is really an inflated bauble, an architectural symbol rather than a house. The craving to objectify some symbolic or genealogical or merely geometrical idea is an essential aspect of the Elizabethan genius and there are analogies in poetry. In architecture it comes out so strongly at times that a certain number of buildings may be grouped in a category of their own as having been built primarily with this end in view.

John Thorpe's book contains several plans of this description, notably a silly plan based on his own initials. Thorpe also gives the plan of Longford Castle, Wilts., a house actually built (1580) in triangular form with three corner towers, following the medieval symbol of the Trinity in which *Pater, Filius,* and *Sanctus Spiritus* (the towers) are joined by repetitions of the word *est* (the three main blocks) and by similar repetitions of *non est* to the central *Deus* (not expressed in the plan, though Thorpe gives marginally the complete symbol). There are two other very curious and complex triangular plans in Thorpe, while in the Hatfield collection is a design for a house on the plan of a Greek cross with very long arms, an exaggeration of a similar plan by Serlio.

Certainly the most interesting case of an Elizabethan builder indulging this passion for architectural symbolism is that of Sir Thomas Tresham (? 1543–1605) of Rushton, Northants. Tresham did not actually build a new house, but altered two old ones and built a market-house and a number of 'lodges' on his property. He was a passionate convert to Catholicism and, on that account, lived a difficult and dangerous life, some of it in captivity. His building exploits seem eccentric, but in the context of the Elizabethan mania they are not quite so eccentric as, *prima facie*, they appear. Tresham only made an cult of what, to others, was an intellectual game.

Tresham's first recorded building adventure, begun when he was about thirty-five, was Rothwell Market House, erected manifestly for the public weal but more truly as an heraldic monument to Tresham and his local contemporaries. It is a wonderfully tasteful two-storey structure on a rectangular plan, rendered cruciform by four projecting arms. There are two orders, in pilaster form, and the upper frieze contains a series of carved shields whose display is, no doubt, the essential purpose of the whole.

The Market House is a secular conceit and its symmetries are those of the banqueting-house type. Tresham's next undertaking, however, sixteen years later, was strictly symbolic. This was the 'garden lodge', usually known as the Lyveden New Bield (Plate 24A), erected from 1594 onwards and surrounded originally by carefully planned gardens. Here the plan is an equal-armed cross with a five-sided window-bay added to each arm.

The symbolic intent of the building is underlined by the presence of roundels containing instruments of the Passion.

In the same year, 1594, Tresham began another structure, the Warrener's Lodge or Triangular Lodge at Rushton. This, one of the most eccentric buildings of the Elizabethan age, is a trinitarian symbol of great complexity. The plan is a triangle and each of the three sides is surmounted by three triangular gables, while from the roof emerges a triangular chimney-shaft. All the windows are trefoils or built-up of trefoils; the door-head is a trefoil and an inscription announces the theme of the whole in the words *tres testimonium dant*. The architectural treatment is nearer to Gothic than one would expect from the builder of the New Bield.[10] There is a classical main cornice, but the crocketed gables and trefoil windows are near to medieval tradition, lending themselves the more readily thereby to the three-fold symbolism required. Eccentric though the Triangular Lodge most certainly is, it accords with the eccentricity of its time and is paralleled, as we have seen, by the trinitarian plan of Longford Castle, built by Sir Thomas Gorges, who was not a Catholic.

The Triangular Lodge was completed in 1596, in which year Tresham began the Hawkfield Lodge. This no longer exists, but there is a contemporary drawing which shows a twelve-sided figure with four projections giving a cruciform character to the whole. The symbolism intended here is unexplained.

Tresham built also at his own house, Rushton Hall, and at Lyveden Old Bield, but here his activities were more conventional, and it is for his symbolic toys that he is chiefly remembered. Of his real interest in architecture (as distinct from symbolism) and of his capacity to design we know little. The Market House, a remarkably pure work for 1578, was built by a mason named William Grombald (or Grombold or Grumbold – we shall meet the family again, p. 194), and there is a contract mentioning a 'plott… drawn by the said William, showid unto the said Sir Thomas Tresham'. The Grombalds again contracted for the New Bield, but the Triangular Lodge and the Hawkfield Lodge were built by a family of masons called Tyrroll, a special mason, Parris, being called in for the finer decorative features. The drawing of the Hawkfield Lodge is signed R.S., and at the New Bield a certain Roland Stickles (surely a relative of the celebrated Robert Stickelles, p. 27) is mentioned.

Very personal though Tresham's building projects are, they are scarcely more so than any of the other buildings we have dealt with in this chapter. Longleat, Kirby, Wollaton, and Burghley are all extremely personal, even arbitrary, enterprises. They are in no tradition and are perhaps the first English buildings of which that can truly be said. Each is a prodigy, an individual romance. It is not until we have crossed the threshold of the new century that the innovations they instance begin to become part of the vernacular.

NOTES TO CHAPTER 4

1. Veblen, T. B., *Theory of the Leisure Class*, 1899.

2. The exterior of Longleat has no very significant relation to the interior, and this is the case with most Elizabethan and Jacobean houses. There are the usual hall, long gallery, and parlours, and they are fitted in so as not to detract from the uniformity of the exterior. Of the original interior decoration of Longleat almost nothing remains, since it was remodelled in 1683 and again about 1860. The hall, however, has a hammer-beam roof closely related to that of Middle Temple Hall (1558–70) on the one hand and Wollaton (1580–8) on the other.

3. In a letter to Lord Carlisle (*Wal. Soc.*, xix, 126).

4. Preserved in the Nottingham University Library.

5. There are house plans by Robert Smythson among the Smythson drawings at the Royal Institute of British Architects which suggest that he may have created several important and widespread types. That he was respected as a master outside his own Midland area is proved by the inclusion of a drawing of Wollaton in Thorpe's book.

6. The interior of Hardwick, consisting of all the usual Elizabethan apartments, is notable for many things, chiefly perhaps the plaster friezes of Abraham Smith, the great heraldic cartouche over the hall fireplace and the Doric screen at the entrance end of the hall, resembling the design for a screen at Worksop among the Smythson drawings, given in Plate 17B.

7. There is a most striking resemblance between the Kirby pilasters and those of the church tower at Chars (Seine-et-Oise), attributed to the Lemercier family of masons. Hautecœur, *op. cit.* i, p. 391.

8. It was then bought by Sir Christopher Hatton, whose successors made many alterations up to 1632. The house is now a ruin.

9. Billingbere, Berks., built for Henry Neville, perhaps with John Thorpe's advice, may be a little earlier, but is tentative compared with Wimbledon.

10. This arrangement of gables, however, on a small building can be paralleled in the conduit-house at Bristol, mentioned on p. 17, and illustrated in J. S. Prout, *Picturesque Antiquities of Bristol*.

CHAPTER 5

PRODIGY HOUSES: THE JACOBEAN SEQUEL

BETWEEN the architecture of Elizabeth's reign and that of James I there is unbroken continuity. The new king, wisely and cautiously and much to the relief of his English Court, swam with the Elizabethan stream. In the person of Robert Cecil he maintained the Burghley dynasty in high office; he regularly progressed through his kingdom, after a fashion necessarily less romantic but at least as expensive as Elizabeth's. Elizabethan architecture became Jacobean without the least symptom of crisis. And yet there was a change: it is reflected in our instinctive use of 'Jacobean' as distinct from 'Elizabethan' as a stylistic and not merely a chronological expression, and the fact is that, although, as we have seen, the 'Elizabethan' style has no very solid existence, the 'Jacobean' style has. From the last decade of the sixteenth century, we begin to recognize a widespread constancy to certain plan-shapes and silhouettes and to a vocabulary of detail which varies little throughout the country, and is characteristic only of the years of James's reign and the decade immediately preceding it.

All these characteristics are, indeed, merely intensifications of certain aspects of Elizabethan architecture, as seen, for instance, in Longleat, Worksop, and Wimbledon. After those houses, which must have been enormously influential, the conception of a great house as a romantic pile, full of incident and surprise from every point of view, had not much further to go, but it could and did crystallize into many variations and re-combinations; and the Jacobean generation exploited it to the full. Striking mass arrangement and silhouette were the main objectives; the actual disposition of the rooms within a house excited little imaginative interest. The only really notable tendency was to abandon the traditional placing of the hall lengthwise to the main front and entered indirectly through a screened passage. From Hardwick onwards we find that a number of larger houses have the hall placed at right angles to the main front and entered directly on its long axis. That was a highly important innovation. Apart from it, however, planning remained traditional or empirical, and we find rooms packed, often rather grotesquely, into predetermined plan-shapes – 'uniform without, though severally partitioned within', as Francis Bacon[1] puts it. Thus, the bay-window of a summer parlour may match exactly the window of the dry larder in the opposite wing.

The general character of the Jacobean house owed much to the increasing employment of Flemish carvers and other foreign craftsmen. As the sixteenth century passed into the seventeenth, the number of immigrants at work on tombs, fireplaces, entrances, and other distinct architectural features was considerable. There were the families of Holleman, Johnson (or Janssen), Stevens, Cure, and Colt, most of them working in London, all of whom erected tombs in the first quarter of the seventeenth century and many, if not all, of whom were engaged on parts of houses, such as fireplaces and entrances. We have already seen how Gerard Holleman supplied the fireplaces for Kyre Park (p. 28). In the

1590s a certain Giles de Witt built the elaborate entrance features at Cobham Park, Kent. The name of Bernard Johnson is associated (by Vertue) with the designing of Audley End and Northumberland House; while Maximilian Colt, who made Robert Cecil's tomb in Hatfield Church, had previously been responsible for fireplaces in the great house near by. Two Cures, father and son, even filled the office of Master Mason to the Crown for many years.

There were, of course, English craftsmen, besides; and, indeed, the style had always a strong English inflexion, for which the influence of Nonsuch is very probably account-able. Slight as our knowledge of Nonsuch is, it is sufficient to suggest that the interior decorations of that Palace are as important a source for the Jacobean style as either foreign books or foreign craftsmen of a later date.

This ornamental style, so dazzling and provocative an attribute of Jacobean houses, requires explanation. Its extreme impurity makes this a little difficult. It is, essentially, a version of Italian Mannerism brought to a pitch of stylization, beyond that to which Rosso brought it at Fontainebleau. It is at once more scholarly and more outrageous than the strap-work of de Vries, and owes much to the candescent imagination of his German follower, Wendel Dietterlin, whose famous book has already been mentioned (p. 25). Dietterlin took as his starting-point the work of advanced Mannerist designers of late sixteenth-century Italy. Of their style he produced a grotesquely exaggerated version, working in the spirit of a decorative engraver or theatrical designer rather than an archi-tect. There was no Mannerist contortion which he would not doubly or trebly contort; no conceit to which he would not add some grotesque whimsy. He would leave no single classical element unmutilated: a column must be banded with mouldings, the lower part wrought with arabesques, the upper part hung, perhaps, with a fringe of stylized tassels; the leaves of the capitals must swarm and twist, while every member of the entablature must be notched or snipped, enriched and counter-enriched with tablets, garlands, and masks. His designs squirm with an erotic intensity and, here and there, the ornament passes beyond the border-line of suggestiveness.

The designs of Dietterlin are the last word in a particular kind of aesthetic sophistication. What we are concerned with, however, is not so much the designs themselves as their effect on artists who were the reverse of sophisticated – the simple Protestant craftsmen of Flanders and England who found the greatest delight in Dietterlin's intricate patterns while having little or no knowledge of the architecture on the basis of which these patterns were devised. The ornament of Jacobean architecture shows us a style derived from a brilliant caricature of a style – strange progeny indeed. In England it never touches the virtuosity of Dietterlin himself and is, perhaps, most felicitous when its prototypes are least in evidence. Jacobean ornament can be crisp, rhythmical, and delightful in contrast to the plain surfaces against which it is set. It can, on the other hand, be disingenuously vulgar.

It is important to realize that the Dietterlin style was brought into England through craftsmen and not through books. That is to say, in a more or less digested form. Dietter-lin's books were not, to any extent, used as copy-books, and only one case of literal copy-ing from them is at present recorded (see p. 48). Thus, in Jacobean houses like Audley End and Hatfield we shall look in vain for quotations either from Dietterlin or from

Serlio or de Vries. Therein is one of the essential differences between what is 'Elizabethan' and what is 'Jacobean'. In Elizabethan architecture the native vernacular tended to borrow its ornaments from foreign books; in Jacobean architecture it took the infection of a foreign style which rapidly coloured the whole of the country's building output. The distinction is not a fundamental one, but it gives some meaning to two terms which have long been in currency as stylistic labels.

A Group of Jacobean Houses

Right at the beginning of the new reign we come upon a group of great houses, linked in various ways. Two of them are associated with the name of Henry Howard, a nobleman who, having lived under various disabilities during Elizabeth's reign, found himself esteemed by James and elevated, in 1604, to the Earldom of Northampton. Reputed the most learned nobleman of his generation, Northampton's first opportunity for architectural patronage came when his nephew, the newly-created Earl of Suffolk, started to build a new house on his estate in Essex. Having supervised Suffolk's early education, Northampton continued it by supervising the design and construction of his house.

Audley End, Essex, begun soon after 1603 and finished in 1616, remains, in spite of partial demolition, the most powerful and impressive of Jacobean houses. As originally built, it was calculated to give an effect of almost limitless size; for, although designed round two courtyards, the relative heights of the component masses were such as to permit the whole building to reveal itself from the approach side in a succession of planes falling back to the turreted silhouette of the furthest block. This grand recessional drama was most skilfully handled, as Winstanley's engraving shows (Plate 25). Most of the elements in the composition we have met before in Elizabethan houses. The turreted masses recall Burghley; the shallow rectangular bays go back to Longleat; the angular windows in the entrance front are from the late Gothic of Henry VII. But the composition as a whole shows a more original and determined exploitation of variety within symmetry than any Elizabethan house, or, indeed, than any house which may be found in the plates of du Cerceau.[2] The arrangement of the inner (and now only existing) court is particularly interesting. The hall occupies the low front block, of which its oriel is made the central feature. To left and right are projecting two-storey porches, the left-hand one of which is the entrance to the screens-passage. The right-hand porch is an arbitrary duplication of this traditional feature, purely for the sake of the symmetrical build-up. Within the court (now spoilt by eighteenth-century additions), symmetry was again emphasized by the placing of a projecting bay in the centre of each side.

As a composition, Audley End is a wonderful study in what the eighteenth century was to call 'movement', that distribution of contrasting masses which both Vanbrugh and Adam were to seek to recapture, a quality which has always made Audley End recognized as a very considerable work of art.

Its ornament and interior treatment are rather coarse Anglo-Flemish work. There is not much external ornament, beyond the richly fretted balustrades and the porches of superimposed orders with pedestals and spandrels, again intricately fretted in relief.

The hall has a flat, panelled ceiling with vestigial hammer-beams in the form of brackets and a huge screen, with male and female terms and some finely executed *grottesche*.[3]

Who designed Audley End? Vertue, on the good authority of Charles Stoakes, the great-nephew of Nicholas Stone, tells us that 'Bernart Janssen' was the surveyor – 'a great imitator of Ditterling'. Probably a son of Gerard Johnson (Janssen), he was, like the latter, chiefly a tomb-maker. It is all very well for Stoakes to say that he was an imitator of Dietterlin, whose name got loosely attached to almost anything Jacobean. The fact is that Audley End cannot show a single derivation from Dietterlin's plates; all, in detail as in composition, comes from the Anglo-Flemish repertory, stretching back to Nonsuch.

Bernard Johnson, again, was the surveyor for Northumberland House, Charing Cross, built for himself by the same Earl of Northampton who supervised Audley End.[4] It must have been begun about 1608 and was destroyed in 1870. Within the limitations of an urban site, the plan of Northumberland House resembled Audley End in many ways. It had corner-turrets, and on the garden front and in the courtyard were the same centrally projecting bays. In the centre of the Strand front of Northumberland House, however, was a great carved frontispiece of three orders of term-like pilasters in the Dietterlin taste, at the top of which occurred the inscription C Æ, which is reputed to have stood for *Christmas Aedificavit*, the carver Gerard Christmas (d. 1633) being perhaps responsible solely for this ornate and conspicuous feature of the house.

Although we lack detailed knowledge, the over-all picture is clear enough. The plans of these houses develop from the great Elizabethan examples. Some inspiration comes, perhaps, from du Cerceau's plates of the great French châteaux, but far more is borrowed from houses like Burghley and Theobalds. The ornamental parts, however, originate in the school of Flemish carvers and their imitators, by now well established in the London area. As in the case of the Elizabethan houses, no single mind controlled the work, and it is therefore not surprising that no names of outstanding 'architects' have come down to us in association with these buildings.

Gerard Christmas's portal at Northumberland House reappears in another edition at the vast house of Bramshill, Hants. (Plate 26), built by Lord Zouche between 1605 and 1612. Here the plan was to some extent controlled by the presence of an older structure, partly incorporated in the new. The long mass with corner projections suggesting pavilions is unique to Bramshill. But the entrance front, where the Christmas portal stands between two 'extruded corners' to which it is linked on each side by a loggia arch, the whole framed by two square projecting wings, is a thoroughly Jacobean composition. Again, as at Audley End, we have a study in recession, but this time localized in a single elevation. There are five main planes in this composition, while subsidiary planes are created, if we count those established by the projections of the pilasters and the semi-circular bay over the entrance. It is an exciting 'set piece', strongly contrasting with the quiet unworried side elevations of the house, which are little different from those built during the early years of Elizabeth or even the later years of her father. Here again we have the feeling that the plan is the work of one (or several) minds and that the architectural 'gestures' were supplied by another (or others).

Audley End, Northumberland House, and Bramshill are in various ways related to one another and with them must be grouped Charlton Park, Wilts., built about 1607, by the builders of Audley End, Lord and Lady Suffolk. Charlton telescopes some of the pictorial qualities of Audley End into a small compass and on a plan much employed at this time – an H, to which variety is given by 'extruded corners' which rise into ogee-capped turrets, a projecting two-storeyed porch and a loggia along the ground-floor of the centre. This is, of course, an elaboration of the Wimbledon plan (p. 40). It is, if such a thing can be

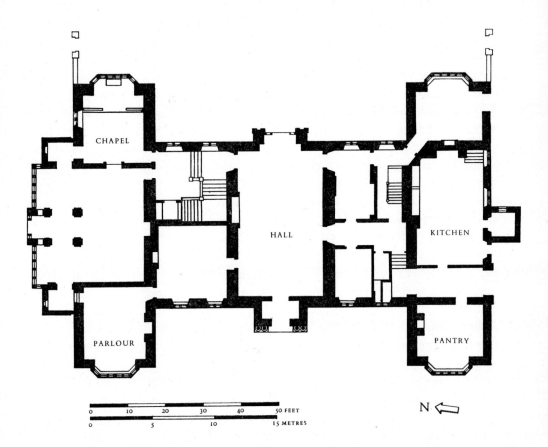

Figure 8. Charlton House, Greenwich

postulated, the standard plan of the Jacobean period and appears with every sort of variation in the greater houses of the time. An excellent example is (rather inconveniently) another Charlton – Charlton House, Greenwich (Plate 27; Figure 8), built, also in 1607, by Adam Newton, tutor and secretary to Henry, Prince of Wales. Here, however, there are no 'extruded corners' and the towers rise from the flanks of the house.[5] Here, as at Northumberland House and Bramshill, there is a richly carved 'Dietterlin' entrance-piece and, on this occasion, the artist has borrowed directly from Dietterlin's book: this is the only recorded instance of such direct derivation. Charlton, Greenwich, also presents

48

us with a notable instance of the axially-entered hall, while the plan as a whole closely resembles one in John Thorpe's book, almost certainly designed by him. This suggests, at least, that the themes involved were favoured by the officers of the King's Works, of whom Thorpe had been one.

The Houses of Robert Cecil, Earl of Salisbury

Just as Lord Burghley was, in Elizabeth's time, the greatest builder and most assiduous of patrons, so his son and successor exerted his mind and depleted his purse in the cause of Jacobean architecture. The year before his father's death, in 1597, he was already remodelling Beaufort House, Chelsea, into a broadened version of the H type with very short wings. From 1601 he completely transformed Cranborne Manor, Dorset, giving it a charming loggia adorned with crisp and lively Flemish detail. In London, a little later, he built Cecil House in the Strand, employing Simon Basil, who became the King's Surveyor in 1606. Finally, having been induced by James I to exchange his inherited seat of Theobalds for the old episcopal palace of Hatfield, he began, in 1607, to build (near the old palace but on higher ground) the new house which to-day survives intact in the ownership of his lineal descendant.

Hatfield House (Plates 28A and 28B; Figure 9) has a curious plan, not really characteristic except in so far as it is basically an H; the centre stroke, however, is pushed so far down as virtually to make the figure a rectangular U. The outline of the plan is extraordinarily inelegant and it looks as if an effort had been made to unite two rather different conceptions of grandiosity into one plan. The entrance front is a thing by itself. It boasts extreme squareness of silhouette, the sky-line stepping up and down where the projecting bays are carried into towers. The garden front, on the other hand, is more familiarly Jacobean, with ogee-capped corner-towers and a suggestion of 'extruded corners' between which runs a loggia, with a storey above containing a long gallery. This is interrupted in the centre by a frontispiece of three storeys, while set back on the roof is a clock-tower recalling the similar feature at Nonsuch. We know that the loggia and frontispiece, finished in 1611, were the work of Robert Lyming, carpenter, who drew the 'upright'. But it would be rash to ascribe the whole building to his or any other single mind. Robert Cecil, like his father, took an active part in his own building works, and we know that he consulted Simon Basil and probably others about Hatfield, so that the house will have grown, like others of its kind, as the result of discussion and compromise. This one can realize by looking at the flanks which ramble (in a wonderfully happy, picturesque way) between the two distinct and emphatic concepts embodied in the two main fronts.

Whatever part Robert Lyming played at Hatfield, we do know that he played a part of major importance, some fourteen years later, in the building of Blickling Hall, Norfolk, for Chief Justice Hobart. Here he carved his cipher on various parts of the house, and the burial register at Blickling describes him as 'architect and builder' of the hall. Blickling, a great oblong with corner-towers, is reminiscent of the garden front at Hatfield and here we see the ornate Flemish style of classicism completely digested by an English artist who has become equally adept at handling masses and adorning them. Blickling is one of the

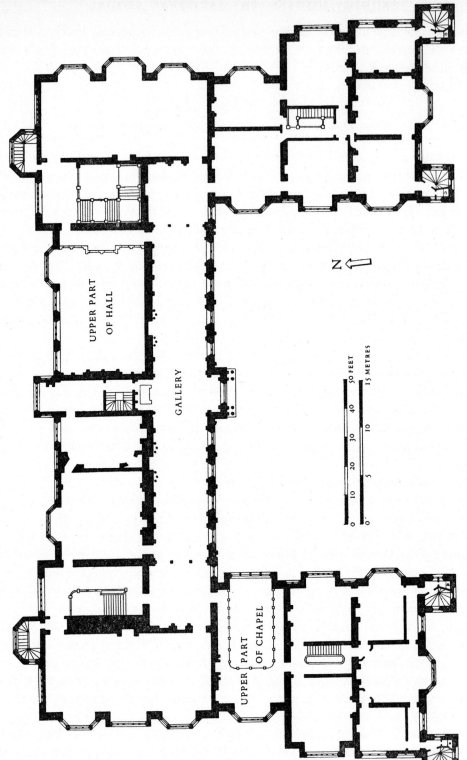

UPPER PART OF HALL

GALLERY

UPPER PART OF CHAPEL

N

50 FEET

15 METRES

Figure 9. Hatfield House: first floor

last houses of its kind. When it was building, Inigo Jones's Banqueting Hall was already six years old and had sealed the doom of Flemish ornamentalism and picturesque invention in plan and silhouette.

John Smythson's Work at Bolsover

To the reign of James I belongs the older part of that unique, eccentric, and extraordinarily attractive building, Bolsover Castle, Derbyshire (Plate 31). Built by Sir Charles Cavendish from 1612 onwards, it consists of a massive square house, built on the site of the donjon of a medieval castle and itself deliberately partaking of the character of the building it replaces. It is, in fact, a 'sham castle', and as such it is the most prominent and complete manifestation of that curious poetic dualism which seems to have become attached to the castle idea even before castles became obsolete as means of defence. In embryo we found the idea present at Nonsuch and its banqueting house (p. 10). At Wollaton and Barlborough (p. 36) we met it yet again, in different guises; while towards the end of the sixteenth century it was emphatically expressed in Lulworth Castle, Dorset. At Bolsover it is exploited to the full. The house boasts itself a castle by its massiveness, its corner-towers, and its crenellated sky-line; and it is approached by way of a 'fortified' forecourt. It is not easy at once to understand the frame of mind in which such a house was designed at a period when the whole trend of taste was towards the realization of Flemish, French, and Italian classicism. But it becomes easier if we recall, as we did when we were considering Wollaton, how the figurative castle comes into contemporary poetry;[6] if we recall, too, the castellar buildings in Italian theatre designs; and, moreover, if we recall that already historical and topographical writing was colouring the old castles of Britain with an heraldic glamour. This was the age of Camden, of Norden, and of Speed; the perspective of historic time was already aglow.

The designer of Bolsover was John Smythson (d. 1634), son[7] of Robert Smythson, of Longleat and Wollaton fame, and one receives the impression of a very distinct personality controlling the design of the whole. When Bolsover was approaching completion we know that Smythson travelled south (1618–19) and saw Theobalds and many of the newer buildings of London, including Arundel House and the beginnings of Inigo Jones's Banqueting House in Whitehall. The drawings he made on this occasion exist. They betray the reaction of a provincial mind, unable to grasp the essentials of the newer classicism but eager for its crisp and mechanical character. He drew some of the intricate Flemish wall-panelling at Theobalds and reproduced it at Bolsover. He drew the new Italian 'pergula' (balcony) at Sir Fulke Greville's house in Holborn (p. 59) and a new Italian gateway in the garden of Arundel House (where Inigo Jones was probably then at work) and adapted these, too, as features for his castle (Plate 37). The adaptations are unscholarly, but dramatically placed and not at all lacking in artistic feeling.

Bolsover is unique and the product of a unique personality rather than of a school. Great additions were made to it by Cavendish's son, who became Duke of Newcastle. These were designed by Smythson's son, Huntingdon Smythson, and betray a different sort of influence, which we shall discuss in another chapter.

Jacobean Houses in General

It is easier to generalize about Jacobean houses than about Elizabethan. A fabulous number of large and medium-sized houses was built, and from the over-all picture we can abstract distinct types, which are really the product of the whole Elizabethan-Jacobean phase of evolution. Easily the most popular types were the time-honoured rectangular U and the more recently evolved H, whose origin we have discussed. The attraction of the H-plan was that it gave opportunity for varied pictorial arrangement and elaborate recession on both sides of the house, with turrets running up either from 'extruded

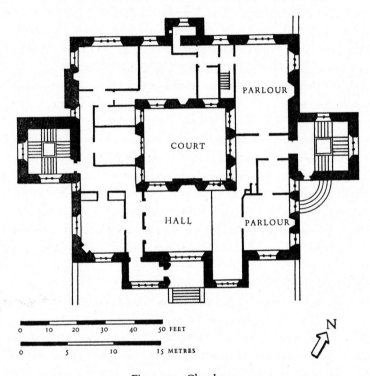

Figure 10. Chastleton

corners' or elsewhere on the plan. Holland House, Kensington (Plates 30A and B, for Sir Walter Cope, a friend of Lord Salisbury, c. 1606–7), is a good example of the H-plan fully developed for pictorial effect. Quenby Hall, Leicestershire (finished 1621), and Temple Newsam, Yorks. (begun 1622), are larger and more expansive houses on the same theme.

Another Jacobean type is the square or rectangular house which avoids the corner-pavilion idea but has projections on all sides running up either into gables or towers, somewhat like Smythson's Barlborough. Such a house is Chastleton, Oxon. (Figure 10), begun in 1603 by a wool merchant of Witney. Chastleton has few classical features, but its designer was intensely alive to the new feeling for symmetry, recession, and silhouette.

The accommodation in these houses and its disposition has little relation to the choice of plan-shape, since many different and equally convenient arrangements could be contrived within the same outline. The *Hall* for a long time preserved its traditional place to left or right of the main entrance, so that the approach was through a screened passage. But, as we have seen, an important innovation of James I's time was the placing of the hall on the central axis, so that it was entered either in the middle of one end or the middle of one of its sides. This meant that the hall lost its old sense of 'direction' and began to be more like what it was soon to become – simply an entrance vestibule leading to other parts of the house. We find this arrangement at Holland House (where the hall is entered on its short axis) and at Charlton, Kent (on its long axis).

With the decline in the importance of the hall, the rest of the accommodation became more ample. The *Long Gallery* was almost invariably on the first floor, occupying (in an H-plan) either the whole length of the centre block or the whole length of one of the wings. Often there was an open loggia under the long gallery, the loggia and the gallery being intended for taking gentle and sheltered exercise in summer and in winter respectively.[8]

Every fair-sized house had at least two *Parlours*, one for summer and one for winter. These adjoined the hall and were soon to become drawing-rooms and dining-rooms, their importance increasing with the disintegration of the hall and its functions. The *Kitchen* usually occupied a wing fairly remote from the hall; adjoining it were wet and dry larders and a room for pastry-making. The *Great Chamber*, often above the hall, was an important room where the master and mistress of the house would receive guests; it was the prototype of the principal drawing-room of later houses. Bedchambers were given little thought or prominence, but a certain number of *Lodgings* were provided consisting of a suite of two rooms for day and night use respectively. Every member of the household, other than servants, had his or her lodging, and in houses where entertaining was done on a great scale, many lodgings were provided for guests.

The *Staircase* had claimed some importance in Elizabeth's time. The wooden stair within a square or rectangular tower and with landings at every turn had already displaced the old breathless spiral; and at the Duke of Norfolk's Charterhouse (1571) there was a 'dog-leg' stair with open balustrades; a similar stair was at Theobalds. Lord Burghley, it is true, had built a stone-vaulted staircase of great richness, perhaps before 1570, in direct imitation of French examples. But his pioneering was not followed. The wooden staircase held the field and in the first few years of the seventeenth century developed majestically. At Audley End (p. 46) the two staircases are still tightly planned round wells no bigger than 3 ft by 2 ft, but the balustrades are highly enriched and in one case the newels, decorated with frets, go continuously up the well. At Knole (*c.* 1605) we find the staircase treated, for the first time, as an architectural spectacle and constructed in an open well for this purpose. At Hatfield (Plate 29) a few years later, we find another completely open staircase. Here the stair occupies a very large space, so that it can be viewed as a whole and is superbly lighted. Robert Lyming was, it will be remembered, a carpenter (p. 49), which may account for this special feat of timber construction. His staircase at Blickling is rather similar and so is that at Temple Newsam; in both these cases the newel-posts are used as opportunities for the display of sculpture. The wholly visible staircase, occupying a very large cubic area, was an extremely important departure in planning, maintaining its importance for the whole of our period.[9]

Panelling and Plaster-work enter the Jacobean picture under the head of 'seeling' (our modern 'ceiling'), which word was used to denote both the plastering of ceilings and the panelling of walls. To this work joiners and plasterers brought their respective techniques. In joinery, the English tradition passed from the native linen-fold of the time of Henry VII to the flat relief portrait medallions and dolphins which usually denote a date around 1540–50. Thereafter, the craft was revolutionized first, perhaps, by the decorations at Nonsuch and then by the influx of Flemings bringing their tortured pilasters, affluent mouldings, and carved panels with scenes of myth, allegory, or biblical history copied from the engravings which issued in such numbers from the Antwerp presses. At Hardwick Abraham Smith showed how perfectly an English craftsman could master the style.

In plaster-work foreign influence is not quite so obvious, and the native tradition remained very strong. Already, in the watching-chamber at Hampton Court (1536), the idea of a plaster-vault with pendants had been exploited, and at Hengrave (*c.* 1538; p. 15) it was specified that a ceiling should be executed 'vault fashion'. From this idea the later intricate patterns of moulded ribs developed naturally enough and the enrichment of ceilings often exhibits a good deal of naïf floral invention. Here and there we find Flemish strap-work, *compartimenta*, and scenes copied from engravings; and at Deene, Northants., a Jacobean plasterer used one of the ceiling designs given in Serlio. But of foreign plasterers we hear little or nothing and the craft certainly did not depend on their influence.

The *Siting* of houses and the treatment of their immediate surroundings developed rapidly at the end of Elizabeth's reign. The builders of Wollaton and Hardwick chose sites of extreme prominence for their houses, and when Sir Robert Cecil entered into possession of Hatfield he deserted the old Palace and built on the highest part of the estate. These positive, assertive monuments made no compromise with nature and sought no protection.

The land around the house began to be treated in a formal way as soon as the 'outward-looking' house was well established. On the entrance side was often a walled forecourt, a vestige of the courtyard plan, with an ornamental gateway and, perhaps, lodges. On another side was usually an orchard and on another a formal garden set with flowers and herbs. The fourth side, adjacent to the kitchen, was a woodyard. The favourite plan for a garden was a square with four paths leading to a little square in the centre, where there was a statue or a fountain. The beds were laid out in designs as extravagant and intricate as the panelling and balustrades of the house itself. The courtyards and gardens bore a strict relation to the house but fell short of participating in a single organic plan for the whole of the terrain. That idea was yet to be discovered.

NOTES TO CHAPTER 5

1. Essay XLV, 'Of Building'.

2. The plan of Charleval, however, is worth studying in connexion with Audley End.

3. This screen is related to the one at Knole, Kent (c. 1605), and to much earlier screens such as that of the Middle Temple Hall (c. 1570). There is a whole family of Elizabethan-Jacobean screens, the prototype of which may have been the hall screen in old Somerset House or even a screen at Nonsuch. The Audley End screen is a good example of the persistence of motifs which we know to have existed in the Nonsuch decorations – e.g. the cipher-and-square and square-in-square panels, the panel containing an arch in perspective (such a panel, from Nonsuch, exists at Loseley) and the terms with protruding feet.

4. Syon House, Middlesex, remodelled by the same Earl of Northampton, will have been another of this group of houses. Here is preserved an estate map signed by Moses Glover, 'painter and architeckter', 1635, and this has given rise to the suggestion that Glover was the architect of this and Northumberland House.

5. The placing of narrow towers in the centres of the long and short elevations of a house goes back to Smythson's Worksop which, as a very famous and influential house, may be the point of departure of this theme.

6. 'Leave the goodly fabrics of houses, for beauty only, to the enchanted palaces of the poets' wrote Bacon.

7. The relationship has been regarded as uncertain, but in Robert Smythson's will, in the York Registry, his principal legatee and executor is his son John.

8. The Long Gallery is a peculiarly English feature. There were, as we have seen (p. 3), early Tudor prototypes at Richmond, Thornbury, and Whitehall, but it is probable that the Galerie François Ier at Fontainebleau had a more decisive influence, possibly through Nonsuch.

9. The open staircase seems to have taken its origin in Spain at the beginning of the sixteenth century (N. Pevsner, *Outline of European Architecture*, 2nd ed., 1945, pp. 151–3), but nobody has yet traced a connexion between the Spanish and the much later English types.

CHAPTER 6

BUILDING IN TOWN AND COUNTRY
⟨1570–1640⟩

(a) Town-Houses

THE Gothic age left to the Tudors several types of town-house. The largest type was that which was in all essential respects the same as a country manor-house, having a hall, buttery, and solar, and lodgings arranged round a courtyard. That type was gradually eliminated from the towns with the passing of the class of people who had built it – either members of the feudal ruling class or else merchants whose exceptional wealth qualified them to adopt the manners and style of that class.

The successor to that 'manorial' type was the very rare formal courtyard type, instanced by the great house which Sir Thomas Gresham built for himself in Bishopsgate, London, shortly before 1566 and, later, by such town palaces as Northumberland House (see p. 47) and the Derby town-house in Cannon Row, Westminster, recorded by Thorpe.

But the Middle Ages bequeathed also a much simpler type – a type essentially of the town: the house with a narrow frontage to the street, rooms back and front on each floor and a long court or garden at the rear. That type of house, which we may conveniently call the *unit-house*, was dominant in all towns where space was a great consideration; and its plan remained dominant for the whole period covered by this book.

The unit-house must have originated as a hall with a solar or chamber above, a mere two-cell dwelling. Long before Tudor times it had developed considerably, and been doubled in depth. The ground-floor, instead of a hall, had a shop in front and a kitchen or parlour (or both) behind. The hall was promoted to the first floor, which meant, of course, that it was no longer a hall in the historic sense, with entry and screen at one end, but simply the main living-dining-room. The use of the word 'hall' for such a room in a town-house survived till far into the seventeenth century, but the hall as the main component was already obsolete before the century had started.

This unit-house, with its shop and kitchen at ground level, a cellar below and one, two, or perhaps three floors above with a garret in the gable and various projections in or over the court was already, in early Tudor times, a flourishing type of town architecture. There were, moreover, several sub-types, notably that which had a side-entry and long narrow open passage, enabling the whole depth of the house on one side to be windowed. Other sub-types were determined by the position of the single massive chimney-stack, structurally the most substantial part of the house.

The unit-house by itself, however, was not capable of rising to the requirements, either as to accommodation or stateliness, of the merchant princes of Elizabethan England. It might perhaps have done had they been inclined to copy the merchants of the Baltic towns in building houses of great width rising into perfectly enormous single gables. This they never attempted. What they did do was to *multiply* the unit-house by two, three, or even four and to build mansions of great size which, externally, may often be mistaken for rows of unit-houses of identical, or at any rate balanced, design.

The double-fronted, triple-fronted, or even quadruple-fronted house, with a row of gables to the street is the characteristic creation of the Tudor town. Under Elizabeth its character became set and is usually austere. Under James I it became subject to all sorts of variations and enrichments, but persisted very distinctly up to the Restoration and beyond.

Tudor town-houses of any importance datable before the year 1580 are uncommon.[1] In London (where we should naturally look for important evidence) not a single Elizabethan house of the type described survives,[2] and owing to the incidence of the Great Fire only a few lasted into the period of topographical recording. We have to go to towns like Chester or Shrewsbury to find existing or adequately recorded specimens.

At Shrewsbury there is a notable series, dating between 1570 and 1590, and built by clothiers who held office as Bailiffs of the town. Sherar's Mansion (Plate 32A; before 1573) is the perfect Elizabethan type, a triple house of three storeys, the top storey rising into gables. Both the upper storeys are 'jettied' (i.e. cantilevered out towards the street), and both have broad, shallow bay-windows. The style and construction (timber) are Gothic, except where carved Renaissance consoles are tucked under the jetties to give apparent support. Ireland's Mansion (about the same date) is quadruple, and here the gables are condensed into dormers lighting a garret, while the shape of the outer bay-windows is varied to give a sense of symmetry to the whole. A third house, Owen's Mansion (dated 1592), introduces gables only to gain head-room above the top windows.

Few towns have as satisfactory examples of early and mid-Elizabethan houses as Shrewsbury. In most towns of 'Elizabethan character' most of the work is found to date from 1590 and later, going well into the seventeenth century. At Chester, for instance, Stanley Palace (Plate 32B; a good example of the side-lit type) is dated 1591 and shows in its enrichments the onset of Flemish influence, though the main lines are still thoroughly traditional. The timber-gabled houses of Bristol and the many-dormered houses of Norwich are nearly all seventeenth century, though they are, generally speaking, pure-bred from Elizabethan types.

It is to the early seventeenth century that all the most adventurous and sensational town-houses belong. During Elizabeth's time the status of the merchant had ascended very steeply, and the success of the great trading companies had invested him with an almost romantic glory. It was no shame for younger sons of the landed class to serve apprenticeships in the towns nor to marry the daughters of city men; and the larger town-houses of King James I's time reflect very eloquently this new colouring of the mercantile status.

The London houses of this time were often very splendid and of these we do know something, since many of the greatest of them were built in outlying parts of the capital which escaped the fire – notably Bishopsgate, Fleet Street, Holborn, and around Charing Cross.

In Fleet Street still survives a fine town-house of 1610–11 (No. 17, much restored and, now, for no adequate reason, called 'Prince Henry's Room'). Built probably as a tavern, it is double-fronted, with two tiers of jettied bays, and above them a balustraded gallery, a Jacobean innovation tending to obscure the gables and introduce a new horizontality into town architecture.

Finer than this house was the one built in Bishopsgate by a great figure in the trading world of Jacobean London, Sir Paul Pindar (*c.* 1565–1650). Pindar came of a good family and was intended for the University but 'rather inclyned to be a tradesman'. After a fabulous career in the Levant as factor, consul, and, finally, ambassador he returned to London, living in Bishopsgate from 1624, which must be the date of his house. Its carved timber front (Plate 33) was re-erected, in 1890, in the Victoria and Albert Museum.

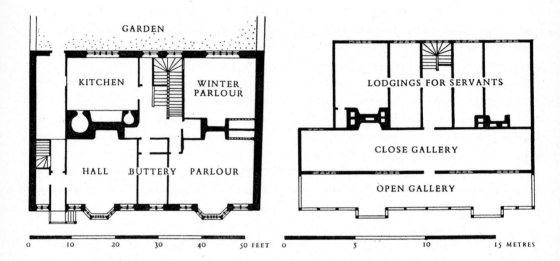

Figure 11. Ground and Upper Floor Plans of Sir Thomas Lake's House

The superimposed bay-windows are given fanciful plan-shapes and the whole thing is superbly carved. Again, there was a gallery above the bays, the gable being dismissed so far as external effect is concerned.

Thorpe gives us several plans of London houses, including one 'at the hither end of Holborn' whose shaped bays remind one of the Pindar house. He also gives plans (Figure 11) of Sir Thomas Lake's house,[3] near St Martin's-in-the-Fields, noting it to be 'the breadth of three ordinary tenements'. Here we find a hall, parlour, kitchen, and winter parlour on the ground-floor, chambers above, and, on the top floor, an open gallery (as at No. 17 Fleet Street), and behind it, in the roof, a 'close gallery', in other words a London version of the Elizabethan long gallery, by now an essential feature of a patrician or first-rate mercantile house.

In provincial towns, existing examples of Jacobean houses are so numerous as to out-shine even the many London houses we know from records. The finest groups are in the west and south-west. At Exeter is a five-storey example (built probably by Simon Snow, Mayor in 1653) in which two tiers of boldly projecting bays support the two upper storeys. This is paralleled at Tewkesbury where, however, the gable is set back and the visible part of the composition is crowned by a great cornice, prophetic of the change which was about to take place in English street architecture. But nearly every old town has its Jacobean specimens, small or great, and the variations in type are beyond the scope of this book.

So far, I have spoken only of timber houses. Stone or brick town-houses were uncommon before 1600. At Norwich, York, and Bristol there appear to be no brick or stone houses earlier than that date, except for those dating well back in the Middle Ages. Even in London, where royal proclamations[4] of 1605, 1607, and 1608 had positively ordained brick or stone fronts, timber-building continued. Indeed, it is wonderful how persistently it was possible to ignore royal injunctions in this matter.

Brick and stone town-houses of the early seventeenth century tend to be exceptionally large and for exceptional people. Thus, Bampfylde House, Exeter (c. 1600; destroyed 1942), built for a Sheriff of Devon, was a U-shaped stone house, with a small entrance-court. Its design is paralleled in a remarkable set of drawings in the Bodleian, dated 1600 and showing a town-house comprising hall, lodgings, great chamber, long gallery, and all the amenities of a country-house packed on to a town site. Rowley's Mansion, Shrewsbury (1618), is a stone house on an L-shaped plan with a walled court in the angle of the L.

Of the progress of the brick or stone front in London we get an interesting glimpse in the drawings made by John Smythson (see p. 51), when he visited the capital in 1619 (Plate 34). In Holborn he found two (apparently brick) fronts surmounted by curved gables, topped by pediments. In the Strand he found another similar house, in stone. Those houses we may fairly regard as being conspicuous and novel in the London of their time – pioneers in the 'Artisan' Classicism which, from about 1615, began to supersede the earlier mixture of native and foreign motifs. And we shall see later that these houses were probably responsible for starting a nation-wide vogue for this type of gable. Their salient features were, first, the shaped gables with scrolled sides and a pediment above, and, second, strong cornices of classical profile at various levels. 'My Lady Cooke's house' in Holborn and the house in the Strand have cornices at all floor levels. 'Sir Fulke Greville's' in Holborn has a main cornice and a distinct attic storey below the gable. This latter house has also a feature which Smythson calls 'a pergula', but which we would call a balcony, projecting at first-floor level – a feature which Inigo Jones had introduced at Arundel House and also at another house in the Strand, belonging to one of the Cecils.

This Netherlandish type of front, in brick or stone, must have become very common in London before the Civil War, but not a single example survives, the nearest approaches being a fragment of a house in Bermondsey, and the 'Dutch House' at Kew (1630), whose gabled front (Plate 54B) gives an excellent impression, in triplicate, of the kind of street front which was a novelty when Smythson visited London in 1619.

We cannot discuss, at this stage, the critical changes which were introduced into London house design in the years 1636–41, for those changes were the result of the influence of Inigo Jones, whose life and work will engage us in the three chapters which follow. Here, it must suffice to say that, whereas those changes were revolutionary (see p. 102), involving nothing less than the subjection of the London house to a formula derived from the Italian Renaissance, the full effect of those changes was not widely accepted till long after the Restoration. In London, timber houses on the Jacobean model with jettied storeys, and brick or stone houses in the 'Artisan' style, continued to be built throughout the Commonwealth. While, in the provinces, the tradition lasted even longer. Up to 1941, the noble 'Dutch House', Bristol, a corner building of five storeys, all timber and thoroughly Jacobean in spirit, survived to show that the old taste was still alive in 1676; while the row of four houses in King Street, in the same city, one of which is the Llandoger Trow, still stand and are said to date from about 1664. In the north of England conservatism was even more pronounced, and in Settle, Yorks., is a majestic house of stone ('The Folly') built in 1679 but exhibiting not the faintest sign that, at that date, Inigo Jones's greatest work was sixty years old and Sir Christopher Wren in mid-career.

(b) Building on the Land

The country buildings of late Tudor and early Stuart England are the visible evidence of a revolution in the Englishman's attitude towards land, which had been proceeding since the fifteenth century. The enclosures of Henry VIII's time and the virtual extinction of villeinage opened a new epoch in which land, which from time immemorial had been thought of as every man's direct and immediate means of subsistence, came to be considered as an asset which could be exploited and converted into other sorts of wealth, to be spent in a variety of markets. The change in outlook was the accompaniment of a corresponding social change, which by Elizabeth's time was complete. The old manorial system, with its villeins and serfs tied to the soil, had given place to a broader and more fluid rural society. At the top of it were the great and increasing landowners; below them came a middle class consisting partly of small gentry, partly of tradesmen, partly of yeomen; below them again were the husbandmen and labourers.

It was that middle class, recruited partly from families of gentle stock, partly from the old villeinage, and partly from the mercantile element in the towns, which gave to rural England of the period much of its most characteristic architecture. That architecture includes the manor-houses of gentlefolk who by prudent management had rendered their estates profitable in the changing conditions of the period. It includes also the farmhouses of the yeomanry – a yeoman being definable as any small farmer (whether leaseholder, copy-holder, or tenant-at-will) holding property of substantial value. And, thirdly, the houses of men who had made money in trade and invested it in land as the only stable form of wealth, a form, moreover, conferring a certain status on the owner and preparing the way for social advancement in the next generation.

Between the larger types of buildings built by these different sorts of people there is no fundamental difference. The wealthier yeomen were better off than many gentry and built houses indistinguishable from small manor-houses. The less prosperous yeomen naturally built smaller houses and among these certain types emerged which one naturally classes as 'yeoman' types. But it would be rash to connect distinct types of house with particular social categories, for all categories required much the same sort of accommodation, the only differences being those of wealth and, thus, of the amount of accommodation involved.

Building below the yeoman status consisted of cottages for husbandman and labourers. These were, for the most part, built by the holders of the land and rented. They consisted of the simplest types of mud, clay-lump, or turf cabins, and it would be hard to find any certifiable examples of Tudor cottages of this kind, the 'cottages' of the country-side of to-day being either small yeoman houses, yeoman houses which have at some time been subdivided or else structures of much later date. Cottage-building, moreover, received a severe set-back as the result of the Act of 1590 which forbade the erection of a cottage unless four acres of land were laid to it. The purpose of the Act was to keep up the agricultural population and maintain land in tillage. But as many yeomen were unwilling to part with four acres in order to accommodate a married labourer, one of its results was to check cottage-building. Probably this Act also led to much subdivision of existing tenements in villages.

By and large, the period 1570–1630 was a prosperous one for the country-side. In spite of the growing spirit of exploitation, rising rents, and frequently greedy landlords, the condition of the yeoman class in most parts of England was good. William Harrison, in a famous chapter on English houses, first published in 1577, makes a great point of the way circumstances had changed within the memory of people living in that year. Whereas in the earlier part of the century, he says, there would not be more than two or three chimneys to a village (apart from manor-houses and monastic buildings) they were now seen everywhere. The villager's whole standard of living was rising; logs as pillows, for instance, were giving place to bolsters, treen platters to pewter. And the wills of the period show us that even husbandmen and labourers could have some quite valuable household equipment and a fair sum in cash to leave to their children.

★

Common to all types of country-dwelling in Elizabethan England was the hall, 'house-place' or 'house-body', entered, as it had been for hundreds of years, at the end of one of its long sides where, in the larger houses, a wooden screen formed a passage across the end of the room; while smaller houses had simply a 'speer' or partition forming a rudimentary internal porch.

The house developed at either end of this traditional nucleus, as well as above it, and the accommodation of a typical Elizabethan manor-house or farm-house was as follows:

> *Ground-Floor:* Hall, parlour, kitchen, larder, pantry, etc.
> *First Floor:*   Chambers throughout.
> *Garret:*   Rooms for servants and labourers, apple store, etc.

The hall invariably occupied a more or less central position. The kitchen developed at one end and the parlour or parlours at the other. This resulted in several sorts of plan:

61

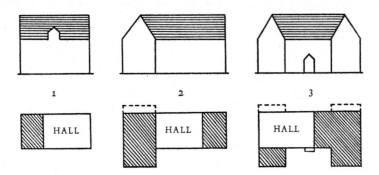

Figure 12. Sixteenth-century House Types

Most houses of the period are reducible to one or other of these shapes, though there are infinite variations in the handling and elaboration of them, such variations being dictated partly by convenience and partly by taste.

In so far as taste affected the planning of the smaller Elizabethan house, it tended to impose symmetry. At the beginning of the sixteenth century symmetry was already appreciated as an expressive and striking characteristic even in comparatively humble buildings. Symmetry ran against the natural planning of a house, the traditional arrangement of the hall and its entry being unsymmetrical in essence; but this, no doubt, gave additional point to the deliberate imposition of symmetry and the arrangement of a plan in such a way as to disguise the commonplaces of its internal arrangement.

Plan-type No. 3 lent itself most readily to symmetrical expression and is the shape most characteristic of the Elizabethan manor-house. The hall could be so placed in the centre block that its entrance came on the main axis; and the addition of a porch at this point gave the plan the shape of the letter E, while extensions at the rear tended towards the familiar H. The two wings accommodated the parlours, the kitchen, and various other service rooms.

A less ambitious type of house was No. 2, which had a wing on one side only making an L-shape or T-shape. The simplest type of house was No. 1, which, however, was often elaborated by the addition of one or more dormers to light the garret. These three types of houses are found in every part of England, the proportions and style varying with the locality and the materials used.

The effect of materials on the external design of houses was, of course, considerable, and when Harrison wrote in 1577 he noted, already, the rapid passing of timber in favour of stone or brick or a mixture of both. The reason for this was the destruction of timber which had taken place without provision for its replacement. As a result of this the price of timber rose to the point where to build in stone or brick was no more costly than to build in timber. The more durable and traditionally more luxurious materials were, very naturally, preferred, and in many parts of the country the art of building had passed out of the hands of the carpenter into those of the mason or bricklayer by the end of the sixteenth century.

The interiors of houses underwent a considerable change in Elizabethan times. It became common for both the hall and the parlour of a yeoman house to be 'ceiled' (i.e. panelled) either with native oak or imported wainscot and for the ceilings to be finished in plaster of Paris, whose 'delectable whiteness' is noted with approval by Harrison. Both these features had been privileges of the wealthiest builders under Henry VIII. Plastering also became common on the outsides of houses, partly for ornament and partly as an effective protection against fire.

The materials provided by the different geographical regions of England make the most natural divisions for the study of rural building. Other factors, however, must be taken into account, notably the distribution of the cloth-making industry, which had the effect of producing not only wealthy house-building clothiers but those well-built villages where the spinning and weaving for the clothiers was done. The following notes, under regional headings, give only an approximate indication of the localities where rural building flourished with special vigour or distinct character in the period 1570-1630.

★

SOUTH-EASTERN COUNTIES. Throughout Kent, Surrey, and Sussex timber building continued through the whole period, little stone being used except in parts of Sussex. Middle House, Mayfield, Sussex (dated 1575; Plate 35A), is a magnificent example of type No. 3, wholly Gothic except for carved details in a bucolic version of the Anglo-French style. Type No. 2 is represented in a splendid dated example (1610) at Penshurst, Kent. Type No. 1 is common, and there is a good example dated 1604 near Sedlescombe, Sussex. All these are of timber, exhibiting only very slight ornamental deviations from medieval tradition. Houses entirely in brick are rare before 1630.

★

EAST ANGLIA. In most of Norfolk, Suffolk, and Essex timber was replaced almost exclusively by brick, owing to the distance from supplies of stone. Flint, carstone, and clay lump were also used. Brick had been used in the area since medieval times, for special buildings, but it was common by 1570. Little Hautbois Hall (plan-type No. 1) is entirely in brick with brick dormers and finials and dates from c. 1555. Stanfield Hall, Norfolk (c. 1575), and Eastbury Manor House, Essex (1572-3; Plate 36A and Figure 13), are on plan-type No. 3 and these again have brick dormers with moulded finials. Two types of brick gable are frequent in Norfolk. One is the double-curved gable which made an early appearance in this county (at Carrow Manor, near Norwich, such gables are dated 1578). The other type is the 'crow-stepped' gable, which appears to belong to the seventeenth century (Kirstead Hall, Norfolk, dated 1614, and many others about that time).

All three plan-types occur commonly in Norfolk in brick or brick-and-flint with double-curved or crow-stepped gables and rudimentary brick pediments over all the windows.

The brick architecture of East Anglia is often held to be the product of direct Flemish immigrant influence, but that theory needs considerable qualification. It is a fact that

63

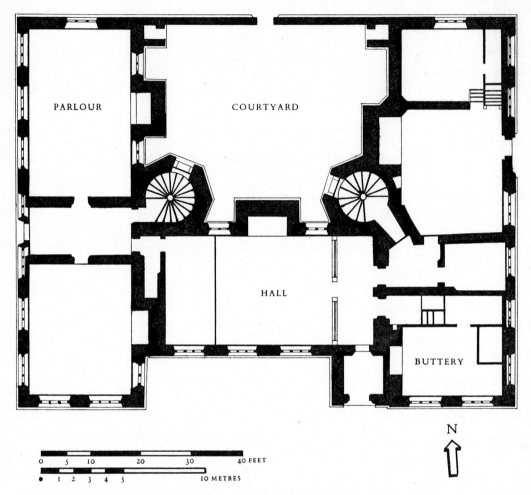

PARLOUR

COURTYARD

HALL

BUTTERY

N

0   5   10   20   30   40 FEET

1 2 3 4 5   10 METRES

Figure 13. Eastbury Manor House

English brickwork of the sixteenth century, wherever it is found, bears the stamp of Flemish sources, and in the brickwork of Norfolk this is neither more nor less pronounced than elsewhere. A large proportion of the foreigners in Elizabethan Norwich had, in any case, arrived there not across the North Sea, but from the south, via Sandwich. Moreover, the curved brick gables of Norfolk are precisely similar to curved brick gables found in Kent and Essex and even at places much further inland like York and Derby. Norfolk, therefore, must not be considered specially accessible to Flemish influence. It is the accident of its poverty in timber and stone and the consequent widespread use of brick, with details characteristic of the Netherlandish use of that material, which gives its architecture an occasionally notable Flemish or Dutch cast.

★

NORTHERN COUNTIES. In Yorkshire and most of the North, timber was superseded by various kinds of local stone. The most remarkable developments are in South Yorkshire, in the cloth-manufacturing districts around Bradford and Halifax. Here are a number of houses built for the most part by clothiers. They are of millstone grit, very broad and low in proportion, mostly on the type No. 3 plan with the hall (in early examples) extending the full height of the centre block. Oakwell Hall, near Birstall, is a good example, built by Henry Batt in 1583. The type extends well into the seventeenth century, and a group built between 1630 and 1650 (of which East Riddlesden Hall, 1640, is a good example; Plate 35B) has the curious feature of one or more traceried rose-windows, usually set in the upper part of a porch. Drawings of two such windows occur in the Smythson collection.

The north was somewhat inaccessible to the influence of the fashionable Flemish detail and curiously stylized versions of late Tudor ornament are found right through the seventeenth century, in combination with the low, broad proportions already mentioned which pervade the whole vernacular of north England.

*

MIDLAND AND SOUTH-WEST COUNTIES. Counties situated near the great limestone belt which runs approximately from Peterborough to Bath enjoyed the availability of fine stone quarries, and Northamptonshire in particular produced a stone vernacular of high quality. Manor-houses on plan-type No. 3 are common. The yeoman houses are most frequently on the basis of type No. 1 with one or more stone dormers jutting into the roof to light the garret (Plate 36B). We find these dormers on quite large houses, carefully placed to produce exact symmetry.

In Oxfordshire, Gloucestershire, and parts of Wiltshire and Somerset there is more excellent stone-building, mostly of the seventeenth century and stimulated in certain districts by the prosperity of the cloth industry. This industry relied, for weaving, on the domestic system. Cottages for weavers being indispensable to its success, many were built by the clothiers themselves. This resulted in the development of villages such as Bibury, Glos., where the row of gabled cottages known as Arlington Row is a famous example of housing built under these conditions. At Burford, Oxon., a clothier and mercer, Simon Wisdom, built many cottages, bearing his cipher, and some of them survive.

In this south-western area, which includes the Cotswolds, the large, broad gable, even on small dwellings, found greater favour than the dormers characteristic of Northamptonshire. Manor-houses and large yeoman houses were built on plan-type No. 3, but quite as often on a square or nearly square plan with each of the four walls rising into two or three gables, as at Boyton Manor, Wilts., or several of the clothiers' houses around Painswick, Glos.

*

The variations in vernacular building throughout Britain, their geographical distribution, and their relation to social conditions is a subject which, in spite of the enormous prestige of English rural building, has been almost totally neglected. Much more field-work is needed before an adequate survey of the subject can even be attempted, and one can only hope that it will be done before the still plentiful material is reduced by the operation of planning and rehousing legislation.

NOTES TO CHAPTER 6

1. One of the very rare early Tudor examples to survive is the house at Southampton built before 1535 by Henry Huttoft, King's Customer, and now the Tudor House Museum. It has four gables, one slightly larger than the other three. In Leland's time it was the 'Chiefest' house in the town.

2. The nearest to the type is the range of timbered houses at Staple Inn, Holborn, built 1545–89, but they have been so much altered and restored as to be of little illustrative value.

3. This house appears to have been built for himself by Thomas Fowler (d. 1596), Comptroller of the Works for forty years.

4. The Proclamation of 1605 called attention to the waste of wood in building and required that brick or stone be used instead. No new house was to be built within one mile of the suburbs of London unless its walls, windows, and forefront were made of brick or brick and stone. Moreover, the forefront of all houses were to be 'of that uniform order decreed by the magistrates for that street'. Steele, R. R., *Tudor and Stuart Proclamations*, 1910.

PART TWO
INIGO JONES AND HIS TIMES
⟨1610–1660⟩

CHAPTER 7

INIGO JONES AT THE COURT OF JAMES I

THREE generations participated in the Elizabethan age. First there were the men already middle-aged when it began, men who had travelled through the years of the Reformation and the uncertain times of Edward and Mary. These were the men of the Burghley generation who, if they had an eye for architecture, would look back to the time when Henry VII's Chapel was still a recent marvel, who remembered the building of Nonsuch and the way that Somerset House had seemed to open up a new and charming future for English building.

Second, there was the generation born within a decade, either way, of 1540. They were the real makers of the age, the contemporaries of the Queen herself, of Christopher Hatton, and of Robert Dudley, Earl of Leicester. They were the builders of the prodigy palaces, of Kirby, Holdenby, and Wollaton.

Third, there was the generation born in the region of time lying around 1570. They came in on the crest of the wave and Shakespeare was among them. To them, the Reformation was already history. To them, architecture was already a living art rather than a 'new fashion'. They were the builders of Audley End, Bramshill, Hatfield, and Blickling: houses in which the discoveries of the previous generation were exploited with supreme confidence and lavish elaboration.

Now, it is precisely to this generation that Inigo Jones (1573–1652) belongs. The fact needs underlining, because the character of his art and the circumstance that many of his patrons were considerably younger than he makes him seem the product of a generation ahead. Yet Inigo Jones was already thirty when Elizabeth died. He was only nine years younger than Shakespeare and the very near contemporary of all those lesser poets and dramatists whom we habitually call 'Elizabethan'. Donne and Ben Jonson, for instance, were born in the same year as Jones; Heywood and Webster two years later, Dekker and Middleton only three years earlier.

Inigo Jones comes into the architectural history of his time in an oblique and slightly mysterious way: neither by rising from a craft, nor by early introduction to the Works. The very moment we hear of him as an architect, he is head and shoulders above anybody else. Who, for instance, would think of comparing the drawings of John Thorpe with those of Jones? Yet Thorpe and Jones were but ten years apart in age, and their

67

employments were, for a time, somewhat similar. Neither is there in painting any remotely comparable character: only the flat figure of the Fleming, Paul Van Somer, whose portraits hang happily enough in Hatfield or Audley End, but would be absurd company for the architecture of Jones. The truth is that Jones's proper companion is Rubens. To place him intelligibly one must think of him not in an English but a European context; one must see him, let us say, as an architectural Rubens – an individual of altogether exceptional genius whose vision and energy transferred a Mediterranean phenomenon to the still half Gothic north. His architecture challenges not merely the English but the European achievements of his time.

Of the early life of Inigo Jones we know less than enough to explain his prodigious later success. He was born in London in 1573, the only son of a Smithfield clothworker of moderate means. We know nothing of his education and, indeed, nothing whatever about him until, in 1603, he is mentioned in the Earl of Rutland's household accounts as 'Henygo Jones, a picture maker'. At that time the Earl was just about to depart on an embassy to King Christianus of Denmark, bearing with him the Order of the Garter as a gift on the occasion of the christening of the Danish King's heir. Inigo Jones may have accompanied the embassy, for it is certain that he visited Denmark. Nor was that his first journey abroad. He had already been to Italy; for John Webb,[1] writing in 1665, says that King Christianus 'sent for him out of Italy and engrossed him to himself'. The statement is unsupported, but it does look as if Jones had been in Italy before he went to Denmark. It is this first visit to Italy, a visit Jones must have made while still in his twenties, which is the most obscure part of his career. The most likely way for him to have got there would have been in the company of some travelling nobleman – possibly, indeed, the Earl of Rutland himself, who was certainly in Italy in 1596.

In any case, it is clear that Inigo Jones had been in Italy before 1603 and, what is immensely significant for our purpose, had come in close contact with Italian art and had learnt to draw.[2] Jones's very considerable capacity as a draughtsman at once marks him off from all his English contemporaries. They might be exquisite calligraphers and capable of producing the neatest possible 'platts' and 'uprights', but they had no conception of the free, suggestive draughtsmanship which had now for a hundred years been the instantaneous medium of expression for Italian painters, sculptors, and architects. It is not simply the ability to draw which is significant, but the state of mind, the sense of control of which that ability is the outward sign. It represents, indeed, a revolution in architectural vision, and when we meet with Inigo Jones's earliest surviving sketches in 1605 we know that we have finally crossed the threshold from the medieval to the modern.

These first sketches were not, however, architectural. They were costume designs for the Queene's Masque of Blacknesse, performed on Twelfth Night, 1605, the first of a long series of similar spectacles with which Inigo Jones was associated as designer and contriver of effects.

These Court Masques mark very distinctly the function of James's Court and that of his Queen as the centre of artistic patronage – a centre of an un-Elizabethan kind, lacking the dominant personality of the old Queen and rapidly resolving itself into an exclusive circle of noble families, nearly related to one another, and bent exclusively on the pursuit of pleasure and self-interest. Elizabeth's Court had been economical and, latterly, dull. James and Anne started their reigns with unlimited confidence in the resources of the English exchequer and spent without reflection. And whereas Elizabeth had fallen into the habit of being royally entertained by her subjects in their own great houses and at their expense, James entertained his subjects at Whitehall and his other palaces at *his* expense. It was natural that a King should thus reverse a tradition appropriate to the reign of a virgin Queen, and an equally natural result was the gravitation of artistic talent to the one centre where the arts were constantly and open-handedly cultivated.

The Masque was, of course, nothing new in Court life, but after 1603 it was rapidly lifted from something in the nature of an elaborate peripatetic charade to a highly finished dramatic performance. Probably Queen Anne had more to do with this than the King. She loved amusement and was not without ideas, and the Queene's Masque of Blacknesse was written and performed on her initiative. The 'book' was by Ben Jonson, who shares with Inigo Jones the distinction of having brought the Jacobean and Carolean Masque to its finest pitch. Jonson was born in the same year as Jones and came of much the same class, but had advanced more rapidly to fame, so that it was natural for the Queen to command his services. Jones may have recommended himself to her on account of his acquaintance with her native country, and (if Webb is to be trusted) the favour he found with her brother, the King of Denmark. In any case, this was the first occasion on which Jonson and Jones collaborated, and they continued to collaborate until Jonson's jealousy of the architect got the better of him and relations were broken off, with much bitter rhyming on both sides, in 1631.

Jones's contribution to the development of stage-craft cannot be dealt with fully here, but the earlier masques are important to us because they provide evidence of his taste as a designer some ten years before the earliest evidence of his work as an architect. The Masque of Blacknesse was very magnificent, very expensive, and very new – probably, indeed, the first Court masque in which the contemporary Italian *intermezzo* was imitated in England. Jones not only concentrated the setting (an innovation only recently effected), but provided the dramatic preliminary of a landscape curtain which, at a given moment, fell and revealed a sea-scene of great elaboration, with a giant shell rolling on actuated billows.

Clearly, Jones had made a study of the Italian theatre part of his business in Italy and was able, at one stroke, to introduce a great novelty at Whitehall and to make his name. In August of the same year he was employed on some entertainments for the King at Oxford, for which, although they were not a pronounced success, he was lavishly paid. In January 1606, at Whitehall, he was responsible for the Masque of Hymen, in which there was a globe or *microcosmus*, with moving clouds, a feature which has been suggested, with good show of reason, as the source of Shakespeare's imagery in one of the most famous lines in *The Tempest*.

In 1608 came the Hue and Cry after Cupid, to celebrate the marriage of Viscount Haddington. Here there were rocks which clove in twain, possibly on the Vitruvian principle of the *scena ductilis* (moving shutters), a new departure in English stage design.

69

This was followed, in 1609, by the Masque of Queens, wherein was, probably, the first attempt at a genuine change of scene. A 'Hell' disappeared, suddenly giving place to a 'House of Fame', perhaps by means of a revolving platform. A similarly striking transformation occurred in Tethys' Festival of 1610, this time probably by means of *periaktoi*, upright columns of triangular section which gave three different scenes according to the positions to which they were rotated. Oberon, the Faery Prince, followed in 1611 and, in 1613, the Lords' Masque, which contained the most impressive transformation scene yet achieved, as well as superb costumes and a great deal of architecture.

In the case of all of these early masques (excluding the entertainment at Oxford) some of Jones's designs have survived. Most of them are for costumes; but we have a sketch for the House of Fame in the Masque of Queens and several for the Faery Prince's Palace in Oberon. These give us a few rough hints about Jones's architectural taste in 1609–11. The buildings are, of course, deliberately fantastic and combine castellated with classical features (as was done in the contemporary Italian theatre); they also contain a few details (such as the pendant keystones in Oberon's Palace) reminiscent of work of the current vernacular in England. But there is a sensibility to proportion and detail which only a man with Jones's italianized eye and hand could have produced. Unluckily, there is no record of the architecture in the Lords' Masque with its golden, gem-studded pilasters, its capitals 'composed and of a new invention' and its upper 'bastard order with Cartouses reversed, comming from the Capitels of every Pillaster ... rich and full of ornament'. This must have represented Jones's most elaborate architectural achievement in the paint and canvas of the first series of masques.

Did he exercise his powers in anything more substantial than this medium at this time? The legend of Jones as a 'Jacobean' architect, working in the style of Audley End or Hatfield before his conversion to strict classicism, is now usually dismissed. Too peremptorily, however. For a design (Plate 38) for Oberon, a masque of 1611, is not only decidedly 'Jacobean' but bears some resemblance to the arcade leading to the staircase at Knole (*c.* 1605). Obviously, in so far as Jones designed architecture at this early period he did so much in the spirit of such contemporaries as Simon Basil and Robert Lyming. Unlike them, however, he could, in the new sense, draw; and that freedom of hand represented a freedom of mind which placed him in a different class.[3]

At least until 1610 Jones's main work was as the designer for the theatre at Whitehall. At the beginning of 1611, however, he was appointed Surveyor to Prince Henry, the heir apparent to the throne, who, in the previous year, had been created Prince of Wales. Jones had already (1609–10) designed the setting for The Prince's Barriers, a kind of tourney with mock fortifications and verses by Ben Jonson, the whole conceived in an Arthurian spirit and set in the Banqueting House. He can have done little else for the Prince, though he is supposed to have built a 'cabinet room', for his collection of pictures, in Whitehall. Apart from that, we hear only of some reinforcing operations to three islands at Richmond, where the Prince often kept his Court.

As one of the officers of Prince Henry's Court, Inigo Jones was in excellent company, for the Prince was, in the eyes of his contemporaries, something near the ideal 'universal man' of the Renaissance – athlete, warrior, and scholar; and although he was only sixteen when he was given a separate establishment, this immediately became a centre of artistic activity. His collection of pictures was to become the nucleus of the great collection eventually formed by his brother, Charles I. He retained the services of a drawing-master, Salomon de Caus (1576–1626?), who built him a picture-gallery at Richmond, while in 1612 he appointed Abraham van der Doort Keeper of his pictures. He also acquired an important collection of medals.

Around the Prince revolved a number of young noblemen who shared some at least of his interests, and among these was Thomas Howard, 2nd Earl of Arundel, destined to become one of the most important patrons in the history of English art, and to have a particularly close association with Inigo Jones. Howard was born in 1586, the only son of the 1st Earl, a Catholic who had died miserably in the Tower. From a childhood overcast by this tragedy and the pathetic circumstances in which his mother was left, Howard grew up to be a man of uncommon ability and integrity – haughty, reserved, and, at times, irascible but as a character head and shoulders above most of the people among whom he moved. King James restored him in title and blood in 1604, and at the age of twenty he was already conspicuous at Court. He took part in the second of the great masques, the Masque of Hymen, and thereafter he and his Countess were often included in the castes of these shows. Arundel will thus have been familiar with Inigo Jones and his work from the time that he came to Court and will probably have learnt much from him about architecture and the arts. Jones was thirteen years older than the young lord and probably the only man in England with anything like an intimate first-hand knowledge of Italian art.

With such a man as Arundel for his friend and Inigo Jones for his Surveyor, Prince Henry might have become a superlative promoter of architecture. But in little more than two years after his investiture as Prince of Wales he was dead. Typhoid fever carried him off on 6 November 1612, and Inigo Jones's office came abruptly to an end.

Mourning for the Prince did not last long, for arrangements were already in hand, and could not well be postponed, for the marriage of the King's daughter, Elizabeth, to the Prince Palatine, heir to the Throne of Bohemia. The marriage took place in February 1613, and it was on this occasion that the Lords' Masque was performed. Thomas Campion, the author, described his collaborator as 'our kingdome's most Artfull and Ingenious Architect'. Jones had still built scarcely anything but stage sets, yet the tribute was well timed, for on 27 April 1613 he was granted the reversion of the highest office in the world of building – that of Surveyor of the King's Works.

In April the bride and bridegroom, with an immense retinue, started on the journey to Heidelberg, which they reached in June. With them were Lord and Lady Arundel, travelling with the Duke of Lennox; and among the Arundels' suite of thirty-six persons was Inigo Jones. It seems that Arundel had at the back of his mind when the expedition started the possibility of going on from Heidelberg to Italy, which he had visited once and wished to see again. It seems, also, that he secured Inigo Jones's company in order to have the advantage of his experience beyond the Alps. So at Strasburg the Arundels parted with the Duke of Lennox, made for Basle and then for Milan, where they arrived in mid-July, passing almost at once to Parma and thence to Padua, where the household installed itself in a country villa. At Venice the Earl and Countess were entertained with much formality, but in September the Earl cut adrift from the almost royal dignities attributed to him and after visiting Vicenza and Bologna went to Florence and then to Siena where Lady Arundel joined him. From Siena he went to Rome in the winter of 1613–14. This was a step which few Englishmen of Arundel's standing would have dared to take unless (as was possibly the case with Arundel) he had obtained King James's formal or informal consent. Rome was practically out of bounds for Englishmen, being the natural seat of every kind of Catholic intrigue. There, however, Arundel went and Inigo Jones with him. He obtained permission to excavate some ruins and discovered a number of antique statues which he despatched to England. From Rome, the party went on to Naples, was probably back in Rome in May and June, but spent most of the summer of 1614 at Genoa, where they were detained by illness. In September they travelled north again and eventually home by Turin and Paris.

During a great part of this tour, lasting one year and seven months, Arundel was travelling *incognito* and apparently for no other purpose than the exploration of the painting, sculpture, architecture, and landscape of Italy. Although Inigo Jones was in his suite, we cannot be sure how constantly he and his patron were together. Jones seems to have paid an additional visit to Vicenza and Venice while the Arundels were in Genoa; and there is no doubt at all that he had ample opportunity for concentrated study of the architecture which preoccupied him. This is proved by the notes he made in the copy of Palladio's *Quattro libri dell' architettura* which he had with him all through the tour. This copy, which still exists in the library of Worcester College, Oxford, is a document fraught with great significance for English architecture.

Palladio's famous tetralogy was first published in complete form in Venice in 1570, though parts had appeared earlier. The work takes its general form from earlier treatises, going back to Alberti and thus ultimately to the grand prototype of Vitruvius. The four books deal, respectively, with the orders and elements of construction; Palladio's own designs; public works; and Roman antiquities. The section on antiquities was, in its time, by far the most careful study of these things and was based largely on Palladio's own measurements. Probably it was this part of the book to which, in the first instance, Jones attached principal importance; for there is no question that in his Italian journeys he consistently gave priority to Roman antiquity over contemporary fashion. He was in Italy to see the remains of Rome, not to gather hints from recent or contemporary masters. The Roman versions of the orders were to give him his criterion of classical excellence and these he studied with the most minute attention. From his notes we gather that his method was to take his Palladio to the sites and check the engravings against the originals, amplifying Palladio's information and noting variations between the different examples.

It is more than doubtful if any Englishman had attempted this method of study before, or paid any really close attention either to antique buildings or antique sculpture. Hitherto, antiquity at second hand, through Serlio, or at third or fourth hand through Flemish and German ornamentalists had been deemed a sufficient acquaintance. Jones, by his insistence on first-hand examination of Roman monuments, brought a completely new factor into English architecture – a critical appreciation of Antiquity.

Jones's notes are tantalizing in their brevity, but we do learn that he met old Scamozzi in Venice and discussed some technical matters with him; also that he had seen some of the architecture of France, including the Maison Carrée at Nîmes and the Château of Chambord.

Besides the annotated *Palladio*, there exists an Italian sketch-book by Jones, the survivor of many which he may have filled. It contains mostly studies of figure drawing, taken from paintings or prints by Italian masters, but it has one direct reference to architecture which, since it clearly illuminates his point of view at the time, must be quoted in full. The date is 20 January 1615.

And to saie trew all thes composed ornaments the wch Proceed out of ye aboundance of dessigners and wear brought in by Michill Angell and his followers in my oppignion do not well in sollid Architecture and ye fasciati of houses, but in gardens loggis stucco or ornaments of chimnies peeces or in the inner parts of houses thos compositiones are of necessety to be yoused. For as outwarly every wyse mā carrieth a graviti in Publicke Places, whear ther is nothing els looked for, yet inwardly hath his immaginacy set on fire, and sumtimes licenciously flying out, as nature hir sealf doeth often tymes stravagantly, to delllight, amase us sumtimes moufe us to laughter, sumtimes to contemplation and horror, so in architecture ye outward ornaments oft [ought] to be sollid, proporsionable according to the rulles, masculine and unaffected.

That is the only general comment by Inigo Jones on the art of architecture which we possess. It is extremely valuable, because it implies the same criticism of Italian Mannerism which, as we shall see, is implied in his executed works. Does Jones echo, in this expressed opinion, some conversation with Scamozzi, or does it simply crystallize his own temperamental reaction to Italian architecture as he saw it – and English architecture as he had known it? Whatever the case, the statement appropriately closes the preliminary phase of his career. In the same year that it was written, his active career as an architect began.

NOTES TO CHAPTER 7

1. John Webb, Jones's pupil, eventual deputy and successor, will be considered in Chapter 9, but it is necessary here to mention the book which he produced, 'from some few indigested notes' of his master's, on the origin of Stonehenge. *The most notable Antiquity of Great Britain, vulgarly called Stone-Heng ... Restored, by Inigo Jones, Esq; Architect General to the King* is dated 1655. Its thesis, that Stonehenge was Roman, was challenged by Dr Charleton in *Chorea Gigantum*, whereupon Webb published the *Vindication of Stone-Heng Restored* (1665). He devotes some space in this last book to eulogy of Jones and some brief notes on his life.

2. The subject of Jones's draughtsmanship still requires a great deal of research, but it is pretty certain that he learnt from no particular master but from persistent copying of Italian or French drawings and engravings. Parmigianino was one of his

principal models. Among the masque drawings are many obvious references to Callot, while some of the masque scenes derive almost entirely from engravings after Alfonso and Giulio Parigi, scenic artists in the service of the Grand Duke of Tuscany. Jones was a perpetual borrower, both in his masque work and, as we shall see, in his architecture.

3. It would be hazardous to assign any 'Jacobean' buildings to Jones on purely stylistic grounds, but it is perhaps worth mentioning, as a subject worth further inquiry, the great house which Anne of Denmark built at Byfleet. The one slight surviving record of the house shows an uncommonly 'classical' frontispiece and shaped gables not unlike those of a design for a pavilion in which Queen Elizabeth is shown enthroned and which can hardly therefore be later than 1603.

CHAPTER 8

THE SURVEYORSHIP OF INIGO JONES

INIGO JONES became Surveyor of the King's Works on the death of Simon Basil in September 1615, his pay beginning on 1 October. Between that date and the beginning of the Civil War in 1642 – a period of twenty-seven years – he was continuously engaged on the supervision of works at the royal residences. Much of this work consisted simply of maintenance and minor alterations and will have been left to the Clerks of Works at the various residences; but scarcely a year passed without something being undertaken which required skill in design. And although Jones's Patent by no means obliged him to set his own hand to all this work, the evidence we have shows that little, if anything, came out of the Office which was not in fact the personal architectural work of the Surveyor himself.

In the first year of Inigo Jones's Surveyorship, 1615–16, a substantial work at Greenwich, for Queen Anne, was brought to its conclusion. It was an extension to the Queen's lodgings and the accounts suggest that it was in the style of the wing recently added to Somerset House, which is to say, something like the style of Audley End. No doubt it represented the work of Simon Basil.

But while the finishing touches were being put to this purely 'Jacobean' work, another building at Greenwich, of a very different kind, was being begun. In June, 1617, a correspondent of Sir Dudley Carleton's wrote to him that 'the Queen … is building somewhat at Greenwich wch must be finished this sommer, yt is saide to be some curious devise of Inigo Jones, and will cost above 4000^li'. There is no doubt that this was what we now know as the Queen's House. The accounts tell us that an old building on the site was removed and the new foundations laid in 1616. But the house was not finished in the summer of 1617, nor for another twenty summers. The work must have been stopped soon after the above-quoted letter was written, and in 1619 Anne of Denmark died. Work on the 'curious devise' was not resumed for ten years.

The Queen's House is usually considered to be Inigo Jones's first important building and thus the first strictly classical building in England. This estimate is probably correct for, the foundations once laid, Jones was committed to the plan, and the work seems to have been taken up to first-floor level before being abandoned. He had submitted two designs, for which he was paid the large sums of £10 and £16 respectively. We cannot know, however, what modifications were introduced in 1629 and it is probably wiser to consider the general appearance of the Queen's House as a product, more decidedly, of 1629–35 than of 1616. The plan in itself, however (Figure 14), is remarkable enough and calls for comment, in principle, at this stage.

The house was designed to meet very peculiar circumstances. At Greenwich the gardens of the palace were divided from the park by a public road, running from Deptford on the west to Woolwich on the east. This meant that a royal party proceeding into the park had to cross the road; it also prohibited any effective architectural link, short of a bridge, between palace and park. In conceiving the Queen's House, Jones converted this difficulty into an opportunity and designed a double house, half in the garden, half in the park, the two halves connected by a covered bridge. He did not attempt to make anything spectacular out of the bridge and packed the whole design into an approximately square figure, so that when, in 1661, two further bridges were built, on the perimeter of the

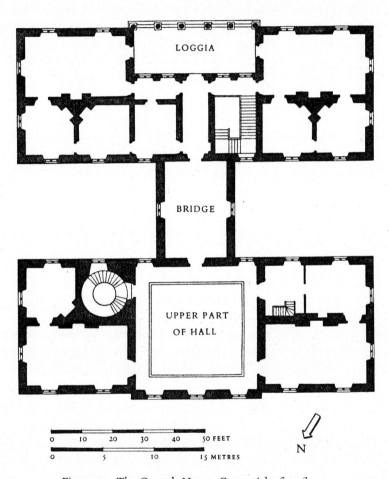

Figure 14. The Queen's House, Greenwich: first floor

square, and flush with the outer walls, the division in the design ceased to be apparent without any violence being done to the conception as a whole. To-day, with the road diverted, it is hard to believe in the duality which was such an essential and curious feature of the original conception.

While the foundations of the Queen's House were being laid, a less ambitious work was being carried out for Queen Anne at her other favourite seat, Oatlands in Surrey. Here, as at Greenwich, was a Tudor palace with a garden and a park; and here again it was desired to provide a formal architectural entry from the one to the other. There being no intervening road and no desire for a new residence, it was simply a matter of erecting a formal gateway. The rusticated gateway which Jones designed in 1617 is plainly inspired by one of the arches in Serlio, and it is interesting to note that Jones had no aversion to this source, even after his acquaintance with better things through the eyes of Palladio and Vignola. But, as always in Jones's borrowings, the details are most carefully revised and the finished result is a much more refined thing than its prototype.[1]

A lodging for the Marquis of Buckingham, in Whitehall Palace, was built by the King's Works in 1617–20, presumably on the strength of Buckingham's holding the office of Master of the Horse. Of the lodging, which faced the Privy Garden, we know little except that it was timber-framed and had 'four great pillars' under it, but there is a design for a ceiling at Worcester College[2] which may be identifiable with 'a roufe for a dyninge roume' mentioned in the accounts for 1619–20. It is a beautiful design, elaborated and refined from a Roman ceiling given in Palladio, and painted in gold, silver, and blue.

This house for the King's young favourite was Jones's first addition to the great rambling Palace of Whitehall. His next work was in the same palace, but of a very different calibre, being indeed his greatest work – the new Banqueting House, built to replace the old structure which one of Jones's predecessors had built in 1607, and which was destroyed by fire on 12 January 1619.

The building of the new Banqueting House (Plates 40 and 41) was placed in the hands of five commissioners, including Jones's special friend and patron, Lord Arundel. An estimate was submitted on 19 April 1619, signed by Jones, the Comptroller, the Master Carpenter, another carpenter, and one of the Clerks of the Works; and it amounted to £9850. The Paymaster was appointed, under two privy seals, to receive and disburse the necessary sums of money, and between 1619 and 1622 £14,940 1s 1d was spent. In addition, money was spent on the construction of a pier at Portland to obtain stone for certain parts of the building. The Banqueting House was begun on 1 June 1619, and in the same month Jones was paid for the 'model'. The building was finished in 1622.

The chief workmen were the best of their kinds. The elderly King's Master Mason, William Cure, was for some reason dismissed, and Nicholas Stone, aged thirty-two, appointed to replace him for this particular task (Stone did not become King's Master Mason till Cure's death in 1632). Portington, the Master Carpenter, had been in the Works for over twenty years, and George Weale and Andrew Durdant, the Clerks of the Works, were men of long experience. The accounts were managed by Tobie Samways, who, oddly enough, had drawn the plans for the old Banqueting House of 1607.

Jones himself was close on forty-six, an experienced architect in wood and canvas, far less experienced in the execution of monumental buildings. So far as we know he had to his credit only those few minor buildings we have mentioned, when he set about designing the greatest London building of his time.

The designing of the Banqueting House was evidently done within about three months. In that space the ideas which were uppermost in the architect's mind coalesced, modified one another, and finally resolved themselves into the building we know to-day. What these ideas were and how their co-ordination proceeded we can trace with some certainty, thanks to the survival of two preliminary designs (Plates 40A and B) and our knowledge of Jones's then rather restricted sources of inspiration. Nearly the whole of the Banqueting House, both in mass and in detail, derives from Palladio – either from his own designs or from his exposition of Vitruvian theories and formulas. But nothing about the building is more remarkable than the way in which these derivations have been transmuted and combined into a final result which is detached from the spirit of sixteenth-century Italy and has a character which, if you are so inclined, you may truthfully call English.

In the early stages of the work, Jones seems to have been obsessed with two quite different conceptions which he proceeded to combine. The leading idea was to build a hall on the model of a Roman basilica, as described by Vitruvius and interpreted by Palladio. Such a hall, to be strictly loyal to its model, would have to consist of what, for convenience, we may call nave and aisles – a high nave, with colonnades supporting a clerestory, and low aisles on either side beyond the columns. Aisles, however, had been ruled out by the time the first surviving sketch was made. Perhaps King James, who had objected to the columns in the old Banqueting House, insisted on their absence in the new one. Perhaps Jones's own experience of masques in the old House was enough to condemn them. Anyway, the aisles were suppressed, though the colonnades remained in vestigial form, as the lower pilaster order of the interior; while a cantilever balcony (the only un-Palladian feature of the building) was introduced at the level of the cornice of this lower order.

Jones's second idea, which suggested itself, perhaps, at the moment that the basilican aisles were discarded, was to treat the two exposed exterior elevations on the lines of some of Palladio's designs for town-houses – that is to say, with superimposed orders of columns, the centre bays of each façade being slightly advanced and crowned by a pediment, betokening a portico.

Now these two ideas, as first combined by Jones, fundamentally contradicted each other. The main axis of a basilica is, quite obviously, the centre line of the 'nave'. The main axis of a Palladian house is, equally obviously, the line through the pedimented centre of its entrance front. To apply the Palladian *front* to the *side* of the basilica is to make a flatly contradictory statement. Jones must have felt this; for the steps he took to reach the final design all involved a reduction in the central emphasis of the Palladian elevation.

The first Chatsworth design (Plate 40A) adheres very closely to the lines of one of Palladio's diagrams, with a plain basement substituted for the columned ground-floor. In the second design (Plate 40B), the flow of emphasis to the centre is checked by break-ing the entablatures outwards over each column in the lateral bays, in the manner of the Palazzo Porto. Jones's pencil has hesitated as to the propriety of breaking the entablature in the centre bays also. That step, obviously, he could not take while preserving the integrity of his pediment. But a ghostly line through that obstructive feature shows what is coming, and in the design as executed the pediment no longer obstructs, for it has vanished. The entablature breaks over all the columns, and the façade, instead of con-verging to an emphatic centre, flows rhythmically from bay to bay, the slight projection of the three centre bays serving merely to give that fullness to the façade which so enhances the effect of mass.

As the conflict between those two ideas was gradually eliminated and the design assumed its unique character, the details gradually worked themselves out in Jones's mind. The 'vocabulary' is, as I have said, Palladian throughout, and for every single feature of the exterior and most in the interior a page in Palladio's book can be quoted. Yet the *combinations* are original and their totality makes the building a thoroughly personal work.[3]

When all borrowings have been marked up, there remains the all-important matter of proportion. In this, the interior follows the Vitruvio-Palladian basilica in so far as it is to all intents and purposes a double cube. But the spacing of the window bays and of the columns and pilasters inside and out departs emphatically from the spirit and practice of Palladio, the bays being considerably broader (in relation to their height) than any that Palladio used, except when he introduced an arch between the columns. This feeling for breadth, both here and in Jones's other works, is extremely interesting. It is, I think, the result of intuitive modification on the part of an artist who, while he admired the work of the *Cinquecento*, felt out of sympathy with the strained, nervous character of Italian Mannerist architecture. Palladio's Vicenza palaces are all ever so slightly top-heavy; deliberately so, for in the mounting peril of order upon order was part of their attraction. Jones's classicism discounted this; he was in search of a finality, a balance, more akin to the age of Bramante, and to this all his revisions of Palladio tend. In this, too, he showed, all unconsciously, the phlegmatic Englishness of his mind and its appropriateness as the source of the English tradition in classical design.

To-day, the Banqueting House stands in nearly perfect conformity with the original design, except that the modern window-sashes are of a design quite different from the four-light mullion-and-transome casements which Jones used in this as in all his buildings. And there has been one other important change – nothing less than the material of the exterior. In spite of the fact that elaborate provision was made for obtaining Portland stone, the Banqueting House was faced with Northamptonshire stone, except for the basement which was in Oxfordshire stone and certain details only in Portland stone.[4]

The purpose of the Banqueting House was, of course, as a setting for State banquets, the reception of ambassadors, and the presentation of masques. The use of the vaulted basement is not quite clear but it was evidently not severely practical, as an ornamental 'rock' was installed there and equipped with shell ornaments by Isaac de Caus: evidently some kind of grotto. The final adornment of the building came when the ceiling panels by Peter Paul Rubens, representing the apotheosis of James I and an allegory of the birth of Charles, were installed in 1635. These precious additions to the building (Rubens's fee was £3000) induced Charles I to exclude the presentation of masques, with the smoky risks accompanying them, from the building's functions. He built a wooden structure of nearly equal size in the adjoining court, which survived until demolished by the Parliamentarians in 1645.

During the years 1619–22 when the Banqueting House was rising, Jones produced little else of architectural importance. Of the Prince's Lodging at Newmarket, an addition to the palace there, no pictorial records survive, and the accounts conjure up only a vague picture of two storeys of classical windows with a crowning entablature.

In spite – or, indeed, because – of its probable simplicity the building may very well have been important and influential in its time.

In 1623 the need suddenly arose for several Chapels Royal for the Catholic Infanta of Spain, whom Prince Charles sailed out to fetch as his bride in February. In May a warrant was issued for building the first of them at St James's Palace, and on the 16th the foundation stone was laid in the presence of the Spanish ambassador. The Queen's Chapel at St James's (Plates 42B and 43), thus begun, was not completed till 1627 when, the Spanish marriage having miscarried, it served the Court of another Catholic Princess, Henrietta Maria. The building still stands to-day as the Chapel of Marlborough House.

This was Jones's first ecclesiastical building. The conception of a large domestic chapel of strictly classical character was something new for England, and Jones, as one would expect, considered the problem afresh in the light of his knowledge of, and belief in, Roman antiquity and the theories of Palladio. He designed what may be considered the *cella* of a Roman temple, but with a strong horizontal division as of a Palladian house, the lower part rusticated. The cornice is a corbel cornice of the Pantheon type. The east end is lit by a Venetian window such as Scamozzi occasionally used. The west front has a door and two windows in the rusticated part and, above, a trio of windows – one round-headed, between two flat-headed – an arrangement not strictly Palladian, and one which, here and elsewhere, gave Jones a certain amount of trouble in determining the proper relationships. The interior of the Chapel, though somewhat altered, retains the segmental ceiling, coffered somewhat in the manner of the ceiling for the Duke of Buckingham already mentioned.

An elaborate new east window for the Chapel of Greenwich Palace also belongs to 1623, but there are no records of it. Nor are there any of the new Banqueting House at Theobalds, a kind of summer-house for King James to spend quiet hours in, but hardly finished by his death. He died in 1625, and in May of that year Jones designed for his funeral the magnificent Hearse of which there is a fine drawing at Worcester College. Inspired by Bramante's tempietto, the eight Doric columns are attached to as many square Doric piers in a manner which makes it clear that the works of Fontana and Vignola were in Jones's mind. The use of sculpture is also in a later style than Bramante's. The hearse was richly decorated, painted by Matthew Goodrich, with sculpture by Maximilian Colt and Hubert Le Sueur.

With the accession of Henrietta Maria to the consort's throne and her entry into possession of Somerset House, Jones was almost continuously employed on that palace for thirteen years or more. Between 1625 and 1639 we hear of new decorative features for the Queen's closet, an ornamental seat in the Bowling Alley, a new cabinet room, an arbour, and a new river-gate and stairs.[5]

It is useless to attempt to visualize, from the meagre evidence of the accounts, the interiors which Jones designed for the Queen at Somerset House. Some of the fireplaces alone are given among the drawings at the Royal Institute of British Architects; they are dated 1635 and 1636. It is almost equally difficult, unfortunately, to obtain a clear picture of the Queen's Chapel, a lavish setting for the Mass with which Charles I most unwisely indulged his French queen. It was an important work, and one can only regret that neither the Palladian enthusiasts of Burlington's time nor Sir William Chambers', who built over the site, thought it worth while to publish a complete survey of it. All the records we have are a few beautiful details among the Jones drawings (Plate 44A), an adequate measured drawing of the ceiling, an engraved elevation by Ware of the screen (Plate 44B), and distant glimpses in views of the palace taken from the river.

The Chapel was commissioned in 1630 and inaugurated in 1635; £5050 was spent on it. It was a hundred and four feet long and thirty-six feet wide, with shallow transepts, each containing a side-chapel. The body of the building formed a double cube of thirty-six feet with, at the west end, the 'Queen's closet', supported gallery-wise on columns and having a ceiling of enriched octagonal coffers. The exterior, largely concealed by surrounding buildings, was unimportant, and everything was lavished on the inside. Here, the details, as at St James's, were far from Palladian. A large window, of which a drawing survives, is adapted from one given by Domenico Fontana; a niche, also shown in a drawing, is reminiscent of Vignola; while the screen consisted of a Doric order with terms above, supporting a scrolled cresting resembling some of the fireplace designs and close to Jean Barbet. Everything about the Chapel was rich and lavish, and the altar arrangements (all smashed by the Parliamentarians) were on the level of Jones's most magnificent masque scenes.

Parallel with the Somerset House Chapel came the resumption of work at the Queen's House at Greenwich (Plates 39A and B; Figure 14). The accounts for this are lost, but we know that the arch over the highway was still protected by a temporary roof in 1629–30. Building was proceeding in 1632, and in 1635 a tablet recording the house's completion was put up. Four years later decorative details were still being added. Inigo Jones, as we have seen, committed himself to the general lines of the building, when the foundations were laid in 1616–18. So the plan necessarily belongs to those years. It consists of two elongated rectangles connected by the bridge, but apart from this curious division, dictated by the site, the plan is strictly Palladian. It is as if one of Palladio's square villa plans had been bisected along the central cross wall, the two halves drawn apart and somewhat elongated. One design, in particular, in Palladio's book, lends itself quite nicely to this process. In that design a great square hall occupies the centre part of one half, while the corresponding part in the other half consists of a loggia with rooms behind, the columns of the loggia forming part of an attached portico on the elevation. These are precisely the essentials of the Queen's House, and it is quite likely that here, as in the Banqueting House at Whitehall, Jones originally designed a pediment at least on the south (loggia) side. On the north side he introduced that trio of windows – the centre window round-headed, the others flat – which he had introduced in the St James's Chapel.

Another design in Palladio gives the south elevation (Plate 39B) very nearly, if the pediment is removed, the ground-floor loggia walled up, and the whole ground storey rusticated, and there is very little in the Queen's House for which authority cannot be found in Jones's main source-book. But, as in the case of the Banqueting House, the proportions are un-Italian; the columns in the loggia are more widely spaced than in Palladio and the whole effect of the building is long and low – there is no gravitation to the centre. Here again, we find Jones's native inclinations profoundly modifying a design which, in plan and detail, adheres closely to authority. Of the two 'halves' of the house, that facing north towards the river contains the most important rooms. Here is the hall, a forty-foot cube with a cantilevered gallery at first-floor level, a ceiling with enriched beams and a floor laid with black and white marble, all reminiscent of the interior treatment of the Banqueting House. There is something bleak about a cubic room and neither this interior nor indeed the double-cube interior of the Banqueting House itself can be numbered among Jones's great successes. The Cabinet Room, the Queen's Cabinet, and the Queen's Bedchamber, all on the first floor, are more humane. The first two have beamed plaster ceilings of considerable richness, while the Bedchamber has a coved cornice and ceiling superbly painted with what, in the language of the time, was called 'grotesk-work': it is almost certainly the work of John de Critz, the Serjeant Painter, or of another painter, Matthew Goodrich, who is recorded as having done 'grotesks' for the Queen at Somerset House. For this bedroom, Jones designed a fireplace of which, with others, we have his drawing; the details echo exactly the terms and frieze in the screen in the Queen's Chapel at Somerset House. Finally, there is the novel and daring circular staircase, modelled on one given by Palladio, but for England a new departure in masonry design.

It was in 1638, when the last details for Greenwich had been designed, that Inigo Jones produced the design for (apparently) a complete new palace at Somerset House, a design which leads on to the Jones-Webb series of designs for rebuilding Whitehall, and will be discussed with them.

But we must retrace our steps, for the work for Henrietta Maria has carried us past a number of less important buildings which belong to the first decade of Charles I's reign. Thus, there was a Clock-House at Whitehall, built in 1626–7 and, at the same palace, a new gallery with an outside staircase, known as the Park Stairs, leading into St James's Park. This staircase, shown in several seventeenth-century paintings, was all in timber and connected with a double colonnade of superimposed Corinthian and Composite columns, with a scrolled cresting, the effect of this being not wholly unlike the screen at Somerset House Chapel. This was built in 1629–30, and about the same time the old Tudor cockpit was converted into the Cockpit Playhouse. Here, Jones erected a permanent scene, recorded in a drawing by Webb at Worcester College: a segmental concavity, divided into bays by superimposed Corinthian and Composite orders, with pedimented openings in the centre.

In 1631–2 an extension to the King's Lodge at Bagshot, which appears, however, to have been a self-contained building, was completed. It was all of timber, painted stone-colour and seems, from the accounts, to have been a miniature Palladian villa with four columns prefacing a 'pergula' or loggia as they do at the Queen's House. In 1634–5 a Lodge in Hyde Park, with four composite columns between pilasters, was built.

During the six years immediately preceding the outbreak of Civil War in 1642, Jones built nothing of great importance for the King and Queen. We hear of a balcony and a new cabinet at Oatlands, an open wooden gallery in one of the courts at Whitehall, a new bedchamber for the Queen at the same palace, and sundry fireplaces here and there, but of the appearance of all these we are ignorant.

The Restoration of St Paul's

To the period of the Surveyorship belong several very important works, not royal buildings but works of public importance with which Jones became involved either directly or indirectly because of his office. The chief of these was the restoration of St Paul's Cathedral (Plate 45).

A Royal Commission of nearly seventy persons, of whom Jones was one, was appointed to initiate the restoration of the Cathedral in 1620, but there was difficulty in obtaining funds and the matter was dropped. It was resurrected, however, under Laud, who became Bishop in 1628, and another Commission, not including Jones, was appointed in 1631. A report was obtained from Jones in that year, but it was not until 1634 that he was appointed Surveyor to the Commission, an appointment which he undertook without fee. The work was started without further delay.

The old Cathedral, which had been in a deplorable state since a conflagration in Elizabeth's time, presented an awkward problem, and Jones's attempt to classicize it by casing up much of the exterior in rusticated masonry must be judged as a piece of architectural juggling in almost impossible circumstances. It was on the west front that Jones made his most determined attempt to produce a new, complete, and effective composition. A preparatory drawing at the Royal Institute of British Architects shows that he had Vignola's and della Porta's Church of the Gesù in mind. From this he took the superimposed orders and the giant scrolls which fill the angles between high nave and low aisles; but he had to extemporize boldly to reform the old Gothic gable and was obliged, also, to incorporate and classicize the Gothic tower of St Gregory-by-St Paul's on the south and, moreover, to repeat it for symmetry on the north.

The executed design dispensed with all the Gesù details except the scrolls and turned rather towards Palladio's restoration of the Temple of the Sun, the main feature of which is a great Corinthian portico, without pediment, projecting from its lower storey, the upper part of the temple, with round-headed windows, being seen above and behind the portico. Whatever the effect of the whole new west front (it was destroyed, of course, in the fire of 1666) there is no question that in this portico Jones scored a great triumph. It was the first thing of its kind to be built in Britain and remained, till its destruction, the most completely *Roman* structure in the country. Apart from that there is little to be said about this work of pure scholarship, attached to a façade which can be admired only as a gallant attempt to make a Classical silk purse out of a Gothic sow's ear.

The Commission on Buildings

There is one side of Jones's work which was very extensive and very important, but which cannot be dealt with here in detail. That was his share in the administration of controls aimed at the improvement of building in London and the limitation of abuses, such as building in timber contrary to the several proclamations on this issue, the regulation of brick construction, and overbuilding in already crowded areas. A Commission on

Buildings was set up in 1618, re-formed and enlarged in 1620. It included the names of the Earl of Pembroke, the Earl of Arundel, and among many others that of the Surveyor-General, who was the Commission's executive officer.

It was this Commission, as first appointed, which proposed to lay out Lincoln's Inn Fields as a formal open space, and it has sometimes been assumed that the regularity of this, the first of London's squares, dates from the recommendations of 1618. Actually these recommendations, which referred to 'fair and goodly walks' and had nothing to do with buildings, were dropped; and the later enclosure of the Fields by regular masses of buildings is another story and not a very clear one. Jones's connexion with Lincoln's Inn Fields is an assumption of the early eighteenth century.

Jones certainly was, however, associated with the geometrical planning of London's developing fringes in the notable instance of Covent Garden (Plate 46A), and the story of this is clear enough. The 4th Earl of Bedford possessed houses and lands north of the Strand and obtained in 1630 a licence to demolish some of the old buildings and erect new ones. 'Thereupon', says a document issuing from the Earl's son during the Common-wealth, 'many ancient buildings were demolished and other new buildings erected by special direction of the then King and his Council with much ornament and beauty and to a vast charge.' This statement seems to suggest that the King and Council brought pressure or persuasion on the Earl to the intent that his new buildings should be of special architectural character. They were. For in developing the land called Covent Garden the Earl created London's first formal open space and lined it on two sides (north and east) with buildings of strictly uniform and classical character. On the west side he provided a church, linked to two separate houses. The south side, adjoining his own private garden, was open.

Inigo Jones's name has been connected with Covent Garden since the seventeenth century, and there is no reason whatever to doubt that the church was his. We may also trust the tradition to the extent of believing that he imposed the general character of the whole scheme. But the executant architect of the houses on north and west seems to have been Isaac de Caus,[6] who had worked with Jones at the Banqueting House (p. 78) and was to do so elsewhere; and this may account for the faintly French character which these buildings had, recalling Chastillon's Place Dauphine and Place des Vosges of thirty years earlier; it would also account for the lack of harmony between these houses and those (presumably by Jones) flanking the Church.

The houses had loggias ('piazzas' as they became called) on the ground-floor, vaulted much like those of the Place des Vosges, with a two-storey superstructure of brick with stone pilaster-strips, and dormers in the roof. All have been demolished, but a passable reproduction (built in the 1880s), remaining at the north-west corner, records their scale and general character.

The Church, finished in 1631, is also lost to us, having been burnt in 1795, though this again is represented by a tolerable copy on the old foundation. It is a study in the rarely used Tuscan order and Jones availed himself of plates in Vignola and Zanini for his Tuscan portico of two round and two square columns, the latter linked (as in Vignola) to the body of the Church by walls pierced by arches. The Church is correctly oriented and the eastern position of the portico, making a scenic focus for the square, is anomalous; the doorway in the east wall is (and perhaps always was) a sham. The interior of the present building is a mere box, but the original had a painted ceiling and arabesque decorations by Matthew Goodrich, who worked on several of the royal buildings.

It is doubtful if, even in its original form, the Covent Garden group was altogether successful. De Caus's houses, high and narrow, must have gone ill with the exaggerated sturdiness of the Tuscan Church and the openness of the south side will have detracted from the effect which the exact symmetry of the lay-out was intended to produce. Nevertheless, both Church and houses were, in themselves, excellent, as well as extremely novel. Both became classics and entered into the vocabulary of English architecture.

The Designs for Whitehall Palace

Finally, in this account of the products of Jones's Surveyorship, we come to designs made for the King but not carried out. Those which survive include, principally, an elevation, dated 1638, for a large new building at Somerset House and a great number of undated designs for a complete rebuilding of the Palace of Whitehall (Plates 47A and B).

These designs for Whitehall have, in recent years, been the subject of some confusion.[7] There are several distinct sets and the presumption now is that some at least of the early sets were done under Jones's immediate direction; that the 1647–8 set was done by Webb at Charles I's command; and that the remainder represent a resumption of the scheme, again by Webb, after the Restoration.

The early sets are of first-rate importance in the history of English architecture, partly because they fill out our knowledge of Jones as an artist, but also because the two which were engraved (by Campbell in 1717 and by Kent in 1727) were among the most important documents in the Inigo Jones revival which occurred, as we shall see, in the first quarter of the eighteenth century.

The set of drawings engraved by Kent is unquestionably the most important of the early schemes and the one most easily integrated with Jones's stylistic development as we know it. It represents a vast rectangular palace comprising one great oblong court in the centre and three smaller courts on each side of it, the middle court in each three being specially treated, one with a circular, the other with a square, loggia. The palace was to be symmetrical about its east-west axis and to lie across the whole site of the old palace, with the state apartments looking on St James's Park and a grand entrance towards a Thames embankment. The existing Banqueting House was to be incorporated at the south-east corner of the centre court and repeated three times to fulfil the symmetry of the whole.

This scheme appears to have developed out of one prepared nearly at the same time for a site further west and involving the demolition of the Banqueting House. The plan of that scheme seems to suggest that Jones attacked this gigantic and (for England) unprecedented problem in the true spirit of the early sixteenth-century Italian theorists, starting with a square central court and developing ten further courtyards around it, giving an approximately square totality.

As one scheme developed into the other (the King's objection to deserting his Banqueting House being the likely motive), it looks as if Jones had cast his eye on de l'Orme's plan of the Tuileries, deriving from this a freer conception of a great modern palace and a distincter notion of the value of pavilions in such a design; deriving also the happy idea of introducing a circular court within the rectangular pattern. The design has square pavilions at all the points where the main lines of building join one another. Thus, the north and south elevations (the flanks of the palace) have four pavilions, all of three storeys and identical in design. The centre and park fronts (the ends of the palace) have only two pavilions each, at the outer angles. Both side and end elevations are broken up into unequal sections, some of two, some of three storeys and the centres are in all cases flanked by towers, rising into domed turrets.

The resultant composition is, one is bound to confess, not overwhelmingly impressive. And it is not difficult to see why. Inigo Jones had trained himself to think not in mass but in detail. Out of a single bay of a classical design he could, by accurate and sensitive adjustment of every detail, make a personal work of art. This faculty he could extend to a single façade of some magnitude. But Whitehall Palace involved not only relationships of detail but relationships *between façades* – i.e. relationships of mass. Here Jones's powers proved unequal to the task and although the mass relationships in the Whitehall designs have no conspicuous faults they simply do not carry conviction. The modulations from mass to mass are beautifully studied, the rhythms are carefully preserved, the textures nicely contrasted. But in no single part of the design does mass *tell* against mass, and one leaves the drawings with an impression of monotony, in spite of the faultless beauty of each component in the design.

No stylistic analysis of the Whitehall drawings has yet been undertaken, but it is obvious that even at the age of sixty-four or five Jones leaned conscientiously and all the time on his knowledge of Italian theory and engravings. One easily detects references to Palladio and Scamozzi and here and there to Serlio; Zanini has inspired some of the rusticated work and from Rusconi have come the caryatid figures which Jones, in one of his rare moods of fantasy, distributed in two ranks around the circular loggia. From sources other than Italian come the French character of the plan and, just possibly, a certain likeness in the domed turrets to the tower of the Jesuit Church at Antwerp.

In a sense, the Whitehall drawings are the fulfilment of Jones's career. They prove to us that his greatness is appropriately and adequately enclosed within the limited dimensions of the Banqueting House, and that had his opportunities been as great as his royal master would have wished the beauties of that building might have been multiplied but would not necessarily have been deepened or enlarged.

NOTES TO CHAPTER 8

1. Two other plainer gateways were built at Oatlands about this time and Jones designed several elsewhere. A fashion for these architectural toys had been established in the previous century (see Holdenby, p. 38) and designs for them were available in Serlio, Vignola, and elsewhere. They served no particular purpose except as exercises in taste and ingenuity on the attractive theme of the triumphal arch.

Jones's great gate at Oatlands was Serlian, but one of the gates he built for Lord Arundel at Arundel

House derived (perhaps through Serlio) from Michelangelo's Porta Pia. For Beaufort House, Chelsea, he designed the very simple Doric gateway (for Lionel Cranfield, 1621) which is now at Chiswick Park, having been moved there by Lord Burlington in 1740. There are designs for several gateways among Jones's drawings, dating from the early 1620s, and in 1623–4 he built a heavily rusticated Doric gateway in the Park wall at Greenwich.

2. Gotch describes and illustrates this as a ceiling for Buckingham House, Strand, with which, however, Jones probably had nothing to do (the watergate must, as we shall see later, be attributed to Gerbier).

3. Here are some of Jones's Palladian borrowings. Pilasters and columns against a rusticated background come from the Palazzo Barbarano (ground-floor); but the coupled pilasters at the outer angles are from the Thiene, while the breaking of the entablature over each column or pilaster can be from the Porto or the Basilica. The idea of the high basement forming a podium for the superstructure is a brilliant intrusion of Palladio's country-villa style into his town-house formula; its rusticated treatment, however, is suggested by the ground-floor of the Barbarano. The treatment of windows derives from the Chiericati and the Porto. The balustrade, like the basement, is foreign to the Palladian townhouse; it does occur in the Basilica, but its enormously effective triple plinth, which Fergusson criticized but which surely gives the building just that extra 'lift' and vitality, seems to be a pure Jonesian inspiration. Both the Ionic and the Composite orders are select combinations of Palladio and the antique, the caps being original variations in both cases. The interior is slightly less complicated; for Jones stuck to the basilican theme, combining it with Palladio's interpretation of the 'Egyptian Hall', which Vitruvius described as a kind of basilica.

4. The basement decayed rapidly and was refaced with Portland in 1773. In 1829, Sir John Soane, charged with the restoration of the whole building, found the balustrade and cornices in tatters and replaced them all, with Portland stone; and he cut away the old rusticated surfaces in Northamptonshire stone (his mason identified it as Ketton) and introduced a new outer skin, all of Portland. Any portions of the original Ketton which Soane left must have been replaced by Portland since his time, for to-day there is neither Oxfordshire nor Northamptonshire stone to be seen, and the legend has quickly grown up that, in the Banqueting House, Inigo Jones gave London its first great Portland stone building.

5. The appearance of the river-gate is preserved for us in Canaletto's famous painting of London which shows it in the foreground. Jones at first proposed obelisks to mark the entry but changed these to tall piers carrying vases, or 'potts' as they are called in the accounts. These were flanked by scrolls, while below the parapet and seen only from the river were two carved stone figures, representing 'Thames' and 'Isis'. Behind the figures was 'sedge-work' rustication, while below them the water lapped against masonry cut rockwise. Wooden gates were hung between the piers and painted white, with gilded metal fleurs-de-lis as a defence along an arched crosspiece at the top. Gate-piers had, of course, been common features in Jacobean design.

6. Assuming him to be identifiable with the 'Mr Decause' whose name appears in the accounts for some of these buildings in the Duke of Bedford's archives at Woburn.

7. There are in all, some seventy drawings, distributed in three collections and comprising a number of distinct designs. Two sets were engraved and published over Inigo Jones's name in the eighteenth century, and up to 1912 all the drawings were loosely assumed to be the work of Jones. In that year, however, J. A. Gotch noticed that the bulk of the drawings appeared to be in the hand of Jones's pupil and assistant, John Webb. As the only dated drawing was inscribed 1661 in Webb's handwriting and as Webb stated that he had been commanded to design a new Whitehall a few years before Charles I's death, Gotch challenged the whole force of tradition and assigned everything to Webb, and to dates during and after the Civil War. Subsequently, however, decisive evidence came to light that Jones had received instructions for a new palace in the late 1630s. The drawings were then thoroughly re-examined by Margaret Whinney (1946), with the result that three sets, with various related drawings, are now allocated to c. 1637–9, one set to 1647–8, the one dated drawing alone to 1661, and a small scheme to c. 1661–5.

CHAPTER 9

INIGO JONES, HIS CONTEMPORARIES AND
FOLLOWERS

As Surveyor to the King, Inigo Jones was in no way inhibited from making designs for private persons. Those persons were, however, almost without exception, closely connected with the Court and the circles where the Surveyor's talents were available were probably extremely limited. Tradition, or the guesswork of optimistic historians, has assigned more than one hundred and twenty buildings (not including royal works) to Jones! Of these less than a dozen are certainly associated with him, half a dozen more possibly. Of the remainder it may be said that tradition is occasionally valuable as a pointer to the origin of a design in Jones's entourage; it may be the work of one of the under-officers or patent artificers of the Works. But many attributions have been made on no better evidence than that the work is of Jones's time (or ten years after it) and more or less respectably classical.

We have already seen that Jones, acting in a private way, built gateways and other things for Lord Arundel, and the gateway at Chelsea for a personal friend, Sir Lionel Cranfield. In 1617 he was probably approached by another personal friend, Christopher Brooke, on behalf of the Society of Lincoln's Inn to furnish the model for a new chapel, but nothing came of this.[1]

More important are a number of large country-houses with which he was reputedly concerned after 1630. Stoke Bruerne Park, Northants. (Figure 15), was built between 1629 and 1635 by Sir Francis Crane, who 'brought the design from Italy, and in the execution of it received the assistance of Inigo Jones'.[2] Crane was the man who established the Mortlake tapestry factory under James I. He succeeded in building only two lateral pavilions and curved colonnades before his death in 1635 and the centre block was added after the Civil War by another hand. The alleged Italian provenance of the design may mean nothing more than that the main theme (judged from the existing pavilions) derived from Michelangelo's Palazzo dei Conservatori, a giant order with a secondary order laced through it at ground-floor level. This theme is very deftly applied to the junction of the pavilions and the colonnades. The plan, of which these features are part, is also thoroughly Italian and, in fact, a type of plan favoured by Palladio and (in his thesis drawings) by Inigo Jones. Stoke Bruerne is the first case, in England, of a house consisting of a main pile, connected by curved colonnades with forward-standing pavilions. The popularity which this plan enjoyed in the eighteenth century was part of the Jones-Palladio revival and in this the publication of Stoke Bruerne, in *Vitruvius Britannicus*, played its part.

Another house with which Jones has been traditionally associated since the early eighteenth century is Castle Ashby, Northants. (Plate 48B), an Elizabethan building with additions of various dates, including a two-storey screen or loggia, closing the courtyard. This screen, although it picks up the lines of older work, almost certainly dates from 1635 or later and will have been done for the 2nd Earl of Northampton. It has superimposed pilaster orders and a pedimented entrance with coupled columns, a charming and techni- cally expert design which one readily gives to Jones – the more so because it is echoed in the Whitehall and Somerset House projects on which he was working in 1638.

A third house attributed to Jones on the rather slender evidence of family tradition (even to the optimistic Colen Campbell in 1717 it was only 'said to be designed' by him)

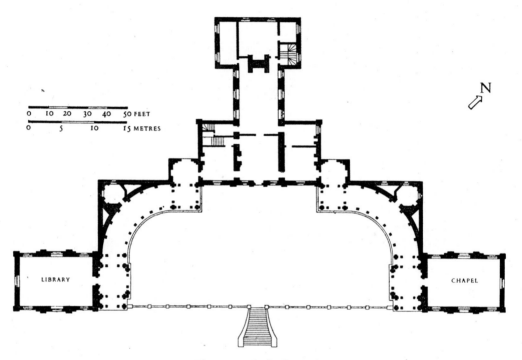

Figure 15. Stoke Bruerne

is Chevening, Kent (Plate 46B). The same tradition makes the 13th Lord Dacre the builder of it, and he died in 1630. The house was completely transformed in the eighteenth century, but, in origin, was a pioneer or at least among the very first of its kind. It con- sisted of a single rectangular block, two rooms deep – a type which we may follow Pratt in calling a 'double pile'. There was a crowning entablature at the eaves, from which a hipped roof rose steeply to a platform, emphasized and protected by a balustrade.

The directness of such a design as this was, for England, revolutionary. It opposed the whole Elizabethan-Jacobean tradition of plan-form and silhouette. It was a single massive block, no romantic effects being elicited by recession or projection, by flanking towers or extruded corners. For effect it relied on mass, on the careful spacing of windows, and their nice diminution from storey to storey, and on the bold treatment of the roof with its balustraded summit.

Roofs of this kind, but without the balustraded platform, occur among Jones's draw-ings, and it is possible, moreover, that the Prince's Lodging at Newmarket (1619), which had a crowning entablature, was the prototype of this sort of elevation. The plan shows a hall and a saloon, back-to-back, each centrally entered from the centres of the long façades. The stair climbs up the walls at one end of the hall, to which it is perfectly open – another striking innovation in an age when stairs were invariably enclosed in rectangular compartments of the plan.

In the absence of firm evidence, we must not hang too much on either the reputed date or the reputed authorship of Chevening. But as it can hardly be much later than 1630 and as no other houses of similar type are recorded till Roger Pratt began Coleshill in 1650, it is obviously something of a landmark. To Coleshill and its author we shall come in due course, but for the present we must follow Inigo Jones through the last part of his career.

The Last Years of Inigo Jones

In 1642 the Civil War put an end to the Court life in which Jones had been such a brilliant figure. He left London and appointed his pupil and relation-by-marriage, John Webb, as his deputy. This he was entitled to do under the terms of his patent. In July 1642 he was with the King at Beverley, where he lent Charles I £500. From that date, we hear nothing of him till 1645 when he was involved in the siege and burning of Basing House. 'There', says a contemporary news-sheet, 'was the famous Surveyor. ... Innico Jones, who was carried away in a blanket, having lost his clothes.'

What was happening in Scotland Yard during these years we do not know; for there is a gap in the accounts from 1640 to 1644. Webb will have been in charge for little more than a year, for the Surveyorship of his master terminated with the ordinance of 20 September 1643, 'for seizing ... all His Majesty's, the Queen's and Prince's Houses, Manors, lands etc.' Under the same ordinance Edward Carter,[3] a man whom Jones had nominated his deputy on at least one occasion, was erected in his stead. He continued as Surveyor-General till about 1653 when, according to Webb, his 'double-dealing' caused his removal.

Jones, after his adventure at Basing House, returned to London, perhaps as a prisoner. His property was sequestrated, but he pleaded to the Committee for Compounding that he had never taken up arms against the Parliament nor given information to the other side. He was heavily fined and made to yield his 'fifth-and-twentieth part'. In 1646, however, his pardon was confirmed and his estate restored.

From that year till his death in 1652 Inigo Jones seems to have swum, not uncomfort-ably, with the prevailing political tide and in the year of his royal master's execution he was assisting the 4th Earl of Pembroke (brother of the Earl so closely associated with Arundel and Jones in earlier days) with the rebuilding of part of his great house at Wilton. This Earl was one of those noblemen who had adhered to the Parliamentary cause throughout the Civil War and were able, after the struggle was over, to live in great state without criticism or hindrance. There is, to modern feelings, something a little incongruous in finding the deposed Surveyor serving one of the new rulers of England in this way, but it only serves to emphasize how indistinct was the social cleavage caused by the Civil War.

Wilton House (Plates 48A and 49) was a Tudor building to which additions are said to have been made by Salomon de Caus. These were burnt in 1647 and an opportunity was provided for Jones to rebuild the whole of the garden front, with a magnificent suite of State rooms on the first floor. Externally, the design is simple, comprising a ground-floor treated merely as a base, a lofty first floor, and a shallow second floor which in fact is only partly real, for the State rooms borrow it to achieve their great height. In the centre of the exterior, double flights of steps lead up to a doorway modelled like a Venetian window of the type which Jones had used at St James's Chapel. Pavilions are marked by slight projections at either end of the façade and these rise into additional tower-like storeys with pediments. Their effect is curious. Without them, the front would be unusually, and rather mournfully, long and low; their striking vertical emphasis gives tension to the horizontals and reinforces the importance of the central window.

The conception of Wilton seems to come from a design in Scamozzi with similarly wide spacing and corner towers, but Jones's rendering has produced a wholly different and much more economical and compact result; the pedimenting of the towers is an important stroke of invention.

Behind this front are two superb State rooms – the 'cube' room and the 'double cube' room (Plate 49), one opening into the other. They are decorated in a style of extreme richness, whose origin is quite obviously French. Indeed, Jones here availed himself of Jean Barbet's *Livre d'architecture*, published in Paris in 1633 and again in 1641. Influence from the same source had already appeared at Somerset House, and the taste of Henrietta Maria's Court would render it appropriate enough.[4] Here, at Wilton, the French taste (with, here, a strong Flemish element) is lavishly and even rather heavily deployed about the mantelpiece and the door-cases. On the walls, thick clusters of fruit and foliage hang from scrolled cartouches between the inset Van Dyck portraits. A vast cove, superbly painted by Thomas de Critz, sweeps up to the flat ceiling whose panels are filled with allegorical paintings.

Inigo Jones died on 21 June 1652, 'through grief, as is well known, for the fatal calamity of his dread master', as Webb tells us. But as he died at Somerset House, a building reserved under the Protectorate for high officials and members of the Parliament, it is by no means certain that the former Surveyor foundered in the poverty and despair which some of his biographers have thought appropriate.

John Webb

In following the career of Inigo Jones it has been necessary to mention from time to time the name of the man who was, for some twenty-four years, his pupil and assistant and who must now be introduced in his own person. John Webb (1611–72) was a Somerset man, born and educated in London, and appears to have come to Jones as a pupil when he was about seventeen. He married a kinswoman (probably a niece) of Jones and records that Charles I was interested in his being trained as Jones's successor in the office of

Surveyor-General, not only in architecture but in the design of settings for masques. We have no information about the exact relations subsisting between Jones and Webb, but it appears that during the 1630s Jones increasingly used his pupil as an architectural amanuensis. There are far more 'Jones' drawings by Webb than by the Surveyor himself, and, as we have seen, the whole of the Whitehall Palace drawings are in Webb's hand. There are also, at Worcester College and the Royal Institute of British Architects, a large number of purely theoretical drawings by Webb which, studied as a whole, give the impression of having been prepared for some kind of treatise on the lines of Scamozzi's. The making of these drawings, in which it is clear that a great deal of Jones's thought is embodied, will have served the double purpose of training Webb and building up a corpus of illustrative material for the book.[5]

Up to within a few years of Jones's death, Webb's career is inseparable from that of his master, but we have his own statement that, between 1647 and 1649, he was called upon by Charles I to design a new Whitehall Palace; and there is a design in his hand for a rebuilding of Durham House, Strand, which must date from 1649 and is probably his own production. After 1652 his independence is unambiguous. He designed Lamport Hall, Northants., for Sir Giles Isham in 1654–7 (the wings are later), Belvoir for the Earl of Rutland in 1654 (since rebuilt) and added, in the same year, the portico of The Vyne, Hants., for Mr Speaker Chaloner Chute. After the Restoration he designed two more great houses, Amesbury, Wilts. (1661), and Gunnersbury, Middlesex (1663), and his one public building, the King Charles block at Greenwich (p. 117; Plate 68B). In addition, there is some reason for connecting him with Ashburnham House, Westminster, built before 1662 and important because of the unusual arrangement of its staircase and the open cupola which rises above it. The details here, however, are very awkward and do not conform with the high technical standard of Webb's authenticated work.

There are enough buildings here to enable us to assess Webb's powers. They were not intrinsically great. Inevitably, his unique, long, and laborious training under Jones comes out in everything he designed, with the result that from the point of view of technique and scholarship he was head and shoulders above all other designers practising at the date of the Restoration. The only personal trait seems to be a tendency to a rather depressing emphasis on horizontals, a psychological clue, perhaps, to a nature dominated by loyalty to the great genius whose right hand it was his pride to have been.

The measure of Webb's intellect can be taken from the book on Stonehenge (see p. 73 n.), which he published under Inigo Jones's name in 1655, and the later *Vindication* of the work. In both books he quotes liberally from the classics, but shows himself singularly lacking in imagination, and becomes animated only in the encomiums he bestows on Jones in the second of the two productions.

Architect Contemporaries of Inigo Jones

Apart from Webb, Inigo's effective contemporaries in the building world were nearly all either working masons and carpenters of the type of Nicholas Stone and Robert Lyminge or clerks and surveyors like Robert Stickells or John Thorpe. And, so far as we know, none of these people seriously attempted to follow Jones in his loyalty to a selective and critical version of Italian design. Even in the Office of Works, Jones seems to have inspired nobody to follow his lead very closely, and the prevailing style in England during the whole of his career is the style which we shall examine in the next chapter under the title of Artisan Mannerism. First, however, it is necessary to dispose of the question whether Jones was, in truth, the only man to detach himself from the main stream in this way. There are a few other names to be considered. Salomon de Caus has already been mentioned (p. 71) as having served at the Court of Prince Henry and built a gallery at Richmond and possibly the old garden front at Wilton. As he left England in 1613 his importance is negligible. A son or nephew, however, Isaac de Caus, was certainly closely associated with Jones, both at the Banqueting House and at Covent Garden. He was primarily a garden architect and designer of grottoes in the Italo-French manner. The grotto at Woburn, Beds., may well be his, and if he designed the 'piazzas' at Covent Garden (p. 83) his importance as an architect is undeniable.

Then there is the Dutch-born Huguenot, Sir Balthazar Gerbier (1591?–1667), a curious character – courtier and diplomat, miniaturist and architect, pamphleteer and promoter – whose career threads grotesquely through the events of the seventeenth century up to the Restoration and beyond. It is very nearly certain that Gerbier designed the York Water-Gate (Plate 50A; now in Embankment Gardens) as part of his work at York House for the Duke of Buckingham, in 1626–7. Usually attributed to Jones, on the strength of a drawing by Webb at the Royal Institute of British Architects, and certainly executed by Nicholas Stone, the Water-Gate is a direct but rather feeble imitation of the Fontaine de Médicis at the Luxembourg in Paris (c. 1624).[6] It is exceptional as being of direct Parisian inspiration, and important because of the great respect paid to it (as a work of Jones!) in the eighteenth century. Gerbier wrote two books on building, neither important, and attempted to form an Academy in his house at Bethnal Green. We shall meet him again as the designer of Hampstead Marshall and the master of one of Wren's contemporaries, William Winde.

These few names and their relative unimportance serve merely to emphasize Jones's long and complete isolation in his task of Italianizing English architecture on the highest technical level. Nor do imitators and successors follow hard upon him; and apart from Webb, the first man to carry forward Jones's work in a series of important buildings was one nearly fifty years his junior. His name was Roger Pratt.

Sir Roger Pratt

Roger Pratt (1620–84) came of a good Norfolk family and was educated at Magdalen College, Oxford, and the Inner Temple. The outbreak of the Civil War induced him to go abroad and from 1643 to 1649 he was travelling in France, Italy, Flanders, and Holland. At Rome (1644–5) he lived for a time with John Evelyn, a man of exactly his own age, whose interest in the arts had been stimulated and guided by Lord Arundel. We do not know when Pratt's serious application to architecture began, but he certainly made industrious use of his time abroad, for his copious notes on French and Italian buildings are shrewdly analytical.

Returning to England in the year of the King's execution, Pratt lived a fashionable life of such sort as the times afforded until in or about 1650 (the date is very uncertain) he undertook to assist his cousin, Sir George Pratt of Coleshill, in rebuilding his house, which had been burnt down. Thus Pratt opened his short but very remarkable career as a private architect. That career lasted only until, having come into his own inheritance in 1667 and been knighted in 1668, he retired to his native Ryston and built only for himself.

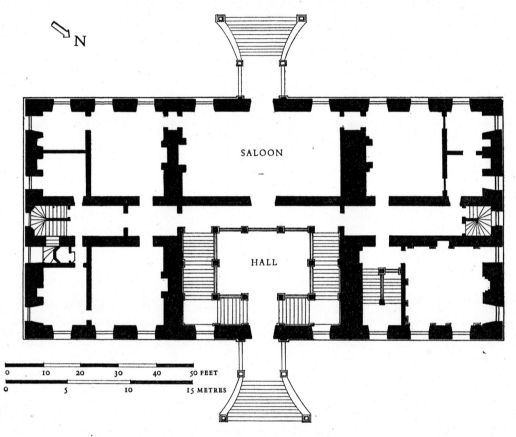

Figure 16. Coleshill House

Pratt built five large houses and, so far as we know, nothing else. His houses are very similar to one another in composition, and although each advances from the last in important particulars, it is clear that Pratt had one ideal in mind and cultivated it with all the methodical thought of which he was capable. A great lover of detail, his notes show him to have been fond of committing his mind to paper, as if to clarify his thoughts, at every stage of a building enterprise.

Until the publication of Pratt's note-books in 1928, Coleshill, Berks. (Plates 51A and B; Figure 16), was confidently attributed to Inigo Jones or Webb. There is no doubt that

Jones did know Pratt and that he contributed to the design and visited Coleshill with him. But it is equally certain that the house as it stands is substantially the work of Pratt.

The general form of Coleshill is what Pratt called a 'double pile'. That is to say, it is a simple rectangular block divided down its length by a corridor, with important rooms on either side of it, the centre rooms on the short axis being, respectively, the staircase hall and great parlour (on the ground-floor) and the hall void and great dining-room (on the first floor). This type of plan, as we have seen, emerged first, so far as we know, at Chevening (p. 88) and is thus probably due to Jones. It is, in essence, Palladian, as regards both the proportions of each room and their relations to one another. But the general conception of the whole of Coleshill cannot be called Palladian. Palladio never gave two principal storeys so nearly equal importance, unless the ratio was controlled by superimposed orders, nor used dormer windows or visible chimneys, which at Coleshill are important parts of the design; nor did he ever envisage a stair such as that at Coleshill, whose double flights and uniting gallery belong rather to seventeenth-century Italian Baroque.[7] Coleshill is not Palladian. It is a mixture of Italian, French, English, and possibly Dutch themes. Jones, we have shown, never designed without specific models in his mind and probably before his eyes. No specific models are reflected in Coleshill. The 'double-pile' is mentioned in Pratt's notes as one of the fundamental house plans, all questions of style apart. The details of the windows and cornice are very much what Palladio or Jones might have done. The rustic basement is likewise near to Jones, but nearer to du Cerceau's work at Verneuil, while the rustic quoins suggest Verneuil or Richelieu, and French influence is paramount in the grand architectural chimneys, with their sunk-and-raised panels. The balustraded platform on the roof echoes Chevening and so do the dormers; while the lantern on the roof is, again, French, recalling a similar feature surmounting the central pavilion at Richelieu.

Thus, in this remarkable house Pratt combined the fruits of his travel experience with much learnt from Jones and the usual Italian books. Massive, serene and thoughtful, absolutely without affectation, Coleshill was a statement of the utmost value to British architecture.[8] It was probably widely imitated, though (being remotely situated) not to the extent of one of its architect's later works.

In 1663–5 Pratt was building two houses, at Kingston Lacy, Dorset, for Sir Ralph Bankes and Horseheath, Cambs., for Lord Allington. The Dorset house (somewhat altered by Barry in 1834) has much in common with Coleshill, but the main façade has the important difference that the three middle windows, instead of being *more* widely spaced for emphasis, are *less* widely spaced. The centre section of the façade, moreover, where they occur, is slightly advanced, with rustic quoins emphasizing the breaks.

The greater definition of the centre section was even more decisive at Horseheath (destroyed in 1777), where it was surmounted by a pediment, and in this house Pratt arrived at a type which became common throughout England up to 1715. It is the type often misleadingly designated the 'Wren' type, although when Horseheath was built Wren had scarcely begun to be an architect at all. It is, in fact, an English type deriving from Inigo Jones, perhaps slightly modified by acquaintance with such Dutch buildings as the Mauritshuis at The Hague, and popularized by a few architects, of whom Pratt was the chief, immediately after the Restoration.

After Horseheath, it still remained for Pratt to build his greatest house and one which, being in London, proved to be his most influential. This was Clarendon House in Piccadilly (Plate 52) for the great Lord Chancellor, Edward Hyde. Built between 1664 and 1667, it stood back from the north side of the street, opposite St James's Street. It existed only for some sixteen years, being demolished in 1683; and records of it, apart from one fine engraving of the front, are scanty. Of the plan we know nothing. The engraving, however, shows us a front very close to Horseheath, but with wings projecting forwards at right angles to the main pile. As at Horseheath there is a pedimented frontispiece; as at Coleshill, Kingston, and Horseheath, the roof rises to a balustraded flat, and this treatment continues over the wings. Again, as in the precedent houses, there are rustic quoins, the two main floors are of nearly equal height and in the centre is a domed lantern. In fact, Clarendon House represents *the* Pratt idea of a house in its most fully-developed and refined form.

Clarendon House was among the first great classical houses to be built in London and easily the most striking of them. It was imitated far and wide, both closely and loosely. Belton, Lincs. (Plate 53), built for Sir John Brownlow by the London mason, William Stanton (1639–1705), is probably the most famous imitation and one of the closest.

Evelyn called Clarendon House 'without hyperbolies, the best contriv'd, the most usefull, gracefull, and magnificent house in England', and although he somewhat modifield that opinion later, it did indeed represent a milestone in the history of English domestic architecture. It is only because its life was so short that its importance has been so scantily appreciated.

After one or two brief appearances in official capacities connected with St Paul's and the City (see pp. 122 and 125), Pratt disappears to enjoy a knighted retirement at his native Ryston, where he rebuilt his own house in a rather novel fashion, reflecting his French sympathies in a central high-roofed pavilion. But his main work was done. It had been to create a type of house perfectly acceptable to the noblemen and gentlemen of the later Stuart epoch – a type which, in spite of much indebtedness to the Continent, we may, without much exaggeration, call essentially English.

NOTES TO CHAPTER 9

1. The attribution to Jones of Lincoln's Inn Chapel is due to a slip made by Dugdale, enlarged into a blunder by Vertue. A careful reading of the Black Books of the Society makes it abundantly clear that Jones had nothing to do with it. The chapel was designed and built by a mason, John Clarke.

2. J. Bridges, *History of Northants*, 1791.

3. Son of Francis Carter (d. 1630), who had been a clerk in the Works and a designer of some repute before becoming Clerk of the Rolls. See p. 29.

4. There may indeed have been some pressure on Jones, from the Queen's circle, to pay attention to the latest French style. Some 'chimneys from ye French embasador' are included in the Burlington-Devonshire Collection.

5. In connexion with these drawings, it has been shown by W. G. Keith (1925) that some are studied from original drawings by Palladio, which goes to prove that a number of the master's drawings (usually assumed to have been all collected by Lord Burlington) were in Jones's possession.

6. The main reasons for this attribution are the fact that Gerbier is known to have been in charge of York House, the resemblance of the water-gate to the Fontaine de Médicis, which Jones never saw and Gerbier certainly will have seen in 1625, and the re-semblance of the design to an indubitable drawing by Gerbier in the Bodleian (Plate 50B).

7. Baldassare Longhena's staircase in the monastery of S. Giorgio, Venice, completed while Pratt was in Italy, is similar in plan, but a masonry structure with all its parts supported on walls or arcades. The Coleshill stair was a framed carpentry structure with cantilever supports.

8. Sadly I must record that, since this was written, Coleshill has been destroyed by fire.

CHAPTER 10

ARTISAN MANNERISM
⟨1615–1675⟩

INIGO JONES was a Court artist. With few exceptions his genius was employed only on royal buildings, and his influence in his own time was restricted and (as we saw in the last chapter) clearly definable. Although to us he seems to dominate his period, not all his contemporaries will have felt that to be the case. Jones's architecture was in no sense popular. English building proceeded at its own pace and, quite independently of the great man at Whitehall, drew influences from abroad and incorporated them in a style which not only outlasted Jones's surveyorship and enjoyed a mild triumph during the Commonwealth, but persisted till the last quarter of the century.

This style, the natural successor to the 'Jacobean', has never been given a name. Artisan Mannerism may perhaps serve, for the style in essentially that of the best London craftsmen – joiners, carpenters, masons, bricklayers. It is not hard to recognize. In feeling, it is broad and coarse and has none of the naïf intensity or exciting contrasts of the preceding style, nor the fine taste and exquisite balance of Jones. It is strongly Mannerist in character and related to types of Mannerism flourishing in France and, more particularly, the Netherlands after the year 1600. There appear to be no 'masters' of the style and, as far as one can judge, it was sponsored by the abler masons and carpenters, especially those in and about the City of London. Masons and carpenters are, at this time, still extremely important figures, and before going further with the question of the Artisan style, we must consider who some of them were and how they worked.

The London Masons and Carpenters

In the City of London a monopoly was exercised by the Masons' Company and all the important masons working in the metropolitan area were members of it. The Company had two principal functions; first: to maintain standards of material and execution by periodical 'searches'; second: to control the operations of 'foreigners'. Apart from these functions, the activities of the Company do not loom large in a history of English architecture. More important are the divisions between the functions of the masons themselves. These are not clear-cut, since one mason might, from time to time, fulfil different functions. Nevertheless, we can distinguish (a) the 'shop-keeper' mason, who was principally a statuary and tomb-maker and whose main work was supplying church monuments; (b) the 'mason-contractor', who undertook the performance of large works, sometimes even to the extent of contracting for a complete building and sub-letting those trades which were not his own; (c) the stone-merchant; and (d) the foreman or supervisor or salaried mason constantly employed to keep some large work in repair. An important

97

mason might easily combine the first two and the last of those functions, and even all four, at various times in his career.[1]

The carpenters were similarly organized in a Company, incorporated in the fifteenth century. Up to Elizabeth's time, the main division within the Company was between the constructional carpenters who were in effect the chief house-builders of the City and those who executed 'joined stuff', such as furniture and panelling. These 'joiners' became separately incorporated in 1571, but the division between the two trades was never hard and fast. The carpenter-contractor was even more important than the mason-contractor until stone and brick took the place of timber as London's chief building material. Even then, it was often a carpenter who was retained by corporate bodies to look after their premises and provide designs for new buildings, even though executed mostly in brick and stone.

The bricklayers were also organized, in the Tylers' and Brickmakers' Company, which had obtained its first charter from Queen Elizabeth and whose objects were comparable to those of the Masons. Types among bricklayers are not easily distinguishable. Most of them probably made their own bricks, and it would be hard to find evidence of any division between those who wrought ornamental work and the merely routine builders.

Masons, carpenters, and bricklayers were in the habit of leasing land and building houses on their own account as investments. In the period with which we are dealing the bricklayers had the advantage in this profitable field owing to the relative cheapness of their material in the London area. Their triumph, however, was to come after the Great Fire.

For us, the importance of all these people is that they continued, from the Tudor period, the old functions of the artificer in combining design and execution. The chief of them were very notable artists.

Easily the most distinguished mason in the thirty years preceding the Civil War was Nicholas Stone (1586–1647). Born in Devonshire, he was apprenticed in London, but at the age of twenty attached himself to the famous Hendrik de Keyser, Master Mason and Sculptor to the City of Amsterdam. He executed a (still existing) gateway at the Wester Kerk there, married de Keyser's daughter, and returned to England in 1613. Taking premises in Long Acre, he immediately became active as a sculptor and tomb-maker, and during the next three decades executed over eighty monuments, distributed in twenty counties, as well as chimney-pieces, statues, dials, and some entire buildings. From 1619, as we saw in a previous chapter, he fulfilled another function of his craft by working as principal Master Mason on the Banqueting House. He did much more for the royal buildings, was Master Mason at Windsor from 1626, and on the death of William Cure in 1632 became Master Mason to the King. He was Master of the Masons Company in 1633 and 1634.

Nicholas Stone's association with Inigo Jones has made it somewhat difficult to form a just estimate of his own architectural work. His monuments, however, are firm evidence. Some of them represent a clean break with the Jacobean; they are competent productions in which strap-work and arabesques have given place to a flowing combination of architecture and figure sculpture not so distant in spirit from the work of Italy itself, and often of considerable beauty.

Stone's known architectural works include the gateway to the Physic Garden at Oxford (1632–3) and the Goldsmiths' Hall (1634–40). Both are decidedly Netherlandish, and the fenestration of the Goldsmiths' Hall was perhaps indebted to Rubens's *Palazzi di Genova*.

Of Stone's mason contemporaries we know little except their names, which stand in the records of the Masons' Company, and much work remains to be done in the elucidation, through building accounts, of the precise contribution each of them made. Next in importance to Stone, however, was the man who eventually succeeded him as Master Mason to the King. Edward Marshall (1598–1675) was apprenticed to the John Clarke who built Lincoln's Inn Chapel (p. 95 n.); he became one of the principal tomb-makers of his time and is a potentially important figure in connexion with the many buildings, from the 1630s onwards, whose authorship has not yet been settled.

In the provinces were masons of much distinction, notably John Jackson (d. 1663) of Oxford, who executed, if he did not design, the south porch of St Mary the Virgin and was also concerned with the Canterbury Quad at St John's, two Artisan works of the first importance (p. 110).

Among the carpenters, none in the first half of the century rises to the importance achieved by Nicholas Stone among masons, though there is evidence that William Partington, Stone's carpenter colleague in the Works, was a man of artistic as well as technical ability, and the influence of carpenters on the emergence of the Artisan style may have been at least equal to that of the masons. Of bricklayers the same could hardly be said, though it does happen that one of the most conspicuous designers in the whole school, Peter Mills, was a bricklayer by trade.

The Artisan Style and the 'Holborn' Gables

Among the first buildings symptomatic of the new developments in English architecture were the two houses in Holborn, those of Lady Cooke and Sir Fulke Greville, mentioned previously (p. 59). John Smythson drew them when he visited London in 1619, and we may infer from that that they were recent then, and strikingly new in character. Both were narrow street-houses and both had gables of a hitherto unfamiliar type, with curved (concave) sides and flat tops carrying pediments. Further, the moulded edges of the gables were voluted at their lower ends, giving a suggestion of classical consoles. Gables of this kind had already appeared in Amsterdam, and it is tempting to connect their migration with Nicholas Stone's arrival from that City in 1613, especially as Stone certainly erected a dial, some years later, on the Greville house and executed monuments for the Cooke (Coke) family.

If we are right in accepting these Holborn houses as pioneers we can see them reflected in many later buildings of the period. Smythson himself and his son, Huntingdon Smythson (d. 1648), borrowed them for their new buildings at Bolsover (1629–33) and later introduced versions of them at two Yorkshire houses, while they reappear unmistakably at Raynham (*c.* 1635–8) and Swakeleys (*c.* 1638), and even (in the stables) at Thorpe (1653–6), houses to which we shall come in due course.

Apart from this new sort of gable, the Artisan style was distinguished by certain other emphatic traits. One was a tendency to abolish mullions of brick or stone and introduce wood window-frames in large rectangular openings – a far-reaching revolution. Another was a tendency to stress the horizontals in a façade with heavy cornices at certain levels and to diminish the importance of the roof except where it stood forward behind gables of the kind I have just described. In the 1630s the style developed further conspicuous characteristics, notably pilasters with cartouches a third of the way up their shafts, and architraves with enormously exaggerated 'lugs' at several points, sometimes in combination with three-quarter pilasters tucked against the architrave and ending, below, in a volute. Finally, the broken pediment came into the greatest possible favour, especially in that peculiarly perverse version where a bust, shield, tablet, or other feature is interposed between the two broken segments.

The advent of the new style coincided with the greatly increased use of brick, and many of its earlier manifestations are entirely in this material. In the 1630s the brick-layers seem to have made a determined effort to bring the prestige of their craft level with that of the masons, to the extent that a bricklayer-contractor could provide a completely architectural house without having to bring in a mason for the ornamental parts. This challenge on the part of the younger trade produced such houses as West Horsley and Slyfield Manor, both in Surrey and dating from about 1630. Both have Dutch gables, though not quite of the Holborn type; and both have pilasters executed entirely in brick. The 'Dutch House' at Kew (1631; Plate 54B) is a magnificent example of this brick virtuosity, but perhaps the finest of all is Broome Park, Kent (1635–8), where a well-proportioned scheme of pilaster-strips leads up to gables of extreme complexity, curved broken pediments and all, done with the most admirable technical skill. To the same group belongs the many-gabled Swakeleys, Middlesex (1638), though here the design is helped out with stone.

Swakeleys was built by Sir Edmund Wright, a Cheshire merchant who became Lord Mayor of London in 1640. Remembering that it was built towards the end of Inigo Jones's Surveyorship, we can see what a gulf there was between the taste of the Court and that of the City, which Swakeleys very fairly represents. In plan it is wholly traditional, the hall being entered in the old asymmetrical way. In general treatment it is modern only in its boastful display of 'Holborn' gables, and even those were, by 1638, not particularly novel.

Swakeleys naturally leads us to a similar but much more remarkable house, begun rather earlier but still unfinished in 1638 – Raynham Hall, Norfolk (Plate 55B). Raynham was built by Sir Roger Townshend, a Norfolk landowner with an interest in architecture so great that he took his mason with him to London and thence to the Continent before starting to build. He made a false start in 1619–22, and we do not know exactly when the present house was begun. Although adopting something like the traditional H-plan, the main apartments at Raynham are arranged in a manner sanctioned by one of Palladio's designs. The hall (as originally designed) compromised with tradition by having entries at *both* ends. Again we have the 'Holborn' gables, but otherwise the treatment of the façades is wonderfully close to Inigo Jones, especially in the narrow pavilion with an applied Ionic portico which so surprisingly occurs in the centre of the east front. Even allowing for the fact that alterations by Kent in the eighteenth century made this feature look much more like Inigo than it should, Raynham is an exceptional work for its time and something of a freak. We do not know who designed it, but may infer that Townshend had the assistance of somebody who had worked in close proximity to Inigo Jones.

The Artisan Style in London

It was among the City of London artificers that the Artisan style originated. An early and important example was a service block at Leathersellers' Hall, off Bishopsgate Street, built in 1623, together with a grand porch to the old hall with columns and a broken pediment (Plate 54A). Master Clark, the Company's carpenter, was evidently the designer. His pupil and successor, Anthony Lynnett, added some buildings in the same style in 1632. All this work was destroyed in 1799, but Lynnett may well have been associated with the existing porch at St Helen's Church near by.

A further development in the style comes with the so-called Cromwell House, Highgate Hill (Plate 55A), built for Richard Springnell, a Captain of Train Bands, in 1637-8. This house, which suggests a *tour de force* on the part of some bricklayer-contractor, has rich moulded brick cornices and, in the centre window, a double-lugged moulded architrave with console ornaments, all, apparently, carved in the brick-work *in situ*. The regularity of the five-window front is perhaps a tribute to Jones's widening influence, but the plan follows the old fashion. The interior is richly fitted up; some of the joinery is designed in sympathy with the front, but one of the plaster ceilings harks back to a Jacobean pattern, and the staircase, with its military statuettes (allusive to the owner's profession), is a thing with a character all its own, these varieties proving the house to be the joint production of good craftsmen (probably co-ordinated by the bricklayer) rather than the single-minded work of an architect.[2]

The Buildings on William Newton's Land

Exactly at the time that Cromwell House was built, a great house-building project was afoot in the suburban parish of St Giles-in-the-Fields. This is represented by the activities of William Newton, a Bedfordshire man who from 1629 till his death in 1643 interested himself in land development in Great Queen Street and Lincoln's Inn Fields. In its architectural aspect his work was of great importance.

In 1636 Newton obtained a licence to build fourteen large houses (each with a forty-foot frontage) on the south side of Great Queen Street (Plate 56A); some, at least, of the houses were built in the following year. In 1638 he obtained another licence, to build thirty-two houses on the west side of Lincoln's Inn Fields, and these were mostly built by 1641. Some houses he built himself, but in most cases he merely sold the sites for others to build on. The important thing is, however, that both these long rows of houses were built to a regular, and classical, design.

The Queen Street houses, which came first, had Corinthian pilasters, rising from first-floor level to an eaves cornice; there were coupled pilasters at each party wall so as to give the houses separate identities. In Lincoln's Inn Fields a more ambitious scheme was envisaged, involving a symmetrical composition with a great house in the centre, two slightly lower houses on each side and more houses, lower still, filling the remaining plots to left and right. In execution, this symmetry proved, for various reasons, impracticable. All the houses had Ionic pilasters, those in the centre house being raised on squat pedestals, to give the additional height required.

Obviously the recent building of Covent Garden (1630–1) was the inspiration for this bold imposition of classical formality on London house-building, and, inevitably, Inigo Jones's name has become associated with it. There may, indeed, have been pressure or persuasion here as there was at Covent Garden (p. 83), but there is not a scrap of evidence. Gerbier mentions Webb as the architect of the Great Queen Street houses, but Vertue implies that Peter Mills, the City bricklayer, built them. In the case of the centre house in Lincoln's Inn Fields, now known, from a later owner, as Lindsey House (Plate 56B), there is some reason to connect it with the name of Nicholas Stone, since it was built for a friend of his, Sir David Conyngham,[3] for whom he executed monuments in 1631 and 1639. It is, in any case, an example of the purer type of Artisan classicism, of which Stone was certainly master. As the sole intact survivor of the entire Lincoln's Inn–Great Queen Street adventure it is perhaps, historically, the most important single house in London (see p. 230).

From these new houses on Newton's land the new style of house-front spread about London. Conyngham's house was closely followed in the Earl of Thanet's house in Aldersgate Street. In Great St Helen's in the City was a brick house with Corinthian pilasters, dated 1648, and there were other houses of the type in Winchester Street. None of these houses survives. All had, in greater or less degree, the idiosyncrasies I have described, and the theme of the pilaster order running through two storeys became common even among designers who clung to the Jacobean fashion of gables and bay-windows. A trio of houses in Bishopsgate, combining all these features, was dated as late as 1657.

Country-Houses during the Civil War and Commonwealth

From 1642, the year in which hostilities between King and Parliament broke out, the stream of English architecture begins to run very thin. Certain houses built on the eve of the war show that the Artisan style was all ready to conquer the country as it was already conquering the town. Thus, Lees Court, near Faversham (Plate 57), is a building one would like to attribute to the same hand as Lindsey House, on account of the grandiloquent parade of fourteen giant Ionic pilasters, adorned, like those of Lindsey House, with garlands on the capitals. The house belonged to the Royalist Sir George Sondes and was perhaps incomplete when the war began. Balls Park, Herts., was built in 1638–40 by Sir John Harrison, who had a house in Bishopsgate. It is a singularly reckless example of Artisan affectation, executed in brick and stone, with all the usual pilasters, lugs, and cartouches, all badly misplaced and recalling the kind of architecture then proceeding in the City. These two examples show the style respectively in a sophisticated and a less intelligent application.

As the war proceeded, country-house building became an impossible adventure for Royalists and Parliamentarians alike. We saw in the last chapter how the Earl of Pembroke, with arrogant promptitude, set Inigo Jones to work on Wilton as soon as the military struggle had been decided; and we saw how, about 1650, Inigo discussed with Roger Pratt the plans for Sir George Pratt's house at Coleshill. Those two great houses are salients from the Court style of old Whitehall, and they serve to bridge a period of ten years during which few other houses were built and those few were strongly characteristic of the less courtly style.

The houses in question were all built by men in high office, or at least in favour, under Oliver. Sir Anthony Ashley Cooper, the future Lord Shaftesbury, that man of innumerable disloyalties, built Wimborne St Giles about 1650, during his temporary adherence to the Parliament. Thorpe Hall, Northants., was built by Chief Justice Oliver St John, 1653–6; Wisbech Castle, Cambs., by John Thurloe, Secretary of State, 1655–7; and Thorney Abbey House, Cambs., by the 5th Earl (eventually 1st Duke) of Bedford, in the year of the Restoration. To these we may add certain features at Forde Abbey, Dorset, for Edmund Prideaux, the Attorney-General, and Tyttenhanger, Herts., built in 1654 for Sir Henry Blount, the traveller, who served on several Commonwealth commissions.[4]

Of these houses, three – Thorpe, Wisbech (demolished), and Thorney – are very close in style. Thorpe is the earliest and most important and we now know, thanks to Mr. Howard Colvin's research, that it was designed by Peter Mills, the same City of London bricklayer who built houses in Great Queen Street.

Thorpe Hall, Longthorpe, Northants. (Plates 58A and B), is a great rectangular block, a 'double-pile' house, but so thickened as to be nearly square. It belongs to the class of house which, we saw in Chapter 9, emerged (so it seems) with Chevening before 1630. It has the characteristic eaves-cornice with a steep roof rising to a platform, perhaps at one time balustraded. The general conception is classical enough for the house to have been ascribed (dreary inevitability!) to Inigo Jones and subsequently to John Webb. But it quite clearly belongs to another school. Even if we allow that this kind of house was Jones's invention (which is doubtful), the handling of Thorpe places it distinctly in the Artisan category. The formality of the north and south fronts, with their three ranges of seven windows and rustic quoins, is deceptive. There is none of the Jonesian feeling for profile and textural contrast, while on the west front there are mullioned windows which send one back to the period of Swakeleys and Raynham. Moreover, in the stable wing and one of the garden buildings, we meet once again the 'Holborn' gable. Add to this the fact that, in its plan, the house adheres to the obsolescent entry to the hall through a screen, and it is clear that we are dealing with a building for which nobody in full sympathy with Inigo could have been responsible.

Thorpe is as lavish, though not nearly as artistic, as Coleshill. The sympathy between the masonry, the joinery, and the plaster-work gives the impression that Peter Mills' pencil has controlled everything. The decorations, particularly in the drawing-room, reflect the contemporary French manner and appear to have been studied with the help of French engravings. The staircase is very remarkable. It is not open to the hall as at Chevening or Coleshill, but the compartment of the plan which contains it is generous, forming in effect a separate staircase-hall and allowing for a wide open-well stair. The balustrades are of the type we found at Cromwell House (1637–8), which is to say, that instead of balusters they have continuous panels of pierced carved work, consisting, in the case of Thorpe, of scrolls of acanthus foliage, while each newel is surmounted by a vase of fruit on an ornamental base. The plaster-work has something in common with the rich Italo-French style of the great rooms at Wilton.

Thorney Abbey is a humble imitation of Thorpe by a Peterborough mason, and Wisbech Castle had the reputation of being a near duplicate of Thorpe. At Forde Abbey the joinery in the rooms built by Prideaux establishes its close relationship with the others.

Tyttenhanger does not quite belong to this group, though it shares some of its characteristics. It is a brick house, comparable, in some details, to Cromwell House and built originally on a quadrangular plan. Its most remarkable feature is the internal joinery which grossly exaggerates that particular mannerism, the heavily lugged architrave. The staircase is of the Thorpe type, though evidently interpreted by another hand.

These Commonwealth houses betoken the establishment in England of a mannered classicism closely related to that of France and Flanders. Inigo Jones had nothing to do with the introduction of that style, and his influence modified it in only a few particular cases. Probably English builders would have reached very much the same results as Thorpe and Tyttenhanger, if Inigo Jones had never lived.

The subsequent history of the style belongs to the chapters which follow. If in London French influence and the mature Dutch school, deriving from van Campen, tended to flatten it out of existence, it retained its hold undiminished in many parts of the country. The works which Samuel Marsh (d. 1686 or 1687), a Lincoln mason, carried out for the 1st Duke of Newcastle at Bolsover (c. 1670) and Nottingham Castle (1674–9; Plate 59A) are of the Artisan school and among the most remarkable manifestations of the style.[5] The Bolsover work consists of additions to the buildings of John and Huntingdon Smythson (themselves an earlier example of the style) and includes a portal reminiscent of Clark's work for the Leathersellers, conceived in a sculptural spirit and very cleverly detailed. Nottingham Castle is a great rectangular mass, heavily rusticated, with pilasters and richly detailed windows, some framed in cartouches. Here again the sculptural character of the work is pronounced, while in general composition there is a decided indebtedness to Rubens's *Palazzi di Genova*. It should be added that the Duke, in his will, alludes to the 'model' having been 'laid and designed' by himself.

One of the best late examples of the style is the great gateway of the Citadel at Plymouth (Plate 59B), dated 1670. Probably the work of the Dutch engineer-general, Sir Bernard de Gomme (1620–85), it is close in style to the kind of gateways found in Dutch cities and fortresses, and its ornate character and foreign authorship mark it off somewhat from contemporary English developments.

Sources of the Artisan Style

It is evident that the Artisan style developed, just as the Jacobean had done, rather from contact between England and the Continent than from the circulation of engraved and printed works. Nicholas Stone's training in Amsterdam is the classic instance of such contacts. There may have been others as direct, and we know that several of the de Keyser family and many other foreigners worked as sculptors in England.

There are, however, two or three books which ought to be mentioned. Jacob Francart's *Premier Livre d'architecture*, 1616, is suggestive of many of the mannerisms we find in English work. *Architectura Moderna*, a book of designs by Hendrik de Keyser, was published in Amsterdam in 1631. No direct 'quotations' from either have been found in English buildings, but they may have had a certain influence. More important was the *Palazzi di Genova*, published over the name of Rubens in 1622. This book, containing fine and accurate engravings of Genoese palaces, undoubtedly had a great reputation corresponding with the enormous esteem in which Rubens's name was held in this country; we have just observed its relevance in the case of Nottingham Castle. But the part played by books was not conspicuous in the development of Artisan Mannerism. It is, indeed, the last English style in which influences circulated in the impenetrable anonymity of masons' yards and joiners' shops.

NOTES TO CHAPTER 10

1. For much concerning the work of London masons I am indebted to the work of Messrs Knoop and Jones (see Bibliography).

2. The staircase at Cromwell House, which has, instead of balusters, panels of foliated carving, may be compared with the staircase, similar in principle, introduced at Ham House, Petersham, Surrey, in 1638. The staircase, long gallery, and other rooms at Ham bear a relationship to the best Artisan classic of the period, though rather closer to the Court style of Inigo Jones. This type of staircase is found during the Commonwealth and for some years after the Restoration.

3. This Sir David was *not* the same Sir David Conyngham who was Surveyor from 1603 to 1606. The Surveyor was Sir David Conyngham of Robertland and a relative of the Sir David who built Lindsey House, as we see from the latter's will (1659) wherein 'my honoured kinsman, Sir D. C. of Robertland', is the chief beneficiary. The two men (both knights and baronets) are confused by no less

an authority than G. E. C. (*Complete Baronetage*). Nor is this the worst. It is distinctly stated in a Scottish document (McGibbon and Ross, v, 548) that D. C. of Robertland, the Surveyor, was deceased in 1607; another Scottish document, however (*ibid.*, p. 547), refers to D. C. of Robertland, *architectus regius*, as living in 1614, and it is he, presumably, who crops up again in the English Declared Accounts in 1615–16. The Declared Accounts also mention a D. C. acting as one of the clerks in 1604–5; he may be either, or neither, of the other two. What to make of all this, I just do not know.

4. The stylistic grouping of these houses was first indicated by Professor Geoffrey Webb in 1927 (see Bibliography).

5. Nothing whatever is known of Samuel Marsh, but he evidently was the designer of these buildings; for a model of Nottingham Castle, designated 'Mr. March's Model', exists (*R.I.B.A. Journal*, 3rd series, xxxii (1925), 520). His work is of a very high order and argues a London apprenticeship.

CHAPTER II

CHURCHES AND COLLEGIATE BUILDINGS
1530–1660

In all previous chapters interest has been directed towards, and almost limited to, either the operations of the royal Works or houses in countryside or town. Various important types of buildings have been ignored. These include churches; college and university buildings at Oxford and Cambridge; grammar schools and almshouses; buildings at the Inns of Court; and buildings for municipal and mercantile corporations. It is natural to group these buildings subordinately. The promotion of architecture from the Reformation onwards was, in the main, the promotion of palace-building and house-building. Churches, colleges, schools, and almshouses were collateral and occasional products of the same sources of patronage and wealth, but only rarely do they represent any striking architectural innovation. They were paid for by founders and benefactors who in most cases had already furnished themselves with characteristic architectural backgrounds. They represent, in short, the architecture of individual munificence, of benefaction.

This is not the case with two of these categories – the Inns of Court and municipal and mercantile corporations; but this corporate patronage has no distinct colouring and is therefore grouped with the others for convenience. The Inns of Court, though in many respects comparable to Oxford and Cambridge Colleges, were financially stronger and thus able to build for themselves, while in the case of the municipal corporations and city companies they were certainly not objects of benevolence and their architectural adventures were undertaken at the instigation of their own necessities and vanities. Even in these cases, however, benefaction enters in, individual benchers or individual burgesses contributing very often that margin of luxury which enabled common needs to be satisfied in an uncommon way.

Church-Building

After the last great Gothic wave of building and rebuilding in the fifteenth and early sixteenth centuries, England's vast stock of churches hardly admitted of expansion, and with the dissolution of colleges, chantries, and free chapels in 1545 almost the last source of church-building initiative was destroyed. Four years later came the Book of Common Prayer; and the Gothic church was obsolete.

The history of English church-building from 1545 to the Restoration of 1660 is a curious by-way in the story of our architecture. It is not without incident. Up to Elizabeth's reign there must have been virtually no church-building at all, except indeed an occasional private chapel in a great house or a college. The old churches stood as they were, except that images were destroyed or covered, the stone altar removed and the 'Lord's Board' brought in. Screens were not, as a rule, destroyed and the prayer-book of

1552 had the effect of preserving the old divisions of the church. Mary's short-lived attempt to countermand the Reformation brought some hasty replacements and re-furbishings, but the prayer-book returned to stay in 1559, and thereafter the character of the English church settled down to what it was to be until the Victorian revolution of the 1840s.

There are examples of Elizabethan church-architecture – mostly partial rebuildings – scattered over the country, and the Earl of Leicester even laid the foundation stone of a large new church, in Denbigh Castle, in 1578. The interiors of churches continued to undergo a certain amount of change. With the emphasis on corporate worship and on the audibility and intelligibility of its conduct it was necessary to bring the officiating minister into the nave (except for the Eucharist) and to provide for him a reading pew and a pulpit. The parcloses of the family chantries were rearranged to make family pews – the prototypes of the great box pews which were built in two succeeding centuries.

Throughout the reigns of Elizabeth and James I this moderate and conservative re-arrangement proceeded, witnessed to-day by the very large number of Jacobean pulpits which have survived the Victorian restorers. Then came a new movement, initiated by William Laud, but felt and supported by other great churchmen, towards a rehabilitation of the transcendental character of the liturgy and the intrinsic importance of its setting. This movement – the 'Laudian Revival' – took its effective start with the accession of Charles I in 1625 and the elevation of Laud to the Bishopric of London three years later. The architectural products of this revival are highly curious. In some instances there is a faint flavour of stylistic revivalism, in most cases none. Laud himself does not seem to have had any stylistic prejudices. He pressed ahead Inigo Jones's classicizing of St Paul's Cathedral in 1633. The Church of St Katherine Cree, however, which he consecrated with great pomp in 1631, is only partly classical, has a flat Gothic vault and, in its east window, makes deliberate reference to the east end of the medieval St Paul's Cathedral.[1] The work which Laud initiated at St John's College, Oxford, and the porch at St Mary-the-Virgin in the same city, built under his influence, are both examples of Anglo-Flemish Mannerism, with few medieval recollections and those accidental rather than deliberate. Clearly there was no very determined Gothic revivalism here, and if we find Gothic churches being built in country places at this time, the fact that they are Gothic is neither more nor less significant than the fact that they are churches. To build a church was an act of conservative colour; and the conception of a church was by the overwhelming force of tradition a Gothic conception.

The main characteristic of churches built at this time is the omission of anything emphatic in the way of a chancel. Groombridge Church, Kent (1623), for instance, built by Lord Camfield in pious thankfulness for the return of Prince Charles from Spain without the Catholic bride he went to fetch, is a simple rectangle with 'Perpendicular' windows and a little bell-cote. Leighton Bromswold Church, Hunts. (1626–34), rebuilt during the incumbency of George Herbert, the poet, is cruciform only because it is a reconstruction of an older church. The style, again, is 'Perpendicular' (except for the rather later round-arched tower) and the fittings are 'Jacobean' with many turned colonettes and pendants.

In the early 1630s we find a small number of churches built under the immediate influence of Laud and his friends. Easily the most remarkable is St John's, Leeds (1632–3; Plate 60A), a large 'Perpendicular' church with a single nave arcade down the centre and a tremendously rich 'Jacobean' screen across the whole width of the interior. The church represents the munificence of one man, John Harrison, 'a Native and Chief Glory of this populous Town'. A screen in similar style and attributed to the west-country carpenter John Abel, is at Abbey Dore, Herefordshire, its date (1634) coinciding with the elevation of Bishop Wren (uncle of the architect and a loyal friend of Laud) to the see of Hereford. In Durham a phenomenal revival of Gothic tabernacle-work took place under Bishop Cosin, another member of the Laud circle. It is to be seen in the church at Brancepeth, where he was Rector from 1626, and later at Sedgefield, in Durham Cathedral and in the Bishop's Palace at Auckland (1662–3). Early specimens are wonderfully true to Gothic precedent; later ones, like the Durham font-cover (Plate 60B), which compromises so quaintly with 'Jacobean', are typical stylistic curiosities of the Laudian movement.

Cosin's work carries the effects of that movement beyond 1660, the date of his elevation to the see. The Commonwealth had seen no church-building except for a few rare freaks in remote parts of the country. One of these, the Gothic church of Staunton Harold, Leicestershire, begun in 1653, is an almost incredible salient of the Laudian ideal into the anti-Laudian Commonwealth. It has nave and aisles, chancel and west tower, and is 'Perpendicular' throughout, except for a western door-case with Flemish terms and swags. This challenge to puritanism did not pass unnoticed, and its builder, Sir Robert Shirley, who so gallantly (as his epitaph says) 'did the best things in the worst times and hoped them in the most calamitous', ended his days in the Tower of London.

Buildings at Oxford and Cambridge

The Chapel of Trinity College, Cambridge, was completed in 1564, eighteen years after the foundation of the College by Henry VIII. It is a Gothic building, on the model of King's College Chapel, but with all the splendour and technical prowess extinct. Within a year of its finishing buildings of a very different sort were rising at the college which John Caius founded on the basis of the Hall of Edmond Gonville and now called Gonville and Caius. In Dr Caius we find one of the first of those Renaissance scholars to whom antique architecture was important, and who deliberately stimulated its introduction into the buildings of the two University towns. There were not many such men, but they occur periodically in the sixteenth, seventeenth, and eighteenth centuries, and constitute a particularly interesting thread in the history of architectural patronage.

Dr Caius had studied and taught in Padua and travelled in France and Germany. Returning to his old university, he started, in 1565, to add a new quadrangle to Gonville Hall. In doing so, he planned the approaches to form an allegorical 'progress', first through a Gate of Humility (a mere doorway in a low wall), then through a more elaborate Gate of Virtue (Plate 61A) incorporated in one of his new wings, and finally, turning south in the new quad, through a Gate of Honour (Plate 61B), an impressive little building in three richly carved storeys terminating in a domed hexagon and leading towards the Schools.

Caius died (1573) before this last building was built, but it is recorded that he made the design. The gateway has been presumed to be based on a Roman tomb which Caius saw in Italy, but a simpler and more probable explanation is that it is a free rendering, in miniature, of a design for a palace given in Serlio.[2] We need not doubt that Caius himself was the second begetter of the design, but we know also that he employed a Fleming, Theodore Haveus or De Have, a man who had settled in King's Lynn in 1562 and was 'a skilful artificer and eminent architect'. Haveus certainly designed the (no longer existing) column with dials in Caius Court and did carving on Caius' remarkable tomb in the chapel (1573–5). His portrait hangs in the College.

In 1584 Sir Walter Mildmay founded Emmanuel College and introduced to Cambridge Ralph Simons, whom we first hear of setting up the hall screen at Whitehall thirteen years earlier.[3] Simons built the original Emmanuel, which has mostly disappeared. He was then employed by Thomas Nevile of Trinity College, during whose mastership (1593–1615) the College underwent a thorough architectural reformation. Nevile was possessed of the growing passion for 'regularity' and formed the present roughly symmetrical Great Court of Trinity out of a chaotic miscellany left over from two of the earlier foundations of which the College was composed. As part of this court he built (indirectly at his own expense) the hall, for which Simons provided a model in 1604. Deliberately based on the thirty-year-old precedent of Middle Temple Hall (p. 113), it is a somewhat too spare and airy example of its kind. Simons was likewise responsible for Nevile Court with its Doric arcades and a pilastered upper storey (altered 1755). At Sidney Sussex College (founded 1594) he designed the original buildings in 1596–8 and at St John's College the still existing Second Court (1598–1602), plain brick with dormers. He was not a very important designer, judged by his works, though on his portrait, which hangs at Emmanuel College, he is called *architectus sua aetate peritissimus*. He was, in any case, one of those artificers who were gradually creating the professional rôle of architect by taking a large view of the problems connected with building and ministering to the new taste for 'regular' planning.

With the opening of the seventeenth century Oxford succeeds Cambridge as the University of chief architectural interest. There, Sir Thomas Bodley began building the Schools (Plate 62B) in 1613. The work proceeded till the whole quadrangle was finished in 1636. Unlike Caius and Nevile, Bodley took little personal interest in the architecture of his great benefaction. He entrusted the work entirely to Yorkshire masons, and the epitaph of Thomas Holt (d. 1624) tells us categorically that he was *scholarum publicorum architectus*. In view of the fact that Bodley's correspondence with his librarian, Dr James, contains not a single reference to Holt, this is rather curious; and the probable truth is that Holt was *architectus* simply by courtesy and in fact nothing more than the principal carpenter. The executive masons were John Acroyde (d. 1613), John Bentley (d. 1615), and his brother Michael Bentley (d. 1618), all Yorkshiremen.

The Oxford Schools, three-storey buildings ranged round a quadrangle, are far behind most of the greater houses of the time in architectural skill and taste, and the Yorkshire masons brought to Oxford a retrograde mixture of the 'modern' and the 'antique'. The most ambitious feature of the Schools is the tower, a composition of the traditional gatehouse type to whose five storeys the five orders, heavily crusted with antic-work, are pedantically and precariously applied.[4]

While the Schools were in progress, Wadham College (1610–13) was begun. Here again the design is traditionally attributed to Holt, but the accounts show him only as the carpenter, while William Arnold, from Somerset, was the man in charge. Wadham is as Gothic as the Schools, but insists more elaborately on symmetry, the hall and ante-chapel being designed to balance each other on the main axis and being in fact externally indistinguishable.

The Laudian Revival left its mark at both Universities. The south porch of St Mary the Virgin, Oxford (1637; Plate 62A), has already been mentioned. It is a florid composition, with twisted Corinthian columns supporting the two split halves of a pediment, in the middle of which a great niche is inserted. Within is a purely Gothic vault. It was built at the expense of Dr Morgan Owen, Laud's chaplain, and was early ascribed to Nicholas Stone. Actually, Laud stated that it was done by a Mr Bromfield, and the accounts tell us that John Jackson (p. 99) was the carver. Jackson was certainly associated with the Stones, but the actual provenance of the design remains doubtful. With the carved Virgin and Child and the angels in the spandrels and on the pediments the porch is boldly representative of the Laudian spirit and, not surprisingly, formed an item in the indictment which led to his execution.

Still more intimately associated with Laud is the new quadrangle he helped to build at his own college, during the time that he was Chancellor of the University. Canterbury Quad at St John's (Plate 63) was built between 1632 and 1636. Two sides of it are in a modest Tudor style, but there was a change of masons while the work was in progress, and the east and west sides embody cloisters in rich and pronounced Artisan classic. The designer may have been a Mr Brown, who figures here and there as Laud's 'joiner', but John Jackson, here as at St Mary's, did the carved work, except for the two fine statues of Charles I and his Queen which are by Le Sueur.

At Cambridge, Peterhouse, during the mastership of Matthew Wren, 1625–34, was the great centre of the revival. In 1628 Wren began to build a new chapel and cloisters there, and the work was sympathetically continued by Cosin who succeeded him. The chapel, not completed till after the Restoration, can be classed with St Katherine Cree and Cosin's later work at Auckland Castle as a Classic-Gothic hybrid. The east end combines a purely Gothic window with a pedimented gable, a heraldic cartouche with crocketed niches.

The persistence of Gothic building at the two Universities has often been regarded as in some way symbolic of the conservatism of academic circles. This is hardly the case. The only reason why Gothic lingered at Oxford and Cambridge was that ecclesiastical and collegiate architecture had a tradition too strong to be easily displaced, nor was there any particular reason why it should be displaced. The classical movement was associated in the first place with the Court and in the second with great houses usually built with a view to the reception of the Court. Patronage of this kind did not find a place at the Universities. The building of the hall staircase at Christ Church, Oxford, in pure Perpendicular Gothic as late as 1640 was simply a matter-of-course continuation of the

College's building programme in the normal collegiate style. And the history of Brasenose College Chapel shows that the construction of Gothic traceried windows there in 1666 was simply the delayed completion of a scheme prepared before the Civil War.

It was only with the general latinizing of the English vernacular that Church and University architecture forsook the Gothic. And even then Wren and after him Hawksmore reverted, without surprise or controversy, to the older style on occasions when the spirit of continuity seemed to demand it.

Almshouses

The building of almshouses, during Elizabethan and Stuart times, was widespread among the official and propertied classes. Its social importance since the dissolution of the monasteries was considerable, but the motives involved were not entirely those of social or religious conscience. Almshouses were almost always personal memorials of their founders, and in this respect are comparable to the costly church monuments which the same persons usually prepared for themselves or for which they left provision in their wills. It is significant that the chief builders of almshouses were merchants, people who had not the same dynastic status in society as the landed aristocracy. To such people the foundation of an almshouse offered the opportunity of investing in a living memorial to themselves and one likely to be cherished by posterity. Hence the innumerable almshouses throughout England, bearing the name and displaying the arms of some gentleman or merchant of the sixteenth and seventeenth centuries, often a mayor of the town, but nearly as often a man who had left the town as a youth to make his fortune in London and was pleased to signalize his ascent to wealth by a public benefaction, which was also a personal monument, in his native place. To cite two such cases, there are the almshouses at Nantwich, Cheshire, built in 1638 by Sir Edmund Wright, Lord Mayor of London and the builder of Swakeleys (p. 100). And there are the three tiny cottages at Kingscliffe, Northants., built probably from a bequest by John Thorpe, the surveyor, in 1668. It is characteristic that an inscription on this very lowly structure asserts, with an optimism which time may be said to have justified, that it will 'endure for a whole age'. Such was the desire, in a period not wholly convinced of transcendental values, for immortality in a solid form.

As an architectural type, the block of almshouses varies a good deal. The larger examples are built round courtyards, with hall and chapel placed much as they were in colleges. Others have forecourts with a low wall and a gateway, bearing heraldry and inscriptions, in the centre. Others again are simple rows of cottages with a central inscribed feature. In almost all the larger examples the monumental character of the building is emphasized by the exhibition of three gables towards the street, whether functionally necessary or not, a grouping which goes back to the early sixteenth century. Ford's Almshouses, Coventry (1529), have three equal gables over the street front. The important Leicester Hospital at Warwick, refounded by the Earl of Leicester in 1571, has a large central gable with two smaller gables on either side and the Penrose Almshouses at Barnstaple, Devon (1627), have a gabled gatehouse linked to a gabled hall on one side and a gabled chapel on the other.

Some of the more conspicuous foundations are those of Bishops and Archbishops. Whitgift Hospital, Croydon, where Archbishop Whitgift himself had apartments and installed his library, was built in 1596–9. Abbot's Hospital, Guildford (Plate 65), was begun by Archbishop John Abbot in 1619. This is a splendid brick building with Flemish gables of the Surrey type (p. 100), moulded chimney-stacks, and a gatehouse which, considering its date, must surely represent a deliberate reversion to Tudor models. Its octagon turrets with ogee caps are a strange reflexion of Henry VIII's taste for the year which saw the beginning of the Whitehall Banqueting House.

Great landowners sometimes founded almshouses, as in the case of Sackville College, East Grinstead, built in 1619 from a bequest by the 2nd Earl of Dorset. But it was the merchants who provided the majority of these institutions either by gift or bequest. In the London area members of the city companies built almshouses for the poorer members of the craft, to be administered by the companies; a case in point being the Jesus Hospital at Bray, built in 1609 by William Goddard, for forty freemen of the Fishmongers' Company.

Grammar Schools

The last acts of the Dissolution having reduced the nation's educational system to ruins, an immediate attempt to reconstitute it was made by a Commission of Edward VI in 1548, the result being simply the resuscitation of a number of the schools as 'King Edward VI Grammar Schools' after the Corporations to which they owed their existence had been extinguished. The real initiative in the Tudor rehabilitation of education came from individuals and local groups who sought and obtained charters for the foundation of Free Grammar Schools – 'free' in the sense of owing no obligation to a superior Corporation.

These Grammar Schools had as their prototype Colet's foundation of St Paul's School in 1505. The administrative arrangements of most of them were closely similar and so, naturally, were their building requirements. One long schoolroom was the main item, with seating provision for two classes, the Master sitting at one end, the Usher at the other. Living space for Master and Usher were also needed and, sometimes, a library and gallery.

Even less than in the case of almshouses does any pronounced type emerge among the many school buildings of late Tudor and early Stuart times, and much less care was lavished on their ornamentation. An early post-Reformation example (destroyed 1864) was Tonbridge School, built in 1553 and consisting of a very long building with a forty-foot schoolroom in the middle and Master's and Usher's lodgings at either end, all under one roof. Sixty years later, the 'fayre and convenient school howse' provided for by Peter Blundell at Tiverton and dated 1604 is, similarly, a very long rectangular structure in which similar accommodation was comprised. In other cases, the lodgings are omitted and the schoolroom stands by itself, as at Archdeacon Johnson's two foundations (1587) at Uppingham and Oakham, or the little schoolhouse at Burton Latimer, Northants. (1622; Plate 64A).

On the other hand, there are examples of more varied planning. The school at Guildford, Surrey, begun in 1557 and completed at intervals up to 1586 is built round a tiny courtyard, thus somewhat resembling a Tudor type of large town-house, with the great schoolroom in place of the hall; while among the archives of Harrow School is a 'platt' by a surveyor named Sly, showing a T-shaped building geometrically set out, the school-room (fifty-six feet long) being a double square and the schoolmaster's and usher's lodgings symmetrically disposed in the head of the 'T'. The plan appears to date from before the founder, John Lyon's, death in 1592; the executed building (1615; partly incorporated in the present Old School) was different, having the lodgings in a low ground-floor, with two storeys and an attic above.

At Shrewsbury, a grammar school of more than usual wealth (Plate 64B), a substantial block containing a library above and a 'gallery' below, was added to the school in 1594–6, while the school itself was rebuilt in 1627–30. As at Harrow, there are three main storeys, but here the lodgings were on the first floor and the schoolroom (eighty feet long) was on the second, while a slight degree of ceremonial distinction was added by a pilastered doorway surmounted by two figures, 'Polymathes' and 'Philomathes', with a Greek inscription.

The Inns of Court

The Societies of the Inner and Middle Temple, of Lincoln's Inn, Gray's Inn, and the other Inns of Court occupied a favourable position in England after the Reformation, with the result that several of them were able to rebuild their halls. Hence we have Gray's Inn Hall (gutted 1941), the Middle Temple Hall, and Staple Inn Hall (destroyed 1944), each with an open timber hammer-beam roof, a feature of some rarity after the middle of the sixteenth century. At Gray's Inn (1556–60) the roof was wholly Gothic but for some classical mouldings and pendants on the hammer-beams. At Middle Temple Hall (1562–1570; Plate 66B), however, the double hammer-beam roof has a distinct relationship to the hall roof at Longleat, and it appears that the Longleat carpenter may have been engaged on it. The roof at Wollaton Hall, incidentally, makes a third in a group of related Elizabethan roofs, while the roof of Trinity College hall, Cambridge (p. 109), imitated from Middle Temple, makes a Jacobean fourth. But the Middle Temple example is the largest. Unlike those at Longleat and Wollaton it is fully open instead of being ceiled half-way up to the ridge. The Staple Inn roof (1581) was a curiosity, a naïf little work with ornament of rustic simplicity surprising in a London building.

Mercantile and Municipal Buildings

The foundation by Sir Thomas Gresham of the Royal Exchange, London (Plate 66A), in 1566 (it was opened by Queen Elizabeth in January 1571) resulted in a building of unique character and considerable importance and one of the first to be wholly Flemish in style. Gresham 'bargained for the whole mould and substance of his workmanship in Flanders'. Not only was his principal workman, Henryk (see p. 20), a Fleming, but much of the material seems to have been brought, ready cut, across the North Sea. The main feature of the building was its courtyard, surrounded by a loggia whose arches were carried on Doric columns, with an upper storey having Ionic pilasters, and niches with statues of the English Kings. It is difficult to assess the influence of this conspicuous building and its detail, but it may well be that such an arcaded structure as Nevile's Court at Trinity College, Cambridge (p. 109), derives from it.

A New Exchange was built in the Strand in 1608 at the expense of the Earl of Salisbury. The records of it are confusingly unreliable, but it should probably be classed with Hatfield as a building of that fairly advanced classical character which we may be right in associating with the name of the probable designer of the New Exchange, Simon Basil.

Among the fair number of market-houses built during the period, Sir Thomas Tresham's at Rothwell (p. 42) stands out as the only one of real architectural consequence, and its two orders of pilasters, and open arcades, may well be a deliberate echo of Gresham's building in London, though the style of execution is French rather than Flemish. The market-houses at Shrewsbury (1595) and Chipping Campden (1627) embody the same principle of an open ground-floor with a great room above and so do the octagonal timber structures at Wymondham, Norfolk (1617), and Dunster, Somerset (before 1629). In the west country, John Abel (1577–1674) built a series of timber market-halls at Brecon, Hereford, Weobley, Kington, and Leominster.

The upper parts of most of these buildings formed council-chambers for the governing body of the town. Town Halls in the more restricted sense existed only in the form of Guildhalls and these, inherited from an earlier epoch, were rarely rebuilt. At Exeter, however, a highly curious extension to the old Guildhall was built out into the highway in 1592–4. In principle, its three bays are comparable to the design of Tresham's building at Rothwell, but there are coupled columns instead of pilasters, while to avoid undue obstruction to traffic the lower order is suddenly truncated below the caps and corbelled inwards towards the cylindrical columns from which the arches spring. The result is quaintly barbarous.

NOTES TO CHAPTER II

1. The designer of this church is unknown, but the design of a City Church at this time is likely to have emanated from the King's Works. Jones cannot be entirely ruled out. Geoffrey Webb (G. Cobb, *The Old Churches of London*, 1941–2, page 7) has suggested the Comptroller, Baldwin, as a possibility.

2. Book IV (page 180 in 1584 edition). Since writing this, I am able to suggest as an intermediate source the Spanish arch in C. Graphaeus, *La Très Admirable … Entrée du prince Philipes … en la ville d'Anvers*, 1550. This converts the Serlio palace into an arch and shows it as part of a processional way.

3. PRO. *Declared Accounts*, E 351/3206.

4. I suggest that the conception of this tower was prompted by Caius's Gate of Virtue at Cambridge, and that the ultimate English source of this and other columned gate-towers is Somerset House.

CHAPTER 12

THE RESTORATION:
HUGH MAY; DR CHRISTOPHER WREN

KING CHARLES II was solemnly proclaimed in Westminster Hall on 8 May 1660. The Roundhead administration of the Office of Works had lasted for seventeen years, and it is surprising how completely it was possible, on the instant of Charles's return, to revert to old forms and methods. The declared accounts for 1660–1 are precisely on the model of those of 1639–40. Expenditure mounted again to its old level and, in 1661–2, was over £14,000. All the former offices were restored, though the names filling them were necessarily new ones. Not a single senior official of the old establishment survived to enlist in the new. Inigo Jones had died in 1652, Baldwin the Comptroller in 1641, Nicholas Stone the Master Mason in 1647, and William Portington the Master Carpenter in 1651. Wicks, the Paymaster, and the Clerks and the minor artificers were, it must be presumed, either dead or past their work. The Serjeant Painter, John de Critz, had been killed at Oxford in 1642. As for the lesser office-holders under Cromwell, only one, the Carpenter, was allowed to retain his post.

The most important vacancy to be filled in 1660 was, of course, the Surveyorship, and for this post it might well seem that there was only one possible candidate – John Webb. Webb lost no time in putting his case before Charles II; but Charles, during his exile, had incurred many obligations and these were to cavaliers who had risked their necks or fortunes in his own service rather than to professional men whose loyalty had been expressed to his father and who had (like Webb) worked for the Commonwealth. Moreover, Clarendon advised him that a certain John Denham should be awarded an official appointment. So Denham, forthwith, was installed as Surveyor.

Sir John Denham (1615–69) was the son of an Irish Judge who had an estate at Egham and had sat in a manor court there with his neighbour John Thorpe. In 1640 or a little later Denham wrote a poem, 'Cooper's Hill', which takes the countryside round Egham for its theme, and has the reputation of being the first English descriptive poem of its kind. At the outbreak of the Civil War Denham was entrusted with the defence of Farnham Castle, whence he was evicted by Waller and carried to London. Soon released, he was permitted to retire to Oxford, but his estate was sequestrated. He evidently continued to intrigue for the royal cause; for in 1649 he carried to the future Charles II, in Holland, a letter from his father. As a poet, Denham was distinguished; as the successor to Inigo Jones's office scarcely so. Of his experience of building Webb was, no doubt, right in saying that 'though Denham may have, as most gentry, some knowledge of the theory of architecture, he can have none of the practice'; and the house he built in Piccadilly (even if we can be sure that it was his own design) was respectable and nothing more.

Of the other senior officers under the new administration, the Comptroller, Francis Wethered, was inconsequential.[1] The Paymaster, however, was Hugh May (1622–84), and his participation in the early years of the Restoration cannot be dismissed so briskly.

Hugh May and Dutch Palladianism

May's chief importance is as exponent of a style which, at the Restoration, was rapidly to displace that Anglo-Netherlandish manner which had been the national idiom since the time of Charles I. The provenance of this style, Dutch Palladianism, is simple. Two Dutch architects, Jacob van Campen (1595–1657) and Pieter Post (1608–69), had, in the thirty years prior to 1660, revolutionized the architecture of the Dutch Netherlands. Against the ornate and more or less Flemish style of de Keyser they had set a style based directly on Palladio. In 1626 van Campen had built the Coyman House in Amsterdam with superimposed pilaster orders to its upper storeys. Then, in 1633–5, he had built, for Prince Maurice of Nassau, the Mauritshuis at The Hague, this time with a giant pilaster order raised on a low ground-floor, the three centre bays rising to a pediment. Pieter Post's 'House in the Wood' (De Saal van Oranie), near The Hague, followed in 1645–51; and van Campen's great Town Hall at Amsterdam, with superimposed orders, each embracing two storeys, in 1648–55.

Common to nearly all these buildings was the use of brick, mixed with stone, and to all of them the straightforward almost diagrammatic use of pilasters. Here was a version of classicism at once agreeable, easy and economical to build, and it is hardly surprising that it found its way readily across the North Sea to a people of frugal habits, accustomed to brick. Moreover, at a time when numerous repatriates were arriving in England after a period of exile largely spent in Holland, the style had many ready sponsors, and of these Hugh May was probably the chief.

May was the son of a Sussex gentleman and a cousin of Baptist May, a prominent Court official at the Restoration. He had been in the Duke of Buckingham's suite during the years of exile, most of which the Duke had spent in Holland. He was employed by Lord Clarendon at Cornbury, Oxon., soon after the Restoration and in 1663–4 built the only completely surviving building known to be by him – Eltham Lodge, London, for Sir John Shaw (Plate 67). This is a 'double pile' house in the plan tradition of Coleshill, but built of brick (which Pratt rarely used), with a centre pediment in the main front beneath which are four Ionic pilasters (and Pratt never used pilasters). Eltham is Palladian in character, but not of the Jones School. It is far nearer to the Dutch Palladianism of Pieter Post and van Campen, and it seems rather likely that May had studied that kind of architecture while with Buckingham in Holland.

His next work, probably his most important, was a house in Piccadilly, near to Pratt's Clarendon House, for Lord Berkeley. Berkeley House (c. 1665) was burnt down in 1733 and the only glimpse of it we have is in Ogilby and Morgan's map of 1681–2. From this it seems to have been very like Eltham Lodge but bigger, and with the addition of curved passages in the Palladian manner linking the *corps de logis* to service wings on the Piccadilly frontage. The importance of its influence, arising from its conspicuous situation, may well have been as great as that of its fine but equally ill-fated neighbour, Clarendon House.

May built several other houses, of whose architecture we know practically nothing. He remodelled a great part of Windsor Castle for Charles II, adopting for the new exteriors a 'castellated' style which gives May some right to be called an early medieval revivalist. More important, he designed St George's Hall which Mr Geoffrey Webb has shown to be the probable prototype of Wren's great hall at Greenwich. Here and at Cassiobury (c. 1677 for the Earl of Essex) he employed his friend John Evelyn's discovery, the carver Grinling Gibbons (p. 144).

May was a prominent figure among the virtuosi of the Restoration, was intimate with Pepys, Evelyn, and Roger North and an executor of Sir Peter Lely's will. Not necessarily a great or original artist, his importance is in having erected a handful of Dutch Palladian houses which proved the usefulness of that style in a country where brick was one of the principal building materials. With Pratt, he helped to introduce the type of house which, as we have said, is so often and so misleadingly called the 'Wren' type, although Wren designed only one or two country-houses and those long after Pratt and May had done their best work.[2]

It will be observed that most of May's important works were for private patrons, though Eltham Lodge, which belonged to the Crown, was perhaps designed in his official capacity. Apart from Windsor, he left no mark on the royal palaces, where building was, however, resumed very soon after the King's return.

Royal Palaces, 1660–1666

Of the royal works put in hand during the early years of the new reign, two are important. The New Gallery at Somerset House (Plate 68A) was built in 1661–2, on the instructions of Henrietta Maria who, as Queen Mother, returned to her old riverside home. The design was by Inigo Jones and had perhaps been prepared by him for this site. It consisted, externally, of an interpretation of the Bramantesque theme of an order raised on open rusticated arches. As executed it seems to have been a building fully worthy of Jones, and it maintained its reputation long after it was demolished to prepare the way for Sir William Chambers, in 1778. Sir William himself imitated it in the Strand front of his new building (p. 259) and John Nash designed, or sponsored, a stucco version of it in Piccadilly Circus.

More important for the future of English architecture was another riverside palace – the new block built in 1665 at the ancient Palace of Greenwich. The work here was given not to Denham but to John Webb – this, with a salary of £200 and the reversion of the Surveyorship (a guarantee never honoured), being a means of compensating him for being passed over in 1660.

King Charles Building, as this block is now called (Plate 68B), was designed as the west side of a quadrangle open towards the river. It is a two-storey building, with an attached Corinthian portico at the centre and pilastered pavilions, with high attic storeys, at the ends. Both main storeys are rusticated, and there is a plain horizontal band between them, which makes a lively contrast and stresses the horizontal feeling of the block. The design is closely related to a drawing of Webb's, dated 1649, for Durham House, in which it is possible that Jones had a say. In any case the Greenwich building is very definitely a flower from the Jones garden and, in some minor details, links up with the Whitehall designs of *c.* 1638.

These two royal buildings and the fact that Webb, though excluded from the Surveyorship, was not wholly overlooked at the new Court, show that the tendency after 1660 was, as one would expect, to pick up the threads broken off in 1642 and to realize something of the magnificence which Jones had been elaborating on paper in the years just before the Civil War.

But the course of English architecture was not destined to travel in quite so straight a line. And while the new blocks at Somerset House and Greenwich were going up, a young man at Oxford, who had no more experience of building than Denham, was turning himself from an astronomer into an architect. His name was to become the greatest in English architecture.

Christopher Wren (1632–1723)

In the year of King Charles's Restoration Dr Christopher Wren, Gresham Professor of Astronomy, was twenty-eight. The son of the Rev. Christopher Wren, Rector of East Knoyle, Wilts., he was born in the Rectory there on 20 October 1632. The Rector's family was large, but Christopher was the only son to survive. Two years after his birth his father became Dean of Windsor and Registrar of the Order of the Garter and, in addition, was presented to the living of Great Haseley, Oxon. Christopher was sent to school at Westminster, under Dr Busby, arriving there in 1641 or 1642 and leaving in 1646. While he was there his family were caught in the troubles of the times. The Deanery at Windsor was raided by a Roundhead officer and the Dean's personal effects were pillaged. The family went to Bristol, remaining there till its surrender to Fairfax, when they returned to East Knoyle. Christopher's uncle, meanwhile, Matthew Wren, successively Bishop of Norwich and Ely and an implacable foe of Puritanism, was imprisoned. He remained in prison for eighteen years, to emerge, an old and much tried man, in the year of the Restoration.

After 1646, when he was fourteen, Wren seems to have spent three years partly at Bletchington, near Oxford, where his brother-in-law, William Holder, held the living, and partly in London, where he studied with Charles Scarburgh, the physician, disciple of the great Harvey. Both from Holder and from Scarburgh he learned much. At the Bletchington parsonage he explored arithmetic and geometry and by constructing dials with his own hands entered into the realm of astronomy. Under Scarburgh he invented a 'weather-clock'. It was Scarburgh, too, who induced him to translate Oughtred's treatise on Geometrical Dialling into Latin, and with Scarburgh he began to interest himself in medical science.

In 1649 Wren's name was entered as that of a Gentleman Commoner at Wadham College, Oxford. It was the year of the King's execution, and the University was recovering from the turmoil of purges and intrusions which had taken place since the City was lost to the Royalists. Puritanism was in the saddle, but it was, on the whole, a tolerant Puritanism, well represented by such a man as John Wilkins, the Warden of Wadham, who, having adapted his politics to the Cromwellian situation, did much to avert Parliamentary interference with the University. Wilkins became the leader of a group of men, mostly of rather indifferent political colour, who at this time bent their energies to scientific work rather than dissipate them in the clash of two equally indistinct lay philosophies. They were, in the words of Bishop Sprat, looking back on them from a safer period, 'men of philosophical minds, whom the misfortunes of the kingdom and the security and ease of a retirement amongst gown-men', had drawn to the University. From among them arose 'a race of young men provided against the next age, whose minds... were invincibly armed against all the inchantments of enthusiasm'.

These young men (Wilkins, the eldest, was but thirty-five in the year of which I am writing) included some of the best minds which were to flourish after the Restoration. They included John Wallis, the mathematician, Seth Ward and Ralph Bathurst, to become respectively a Bishop and a Master of Trinity, Thomas Willis, the physician, Lawrence Rooke, another mathematician, and the physicist Robert Boyle. Thomas Sprat, the eventual historian of the group, joined them in 1651.

That was the circle in which Wren moved from 1649 onwards. He took his degree in 1651, but remained at the University for another seven years. In 1657 he succeeded Lawrence Rooke as Gresham Professor of Astronomy. This took him to London, where he will have lived, for the better part of four years, in Gresham College, Sir Thomas Gresham's old palace in Bishopsgate. There he will have witnessed the triumphs of the Restoration. In the year after that event, however, he returned to Oxford as the new Savilian Professor of Astronomy, the successor of Seth Ward.

Since 1649 Wren must have been wholly engrossed in scientific affairs. He continued to be mainly so until 1665. That means that from the age of seventeen to that of thirty-three, a period during which the foundations of a man's career are usually laid, he was immersed in subjects almost entirely foreign to that which he was eventually to make his own. Indeed, had he died at thirty, he would have remained to posterity a figure of some importance in English scientific thought, but without the word 'architecture' occurring once in his biographies.

Wren's scientific achievement is difficult to assess, partly because his work was so diffuse, but mainly because no thorough study has ever been made of it. Clearly, his most important work was in the realm of astronomy. He helped to forge the essential link between the Keplerian and Newtonian conceptions; indeed, Newton himself considered Wren to be one of the three best geometricians of the time. He followed up Descartes' work on moving bodies and suggested to Boyle a means for testing the Cartesian hypothesis that the moon exerted a pressure on the atmosphere – a suggestion which led to the invention of Boyle's barometer.

But in addition to these main lines of research, Wren was constantly throwing off inventions of a purely practical and empirical kind. There were meteorological instruments for measuring rainfall and recording changes in temperature, improvements to telescopes, experiments in etching, studies of the mechanics of rowing and sailing, and suggestions for the design of water-works.

Few of these inventions proved of much importance; but they illustrate Wren's particular flair for the solution of crude problems of everyday life. Was there in this something of the New Learning's socially conscientious desire 'to assist familiarly', as Sprat puts it, 'in all occasions of human life'? Was there, perhaps, the fascination of the *visual*, of the functioning apparatus, the working model? Certainly one feels that the miscellaneous, empirical inventions of the Oxford period represent that part of Wren's mind which gradually drew him away from astronomy into architecture. The boy's delight in making dials at Bletchington, the youth's invention of the 'diplographic pen', the young graduate's experiments on the collision of bodies, by means of suspended balls – all these mark the development of the mind which was to turn with little preparation but complete confidence to the design and construction of buildings.

Exactly at what point architecture began to be of serious interest to Wren we cannot tell. But as early as 1661 he was offered an appointment surveying and directing harbour works and fortifications at Tangier. With the appointment was to go a large salary and – what is very significant – it was suggested that it would carry with it the reversion of the office of Surveyor-General of the Royal Works. Thus before Wren had built a single building he was considered, in high quarters, to be the type of man fitted for that office. That he should be so is in accord with sixteenth- and seventeenth-century tradition. Architecture was an affair of calculation, of rules, and of ingenuity in working those rules. A man who was a known master of mathematics and famous for his ingenuity was qualified for the Surveyorship on those grounds alone.

Wren, however, declined the Tangier offer, nominally, at any rate, on grounds of health, and continued to work at Oxford. But he must have been thinking much about architecture. It was probably at this time that he was first consulted about the repair of St Paul's Cathedral, a subject to which we shall return in a moment. And in 1662 he addressed himself to the real business of architecture. For in that year he undertook the design and construction of a new building in Oxford – the first, and by no means the least important, of his long career.

The Sheldonian Theatre (Plates 69A and B) was a gift to Oxford from one of its alumni, Archbishop Sheldon, and its purpose was to provide a formal setting for University ceremonies. Wren produced a model and exhibited it to the Royal Society in April 1663. His reason for doing so was that it embodied a trussed roof to carry a ceiling over a considerable span. This was a feature of the design thoroughly in keeping with Wren's previous scientific work and that of his circle. The architectural conception of the theatre, however, represented a departure into a very new field.

The latinity of the Sheldonian is inherent in its name – it was to be, not a hall, but a *theatrum*, analogous to the theatres of Roman antiquity. Hence, Wren took as his point of departure the Theatre of Marcellus, described and engraved in Serlio's *Architettura*, that hoary classic in which Elizabethans and Jacobeans had found so much to help them. A Roman theatre was, of course, a building open to the air, with a banked semicircle of seats facing the *scenae frons*. It was protected merely by a roped canvas covering. Wren set himself the problem of designing such a building with the addition of a permanent roof – hence the need for the large self-supporting ceiling; the ceiling, incidentally, was painted, by Robert Streeter, in such a way as to recall its canvas prototype.

The exterior handling of this roofed theatre was a very difficult matter indeed, and here Wren transferred his empirical ingenuity from the sphere of construction to that of classical design. The plan, of course, was that of the Roman theatre, though Wren substituted a multangular for a semicircular form, perhaps to avoid turning arches in a curved plane. The elevations have for their main theme, externally, an order surmounted by a high attic. In the 'round' of the theatre the order does not appear, there being only rusticated piers and arches; on the flat façade, however, there is an order, with another order above (in the three centre bays only) carrying a pediment into the apex of the roof. To left and right, half-pediments carry the roof-line down. The result is a somewhat mechanical composition, for which an engraving in the Como Vitruvius may be accountable.

Exactly contemporary with the Sheldonian was Pembroke College Chapel, Cambridge (Plate 70A), a gift by Bishop Wren to his old University. It is almost certainly by his nephew, Christopher, though there is no documentary evidence for this. Begun in May 1663, it was the first college chapel in either University to be completely void of Gothic features. The principal (street) elevation, based on an engraving in Serlio, has four Corinthian pilasters supporting a pediment, and there are panels and other details which recall the design of the Sheldonian.

In 1665 Wren provided a design for a block of rooms for Trinity College, Oxford, a drawing for which is preserved and shows an unusual feature for English architecture of the time – a French 'Mansard' roof. This inclination towards a new source of influence is accompanied – and explained – by Wren's decision, in the spring of this year, to visit Paris.

As far as we know, this visit to France was the only occasion on which Wren ever left England. He probably arrived in Paris in July 1665 and was certainly in England again before March 1666 – so the visit lasted perhaps eight or nine months. Now, considering that Wren went to France not as a student, working in one place under a master, but purely and simply as a touring visitor, collecting facts and impressions, the stay was a fairly long one. He must have seen a great deal. Unfortunately, all we know of the visit is contained in one letter written, probably in the autumn of 1665, to an English friend. This refers only to Paris and to places about a day's journey distant and is as striking for its omissions as for what it includes. There is, for example, no reference whatever to the domed churches of Paris, in which Wren certainly took the keenest interest. The letter is, therefore, a totally inadequate indication of how the whole period abroad was spent and it is certainly not impossible that he visited Flanders, and perhaps Holland as well, on his way to or from the French capital. The possibility will seem a very real one as soon as we begin to look at the City Churches.

The Paris letter does contain some very interesting information about what Wren saw in France. He was immensely impressed by the works at the Louvre, proceeding under the cultural dictatorship of Colbert. He visited many of the royal châteaux, including Fontainebleau, St-Germain, and Versailles. He saw Vaux-le-Vicomte, Maisons-Laffitte, Rueil, Courances, Chilly, Essones, St-Maur-les-Fossés, St-Mandé, Issy, Meudon, le

Raincy, Chantilly, Verneuil, and Liancourt – buildings which embodied some of the finest work of the French Renaissance of the sixteenth and seventeenth centuries, from de l'Orme to de Brosse. He also met many of the artists concerned, including possibly Mansart himself and, more probably, Louis Le Vau, then the architect in charge both at the Louvre and at Versailles and the author of the great Collège des Quatre Nations (now the Institut de France) by the Seine.

Moreover, Wren was introduced to Bernini, then in Paris by royal invitation to give a design for the rebuilding of part of the Louvre. Bernini was then sixty-seven (exactly the age of Mansart) and Europe's most distinguished architect. 'Bernini's design of the Louvre I would have given my skin for, but the old reserv'd Italian gave me but a few minutes view ... I had only time to copy it in my fancy and memory.'[3]

Wren left France with his baggage full of all the graphic material he could get – no doubt the books of Du Cerceau and de L'Orme (if he did not already possess them) and the engravings of Perelle. 'I shall bring you almost all France on paper', he wrote, and 'I have purchas'd a great deal of *Taille-douce* [engravings], that I might give our countrymen examples of ornaments and grotesks, in which the Italians themselves confess the French to excell.' The visit represents a lading up of Wren's phenomenal mind with the architectural riches of France (and, maybe, of the Netherlands). In later chapters we shall see how the material and sensations he thus got modified the architect's work and that of his age.

Old St Paul's

On his return from France Wren immediately became involved in the discussions which were going on about the repair of St Paul's Cathedral. The building was in a sad way. Inigo Jones's restoration had been interrupted by the Civil War, and during that period the Cathedral had been occupied by the Parliamentary forces. It had been badly treated and, in parts, deliberately mutilated. But the worst trouble was deeper; it was the unsound state of the medieval fabric as a whole, particularly in regard to the central tower which, having been shored up at various periods, was now once again showing signs of impending collapse.

Wren, as we have seen, had been concerned with the St Paul's problem as early as 1661, but he can hardly, at that time, have been officially briefed. It was only in April 1663 that a Commission was constituted to undertake the restoration, and it was natural that the Commission's first step should be to obtain a report from the highest authority, namely the Surveyor-General, Sir John Denham. Denham, with the necessary help of Webb and Marshall (the Master Mason), reported in favour of demolishing the steeple and nave vaults and effecting a decent compromise with what was left.

The Commission did not act on this advice, and obtained at least two further opinions. One was from Roger Pratt, who was for letting well alone, even to the extent of waiting for the tower to collapse rather than pay for its demolition. A third report was obtained from Dr Wren and this, much longer than the others, was of quite another character. Wren, after diagnosing the maladies of the old building, put forward a reconstruction more ambitious than had been envisaged either by the official men or by Pratt. Agreeing that the tower must come down, he led on to a suggestion for a reconstruction of the crossing on new lines and in the following words the future crown of the City's sky-line emerges for the first time:

> I cannot propose a better remedy yn by cutting of ye inner Corners of ye Cross, to reduce ye middle part into a spacious Dome or rotunda with a Cupolo or Hemispherical Roof and upon ye Cupolo for ye outward Ornament, a Lantern with a Spire. ...

To this proposal Wren added an ingenious suggestion whereby the legs of the old tower should be temporarily retained to reduce the amount of scaffolding required for the new structure. And he concluded the Report by mentioning that he had had the opportunity of studying the construction of such work, 'by ye best Artists, French and Italian'[4] and had, moreover, himself conceived improvements on their methods.

Wren produced drawings of this domed crossing, and they exist (Plate 70B). They show a drum, attic, dome, and lantern remarkably close, in general idea, to the realized structure of forty years later, but rather inartistic in treatment. It combines the Bramante design for St Peter's dome, given in Serlio, with memories of the Val-de-Grâce at Paris. There is a separate inner dome, as there was in some of the Paris churches. The lantern is surmounted by a monstrous elongated pineapple, a naïf apology for the absence of the spire which the Cathedral had once possessed. The interior details look like a beginner's attempt to be florid. The plaster swags and drops in the interior are, however, closely similar to some of the coarse Anglo-Flemish stuff which English plasterers were producing in London at the time – close, in fact, to Lord Mayor Lawrence's house just then building in Bishopsgate. This is an important point, as Wren's assessment of what kind of ornamental work English artificers were capable of producing continued to be an important factor in his work. The nave of the old Cathedral Wren proposed to recase in new masonry 'after a good Roman manner' to correspond with the exterior already so dealt with by Inigo Jones.

In August 1666 John Evelyn who, with two others, had been deputed by the Commission to determine a course of action, tells us of a meeting at St Paul's with the Bishop, the Dean, Wren, Pratt, May, the Master of the Ordnance, and the Master of the Mint. Pratt had already declared his opposition to Wren's scheme, chiefly on the ground of expense. But at this meeting he was over-ruled, and after some argument Wren's plan was, in principle, agreed to. This included the dome, 'a form of church-building', says Evelyn, 'not as yet known in England but of wonderful grace'.

That was on 27 August. Six days later, about 10 o'clock in the evening, the Great Fire of London began to burn.

NOTES TO CHAPTER 12

1. The principal artisans and clerks appointed were as follows. The Master Mason was Edward Marshall (p. 99), who had, apparently, been guaranteed the post by Charles during the Commonwealth. He and his son Joshua Marshall became important figures, both as makers of monuments and for the part Joshua played under Wren in the City Churches and the early stages of St Paul's. John Davenport, the carpenter, and John Grove, the plasterer, became important in the same business. The Clerk Engrosser was William Dickinson (d. 1702). Another Clerk was Richard Gammon, a relation by marriage to Inigo Jones, under whose will he had benefited; with him was Leonard Gammon, his son. Finally, the Serjeant Painter was Sir Robert Howard, a cavalier warrior whose qualifications in the art were probably as doubtful as Denham's in architecture. He was responsible for some 'painted and coloured works' in the King's Closet at Whitehall and in Denham's new lodgings there, but relinquished his post in 1662–3, flourishing subsequently as Auditor of the Exchequer and, more conspicuously, as a poet and dramatist. He was succeeded by Robert Streeter, whose career proved more productive.

2. Comparable to May as a designer (if we judge by the slight remains of his work) was William Samwell (1628–76). He was a Northamptonshire gentleman, and his eminence may be measured by the fact that he designed a town-house at Newmarket for Charles II. He never held office in the Works. Of his Newmarket building we know only that Evelyn found it 'mean', but the simple, well-proportioned brickwork of Felbrigg Hall, Norfolk (1674, for William Wyndham), does him great credit, and he also designed the original Eaton Hall, Cheshire, for Lord Grosvenor (1675–83). This, like so many other houses of the time, derived from Pratt's Clarendon House and it is impossible to determine whether Samwell stood on his own feet as a designer or was merely a prompt follower of Pratt and May.

3. This meeting with Bernini was not Wren's only contact with the living Baroque of seventeenth-century Italy. No less an exponent of Baroque than Guarino Guarini (1624–83) had begun to build the domed Theatine church of Ste-Anne-la-Royale at Paris in 1662, and during Wren's visit it will have reached an interesting stage. That Wren studied this church in progress is borne out by the remark, in a letter of 1666, that he had had the opportunity 'of seeing severall Structures ... while they were in rising, conducted by ye best Artists, French *and Italian* and having daily conference with ym and observing ye Engines and Methods'.

4. See preceding note.

PART THREE

WREN AND THE BAROQUE
⟨1660 – 1710⟩

CHAPTER 13

THE REBUILDING OF LONDON:
THE CITY CHURCHES

THE flames of the Great Fire were under control on 5 September 1666. On 11 September Dr Wren submitted to the King his sketch-plan for the rebuilding.[1] On 13 September John Evelyn submitted another plan, and on the same day a royal Proclamation was issued announcing, among other things, that the City would be rebuilt in brick and stone with wider streets, that a survey was to be made, and that a new plan for the burnt area would be adopted.

To implement this Proclamation, six men were immediately given instructions – three acting for the King in Council and three for the City. The King's three men (called 'Commissioners for Rebuilding the City of London') were Dr Christopher Wren, Hugh May, and Roger Pratt. The City's representatives were Robert Hooke, Edward Jerman, and Peter Mills. This joint committee had two main tasks. First, to get the burnt area surveyed. Second, to formulate proposals for future procedure in such a way that they could be embodied in legislation. In their first task they failed. For a variety of reasons, which need not detain us, the making of a Survey, with a view to a fundamental redistribution of sites, was simply not possible. For technical, economic, and psychological reasons it failed.[2]

The Committee's second task, to formulate methods of rebuilding, was consummated in the first *Act for Rebuilding the City of London*, passed in 1667. This Act provided, in the first place, for the structural standardization of the new houses in three types – all of brick and all with specified floor-heights and wall-thicknesses. In the second place, it provided for a certain number of public improvements, notably for the conversion of part of the Fleet River into a canal and for the provision of a Thames-side quay. In the third place it authorized the collection of a tax on coals coming into the Port of London, the proceeds to be applied to compensation connected with the improvements and to the building of gaols, as being the most essential of public works. The Act made no provision for either the City Churches or St Paul's Cathedral, nor were the proceeds of the tax adequate even for compensation. Accordingly, a further Act was passed in 1670, trebling the tax on coal and allocating specific proportions of it to the Churches, the Cathedral, and the City's own public works.

The Act of 1667 provided for the employment of Surveyors by the City. Very naturally, the same men who had acted in the interim period were invited to serve and, in addition, John Oliver. He and Jerman at first declined the invitation; Jerman died in 1668, and Oliver finally accepted in that year, so he and Robert Hooke and Peter Mills were the three men on whom the technical problems of the rebuilding devolved. It seems that the Royal Commission, consisting of Wren, May, and Pratt, ceased to function with the passing of the Rebuilding Acts. May, thereafter, had only a passing connexion with the rebuilding, Pratt none at all. Wren's connexion was limited, as we shall see, to certain specific undertakings.

The three Surveyors deserve some notice. Robert Hooke (1635–1703) was easily the most remarkable of them. As a boy he had been sent to Peter Lely to learn portraiture, but sickening at the smell of paint he went to Westminster School, where Busby took a particular interest in him. He went on to Christ Church, Oxford, and there mixed with the same intellectual set which Wren had joined a few years earlier. His bent was rather like Wren's – mechanical. He invented the balance-spring for watches and assisted Robert Boyle in some of his most important work. In 1662 he left Boyle to become Curator of Experiments to the Royal Society, an office which he retained for the rest of his life. He was an odd, introverted person, chronic ill-health and a slight deformity having detached him somewhat from the currents of ordinary life. When the Great Fire occurred he had been elected Gresham Professor of Geometry, had set out his theory of combustion and just published his *Micrographia*, the first important work on the microscope. From the time of his appointment as one of the City Surveyors he combined this work with his scientific duties, somewhat to the disadvantage of the latter, though he published occasional works till 1678. He was, as we shall see, the designer of several buildings in the City and elsewhere.

Peter Mills (*c.* 1600–70) was the bricklayer whom we met in Chapter 10 as the designer of Thorpe Hall and, no doubt, other important Commonwealth buildings. He had built much on his own account and suffered severe financial loss through the Fire. John Oliver (1616–1701) was probably brought up a mason but practised surveying from about 1647. In 1686 he succeeded Joshua Marshall as Master Mason in the Works and was Wren's deputy at St Paul's.

Under the direction of these men the rebuilding of the City proceeded in conformity with the Acts. It was a slow and laborious undertaking, for it must be remembered that almost the whole of it was the result of private enterprise and private wealth. There was no insurance, no compensation of any kind; and public money, in the shape of the proceeds of the Coal Tax, was available only for certain public works. The City Companies' Halls, colleges, institutions, and all private houses were rebuilt out of such wealth as had escaped the Fire, either in the shape of cash hastily removed or of investments outside the burnt area.

The symbolically important Guildhall, only partly destroyed, was rising to its new roof by the end of 1667; three Compters, Ludgate, and Newgate followed. The Gresham trustees, encouraged by the King, had the new Royal Exchange ready for occupation by 1671. Most of the Companies had at least a new hall by 1672, with ancillary buildings to follow. Christ's Hospital started rebuilding in 1667 and continued at various times for thirty years. A new Customs House was begun in 1669 and a new College of Arms in 1671.

Of these buildings, the Royal Exchange (Plate 71A) was, architecturally, the most important. Mills, who was considered to have too much on his hands already, was passed over in favour of Edward Jerman (d. 1668–9), a carpenter whom the City people esteemed the next best artist among them. The design, claimed after Jerman's death by Thomas Cartwright, a mason, reproduced the arcaded courtyard plan of Gresham's building but seized the opportunity of street improvements to give the building a grand entrance façade, with a triumphal arch, rising through two storeys, as its centre. Over the arch was a three-stage tower recalling Gresham's original but with elaborations prompted, no doubt, by the cognate example of Hatfield. The handling of the building as a whole was as typically mannered and coarse as one would expect from the City artificers.

The Customs House (Plate 71B), on the other hand (burnt, 1718), a building enclosing three sides of a courtyard, was pronouncedly Dutch and might have been designed by somebody familiar with Jacob van Campen's Town Hall at Amsterdam (1655). As 'Mr Wren's model' is mentioned in the Treasury Books he was evidently responsible, though it would not be surprising to find that the design was made by deputy.

The City Companies' Halls, forty-five of which were burnt, were rebuilt under great financial difficulties, so much of the invested capital of their builders having disappeared in the Fire. The new buildings were therefore simple, and relied on private munificence to provide them with the carved work which, in due course, made them seem lavish. As far as we know, no Company went outside the City for its architect. Jerman's name is connected with the Fishmongers', Merchant Taylors', Haberdashers' (Plate 72B), and Drapers' Halls, all altered or destroyed since. Such records as there are of their original appearance confirm one's opinion of his style as being typically 'Artisan', with most of the mannerisms we observed in discussing Thorpe Hall, Tyttenhanger, and other Commonwealth houses. The only exception was Fishmongers' Hall, whose façade showed something of the new Dutch Palladian influence.

John Oliver designed Skinners' Hall, and in this, the only work so far assigned to this designer, we again find Anglo-Flemish characteristics. A third designer of City halls was Captain John Caine, a bricklayer, who was responsible for building Brewers' Hall (Plate 72A; destroyed 1941) and Tallowchandlers' Hall. The designers of all the halls could probably be discovered, if the Companies' records were accessible, but for our present outline the available evidence points clearly enough to the essentially intra-mural character of the work.

Heralds' College might, one would think, have looked to Whitehall for a design, but in fact the Heralds were content with the rather crude work of a bricklayer, Morris Emmett (1646–94), whose pilasters declare themselves old-fashioned by the Flemish brooches pinned to their shafts.

In the Great Fire, no fewer than 13,200 houses were destroyed, and the replacement of these was long-drawn-out. Only a very few unimportant specimens of immediately post-Fire housing survive, but we can gain a fair picture of the rebuilt City from prints and photographs. Two points are worth noting. One is that the provisions of the Rebuilding

Act left so little scope for fanciful arrangement that the houses tended to conform closely to three basic types, differing only in size (according to the class of street in which each was built). The other point is that, in spite of this, the streets were by no means uniform and much ingenuity was shown in giving houses distinct individualities according to the trade of the builder – ornamental rubbed-brick from the bricklayers, stone dressings from the masons, balustraded balconies from the carpenters, and so on.

The plainest houses had no features at all except projecting brick bands at each floor-level and a moulded wood cornice. The richer houses had robust 'Artisan' ornaments according to taste. An exceptional house, built in 1668, was Lord Mayor Sir William Turner's stone-fronted residence in Cheapside (demolished), richly carved with swags and terms as a gesture of encouragement to his fellow-citizens.

One of the major effects of the rebuilding was that a new structural standard of brick domestic architecture was set up *for the whole country*. The Rebuilding Act was quoted in building agreements far outside the London area. Moreover, the rebuilding emphasized that the gabled street-front was a bygone thing, for although gables did appear here and there in the new City, the floor-heights given in the Act made them uneconomic, and fashion had already condemned them for near thirty years.

The City Churches

Eighty-seven parish churches were destroyed in the Fire. Only fifty-one were rebuilt, the Act of 1670 providing for the uniting of many parishes. The building of the new churches was made possible by the increased tax on coal authorized under the same Act, and three Commissioners (the Archbishop of Canterbury, the Bishop of London, and the Lord Mayor) were appointed to approve designs and govern the procedure generally. Wren, as Surveyor-General, became their executive officer.

The coal dues were paid into the Chamber (i.e. the treasury) of the City of London. The money accumulated very slowly, but the parishes were able to raise money themselves out of revenue, subscriptions, and the sale of old materials, pay it into the Chamber and reclaim it at a later date. Thus the rebuilding of the churches started immediately after the passing of the Act.

The churches were designed, their construction was supervised, and the accounts were passed by Wren, who had the assistance of three Surveyors. These were the Surveyors under the 1667 Act, Hooke, Oliver, and a certain Edward Woodroffe (d. 1675) who no doubt filled the place of the lately deceased Peter Mills. Wren's clerk, Andrew Phillips, was also much concerned with the work.

In each case the parish took the initiative. Having obtained a warrant for the rebuilding, signed by two of the Commissioners, they approached Wren for a 'model'. The next step was to persuade him to get the church built, and this was not always easy. Throughout the parish accounts we find gifts of money or wine or entertainment charges being paid as incentives to Wren, the Surveyors, and Phillips to get the work started and keep it going. This was the regular seventeenth-century way of doing things, and as further gifts – tokens of appreciation for services rendered – often followed we need not assume that Wren and his colleagues were greedy or inefficient. The parishes were expected to pay for most of the fittings, altar-pieces, wainscoting, and fonts themselves, but, very naturally, they pressed for as much as possible to be set against the public account.

In 1670, right on the heels of the Act, fifteen churches were started and by 1677, the peak year, there must have been nearly thirty at some stage of construction. By 1686 the rebuilding was virtually over, apart from certain steeples which were added about the end of the century.

Wren, as everybody knows, designed the churches and they form one of the most fertile sections of his work. But, in considering them, there is a preliminary difficulty. Hardly a single church would one accept, on the instant, as the work of the man who was simultaneously producing the preparatory drawings for St Paul's Cathedral. Their loose handling of classical forms, casually spaced openings and crudities of detail seem to be on a different plane from the precision and scholarship of St Paul's. But this difficulty becomes to some extent reducible after a study of the City Church drawings at All Souls and the Royal Institute of British Architects.[3] Two explanations present themselves. The first is that Wren quite deliberately conceived the churches on a less formal and more experimental plane than his Cathedral; and the second is that he neither detailed them as fully nor supervised their erection as closely, so that an aggregate of minor freedoms on the part of the artisans gives an over-all impression of roughness and insensitivity. It is not difficult to distinguish churches, or parts of churches, where Wren's control has been absolute, from those where it has not. It might be added, moreover, that whereas Wren himself was an elegant and precise draughtsman, his colleagues were capable of producing drawings of detestable crudity. Hooke's drawings are singularly insensitive.

The style of the City Churches presents deeply interesting problems, especially in 1670 and the following years when, for the first time in his life, Wren was fully immersed in the practice of architecture. Let us remember that, faced with this unprecedented church-building programme, he had almost no recent English classical examples to which to refer. There were, to be sure, Inigo Jones's Chapels Royal and Covent Garden Church. But the non-parochial (and papistical) character of the first and the exceptional siting conditions of the second limited their value as points of departure. His own two collegiate chapels at Cambridge were, like the Chapels Royal, mere rectangular cells for small congregations; while that singular hybrid, St Katherine Cree (p. 107), the latest and most 'advanced' City Church in existence, was scarcely a model on which a mind of the calibre of Wren's would willingly lean.

And what else? One local precedent there was, of considerable fruitfulness – Inigo Jones's remodelling of old St Paul's. Here was a case where Jones had been forced away from his Italian models and obliged to extemporize. There were elements here for an appropriate modern church-building vernacular – the plain round-headed and circular openings, for instance, the giant scrolls assisting the silhouette of a façade, the towers with their octagon lanterns,[4] the obelisks used as pinnacles. All these ideas Wren absorbed and, on occasion, imitated rather closely.

But they did not assist the plan-conception of a modern church. For inspiration on this major problem, Wren seems to have gone straight to Rome – that is, to Vitruvius and

Serlio. The Roman basilica Wren probably considered as a fundamental type, and whenever he designed a nave-and-aisles church the basilica was present in his mind as a model and corrective. It is significant that all but one of his nave-and-aisle churches are of five bays – the number in Vitruvius' Fano basilica; and among the drawings are several cases of approximation to that model more explicit than in the executed buildings.

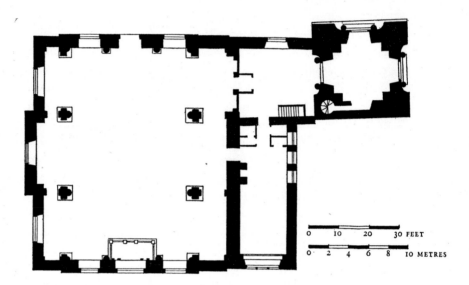

Figure 17. St Mary-le-Bow

Then there was the *Templum Pacis* (Basilica of Maxentius) as given by Serlio. This is acknowledged in *Parentalia* as the model for St Mary-le-Bow (Plate 73A; Figure 17); and the conjunction of columns, piers, and arches occurs in other churches and was a valuable source of inspiration at St Paul's.

But these and some other Roman precedents were merely the background against which Wren exercised his own practical, empirical inventiveness, so that one is rarely conscious of the attachment to Rome and the churches have a stark, sometimes startling, originality.

It is customary to divide the churches into categories according to their plan-shapes but it is noticeable that nearly all the shapes occur together in the first group of churches, which must have been designed in 1670–1. St Dionis Backchurch, St Mary Aldermanbury, and St Magnus the Martyr all have⁵ the simple basilican plan without galleries and with the merest suggestion of a transept on the short axis. St Mary-le-Bow, as we have seen, imitates the *Templum Pacis*. St Mary at Hill (Figure 18) brings in the Greek cross plan, which may conceivably have been inspired by Vitruvius' description of the *cavum tetrastylum*. A more obvious derivation would be the churches of de Keyser in Amsterdam, if we could feel sure that Wren had information about them. But even if he did, a scrutiny of Vitruvius remains more characteristic of his thought than the imitation of the very loose and provincial classicism of Holland. At St Lawrence Jewry (Plate 74B; Figure 19), yet another plan appeared – a large, simple pilastered chamber with an annexe on one side, in the opening to which the pilaster order continues in the round. While at St Benet Fink we have a ten-sided figure brought to an inner flattened hexagon marked out by six columns whose connecting arches carry an elliptical dome. That plan is unique and seems to have been suggested by peculiarities of the site – peculiarities which challenged Wren the geometer and produced an outstandingly original result.

Nearly all the later churches repeat and develop the themes of these earlier ones. With St Stephen, Walbrook (1672–87), however, came a magnificent new departure. The church was patronized by the Grocers' Company and there was money and ambition to make a good thing. Early in the proceedings, the churchwardens voted 'twenty guineas in a silk purse' to be presented to Wren 'or his lady', in consideration of 'his great care and extraordinary pains in contriving the design… and assisting in the rebuilding'.

St Stephen's (Plate 75; Figure 20) may fairly be described as an essay on the central theme with which its architect was wrestling in his design for St Paul's – namely, the combination of nave-and-aisles and transepts with a central domed space. At St Stephen's the dome is within the church, resting at no point on the main walls. It is carried on eight arches and these are carried on as many columns. The north, south, east, and west arches run directly into nave, chancel, and transept vaults. The alternate (diagonal) arches have

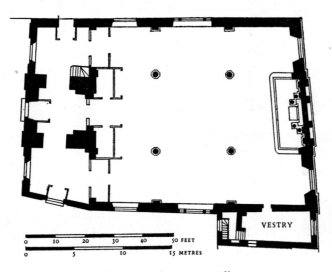

Figure 18. St Mary at Hill

no such obvious destination and so Wren added four more columns, completing the square within which the dome is described, and supplying support for four triangular groined vaults. These, with their awkwardly inserted clerestory windows, are the weakest part of the design. Apart from them, however, the solution is neat and, in plan and section, looks faultless.

The dome of St Stephen's is constructed in wood and plaster and could not, of course, have been built in materials developing lateral thrusts. It is an essay in the solid geometry of the domed church and exposes a difficulty which Wren met again, and only partially solved, at St Paul's; the difficulty of joining an aisled nave to a domed space, while preserving the fundamental idea of a dome carried on eight equal arches. There is, so far as one can see, no perfect solution of this problem which was, to a certain extent, forced on Wren by circumstances arising at St Paul's. But it is eminently characteristic of him that, both in the Cathedral and at St Stephen's, he accepted it and solved it in an empirical way.

After 1673, there was one more new departure in church planning – and it was of high importance. It came with the designing of Christ Church, Newgate Street, about 1677. Wren had, from the first, pitched the bases of his columns on high plinths, to avoid their being concealed by pews. Here, at Christ Church, he pitched them still higher, converting the plinths into tall pedestals with appropriate mouldings. At this height it was possible to rest the gallery fronts on the pedestals, and Wren had arrived at the notion (sanctioned, of course, by Vitruvius) of a two-storeyed basilica, in which the gallery was an organic part of the design. At St Peter's, Cornhill (close in date to Christ Church), he followed the same idea, and in St Clement Danes (begun 1680) took it a step further by making the pedestals yet higher and converting them into square-plan piers of the Doric order.

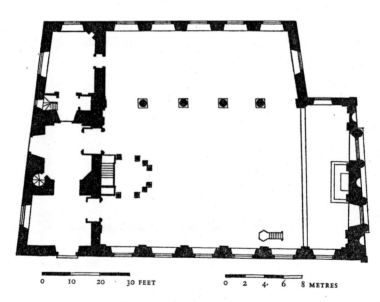

Figure 19. St Lawrence Jewry

Here, a new church-type – the two-storeyed, galleried church with vaulted nave and aisles – stood complete and it only remained for Wren to give final expression to the theme at St James, Piccadilly (Plate 78A), in 1683. This Wren considered a model town church, a type which, he says, 'I think ... may be found beautiful and convenient, and as such, the cheapest of any Form I could invent'.

No less interesting than the spatial formulas invented by Wren for his churches (formulas which echo through the eighteenth century and into the nineteenth – Cockerell's interior of St George's Hall, Liverpool, is the surprising and grandiose fulfilment of one of them) are the designs he evolved for classical steeples. Here again, there was very scant precedent. Inigo Jones had built modest little towers at the west end of old St Paul's

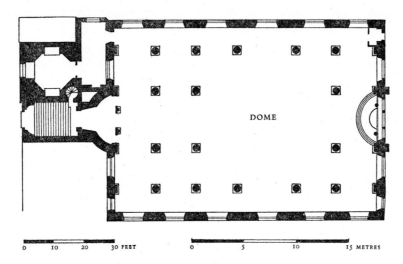

DOME

Figure 20. St Stephen, Walbrook

and Wren will probably have known the towers in Jones's Whitehall designs. De Keyser's Zuyder Kerk at Amsterdam offered a solution of a wholly unintellectual sort; and there were the varied towers and spires of Gothic London, lost in the Fire, but remembered and cherished. It was perhaps such a pre-Fire memory which led to Wren's first grand invention of a classical steeple at St Mary-le-Bow (Plate 76A). To begin with, he thought to build a low tower, surmounted by an octagonal, domed cupola, somewhat like those on Inigo Jones's Whitehall designs and ultimately of Flemish origin. But this he abandoned for a conception of much greater height, magnificence, and originality. In the base of the tower, he set a Doric portal, standing in a rusticated arch – an elegant tribute to Mansart's Palais de Conti. The bell stage he pilastered. Above this he broke into a most original sequence of stages in which there is certainly an element of Gothic paraphrase. The tower of the old church had possessed 'bows' or arches supporting a spirelet and these are echoed in the reversed consoles which cluster round the circular core of the spire above the first (circular) tempietto. Above the console stage is a second (square) tempietto and above this more consoles and an obelisk. At the four corners of the tower are ingenious *pastiches* of classical detail, supplying the effect of Gothic pinnacles; they are like miniature recollections of the top of Bernini's baldacchino in St Peter's.

Among the early steeples, none rivalled St Mary-le-Bow, and the other important examples are all late in date, even if they were conceived, as two certainly were, in the early seventies. The famous steeple of St Bride, Fleet Street (Plate 76B), must be related to the termination shown on the dome of the Warrant Design for St Paul's; and Wren had proposed something similar for St Magnus. It seems probable that this idea of diminishing octagonal *tempietti* springs from the curious notion which possessed early illustrators of Vitruvius that the Tower of the Winds at Athens was of more than one storey. No doubt *turris*, in Vitruvius' very summary description, seemed to suggest height. In any case, the engraving in Jan Martin's editions (1547 and 1572) would be enough to suggest to Wren the possibilities of the theme for a modern spire. St Bride's (built 1702–3) has four stages, each with a pilaster order on a pedestal, and at the top is an obelisk. A brilliant subtlety is that while the pilasters diminish in height from stage to stage, the pedestals actually *increase* in height. Hence the sense of 'lift' and poise in this charming spire.

Another late steeple, utilizing an old idea, is that of St Magnus (1705) where the Flemish type of lantern originally proposed for St Mary-le-Bow is magnificently interpreted (Plate 77A). At St Vedast's (Plate 77B), on the other hand, built in 1697, we have a tower which cannot have been conceived much before the date of erection since it is one of those Wren designs which owes its inspiration to Borromini. The concave face and convex balustrade of the tower of the Philippine Convent in Rome seem to have provided the germ of this remarkable design which, in its further development, proceeds with a sobriety and elegance remote from Borromini and allied to such earlier steeples as, say, that of St Stephen, Walbrook (about 1676). To compare this latter steeple with St Vedast's is to appreciate vividly the change which came over Wren's style soon after 1690 – a change of which we shall have more to say.

Four of the City Church steeples are Gothic, the most important in this style being that of St Dunstan-in-the-East (1698), a direct imitation of old St Mary-le-Bow.

Apart from the steeples, there is little enough to say about the exteriors of the churches which, more often than not, are so hemmed in as to render any but the plainest treatment superfluous. A few, however, are important. The pilastered east end of St Lawrence Jewry (Plate 74A), for instance, is a show-piece, based on the east elevation of the Model design for St Paul's. The west end of St Magnus has a scheme of pilasters under a pediment, recalling Pembroke Chapel, Cambridge. It is the only case where Wren ventured to suggest the anomaly of a tower 'riding' on a portico, though he did make a design, possibly for St Clement Danes, which has the same combination in a more emphatic form and may have supplied James Gibbs with a hint which was to have far-reaching consequences.

St Clement Danes, as executed, has an inconsiderable west front (apart from Gibbs's steeple), but the east end is highly unusual. Apparently to make the best use of the site, Wren swept the aisle walls round in two segments to meet the curve of the apse. The early design shows that this boldly original stroke originated with a very modest rounding-off of corners, so that we need not look for an exotic source for this Baroque gesture. It was unique in English architecture until imitated, here and there, in the next century.

The churches were pewed and fitted and the vestries furnished by the parishes independently, though often with the advice of Wren. The altars and altar-pieces, fonts, screens, and wainscoting represent, in design and execution, the work of joiners and carvers such as Thomas Creecher, Richard Kedge, or William Newman, who sent in drawings with their 'offers'. All belong to the Anglo-Netherlandish school of carving in which Grinling Gibbons was the principal figure. In view of the persistent legend that Gibbons executed most of the carved work in the City Churches it is necessary to add that nowhere in the building accounts or parish minutes does his name occur. Nor do the works themselves justify any such legend, with the exception of the really superbly designed altar-piece in St Mary Abchurch. And in that case, rather oddly, the carver's name is missing.

Generally, the City Churches give a wonderful picture of Wren's mind during the central period of his career. It is an energetic, adventurous mind, proceeding by intellectual argument rather than by the intuitive conception of aesthetic entities to which all argument must be subordinated. Wren was, through and through, an empiricist. A design of his never *grows*: it is stated at once, then abruptly altered or wholly superseded. His strength was the discipline of the geometer, but it was also his weakness, and among the City Churches, by no means all of the experiments succeed. In many there are relationships which have evidently not been 'felt' in the designer's mind; and even in St Stephen, Walbrook, the space problem is solved mechanically rather than by pure judgement of the intuition. On the other hand, there is abounding invention, and none of the churches fails to show some fascinating stroke of ingenuity and freshness of thought.

NOTES TO CHAPTER 13

1. Wren's plan seems to reflect both the Rome of the Popes and the principles of large-scale French garden design which Le Nôtre had begun to develop at Versailles. It consists of a skeleton of main streets linking up several 'ronds-points' whence secondary streets radiate, while a grid of still narrower streets fills the spaces. Evelyn's first plan (he later made two others) is enough like Wren's to make it obvious that there was mutual discussion, but it is less accomplished and the symmetry of it is forced. Robert Hooke also submitted a plan, probably of a regular grid-iron type.

2. For this and other aspects of the subject of this chapter, I am indebted to Mr T. F. Reddaway's book, noted in the Bibliography.

3. The All Souls' drawings, of which there are forty-five relating to City Churches, formed part of the Wren family collection, sold in 1749. Another great part of this collection came to light in 1951 and was sold at Sotheby's. The Royal Institute of British Architects acquired (through the National Art Collections Fund) thirty-four drawings, all relating to City Churches. There are further church drawings,

of late date, in the British Museum, and there is one in the Soane Museum.

4. One of these Wren would willingly have purchased for Chelsea Hospital, but the Dean and Chapter would not allow its re-erection on a secular building.

5. The present tense is used for all the churches mentioned here, whether existing or wholly or partly destroyed. The actual position (1952) is as follows. Of Wren's fifty-three churches in London, thirty-three survived in 1939. Of these seventeen were gutted or destroyed in the war of 1939–45, leaving sixteen more or less intact, viz.: St Anne and St Agnes; St Benet, Thames Street; St Clement, Eastcheap; St Edmund, Lombard Street; St James, Garlickhithe; St James, Piccadilly; St Magnus the Martyr; St Margaret, Lothbury; St Margaret Pattens; St Martin, Ludgate; St Mary Abchurch; St Mary at Hill (largely rebuilt, however, in the eighteenth century); St Mary Aldermary; St Michael, Cornhill; St Peter, Cornhill; St Stephen Walbrook. Substantial remains, including the steeple (if any) of the following churches survive: St Alban,

Wood Street; St Andrew, Wardrobe; St Andrew, Holborn; St Augustin, Watling Street (lead spire destroyed); St Bride, Fleet Street; Christ Church, Newgate Street; St Clement Danes; St Dunstan-in-the-East (steeple only by Wren); St Lawrence Jewry (lead spire destroyed); St Mary-le-Bow; St Mary Aldermanbury; St Michael Royal; St Nicholas Cole Abbey (lead spire destroyed); St Swithin, Cannon Street; St Vedast, Foster Lane. The tower of All Hallows, Lombard Street, was rebuilt at Twickenham in 1937.

CHAPTER 14

ST PAUL'S CATHEDRAL

THE architectural history of the present Cathedral of St Paul really begins with the design Wren made for a domed remodelling of the old structure, just before the Fire, in the summer of 1666 (p. 123). There, as we have seen, was a crude forecast of the conception to which Wren, in spite of many detours, remained loyal – the cruciform plan, the high colonnaded drum over the crossing, the dome and lantern.

The Fire did not immediately precipitate an entire rebuilding, and in the atmosphere of paralysis after the disaster it seemed as if one generation at least would have to content itself with a Cathedral fashioned, with such decency as might be, within the shell of the old. Wren, asked to report on some such expedient, reluctantly conceded to the compromise of pulling down the old choir and tower as hopeless wrecks, and forming a new choir and 'auditory' in the still more or less stable nave. This suggestion was adopted, and work proceeded, until, in April 1668, a chunk of old masonry fell on one of the aisle vaults, brought down one of the newly cased nave piers and threatened still further ruin. 'What you whispered in my ear', wrote Dean Sancroft to Wren, 'is now come to pass.'

The collapse cleared the air and the minds of the authorities. In the following July the Dean, writing in the name of the Archbishop of Canterbury and the Bishops of London and Oxford, told Wren that it had been resolved 'to frame a Design, handsome and noble, and suitable to all the Ends of it, and to the Reputation of the City, and the Nation, and to take it for granted, that Money will be had to accomplish it'. In short, a new Cathedral was to be built; and as a first step a choir was to be designed which would be complete in itself until the greater whole could be accomplished.

This decision led directly to the preparation of the so-called *First Model*. Unfortunately, no drawings of it survive, though there is a fragment of the wooden model itself; this, with some other scraps of evidence, enables us to envisage Wren's intentions at this stage clearly enough. He designed a cathedral consisting solely of a rectangular choir, with a large domed vestibule at the west end of it – a very curious conception, which may just possibly have been suggested by the Temple Church. The choir was a simple arcuated design with two external orders, probably based on Serlio's engravings of the Theatre of Marcellus. The lower arcade, however, was an open loggia, so that the church had no internal aisles – a most eccentric arrangement. The vestibule had porticoes on north, west, and south. The dome had a peristyle of columns, perhaps like those of the pre-Fire design, but apparently two deep.[1]

This model, completed in the spring of 1670, received the King's approval. Throughout 1671 and 1672 demolition of the old Cathedral proceeded, and the materials were disposed of. During those years London's prospects brightened. The City Churches, halls, and houses had begun to rise; and as they rose the scale and character of the First Model may have come to seem unduly modest. Anyway, by September 1673 Wren had prepared a much bolder project, the design known as the *Great Model* (Plates 79A and B), on account of its having been presented in the form of the large and magnificent model still preserved in the Cathedral. This Great Model design is something altogether different from the First Model, which was hardly more than a very large City Church. It is a design for a domed structure on a Greek cross plan, comparable in dignity, unity, and elaboration (though not in size) to Michelangelo's St Peter's.

Like St Peter's, the Great Model plan consists, in principle, of a domed area with four lesser domed areas round it. But, unlike St Peter's, the great dome is supported not on four but on eight equal piers. Moreover, the plan seems to derive equally from St Peter's and from a thesis design for a church in the collection of plans drawn by John Webb for Inigo Jones. It is scarcely possible to believe that Wren did not know this plan, and, as we know that he did at some period have access to Jones's drawings, there is no need to doubt that this study by the earlier master was his inspiration. The main originality in Wren's plan is the joining of the arms of the cross by four segmental curves – a proceeding neither strictly logical (since it curtails the full development of some of the sub-piers) nor likely to be harmonious in perspective.

The elevations of the design, with a giant order and high attic, are equally indebted to Jones, except for the dome, for the character of which Wren evidently turned to Serlio again and the engraving he gives of Bramante's design for the dome of St Peter's. This design Wren inflated to give something approaching the Michelangelesque silhouette.

The Great Model Design was an intellectual excursion with the whole emphasis on the aesthetic and statical problems of a vast domed monument. It was, to be sure, presented as a church and to strengthen the axis of orientation Wren added, as an afterthought, a domed vestibule at the west end. But in the light of Anglican tradition the Great Model was not a church at all. Neither the prayer-book nor popular opinion had ever discarded the old conception of a church as a *directional* building, consisting of a nave proceeding to a choir; and it was hardly likely that a cathedral which totally and arbitrarily rejected this conception would find favour except among some of the lay intelligentsia. The chapter and clergy could not accept it, and although the Great Model had the authority of the Royal Commission issued under Privy Seal in November 1673, the design must have been abandoned almost at once. It was a disappointment to Wren. It meant that he had to go back very nearly to the beginning and pursue yet again the problem of placing a dome over the crossing of what was, in essence, a Gothic aisled cathedral. From 1674 he had to go back to 1666.

The result of this reconsideration was the third design for the new St Paul's – the *Warrant Design* (Plates 80A and B), so called because it is specifically related to the Royal Warrant of April 1675, the document which, following upon the second Rebuilding Act with its provision for adequate finance, directed an immediate start on the building of a new cathedral.

Historians have not always been disposed to take the Warrant Design very seriously, yet there is no question that it represents a sincere attempt to formalize the Gothic cathedral shape and render it into what Wren, on an earlier occasion, called 'true Latin'. Admittedly, the elevations merely repeat and continue, in revised form, Inigo Jones's design for recasing the old structure, while the cupola, rising into a spire, is immature. But the great thing is the plan, and this is very close indeed to the executed structure.

In 1675, the date of the Warrant Design, Wren had already begun St Stephen Walbrook, where, as we have seen, he attempted to combine a domed central space with nave and choir, aisles and transepts. At St Paul's he faced this problem again, with all the added difficulties involved in a masonry structure. The solution he produced was clear-cut. As at St Stephen's, the dome was to rest on eight equal arches – four on the main axes, four on the diagonals. These arches sprang, not from the slender columns of St Stephen's, but from immense masonry piers capable of supporting the weight of the superincumbent dome. The piers, however, were strictly aligned with the nave and transept arcades, thus leaving the aisle vistas perfectly clear from east to west and from north to south. As for the spaces behind the upper parts of the diagonal arches (where, at St Stephen's, we noticed the uncomfortable groined triangle), Wren filled them with semi-domes, so that each diagonal arch was, in effect, the face of a gigantic niche.

Over the central space in the Warrant Design, a dome springs from the level of the crowns of the arches and rises to a great circular opening, above which is the cupola. The cupola concludes the internal space, but supports, for external effect, an additional timber dome surmounted by a spire.

Between the Warrant Design and the design executed the changes are very remarkable indeed and require careful analysis (Plates 80 and 81). The ground-plan was not altered in principle, but modified in several important respects. In the first place, the nave was revised to consist of three bays balancing exactly those of the choir, with an additional compound bay at the west forming a token vestibule and opening into two lateral chapels. This gave the plan a more nearly classical unity by making it consist of a cross symmetrical on both axes, but approached by a western addition and terminating in an apse. It was an approximation, in fact, to the Greek-cross-*plus*-vestibule plan of the Great Model.

Rendering his plan thus more compact and articulate, Wren had in mind a most original and adventurous revision of the superstructure. This amounted to building up the aisle walls the full height of the church *as screens* and introducing behind them flying buttresses on the Gothic principle, to take the thrust of the nave vaults. This scheme had enormous advantages, both aesthetic and structural. Aesthetically, it offered the possibility of a cathedral of massive external uniformity capable of full classical treatment. Structurally, it had these three salient merits: (*a*) Flying buttresses of purely utilitarian form could be used (unseen, behind the screen walls); (*b*) the screen walls added sufficient weight to the walls below them to provide adequate abutment for the flying buttresses; and (*c*) the aisle walls, together with the screen walls, being in line with the main arches carrying the dome, made excellent counterforts for the latter. So far, so good. But there were repercussions. If the aisle walls were going to carry the screen walls and, at the same time, receive the flying buttresses, they would have to be thickened. The aisles, anyway, for the sake of the flying buttresses, would have to be narrowed. The nave piers could be reduced (the flying buttresses having relieved them of much of their responsibility for the vault thrusts), but anything saved here could only be given to the nave. In short, if the total width was to be maintained, the ratios of the Warrant plan were going to be upset. We cannot reconstruct Wren's own analysis of the situation, but the upshot was that he gave an extra two foot to the nave and took one foot off each of the aisles, at the same time narrowing the piers and thickening the aisle walls. In doing this, he deliberately wrecked the elementary logic of the Warrant Design. Not only did arbitrary dimensions take the place of multiples of ten foot for the main heights and breadths but, in respect of the entry of the aisles into the central space, he torpedoed the whole basic idea. In the Warrant Design, the dimensions of nave, piers, and aisles are such that the openings they produce in the central space are *all equal*. As a result of the revisions this was no longer the case. The nave, choir, and transept openings became larger and the four (diagonal) aisle openings became smaller. The original notion of a dome carried on eight equal arches would seem to have gone for good.

How Wren worked his way out of this dilemma is interesting. He had already, perhaps, abolished the tall plinth under the main order of the Warrant Design, bringing the base of the order almost to floor level. Such a revision was, no doubt, aesthetic, for it brought the design closer to its avowed prototype, the *Templum Pacis*. To restore the height of the vault he had inserted a blind attic storey over the entablature. This new arrangement facilitated the solution he finally adopted for the problem of the central space. The four major openings presented no difficulty. The narrower diagonal openings Wren now arched over, with segmental arches, at entablature level, allowing these arches to ride up into the attic storey (as do the arches in the Baths of Diocletian). This had the useful effect of binding the eight dome piers into four sturdy couples. Then, above the attic storey he formed four tribunes or galleries. Above these, each opening was again closed by a segmental arch. With these latter arches, however, Wren played a most ingenious trick. Making the segments exactly comparable with the middle segments of the adjacent (semi-circular) arches, he continued the arch-line as an architrave moulding in relief right across each pier, bringing it down to meet exactly the springing of the architraves adjoining (Plate 87A). Thus, although in actuality the dome rises from four semi-circular arches and four (narrower) segmental arches, the illusion is given of a perfectly regular ring of eight semi-circular arches.

It must be admitted that the 'mechanics' of the illusion are evident; the effect is strained. Why, one wonders, did Wren create these prodigious problems for himself? Could not a more direct solution really have been achieved? Or did Wren, the philosopher, so much relish the challenge of an 'impossible' architectural situation as to seek one in spite of himself. Remembering the Sheldonian and remembering how much else at St Paul's represents a battle of wits between constructor and technician, the possibility is not unreal.

Now, as to the exterior treatment of the aisle walls and their superincumbent screens. If Wren ever considered a giant order or an order with pedestal (such as he had used in the Great Model), the idea was soon abandoned. The earliest drawings show two superimposed orders and there can be no doubt that just as the Warrant Design leans on Inigo Jones's remodelling of the old Cathedral, so the executed design leans on the very masterpiece of Jones – the Whitehall Banqueting House. The extent to which that building (by far the most important classical building then existing in England) influenced the final elevations of St Paul's nave and choir is not always fully appreciated. But the fact surely is that they derive from it in several fundamental respects. From Whitehall comes the idea of a two-storey design rising from a high basement. From Whitehall, again, come the pilasters placed against a rusticated wall-face; and from Whitehall the coupling of those pilasters and the enrichment of the orders by an additional frieze on the line of the capitals. It is true that Wren might have found all these things in the place where Jones had found them before him – Palladio's *Quattro libri*. But the St Paul's elevations do not recall Palladio nearly as much as they recall Jones's great Palladian essay. Wren borrowed not merely the Palladian elements but the Palladio-Jones amalgam. Having absorbed the Jones idea, Wren immediately proceeded to expand and elaborate. The St Paul's elevations are much higher than the Banqueting House:[2] the bay unit is much broader. So, where Jones made single pilasters the divisions of his bays, Wren made them coupled pilasters. Where Jones 'stopped' the ends of his design with a pair of coupled pilasters, Wren 'stopped' his with two pairs of coupled pilasters with niches between. The window openings and their equivalents, too, had to be elaborated in order to keep pace with the new scale; hence the aedicules which surround the niches in the upper storey. The entire conception of the St Paul's elevations is, in fact, a 'working up' of the Banqueting House to a new plane of monumentality.

So much for the problems connected with the structure as a whole. The detailing throughout is rich and brilliant and the transept elevations (Plate 85), which seem to echo Mansart's sketches for the Louvre, are among Wren's most splendid successes; their curved porches (one of the rare incursions of Roman Baroque[3]) establish a wonderful harmony between the great square masses of the church itself and the sweep of the dome above.

The Dome

It is to the dome that we must now give our undivided attention. This gigantic feature of the design passed through a number of phases and was probably not finally settled till the Commission gave the word for it to proceed in 1697. An examination of the several different designs preserved suggests that Wren was constantly vacillating between two distinct types of dome. One of these was the Bramante type with its uninterrupted peristyle. The other was the Michelangelo type, in which columns occur in couples to form a series of buttress-like projections. In the pre-Fire design Wren had taken Bramante for his guide and was no less loyal to him in the Great Model. In the Warrant Design, however, the twin-column buttresses appear for the first time and many variations on this theme follow. In due course, however, the two western towers came under consideration and here (in the early designs) Bramante reappears, as the author not, indeed, of the design for St Peter's but of that for the Tempietto at S. Pietro in Montorio. There, again, we have the uninterrupted peristyle and the circular *cella* rising into a dome – the germ of the final design for the central feature of St Paul's. But Bramante did not triumph absolutely. For the final stroke in the composition was the introduction of the Michelangelesque buttress-theme into the Bramantesque peristyle, a deft conciliation effected by the simple expedient of filling every fourth intercolumniation with solid wall.

The free columns become, in effect, columns *in antis* between solid piers, and the effect is to introduce in the quick rhythm of the peristyle a series of slow beats which give the whole a monumental stability and a relationship to the static mass of the Cathedral below (Plate 82).

If the evolution of the silhouette was gradual, so was the evolution of the section, with the obligations to internal effect which it implied. Wren had always been aware that a single dome, rising prominently over the Cathedral, could not be effective internally, and that a secondary, internal dome was necessary. Bramante had been content with a low dome of the Panthéon type, but Michelangelo had pitched his dome high and given it a double skin. Mansart in his church of the Val-de-Grâce (begun 1645) had gone further and designed two completely separate domes, an inner dome of masonry and an outer dome of timber and lead; while the same architect in his design for a Bourbon Mausoleum (1665, the year of Wren's visit) had shown an inner dome ascending to a circular opening through which light came from invisible windows in an outer dome. This latter scheme really amounts to constructing a 'Panthéon' dome, with its open *oculus*, and then raising a second dome over it; and Wren was clearly thinking on these lines at the Great Model stage. The Warrant Design departs momentarily in a new direction altogether, but Wren soon returned to the old form of the problem and, for some time, was intent on the idea of two masonry domes – an inner dome to ceil the church and an outer dome to support the lantern, and provide for external effect (Plate 84A). The great weight of the lantern tended to control the shape of the outer dome and at one stage we find Wren giving this outer dome a 'cladding' of timber and lead to produce the required silhouette (Plate 84B). From that idea, verging on a triple series of domes, it was a simple step to the final solution – an inner masonry dome with an *oculus*; an intermediate cone, likewise of masonry and designed solely to support the lantern; and an outer 'cladding' of wood and lead strutted out to give the ideal silhouette for external effect. In that structural-aesthetic combination Wren found the complete solution of his problem and produced a dome of vertiginous interior grandeur and one whose external effect has never, in the opinion of Englishmen (and even of some foreigners), been equalled (Plate 86).

Completion of the Cathedral

In 1698 the Cathedral was finished except for the dome, the west front, and the western towers. In 1700 the drum was well in hand and, at the west end, the bases of the towers had been reached. About this time or a little later certain changes were proposed and partially adopted. Drawings suddenly occur for a western portico with a giant Ionic order instead of the two-storey portico which is the more obvious solution. This proposal, a momentary reversion to the character of the Great Model, was abandoned.[4] Some years later, the Bramantesque design for the west towers was discarded in favour of the more Baroque towers with which we are familiar. These are very materially indebted to Borromini's west towers at S. Agnese, Rome.

During much of the latter part of the Cathedral's construction, Wren was working against considerable difficulties, material and psychological. In 1697 the House of

Commons suspended one-half of his salary as an inducement to hasten the work. The arrears were not paid for fourteen years. Then, just as the Cathedral was structurally complete, in 1709, two minor issues which should have been decided solely by Wren were taken out of his hands. One of these was the painting of the dome by Sir James Thornhill, a project of which Wren disapproved. The other was the perfectly trivial matter of a fence round the Cathedral enclosure. The contract for this was given to a deplorable person named Jones. Wren, knowing or suspecting a job, objected but was over-ruled, and after a meeting at which £1000 was ordered to be paid to Jones on account, Wren never attended again during the Commission's existence. He did attend the new Commission of 1715, but only to be snubbed by the appointment of Thornhill. Finally, in 1717, the Commission offered yet another grotesque insult to their aged Surveyor by deciding, in face of his reasoned opposition, to place a balustrade all round the parapets of the building. This extraordinary treatment of Wren by a younger generation[5] with very decided ideas of its own about architecture and no particular liking for the days and characters of Charles II's reign culminated in the dismissal of the architect from the post of Surveyor-General in 1718. The dignified and beautiful letter in which he accepted his dismissal is well known.

The Craftsmen of St Paul's

We cannot leave St Paul's without considering for a moment the craftsmen whose work, under Wren, it is, and who, in this great work, made something resembling a national school of building and decoration – a school of incalculable advantage to the next generation of English builders. Masons, carvers, carpenters, joiners, plasterers, iron-workers, plumbers, and glaziers – all carefully selected for their special competence – here put forth their best endeavours, setting a standard as high as, or perhaps higher than, had existed among the small circle of fine craftsmen working for Inigo Jones.

Masons were, of course, the principal people employed; and in the initial stages of the work, Joshua Marshall (1629–78), son of Edward Marshall (p. 99), seems to have been the foremost. Wren, in the early days, must have leaned much on his experience. Besides working at St Paul's for a few years up to his premature death, he built the Monument and half a dozen City churches.

But the chief names among the fourteen mason-contractors employed during the Cathedral's erection are those of Thomas Strong (d. 1681) and his brother Edward Strong (c. 1652–1723) who, between them, saw both the beginning and the finishing of the work. They came of a family of quarry-owners at Taynton, Oxon., the lifting of restrictions against 'foreigners' after the Fire no doubt drawing them to London. Edward, who spent nearly his whole career on St Paul's, Greenwich, and Blenheim Palace, was the greatest of all the mason-contractors connected with the Cathedral. In 1694 he had as many as sixty-five masons working under him. He became rich and, dying at St Albans, lies under a magnificent marble monument in St Peter's Church.

Christopher Kempster (1626 or 27–1715) was another 'foreigner' attracted to London after the Fire. He came from Burford, Oxon., and built, besides several City churches and a substantial part of the dome of St Paul's, the fine Town House at Abingdon (*c.* 1677), a building so clearly inspired by the wings of Le Vau's Collège des Quatre Nations at Paris that Wren must surely have been concerned in the design. Edward Pearce (*c.* 1630–1695) was a man of a rather different type in that he was the son of a painter-stainer and a good portrait sculptor, and we owe to him not only parts of the south side of the Cathedral, but the bust of its architect.[6]

The border-line between the finest masons and the men who were more strictly carvers and sculptors was never hard and fast, but men of the second category were often accustomed to work both in stone and wood. At St Paul's the principal carver in both materials was Grinling Gibbons (1648–1720). Easily the most famous of the craftsmen associated with Wren, Gibbons was born in Amsterdam, probably of English parents, and came to England as a youth. When John Evelyn discovered him in 1670 he had already developed that astonishing facility for naturalistic carving in soft woods which accounts for the universal and continued popularity of his creations. His aim, quite evidently, was to emulate the effects of the Dutch flower-painters in his own medium, and he succeeded to a miracle. Moreover, his works, illusionist though they sometimes are, have style; and as a figure-sculptor in stone and bronze as well as wood he was a considerable artist.

Gibbons was taken up by Hugh May (p. 117) before Wren had occasion to use him and made his reputation with interior decorations at Windsor Castle and Cassiobury before he began to provide ornaments for St Paul's. These include some stone-carving – notably the festoons under the lower windows (exterior) and the heraldic panel in the north pediment (1698). But the carved ornaments of the stalls, organ-case, and Bishop's throne (1696–8) are his finest work (Plate 87B). These fittings were, of course, designed in Wren's office and, moreover, executed by the Cathedral joiners, only the richest and most intricate work being left for Gibbons. Their complete plastic unity and elegance of movement are remarkable. The French (and not particularly Wren-like) style of their design exactly suits Gibbons's feeling, nor does the intervening presence of the joiners interfere with the unity of the whole. The surviving drawings, which go only part of the way to the final results, suggest that there must have been close collaboration between all concerned.

Another carver (only in stone) was Caius Gabriel Cibber (1630–1780), a Dane who had studied in Italy and Holland. He is represented at St Paul's by, among other things, the carved keystones of the dome arches. He was Sculptor in Ordinary to the King and designed the domed Danish church in Wellclose Square (1694; destroyed). After his death, Francis Bird (1667–1731) became the Cathedral's principal sculptor. He had studied in Brussels and Rome and worked both for Gibbons and Cibber. It fell to him to execute the relief of the Conversion of St Paul in the west pediment, as well as the figures standing at various points on the Cathedral sky-line and the statue of Queen Anne, with its supporting figures, in the churchyard. Bird's work has always been condemned as inadequate to the occasion and it is, indeed, superficial and lacking in any original feeling for design.

Next to the masons, carvers, and sculptors, the carpenters were the chief participants in the work, but their tasks being of a more mechanical kind scarcely concern us, and it must suffice to mention the name of John Longland, who was Master Carpenter for thirty-one years from 1675. The joiners, of whom the principal was Sir Charles Hopson (he was also Purveyor to the Office of Works and made a large fortune), were responsible for model-making and, as we have seen, for the structural part and repetitive ornaments of the stall-work. The plasterers' contribution to the Cathedral was not very conspicuous, but the names of John Grove and Henry Doogood are worth mentioning for the big part they played in so many City churches and in many of the royal Works.

Finally, there was Jean Tijou, the French ornamental iron-worker, who supplied most of the screens and grilles in the choir (many of his panels are now made up into a single grille in the north choir aisle), and the rich flourish of iron-work at the foot of the circular staircase in the south-west tower.

The organization of the crafts for St Paul's Cathedral naturally overlaps the organization of the Office of Works to some extent. Many of the Cathedral craftsmen held offices by Letters Patent under the Crown, and their work is to be met with at Hampton Court, Greenwich, and elsewhere. St Paul's, nevertheless, provides a particularly striking cross-section of the English crafts at the period and demonstrates those standards of workmanship which, once attained, remained the pride of English building for a century.

NOTES TO CHAPTER 14

1. Sir Roger Pratt had nothing to say for this model, of which he had a 'shorte and confused vewe of an hour onely' in 1673. 'The two side aisles are wholly excluded from the Nave of the Church and turned into uselesse Porticos without, instead of adding a spacious gracefullnesse … within'. He disliked the placing of the dome at the west end instead of over the crossing, 'which hath most … ungracefully shortened it', and the placing of three identical porticoes round the vestibule, where only one was needed. As for the elevations, 'how ungracefully and weakly do the Lucarnes stand … over the Portico of the East end … what ornament of the windows to the Porticos etc.' In the dome, 'the Pillars stood two thick and consequently the windows between too crowded'.

2. From base of lower order to cornice of upper order: Banqueting House, fifty-eight feet; St Paul's, ninety-two feet.

3. Compare the façade of S. Maria della Pace (Pietro da Cortona, 1655–67).

4. It is interesting that this giant order proposal should be close in date to the *c.* 1699 designs for a new Whitehall Palace (see Chapter 17, p. 167) where, as we shall see, a proposal of similar dramatic abruptness was made in connexion with the Banqueting House.

5. The generation which, as we shall see, brought in Palladianism. Their balustrade was, no doubt, inspired by their Jonesian loyalties.

6. Mr Colvin has discovered that Pearce designed the Bishop's Palace at Lichfield in 1686–7 and that drawings for monuments given in *Wren Soc.*, XVII, Pls. 22–26 and 28, are by him.

CHAPTER 15

THE ROYAL WORKS
1660–1702

THE first royal building projects after the Restoration were, as we have seen, the New Gallery at Somerset House and the first block of the new quadrangle at Greenwich. The latter was barely finished when the Great Fire abruptly reduced palace-building to an unthinkable luxury. For nearly a decade no new royal buildings of any account were proceeded with. Hugh May set about remodelling Windsor in 1675, but that involved no great novelty of conception, and it was not until the King's decision to found Chelsea Hospital, in 1681, that royal initiative again opened the way for architecture on a grand scale.

Chelsea Hospital (Plates 88 and 89) was inspired, as an institution, by two somewhat older ones of the same kind, Kilmainham Hospital, Dublin (founded 1680), and the Invalides, Paris (founded 1670). The main promoter was Sir Stephen Fox, who had acquired great wealth as Paymaster-General of the Army. The building was paid for partly out of the Privy Purse and partly out of a fund formed by Fox out of deductions from Army pay. The expense did not, therefore, fall on the Exchequer. The site at Chelsea was chosen by Wren, and in February 1682 the King laid the foundation stone.

The conception of the Hospital was one of monastic austerity. It was so described by Evelyn, and this intention is reflected in the bare simplicity of Wren's plan and his choice of the Doric order as the dominant theme. Initially, the plan consisted only of a quadrangle enclosed by buildings on three sides and open to the river. The centre block contains the hall and chapel, with an octagonal vestibule between them, ceiled by a dome and surmounted by a lantern, raised on a concealed brick cone. The two side-wings contain 'galleries' or wards with cubicles, while at each corner is a square pavilion assigned to official residences and other administrative purposes.

The building is essentially a barracks, with three main floors of equal importance and another, lit by dormers, in the roof. The general composition owes, perhaps, something to Libéral Bruand's plan of the Invalides, especially in regard to the massive corner pavilions. The general handling, however, is Dutch rather than French, while the architectonics are very much Wren's own. He set himself the hard problem of controlling this great barrack building by the use of a giant Doric order. The theme is announced in the noble portico (Plate 89) projecting into the courtyard, with its applied counterpart on the landward façade of the same block (Plate 88B). The cornice of this order travels round the entire building at eaves level. The full order, however, reappears only in the centre pavilions of the wings, which, pilastered and pedimented, are, in effect, flattened porticoes. Here, the introduction of the order makes serious trouble with the fenestration and the pavilions seem too like forced answers to the portico.

Wren's uncertainty of control is still, even at the age of fifty, conspicuous here in Chelsea Hospital. The building has admirable directness and dignity, and the corner pavilions, which follow the pattern set by Inigo Jones for the treatment of a single fenestrated block, are excellent. The barrel-vaulted chapel and the flat-ceiled hall are straightforward if unsubtle, but the high octagonal vestibule between them, with its bent Doric angle-pilasters, is too tower-like for its function and too ill-lit for effect.

Yet Chelsea Hospital is of great importance. The use of a giant order on this scale foreshadows the Baroque of Queen Anne's reign. The Doric pavilions in the wings, though not perfectly harmonious, are provocative and memorable. The cupola proposes a type imitated for a hundred years and more, while the grand simple lines of the composition as a whole we shall find echoed in many of the finest collegiate and hospital buildings of the next century.

The main buildings at Chelsea were in progress from 1682 till the close of King Charles's reign. James II continued the work, adding the four low wings which form lateral courtyards and contribute greatly to the dignity of the whole group. The central lantern was finished in 1689 and the Hospital opened in 1692. In the following year Wren was paid £1000 for his work.

Nearly parallel in time with Chelsea Hospital a building of equal size and greater pomp was proceeding at Winchester. Charles II had decided to build a palace there, on the site of the old castle, ostensibly because of the climatic and sporting amenities but perhaps also with one eye on the easy opportunities afforded, via Portsmouth, of liaisons with France. Wren produced a design and the foundation stone of Winchester Palace was laid in March 1683. Building proceeded rapidly until Charles II's death in 1685 when, although nearly complete, it was stopped, never to be resumed. It became a barracks in the eighteenth century and was burnt down in 1896.

We have such poor records of Winchester Palace that no fair estimate of the building can be made. The plan (Figure 21) resembled Chelsea in that it consisted of buildings enclosing a court with one side open. But the court receded in three stages, narrowing to the centre occupied by the main portico – an idea almost certainly derived from Versailles as remodelled by Le Vau and seen by Wren in 1665. In the preliminary elevation (Plate 90A) the portico is insignificant, being applied to the first floor only. In execution it extended the full height of the building and was answered by similar columns on the two pavilions formed at the salient angles of the inner (narrower) court. These pavilions marked the positions of the two chapels – the King's Church of England chapel and the Catholic chapel of Catherine of Braganza. Though richer than Chelsea, the palace was somewhat barrack-like, with three closely fenestrated storeys in brickwork with stone dressings, balustrades, and quoins. Octagonal cupolas were to rise over the central portico and from the two chapel pavilions.

So far as one can judge, the loss of Winchester Palace neither adds to nor detracts from one's estimate of Wren's powers in his middle period. The plan is without very much grace of proportion or disposition, and it is difficult to imagine that the superstructure would have composed successfully. Winchester Palace is, however, an interesting link between Chelsea, on the one hand, and the later work at Hampton Court and Greenwich

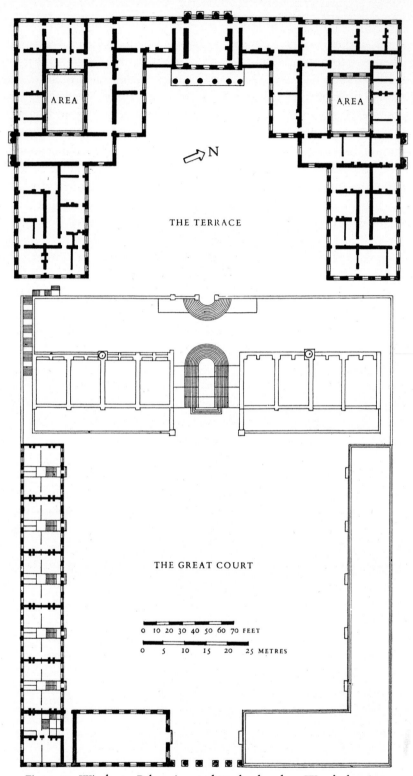

Figure 21. Winchester Palace: incomplete plan based on Wren's drawings

148

on the other. The elevations, for instance, show us the readjustment of the Chelsea fenestration to façades enclosing *un*equal storeys with a *piano nobile* at first-floor level – the main theme of Hampton Court – while the chapel pavilions are prophetic of an important feature in the first Greenwich plan which, though not executed, was to be of considerable use to Vanbrugh at a somewhat later date.

Winchester was incomplete at Charles II's death in 1685. His successor displayed no interest in it but turned his attention immediately to Whitehall Palace, where Wren rebuilt for him a considerable section, starting near the Holbein Gate and going nearly to the river. This long block of buildings faced the Privy Garden, and there was a chapel projecting into the garden near the gate. Behind it, close to the Banqueting House, more buildings enclosed a small court and one of them contained a Council Chamber. All this work was destroyed in the great Whitehall fire of 1698, but we can envisage something of it thanks to a half-finished pencil-drawing, probably by Knyff. The buildings were of brick, in three storeys with windows in the roof – again, rather like Chelsea. The chapel came forward into the garden and had a pediment, its externally undemonstrative character recalling Inigo Jones's similar work at St James's. The Council Chamber stood on open stone arches, had tall first-floor windows and square second-floor windows. The buildings cost the very large sum of £35,000 and were lavishly fitted up, the chapel in particular having a Romish sanctuary of the most sumptuous kind, with carvings by Grinling Gibbons and Arnold Quellin.

These buildings were built with great speed and were followed by another facing the river and containing 'the Queen's new Apartment'. Of this, built in 1687–8 and also shown in the Knyff view, we have Wren's own original sketch. Here, he tried the characteristically French experiment of grouping two windows together (with a niche between them) under a pediment to form the central feature of the two main façades.

Barely was this last building complete than Prince William of Orange landed in England; James made his escape, and Wren found himself Surveyor-General to the third of the five sovereigns whom he was to serve in that office. William was no great patron of the arts, but his Queen had some taste and enthusiasm, and it was she, rather than the King, who forwarded the rebuilding of a great part of Hampton Court Palace. The adoption of Wolsey's long-neglected house as a principal residence must have been one of the earliest decisions of the new reign, for provisional alterations were taking place three months after the Parliamentary settlement of January 1689, while in June foundations were being dug for the new works. They proceeded with little interruption from that date until Queen Mary's death in 1694, when everything was stopped. It was not until after the burning of Whitehall Palace in 1698 that work at Hampton Court was resumed and the Wren apartments were completed.

Wren's work at Hampton Court, as it exists to-day, is only a portion of a comprehensive scheme involving the demolition of the whole of the Tudor palace, except the Great Hall. This scheme, which must have been worked out provisionally in 1689, is recorded in a few sketch plans and elevations in Wren's own hand. These do not correspond with the executed work but approximate to it in a general way, so that we can follow the growth of Wren's ideas and speculate on their sources.

The only part of this sketch-design for Hampton Court fully worked out on paper is a great square of building round a courtyard, but the general block-plan was among the Wren drawings recovered in 1951 (Figure 22). The accommodation balances in the typical seventeenth-century manner, the 'King's Side' on the south, the 'Queen's Side' on the

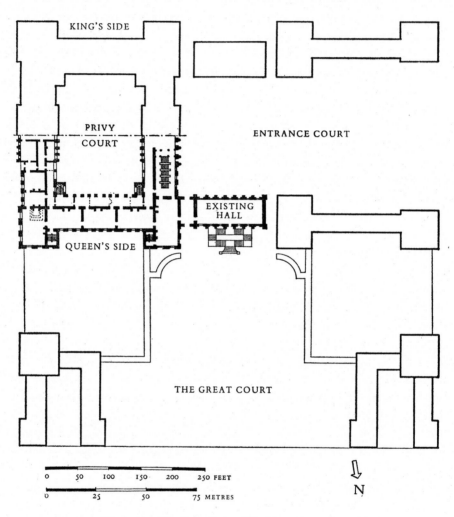

Figure 22. Hampton Court: Wren's project of 1689

north, each with its gallery, presence chambers, drawing-rooms and so forth, the exactitude of the symmetry in this case symbolizing the equal dignity of the two crowned heads. On the east-west axis of this square and to the west is an Entrance Court with blocks on either side of it, while on the north-south axis and to the north (on the axis, that is, of Bushey Avenue) is a Great Courtyard, flanked by barracks and offices.

In making this plan Wren was probably thinking (as he must often have done) of the

Louvre as he had seen it during his Paris visit of 1665. In scale and proportion, however, the first Hampton Court plan worked out very differently, the pavilions becoming broad masses instead of high ones, entirely overmastering the intervening sections. As in the plan so in the elevations (Plate 90B), Wren drew on his Paris memories. The design for the grand entrance front has an attached portico and attic which is an expanded version of the south front of Versailles as completed by Le Vau in 1664. From Le Vau, again, he borrowed shaped mural panels similar to those which that architect introduced between the Versailles windows. And he crowned the 'grand' front with a bell-like dome, a French *lambrequin* surrounding its sloping base. The composition of the main blocks, in this design, is complicated and restless: the fenestration changes constantly in proportion and rhythm, and the silhouette is always on the go. In this, the design is singularly unlike Chelsea; it is wholly free of the placid spirit of Dutch Palladianism and, on the other hand, very close to Mansart and Le Vau.

But Wren was not destined to build Hampton Court in such a manner. Perhaps William and Mary, or one of them, disliked it. Anyway, he proceeded to work his way to something very much more like the new Versailles of Jules Hardouin Mansart. In this process, almost the only part of the first design to be salvaged was the scheme of fenestration belonging to the pavilions. This scheme, consisting of ground-floor, *piano nobile*, and attic storey, furnished the basic unit of the executed design.

In the final drawings, the mobile silhouette, the changeful fenestration, and the decorative intricacies have all disappeared, and the corner pavilions cease to have much importance; indeed, on the Park front they are not expressed at all. The sky-line is dead level throughout and from an excess of variation Wren has passed over to something bordering nearly on monotony. In the uncompromising rectangle of the Park front, the centre pavilion of the first scheme is still traceable, though only as a decorative frontispiece through which the now continuous attic and the *piano nobile* remorselessly march.

Wren's Hampton Court as we know it to-day (Plate 91) is, of course, a fragment, consisting only of the Park façade and the Privy Garden façade and the Fountain Court lying within the angle of the two. The Park façade is an overbearing mass, the uniformity of the attic storey emphasized all too effectively by the range of *œils-de-bœuf* interposed between it and the *piano nobile*. The Privy Garden front, with its strong and simple vertical divisions, is better. The Fountain Court is a rather apologetic substitute for the Privy Court originally proposed, and the crowded fenestration gives an uncomfortably restricted sensation.

In spite of much lovely craftsmanship[1] in brick, stone, and iron and some beautiful passages of detail design, Hampton Court is not a very great success. It must have been designed in a hurry, and if the story is true that Wren was prevented from executing his favourite design, one may guess the reasons for the transformation and its relative failure. It looks as if, for some reason, Wren had to switch suddenly from a design full of lively intricacy and the interplay of varied elements, to a design of stolid, prosaic massiveness. He had not time to visualize the problem again from the beginning, and in the too-hasty transition the vitality of the first design disappeared into the heavy necessity of the second.

A few months before Queen Mary's death, when the work at Hampton Court was stopped, she had become the foundress of a building project as great in extent but to serve a very different purpose. This was the Royal Naval Hospital at Greenwich, for which she and King William granted the site of Greenwich Palace, with the forsaken beginnings of Webb's new court, in October 1694. It was to be the naval counterpart of Chelsea, and it seems to have been due to Queen Mary's 'fixt intention for Magnificence' that it should outstrip Chelsea in architectural splendour and, indeed, be conceived in a spirit as royal as the site.

A Commission was set up in 1695, Wren as Surveyor-General being a member of it and its honorary architect. In the next year a start was made on the first new building – a modest block lying alongside the Charles II building on its west side (i.e. the side away from the proposed great courtyard of the Palace). This new building, containing living accommodation for pensioners, committed the Commission to no over-all lay-out. But at the same time Wren prepared a scheme for the whole site. This involved the duplication of the Charles II block on the other side of a courtyard, just as Webb intended; but instead of closing the courtyard along the south (as in Webb's plan), Wren made it proceed into another, narrower, courtyard, rather on the lines of Winchester Palace. Even this courtyard was not abruptly terminated but led into a space closed, left and right, by quadrant colonnades meeting, in the centre, the porticoed vestibule of a long building lying at the back, right across the whole site. This building, seen over the curved colonnades and culminating in a central drum and dome, was to contain the hall and chapel (Plates 92A and B).

This plan was one of Wren's most important creations. The succession of courtyards receding and narrowing away from the river front comes from his Winchester scheme and, ultimately, from Versailles. The quadrant colonnades, leading to a portico surmounted by a dome, are perhaps a combination of Palladian and French inspiration. Le Vau's Collège des Quatre Nations (another riverside building) has portico and dome in similar relationship, while curved pilastered walls link the portico with the forward-standing wings.

But Wren's borrowings are never literal, and the composition as a whole is a remarkable invention. That this design was never executed is of little consequence, for, on the one hand, it contains the terms of the ultimate Greenwich scheme, while on the other it was to provide Vanbrugh (perhaps through Hawksmore's collaboration) with the basic idea both for Blenheim and for Castle Howard.

The reason why this scheme was almost immediately abandoned was, no doubt, a reluctance to close the vista, which Webb also would have blocked, on the axis of the Queen's House. This old building of Inigo Jones's (see p. 74) was something of an embarrassment to the Greenwich planners; although too small and too far away ever to close the vista with real emphasis, it was a consequential structure which could hardly be ignored. Wren evaded the problem by producing a second lay-out in which the vista was kept open and in which, for the first time, *two* domed structures appeared, marking the hall and chapel and facing each other across an open space in which the Queen's House was framed.

This second design is, of course, the basis of Greenwich as we know it. The idea of successive narrowing courtyards is retained and the domes come exactly at the points where, in the Winchester Palace plan, Wren had placed the cupolas of the chapels. But the second (narrower) courtyard is altogether transformed, becoming, in effect, an avenue flanked by a succession of pensioners' dormitories placed end-on to it and screened by a continuous Doric colonnade. And at the end of the avenue is nothing – except, in the distance, the Queen's House.

How Greenwich Hospital developed from this design of Wren's to the present buildings is a story which we must leave in mid-air and resume in a later chapter. To the early history of the buildings we can only add that the duplicate of the Charles II block was begun in 1697, and that in the following year Wren designed the Hall (Plate 93), an interior of grandiloquent simplicity with composite pilasters ranged round the walls, interrupted only where, at each end, the arches of the entrance and dais occur, like proscenium openings. The solid architecture flows into carved detail designed by Hawksmore and into the clever artificialities of James Thornhill who, when he had finished painting the whole interior, left it the most splendid thing of its kind in England.

NOTE TO CHAPTER 15

1. Most of Wren's best craftsmen are represented here. The Master Bricklayer was Morris Emmett (see p. 127). Much of the stone-carving, including the œils-de-bœuf and keystones, is by William Emmett, but the sculptor for the great pediment and the heraldic cartouches on the garden front was C. G. Cibber (p. 144). He also executed statues and vases for the gardens, planned by Henry Wise. Grinling Gibbons (p. 144) contributed some carved woodwork to the royal apartments and Jean Tijou the great iron gates to the Park. The great staircase and certain ceilings are by Verrio.

CHAPTER 16

WREN AND HIS CONTEMPORARIES

By far the greater part of Sir Christopher Wren's work was done in his capacity as Surveyor-General or in an *ex-officio* capacity amounting to the same thing. As in the case of Jones, all attributions not vouched for by an association with the Office of Works should be regarded with grave suspicion. The grand exceptions to this rule are certain buildings at the Universities and one of the Inns of Court, and there are a few other instances where Wren is known to have supplied designs on the strength of friendship or by special request. But, generally, his work was confined within the sphere of his office; and in dealing with St Paul's and the City Churches and the undertakings of the King's Works we have covered nearly everything that is important in his work. The exceptions remain, and among them, his works at Oxford and Cambridge take precedence.

Wren's Work at the Universities

We have already seen that it was at Oxford and Cambridge, almost simultaneously, that Wren made his début as an architect, designing the Sheldonian Theatre at Oxford and Pembroke College Chapel, Cambridge, both in 1662–3 (pp. 120–1). The Chapel at Emmanuel College, Cambridge, with two flanking blocks of chambers, followed in 1666–73. As at Pembroke the end elevation of the Chapel is Serlian, with a giant order in three bays, but here the centre bay is distinguished by a break, the inner pair of columns being made to support a substantial square pedestal surmounted by a cupola[1] – a thoughtful revision of the purely incidental treatment of the cupola at Pembroke.

In 1674, Wren made a design for a Senate House for Cambridge, a project similar in purpose to the Sheldonian and consisting of a great Corinthian hall with barrel-vault and clerestory lighting through lunettes; and a lower library adjoining, the whole carried on a ground storey partly consisting of open arcades. Themes from Serlio and Palladio are combined here, but the composition is markedly pragmatic, and closely fitted to a rather unusual programme.

This Senate House was not built, but Wren's employment led directly to one of his greatest works, the Library of Trinity College (Plate 94A), initiated by Dr Isaac Barrow, the energetic Master of the College. Wren first tried out a circular design, related to that Inigo Jones thesis design which will then (1675) have been much in his head, if we are right in supposing that it affected the Model design for St Paul's. But he discarded this in favour of a long rectangle. The final design (executed 1676–84) is, in fact, a development of the library portion of the Senate House design, a design in which the treatment of the façade to Nevile's Court is also foreshadowed. The superimposed Doric and Ionic colonnades also remind one forcibly of the First Model for St Paul's, and here is another case of Wren using a discarded portion of the Cathedral designs for another purpose. The provenance of the theme, however, in both cases is, no doubt, the Theatre of Marcellus as given by Serlio.

Towards Nevile's Court the Library displays eleven bays of this Roman design with no relieving breaks or features whatever except four statues over the four centre columns. Wren avowed, in a letter to Barrow, that he would consider any further elaboration 'impertinent, the entrances being endwise and the roof not suiting it'. The result is one of complete, magnanimous serenity. A fixed condition of the programme was the level of the Library floor, dictated by adjoining buildings, and this induced Wren to carry the floor at impost level of the lower arches, making the tympana solid and enriched by cartouches. He justified this device to Barrow by telling him that he had seen it success-fully employed abroad.[2] Towards the river the design was modified by the omission of the orders, the framing of the upper windows in shallow recesses, and the introduction of two great portals based on an engraving in Barbaro's Vitruvius; while the interior is sur-rounded by book-cases up to cill level, where a Corinthian order in plaster begins and rises to the beamed ceiling.

These Cambridge designs, culminating in the Trinity Library, belong to the years during which Wren was hammering out the preliminary alternatives for St Paul's – the First Model, the Great Model, and the Warrant Design. Trinity Library, related in one way or another to all of these, is perhaps the first executed design in which he is confident enough to forget the 'machinery' of classical design and to allow a single idea, simply stated, to be the end and aim of the work. It is, of all Wren's buildings, the most direct, the least mannered. Nor does it give a hint of the changes to come, the struggles with the Mansart idiom and the interpretation of Roman baroque. It is the turning-point between 'early' and 'late' Wren, the serene resting-place between the busyness of immaturity and the more ambitious complexity of his later years.

At Oxford, Wren executed no very important work between the completion of the Sheldonian and the building of the upper part of Tom Tower, Christ Church (Plate 95) in 1681–2. Of this, he tells us that he 'resolved it ought to be Gothick to agree with the Founder's [Wolsey's] work. Yet,' he adds, 'I have not continued so busy as he began.' Wren brought the (nearly) square base to an octagon, filling the splayed corners with semi-octagonal features, borrowed from Wolsey's buttresses and crowning the whole with an ogival dome, an enlargement of the same Tudor theme, but on a bigger scale than ever the Tudors thought to use it.

Tom Tower bears almost no relation to the Gothic which had been practised in Oxford continuously during the seventeenth century. That may legitimately be classed as a still surviving style. Wren's Gothic is certainly not in the nature of a survival; but neither is it exactly 'revivalist'. His approach was objective and analytical. He could choose to be Gothic, just as he could choose, on occasion, to be Roman (Trinity Library), Anglo-Dutch (the City Churches), or French (the early Hampton Court design). Here at Christ Church Gothic was obviously appropriate. So he selected a certain number of Gothic elements and then argued them into a whole conformable to his own classical taste. He seized on the Tudor ogee capping as the equivalent of a classical dome, then composed an octagonal lantern supported by semi-domes and surmounted by a full dome of the same character. The result does not and was not intended to evoke the Middle Ages; it has its own peculiar character, as an abstraction effected by the essentially classical mind of its author. It is a dignified work and important also because it established a point of view, in relation to Gothic, which was adopted by Hawksmore and eventually shared by most architects of the first half of the eighteenth century.

Wren's last important work at the Universities was the Library at Queen's College, Oxford, designed probably in 1682 but built only in 1693–6 and possibly modified in erection by Hawksmore. The main lines are wholly typical, the details more distinctly French than in earlier works. We recognize the open loggia, the panels under the windows, the high attic and the steep pediment mounted against it as features which had been favourites of Wren's for twenty years.

Wren's Other Works

Among the large number of buildings attributed to Wren with more or less certainty, we can deal only with a few of the more conspicuous. At the Middle Temple he designed the Cloister (1680; destroyed 1941), introducing his favourite loggia theme in a simple form. The Gateway to Middle Temple Lane (1683) is probably his in detail, but the rather clumsy idea of a huge pilaster-portico is that of one of the benchers, Roger North. Temple Bar (1671; re-erected at Theobalds Park, 1888) is a peculiar invention which may be Wren's in idea though surely not in detail. Greenwich Observatory (1675; Plate 94B), on the other hand, is like nothing so much as a Serlian palace on a reduced scale; it was built for the Ordnance Department, to house the Astronomer Royal and, in Wren's words, 'a little for Pompe'. Drury Lane Theatre (1672), known only through one doubtful drawing, appears to have had an auditorium (not, as in Palladio's famous theatre, a stage scene) designed to afford a perspective effect from one point of view, presumably the royal box.

Of many town- and country-houses assigned to Wren not a single one can be authenticated,[3] and most of them are merely good examples of the Dutch Palladian manner which flourished after the Restoration and owes nothing to Wren's influence. That one of the most obstinate attributions should be Belton House, Lincs., a building quite evidently deriving from Pratt's Clarendon House and thus of a different school altogether from Wren, shows how uncritically his name has been used merely to glorify some outstandingly good building of the period.

Wren's Contemporaries

The personal achievement of Wren so dominates the Restoration period that many writers have been tempted to relate nearly every building of the time to him and to make his influence accountable for every idiosyncrasy of English architecture after 1670. Nothing could be more mistaken. The general character of Restoration architecture owes nothing to Wren, who, indeed, had very little to show before St Paul's and the churches began to rise. It owes far more to his older contemporaries – to Roger Pratt, whose

Clarendon House was imitated, large and small, well and ill, throughout Britain; and to Hugh May, who assisted more than anyone, perhaps, in propagating that style of architecture which may conveniently be called Dutch Palladian. It was this style which set the new English vernacular. By the time the streets of the City were rising again after the Great Fire, it is evident that the plain brick Dutch manner was already accepted. Wren showed himself familiar with its simple virtues when he designed the City Churches: the round-headed and oval brick windows and the carved stone swags planted above or below them are evidence of this. Moreover, the standard post-Fire house, as exemplified in the ubiquitous speculations of Nicholas Barbon (p. 230), has Dutch as well as English antecedents. Barbon had, indeed, spent most of his early manhood in Leyden and Utrecht before coming to London in 1669.

These influences, through Pratt, May, and others, were of the first importance – of greater importance than any influence exercised by Wren's closer contemporaries. Indeed, from the Restoration until the early years of the eighteenth century the number of men who can properly be classed as 'architects' is extremely small. Roger Pratt, in his later years, stands out prominently as a man who may be said to have 'practised' architecture, without having held any office in the Works, and without, on the other hand, pursuing any other of the occupations suitable to a gentleman until, indeed, his inheritance of Ryston claimed him from the profession.

Pratt's concern with architecture was far more intense and methodical (as far as we know) than that of any other person of his class at the time. Thus, John Evelyn (1620–1706), Pratt's friend and exact contemporary, although interested enough in architecture to translate Roland Fréart's *Parallèle de l'architecture antique avec la moderne*, to prepare a plan for London after the Fire, and to direct considerable 'improvements' on his estate at Wotton, was in no sense an architect, but simply a cleverer virtuoso than most, and, indeed, the model of the entire virtuoso class. As a young man he had been acquainted with Arundel, and he brought something of the great connoisseur's breadth of mind into the Restoration epoch.

A humbler virtuoso was Robert Hooke, whom we have already met (p. 126) as one of the Surveyors for the City. Hooke is remembered as a physicist rather than as an architect, but that he designed a number of buildings is established by entries in his personal diary. They include the Royal College of Physicians (1672–6), Bethlem Hospital (1674–6; Plate 96), Montagu House[4] (1674–80), and Aske's Almshouses, Hoxton (1688–93), all large and important works. He made a determined attempt to copy the French, introducing high pavilion roofs and, at Montagu House, a square domed roof. In detail, however, he was content to borrow from the Dutch. Apart from the Monument on Fish Street Hill, which he must have designed under Wren's surveillance, the only surviving building certainly by him is Willen Church, Bucks., built for Dr Busby in 1678–80: a modest country church whose west tower stands stiffly in the embrace of Corinthian pilasters. Hooke was not a sensitive designer, nor did architectural design take an important place in his life, which was occupied with many other subjects, in some of which his thought led to great results.

More significant among Wren's contemporaries were two younger men – William

Talman and William Winde, two very different designers whom it is not easy to place with precision. Both seem to have sprung from moderately well-to-do families and neither graduated from the building trades.

William Talman (1650–1720) is a particularly problematic figure, especially if the date given by Campbell for Thoresby, Notts. (destroyed; Plate 97), is correct. If Talman designed Thoresby in 1671, when he was but twenty-one years old, he was indeed a phenomenal beginner, for its composition was startlingly new. Built for the Marquis of Dorchester, it was a three-storey house with a main front of thirteen windows, and sides of nine windows, the whole surmounted by a balustrade. No classical country-house had as yet bulked so large, nor suppressed the roof in favour of an open balustrade.[5] The main façade, too, was unusual, for the three centre bays were framed by two isolated Corinthian columns, the cornice only being carried across unbroken between them. Clearly, its designer had first-hand experience of the palace façades of Rome or Milan.

Talman's later works were no less individual. They include the south front and other parts (the famous west front is not his) of Chatsworth, Derbyshire (1687–96), for the Earl of Devonshire, the whole of Dyrham,[6] Glos. (1694–8), and Sir John Germain's south front at Drayton, Northants. (1703). Chatsworth and Dyrham are, like Thoresby, great rectangular masses, topped by balustrades, though otherwise the treatment varies in each case.

Talman must be regarded as a designer with an unusual background whose mixed French and Italian Baroque character cannot at present be explained satisfactorily. His early houses made him a great reputation, and in 1689 he succeeded Hugh May as Comptroller of the Works. In this rôle he was intimately concerned with Hampton Court, and it is impossible not to consider whether the final design of that Palace, so different, as we have seen, from Wren's original project, should reflect in its massive silhouette, its close fenestration, and even in some details the style of the Comptroller as already expressed at Thoresby and Chatsworth.

Talman's houses, being among the most lavish of their time, were extremely influential. The centre-piece of Thoresby, with its two Corinthian columns, widely separated to form a mere frame, instead of a portico, was much imitated and the principle it embodied spread far and wide. By the end of the century a favourite treatment for the façade of a large town-house was to frame the whole thing between giant pilasters, surmounted by their individual portions of architrave and frieze, the cornice only continuing across the façade. A notable example is No. 14, Took's Court, London. Sometimes, instead of pilasters, broad strips of rustication framed the house in a similar way.

Talman's Chatsworth was his most important and influential work. The plan, a great block of apartments arranged round a courtyard, is pedestrian and expressionless (due, in part, to special circumstances), but the giant Ionic order of the exterior, the triple key-stones of the windows, the fine enrichments, and the great staircase, introduced to England a new standard of private magnificence.

Talman lost his Comptrollership to Vanbrugh in 1702 and thereafter continued to practise privately. In 1713 he was employed by the Duke of Chandos at Canons, Middle-sex, but dismissed in the following year after demanding an impudent fee. Both here and at Chatsworth there is evidence of his behaviour being arrogant and arbitrary, and he was perhaps the first English architect to cultivate, as a private practitioner, the pose of infallibility associated with Bernini and Mansart. Between him and Wren there was, not surprisingly, a certain hostility.

Talman's contemporary William Winde (d. 1722) is a less enigmatic and, thanks to Mr Colvin, a better documented character. The son of a Royalist émigré, he was born in Holland. Returning to England at the Restoration, he adopted a military career and led a troop at Sedgmoor. At some period (probably in Holland) he attached himself to Balthazar Gerbier, who dedicated a book to him as his pupil in 1663. The veteran Gerbier was employed soon after the Restoration by the Earl of Craven to build his house at Hampstead Marshall, Berks., but, Gerbier dying in 1667, Winde completed it. Nothing exists now but some fine gate piers by Winde. Lord Craven built two other great houses, Ashdown, Berks., and Combe Abbey, Warwickshire (the completed part dated 1684). Combe, which is certainly by Winde, is an imitation of Pratt's Clarendon House. Ashdown is very different – a very tall house with a steep roof and a lantern on the top, and a neatly arranged forecourt, a house of strikingly Dutch character which may perhaps be by Winde.

His other great patron was John Sheffield, Duke of Buckingham, for whom he designed Buckingham House, London (1703–5; Plate 98A), and Cliefden, Bucks., both now wholly reconstructed, the former as Buckingham Palace. These houses were very different again from either Combe Abbey or Ashdown, and Winde cannot be said to have developed an easily recognizable style. They were also very different from each other, having, however, this much in common, that both had principal façades nine windows wide with parapets, and that in each case a quadrant of Ionic columns linked the house with the out-buildings. Cliefden had three units of vertically linked windows in its façade, more French in technique than Dutch. Buckingham House, on the other hand, was distinctly of the Dutch Palladian school – reminiscent, indeed, of the Mauritshuis, without pediment and with a high attic instead of a visible roof.

Buckingham House was Winde's most important work, if only because, like Pratt's Clarendon House and May's Berkeley House, it was metropolitan and conspicuous. For 1703 it was not, however, a particularly novel production, for by then the Vanbrugh-Hawksmore style was imminent and Dutch Palladianism nearing the end of its period.

Of Newcastle House (No. 66 Lincoln's Inn Fields), built by Winde for the Earl of Powis in 1685–9, much the same could be said. It remains, however (though vigorously reconstructed in 1930), a noble example of its kind and of its architect's work. Winde, it will be seen, does not emerge as a designer of very special distinction, still less as an innovator. Broadly, he may be considered as a competent master of the Anglo-Dutch school whose influence, through Buckingham House especially, he helped to propagate.

Apart from such men as Pratt, May, Samwell, Talman, and Winde, 'architects' of the Restoration and after are rare indeed, and, although a long list could probably be made of gentlemen who designed their own country-houses or claimed to have done so, it is to the craftsman class that we must turn to discover the designers of the majority of buildings of the period.

Among the craftsmen of London there were, as there had always been, masons and carpenters of high quality as artists, whether as sculptors or architects. We have met a number of these already in discussing the rebuilding of the City and the building and equipment of St Paul's. The Strongs, Edward Pearce, Christopher Kempster, Caius Gabriel Cibber were all, on occasion, architects. They worked often at a distance from London and, indeed, were often men with a country background. But besides these, there were craftsmen who were great men in their own localities and who helped to bring the new Restoration styles to the larger provincial centres. There is a specially interesting case at Northampton where local talent appears to have been responsible for All Saints Church (1675–80) and the slightly earlier Sessions House (1673–6). Both were built when the rebuilding of London was at its peak. Jerman's Royal Exchange was evidently the source of inspiration for the Sessions House and one of Wren's Greek-cross churches (perhaps St Mary at Hill) for All Saints, though hints were also gathered from Bosboom's book. Another provincial mason was Sir William Wilson (1640–1710), a man who earned a knighthood by marrying above his station. He came directly into contact with Wren, whose design for Sir John Moore's School at Appleby, Leics., he altered. He was by no means an advanced designer, however, and at his Four Oaks Hall, Warwicks. (1680), we find a late recurrence of the 'Holborn' gable. His rebuilding of Warwick Church (1694–1704) was an excursion into Gothic as remarkable for its success as for its independence in style from other seventeenth-century English Gothic.

Finally, among outlying local designers, there is the remarkable case of Henry Bell (1653–1717) of King's Lynn, Norfolk. The son of a Mayor of Lynn, he twice filled that office himself and belonged, evidently, to the mercantile oligarchy of the town. He designed a number of buildings, among them the Custom House (1683; Plate 98B), a neat square stone building with superimposed pilaster orders, a steep roof, and a lantern on a balustraded flat. Built as an Exchange, it derives clearly from London's Royal Exchange. Less obvious in derivation was the destroyed Market Cross, a domed octagon with short 'transepts' and colonnades, built by Bell in 1707–10.[7]

Scotland: Sir William Bruce

With the Restoration of 1660, it becomes for the first time possible to relate the architecture of Scotland closely to that of England.[8] Lacking a resident Court where standards of taste could be cultivated and maintained, interference from London was, sooner or later, inevitable. It came over the rebuilding of Holyrood Palace. John Mylne, the King's Master Mason in Scotland, prepared a scheme for Holyrood in 1663. Dying in 1667, the project passed to his nephew and successor, Robert Mylne (1633–1710), who was engaged on it in 1670. In the following year, the drawings were submitted to Charles II at Whitehall. He suggested some alterations and ordered a new set to be drawn. The submission of the Holyrood drawings to the King seems to have been the act of Sir William Bruce (d. 1710), the Duke of Lauderdale being the intermediary, and it is to Bruce that the final design (of which Mylne laid the foundation stone in 1671) is always attributed. He was a younger son of a Scottish Baron and, in a private capacity, had intrigued energetically for the Restoration. Like John Denham and many others he had a special right to office when the King came in. The Clerkship to the Bills was his immediate and lucrative reward, but in 1671, on the occasion of the Holyrood project, he was also named the King's Surveyor and Master of the Works, an office which seems to have been, since the time of James I and VI, loosely combined with that of the Master Mason.

In this capacity, Bruce was instructed to pull down some Cromwellian work at the Palace and rebuild 'in pillar work conforme to and with the Dorick and Ionic orders'. The result is the present main fabric of the Palace. Following, it seems, the intention of John Mylne, Bruce preserved the early sixteenth-century tower which was the old building's most conspicuous feature (and by no means old-fashioned, by Scottish standards), repeated it on the far side of his new main axis and joined the two towers by a low building with a Doric gateway in the centre, leading into the courtyard. The buildings surrounding this courtyard are decorated not only with Doric and Ionic but also with (at the third storey) Corinthian pilasters, and there is a steep roof with dormers. There is no subtlety in the design, for which Chantilly, Meudon, or even the Louvre may have provided the inspiration. The interiors have wood-work and plaster-work close in character to early Restoration work in England.

Bruce must rank, unquestionably, as the founder of the classical school in Scotland. The group of large houses which he built after 1671 is very competent, and more interesting architecturally than Holyrood. They include his own house at Kinross (1685) and Hopetoun House (1698–1702; rebuilt), both clearly deriving from great English houses of the early Restoration years. Hopetoun in particular was indebted to Clarendon House, but possessed some points of originality, including horizontal rustication throughout in the French manner, and colonnades linking the main block to the out-buildings in convex (instead of the usual concave) quadrants.

After Bruce, Scotland produced no other architect of importance until after the rebellion of 1715, when the building of classical country-houses started in earnest under the influence of Wren and of that English Palladianism of which a Scotsman in London was the principal propagator.

NOTES TO CHAPTER 16

1. The Como (1521) edition of Vitruvius gives an engraving which may be a source for this, and there seems little doubt that Wren used this book considerably in his early period, in spite of its supersession, from a scholarly point of view, by Barbaro's edition.

2. He was thinking, no doubt, of the arcaded ground storey of Le Vau's Collège Mazarin.

3. Tring House, Herts. (for Henry Guy), was the most probable example of a country-house by Wren. It no longer exists but is engraved in Chauncey, *Hist. of Herts.*, 1700, and there is a plan, probably for this

house, at All Souls. See *Wren Soc.*, XIX, 152. The Wren Society is somewhat liberal with attributions unsupported by documentary evidence and includes, among houses, Fawley Court, near Henley (1684–8), and Winslow Hall, Bucks. (1700); while among other buildings there attributed to Wren are Farley Church and Almshouses, Wilts. (1680–90; for Sir Stephen Fox), Morden College, Blackheath, London (1695), Bromley College, Kent (1672), and the New School at Eton College, Bucks. (1688–91).

4. The house was burnt in January 1686 and, according to Campbell, was rebuilt by a French

architect, 'Mons. Pouget'. This can hardly be the architect-sculptor, Pierre Puget of Marseilles, and, in any case, it has been shown by Miss Batten (see Bibliography) that Hooke's work mostly survived the fire and that the French character of the building was unquestionably due to him.

5. Hawksmore, writing to Lord Carlisle in 1731 (*Wal. Soc.*, XIX, 126), said of Thoresby, 'it never was good, and was burnt down as soon as finished. The attick was added at yᵉ refiting yᵉ house after yᵉ fire.' It is, of course, conceivable that before the addition of the attic, the house had a steep-pitched roof.

6. A passage in a letter from Talman to Wren in 1699 (*Wren Soc.*, IV, 60) seems to suggest that Wren had some responsibility for this house. Possibly he deputed the work to Talman.

7. Other buildings by Bell are the Duke's Head (1689), which may be classed as of the Artisan school and has a broken pediment slightly reminiscent of Raynham; and North Runcton Church (1703–13), which in plan and general character is not unlike All Saints, Northampton.

8. For the earlier history of Scottish architecture, see Appendix I.

CHAPTER 17

ENGLISH BAROQUE:
HAWKSMORE, VANBRUGH, ARCHER

WE have seen that, somewhere about 1692, Sir Christopher Wren began to hand over the designing of buildings to the younger men in his office. After that date, drawings in his own hand are almost non-existent. We know that at St Paul's Hawksmore was 'copying' his designs, which probably means that he was setting up the final drawings under Wren's immediate instructions. By 1702 (when Wren was seventy) it is amply clear that all the work for which the Surveyor was responsible was being drawn, and possibly to some extent designed, by others.[1] This handing-over to a new generation – a generation, in 1692, entering its early thirties – had remarkable and, one may think, unexpected results. Instead of the work becoming a weak, platitudinous, or over-ripe imitation of the master's, it gained gradually in strength and changed in character while never becoming wholly detached from its undoubted main source – the personal work of Wren himself.

The story of how a school which may appropriately and with some pride be called the English Baroque school emerged from Wren's work and flowered into such splendid achievements as Blenheim Palace and the London churches of Queen Anne's and George I's reigns is one of the most interesting and also one of the most difficult episodes in English architectural history. Its difficulty arises from the fact that two main creative personalities were involved whose relative contributions are not at all easy to determine. The resulting style, moreover, is original in a highly complex way, its manifold sources being combined and converted with such power of imagination as to make analysis an extremely delicate matter.

The two chief masters of this style, the prevalence of which in the higher reaches of English building practice extends from 1692 till roughly 1725, were Nicholas Hawksmore and John Vanbrugh. It will be convenient to deal briefly with their careers immediately and then to follow the evolution of the style which must be regarded as their joint creation.

Nicholas Hawksmore (1661–1736), born in Nottinghamshire, became clerk to a Yorkshire justice, at whose house he seems to have been discovered by Edward Gouge, a well-known plasterer. He came to London at the age of about eighteen and, perhaps through Gouge or the circle of artist-craftsmen to which he belonged, entered the service of Sir Christopher Wren as his 'domestic clerk'. By the time he was twenty-one, he was already assisting Wren at Chelsea Hospital. In the following year (1683) he was supervising the work at Winchester Palace, and throughout the 1680s was busy on the City Churches. From 1689 onwards he occupied responsible positions at Hampton Court and Kensington, while from 1691, as we have seen, he was Wren's architectural amanuensis at St Paul's. We hear of him, described as 'Sir Christopher Wren's Gentleman', at Christ's Hospital in

1693 and St Andrew's Wardrobe in 1694. In 1698 he received the appointments of Clerk of Works and Surveyor's Clerk at Greenwich. Seven years later he became Deputy Surveyor at Greenwich.

Hawksmore's connexion with Vanbrugh began in 1699 or rather earlier; he helped him with at least four of his great houses, the association lasting till the end of Vanbrugh's life. He was accepting commissions on his own account by 1707, and in 1712 began to build the great series of London churches which will be described in a subsequent chapter. Simultaneously, he was busy with schemes at Cambridge and Oxford, some parts of which materialized, and in 1715 he obtained the Clerkship of Works at the Palaces of Whitehall, St James's, and Westminster. From this post he was removed, by the same piece of jobbery which disposed of Wren in 1718, and was never reinstated, though he became Deputy-Comptroller to Vanbrugh shortly before the latter's death in 1726. He became Chief Surveyor to Westminster Abbey in 1723, and died, after ten years' martyrdom to gout, in 1736.

It is a worthy but rather colourless record. During a career of nearly sixty active years, during which he was concerned with almost every great building of the time, he attained not a single one of the senior and lucrative posts in the Works. Perhaps for this reason, several writers have set him down as a natural-born second fiddle, a drudge, the willing servant of men abler than himself. That, however, as we shall see, was not quite the case, and there is probably another reason, a temperamental and social one, for the relative obscurity of Hawksmore's official career. He was not, it seems, born a gentleman, and judging from some remarks Vanbrugh made about him, he seems to have lacked the capacity to show himself off and figure as a great artist (as Talman, for instance, did). Though not without a sturdy vanity in his own mastery of architecture, he seems to have been dourly modest. He not infrequently complained of the treatment he received from the men of influence, but no deep bitterness seems to have entered his soul. His fundamental modesty is reflected in the provision in his will that he should be buried in his own 'or any other' country churchyard, under a plain stone slab – an uncommon desire in an age less averse than most to marble immortality.

Between this dour, proud, deep character and that of his chief collaborator there is a contrast which is almost ludicrous, for John Vanbrugh (1664–1726) was neither dour nor proud, and if he was deep, the depths were flood-lit by a wit which had few equals in his time and has had few since. Born in London, the son of a rich sugar-baker whose wife was a daughter of Sir Dudley Carleton, and whose father had been a Flemish refugee from Ghent, Vanbrugh grew up a gentleman. He was apprenticed to no trade and at twenty-two obtained a commission in the Earl of Huntingdon's regiment. As a soldier, he saw something of the world, but resigned his commission in due course and adventured on his own. This led to an unfortunate episode, starting with his arrest at Calais in 1690 and continuing with his detention, for a matter of two years, in French prisons, on suspicion of being a spy. He was for a time at Vincennes, and subsequently in the Bastille, but was treated with distinction and seems at no time to have suffered anything worse than mild discomfort and boredom. On his release he obtained a minor post in the Household, and in 1696 was gazetted a Captain of Marines. At this point, however, he turned to the theatre, for which he had begun to write in his Bastille days. *The Relapse*, a superbly-turned comedy of manners, was produced at the end of the year, and was immediately followed by *Aesop* and, in 1697, by his best play, *The Provok'd Wife*. More plays (there are ten in all) followed in 1700, 1704, and 1705.

But in 1699, when he was thirty-five, Vanbrugh suddenly – 'without thought or lecture', as Swift observed – became an architect, by designing Castle Howard for the Earl of Carlisle. The house began to be built in 1701. The same patron secured for him, in the following year, the Office of Comptroller (in succession to Talman, who was evicted), thus placing him, at one stroke, beside the septuagenarian Wren at the very head of English architecture. This deplorable job, justified only in its consequences, was followed by another, contrived by the same patron; for in 1703 Vanbrugh became a Herald Extraordinary, and in 1704, in spite of his expressed contempt for the whole science of heraldry, Clarenceux King of Arms. In that office he visited Hanover in 1706 to confer the Order of the Garter on the future George II.

Meanwhile, he was selected by the Duke of Marlborough to design the house which Queen Anne was graciously conferring as a gift on the Captain-General of her forces and the victor, in 1704, of the battle of Blenheim. With the beginning of Blenheim Palace, in 1705, came the beginning of Vanbrugh's triumphs and of his troubles. The story of his conflict with the militant personality of Sarah, Duchess of Marlborough, of the difficulties consequent upon Marlborough's dismissal by the Tories in 1711, and of the final rupture and Vanbrugh's exclusion from his own masterpiece, has been twice told with the gusto which such a piece of tragi-comedy deserves. The house was finally completed by Hawksmore a year or so before Vanbrugh's death.

While Blenheim was rising – a period of nearly twenty years – Vanbrugh built much else. First, in 1705, the Opera House or 'Queen's Theatre' in the Haymarket, a project which failed acoustically as well as financially. Then, from 1707, the remodelling of Kimbolton Castle for Lord Manchester, in 1710–11 Kings Weston, near Bristol, for Sir Edward Southwell, and, shortly afterwards, the conversion of his own country box at Esher into the vast Claremont for the young Duke of Newcastle.

Vanbrugh was a Whig, an original and prominent member of the Kit-Cat Club, and at the very centre of Whig society; and the troubles which descended on the Marlboroughs during the Harley administration (1710–14) engulfed him too. A tactless letter which got into the wrong hands lost him the Comptrollership for a couple of years, but on George I's accession he was knighted, restored, and given, in addition, the office of Surveyor of the Gardens and Waters. He succeeded Wren as Surveyor at Greenwich in 1716 and designed the buildings there which will be discussed in the next chapter. His last great houses were Eastbury in Dorset (from 1716) for Bubb Doddington, Seaton Delaval (1720–9) for Admiral Delaval, and Grimsthorpe (from 1722; only partly carried out) for the Duke of Ancaster.

In social class, education, temperament and experience, John Vanbrugh and Nicholas Hawksmore were worlds apart, and it was this, as much as anything, which made a partnership between the two possible. When he participated in Vanbrugh's work, Hawksmore did so as a paid official. There was no question of rivalry and scarcely a trace of jealousy, though a streak of not unnatural annoyance did appear in Hawksmore when Vanbrugh was restored to his Comptrollership while Hawksmore's equally scandalous eviction from his Clerkship was overlooked. The partnership in fact is a partnership only in the perspective of history and must be understood in that sense. How it worked and what it produced it is now our business to inquire.

The Hawksmore–Vanbrugh Partnership

Broadly, what we are trying to investigate is, in the first place, a departure from the attitude to architectural form associated with the two generations of designers preceding the arrival of Hawksmore and Vanbrugh. The change is a fundamental one, a change of feeling, a renewed interest in the *intrinsic* qualities of mass, rhythm, and proportion as opposed to the *extrinsic* management of form by the apparatus of classical design. Since Inigo Jones had concentrated the whole substance of architecture into the play of classical elements, a play of elements it had remained. Wren, from first to last, felt architecture to be an affair of these elements, and of their combination in such a way as to control and, if necessary to disguise, the mere stuff of building. Wren had little feeling for the pure relation of one volume to another, for the spacing of openings in plain masonry or for the effective recession of one surface behind another. To him architecture was a language, the 'true Latin' of building, to be uttered with a correct understanding of its grammar and varied and modified in the spirit of that grammar to suit the exigencies of modern needs. He was embarrassed by sheer mass. His plainer façades are never quite stable but nervously dependent on their columned centres, on the apparatus of quoins, cornices, or window-cases. This is conspicuously so at Chelsea and Hampton Court, where the porticoes rein in the composition with a desperate determination which does not quite bring it to repose. In all his work, even in Trinity Library, there is that margin of *malaise* which reveals that Wren's heart was in the motifs he was deploying and never in the planes and volumes over which he deployed them.

Now, in the style of Wren's two successors this attitude was completely reversed. Mass, sheer mass, became their passion; indeed, the extreme heaviness for which the works of Hawksmore and Vanbrugh have always been criticized is, perhaps, the measure of their enthusiasm for the rediscovery of those intrinsic architectural values which Jones had disciplined away and Wren had not been the man to recall.

How did this rediscovery come about? There is no question whatever that Hawksmore led the way, for we find the new spirit manifested as soon as work in the Wren office began to be delegated to him. That was about 1692. In that year, Wren undertook the design of Sir John Moore's Writing School at Christ's Hospital (Plate 99A); and the Hospital records make it reasonably clear that Hawksmore, 'Sir Christopher Wren's gentleman', was the responsible man.[2] This school building was simple enough: a rectangular three-storey block, with square two-storey pavilions attached at the angles and capped with visible French roofs. This arrangement could have been, and perhaps was, Wren's. But the handling could scarcely be Wren's. Simple as it is, the building expresses a massive stability, foreign to his pencil. This stability is obtained, principally, by a very careful balance of voids and solids; and also by two devices: one, the continuation of the cornices of the pavilions across the façades of the main block, the other, the provision of broad vertical pilaster-strips at each angle of this block.

There is Hawksmore in essence. There is the new feeling for mass which we find in all his work and which enters into Vanbrugh's as soon as he comes on the scene – which is not for another seven years.

The Writing School is valuable as a clear-cut, documented case of Hawksmore's emergence, under Wren's name, as an artist with a developed personal style. His new vision may be accounted for by a combination of natural gifts and the results of that sense of reaction which a new generation always brings to the work of its predecessor; but to this we must add the inspiration of recent French architecture and French books. And, first among the latter, Perrault's annotated and illustrated summary of Vitruvius, the second (enlarged) edition of which was published in 1684. That book set the hoary Roman and his ideas in a new light; for Perrault interprets him not simply as the grammarian of the orders but as the master of a grand arcuated style in solid masonry. Perrault, moreover, adorned his exposition with engravings extraneous to the text, including illustrations of his own Observatory in Paris and of a Roman ruin, of rather impressive character, in Bordeaux. Both these engravings, and the whole spirit of Perrault's edition, had a profound effect on Hawksmore's future buildings – and on Vanbrugh's. But before passing to Vanbrugh and his work we must break off to consider a building which was never built, and for which the surviving designs are at once illuminating and enigmatic.

The Whitehall Designs of c. 1699

In January 1698 the greater part of the ancient palace of Whitehall was consumed by fire, the Banqueting House being almost the only building to escape. The opportunity thus presented was of the first order, an invitation by Providence to embark at last on the great adventure for which Inigo Jones and Webb had in their time made such ample preparations. For reasons we do not exactly know, the opportunity was not taken. But designs were prepared. For years they lay hidden among the Wren drawings in the library of All Souls, but were recovered and published by the Wren Society in 1931.

There are two designs. The differences between them turn chiefly on the way the existing Banqueting House is incorporated. In design No. 2 (Wren Society numbering) it is linked to a giant portico (of a type given by Scamozzi) and repeated exactly on the other side of this portico. The resulting range of buildings faces the river and is attached, at right angles, to long wings reaching eastward to the Thames bank and westwards, for an equal distance, to join the west (landward) front of the palace which encloses the courts and state apartments.

Design No. 1 (Plate 100B) is infinitely more striking. Here the Banqueting House is made the central feature of the whole and, to increase its importance, a giant portico of Corinthian columns is (with what irreverence!) attached to its south front. At either end of the Banqueting House are circular domed towers, composed of the same giant order. These are linked by gateways to the east-west wings stretching from the landward front to the Thames, where they turn north and south respectively, and display magnificent temple-like fronts surmounted by pedimented attics.

The two designs are so different in the degree of boldness and imagination they evince that, although both are evidently by the same draughtsman, one would willingly believe that they spring from different brains. Yet they have much in common, and the common factors are of a kind which make it credible that Wren was associated with both.

The main common feature of the two designs is the vigorous use of a giant order. In design No. 2 this inspiration is from Bernini's design for the Louvre which Wren had had a sight of in 1665 but which was later published in full by Marot. Bernini, the Banqueting House, Scamozzi, and Wren's earlier works supply nearly all the material needed for this design, whose plan is not particularly novel and is related to Webb's small project of c. 1661–5. It would be possible to believe that this design was made, or dictated, by Wren himself.

The design No. 1 is more difficult to explain. The plan is clearly inspired by Wren's 1694 plan for Greenwich (p. 152). It agrees with No. 2 only in so far as it comprises long side-wings joined at half their length by the block containing the Banqueting House and dominating an open fore-court towards the river. The general conception of the design is something entirely new. It achieves effect, not so much by the harmonious design and combination of the various blocks, as by a series of dramatic contrasts, culminating in the central group made up of the Banqueting House with its new giant portico and the two new domed towers which flank it like heraldic supporters; and which, from every point, would have crowned the silhouette.

As in design No. 2, the giant Corinthian order derives from Bernini. The temple-blocks (probably hall and chapel) alongside the river recall Baalbek in the exciting if erroneous versions published by Marot. The service wings are in the Wren manner, but extended to a monotonous length which Wren would surely have abhorred. But whence comes the *bravura* of the circular towers, and whence the majestic treatment of Jones's lower (Ionic) order which, released from its venerable source, courses through the entire design, now in pilaster form, now in an arcuated theme threading through a loftier Doric? In the Louvre and the designs for the Louvre (Marot's own project in particular) some hints for this astonishing design are to be found, but they are only hints, and the conception of the whole is revolutionary.

Whose designs are these? Certainly they come from the Works circle, so that Wren, Talman, and Hawksmore could all be involved and even Vanbrugh cannot be excluded. On grounds of style and presentation, a coalition of Wren and Hawksmore, with the latter at the drawing-board, seems the least improbable answer.

In any case, these Whitehall designs inaugurate the English Baroque School. They are Baroque, not in the sense of any secure attachment to the Baroque of contemporary Rome (there is, however, the one Berninesque thread, through Marot), but in their refreshed sense of a sweeping unity of design, of great, single units placed in theatric contrast to each other. Here, Wren's empiric approach, the conquest of mass by the ingenious deployment of classic units is superseded. Here, mass, silhouette, and the arrangement of receding planes are the uppermost values.

While these projects were being developed, John Vanbrugh, if he did not participate, was certainly close at hand. Hardly had the ashes of Whitehall cooled than he procured from the King a site whereon to build himself a house. This house (Plate 99B) survived, after much alteration, into the present century. Very small and very odd, it was christened 'Goose-pie House' by its contemporaries. Before the wings were added and the triple windows cut down to floor-level it must have looked like a guard-house. Its quaintness

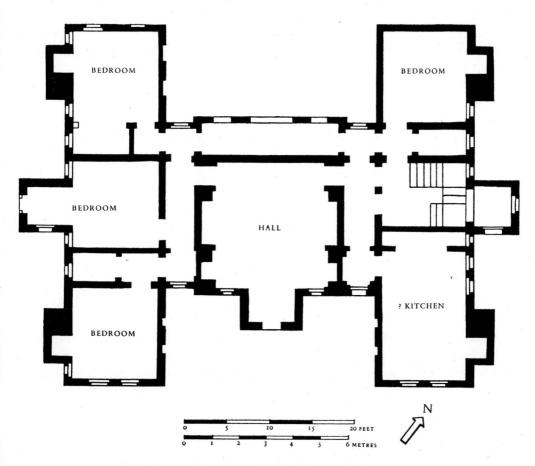

Figure 23. Vanbrugh's House at Esher

presages its owner-architect's wholly unconventional approach to design and if we anticipate events and look at two other houses designed by Vanbrugh for himself, we shall find equally odd humours. His country house at Esher (1711) had a plan (Figure 23) which was perfectly Elizabethan; while at Greenwich he built, about 1717, what he called his 'Bastille' – a little brick fort with round towers and pointed roofs (Plate 140A). To be sure, this sort of thing would not do for great houses like Castle Howard and Blenheim, but however grave Vanbrugh might be, the fantastical imp was always at his elbow reminding him of old castles, strange prisons, and the palaces of the Elizabethans.

Vanbrugh's Houses

Castle Howard, Yorks. (Plates 101A and 102; Figure 24), was Vanbrugh's first and remains one of the greatest of his country-houses. Hawksmore assisted him here, and the plan takes its departure from the Greenwich lay-out of 1695 on which Hawksmore had worked but which had probably been abandoned by 1699. That is to say, the plan consists of a long body of building facing the gardens (at Greenwich, the Park) on one side and on the other side, putting forth curved arcades (at Greenwich, colonnades) to meet fore-buildings forming the sides of an open court and containing the kitchens and chapel respectively.

This theme, at Castle Howard, is elaborated by the addition of lateral courts enclosed by buildings of various heights containing, on one side, stables, and on the other laundry, brew-house, and other domestic services. The central fore-court merges with a greater court, walled, and approached through three monumental gateways.

The garden front with its high centre and low wings, all pilastered, and crowned over each pilaster with a vase or a figure, is almost over-direct in its unrelieved and obvious symmetry to which the domed cupola at the centre adds needless emphasis. To such a flat statement Vanbrugh never committed himself again; nor is there anything flat or obvious about the entrance front at Castle Howard. Here we find Vanbrugh's genius for composition in full play. Here he is at that game of lively but carefully articulated relationships, in height and in recession, which made Reynolds praise him so highly.[3] Each element in the composition – the main block, the curved colonnades, and the little palaces which form the wings – has its own sufficient life, yet by a skilful transmission of units through the entire design absolute congruity is achieved.

At Castle Howard we do not quite lose sight of the Whitehall designs – the close Corinthian spacing of the garden front and the character of the dome seem to derive from them – nor, if we look carefully, shall we fail to find reminiscences of that minuscule essay in the monumental, Goose-pie House: it is echoed in the little rusticated elevation which repeats four times in the range on the entrance side.

Oddly enough it is the 'goose-pie' elevation, with its triolets of windows in the centre of a fully rusticated wall, which leads us most easily from Castle Howard to Vanbrugh's second great house, and his greatest, Blenheim Palace (Plates 101B and 103; Figure 25). At Castle Howard the elevation in question is, in fact, the end elevation of each of the two fore-court wings, and is repeated, for effect's sake (and what an impression of vastness this gives!) in the service and stable wings. At Blenheim it has grown to be something far more important, for it has become the elevation, repeated eight times in all, of the four great corner pavilions on which the whole design hangs. For although the Blenheim plan, like that of Castle Howard, derives from Wren's Greenwich scheme of 1695, the looseness of the original, its rambling plan-silhouette, has been resolved into the clear-cut outline of a rectangular mass with corner pavilions.

Blenheim represents the marriage of the Greenwich idea, introduced at Castle Howard, with this over-all conception of the castellar mass – a conception derived from the French

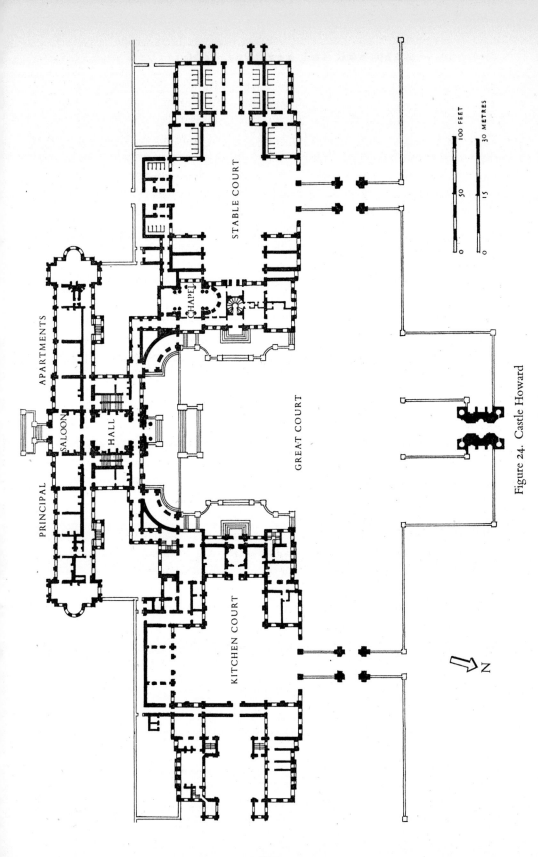

Figure 24. Castle Howard

château plan as we see it at Coulommiers or the Luxembourg. The combination is enormously powerful. Here, again, every relationship is fully articulated. The centre block, with its Corinthian portico (a Scamozzi type, as in one of the Whitehall designs and, indeed, in one version of the Greenwich scheme), is a separate entity, though concealing a subsidiary Doric which emerges in the colonnades which sweep round to the pavilions. These again are entities; the colonnades sink into them and re-emerge in a straight length to meet the entrance elevations of the kitchen and stable courts, where, once again, the theme changes. Knit together by this transmission of the Doric, the drama is wonderfully sustained, mounting to the portico which, robbed of its focal gravity by the presence of the two heavier pavilions, is compensated in height; for above its pediment rises a second pediment dramatically interrupted and recessed. Here on the sky-line we meet those arched attics, dear both to Vanbrugh and Hawksmore and which were the gift of Perrault through his illustration of a little-known Roman ruin at Bordeaux.

At Blenheim the English Baroque culminates. Vanbrugh was to build, or remodel, some seven or eight more great houses, and one or two of them are perhaps even more surprisingly original than Blenheim. But Blenheim is inexhaustible and represents the whole varied mind of its creator – and of Hawksmore his collaborator.

It has often been observed that Blenheim is both a palace and a castle. The massive pavilions with their arched attics give that impression, and it is a true one; for, certainly, Vanbrugh had a feeling, rare at his time, for the qualities of the medieval fortress. When he remodelled Kimbolton Castle for Lord Manchester and Lumley for Lord Scarborough he enjoyed the experience of merging his own weighty classic with the massiveness of a Gothic fortress, and when he built his own country-house at Greenwich he built, as we have seen, a brick châtelet which he liked to pretend was a Bastille.

Vanbrugh never introduced strictly Gothic elements such as tracery or even pointed arches, and his medievalizing certainly takes its origin not so much in the ancient buildings of Britain as in the scenery of the Italian stage, where a kind of bastard Romanesque, well furnished with corbel-tables, was a convention employed to convey the atmosphere of the dark ages. But Vanbrugh's appreciation of the medieval extended, as one would expect, beyond detail, and at Claremont (his own Esher house, expanded to form a country-house for the Duke of Newcastle; destroyed in the eighteenth century) a great castellated pile relied for its effect solely on the disposition of its component masses. As he wrote to Lord Manchester, "tis certainly the Figure and Proportion that make the most pleasing Fabrick, and not the delicacy of the Ornaments'.

At Kings Weston there were certainly few delicate ornaments; it is Vanbrugh's most severe house, though above its level parapet the Bordeaux ruin once more provided inspiration, and the chimney-stacks are composed into a square house of arches through which the wind blows.

In Vanbrugh's last houses, done, apparently, without Hawksmore's help, he was obsessed more and more by the idea of pure mass-relationship as the grand means of effect, with classical elements thrust into the composition at points where they would strike the most telling and even bizarre notes. At Eastbury, Seaton Delaval (Plate 105B; Figure 26), and Grimsthorpe he used, on a great scale, the rusticated Doric which we meet

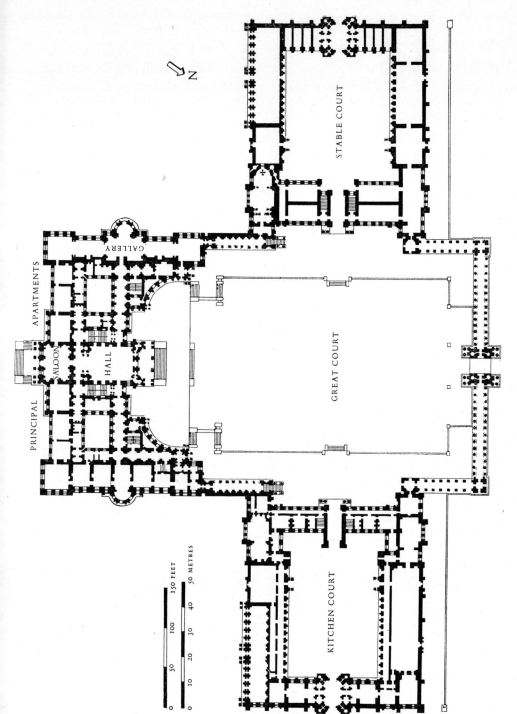

Figure 25. Blenheim Palace

first in the entries to the Blenheim courtyards – a Doric with ringed shafts in the manner of de Brosse at the Luxembourg. At Eastbury there was a hexastyle portico of such columns; at Grimsthorpe (Plate 105A), pairs of them frame the arcuated centre-piece of the house; while at Seaton Delaval (entrance front) three of them embrace each corner of the centre block. In each case they suddenly stamp the bleak Gothic masses with the majestic seal of Rome. All these houses carry on the pavilion theme introduced at Blenheim, the pavilions at Eastbury and Seaton tending to become towers and having Venetian windows in their belvedere-like upper storeys.

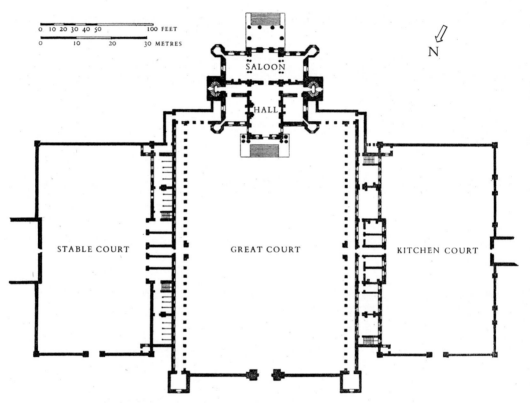

Figure 26. Seaton Delaval

Seaton Delaval is the most concentrated and intense of all Vanbrugh's houses. The main block is comparatively small but comprises an astonishing number of disparate elements, and gives the impression of rapid movement arrested at a dramatic moment. Consciously or unconsciously, the plan, like that of the architect's own house at Esher, is almost purely Jacobean and the octagonal corner towers even recall a favourite Tudor theme, though their immediate inspiration is more likely to have been Perrault's observatory. The different elements are worked together with a complete disregard for convention, enormous technical skill (which Vanbrugh is never supposed to have had), and a magical eye for sheer effect. The result is a superb, a breath-taking exaggeration.[4]

Hawksmore's Share

In this grand serial achievement, from Castle Howard to Seaton, what was Hawksmore's part? The answer can only be speculative, but there can be little doubt that his share, directly in some houses and indirectly in others, was considerable. There are certain themes running through the series which had definitely appeared in his work before 1699 – notably the powerful string-course which we noticed at the Christ's Hospital Writing School. In 1702, moreover, before Castle Howard had been much more than begun, Hawksmore was building Easton Neston, Northants., in a style which cannot possibly be a plagiarism, with a giant order used most grandiloquently all round the house; and a plan of astonishing maturity for its date. While if Hawksmore was not part-creator of the Vanbrugh manner it is surprising, to say the least of it, that he should be able to expand and adapt that manner to church-design in his own churches of 1711 onwards with such absolute confidence.

The truth can only be that *both* Hawksmore *and* Vanbrugh were very exceptional men; that they exploited the same sources in continuous mutual discussion, and shared, more fully, perhaps, than either knew, each other's treasuries of knowledge and invention. It is simply not possible to separate out their individual contributions with any precision, but I will submit my own rough guess. It is that to Vanbrugh we chiefly owe the daring novelties of composition which are outstanding characteristics of the houses I have described; but that it was Hawksmore who discovered (had, indeed, already discovered) the mode of expression appropriate to these adventures. It was Hawksmore, with his deep knowledge of the source-books and of every sort of English architecture, his long experience of practical building, and, above all, his own rediscovery of those intrinsic architectural values I mentioned earlier, who made the Vanbrugh manner possible.

Much additional light is thrown on the subject by Hawksmore's London churches, but these we must leave for a future chapter.

Thomas Archer

We come now to the third name associated with the English Baroque School. Thomas Archer (1668–1743) came of a good Warwickshire family and was, indeed, rather better born than Vanbrugh. After three years at Oxford he travelled for four years, returning about 1693 and, having Whig affiliations, made his way successfully at Court. In 1705 he secured the lucrative office of Groom Porter. He was then thirty-seven and had been assisting the 4th Earl (1st Duke) of Devonshire with his works at Chatsworth for three or four years. He had built the domed cascade-house with its sedge-work rustics, dolphins, and river-gods, and had also given Chatsworth its curved Corinthian-pilastered north front. At the same time he was almost certainly engaged on Heythrop, Oxon., a great house for the 1st (and only) Duke of Shrewsbury. All these works show Archer to have been deeply interested in Roman Baroque and suggest that, unlike Wren, Hawksmore, and Vanbrugh, he had made his acquaintance with the style at first hand.

Therein is Archer's significance. He was the first and almost the only English architect to betray in his work an intimate appreciation of Bernini and Borromini. At Heythrop not only Bernini's Louvre but the same architect's Palazzo Odescalchi have been carefully studied, while Archer's later work is full of reminiscences of the sinister and unbridled style of Francesco Borromini – the *enfant terrible* of Italian architecture and the man whom, in a very few years, English architects were to regard much as a good schoolboy regards a prostitute.

In 1709–12, Archer built two important garden buildings at Wrest, Beds., for the 11th Earl (1st Duke) of Kent. The one which survives, a domed banqueting-house in brick and stone, is built on the curious plan-shape of a hexagon with round and square projections on alternate sides – a rather nonsensical misapplication, perhaps, of the plan of Borromini's Sapienza. In the same year, as one of the Commissioners for the erection of St Philip's Church, Birmingham (now the Cathedral), he designed that building. This and his two London churches belong to a later chapter, for they can only properly be discussed with the larger group of Queen Anne churches to which they belong. But we may note here that all show the Borrominesque influence – notably St Philip's in its doorways and tower, and the Deptford church in its plan, directly derived from S. Agnese, in Rome.

Archer designed two large London houses: Monmouth House, Soho (destroyed), apparently for the widowed Duchess of Monmouth; and No. 43 King Street, Covent Garden, for Admiral Russell. At Monmouth House and also at Roehampton House (1712; now a hospital), built for a Mr Cary, he indulged a curious liking for huge broken pediments on the sky-line. One of his last works was his own house at Hale, Hants. There, he abandoned the Baroque and produced a quiet Palladian villa with which the critics who so denounced his earlier works can have found little fault.

In 1715 Archer acquired another profitable place as Controller of Customs at Newcastle and, thereafter, seems to have designed little or nothing. He died worth over £100,000 in 1743. His creative career extended over scarcely more than fifteen years, but he had made a distinct contribution to English architecture. His originality is unquestionable and his intimacy with the Baroque did not prevent him from benefiting from the Wren-Hawksmore tradition. This will be clearly seen when we come to deal with his churches.

English Baroque

The English Baroque School flourished for one generation. It was the creation of two men, while a third threw his talents into the pool. For a while, these three masters dominated English architecture and the style spread rapidly through the usual channels – official departments, *virtuosi* and local masons. The official style of the Ordnance Office was for a time so close to Vanbrugh that one may well suspect his intermediacy. The Barracks at Berwick-on-Tweed (1719) and the Gun-Wharf at Plymouth (1715) are two notable examples of military architecture in a style close to Vanbrugh's sham-castle style as seen in his own house at Greenwich. Among the *virtuosi* were Dean Aldrich, whom we shall meet later on, and a certain William Wakefield, a Yorkshire gentleman who, from about

1713, built and altered houses in the North in a style close to Vanbrugh's; Duncombe Park, Helmsley, is the earliest known and the most important. Among the masons, William Townesend of Oxford, whom Vanbrugh employed at Kings Weston and Blenheim, ventured on a dramatically heavy classicism when he built on his own account, and a house at Oxford called (not surprisingly) 'Vanbrugh House', with giant Doric pilasters on its humble façade, is attributable to him. Townesend completed the gateway of Queen's College in the same city, taking some liberties with Hawksmore's design (see p. 192).

Of the many palpable allusions to the work of the masters to be found in common building practice up and down the country, many will be subsequent to the publication of designs by them in *Vitruvius Britannicus* (1715–17), a work whose main importance concerns another chapter. Vanbrugh's and Archer's influence, purveyed most probably by this means, is to be found in the imposing little houses of many west-country towns; for example, at Bridgwater, where 'The Lions', built for himself by a carpenter named Benjamin Holloway (*c.* 1724), borrows freely and quaintly from Archer's Roehampton House. Archer's influence, again, may be detected wherever we find scraps of Borrominesque detail, such as the composite capital with inward-turned volutes which the Bastards of Blandford, Dorset, and Nathaniel Ireson of Wincanton, Somerset, used in several of their buildings; while such themes as the double-lugged apron to a window-sill, the triple keystone and the plain heavy architrave with segmental lintel, become part of the fashionable language of the whole building trade. The fashion lasted well into the 1720s. By 1728 it was the subject of a caricature. By 1730 it may be presumed dead.

The Mausoleum at Castle Howard

We cannot leave the subject of English Baroque without noticing a building which dates from long after the style was extinct but which is a major work by the master whose hand was the chief agent of its success.

In 1712, the works on the house at Castle Howard stopped, and Lord Carlisle turned his enthusiasm and his architects onto the gardens and their ornaments. This work went on for years, culminating in the erection of Vanbrugh's Belvedere Temple, which was incomplete when the architect died in 1726. Hawksmore finished it. The design of a mausoleum for the Howard family (Plate 106) took shape three years later. Hawksmore was then sixty-eight. His correspondence with Lord Carlisle from this period has been published and shows Hawksmore's characteristically archaeological approach to the subject. In the early letters he mentions the famous mausolea of antiquity – the tomb of Mausolus itself, the tombs of Lars Porsena and of Cecilia Metella, and he bases a preliminary design on the latter. But that is immediately superseded by a circular design, at first with an arched loggia but then with a peristyle of Doric columns in emulation of Bramante's *tempietto* at S. Pietro in Montorio. That was the design finally chosen, and this great temple, seventy-six feet high and situated on a lonely eminence in the park, was forthwith put in hand. Its progress was not unnoticed by the younger generation of architects and critics. 'I hope', wrote Hawksmore in 1732, 'the poet Mr Pope[5] will not set his satir upon us for it.' He did not; but a few months later the drawings came into the hands of Lord Burlington, who delivered himself of one severe criticism – that the columns were set too close. It must be admitted that they are much closer than Bramante set them and that in antiquity there is no precedent whatever for circular Doric temples. The practical reason for Hawksmore's spacing was the weakness of stone lintels bridging any wider span on the immense scale involved; but he defended himself (copiously but not too effectively) on academic ground. Rules of precedent apart, the Mausoleum needed no defence. But its spirit is the emotional spirit of English Baroque, and it was that which touched Burlington's antipathies. Hawksmore's colonnade is close and tense, a grim palisade. Within, the building is not, as one anticipates, dark, but a great tower of light, which pours in from clerestory windows above a rich Corinthian order. He did not live to finish it. Indeed, it was completed under Sir Thomas Robinson, Lord Carlisle's son-in-law, a friend of Burlington and one of the true Palladian faith. The grand staircase which he added to the upper platform is in the manner of Burlington's at Chiswick House, but it detracts in no way from the splendour of Hawksmore's last great effort, the final affirmation of his own personal and romantic loyalty to the Rome which he never saw.

NOTES TO CHAPTER 17

1. The extent to which Wren personally provided drawings for his buildings is not easily determined and it varied, obviously, from case to case. Thus, the only City Church drawings in his hand are for one or two of the very earliest; much seems to have been delegated. At Trinity College Library, on the contrary, every surviving drawing is his and a letter from him to Barrow gives an idea of the way he liked to carry through a job: 'I suppose you have good masons, however I would willingly take a farther paines to give all the mouldings in great, wee are scrupulous in small matters and you must pardon us, the Architects are as great pedants as Critics or Heralds'. He goes on to say that when the original designs are returned to him he will 'copy out partes of them at large, more proper for the use of the workmen' – in other words, make what we should call working-drawings.

2. 'Mr Treasurer represented to the Committee the great pains and industry that Mr Hawksmore Sr Christopher Wren's gentleman hath taken in making the draughts of the new intended Writing Schoole.' He was granted a gratuity (E. H. Pearce, *Annals of Christ's Hospital*, 1908, p. 151). The building had not yet been begun and a mere copyist of

Wren's design would hardly have merited this favour.

3. 'He had originality of invention, he understood light and shadow, and had great skill in composition. To support his principal object, he produced his second or third groups or masses; he perfectly understood … the conduct of the back-ground; by which the design and invention is set off to the greatest advantage.' (13th Discourse.)

4. In compressing this account of Vanbrugh's work, I have been obliged, for clarity, to omit all mention of the interiors of the houses. His state apartments are always finely organized in contrasting spaces, and as little monotonous as his exteriors. A masterly performance is the hall at Castle Howard (Plate 104), a domed space flanked by corridors and staircases in such a way that the composition is in two vertical planes in all directions and the staircases are seen passing the arches which support the dome. Of Vanbrugh's interior decorations there is nothing to say except that he took full advantage of the various schools of craftsmanship which were a legacy of the church- and palace-building of Sir Christopher Wren.

5. Whose *Epistle to Lord Burlington* had lately been published (p. 221).

THE ROYAL WORKS
1702–1726

VANBRUGH's accession to the Comptrollership of the Works in 1702 was a political job. Jobbery had been common enough in the previous century (Wren's appointment to the Surveyorship, it will be remembered, was rather curiously managed), but from Vanbrugh's time all the places in the Works rapidly take on the character of plums, to be distributed to the clients of the oligarchy in power, irrespective of professional merit. Not only the senior offices, but the clerkships and the places of the Patent Artisans become a prey to nonentities with good connexions; and the prestige of the Office steadily disintegrates. Behind this tendency, and one of its undoubted causes, lies the shift of patronage from the Court to the two great political parties. William and Mary were the last sovereigns to conduct palace-building in the Stuart tradition, and after Mary's death in 1694 it was on Whig aristocrats rather than on the Sovereign at Whitehall or St James's that architecture depended for encouragement and opportunity. It was this new kind of patronage which, broadening down from dukes and earls to baronets, country gentlemen and professional men, converted the occupation of designing from being the amusement of a gentleman, the function of a court official or a craftsman into a profession – the profession of architecture.

Vanbrugh himself designed more for members of the Whig nobility than he did for Queen Anne or George I, and from his time onwards the officials of the Works were, for the most part, successful practising architects who increased their emoluments, but rarely their reputations, by occupying a clerkship or one of the artisan's places in the Works.

Thus the period from 1702 until Vanbrugh's death in 1726 represents the last phase in which the Works occupy the centre of the architectural stage. At the beginning of the period Wren was still in full charge as Surveyor; but he was already seventy, and there are indications that the jobbing and corruption in his department were more than he could handle. Vanbrugh figures, in one instance in 1704, as a vigorous new broom, but in 1713 some kind of reorganization appeared to be essential. It was in that year that Vanbrugh in turn was jobbed out of his Comptrollership. He returned with a knighthood in the following year, and the office of Surveyor was, at the same time, put into commission. Wren was virtually retired, becoming merely one of the Commissioners of the Board of Works, though retaining his title and emoluments. So things continued for four years. But, in 1718, some intrigues about which we are not fully informed had the disgraceful result of procuring Wren's dismissal. He was succeeded, not by Vanbrugh (who, it seems, might have had the post in 1714 but declined 'out of tenderness to Sir Christopher Wren'), but by a poet and pamphleteer with some slight knowledge of architecture, William Benson (1682–1754). Benson proved his incompetence with surprising promptitude and was dismissed in 1719 in favour of another nonentity, Sir Thomas Hewett (d. 1726), who filled the office by deputy. To him succeeded a variety of mere political place-holders, and the lustre of the Surveyorship was dimmed until, upon a further reorganization in 1782, Sir William Chambers was crowned with the title of Surveyor-General. After him Wyatt enjoyed the same title, but proved once and for all the unreliability of artists as administrators. A lay Surveyor-General succeeded him for a few years, but in 1832 the title was finally extinguished.

The royal buildings undertaken by the Office after 1702 are of no great importance unless we include among them the completion of Greenwich Hospital. This we may fairly do because, although controlled by a separate Commission (as was Chelsea Hospital), the personnel were the same. Wren acted, from 1694, as honorary Surveyor to the Commission. Vanbrugh appears as a Director in 1703 and succeeded Wren as Surveyor on his resignation in 1716. And Hawksmore took a big share of the work throughout, first as the man who made the drawings, then in the double rôle of Clerk of the Works and Surveyor's Clerk and finally, from 1705, as Deputy Surveyor.

The Completion of Greenwich Hospital

We have already seen (p. 152) how the Greenwich project developed under Wren, first as confluent great and lesser courtyards dominated by a domed chapel and later with the centre block absent and two domes flanking the main vista – a vista terminating in the low and distant Queen's House.

Of these two domes (Plate 107), that pertaining to the Hall was finished in 1704; the duplicate on the Chapel after 1716. There are drawings, in Hawksmore's hand, which show that the first intention was a lower type of structure, having a drum with eight pedimented openings, somewhat recalling Mansart's Louvre sketches and an early scheme of Wren's for St Paul's. This was felt, perhaps, not to give a sufficiently prominent silhouette; and the executed design is a much steeper affair. The Greenwich domes, though carefully detailed, are not absolutely satisfactory. They suffer from an attempt to reduce Michelangelo's dome at St Peter's to small compass while multiplying some of its parts. The columns of the drum cluster too thickly and restlessly, in too busy contrast either to the simple silhouette or to the broad, serene work below.

The inner court at Greenwich was narrowed, in the executed design, to something more resembling an avenue. Hawksmore, in the legend (characteristically antiquarian) to an engraving of 1728, called it the *columnatio* and showed it flanked on either side by a *porticus*. The avenue is, in fact, defined by colonnades which Wren had first conceived as a way of linking and screening a series of parallel hospital pavilions. By the time they were built (1704 onwards) they screened nothing but the King William and Queen Mary courts and had assumed an intrinsic importance of their own, obviously coloured, in Hawksmore's mind, with a heroic vision of the foregatherings of Roman philosophers.

Of the two lateral courts just mentioned, the first to be closed in was King William's court on the west, where a dormitory block was built, possibly as early as 1702. This is a really amazing piece of work, presumably by Vanbrugh, and certainly wildly amateurish

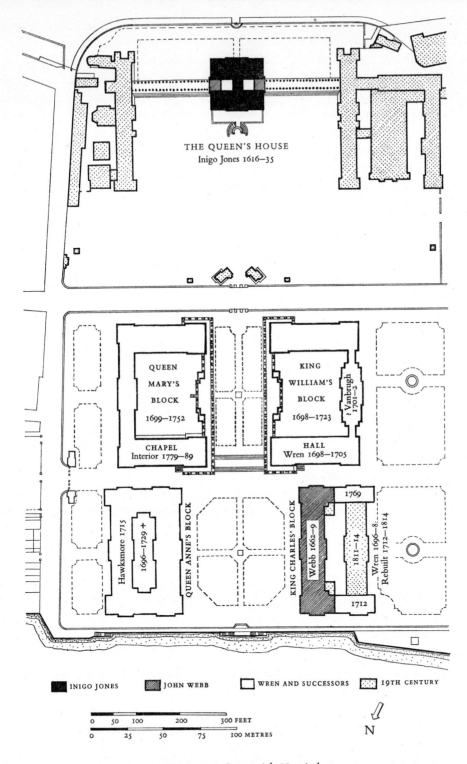

THE QUEEN'S HOUSE
Inigo Jones 1616–35

QUEEN
MARY'S
BLOCK
1699–1752

CHAPEL
Interior 1779–89

KING
WILLIAM'S
BLOCK
1698–1723

? Vanbrugh
1701–2

HALL
Wren 1698–1705

Hawksmore 1715

1696–1729 +

QUEEN ANNE'S BLOCK

KING CHARLES' BLOCK

Webb 1662–9

1769

1811–14

1712

Wren 1696–8
Rebuilt 1712–1814

INIGO JONES   JOHN WEBB   WREN AND SUCCESSORS   19TH CENTURY

0   50   100   200   300 FEET

0   25   50   75   100 METRES

N

Figure 27. Greenwich Hospital

181

in a way that no other participant in the Greenwich business could have been. Towards the court, the elevation is adorned with a grotesque enlargement of the theme of the end (interior) walls of the Hall – an elliptical arch between pairs of composite pilasters. The order is no less than sixty feet high, and its application bears no reference whatever to the fenestration: the windows peep out of the architecture as best they may. The other (west) elevation, with a Doric portico overtopping the main cornice, is no less monstrous, and the building as a whole, though it shows great spirit, can only charitably be explained as a trial of strength on the part of the young, undisciplined genius who had not yet, perhaps, learnt how much Wren, his chief, and his colleague Hawksmore had to teach.

No other building at Greenwich can be assigned so positively to Vanbrugh, though his influence must have been considerable. Wren attended no further meetings of the Building Committee after 1710 and in 1716 yielded his surveyorship to Vanbrugh altogether. Yet the Queen Anne block of 1715 is definitely by Hawksmore. And it was Hawksmore who drew out, with admirable skill, a most elaborate development of Wren's first design, with a central chapel of formidable grandeur rising from colonnades which echo Bernini rather than Le Vau. This was followed by a second design (1711) showing an independent chapel. Vanbrugh's influence may be behind these ambitious drawings; but the schemes can hardly have been official ones nor, so far as we know, was either considered seriously.

Greenwich, as it stands, cannot but suffer from the anomaly of two great domes facing each other across an avenue which leads to practically nothing – like two cats looking at each other in the absence of a king. Knowing and respecting the reason, one appreciates this deference to the Queen's House. But architecturally one must sympathize with the ambition evident in Hawksmore's project to realize Wren's first conception by over-topping the twin domes with a really tremendous climax on the main axis. With a chapel already in proximate existence, however, as the counterpart of the Hall, such a project had nothing except splendour to recommend it. And the day of royal enterprise in building was nearly over. With Anne, last of the Stuarts, it died.

The main works at Greenwich were stopped in 1710, but Hawksmore's services were retained, nominally to look after the conduits and sewers. In 1711 it was decided to take down Wren's brick Base wing and substitute a stone building; as a first step the Webb end elevation, towards the river, was doubled as had already been done on the east.

Vanbrugh remained Surveyor to Greenwich Hospital till his death in 1726, when Colen Campbell succeeded him and carried out some work towards the new road (the present Romney Road) which had been formed to the north of the Hospital. In 1729 he was succeeded by Thomas Ripley. Hawksmore retained his connexion with the Hospital after Vanbrugh's death and, judging by a phrase in a letter of his to Lord Carlisle (1729), considered the whole fabric as to no small extent his work. In 1728 he wrote a valuable description of the foundation and building of the hospital.

Work at Kensington and St James's

When Queen Anne ascended the throne Whitehall had lain in ruins for four years, and Kensington and St James's were the only London palaces fit to receive her. Neither was really adequate for the metropolitan residence of the sovereign, but at Kensington some attempt was made to convert the rambling building and its untidy surroundings into a reasonably fine setting for the Court. To begin with, emphasis was laid on the gardens. A formal lay-out was adopted, and by June 1704 the Queen had approved the design of a greenhouse, the lovely brick building now commonly known as the Orangery (Plate 108). This was probably built under Vanbrugh's direction, and the design is doubtless his or Hawksmore's or, more probably, a joint work, for which Hawksmore made the drawings. The plan consists of a long rectangle with circular chambers at each end. The half-columns applied to the south front are of the ringed de Brosse type which we meet later at Blenheim (courtyard entrances) and, most conspicuously, at Seaton Delaval and Grimsthorpe. Here at Kensington they appear in England for the first time, and the greenhouse is, indeed, one of the first complete manifestations of the style which triumphed, soon after, at Blenheim.

Also at Kensington, about this time was built a summer-house, possibly the brick and stone 'alcove', consisting of a niche under a pediment, which now stands near the north end of the Serpentine. At the Palace itself sundry additions were made and, after the accession of George I, the substantial suite of state-rooms which has acquired some reputation through having been decorated (1724) by William Kent. Kent was not, as is commonly supposed, the designer of the rooms. Three of them were built by William Benson and so badly done that they had to be secured after his dismissal. Others may be by his successor, Hewett, or that gentleman's deputy. None is of much architectural consequence.

At St James's Palace still less was done than at Kensington. Hawksmore was Clerk-of-Works there from 1715 till his dismissal in the year that Wren was thrown over, 1718. During those years he built the arcaded stable block with terminal pavilions with pointed roofs which still exists; and there is a drawing by him of a Doric colonnade which was not, however, executed.

The importance of the Office of Works may be said to cease with Vanbrugh's death in 1726. Already in 1725 the office of Master Carpenter was filled by William Kent who, whatever his brilliance as painter and architect, could hardly be said to be expert with the plane and chisel. Ten years later, his entry into the office of Master Mason was no less inconsequent. The truth is that the constitution of the Office had become an anachronism. The group of artists and craftsmen in the personal service of the sovereign was no longer a reality. Neither, indeed, was the Sovereign a man who considered the conduct of great works a duty and a right. Henceforth the artist and the craftsman sought patronage wherever it was to be found, in the neighbourhood of the Great Men who, of whatever political colour, held the reins of power in England for the next hundred years.

CHAPTER 19

CHURCHES AND THE UNIVERSITIES
1702–1736

JUST as the Great Fire of 1666 marks a new initiative in church-building, so the Act for building Fifty New Churches of 1711 marks another. Just as Wren's was the great designing mind in the first episode, so Hawksmore's was in the second. Between the two episodes there is a lull. Few churches were built in England between 1685 and 1712, and such as there were mostly echoed in one way or another the work of Wren. Two churches, however, belonging to this vacant interval, are of special interest because they show a decided reaction against the style of the post-Fire churches and point a new way.

The first of these churches, All Saints, Oxford (Plate 109A), built in 1707–10, is a remarkable isolated statement, at once an imitation and a critique of Wren and a directive to his successors. It was designed by Henry Aldrich (1647–1710), the convivial, music-loving Dean of Christ Church, an elderly man, almost of Wren's generation, who compiled a careful treatise on Vitruvius and Palladio (published long after his death). He knew Hawksmore, who almost certainly gave him some help. All Saints, though at first sight quite foreign to Wren's mode of church design, is, in fact, closely similar in type to St Lawrence Jewry. It is, that is to say, a great pilastered hall with a flat, beamed ceiling, lit by two ranges of windows, the upper range being in a wonderfully useless attic storey. The main difference between Wren's church and Aldrich's is one of architectural rhetoric. Wren was satisfied that his interior should have pilasters, spaced very openly, and his exterior a columned frontispiece on the one conspicuous elevation, the east. Aldrich, on the other hand, grilled his entire church with a tremendous and strictly disciplined Corinthian order and an answering order within, all without compromise and on a truly handsome scale. All Saints is really a costly revision of St Lawrence's, with everything tightened up and without the slightest ambiguity of emphasis. Aldrich's steeple, similarly, is a bold revision of that of St Mary-le-Bow with much omitted and the emphasis clear-cut.

The enterprise, the sense of power, evinced in Aldrich's church is the keynote of the new school of church design. It is an aspect of the Baroque spirit, in that it conduces to the emphatic dominion of the principal order so that the conception of the whole is understood at a single sweep of the eye. Incidentally, this manner of building cost a great deal more money than was ever available to Wren for a parish church.

Something of this new spirit entered into another church of this period, equally lonely in time and lonelier in its provincial environment. St Philip's, Birmingham (Plate 109B; now the Cathedral), was built to accommodate some of the town's increasing population in 1709–15. The architect, Thomas Archer (see pp. 175–6), was himself one of the Commissioners under the Act obtained for the purpose. The church he designed owes rather less to Wren than does Aldrich's at Oxford, though the plan, with its curved chancel walls, and western tower rising between squares (assigned to gallery staircases), seems to derive from St Clement Danes. The general treatment, however, is, as one would expect from Archer, strongly tinged with Italian Baroque. For the nave arcades he adopted a type of design which Wren never tried, introducing, instead of columns, square fluted piers and bringing the arches directly down on to their (Doric) capitals. Such a treatment he could have seen at Genoa and, perhaps, elsewhere in Italy, though not, as here, with gallery-fronts wedged between the piers. Still more Italian, and more pronouncedly Baroque, is the tower with its concave sides; while much of the detail is Borrominesque. The total result is a curious hybrid, the homeliness of the English plan making an unlikely setting for such sophisticated detail. But All Saints, Oxford, and St Philip's, Birmingham, forecast correctly, in a general way, the kind of church which was to issue from the great State initiative of 1711 – a kind embodying much of Wren's invention, but declaring with infinitely greater force its loyalty to Antique standards, and asserting those standards in orders of great height and uncompromising discipline.

The Act for 'Building... fifty new churches of stone and other proper Materials, with Towers or Steeples to each of them' was passed in 1711. It was a High Church gesture on the part of the new Tory government, aiming ostensibly at the provision of church accommodation in those expanding outer suburbs of London whose little old churches had long been ludicrously inadequate. Had the new administration remained long in power it is conceivable that fifty churches might have been built. In fact, only a dozen new structures owed their existence wholly to the Act, while a few more received assistance, and the funds (deriving from a familiar source – coal dues) were spread over sundry other architectural obligations outstanding from previous reigns.

That the Commissioners under the Act took their work with great seriousness is evident from the number of models which they had made. They obtained a most interesting report from Wren, a classic statement of the functions and form of the 'auditory' type of church. From Vanbrugh, a Commissioner, they had a more rhetorical document, pressing for grandeur of siting, for porticoes, for solidity of construction and adding (rather curiously) a caution against over-lighting.

The Commissioners appointed two Surveyors to design and supervise the churches at a salary of £200 each. They were Nicholas Hawksmore, who worked for the Commissioners from 1711 till his death twenty-five years later, and William Dickinson. Dickinson left in 1713 to take up a post in the Works and built nothing. He was succeeded by James Gibbs who, having built one notable church, was jobbed out in 1715 because of his political affiliations and was succeeded by John James who, likewise, contributed one church and added a tower to another.

Thus, the senior and only continuously effective architect involved was Nicholas Hawksmore, and the six churches he built are the chief works associated with him personally as an architect.

In examining Hawksmore's churches, three influences should be borne in mind. First, it must be remembered that he was trained by Wren and that Wren's work is always the first place to look for constituents of the Hawksmore style. Second, we must understand

Hawksmore's almost morbid passion for classical archaeology, his wide reading, his interest in reconstructions and in the less hackneyed specimens of Roman building; and that slightly childish delight in everything Latin, which induced him to title his drawings with long, far-fetched Latin equivalents for English words.[1] Thirdly, there is a streak of Gothic retrospection. Sometimes, it is evident, Hawksmore is trying to work out Roman equivalents of Gothic compositions, to obtain medieval effects with components as nearly as possible antique. Naturally, it is in his turrets and steeples that this propensity is most evident.

The first two churches built by Hawksmore under the Act were St Alphege, Greenwich (1712–14), and St Anne, Limehouse (1712–24). St Alphege's is a great flat-ceiled rectangular hall (Doric externally) with transeptal projections equidistant from the ends – a shape possibly suggested by a passage in Vitruvius.[2] There is an eastern portico with an open arch in the pediment – a typically late-Roman arrangement which Wren had introduced in the Great Model for St Paul's and hinted at in the transepts of the executed cathedral. St Anne's (Plate 112) is altogether on different lines. It goes to Wren for its four-column plan, but there are east and west 'transepts' and the tower is a wonderful paraphrase of the medieval Boston 'stump'. The receding buttress profiles, the great windows, the lantern, and its attached pinnacles are all effectively emulated in Roman language.

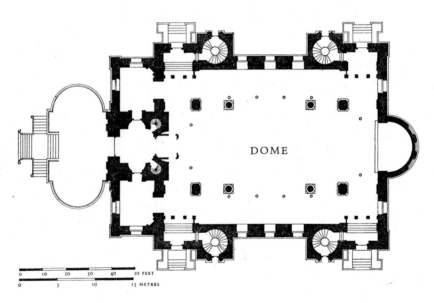

DOME

Figure 28. St George-in-the-East

The next church, St George-in-the-East (1715–23; gutted 1941), also has the 'central' plan (Figure 28) and again the tower (Plate 110B) is on the Gothic theme, though hardly so successful. Four staircase-towers rise above the nave roof into open turrets, almost certainly deliberate paraphrases of those of King's College Chapel; but the doorways at the bases of these towers are among the least explicable of Hawksmore's inventions.[3] St Mary

Woolnoth (Plate 113A), a rebuilding of a City Church which escaped the Fire but fell into decay, followed in 1716–27. Here the plan is most unusual: a square space with triads of columns at each corner supporting the entablature, above which the square space rises in order to provide a clerestory consisting of four great semicircular windows. The exterior of the church has a most interesting relationship to Wren's Mansartesque doorway at the base of the tower of St Mary-le-Bow (Plate 76A). Taking the including arch

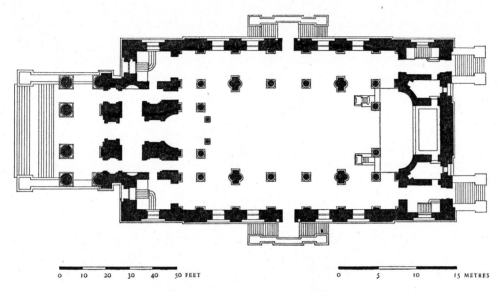

Figure 29. Christ Church, Spitalfields

which frames this doorway, Hawksmore inserts it in his west front, but produces the lines of its rustic quoins right across the façade and repeats them upwards as far as the main cornice, thus creating a frontispiece of funereal grandeur, upon which the Corinthian belfry stands. Then, on the north front, he takes the Wren doorway once more and, reducing the scale of it, converts it into a great window feature, inserting a lunette in the top, filling the centre with a panel and reducing the inner arch to a tiny niche between the pedestals of two columns. This window feature (it is in fact a decorative substitute for large windows), three times repeated, has the grandest possible effect; and it would be hard to find a better illustration of Hawksmore's use of Wrennian material and his power to convert it into something new, something with the powerful unity of the Baroque.[4]

St George's, Bloomsbury (1720–30; Plate 113B), is another square church lit from a clerestory. The Corinthian portico raised on a podium reminds us that Hawksmore was interested in the then hardly known temples of Baalbek (see p. 191), while the upper stages of the steeple, crowned by a figure of George II, embody the idea expressed in Pliny's description of the tomb of Mausolus. The last of the churches is Christ Church, Spitalfields (1723–9; Plates 110A and 111A; Figure 29). Here, the general aspect of the interior is that of the Vitruvian basilica, though heightened in proportion to admit of arches between the entablature and the clerestory, these arches continuing as barrel vaults across the aisle bays, in the manner evolved by Wren at St James's, Piccadilly. The west tower of this church is the most obviously 'medieval' of any, being crowned by a broach spire; though, in perspective, the broad face of the tower and its narrow in-curving sides give an effect of extreme strangeness, without parallel in any church of any age.

Archer's Churches

Two of the 'fifty' churches were designed neither by Hawksmore nor by any of the three architects who were successively his colleagues, but by Thomas Archer. Archer had been made a Commissioner through Harley's influence, no doubt on the strength of having designed almost the only recent large town church in England. For the Commission he

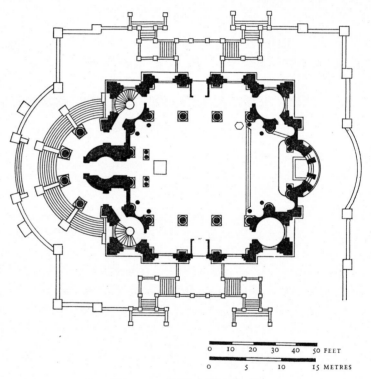

Figure 30. St Paul, Deptford

designed St Paul, Deptford (1712–30; Plate 114A; Figure 30), and St John's, Westminster (1714–28). Both these highly important and interesting churches are closely allied to Hawksmore's style, but show (what Hawksmore's work never shows) the direct influence of the Baroque churches of Rome, which Archer, of course, will have known at first hand. Thus, the plan of the Deptford church, though owing, in outline, something to its Hawksmore neighbour at Greenwich, derives essentially from S. Agnese, Rome. It is not (like S. Agnese) domed but is, all the same, 'central' in type with a giant Corinthian order arranged much on the pattern of the Roman church. The semicircular west portico is also, no doubt, a Roman inspiration, though the charming circular steeple above it is closer in style to such recent English creations as the St Paul's bell-towers and St Vedast. Archer's other church, St John's, Westminster, has always had the reputation of being ugly, which in some ways it is, for it is neither emphatically orientated nor yet as square as its four identical towers would seem to insist. Moreover, the two porticoes (east and west) are surmounted by pediments of unforgettably fantastic form, their raking sides being interrupted and then immediately resumed to meet at the apex, the isolated central section being carried on an arch over two clusters of pilasters in the space where the tympanum of the pediment should be. The theme is, in principle, as old as Rubens's screen in the courtyard of his house at Antwerp, and behind this one suspects the influence of some north Italian Mannerist prototype. The interior of this church, reconstructed after a fire in 1758 and burnt again in 1941, was originally a Corinthian affair, on the four-column plan, in character not unlike the Deptford church.

St Mary-le-Strand

If Archer's churches have certain elements in common with Hawksmore's (due, one suspects, to a certain amount of collaboration among members of the Commission and their Surveyors) the same cannot be said of the single church designed for the Commissioners by James Gibbs. The career of this architect, and his later and more important church, St Martin's-in-the-Fields, will be dealt with in a separate chapter, but it is appropriate to treat of St Mary-le-Strand (1714–17; Plate 114B) among its sister churches, offspring of the famous Act. Gibbs, as we shall see, was unique among his contemporaries by reason of his having studied his art in the studio of a famous Roman architect, Carlo Fontana, and it is not surprising, therefore, to find in St Mary's, his first important commission after his return to England, very distinct reflexions of his Roman studies. It would be wrong, however, to suppose that the church is in the manner of Fontana or even to describe it as Baroque; for, in reality, it is conceived more in the spirit of the Mannerists of the sixteenth century than in that of the Baroque masters (including Fontana) of the seventeenth.

The general proportions will have been fixed by the unusual site allotted to it in a crowded thoroughfare, and a plan had, in fact, already been made by Gibbs's predecessor, Dickinson, very like that of the executed building. The church is a single, barrel-vaulted cell, the walls, internally and externally, being divided into two storeys for the purpose of architectural treatment. The church is thus the only one of the period which deliberately avoids the use of the single giant order, and this gives it a smallness of scale which is in sharp contrast to the essentially big, broad, and bold works of Hawksmore and Archer.

For the theme of his main exterior elevations Gibbs went, not to Wren, nor to contemporary Baroque Rome, but to the early sixteenth century and the Palazzo Branconio dall' Aquila, at Rome, a building attributed to Raphael, destroyed in the seventeenth century, but recorded in an engraving. Its façade was in two main storeys, the upper storey having the series of tabernacled windows with alternate pointed and curved pediments which are the main theme of the north and south fronts of St Mary's. The adoption of this essentially Mannerist design, with its characteristic equivocation between an order used as a colonnade and as a series of tabernacles, detaches the building at once from the Hawksmore school and discovers that tendency to deliberate rhythmical complexity in Gibbs's work which we shall meet again, notably in the Radcliffe Library at Oxford.

St Mary's was designed, originally, to have nothing but a bell-turret over the west front. Some way from the church there was to be a monumental column to Queen Anne, and designs for this, by both Gibbs and Hawksmore, exist.[5] A bronze statue of the Queen was cast in Italy; but on her death the whole thing was abandoned and Gibbs was told to enlarge his bell-turret into a tower. This he most successfully did, carrying up from the west front a tower of three stages, somewhat in the manner of Wren's shorter steeple at St Stephen, Walbrook.

Other Churches of the Period

The only other really important church built under the Act was St George's, Hanover Square (1712–24), the principal work of its architect, John James (1672–1746). James (usually styled 'of Greenwich'), the son of a country parson and a man of some education, had been officially employed at Greenwich since 1705 and Master Carpenter at St Paul's since 1711, when he was employed to give the design for this church. His appointment as Surveyor to the Commissioners (succeeding Gibbs) followed three years later. St George's has the distinction of being the first of the churches to include a full-scale hexastyle Corinthian portico in its design, anticipating Hawksmore's Bloomsbury church and Gibbs's St Martin's by several years. Behind and above this portico, rising out of the church, is a bell-tower, and here again James anticipates Gibbs in producing a new combination of the components essential to a church. This bell-tower, however, bears a relation to the portico more like that of Wren's at Chelsea Hospital (which it resembles in many points) than to that of Gibbs at St Martin's where the bell-tower has grown into a full-size steeple. The interior of St George's approximates to the St James's, Piccadilly, type – an answer perhaps to Wren's instancing this church in his report to the Commissioners as 'beautiful and convenient' and the best solution he had found to the problem of enabling a large congregation 'to hear distinctly, and to see the Preacher'.

The churches of St John, Horsleydown (1728–33; gutted 1941 and demolished 1948), and St Luke, Old Street (1727–33), two more churches of this group, are memorable chiefly for the bizarre attempts on the part of their architects (possibly William Tuffnell in the first case and George Dance, senior, in the second) to substitute a grotesquely distorted column and a Roman obelisk, respectively, for a spire. Other churches assisted under the Act include those of Woolwich (1727–40) and Gravesend (1731–3), both by local builders, and St George's, Southwark (1734–6), a rather clumsy building by John Price (d. 1736) whose work is also recorded at places as far apart as Colchester and Yarmouth (St George's, 1714; a crude imitation of St Clement Danes).

The application of the Act of 1711 was, of course, exclusively metropolitan, and it cannot be said that it was the signal for any great outcrop of church-building in the counties. Probably the initiative of the town of Birmingham in building St Philip's had a greater effect, at least in the Midlands. This seems to be proved by such churches as those at Whitchurch, Salop., and Burton-on-Trent (both by members of the Smith family of Warwick), and by the ambitious and fine church of St Paul's, Sheffield (begun 1720; demolished by the Corporation, 1929), where the mason-architect, Robert Platt (c. 1699–1743), of Rotherham, combined some of the features of Archer's Birmingham church with a steeple based on St Magnus the Martyr. There are many other cases.

From this account of early eighteenth-century church-building one church in particular has been omitted – in some ways the most important of all, St Martin's-in-the-Fields. Its peculiarly personal character warrants this detachment, for it must be seen as part of the whole *opus* of its architect, Gibbs. Along with St Martin's we must omit also for the present that singular brood of churches which owe their form, in whole or in part, to Gibbs's example and the influence of his famous book. St Martin's-in-the-Fields in particular and Gibbs's influence in general we shall return to in a future chapter. Meanwhile we must consider the Universities.

The Universities: Oxford

Both at Oxford and Cambridge there was considerable rebuilding in the first half of the eighteenth century, and in both places it was stimulated and in part conducted by dons who were also *virtuosi* and who promoted on all appropriate occasions the direction of such funds as might be available to the rebuilding of colleges. These rebuildings, rarely called for by any absolute need for expansion or reconstruction, were chiefly rendered possible by bequests and gifts. Energetic heads of colleges solicited such benefactions. Such members of the universities as possessed private fortunes contributed from time to time; while marginal sums were found, when necessary, by the college exchequers. Both Oxford and Cambridge owe many of their handsomest classical buildings to this confident and open-handed period of their history and to the initiative of the amateurs who, without paying the piper, were enthusiastic in calling the tune.

Oxford, on the whole, presents the more interesting picture. The great *virtuosi* were, first, Dean Aldrich of Christ Church, whom we have already (p. 184) mentioned and, after him, George Clarke (1661–1736), Fellow of All Souls, who in addition to his academic and architectural interests, was at various times Secretary at War, joint Secretary to the Admiralty, and a Lord of the Admiralty. As their chief architectural adviser, the colleges employed Nicholas Hawksmore, while the man on the spot, with a hand in every Oxford building project, was the mason-architect William Townesend (d. 1739). These four names stand for a phase in Oxford building with strong characteristics of its own.

Dean Aldrich's All Saints Church we have already characterized as a vigorous revision of some of Wren's church ideas, suggesting that Hawksmore participated. It is certain that Hawksmore knew Aldrich, because both were interested in the publication, at Oxford in 1703, of Henry Maundrell's *Journey from Aleppo*, for which Hawksmore supplied illustrations of the Temples at Baalbek. Those illustrations are borrowed direct from Jean Marot's *L'Architecture françoise* ('le grand Marot'), where, for some curious reason, seventeen plates of Baalbek are given. The plates will have appealed to Hawksmore's passionate love of Roman archaeology, and although one can only guess the extent to which they promoted his (and Vanbrugh's) love of giant orders, it is obvious that their particular kind of colonnaded grandeur (with, here and there, an order embracing two storeys) was exactly in harmony with the new spirit which we find in English architecture from the time of Castle Howard and the post-Fire Whitehall designs.

The Oxford story opens with Aldrich's rebuilding of Peckwater Quad., Christ Church (Plate 115A), in 1705–6. Three sides of the quad. and the return façades are continuously pilastered, following very closely the design of the 'Inigo Jones' house in Lincoln's Inn Fields. In the centre of each side, however, the pilasters become three-quarter columns and the five central bays uphold a pediment breaking through the balustrade. The triple repetition of this theme and the banal junction of the centre with the two side wings, declare the design an amateur's conception. The Palladian restraint of the whole is, however, remarkable for its date.

It was probably as early as 1705 that Aldrich made his proposal to close the open (southern) end of Peckwater with a magnificent library, standing free of the other buildings and adorned by a giant Corinthian order, rising from a low plinth to an entablature at roof level. It is difficult not to associate Aldrich's first design with his interest in Baalbek, whose grandiloquence it forcibly suggests; for it was not till the design had been several times re-cast by George Clarke, after Aldrich's death, that it took on the obviously Michelangelesque character of the building as we know it. It was begun by Townesend, under Clarke's supervision, in 1717 and not completed till after 1729.

These buildings at Christ Church, with All Saints and the Fellows' Building, Corpus Christi College (1706–12; the elevations resemble Peckwater), are the chief works ascribed to Aldrich. He died in 1710, by which year the initiative in Oxford architecture had passed to George Clarke of All Souls and Provost Lancaster of Queen's.

Queen's College (Plate 116A) started, on the strength of a legacy from a former Fellow, to rebuild its front quadrangle in 1709, with Hawksmore advising, and William Townesend as contracting mason. The project, as ambitious as any in Oxford of its time, included the rebuilding of hall and chapel as a symmetrical block, with two residential wings stretching to the High Street and joined by a screen and gateway. No drawings by or payments to Hawksmore are recorded, but the conception is certainly his. Its point of departure is the French college or *hôtel*, as copiously exemplified in Marot, and there are features (particularly the attics marking the centres of the wings) more obviously French than is usual with Hawksmore. But we easily recognize his hand in the hall-and-chapel block where he goes to his master's Chelsea Hospital and gives us a fine restatement of its principal theme, a central Doric portico of four columns, above which is silhouetted a stone cupola. It was not until Hawksmore's very last years that the closing screen and gateway were completed, thanks to a gift of £2000 from Queen Caroline. Her statue stands in the little circular temple over the gate, a temple which, if we are right in associating it with the shrine of Diana in the temple at Ephesus, as engraved in *Parentalia*, once again reflects Hawksmore the archaeologist.

Roman archaeology and the engravings of Marot are, indeed, the pervading influences in Hawksmore's Oxford work, though when we come to All Souls we find a third important influence, that of the Middle Ages, predominating.

All Souls College (Plate 116B) had already considered an ambitious rebuilding scheme, when, in 1708, they obtained a flamboyant North Italian Baroque design from John Talman. In the following year Townesend submitted drawings for a classical building and a 'computation' for rebuilding the hall to match the Gothic chapel. But it was only in 1710, when Christopher Codrington left his library and £10,000 to the College, that impetus was given to a building programme. Hawksmore's services were retained, and in 1714 he produced a design 'showing that ye Colledge ... may be rebuilt after ye Grecian Manner keeping ye old Gothick chapell and Rebuilding ye Hall after ye Gothick'. The design contains no conspicuous provision for a great new library. In 1715, however, the Codrington Library was begun, and in the same year Hawksmore wrote to George Clarke advising, both on practical and historic grounds, against the rebuilding of the front quadrangle. From this date, he appears gradually to have warmed towards a Gothic treatment for the whole of the new buildings, for the Codrington has a Gothic exterior; and although designs for the adjoining cloister (towards Catte Street) dated 1720 are fully classical, the eventual outcome was a new quadrangle entirely in Gothic. The Codrington on the north balances the chapel and (rebuilt) hall on the south; the east side of the quad. has a central feature comprising twin towers in the manner of a Gothic Cathedral front, while the round-arched but strongly medievalized cloister next to Catte Street is interrupted by a gateway surmounted by an ogee dome which Hawksmore described as being 'in ye Monastick manner'. The composition as a whole is a peculiar stylistic compromise, Hawksmore's Gothic readily combining round, four-centred and pointed arches and a French balustrade, while in none of the interiors is there any Gothic at all. The Codrington Library is, internally, an impressively long classical room with the bookcases in two tiers (Doric and Ionic), the Doric entablature projecting as a gallery. The hall has an Ionic screen and a ribbed elliptical ceiling, perhaps as much Townesend's work as Hawksmore's; and the buttery is a neat little essay in geometry consisting of a double-apsed room with two coffered semi-domes and an elliptical dome between them. The Catte Street gate at All Souls, with its 'monastick' cupola, was built as late as 1734 and is thus about equivalent in date to the gate and cupola at Queen's. The choice of a medieval theme in one and a theme from antiquity in the other is typical of that historicism which is such an interesting and often valuable element in Hawksmore's work.

In the years 1712 and 1713 Oxford must continuously have engaged Hawksmore's attention, in spite of his heavy obligations at Blenheim and Greenwich and in connexion with the London churches. The University Printing House (now the Clarendon Building) was built by Townesend, following a Hawksmore design, in 1713–14; its giant Doric portico and the framing of the windows in shallow recesses relate it closely to Queen's. In 1712 or 1713 Hawksmore planned a complete rebuilding of Brasenose. With this, All Souls and Queen's all in his mind together, and yet another great project, a building to house Dr Radcliffe's library, looming ahead, he began to conceive a re-planning of Oxford as a whole. Something of his conception was realized in the placing and general form of the Radcliffe Camera (built eventually by Gibbs, p. 213), and there is evidence that Hawksmore was still interested in this grand and by no means impracticable scheme, within a year or two of his death.

In much that Hawksmore did at Oxford, the vigorous personality of George Clarke is discernible as initiator and promoter, and when Worcester College obtained its charter in 1714 Clarke seems to have been given a free hand in devising a home for it on the site of the buildings of the parent Society, Gloucester Hall. To Clarke, indeed, is attributed the actual design of this college, though there is ample evidence of participation by Hawksmore, as well as, inevitably, Townesend the mason. The college possesses some Hawksmore drawings of special interest in that he names the various sources he has used for his details. On one cornice detail, he quotes the Pantheon and the Arch of Constantine; on another the Farnese Palace and the Bordeaux colonnade given by Perrault; and on a third the 'Tower of Andromachus' (Tower of the Winds) at Athens. His Tower of the Winds, imagined from Vitruvius' slight description, was never built, but it may well be the clue to some features in his church designs. Worcester was begun in 1720, but its completion was long delayed, the north range and the Provost's lodging being completed only in the last quarter of the century.

Clarke died in the same year as Hawksmore, 1736, leaving to Worcester College not only £8000 for buildings but all his books and manuscripts, including those books and drawings which had belonged to Inigo Jones and which to-day make Worcester College a supremely precious repository of architectural history.

Cambridge

Since Wren's time, the principal figure in Cambridge building had been Robert Grumbold (1639–1720), the master-mason for Trinity College Library. Self-trained, presumably, in classical design, he was responsible for parts of Clare College, including the pilastered west (river) front of 1705–6. Grumbold was a fair master of the new vernacular, no more. And the only building project at Cambridge comparable to those undertaken at Oxford was a scheme, of which Hawksmore was the author, for rebuilding most of King's College. The plans date from 1712–13, but nothing came of them, nor of the remarkable re-planning scheme which Hawksmore, on his own initiative, devised at the same time. That scheme, as ambitious and as realistic as his similar project for Oxford, he excused to his employers 'because Cavalier Fontana and others have done the same in cases of like nature', and it is clear that a project in Carlo Fontana's *Templum Vaticanum* was one source of inspiration.

Before anything was done at King's, Hawksmore, too 'luxuriant' and 'exorbitant' for the Fellows, was replaced by James Gibbs. His splendid Fellows' Building we shall discuss in dealing with Gibbs's work as a whole (p. 213). A few years earlier, however, Gibbs had begun the Senate House (1722–30), a building which, for a certain reason, is best dealt with here. The Senate House was designed as one wing of a building forming three sides of an open quadrangle (Plate 115B), with a central hexastyle portico, two similar porticoes facing each other across the court and porticoes at the ends of the wings, the giant order (Corinthian) being expressed in three-quarter columns in the porticoes and continued elsewhere in pilaster form. This rich but somewhat pedestrian composition bears a certain resemblance, in principle, to Aldrich's Peckwater Quad. at Oxford. It has the same faults. It is, moreover, singularly uncharacteristic of the architect of St Martin's-in-the-Fields, so that one is inclined to give some weight to the tradition that the conception originated with the eminent Cambridge *virtuoso*, Sir James Burrough (1691–1764). Burrough was Esquire Bedell from 1727 and Master of Caius from 1754. Dallaway states that 'to all that is excellent in the architecture of the Senate-house, Sir James Borough has the better claim'. Whether it is the excellencies or their converse which should be given to Burrough is a matter of opinion. Standing alone, the Senate House is fine, even if there is some overcrowding of pilasters and windows. But the composition to which it owes its origin one would more willingly give to the young amateur, Burrough, than to the experienced Gibbs.

Burrough came to occupy in Cambridge a position of architectural authority somewhat similar to Clarke's in Oxford. His status, however, developed a professional bias, and at Peterhouse, where he built (1736–41) one wing of the fore-court and its two little entrance portals, he received a professional fee. This and the hall at Queens' College show that Burrough owed more to Gibbs than Gibbs could possibly have owed to him. He was a designer of purely local importance, who 'beautified' chapels and remodelled halls in 'a neat and elegant manner' – which was not far from the manner of James Gibbs.

Apart from Gibbs's works, the most important building erected at Cambridge during Burrough's life-time was the University Library (1754–61), built at right angles to the Senate House with the intention of realizing the courtyard plan (though in another direction) with which that building had begun. To the Senate House, however, the Library makes not the slightest stylistic concession, for its façade has no order and is, in fact, in the style of William Kent, whose Horse Guards was then rising in Whitehall. The explanation is the simple one that its architect, Stephen Wright (d. 1780), an officer in the Works, had at one time been Kent's clerk. The façade of the library is nothing but an expansion of the pavilion units in the Horse Guards, the only pronounced novelty being the carving of a highly effective band of festoons under the main cornice.

NOTES TO CHAPTER 19

1. For instance, *Xenodochii Hemisphaerium Grenwicani* for the dome of Greenwich Hospital!

2. Bk. V, cap. 1, describing the basilica erected by Vitruvius at Fano. Wren probably had this passage in mind when he made the plan of St Magnus in 1670–1.

3. Perhaps they derive from Wren's two doorways (borrowing a theme in Barbaro's Vitruvius) on the river front of Trinity College Library. If they do, the 'working up' is a spectacular performance indeed.

4. There is, incidentally, a Borrominesque twist in the placing of the columns, recalling the windows of the Palazzo Propaganda.

5. In the British Museum (Print Room).

PART FOUR

THE PALLADIAN PHASE
⟨1710−1750⟩

CHAPTER 20

THE PALLADIAN MOVEMENT: BURLINGTON
AND KENT

ABOUT the time that Blenheim was finishing and the Queen Anne churches were rising, when Wren was very old, Vanbrugh and Hawksmore past their prime, and Archer in affluent retirement, English architecture entered a period during which it became increasingly subject to what has appropriately been called the Rule of Taste. During that period, which lasted for about forty years, a set of distinct ideas as to what was good in architecture became widely held, and standards, based on the acknowledged excellence of certain architects and authors, were widely endorsed. This period of consolidation, during which the influence of a small group of architects and amateurs became impressed on the whole output of English building, has long ago become labelled 'Palladian', a description not wholly accurate (as no such labels can be), but accurate enough and secure in acceptance.

How and among whom this Palladian taste became formed it will be our business presently to inquire. The first point to note is that it had nothing to do with Wren, Vanbrugh, Hawksmore, or Archer except in so far as, by excluding the works of these architects from salvation, it was better able to distinguish its own particular sort of grace. The second point to note is that, once formulated, the Palladian taste became the taste of the second generation of the Whig aristocracy, the sons of that Whiggery which dated its accession to power from 1688 and to which, in Anne's time, artistic and intellectual leadership, once centred at the Court, had passed. This second Whig generation had strong beliefs and strong dislikes, conspicuous among the latter being the Stuart dynasty, the Roman Church, and most things foreign. In architectural terms that meant the Court taste of the previous half-century, the works of Sir Christopher Wren in particular and anything in the nature of Baroque.

As spokesmen of that generation, we cannot do better than lend our ear to the Earl of Shaftesbury who, writing from Italy in 1712, expressed himself forcibly concerning English architecture of the age of Wren.[1] 'Thro' several reigns we have patiently seen the noblest publick Buildings perish (if I may say so) under the Hand of one single Court-Architect; who, if he had been able to profit by Experience, wou'd long since, at our

197

expence, have prov'd the greatest Master in the World. But', he continues, 'I question whether our Patience is like to hold much longer', and he consoles himself with the reflexion that a new Whitehall and a new House of Parliament are opportunities still unspoilt. 'Hardly... as the Publick now stands, shou'd we bear to see a *Whitehall* treated like a *Hampton-Court*, or even a new Cathedral like St Paul's.' Shaftesbury was the complete Whig and, according to him, the British people, having solved the fundamental problem of government, were now in the best possible position to develop the arts. To this end, an Academy should be established; and it is with a general plea for such an institution that the letter concludes.

It is noteworthy that Shaftesbury gives no hint as to the character of the reformed architecture of Whig Britain, and although, in another of his writings, he says that it should be 'founded in truth and nature' and 'independent of fancy', he is merely restating an already worn platitude. Shaftesbury's intuition, however, was correct. At the moment he wrote, an architectural movement in Britain was beginning to stir and it did ultimately permeate the whole building capacity of the nation with astonishing thoroughness. Moreover, his notion of an Academy was taken up, as we shall see, almost at once and never quite lost sight of until finally realized in the Royal foundation of 1768. How and when did the new taste begin to appear? To answer this question we must take our bearings from two important books, both published in 1715.

The first of these books was the first volume of *Vitruvius Britannicus*, a folio of 100 engravings of classical buildings in Britain. Volume 2 appeared in 1717 and a supplementary volume in 1725. The author was Colen Campbell (d. 1729).

The second book was a translation of Palladio's *I quattro libri dell' architettura*, in two folio volumes with plates specially redrawn by Giacomo Leoni (1686–1746) and engraved in Holland, and the text translated by Nicholas Dubois (c. 1665–1735), who also supplied an introduction.

These two books have certain things in common. Both are dedicated to George I and thus stamped as Whiggish products. Further, both evince the same distinct architectural loyalties – namely, to Palladio and Inigo Jones as the two modern masters to whom the British architect is to look for guidance, to the exclusion of all others. Further, both books show that their authors knew of the large collections of drawings left by Jones and fully appreciated their importance. That there was no rivalry between the two projects is shown by the fact that Dubois quotes appreciatively from Campbell's introduction in his own.

Here, then, we have two books and three persons – Campbell, Leoni, and Dubois – concerned in the inauguration of a Palladian movement coupled with the name of Inigo Jones. A careful analysis of the contents of Campbell's first volume justifies us in adding a fourth name, perhaps the most important, that of William Benson (1682–1754), the man who was very shortly to succeed Wren as Surveyor of the Works and whose brief occupancy of that office we noted earlier (p. 179). The reason Benson comes into the picture is that in 1710 (according to *Vitruvius Britannicus*) he built for himself Wilbury House, Newton Toney, Wilts. Campbell illustrates it and distinguishes it as being 'in the style of Inigo Jones'. It derives, not from any executed work by Jones but from one of the drawings by him now at the R.I.B.A. It represents, so far as we know, the earliest evidence of anything in the nature of an Inigo Jones revival.[2]

Benson was certainly the most influential of the group. He was Sheriff of Wiltshire in 1710, a prominent Whig writer, and M.P. for Shaftesbury in 1715. He spent some years before 1714 at the Electoral Court of Hanover where, by devising the mechanical parts of the fountains at Herrenhausen, he no doubt prepared his future sovereign's mind for his elevation to the Surveyorship. Giacomo Leoni, a Venetian by birth, had been employed by the Elector Palatine and may conceivably have been picked up by Dubois, who had accompanied Marlborough to Germany as a military engineer. Nicholas Dubois was probably the oldest of the group, having been born about 1665. William III had sent him to Holland as tutor to the son of the Prince of Orange. In 1715 he described himself as one of George I's 'engineers', and in 1719 became (perhaps through Benson's influence) Master Mason.[3] As for Campbell, he was, of course, a Scotsman and launched his *Vitruvius Britannicus* under the patronage of the Scottish nobility in general and the clan Campbell in particular. He had built a house in Glasgow for one of the clan in 1712 and had perhaps come south in pursuit of the large number of Scottish notables who had made for London after the Union of 1707. A document of 1719 describes him as Benson's 'agent'.

In 1718 Benson succeeded Wren as Surveyor-General. He proved his incompetence with so little delay that he was removed (and promoted) in 1719. Already, however, both Campbell and Dubois were associated with the Royal Works and only Leoni (who as an Italian and a Catholic could hardly expect such preferment) was left out of the party. It was in 1718 that, against Wren's wishes, a balustrade was ordered to be built upon the parapet of St Paul's and this was, no doubt, done at the instance of Benson and in imitation of Jones's Banqueting House.

The relations of this group of architects cannot be precisely determined, but it looks as if Campbell, Dubois, and Benson between them initiated both the Palladian movement and its counterpart, the Inigo Jones revival.

Why, and under what inspiration, did these people seek so energetically the diversion of English taste from the French, Dutch, and Baroque models of Wren, Hawksmore, Vanbrugh, and Archer? The motive probably has some connexion with that search for absolutes with which the French Academy had for many years been concerned and which had given rise to much painful argument between 'ancients' and 'moderns', between those who believed that the architecture of antiquity comprehended a *complete* rational system of architecture and those who held that innovation was to a certain extent permissible. Those quarrels, by 1710, had become quiescent in France, but the search for absolutes was open to anybody to resume and in England it had some flavour of novelty, while Vanbrugian Baroque offered a wonderful target for polemics. Moreover, the dawning philosophy of Whiggism was extremely propitious to a thesis which embraced, at one and the same time, a devotion to antiquity, a flexibility authorized jointly by Palladio and common sense, and a strong national loyalty in the figure of Inigo Jones.

One further point. Not only the reputation (and the drawings) of Inigo but that of Palladio were ready to be exploited here in England, for as far back as 1665 Evelyn had published his translation of Roland Fréart's *Parallèle*, a book of pronouncedly Palladian prejudice. The new Palladians had but to select threads from the English past and draw them together.

How far the two publications of 1715 would have affected the course of English architecture without the intervention from an influential quarter which followed hard upon them can only be guessed. A reversion to some kind of doctrinaire classicism would certainly have come about, but the Palladian movement could hardly have attained the momentum it did without the intervention of one particular personality whose name soon became identified with the movement – the Earl of Burlington.

Burlington and Campbell

Richard Boyle, 3rd Earl of Burlington and 4th Earl of Cork (1694–1753), succeeded to his titles at the age of nine, and was thus brought up in an atmosphere of impending responsibility which probably affected his after-life considerably. Before he was twenty the responsibilities began to descend. Appearing to a letter-writer of 1713 simply as 'a good-natured, pretty gentleman', he became in his twenty-first year a member of the Privy Council, *Custos Rotulorum* of the North and West Ridings, and Lord High Treasurer of Ireland. The acceptance of those offices did not, apparently, interfere with a Grand Tour he made to Italy in 1714–15, but the visit must have been brief, for he was back in time to celebrate his coming of age in April 1715. By that date he already had a consuming enthusiasm for architecture. He had (presumably before his departure for Italy) subscribed for two copies of *Vitruvius Britannicus*, and perhaps knew something of its author, who was just then making a great name for himself by building Wanstead (Plate 117A), the great house in Essex (1715–20; demolished 1822), for Sir Richard Child, later Earl Tylney. Wanstead was an enormously long block of building, superficially like the garden block of Castle Howard, but treated in the Palladian manner with a full-scale hexastyle portico which Campbell claimed as the first erected in Britain.

Burlington must at once have recognized in the Wanstead designs and in the general tenor of *Vitruvius Britannicus* a point of view which he was prepared to adopt as his own; and very soon he was employing Campbell to remodel Burlington House in London. Or rather, to take over the remodelling from somebody else, for it seems that when Campbell came on the scene a new stable wing had been built eastwards of, and at right angles to, the original building; and two quadrants of Doric columns of impressive dimensions had also been erected. Campbell carefully excludes the name of his predecessor from his account of Burlington House, but it was almost certainly James Gibbs, whom as a rival Scottish architect (incidentally, in the Tory camp) Campbell probably regarded with hostility. That the stable-block and colonnades have points in common with Bruce's Hopetoun House tends to confirm the attribution to Gibbs who was the only other architect in London, besides Campbell, likely to have known the building.

In any case, the new buildings did not, evidently, accord with Burlington's newly determined criteria and when Campbell refaced the old house (the date usually given is 1717) he modelled the design closely on Palladio, in particular on his Palazzo Porto-Colleoni at Vicenza. Most of the front survives, though embedded in additions of 1866.

Probably through pressure from Burlington, if not through Benson, Campbell was commissioned to build the Rolls House (destroyed) in Chancery Lane, in 1717–18, although the work would normally have been done by the Office of Works. Between that date and his (possibly early) death in 1729 he built a dozen or more country-houses, mostly either around London or in the north, where Burlington had extensive influence. He included many of his own works in the second and third volumes of *Vitruvius Britannicus*, and all share the same rather cringing loyalty to his two heroes – Palladio and Jones. The most obvious derivation of them is Mereworth, Kent (1723; Plate 117B), a version of Palladio's Villa Rotonda, near Vicenza. His plans are always compact blocks of rectangles of the proportions to be found in Palladio and there are few concessions to English usage, apart from the greater amplitude of the staircase and its accompaniment by a service stair going the full height of the house. The Hall, entered centrally, is now simply a grandiose vestibule.

Campbell must have the credit (if credit is the word) of having invented what we loosely call the 'Palladian house' – the great blockish mansion with or without wings, often with a portico but otherwise sparingly adorned with elements drawn from a very limited and frigid vocabulary of ornament. It was not a particularly original invention, only a rather tepid abstraction from Palladio and Jones; but it was successful, because it was exactly suited to the temper of the age. To us now it may seem pompous and artificial; but to the Whig mind of the 1720s it was a good expression of that moderation, that resistance to 'fancy' and 'enthusiasm', that balanced combination of the useful and the beautiful, of prosperity and good breeding which was its ideal.

Campbell's influence was very great, partly because it required no inordinate skill to imitate him and partly, no doubt, because of the circulation of his designs in *Vitruvius Britannicus*. Wanstead, in particular, struck deep into the minds of his contemporaries, accounting not only for direct imitations in several parts of England but, as we shall see in the next chapter, for the conception of the town-house block as a palatial unity.

All this has taken us some distance from Lord Burlington, and it is necessary to explain, without delay, that his way and Campbell's parted very shortly after the refronting of Burlington House. In the summer of 1719, the Earl departed once again for Italy, this time with the direct intention of studying Palladio and collecting all available information about him. He had, two years before, erected his own first building, a bath-house on his estate at Chiswick (wholly dependent, in style, on Campbell), and was now presumably intent on developing his own powers as well as promoting those of others. He also seems to have had in mind the formation of something in the nature of an Academy of Arts or at least of a practising combination of architect, sculptor, and painter, based on Burlington House. An architect he already had in Campbell; a sculptor he had found in the person of Guelfi, who lived for many years in his house; while as for a painter, there was in Rome a young Yorkshireman called William Kent, whom he had met on his first visit and whom he now proposed to invite to complete the decorative painting at Burlington House.

Burlington and Kent

Burlington brought Kent back to England at the end of 1719, lodged him in Burlington House, and set him to work. That was the beginning of an association between the two men which lasted until Kent's death in 1748, a period of nearly thirty years: an association which was to have surprising and far-reaching results, not indeed for English painting, in which Kent proved a negligible figure, but for architecture and, perhaps most of all, for the art of landscape-gardening.

William Kent (1685–1748) was born in Yorkshire, of humble parents, and apprenticed (says Vertue) to a coach-painter and house-painter. He broke his articles, however, and went to London. There he was fortunate in being taken up by some Yorkshire gentlemen who provided the means to send him to Rome, where he went with John Talman and another and where he must have spent about nine or ten years, mostly in the studio of Luti, on copying Guido Reni and Guercino for his English patrons. With childlike faith in young Kent's genius the Yorkshire squires paid out his allowance (it cost them little enough) and plied him with instructions on what to paint, what to collect for them, and, above all, instructions to study, 'donec Raphael secundus eris'.

He met all the English visitors, including Coke of Holkham, whose great house he was eventually to build, and, of course, Burlington.

The relations between Burlington and Kent (the Earl's senior by eleven years) were clearly something rather different from those ordinarily subsisting between a nobleman and his professional retainer. They became extremely fond of each other, as the letters between them show. Kent had vitality and a lack of restraint which went, one imagines, straight to the heart of the young patrician, so formally bred and so early harnessed in the trappings of statesmanship. Kent, in his letters, rambles ungrammatically on to his dear patron, the subject always their mutual enthusiasms in the arts; nor did anything disturb this happy friendship of nearly a lifetime.

Burlington's first attempts to raise his friend's genius to the place where he believed it to belong were not altogether fortunate. Insisting that he was the first great History painter England had produced, he managed to secure for him, over the head of Thornhill, the Serjeant Painter, a commission to execute the wall-paintings in the new rooms at Kensington Palace. This gross intrusion of a favourite (a parallel, no doubt, to the capture of the Rolls House for Campbell) might have been very well if Kent's work had proved of high excellence. But it did not. His *chiaroscuro* architecture was fair, but his figure-groups and trophies were far below what Thornhill had shown himself capable of, and his 'grotesque-work' is inferior to what the serjeant painters of the previous century had done.

The Kensington work proceeded through the years 1721–7, during which time Burlington himself was maturing as an architect. That he was an architect in all but the professional sense, that he did, at any rate, make designs which were entirely the product of his own thought and pencil, has now been proved beyond dispute.[4] And those designs, most of which precede Kent's conversion from painting to architecture, are of the utmost importance. They include, in 1721, the Dormitory at Westminster School, Petersham Lodge, Surrey (destroyed), and Tottenham Park, Wiltshire (rebuilt in the nineteenth century).

These designs were made while Wren was still alive; while Vanbrugh was building Seaton Delaval and Hawksmore completing his London churches. Indeed, Wren and Hawksmore both produced designs for the Westminster building. Burlington turned his back on all these men and worked away by himself, remorselessly adhering to principles, explicit and implied, in Palladio and Jones. These principles were, in the first place, the system of proportion derivable from Palladio's second book; and in the second place rules of precedent, limiting the choice of themes to what the two masters had used or to what they had discovered and recommended in the works of antiquity.

It might be supposed that, working on these lines, Burlington's results would have been more or less indistinguishable from Campbell's. But that was not the case. Infinitely more fastidious than Campbell, he had a curiously pedantic feeling for the separateness of each component in a design, and this resulted in what Wittkower has well called a *staccato* manner, an over-articulation which loved to cap each pavilion, each projecting centre, with a distinguishing pediment, or attic. This tendency is well illustrated in the designs for Tottenham Park, but it recurs throughout Burlington's work, one notable exception being the Westminster dormitory where, logically enough in view of its single uncomplicated function, the building is an unrelieved mass, the openings constituting one unit which repeats from end to end.

Burlington's own personal *œuvre* appears to have consisted of about a dozen works, mostly houses for his friends or public buildings in whose erection he figured as patron, if not donor. In 1725 he began to build, on his estate at Chiswick, an ornamental villa (Plate 118), consisting entirely of state-rooms and attached by a short wing to the old Jacobean family residence. This villa is, superficially, an imitation of Palladio's Rotonda, post-dating Campbell's similar essay at Mereworth by only a couple of years. But there is far more in it than that. Only one façade follows the Rotonda with any faithfulness, the fenestration towards the garden introduces Jonesian features, the plan is developed with reference to the Palazzo Thiene, while the steps to the portico have been traced by Wittkower to a Piedmontese source. Even in this uncompromisingly square design, Burlington's *staccato* is in evidence, in the spacing of windows and niches and in the sudden prominence of the dome, raised on a high octagon drum.

This building and the lovely Assembly Room at York (1730; Plate 119), an exact model of Palladio's Egyptian Hall, based on Vitruvius, are among Burlington's chief works, but his genius as an innovator cannot be assessed by these alone, for there is no doubt that it is from Burlington that Kent derived all that is most significant in his own style. And to William Kent we must now return.

The Works of William Kent

Kent's metamorphosis from painter to architect proceeded gradually, and always, it seems, under Burlington's direction. He had acquired some knowledge of the subject in

Rome, and his painted architecture at Kensington is not unskilful. Then, in 1724, Burlington induced him to undertake the editing of the *Designs of Inigo Jones*, which appeared in 1727. This close contact with Inigo's work formed Kent's style in interior decoration: nearly all his chimney-pieces, ceilings, and door-cases bear the impress of Jones and the people from whom *he* borrowed, such as Barbet. It was not till after 1730 that Kent, then well into his forties, became the complete architect. He had, to be sure, been Master Carpenter in the Works since 1725, and it is fair, perhaps, to date his conversion to architecture from then. In 1735, after several important works had been built under his name, he proceeded to the traditionally greater office of Master Mason and thence, in 1737, to that of Deputy Surveyor (the Surveyor himself being then a mere place-man). Kent's greatest period of activity was from 1730 to 1739 and in 1734 his most representative work, Holkham, was begun.

Holkham Hall, Norfolk (Plates 120 and 121A; Figure 31), may well owe as much to Burlington as to Kent, for it emerges directly from Tottenham Park (in plan) and the Chiswick villa (in fenestration and the relationships of some of the rooms). It consists of a great rectangular block with corner pavilions raised into low towers, attached at the angles to four other blocks each with a high pedimented centre and lower sides, also pedimented. A *staccato* sense of detachment, characteristic of Burlington, runs through the whole. The Venetian window contained under a relieving arch, the main theme of the Chiswick garden front, is conspicuous here again; it is essentially a self-isolating theme, and nowhere in Holkham is a repetitive rhythm of identical openings allowed to assert itself for a moment. Indeed, in the whole design of Holkham there is hardly a single case where two adjacent openings in the same plane are of the same design! Therein is the essential character of this, as of so much of Burlington's and Kent's work. Each section of a design is autonomous, related to the whole only by a general system of ratios and by strict symmetry.

The entrance-hall at Holkham is, in itself, one of the great monuments of the Burlington school. It is an apsidal hall, a combination (as Wittkower has shown) of the Roman basilica and the 'Egyptian Hall' given by Palladio after Vitruvius. Inigo Jones had proposed something of this kind for a Council Chamber in his Whitehall scheme. At Holkham the apse contains a flight of steps, narrowing to the space between the two centre columns, behind which the apse opens into an exedra, with a doorway leading to the saloon. The result is theatrical, though the inspiration is not. The drama is that of a splendid museum, a compilation from antiquity and the Renaissance; and perhaps that was exactly the appropriate kind of drama for Lord Leicester, whose collection of Roman antiquities was the most important to be assembled in this country since the time of Arundel.

Closely related to Holkham is the interior of No. 44 Berkeley Square (1742–4; Plate 121B), designed by Kent for Lady Isabella Finch, a relative of Burlington. Here is the most determined attempt, before Adam, to arrange the interior of a London terrace-house in a palatial fashion, and it is most ingeniously done. The stair ascends in one of the apses of a two-apsed compartment, lit from the top. At first-floor level the apse has columns arranged like those at Holkham, and behind them the next flight of the stair winds up

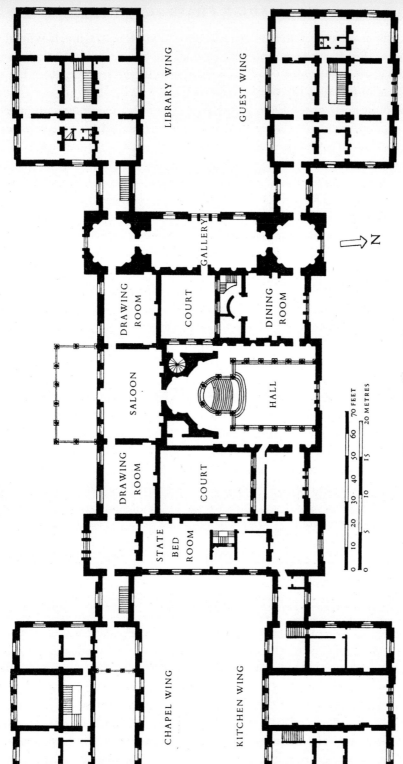

Figure 31. Holkham Hall

against the apse wall, emerging in an open gallery. The effect is, again, theatrical, if rather over-complex. The front drawing-room has, like the saloon at Holkham, a high coved and coffered ceiling, the coffers painted with figure-subjects in grisaille. One feels that one is in the ante-room of a palace.

Kent's various posts in the Office of Works gave him the opportunity of providing designs for government buildings, and in 1732 he produced his first scheme for new Houses of Parliament – that project on which, all through the eighteenth century, were focused the hopes of British architecture. Neither Kent nor Burlington were well equipped to plan a monumental building of this kind, and Palladio's precedents were mostly ecclesiastical or domestic. One would have expected Kent to rely on the Jones designs for Whitehall, which he had published, but in fact he attempted something decidedly original, introducing Jonesian elements only into the plan but not into the elevations. Both in the 1732 design and in those which followed it in 1735–9 (Plate 122B), Burlingtonian square pavilions rising into low towers (sometimes domed) frame and punctuate the composition; the centre part towards the river (and, in one scheme, to Old Palace Yard) was to have a free-standing colonnade on a high rusticated base containing a ground-floor and mezzanine. In all the schemes, the square Hall between the two Houses is covered by a 'Pantheon' dome which, with the portico breaking outwards from the colonnade, would certainly have struck a sonorous Roman note in London's river landscape.

Kent never had the opportunity of putting any of these grandiose and original schemes into execution. He did, however, build the Treasury (1734), where reliance on Jones's Whitehall is evident; and the Horse Guards (c. 1751; Plate 122A) was built from his designs after his death. The Horse Guards is closer to Holkham than anything else in Kent's later work, and the resemblance would be striking if it were not for the clock-tower, which gives such emphasis to the centre of the London building. The broken com-position, with its isolated elements, and the play of Venetian windows are the essential characteristics of both buildings. The King's Mews (1732), on the site of the National Gallery, was another government building for which Kent was responsible – a long, low, plain structure with something very like Campbell's gateway to Burlington House in the centre and square pavilions carrying cupolas suddenly appearing in the centre of each wing. Burlington is reputed to have had a hand in this design and its *staccato* character certainly suggests it.

In all the classical works of Burlington and Kent one feels the effects of that remorseless self-imposed confinement to the two consecrated sources – Palladio and Jones. The Palladian movement could never spread its wings in the Baroque-Rococo air of the European tradition, by now so decoratively fluent. It was a clipped style. Always it was the *unit* which was precious – the single pavilion containing a single Venetian window; the single room, fitted into a jig-saw of other single rooms, all proportioned according to the elementary but strict Palladian code. Burlingtonian design was, in essence, the com-position of these separate units into a single whole, a rigid, inorganic whole whose effect was far from the aims of either Palladio or Jones. It is strange that it so often has qualities of drama and picturesqueness, scarcely the qualities which Burlington set himself to seek.

His mind was essentially classical, anti-romantic; it sought, above all, precedent and method, free from impurity. How deeply Kent shared this view it is difficult to say. Perhaps he shared it because he loved Burlington and had no desire to erect intellectual standards of his own. He was not a thinker; he was only a second-rate artist with a well-developed sense of decoration. He would probably have swum happily enough with any tide of taste.

To assess Kent faithfully, one must take account not only of his decorative painting and his classical architecture, but of his illustrations for the *Faerie Queene* and Gay's *Fables*, his occasional essays in a very personal kind of Gothic, his furniture, and, above all, his landscape-gardening. Kent's Gothic we shall discuss in a later chapter. Of his furniture one need only say that it is singularly variable in style, sometimes affectedly French and at other times (perhaps under his patron's influence) ludicrously architectural. Of his landscape work, though it is not strictly our business, something must be said, because the revolution he effected was a revolution in the relation between a house and its setting, one, therefore, that could not fail to be important for architecture.

It is observable that a strong attraction to a classical point of view instantly admits its antithesis – sentiment. The sentiment for 'nature' in the early eighteenth century was bound up inextricably with the repressive discipline of classical purism; and as the house itself crystallized into something elemental and inevitable, the conception of what its surroundings should be became fluid and accessible to sentiment. The last decades of the seventeenth century had surrendered completely to the French park and garden as the generation of Le Nôtre had understood it: the garden an affair of geometrical *parterres*, the park brought under control by a system of straight lines converging mechanically into *ronds-points*.

The finality of this kind of design bred an aversion. Shaftesbury, whose writings so accurately reflect the mood of his time, confessed (1709) to a preference for the '*genuine* order' of nature over 'the mockery of princely gardens'. Addison and Pope echoed him in different ways. But Kent seems to have been the first to draw plans in which a new kind of gardening practice was implicit. He does not at once discard the traditional geometrical principles (as still embodied, for instance, in the work of Bridgeman), but he blurs them, allows wildness to swim into the pattern. He demolishes the garden walls, substituting sunk fences, and allows the semi-formal garden to merge with the landscape beyond. In the gardens of Carlton House, Claremont, Chiswick, and Stowe, Kent was busy in the early 1730s, re-forming them 'without either level or line'. At Rousham, Oxon., still unaltered, Kent introduced glades, groves, winding paths, and a serpentine stream, running through the woods in a stone-bordered channel; here too may be seen, through the vistas between the glades, rustic cascades, temples, and statues.

In this new gardening Kent was interpreting a literary idea, the sensibility of the man of letters (especially Pope) to his surroundings. The movement was supported by essentially 'literary' discoveries, as for instance that the Chinese enjoyed irregular gardens or, better still, that the Romans had cultivated deliberate wildness and serpentine paths around their villas. Further, the movement was endorsed by the compositions of irregular beauty in the canvases of Claude Lorrain and Salvator Rosa.

The importance to architecture of this new conception of garden-landscape was fundamental, since it reduced the obligation of the house to affirm and command. Vanbrugh's houses, as originally sited, gathered the whole drama of a landscape into their own complex finality of silhouette and recession. The Burlingtonian house is less a command than a statement; it becomes an object not controlling the landscape but seen within it. And such was the nature of the country-house from the time of Burlington onwards. The duller Palladians never understood this and continued to affirm too much, and it was not until the time of Adam, who understood the Burlington manner of composition as perfectly as Burlington himself, that the happiest relation of house-within-landscape was attained.

NOTES TO CHAPTER 20

1. *A Letter concerning the Art or Science of Design.*

2. The present house does not correspond at all closely with Campbell's illustration, but there is no mistaking its architect's intention to imitate Jones.

3. He designed the remarkable circular staircase at Chevening and a large house at Stanmer, Sussex (1722–7), which, while free from any Baroque taint, is not notably Palladian.

4. By R. Wittkower, to whose papers (see Bibliography) I am much indebted in this chapter.

CHAPTER 21

THE INDIVIDUAL CONTRIBUTION OF
JAMES GIBBS

THAT it should be necessary to interrupt the story of Palladianism, its expansion, and its permeation of English architecture, in order to devote a separate chapter to James Gibbs (1682–1754), indicates at once the stature of this architect and his inaccessibility to the more doctrinaire influences of his time. So far, we have met him only as the architect of one of the Queen Anne churches, St Mary-le-Strand (p. 189), a work of very detached and personal character, and as the executive architect of the Cambridge Senate House. It is now time to consider as a whole his long and extremely influential career.

An essential and characteristic fact about Gibbs is that his affiliations were Tory. He is also reputed to have been at one time a Catholic, a fact which, as he was certainly a Scotsman, hints at Jacobitism. He was also a trifle older than most architects of his generation. These facts together place him rather outside the sphere of Whig thought and influence which we discussed in the previous chapter. Born near Aberdeen, of good family, Gibbs was a younger son and rambled off to Holland (where he had an aunt living) and thence through Flanders, France, Switzerland, and Germany to Italy. In Rome he determined to become an architect and obtained admission to the studio of Carlo Fontana, then an old man. He was certainly in Rome between 1707 and 1709, and probably earlier. This was before Kent's time and some fifteen years after Archer's, and he must have been about the only Briton studying architecture in Rome at the time.

Returning to England at a moment when the Vanbrugh-Hawksmore school was paramount, he sought, as we have seen, in St Mary-le-Strand, to make a distinct contribution to English Baroque, a contribution combining elements from Wren's work with fresh ideas from Italian Mannerist and Baroque sources. Those Italian ideas, expressed in London on the eve of the accession of Whiggery, Palladianism, and George I, met with a singularly bad reception, and Gibbs seems to have resolved never again to endanger his reputation by expressing himself in terms resembling those of seventeenth-century Rome. Whether this was professional caution or personal conversion we can only guess, but when Gibbs designed the offices (and perhaps the colonnade) of Burlington House his manner was much more conservative. This would be after the appearance of the first volume of *Vitruvius Britannicus*, which contains a gibe at Gibbs's master, Fontana, and some observations on church-design obviously directed at St Mary-le-Strand. Campbell, as a rival Scot with Whig loyalties, was no doubt hostile to Gibbs. In his third volume, where he illustrates his own work at Burlington House, he is significantly silent about the predecessor whom he had, perhaps, unseated.

Gibbs, however, while abandoning his Italian style, never became a real Palladian, but attached himself more closely than any other architect of the time to the personal manner of Wren. That is to say, he looked not to the 'late Wren' which was, as we have seen, in some part the creation of Hawksmore, but to the Wren of St Bride's and the Cambridge Library. We know that Wren was among Gibbs's 'patrons' and can therefore assume that this loyalty was not a wholly impersonal choice.

To the Wren manner, Gibbs brought his unique experience of the technical skill of Roman *seicento* masters and some idiosyncrasies collected from Palladio and Jones, notably the frequent use of round-headed windows with the architraves regularly interrupted by dies, one of which forms the keystone. Palladio's influence is strong in many of Gibbs's plans and some of his elevations, but the Burlingtonian idea of composition as an aggregate of self-subsisting units never interested him. His compositions consist, as a rule, of broad masses relieved by centre and end projections and uniformly fenestrated, a type of composition familiar in England since Pratt and in Scotland since Bruce.

Gibbs's independence of the Palladian movement is due, presumably, partly to his being a trifle older than the leaders of that movement, partly to his experience of Italian architecture, and partly to temperament, this last factor being connected with certain hostilities of which we are dimly aware. He became the favourite architect of the Tory party and worked for the Earls of Oxford and Mar, Lord Bolingbroke, and the Duke of Bolton; and also for Pope and Matthew Prior. The Palladian movement, on the other hand, was essentially Whig. The Whigs dismissed Gibbs from his Surveyorship to the church-building commission, and he may be forgiven if a distaste for Whig doctrine in architecture helped to modify his stylistic outlook.

Not all Gibbs's patrons, however, were Tories. Indeed, in the Duke of Argyll, for whom he built Sudbrooke Lodge, Petersham (*c.* 1718; Plate 123A), he shared the same patronage as Colen Campbell, while his most important church, St Martin's-in-the-Fields, was built for a predominantly Whig committee.

After St Mary-le-Strand, Gibbs built the Tower of St Clement Danes (1719), a graceful essay in Wren's style and also the first known instance of the occurrence of the Gibbsian window. By that time he was heavily engaged with private commissions. He built most of Cannons (1716–20) for James Brydges, Duke of Chandos, and if we can trust the engraving of its façade commissioned in 1720 by another architect, was still at that time indulging in a few Baroque reminiscences such as terms set against pilasters in a rusticated attic storey.

At Ditchley, Oxon. (1720–2 for the 2nd Earl of Lichfield; Plate 123B), however, the Gibbs manner reached its mature condition. The plan could almost pass for the work of a Palladian. But not quite; for the proportions of the rooms are, on close inspection, not Palladio's, some of them being, for instance, not quite square, yet not a square and a third or a square and a half. The main elevations show projecting centre and ends, the ends advancing further than the centre, a familiar arrangement. The doorway and all the quoins are rusticated, and all the windows, even those in the attic, have architraves and keystones, an indifference of emphasis which a Palladian would have found detestable. Quadrant corridors link the main house to the two service wings, again in a roughly but not exactly Palladian fashion.

Ditchley is typical of most of the houses illustrated by Gibbs in the book of his own work, which he published in 1728 and seems to represent the domestic style he was anxious to propagate. Nor did his manner change between that date and his death. One of his last works was the rebuilding of Hampstead Marshall (begun 1739 and not finished; later destroyed), whose composition is very much that of Ditchley.

But if Gibbs's domestic work is uniformly sober, to the point of tameness, his public buildings show him to great advantage. In 1721–4 he designed the chapel-of-ease on the Earl of Oxford's estate round Cavendish Square, now called St Peter's, Vere Street. Almost at the same time he began the much greater church, for which St Peter's looks,

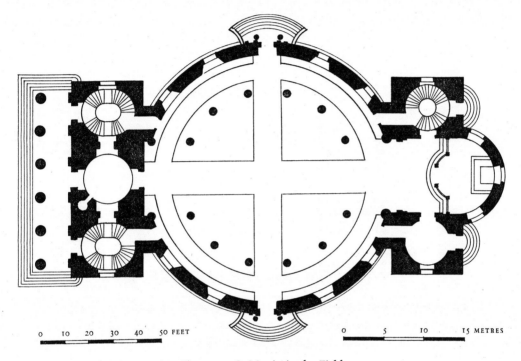

0   10   20   30   40   50 FEET   0   5   10   15 METRES

Figure 32. St Martin-in-the-Fields

internally, like a preliminary model – St Martin's-in-the-Fields (1721–6; Plates 124B and 125; Figure 33). This church is important not only as an achievement in itself, but for its enormously widespread and continued influence. Through the fine engravings of it in Gibbs's book, it became the type of the Anglican parish church and was imitated wherever in the world English was spoken and Anglican worship upheld.

Before building St Martin's as we know it Gibbs produced a different design which was rejected by the Committee on grounds of expense. It was for a circular church (Plate 124A; Figure 32), based partly perhaps on impressions of Bernini's oval church of S. Andrea al Quirinale in Rome, but chiefly on a close study of Sir Christopher Wren's City Churches, St Stephen, Walbrook (Figure 20) and St Antholin, Watling Street (Plate 78B), in particular. Although this very wonderful design was turned down, Gibbs recorded it in his book, with the result that it provided the model for several interesting churches built later in the century: St Paul's, Liverpool (by T. Lightoller, 1765–9; destroyed 1932), All Saints, Newcastle-on-Tyne (by David Stephenson, 1786–96), and St Chad's, Shrewsbury (by George Steuart, 1790–2). None of these however, was as bold or as fully developed as Gibbs's circular St Martin's would have been, and the last two examples are, of course, modified by a very different trend of taste. Even Sir William Chambers borrowed this circular plan when designing a church for St Marylebone.

As executed, St Martin's-in-the-Fields owes as much to Wren as the circular design, while there is a trace of Bernini in the management of the tribunes or state pews adjoining the chancel. It is an aisled church of five bays, and the east and west ends are planned so that there is substantial symmetry on both axes, vestries on the east corresponding with

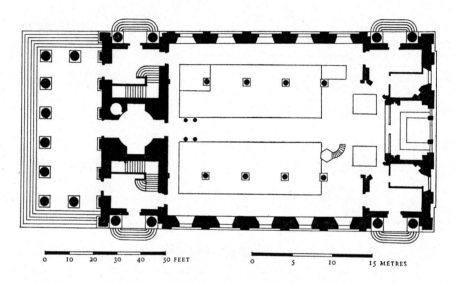

Figure 33. St Martin-in-the-Fields: Preliminary Plan

vestibules on the west. Each of the eight columns carries its own entablature (Wren had never dared this extreme articulation and, in similar circumstances, either doubled the columns or omitted the cornice and frieze), while above the entablatures spring semi-circular arches intersecting with an elliptical barrel vault. The closest parallel to this scheme among the Wren churches was St Andrew's, Holborn. Gibbs's main departure from the principle there embodied is the use of an order standing on a pew-high pedestal and reaching up (with its entablature) to the springing of the vault. Wren had used a diminutive order, resting on the gallery front which, in turn, rested on piers. Gibbs was less tolerant of galleries than Wren and made them appear as an unwanted (though neatly handled) insertion sliding in between the columns and intended to be seen as little as possible. Wren had always hesitated between emphasis on the gallery and on the order (compare St Bride's with St James's, Piccadilly). Hawksmore awarded pre-eminence to the order, and at St Martin's Gibbs agrees with him.

The exterior of St Martin's is, like the interior, dominated by a giant Corinthian order, advancing at the west end into a superb portico and continuing round the church in pilaster form except where, in the end bays of the long façades, two whole columns are recessed *in antis* (an effective device borrowed from the interior of the Pantheon). Then there is the steeple. Wren had always built his steeples as *adjuncts* to his churches in the Gothic way, and in this Hawksmore followed him. Gibbs, boldly attempting to achieve a more compact unity, built his tower *inside* the west wall of the church and made it emerge through the roof. The result has often been criticized, and with some reason, for the incongruity of the temple-like church and the steeple which rushes up through its roof is undeniable. The steeple itself, however, is a masterpiece, based on the fullest sympathy with Wren. Indeed, the whole church may be described as the fulfilment of those ideas which Wren's thought brought to birth in the building of the often crude and rather tasteless City Churches. In those churches, built in haste, with too much participation by their craftsmen, Wren's themes are rarely developed to their full extent or with complete technical competence. In St Martin's several Wren ideas are combined and their implications loyally worked out without hitch or bungle.

A minor glory of St Martin's, and equally of its little prototype, St Peter's, is the plaster ornament or 'fret-work'. This is by Giuseppe Artari and his partner Bagutti, who, no doubt, designed as well as executed it under Gibbs's eye. These two Italians, 'the best fret-workers in England', worked constantly for Gibbs. Their Rococo ornament is of the Italian, not the French, variety and close in character to the plaster-work of Roman churches of the early eighteenth century.

Gibbs's other large church, All Saints', Derby (1725; now the Cathedral), is on the lines of St Martin's, but benefits greatly by the absence of galleries: no tower problem arose as the tower of the ancient church was retained.

At Cambridge Gibbs built the Senate House and the Fellows' Building at King's College. The Senate House we have dealt with elsewhere as a building whose design involved another personality. The Fellows' Building at King's College (1724; Plate 126A) is a far more important witness of Gibbs's genius. It approaches, in its comparative simplicity, his country-house style, but is monumentalized by its central feature, consisting of an open archway framed in a Doric portal, which in turn is surmounted by a great semicircular window with two stone mullions, while a pediment stands across the top of the whole, joining the main cornice where the centre of the façade breaks forward. This decidedly Mannerist composition has a Venetian air, even momentarily recalling the Baroque side chapels of Santa Maria della Salute, though, on analysis, its elements can mostly be traced to Palladio.

It was at Oxford that Gibbs raised the building which, with St Martin's-in-the-Fields, constitutes his greatest claim to fame – the Radcliffe Library (1739–49; Plate 127). We have seen that Hawksmore had, as early as 1715, designed for the Trustees a circular structure with a rusticated base, a Corinthian peristyle, and a dome rising from a circular drum. Since that date many delays had occurred and Hawksmore died in 1736. Before his death, however, he had submitted a new design, and Gibbs had also submitted one, which was chosen. This must have been the long rectangular building of which drawings still exist and which owes much to Wren's great library at Cambridge; but it was abandoned for the design eventually executed, which is clearly based on the Hawksmore project of 1715. Its treatment, however, is very different, and here, in his last great building, Gibbs dared to indulge once again that tendency to Italian Mannerism which we noticed in his first church, St Mary-le-Strand. Here again, as in the centre feature of his building at King's, one cannot help thinking of S. Maria della Salute. The curved buttresses which stand against the drum are the only features which can conceivably derive from that church, but the character of the whole is more strongly Italian than any other English building of its time. Essentially Mannerist is the treatment of the Corinthian order, whose coupled columns separate alternate wide and narrow bays, the difference in width being, however, purposely ambiguous. Again, above the order, the buttresses of the dome come down *between* and not over the pairs of columns, and yet the bays in which they occur are precisely *not* the bays which are strengthened by forward breaks in the rusticated base. Moreover, these emphatic units in the base line up with only *one* of each pair of columns in the bay above them. The rhythms of the whole structure are thus extremely complicated. No emphasis falls just where you would expect it; everything is syncopated. Very rarely in English architecture has the spirit of Mannerism been so pronounced. It can be accounted for here only by the personality of the architect and his thorough acquaintance (so carefully forgotten in so much of his work) with the Italian Mannerist masters.

In the interior these Mannerist traits are absent, and the treatment is more Wren-like, consisting of eight equal piers and arches carrying the drum and dome, the whole richly decorated by Artari and Bagutti.

Because of his strong individualism and in spite of his conservatism, Gibbs's influence proved enormous. This is largely to be accounted for by his books, especially *A Book of Architecture* published in London in 1728 and containing most of his executed works up to that date, as well as an ample treasury of designs, based on English, French, and Italian sources, for small buildings and ornaments. This book was frankly intended as a pattern book for the use of country gentlemen in districts remote from architectural advice; and the designs, says Gibbs, could be 'executed by any workman who understands lines'. As Gibbs intended, so the book was used. Its success was immediate and it was probably the most widely used architectural book of the century, not only throughout Britain but in the American colonies and the West Indies. Its directness and the conservative simplicity of most of the designs probably accounted for its success, which brought its author a handsome financial reward. Gibbs also produced *Rules for Drawing the Several Parts of Architecture* (1732), a fine text-book whose reputation survived well into the nineteenth century.

James Gibbs is one of the most individual of English architects. Not a profound innovator or a man of great imaginative power, he was a superlative technician and possessed an ability to select and combine the characteristics of other architects and fuse them into a style of his own, independent of the trend of fashion. He belongs to no school, and although he was widely imitated[1] his contribution to the further development of English architecture was slight. He is best described as the delayed fulfilment of Wren, as a brilliant continuator of a chapter closed about 1692, when the Vanbrugh-Hawksmore episode began.

NOTE TO CHAPTER 21

1. An interesting case of a provincial designer deriving almost exclusively from Gibbs (probably through his books alone) is that of Thomas Ivory (1709–79) of Norwich, who, trained as a carpenter, built most of the principal Norwich buildings of his time, including the Octagon Chapel (1753; inspired by the circular design for St Martin's), the Assembly Rooms (1754; with a remarkable interior), and the Theatre (1757; demolished).

CHAPTER 22

THE PALLADIAN PERMEATION

IT will have become apparent that the expression 'Palladian', in relation to English architecture, means considerably more than the imitation of Palladio. Three main loyalties were involved – loyalty to Vitruvius; to Palladio himself; and to Inigo Jones. Vitruvius stood for the fundamental validity of the antique and the value of archaeological inquiry. From Palladio came the general mode of expression of a modern architecture – principles of planning and proportion and the rich potentialities of rustication. Finally, Jones supplied extensions and variations of Palladio and, in addition, ways of treating ceilings and fireplaces which were wanting in Palladio. Without the admission of Jones, Palladianism might have approximated to a High Renaissance purity of composition, modified only by the Mannerist streak in Palladio. Jones, however, had been more eclectic than his admirers knew, and, under his name, the Mannerism not only of Palladio but of Vignola and Domenico Fontana, Scamozzi, Rusconi, and Zanini and, later, of French decorators like Barbet (whose sources were in part Flemish) came into the picture.

'Palladianism' in England from 1715 to 1760 is, in fact, a fairly mixed style and expanded very readily into the further eclecticism from which the neo-classical point of view emerged. So far we have dealt only with the initiators and leaders of Palladianism. In this chapter we come to the expansion of the style, its deliberate propagation by the Burlingtonian group, and subsequently its exposition by a second generation of architects in whose hands it reached the cold, elaborate finality from which the late eighteenth century energetically revolted.

Lord Burlington, both as an architect and as an intellectual nobleman, was the great figure in the first phase of the movement. But he was not the only member of the Whig aristocracy who contributed to its success. His own work at the drawing-board was exceptional (and, in Chesterfield's view, rather improper for a man of his caste), but apart from that he was a representative of a type. Many of his noble contemporaries travelled to Italy as part of their education; many, like the Earls of Leicester and Bessborough, collected antique marbles, and for a hundred years it had been considered the ordinary thing for a gentleman to have some knowledge of architecture. Gentlemen and noblemen who did not actually design (in our sense) often claimed to be their own architects and purchased expensive sets of drawing instruments; and it is not always easy to make out whether or not their pretensions amounted to anything more than the general direction of a building project over the head of a professional man.

There is the case, for instance, of Henry Herbert, 9th Earl of Pembroke (1693–1751), a man almost the same age as Burlington, a friend of his and the heir to Inigo Jones's great work at Wilton. Like Burlington, he pinned his early faith to Colen Campbell, and Campbell built him a house at Whitehall soon after 1717. Later he wielded the dividers himself and has been credited with some half a dozen works. In every case, however, there is an alternative ascription to Roger Morris (d. 1749), the Master Carpenter to the Office of Ordnance, and one is inclined to see here a partnership where the technical skill was mostly on the side of the professional man, working, no doubt, under active and well-informed direction. The Pembroke-Morris style was Palladian in the Campbell sense, not the Burlingtonian. A dry, lifeless but charmingly sited example of their work is Marble Hill, Twickenham, built about 1728 for George II's Countess of Suffolk, and reminiscent of the Earl's own house (by Campbell) at Whitehall. By far their happiest joint effort was the reduction of Palladio's idea for a triumphal bridge to the size required for the ornamental Palladian Bridge at Wilton (1736; Plate 126B), a beautiful reconstruction which was copied at Prior Park and Stowe. But perhaps Pembroke's greatest claim to fame is less as an architect than as the promoter of Westminster Bridge (1739–47), the first bridge to be built over the Thames at London since medieval times and the first classical bridge of its size in England. The engineer was a Swiss, Charles Labelye (1705–?62), who seems to have followed, in a general way, the humped round-arch type of bridge introduced in Paris under Henri IV. Neither in type nor in its use of rustication did the bridge attempt to be Palladian.

Patronage forwarded the Palladian business in more ways than one. Direct participation in design was one way. The employment of the right artists to build private houses was another way. A third way, by no means less important, was the indoctrination of the Office of Works. The storming of this citadel where, in 1715, the discredited triumvirate, Wren, Vanbrugh, and Hawksmore, still held office, was by no means easy, for place-holding was more an affair of politics than of aesthetics; and Vanbrugh anyway was a perfectly good Whig. However, Burlington, in securing Kent's employment at Kensington Palace over the head of the Serjeant Painter, showed what could be done, and the similar employment of Campbell for Rolls House (see p. 201) was, no doubt, jobbery with the same intent.

But it was in 1718–19 that the old régime was finally dislodged. Wren's dismissal was secured, Vanbrugh prevented from entering the office to which he had every right, Hawksmore similarly excluded from promotion, and William Benson, who had the backing of the German element at Court, put in as Surveyor with (shortly afterwards) Nicholas Dubois as Master Mason. Thus, in 1719, two of the four principal officers of the Works were true Palladians – perhaps, indeed, the original Palladians. A third office, that of Master Carpenter, fell vacant on the death of Grinling Gibbons in 1721 and was filled by a nominee of Sir Robert Walpole's. That should have made a Palladian majority, but unfortunately Thomas Ripley (d. 1758) had Walpole's patronage for other than artistic reasons, and 'had not the countenance', says Horace Walpole, 'of Lord Burlington'. His Admiralty, Whitehall (1722–6), is scarcely Palladian and nothing but a late and poor specimen of Wren's style, vilely proportioned and adorned with a sort of French quoins which the Palladians had condemned. However, apart from the Admiralty he did little damage, and when he was moved up to the Comptrollership on Vanbrugh's death in 1726, he designed nothing[1] and made room for the Palladians' star performer, William Kent.

The clerkships in the Works were easier to fill with Palladian nominees, and of these the principal were Henry Flitcroft (1697–1769) and Isaac Ware (d. 1766). Flitcroft was the son of a man employed on the Hampton Court gardens in William III's time and was apprenticed to a joiner. While engaged on some work at Burlington House he broke his leg and was taken on by Lord Burlington as a draughtsman. He redrew, for the engraver, most of the Inigo Jones designs published by Kent and in 1726 was given a clerkship in the Works. From that office he proceeded to the offices of Master Carpenter (1746), Master Mason (1748), and, finally, Comptroller[2] (1758), which last he occupied until his death. The Works provided him with few opportunities to show his quality as a designer, and his principal work was done independently. The church of St Giles-in-the-Fields (1731–1733), for which he was both architect and contractor, is a work which Burlington can hardly have approved, being in fact an unflattering imitation of St Martin's-in-the-Fields, without a portico and in every respect less satisfactory than its model. The colossal mansion of Wentworth Woodhouse, Yorks. (c. 1740, for Lord Malton, afterwards Marquis of Rockingham), confirms what the church leads one to suspect, that Flitcroft had no creative ability whatever. The façade of Wentworth owes its splendour to *Vitruvius Britannicus* (the prints of Campbell's Wanstead in particular) and the saloon is modelled on the Whitehall Banqueting House. Woburn Abbey (c. 1747, for the Duke of Bedford) is equally derivative. But Flitcroft was very good up to a point and his town-houses (for example, No. 10 St James's Square, for Sir W. Heathcote, 1734, and the house adjoining) are good examples of the Palladian idea of a London street-front reduced to its barest elements.

Isaac Ware was in much the same class as Flitcroft but started lower. He is supposed to have been a chimney-sweep in whom somebody discovered a talent for drawing. He knew Kent and was given a post in the Works in 1728, and held various offices there till the end of his life, when he was among other things Secretary to the Board, in which office he followed Hawksmore. Like Flitcroft's, his principal works were for private patrons. These included Lord Chesterfield, for whom he built Chesterfield House (1749; destroyed 1934). This consisted of a block somewhat on the lines of Jones's Chevening (and houses of the sort among the Jones drawings), but with Doric colonnades extending from it to left and right and returning along two sides of a forecourt. Some five years later he built Wrotham Park, South Mimms, Middlesex (Plate 128), for Admiral Byng, a house consisting of elements chosen from Palladio and Kent. Again, like Flitcroft, he built a number of London houses, including, probably, Nos 45 and 46 Berkeley Square.

Flitcroft left in manuscript a collection of drawings obviously intended for a comprehensive treatise on architecture. Ware actually produced such a book and *A Complete Body of Architecture* came out in 1756. It was intended to serve as 'a library on [architecture] to the gentlemen and the builder; supplying the place of all other books'. It contains a great deal of information and is ably compiled, reflecting very fairly the solid, unimaginative competence of its author's executed works.

To the names of Flitcroft and Ware may be added that of John Vardy (d. 1765), who appears to have been employed by or under Kent and who held several clerkships in the

Works. As the clerk in charge of Whitehall at the time of Kent's death he was entrusted with the execution of that master's design for the Horse Guards; and as clerk for Westminster Palace probably designed the house which is now Nos 6 and 7 Old Palace Yard. His most important work, however, was Spencer House (1756–65 for Earl Spencer; Plate 129A). General Gray, a prominent member of the Dilettante Society, suggested the design, the park façade of which is strongly Jonesian.

In capturing the best places in the Office of Works for themselves and their candidates, the Palladian group no doubt hoped that a new Whitehall Palace and a new Palace of Westminster (those two national opportunities which Wren had not been able to spoil) might rise to illustrate supremely the true principles of Palladio and Jones. In this they were disappointed. The burnt site of old Whitehall was squandered upon a variety of small houses and public offices; and at Westminster Kent's imagination was exercised only on paper, and his executed work was limited to some reconstruction at the Law Courts. Their one great London triumph was the Horse Guards. Nevertheless, the establishment of Palladianism as the official style of Great Britain was not without its merits, and when the original Palladians were dead, it remained the only standard to which a new generation of designers could rally.

Books and the Palladian Movement

Campbell's *Vitruvius Britannicus* and Leoni's *Palladio* inaugurated a great period of architectural book publishing. They came out in 1715–17. Within ten years a continuous stream of books had begun to flow from the press, so that between 1725 and Chambers's *Treatise of Civil Architecture* of 1759 nearly every year saw the appearance of one or more illustrated books on architecture. The trend of this literature was generally Palladian, but it varied greatly and was inflected by Gibbs's influence after 1730. The principal works were the great folios sponsored by Burlington himself and including Kent's *Designs of Inigo Jones* (1727), Robert Castell's *Villas of the Ancients* (1728; a series of reconstructions of Roman houses and gardens based on passages in classical literature), and Burlington's own *Fabbriche antiche* (1730), a superb book of engravings from Palladio's own drawings, published in a limited edition, with a preface in Italian. The book of Jones's designs proved very influential and was followed by a slim octavo in which Isaac Ware produced some further *Designs of Inigo Jones* (1735), while John Vardy brought out *Designs of Inigo Jones and William Kent* in 1744.

None of these books contained anything much in the way of critical or theoretical writing and, indeed, the literature of the Palladian movement produced no treatise of any depth or importance. Leoni's translation of *The Architecture of L. B. Alberti* (1726) made available a theoretical work of fundamental, if rather archaic, importance, but one does not find it much quoted. Almost the only contemporary theoretical writer was Robert Morris, a relative and pupil of Lord Pembroke's man, Roger Morris. He described himself as a Surveyor, but no executed works of his are known. His first book, *An Essay in Defence of Ancient Architecture* (1728), was an attack on contemporary work of the Vanbrugh-Hawksmore school, an unfavourable example of which he illustrated. Six years later he brought out a series of *Lectures on Architecture* (1734), read to a society which he, apparently, had formed. The lectures include a general historical sketch, an exposition of a somewhat elementary system of proportion, derived at second-hand from Alberti, and an analysis of some of Morris's own designs, of which engravings are given. Morris was by no means a bigoted Palladian; he admired both Wren and Gibbs. It is difficult to assess the influence, if any, of the *Lectures*; but it is certain that his later books of designs, *Rural Architecture* (1750), the *Architectural Remembrancer* (1751), and, above all, *Select Architecture* (1757), were much used, and that the latter had a considerable influence in America in the hands of Thomas Jefferson (p. 342).

John Wood of Bath (p. 234) was the author of a curious quasi-philosophical work, entitled *The Origin of Building: or, The Plagiarisms of the Heathen Detected* (1741), in which he showed, to his own satisfaction, and with the help of Villalpando, that classic architecture had been revealed to the Jews and incorporated in the Temple at Jerusalem. The book is personal and has no particular connexion with Palladianism except that it illustrates in a remarkable way the desire for an absolute sanction, biblical as well as philosophical, for the Vitruvian source of architectural virtue.

Some interesting architectural criticism is contained in *A Critical Review of the Public Buildings of London* (1734) by an author called (in later editions) Ralph, whose identity has never been established. He is often denounced as hypercritical, and with some justice, for he takes exception to every detail which (in his view) would be foreign to the drawing-board of Palladio or Inigo Jones.

Another type of book altogether is that represented by the works of William Halfpenny who, after producing nearly twenty titles, died in debt in 1755. His first production, *Magnum in Parvo, or The Marrow of Architecture*, appeared in 1722 and again in 1728. The title plagiarizes Venterus Mandey's *Mellificium Mensionis: or the Marrow of Measuring* which had appeared as long ago as 1682 but was still in use (a fourth edition appeared in 1727). Halfpenny's book is designed, as was Mandey's, for the use of the artisan, and gives engravings of the orders, mostly in combination with arches, 'according to the proportions laid down by Palladio'. His next book, *Practical Architecture*, ran to seven editions by 1751. In 1725 came *The Art of Sound Building*, concerned with 'arches, niches, groins and twisted rails' and including a frontispiece of Holy Trinity, Leeds (1721–7), of which Halfpenny was the architect. Its dedication to Sir Andrew Fountaine and the presence of the names of many Richmond tradesmen among the subscribers makes it evident that Halfpenny enjoyed patronage at the Court of Princess Caroline.

Halfpenny produced a book on perspective in 1731. Then, after an interval, came his books of designs, including *A New and Compleat System of Architecture*, 1749. In this he acknowledges the critical help of Robert Morris, but the designs are mostly very poor, and far from Palladian. This and his subsequent books were aimed chiefly at country gentlemen and builders, and include several books of Chinese designs, the first of which, *Rural Architecture in the Chinese Taste*, must have appeared before 1750 (the second edition is dated 1750–2). It must be close in date to the Chinese buildings at Wroxton which Walpole, in 1753, mentions (without enthusiasm) as the first of their kind. The engravings are exceedingly poor and, since the designs are as much French Rococo as Chinese, they will probably have been concocted from French prints. This and other of Halfpenny's later books, which included Gothic as well as further Chinese patterns, were produced under the joint names of William Halfpenny and his son, John.

Another famous author was Batty Langley (1696–1751), 'architect, surveyor, builder, measurer', as he described himself. His output was just about equal to Halfpenny's. He started in 1726 with two books on geometry and architecture for workmen and *A Sure Guide to Builders*, containing engravings of the orders, on the lines of Halfpenny's earlier book. Books on gardening and estate improvement followed in 1728, and on the cultivation of fruit-trees in 1729. From 1730 onwards, probably as a result of the success of Gibbs's *Book of Architecture*, Langley started producing treasuries of designs. *Ancient Masonry* (1734 or 35) is a massive compilation, giving designs for all kinds of architectural features, drawn from a wide range of English and foreign sources, including Gibbs. In 1738 came *The Builder's Compleat Assistant*, which ran into four editions. Many similar works followed. They are all competent, with clear and accurate engravings. Many of the designs are pirated from earlier English or French books. The *Gothic Architecture Restored and Improved* (1742), however, in which Kent's version of Gothic is formalized into 'orders', is a work of some originality and will require our attention in a subsequent chapter.

Abraham Swan, carpenter and joiner, published from 1745 books of designs for staircases, panelling, bridges, domes, roofs, and chimney-pieces. They derive from Kent and Inigo Jones and from the Rococo which joiners, cabinet-makers, and plasterers were in the habit of imitating from French models.

The many other books of the period included editions of Palladio, cheaper than Leoni's, in 1733 (by Isaac Ware), and W. Salmon's *Palladio Londinensis* (1734), a general text-book, with a few Palladian designs. The influence of all these books was to a large extent over-ridden by James Gibbs's *Book of Architecture*, already mentioned (p. 214). This had the effect of greatly diluting the Palladian influences, being, in any case, a more suggestive and practical work than the scholarly books patronized by Burlington and far better engraved than those of Halfpenny or Morris. Without Gibbs, the Palladian movement would have achieved a more nearly absolute dominion over English architectural style.

The last important work in the library of Palladian literature was, as we have seen (p. 218), Ware's *Complete Body of Architecture*. But in three years it and many of its predecessors were overshadowed by a book altogether more important, more cultured, and more critical, for with Chambers's *A Treatise of Civil Architecture* (1759), for all its indebtedness to Ware, architectural literature enters a new phase.

The Spread of the Palladian Fashion

The consequences of Burlington's propaganda for a pure Palladian manner were clear enough by 1731 for Alexander Pope to exaggerate and ridicule them. His *Epistle to Lord Burlington*, published in that year, pays tribute to Burlington's own taste and sense, but predicts the vulgarization of his manner.

> You show us, Rome was glorious, not profuse,
> And pompous buildings once were things of Use.
> Yet shall (my Lord) your just, your noble rules,
> Fill half the land with Imitating Fools;
> Who random drawings from your sheets shall take,
> And of one beauty many blunders make;
> Load some vain Church with old Theatric state,
> Turn Arcs of Triumph to a Garden-gate;
> Reverse your Ornaments; and hang them all
> On some patch'd dog-hole ek'd with ends of wall;
> Then clap four slices of Pilaster on't,
> That, lac'd with bits of rustic, makes a Front
> Shall call the winds thro' long arcades to roar,
> Proud to catch cold at a Venetian door;
> Conscious they act a true Palladian part,
> And if they starve, they starve by rules of art.

The prophecy was largely justified. Not only in England, but in Scotland and Ireland, Palladianism spread into local schools mostly of very indifferent quality and far, indeed, from the exquisite richness of Chiswick or the studied classicality of Holkham.

In London, of course, the issue of the movement came thick and fast, Palladianism becoming debased by such men as Edward Shepherd (d. 1747), whose Covent Garden Theatre, built for John Rich in 1732, earned the contempt of Kent, and by George Dance I (1695–1768), a mason turned architect, whose Mansion House (1739–53) is both cramped and over-dressed. A better building in the same area was the Bank of England (1732–4; Plate 129B) by George Sampson, whose design was closely related to the 'Inigo Jones' house in Lincoln's Inn Fields. But Sampson held a clerkship in the Works and thus knew better than most what Palladianism was about.

From London, Palladianism was carried to Bath by John Wood who returned there to pursue his monumental redevelopment schemes in 1727. His career belongs to the next chapter, but it is of consequence here as showing how one energetic and successful man could transplant the style to a new locality. For Wood not only built a great part of Bath, but several country-houses and the Exchange at Bristol (1740–3), while his reputation spread to Liverpool where he designed (with his son) a building of similar purpose, now the Town Hall (1748–55).

Most provincial centres at this time had one leading figure, usually a mason who had 'left off his apron', who led the way in design, who designed and built the bigger houses in the town and district and whose manner was copied by lesser men. Among the first generation of Palladians these local men are not yet of great importance, but with the second generation, to which we are now coming, we shall find that they rank nearly equal with the London men and must be awarded attention accordingly.

Palladianism: The Second Generation

William Kent died in 1748, Roger Morris in 1749, the two architect earls, Pembroke and Burlington, in 1751 and 1753. They were the last of the originating Palladian generation;

for Leoni and Campbell were long dead, and although Ware, Flitcroft, and Vardy lived on into the sixties, their importance passed with the men who made them what they were.

By the middle of the century a new generation of architects was growing up which, although it included two innovators who were to change the course of English architecture decisively, was, in other respects, conservative and consolidating. To this generation belongs a group of men who, for a time (say, 1753 to 1768), dominated the profession, building very many houses for private patrons in town and country and a few, not very important, public buildings. The group in question includes, principally, Sir Robert Taylor and James Paine, practising in London; with John Carr practising in York. Not the least important fact about this group is that some members of it were among the first architects to take articled pupils into their offices. We never hear of Kent or Gibbs or any of their contemporaries doing this, though they had, of course, clerks who, to some extent, enjoyed the advantages of pupilage. But Taylor in particular, and Paine also, had pupils in their offices, presumably bound to them by articles, thus inaugurating a practice which was to continue for two centuries and is indeed still in being. The significance of this is that from this period we can date the real existence of an architectural *profession*, a profession to which young men are trained up and not merely one whose members have all either graduated from a trade or which they have adopted through a combination of circumstance and predilection, often late in life.

Of the group of practitioners just mentioned, the eldest was Sir Robert Taylor (1714–1788). The son of a stone-mason, he became a pupil of Cheere and visited Rome. Left in poor circumstances by his father, he fortunately obtained the patronage of the Godfrey and Heathcote families, both associated with the Bank of England, and through them obtained important statuary commissions at the Bank and the Mansion House (where he executed the pedimental group). For the Heathcotes he built Normanton, Rutland (demolished 1925), probably an early work and closely following Kent. In 1754 he built No. 35 Lincoln's Inn Fields (bombed 1941), again Kent-like but with sundry experimental features including a room decorated with the motif of Bramante's Belvedere Court and windows with octagon panes. Asgill House (Plate 130; for Sir Charles Asgill, the banker), by the Thames at Richmond, is also drawn from Kent, though later alterations somewhat disguise the fact. Asgill's banking-house at No. 70 Lombard Street (*c.* 1756; destroyed) was interesting for the inset Doric order in its ground-floor, an early concession of private banking to the need for architectural expression.

With his appointment to expand the Bank of England in 1765, Taylor executed some of his best work. Here he built a Rotunda, with three halls adjoining, all of similar design; and in 1774 a Court Room and Committee Room Suite. The Belvedere motif was applied in the Corinthian colonnades and porticoes of the exterior elevations, flanking Sampson's block (p. 222), and again in the Rotunda where its effect was to give a plan not unlike Sanmicheli's Pellegrini Chapel. The three halls, on the other hand, rather naïvely availed themselves of St Martin's-in-the-Fields, reproducing its nave, on a small scale, with top-lights introduced in the domes and vaults – and, of course, no galleries.

In 1775, Taylor started to build Stone Buildings, Lincoln's Inn, probably part of a larger scheme for rebuilding most of the Inn. The block towards Lincoln's Inn Fields is an unusual composition for a Palladian, consisting of a mass terminated by porticoed pavilions but with no central emphasis whatever. The explanation may be that a third portico was envisaged on a southward extension. On the other hand, Taylor favoured this composition elsewhere and there may be an association with Gabriel's recent palaces in the Place de la Nation at Paris.

Taylor's last works include the fine bridge at Maidenhead and Heveningham, Suffolk, where the pavilion theme of Stone Buildings reappears, but this time with a massive centre block on the same Paris-inspired lines as Sir William Chambers's Strand front at Somerset House.

Taylor, it will be seen, was a Palladian with eclectic proclivities, which may or may not mean that, in his later years, he relied on 'ghosts'. Nevertheless, his style is recognizable chiefly by the use of certain Palladian themes in a personal way and always with complete technical competence. He had a special liking for rusticated arches (from the Palazzo Thiene through Kent), which he used with telling effect in the Maidenhead bridge, in the Bishop of Ely's house in Dover Street (c. 1772), the Council House at Salisbury (1788), and elsewhere. By far the most original work attached to his name was the Reduced Annuities Office at the Bank, but this was finished after his death, and may be the work of Thomas Malton (1748–1804).[3] This top-lit hall, with its circular clerestory carried on segmental arches, was to lead directly to some of the most remarkable works of Sir John Soane.

Taylor was all his life connected with the City of London, where he was Sheriff in 1782–3 and knighted as a consequence. He amassed a fortune of about £180,000, the bulk of which he left to Oxford to found an institution for the teaching of modern languages.

The career of James Paine (1725–89) runs exactly parallel with Taylor's; for although he was eleven years younger, he tells us that, at nineteen, he was already engaged on one of his largest works. Although he began as a Londoner and studied at the St Martin's Lane Academy, and although London seems to have remained his headquarters, he built little there and is chiefly associated with a number of very large houses in the Midlands and the North. He had already found several patrons in Yorkshire when in 1745–8 he built the Mansion House at Doncaster, a building where the Mayor and Corporation might entertain the county with due honours. The design was based on Inigo Jones's Palace drawings as engraved in Kent's book, and there are ambitious interiors in which Paine put to good use the facility in rococo ornament he had acquired in St Martin's Lane. This building was followed by a long series of great houses, beginning with Nostell Priory (for Sir R. Winn), and including the stables and bridge at Chatsworth (for the Duke of Devonshire), Worksop Manor (a vast scheme for the Duke of Norfolk, only partly built), Wardour (for Lord Arundel; Plate 131), and Kedleston (for Lord Scarsdale: Paine says he abandoned the commission owing to his heavy obligations elsewhere). These and several others were built between 1745 and 1770, during which period Paine was unquestionably the leading house architect in the country. All the houses rely absolutely on Kent, Inigo Jones. and, to a minor extent, Campbell. All are technically competent, planned in a practical way, and superbly built. Both at Kedleston (Figure 34) and Wardour one recognizes obvious attempts to outshine Holkham by modelling the main elements in the plan on antique types. Thus, at Kedleston, Paine conceived the conjoint basilica and pantheon which Adam was to complete and decorate, while at Wardour the staircase rises into a circular temple elaborated from the Pantheon theme. For Worksop, he proposed a gigantic Egyptian Hall. Paine, in fact, brought Palladianism along the road to neo-classicism marked out by Burlington, though by the time he had finished other men and other influences had brought it even further.

Paine never travelled, as far as we know, until in his last years he went to France, as the result of some domestic trouble, and died there. He was not much attracted by the

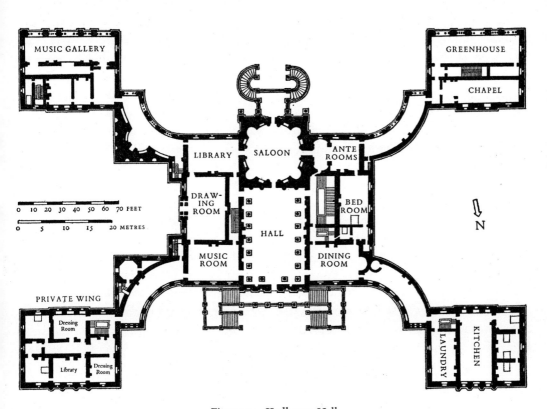

Figure 34. Kedleston Hall

discoveries in Syria and Dalmatia and professed to regard them, generally, as merely 'curious'; and although he admired Piranesi, there are no signs that he was in any way influenced by him. Nevertheless, he could not escape the itch for novelty prevalent in the seventies and his later interiors contain Grecian and Adam features and a variety of mannerisms – as, for instance, the elliptical arches in the staircase at Brocket, Herts. (finished c. 1775). These may, however, be ascribable to his son, who had travelled and who assisted his father on his return.

It was said by an authoritative writer[4] of 1825 that Robert Taylor and James Paine 'nearly divided the practice of the profession between them, for they had few competitors till Mr Robert Adam entered the lists'. This is obviously true, and none of the contemporaries of these two men, before about 1763, had anything like the amount of work which they handled. The one who came nearest to their eminence was John Carr (1723–1807) of York who, strangely enough, rivalled Paine in his own particular field, as a builder of great houses in the Midlands and the North. Carr began life as a working mason and, while still in his twenties, built Kirby Hall, near Boroughbridge, in the design of which Lord Burlington and Roger Morris were associated. After this first-hand experience of high Palladianism he built a long series of houses, the chief of which are Harewood House, Yorks. (1760; for Edwin Lascelles, afterwards Earl of Harewood), Tabley House, Cheshire (1762–9; for Sir Peter Leicester), and Basildon Park, Berks. (1776; for Sir Francis Sykes). These and most of Carr's other houses are as securely in the Palladian tradition as the houses of Taylor and Paine, but in the County Court House, York (1765–1777), he suddenly figures as a pioneer neo-classicist, producing a building which it is hard, indeed, to accept as the work of a provincial Palladian and must surely be attributable to some London 'ghost'. For Carr was not an artist of any calibre, but an able man of business. Like Taylor, he was interested in municipal affairs, becoming Lord Mayor of York twice. And, like Taylor, he left an immense fortune. If we may judge by the inclusion, in Beechey's portrait of him, of a view of the Crescent at Buxton, that was the work which he himself most esteemed. It is, indeed, a notable performance, as we shall see in the next chapter (p. 236), but its conservatism is beyond question and characteristic of its architect.

Apart from Taylor, Paine, and Carr one can mention the names of about a dozen architects similarly employed on the building of great Palladian houses. Most of them are represented by at least one illustration in Woolfe and Gandon's continuation, in two volumes, of *Vitruvius Britannicus*, published in 1769 and 1771. Woolfe was an official in the Works, Gandon a brilliant young designer to whom we shall presently come. Their book gives a wonderfully true picture of the architecture of the period, with its rigid triad of loyalties and cold, triumphant competence.

Palladianism in Scotland

On the death, in 1710, of Sir William Bruce, Scotland's last Court architect, the architecture of the country was in a condition of remote provincialism from which it was not to emerge for half a century. Colen Campbell's respectably classical house for a Glasgow merchant was exceptional, and it was perhaps inevitable that its gifted architect should seek fame and fortune in London. In his *Vitruvius Britannicus* Campbell mentions a Mr James Smith as being 'the most experienced architect in' Scotland and illustrates a rather grim, plain house built by him in 1692. Smith built, besides this, a great house for the Duke of Hamilton which showed him to be a not ineffective designer in a manner derived, perhaps, from Wren or Talman and certainly having English affiliations.

After 1715 and much more after 1745, opportunities for architecture did gradually increase in Scotland, thanks to those noblemen and lairds who began to enclose land and enrich themselves and the country by adopting English methods of agriculture. A large proportion of these opportunities fell to William Adam (1688–1748), a man of some property and standing who held an important official post as Master Mason in North Britain to the Board of Ordnance. Adam enlarged and reconstructed Smith's house for the Duke of Hamilton and succeeded Smith at other great houses. At Hopetoun (Plate 132A) he transformed Bruce's house (p. 161) into a swaggering pile in which the influence of Vanbrugh is apparent. Most of his houses reflect the mixed influence of Wren, the Palladians, and Gibbs, and Adam showed no desire to discriminate between them. His interiors have rich Rococo plaster-work, in some cases of Dutch workmanship. In a general way, he adopted Palladian plan arrangements, while Wren's motif of a pediment against a high attic was a favourite, and heavily rusticated architraves of the Gibbs type give some of his houses a quaintly barbaric richness. Latterly, his eldest son John brought a purer Palladianism into the business. Adam had his works engraved, with those of a few other Scottish architects, and sets of these engravings were eventually (c. 1810) published under the rather presumptuous title of *Vitruvius Scoticus*.

Scotland, shorn in 1707 of Court and Parliament, had not the need nor the means for much public architecture. At Edinburgh William Adam built the Royal Infirmary (Plate 132B; destroyed), with its square French dome, in 1738. The Royal Exchange (now the Burgh Hall), by J. Fergus, followed in 1753–61. To William Adam again is due the Town House, Dundee (demolished), a roughly Palladian mass, on a traditional Scottish plan, surmounted by a Gibbsian steeple. But these are the best of a period in Scottish history when architecture cannot be said to have flourished.

Palladianism in Ireland

In contrast to the economic and cultural poverty of Scotland, Ireland presents the picture of a country poverty-stricken indeed but supporting an alien aristocracy of great wealth and cultural vitality. At Dublin the Parliament and the Viceregal Court provided the focus for a metropolitan life scarcely less lavish and varied than that of Westminster, and with architectural opportunities more obvious because less obstructed by an inheritance of old buildings. Here Palladianism flourished exuberantly for some thirty years, contributing to the movement two or three at least of its finest monuments.

The most interesting Palladian building in Ireland is the old Parliament House, Dublin (now the Bank of Ireland; Plates 133A and B), built in 1728–39 and comprising a House of Lords and House of Commons, behind an imposing colonnaded approach. The Surveyor-General for Ireland in 1728 was Thomas Burgh (d. 1730), whose Trinity College Library (finished 1732) is a simple three-storey mass showing marked French but no Palladian influence. Burgh, however, appears to have delegated the Parliament building wholly to a younger man, Edward Lovet Pearce (c. 1699–1733), and from first to last it was Pearce who was responsible for the provision of drawings and the expenditure of funds.

But Pearce can hardly be the real designer of the building, for the stylistic evidence points emphatically in another direction. The two main interiors, the Lords' and Commons' chambers, are so close in style to Lord Burlington that one is almost bound to assume his participation in them. Pearce, in 1728, was only about twenty-nine, and of his early career we know nothing except that he was a Captain in a regiment of Dragoons.

Burlington, on the other hand, was just completing Chiswick. He was an Irish as well as an English peer, and moreover, Lord High Treasurer of Ireland, and can scarcely have been disinterested where the building of the Irish Parliament House was concerned. His silent but effective influence (to call it nothing more) may be taken for granted. The Parliament House certainly derives from the Burlington circle. The octagonal House of Commons (destroyed 1804), with its dome showing externally, recalls the octagon of Chiswick House, while its internal treatment, with an Ionic order raised on a high plinth, was prophetic of the hall at Holkham. The House of Lords (incorporated in the present Bank) is a simpler apartment with several features which reappear in Kent's designs, some years later, for the Houses of Parliament at Westminster.

The colonnaded approach to the Parliament House (Plate 133B) cannot be so readily assigned to Burlington, but here another member of the Palladian circle seems to be involved. Robert Castell (d. 1729) brought out his *Villas of the Ancients* in 1728, dedicating it to Burlington. In one of his reconstructions we find a colonnaded approach in which a portico develops from the colonnade much as it does in the Parliament House. A suspicion that Castell may have provided this part of the design is to some extent confirmed by an accusation of plagiarism levelled against Pearce in 1736, in which a reference to Castell appears to be intended.[5]

The participation, *sub rosa*, of the Burlington group in Irish architecture extends to the mansion which Speaker Conolly built for himself at Castletown, Kildare, in 1725–30. This has a three-storey, thirteen-window front of stupendous monotony, relieved only by window-dressings and a small porch, while the plan includes a hall manifestly based on part of Inigo Jones's Whitehall designs, on the publication of which Kent will have been working when Castletown was designed. With the execution of the building both Burgh and Pearce were associated.

Castletown, the first all-stone mansion in Ireland, inaugurated the great period of Palladian building, both in Dublin and in the country-side. The leading architect of the period was Richard Cassels (c. 1690–1751), a German. If Summerhill, Meath (burnt 1917), was his the rather continental details of it are no doubt due to his early training, for in his later works Cassels conformed exactly to English standards. Tyrone House (1740–5), the first stone house in Dublin, and Leinster House (1745), also in Dublin, could both have been built by a London Palladian, and the latter is comparable to Campbell's first design for Wanstead, given in *Vitruvius Britannicus*. His greatest country-houses are Carton, Kildare (finishing 1739), and Russborough, Wicklow (1741).

After Cassels's death, the leading architect in Dublin was, for a time, John Smyth, who built two Palladian churches and copied, in his façade of the Provost's House at Trinity College, Burlington's design for the London house of General Wade (copied, in turn, from a drawing wrongly attributed to Palladio). Another architect was Thomas Ivory, who built the Blue-Coat School (1773–80), a centre-and-wings composition like a country-house; a Gibbsian steeple was proposed but never executed.

By 1760 the appearance of the better streets of Dublin was very much that of those in the West End of London, while internally many of the houses were enriched with Rococo plaster-work exceeding anything of its period in England. This was the work of foreign immigrants, notably Paul and Philip Francini and Bartholomew Cramillion. Cramillion's interior of the Rotunda Hospital Chapel, designed (1755-7) by himself within a carcass built from Cassels's design, is a surprising specimen which approaches the full theatrical Rococo of continental churches.

Apart from occasional decorative phenomena of this kind the absence of local variations in Ireland is astonishing. Irish Palladianism is as intimately joined to the London school as if the Irish sea were no greater an affair to negotiate than a couple of English counties. Such was the carrying power of this movement which penetrated to every corner of the British Isles and was carried by British ships even further overseas to the remotest corners of the earth.

NOTES TO CHAPTER 22

1. Ripley did, however, design some important houses outside his official sphere. He carried out Houghton Hall, Norfolk, for Walpole, from Colen Campbell's designs (1722-35), introducing the corner-domes and making other alterations. In 1724-30 he designed Wolterton Hall, Norfolk, which Horace Walpole considered 'one of the best houses of the size in England'. It is compactly planned round a top-lit staircase, going the full height of the house and, although scarcely elegant, does, as Walpole says, 'acquit this artist of the charge of ignorance'.

2. By this time, the Comptrollership was the highest office attainable by a professional architect, the Surveyorship having become a purely political appointment.

3. Malton is best known as a topographical draughtsman of extraordinary accuracy. He began, however, as an architect, winning the Royal Academy Gold Medal in 1782. Two years later he exhibited a design for a bath (now in the Royal Institute of British Architects) which has all the essentials of the Reduced Annuities Office. He was probably employed by Taylor, after whose death he brought out a fine series of aquatints of that architect's works, the Reduced Annuities Office among them.

4. Thomas Hardwick in his life of Chambers, prefixed to Gwilt's edition of the *Civil Architecture*.

5. The accusation is in a scurrilous poem, *The Toast*, by the Rev. William King, where Pearce is said to have used the brains of one *Castellus sive Castles* for his design. Although Castell is, no doubt, intended, commentators on the poem have invariably identified *Castellus* with Richard Cassels, a wholly different character but one who, as we shall see in a moment, was well known in Ireland. See C. P. Curran in Bibliography.

CHAPTER 23

THE HOUSE AND THE STREET IN THE
EIGHTEENTH CENTURY

THE town-house, as we saw in Chapter 10, reached a decisive stage in its conversion to classicism when the houses in Lincoln's Inn Fields and Great Queen Street were built, in the decade before the Civil War. The gable vanished and a classical order was applied (notably in Sir David Conyngham's house) in a wonderfully appropriate way, the ground-floor being regarded as a podium and the order itself embracing the two upper storeys without inconvenience or distortion. At the Restoration this new mode of expression did not have by any means an immediate success, nor, when the City was rebuilt after 1666, did pilastered houses of this kind occur frequently. The reason was, perhaps, that the change of emphasis implied by the proportions of the Conyngham house was not generally acceptable. The idea of treating the first-floor rooms as more stately and more formal than the others and giving them increased height for that purpose did not commend itself either to the rebuilding citizens or to the speculating builders in the West End.

Thus, the typical London house of the Restoration period has windows all the same size, whether on ground, first, or second floors. Its external ornaments consist of key-blocks to all the windows, bands at the principal floor-levels, a modilion eaves cornice, and a wooden door-case consisting usually of a classical portal. Its plan is the old inevitable one of a front room and a back room on each floor with staircase at the side, and, frequently, a small projection at the back providing each floor with a small room or closet. There is a basement (a Jacobean innovation, as we learn from Thorpe), but without a proper area and lit by windows peeping out of the earth at ground level.

Houses of this kind were built in great numbers after 1670, notably by the greatest speculator of the time, Nicholas Barbon (d. 1698), a man of unscrupulous character but outstanding ability as a financier and a pioneer of insurance. So far as one can judge by existing evidence, all Barbon's houses were identical in design and detail, even to the profiles of the staircase balustrades, and his work is a remarkable instance of large-scale house production at an early period.

The larger town-houses of the Restoration period differed little from the others except that, if they extended to a width of five or seven windows, the centre part would be broken forward and surmounted by a pediment; and there might be stone quoins. The last good example in London of a house of this type was Carlisle House (Plate 134A), off Dean Street, Soho, destroyed in 1941.

The uniformity of the Restoration period lasted till the reign of George I, and there are few London houses of that time, existing or recorded, to which the above observations do not approximately apply. Among those few is that interesting freak, Schomberg House, Pall Mall (Plate 134B). Built about 1698 for the Duke of Schomberg, a German by birth, but a Marshal of France as well as an English Duke, it evidently represents an attempt to be continental, an English builder (apparently) having helped himself to a variety of themes given in the engravings recently published by Daniel Marot. It is one of the few buildings which can be set down to the influence of the great French ornament-alist, although he styled himself 'Architect to the King of England' and lived in this country for some, at least, of William III's reign.

Other London houses slightly out of the ordinary are those in Queen Anne's Gate (c. 1705), with grotesque heads for keystones and carved door-hoods of a unique kind; and the earlier houses in Hanover Square and George Street (c. 1718), where the windows are joined by rusticated work into continuous vertical features, rather in the manner of Lemuet's designs, while on the line of each party-wall is a *chaîne*, in the form of a strip of alternate brick and stone (? or stucco) rustication. This curious intrusion of French design in Georgian London has not yet been accounted for.

The vertical connexion of the windows appears again in a fairly common type of house exemplified in Nos 43 and 44 Grosvenor Square, but here the connexion is solely by means of the introduction of *chaînes* of red brick into the ordinary brown. In both Hanover Square and Grosvenor Square the windows have segmental arches instead of flat lintels.

Such variations as these vanish with the onset of Palladian influence; for the movement rapidly established a new formula for the London house. This derived from the old houses in Lincoln's Inn Fields and Queen Street (generally supposed, at the time, to be by, or connected with, Inigo Jones) and insisted on a major emphasis at the level of the first floor. It did not insist on the application of pilasters. It involved not an applied but an *implied* order, standing (with or without pedestal) at first-floor level. This idea, of course, is implicit in any part of a Palladian design (e.g. the sides of a villa) where the order is not expressed; and its application to the ordinary London house is perhaps too obvious a move to be accounted a stroke of genius. Yet the success of the formula makes its introduction important. From about 1730 till well after 1830 the façade of the London house was loyal to this Palladian *schema*. Where there is an order, it rises at first-floor level through two or three storeys to the entablature, above which there may be an attic. Where there is no order, a broad band marks the first-floor level and there is room between the lintels of the top windows and the cornice for the architrave and frieze which are not there. Sometimes an additional (narrow) band runs under the cills of the first-floor windows in token (as in many Palladian villas) of an absent pedestal under the order.

It is impossible definitely to locate the first London houses in which this formula was introduced, but one naturally looks towards the streets round Burlington House, where building began soon after 1717 and where there are houses of the older type adjacent to others of a more Palladian character which must reflect the influence of Burlington him-self. In Burlington Gardens we find Queensberry House (Plate 135; now the Bank of Scotland) with a noble Composite façade by Leoni based on Conyngham's (so-called Inigo Jones's) house in Lincoln's Inn Fields. This façade[1] not only resurrects in a splendid way the theme of 1630, but controls the proportions of the houses in Old Burlington Street, where they meet its return façade. Now the date of Queensberry House is given by Leoni as 1721, so here is the probable birthplace of the Palladian town-house. In Old

Burlington Street a broad stone band, continuing from Queensberry House, emphasizes the primacy of the first-floor level. In the next street, Savile Row, the *schema* is independently introduced and the narrow stone band at cill level is added – perhaps for the first time in a street of plain houses.

Palladian houses of the Burlington Gardens and Savile Row kind are still common in London and we mentioned a few in dealing with Flitcroft, Ware, and Vardy. Representing the later Palladian phase, there are several fine examples by Sir Robert Taylor (p. 224).

The London house naturally led the way in design throughout the country, and there is little to add concerning the provincial town-house except that it developed, all along, much later than its prototype and often with much greater elaboration. There are Palladian town-houses in York, Norwich, Bristol, Derby, Nottingham, and many smaller places, which in the London of their time would have ranked as very conspicuous and even pretentious residences. Usually they overlap in date the next phase of innovation in the capital, but in design and execution they are often equal to the best London work.

The Street and the Square

In the eighteenth century, Great Queen Street was always accounted 'the first uniform street' in London, and the principle of uniformity may be ascribed to the influence of Jones. There, and in Lincoln's Inn Fields, it was probably imposed on the builders. After the Restoration there is no evidence of the official imposition of uniformity, and the rebuilders of the devastated city of 1666 had complete freedom within the requirements of the Rebuilding Act, which dictated only floor-heights and certain structural dimensions. The principle of uniformity, however, was not forgotten, and it operated, naturally enough, when one builder undertook the erection of a number of contiguous houses. This did not often happen, since the speculations of the typical London craftsmen were usually in ones and twos and threes on widely distributed sites. It did happen, however, in the case of Nicholas Barbon, who, we are told, found it 'not worth his while to deal little, *that* a bricklayer could do. The gain he expected was out of great undertakings, which would rise lustily in the whole.' Such 'great undertakings' consisted in the laying out and building of entire streets of houses, like, for example, Essex Street (finished 1682) on the site of old Essex House. There Barbon built a uniform street and closed it, at the river end, with a Corinthian water-gate.

The very obvious connexion between large-scale building operations and uniformity of design accounts for most of the regularity which Georgian London possessed. Where regularity was imposed, it was imposed usually by a head lessee on the smaller men to whom he assigned building-leases. Ground landlords rarely found it practicable to dictate the architectural character of the buildings on their land. They might set out the lines of the streets and squares, but once the building agreements were signed the control of elevations was virtually out of their hands. If they let large blocks of sites to one builder uniformity would probably result; if they did not, a street or the side of a square was liable to be built up in a heterogeneous way.

This we see in the earlier squares of London. The first of these squares to be so called was Bloomsbury Square, laid out in front of his town mansion by the 4th Earl of South-ampton and begun to be built in 1661. St James's Square was laid out by the 1st Earl of St Albans almost at the same time, a lease having been granted to the Earl in 1660. The pre-cedents for these squares were, of course, Covent Garden and Lincoln's Inn Fields, with perhaps a glance at the great *places* of Paris and Lyons. Neither of these squares was archi-tecturally ambitious and it is doubtful if either was ever completely uniform. Hanover Square, promoted *c.* 1717, probably by the financier Sir Theodore Janssen, was certainly not uniform, for two very different types of early house survive, and it is not till the development of the Grosvenor Estate that an attempt was made to endow the sides of a London square with an architectural character over-riding that of the individual house. Characteristically, the attempt was on the part of speculators rather than of the ground landlord. It was not entirely successful, but on two sides of Grosvenor Square (Plate 136) experiments were made which eventually bore abundant fruit.

The east side of Grosvenor Square (*c.* 1725–35; all now rebuilt or refaced) was erected by a single speculator, John Simmons. It consisted of seven houses. The centre house was larger than the others, with rusticated quoins and a prominent centre crowned by a pediment. The end houses were similarly but less emphatically articulated. By this means the block assumed the character of a single palatial building, and an important step had been taken towards a new conception of street architecture.[2]

The north side of the square was the subject of a more daring, if less successful, effort. Here the builder-architect, Edward Shepherd (see p. 222), proposed an architectural treat-ment of the entire block, but as some of the other builders would not fall in with it he had to limit himself to grouping a few houses together behind a façade which was not, even then, symmetrical. Shepherd's innovation, however, consisted in composing the front of a set of houses in a manner strictly imitative of a great Palladian villa like Wan-stead, which, indeed, his houses in Grosvenor Square somewhat resembled; for he rusti-cated the ground-floor and erected upon it an attached portico of six Corinthian columns. Lop-sided, and relegated to one side of the entire block, this adventure misfired, but the great thing was that it had been tried, and almost immediately the experiment was repeated with complete success in a distant town by another architect.

Bath and John Wood I

With the completion of Shepherd's Grosvenor Square houses, about 1730, the develop-ment of urban design in London ceases, for a time, to be of much interest. The story, however, continues and reaches its climax in Bath where street design developed in a most important way for a matter of forty years.

Bath in the first quarter of the eighteenth century was still a small town dependent on a moribund wool industry, but with an extraneous attraction in the qualities of its famous waters. That attraction had drawn royal health-seekers and, in their train, a section of London society in search of a summer centre of amusement, when the Court was out of town. By 1720 the city's social reputation was already high, and its architecture, hitherto indistinguishable from that of any moderately thriving west-country town, began to receive distinguished additions. Of these, one of the earliest and most important was a House in Abbey Church Yard (*c*. 1720) built for General Wade and closely imitating the 'Inigo Jones' façade in Lincoln's Inn Fields. We do not know who designed it, but a local mason with *Vitruvius Britannicus*, I, plate 50, before him would fill the rôle.

The great period, however, of Bath's expansion began in 1725. In that year, 'Beau' Nash as Master of Ceremonies was at the height of his influence, while the brains and capital of Ralph Allen were exploiting the capabilities of Bath stone. In that year also John Wood (1704–54) drew the first plans of those parts of the city with which his name will always be associated.

Now these plans were drawn by Wood not in Bath but in Yorkshire, a county where he enjoyed the patronage of Lord Bingley, whose seat was at Bramham, near Tadcaster. The house at Bramham was built in 1710, possibly by Leoni, and there is evidence that Wood was early associated with that architect. He was certainly engaged on the lay-out of the Park at Bramham, for there is an engraving bearing his name which shows an ambitious design in the Le Nôtre manner; one feature of this plan is highly important (as we shall see) in view of Wood's later planning activities in Bath.

In 1725–7, however, Wood was mostly in London, where he was employed by the Duke of Chandos on some trifling work in Cavendish Square and where he may also have been associated with building activities on the Grosvenor Estate. It was in London that Wood approached two owners of land near Bath with the development schemes he had prepared in Yorkshire. One of these landowners, Robert Gay, accepted his proposal and employed him as his agent. Almost at the same time (1727) Wood undertook a considerable rebuilding scheme in Bath for the Duke of Chandos and was also involved in other projects there, including a Hospital, for Humphrey Thayer.

In 1727, Wood moved to Bath and lived there until his death twenty-seven years later. He soon found himself not only architect and builder but lease-holder of much of Gay's land, on which, at his own risk, he started to build Queen Square (1729–36; Plate 137). In view of Wood's London experience, it is not surprising to find that Queen Square is directly related to the great west London estates of the time. Its north side, with its rusticated ground-floor and attached portico, is, in fact, a fulfilment of Edward Shepherd's thwarted intentions in Grosvenor Square, while the original arrangement of the west side, with a great house set back and two more as salient wings, echoed a proposal (not executed) by the Duke of Chandos for the north side of Cavendish Square. In short, Wood's first work in Bath is the direct outcome of the most recent architectural experiments in London.

But if Queen Square is, for that reason, important in the history of architecture, John Wood's further works at Bath are much more so. He had a curiously original mind, fundamentally unlearned, but steeped in amateur erudition. As his *Origin of Architecture* shows (p. 220), he had read a great deal, and out of this reading had come the conception of an expanded Bath with something of the character of its ancient Roman predecessor. Wood never lived to see the rediscovery of the ancient Baths, but he knew the city had been Roman, and was determined to re-endow it with Roman monuments, including a Forum, a Circus, and what he called an Imperial Gymnasium. This quixotic ambition he partly achieved. In the South Parade (1743 onwards) and the open space in front of it, we see the relics of Wood's Forum; had it been completed according to his desires, it would have consisted of houses with classical palace façades facing on to sunk gardens with rusticated retaining walls related in design to the houses – an original and striking conception. As it stands it is a rather tame composition standing above a patch of drab allotments.

But if the Forum misfired, the Circus (Plate 138) was a considerable success. Although Wood first conceived his Circus as a place 'for the exhibition of sports', the fantastic impracticability of such a project in eighteenth-century Bath must soon have dawned on him. The conception became practicable only when he merged the Circus idea with the idea already embodied in Grosvenor Square and Queen Square – that is to say, the treatment of a row of ordinary town-houses as a monumental unity.

The Circus at Bath is a monumental conception, based on the Colosseum inverted, simplified, and enormously reduced in scale and made to be the frontispiece of thirty-three standard town-houses of moderate size. It has three superimposed orders, their entablatures richly carved, and its effect is quaintly beautiful – as if some simple-minded community had taken over an antique monument and neatly adapted it as a residence.

The plan of the Circus, though at first sight simplicity itself, is remarkable. Three streets enter it, none of them opposite one another; so that no impression is given of the Circus being 'bisected'. The plan is, indeed, that of a *rond-point* in the tradition of French garden lay-out of the Le Nôtre school, and we only have to glance at Wood's engraving of the gardens at Bramham to see where, in fact, this important element in the design comes from. Nor should it be forgotten that J. H. Mansart had built his circular Place des Victoires in 1686.

One of the streets leading into the Circus is Gay Street, the first Bath street planned by Wood on the Gay estate. The other two are short streets leading to the two major works of Wood's son and successor who bore the same name. One of these is the Assembly Rooms: the other is the Royal Crescent.

John Wood II: The Invention of the Crescent

The elder Wood lived only to see his Circus begun. He died in 1754, and it was completed by his son. In 1766 the younger Wood acquired, in partnership with another person, a piece of land eastwards of the Circus and on this he built the Royal Crescent (1767–75; Plate 139A). This great semi-elliptical block, comprising thirty houses, is of very special importance in English architecture, for it introduced a type of urban composition which was used over and over again, with innumerable variations, until well into the nineteenth century.

The creation of this type was a remarkable stroke. Probably it developed out of the Circus by way of the notion of an elliptical 'circus' following, more or less, the true curvature of the Roman Colosseum. That conception was split into two 'demi-colosseums' by the need for a road passing through the structure. The omission of one of the 'demi-colosseums' leaves the Crescent.[3] The younger Wood, however, did not retain in his 'demi-colosseum' the ordonnance which his father had used in the Circus, but adopted the simpler canon which had first appeared in London in the Conyngham house in Lincoln's Inn Fields. The result is a noble sweep of Ionic columns, raised on a high base. The scale is much greater than that of the Circus, the monumentality more effective.

Taken together, the Circus and the Royal Crescent with Gay Street and Queen Square form a highly original complex of urban architecture. Nowhere in Europe had anything with quite this same freedom and invention been executed. In England the influence of these things was naturally very great, Bath having become, by the middle of the eighteenth century, nearly as important a centre of artistic leadership as London. The idea of blocks of town-houses presented as monumental unities was immediately accepted. The Circus, it is true, was rarely imitated, until Dance, followed by Nash, took up the theme for its merits as a way of dealing with a traffic-crossing. But the Crescent had a glorious career.

The first important imitation of the Bath crescent was at Buxton, Derbyshire (Plate 139B), where the 5th Duke of Devonshire employed (1779–81) John Carr of York (p. 226) to build a structure comparable in many ways to Royal Crescent, Bath. But Carr, instead of following the type of Lincoln's Inn Fields in his elevations, went back to another famous classic of the Inigo Jones period – the Piazzas of Covent Garden, giving his crescent a round-arched loggia on the ground-floor. At Bath, Camden Crescent, by John Eveleigh, was built in 1788, to be followed at once by John Palmer's Lansdown Crescent, and by Somerset Place, again by Eveleigh. The fashion soon spread about the country. In London a miniature Crescent and Circus, joined by a short street, were laid out off the Minories by the younger Dance as early as 1768, before the Bath Crescent was complete; and Dance's later planning schemes introduced the feature frequently, though few of his projects were executed. The Crescent arrived at the seaside before the end of the century, and Royal Crescent, Brighton, was built in 1798. Here the theme of a 'demi-colosseum' is quite forgotten. There is no order, nor even the token of one; angular bay windows to each house are introduced and here, too, the verandah makes one of its first appearances in this country.

Street Design: Later Developments

Street design up to the time of the Regency will be found to be loyal, in principle, to what had been developed in Bath. The two most important names in English planning during the period are those of Robert Adam and George Dance II, whose careers will be dealt with in the chapters which follow. Both of them recognized the principle of the monumentally treated block of ordinary houses, with centre and wings emphasized, as the proper solution of the urban street problem. We shall find Adam using this theme at the Adelphi (1768), Portland Place (1774), and Fitzroy Square (1790), London, and Charlotte Square, Edinburgh (1791). For William Pulteney's Bathwick estate at Bath, Adam prepared an extensive formal design in the French manner. Only the classical bridge (Pulteney Bridge, 1769–74) which links it to the city was executed, but the lay-out by

Thomas Baldwin (*c.* 1751–1820) incorporated Adam's diagonal square (Laura Place, *c.* 1788) as the focal point in the scheme. Baldwin also designed the charming Bath Street, Bath (1791), where the fronts of the houses are supported on slim Ionic columns so that a covered promenade is formed behind them.

George Dance II's planning schemes prepared for the Corporation of the City of London exist mostly on paper, but show that he was bent on developing the discoveries of the two Woods. Among other things, he planned Alfred Place (1790) off Tottenham Court Road, London, with two facing crescents joined by a broad street, the fronts of the houses (all rebuilt) being designed by him.

The square, the crescent, and the circus, alone and in combination, formed the basic elements in English town-planning till the end of our period, and in a later chapter we shall discuss their architectural development in the hands of John Nash in London and by other architects elsewhere in Britain.

NOTES TO CHAPTER 23

1. Altered in 1792. J. B. Papworth in Britton and Pugin, *Public Buildings of London*, 1825, implies that it was wholly rebuilt but Malton, in his *Picturesque Tour*, 1792, makes it clear that this is an exaggeration.

2. Among the Gibbs drawings in the Ashmolean Museum, Oxford, is an undated engraving by Colen Campbell for a row of houses on this east side, treated in the manner of Lincoln's Inn Fields.

3. The adoption of this word requires explanation. 'Demi-lune' was a familiar term in fortification and may conceivably have suggested the analogous 'crescent'.

CHAPTER 24

BUILDING IN GOTHIC:
FROM WREN TO WALPOLE

WREN built Tom Tower at Christ Church, Oxford, in 1681–2 and for nearly sixty years after that date the Office of Works produced, from time to time, Gothic buildings which owed much in spirit and often something in silhouette and detail to that beginning. Of Wren's own attitude to Gothic something has already been said (p. 155). Clearly, it had for him no emotional significance whatever. Further, he considered it unscientific and its complexities often meaningless. He despised 'the Flutter of Arch-buttresses', and 'the Normans' for thinking them ornamental, while 'pinnacles are of no use, and as little Ornament'. And yet Wren designed in Gothic, when occasion demanded, without apparent lack of enjoyment or the vivid exercise of thought, or even any great aversion to pinnacles. And to two of his colleagues, William Dickinson (c. 1671–1725) and Nicholas Hawksmore, he transmitted his own peculiar mode of handling the style.

The result is that we owe to the Office of Works of late Stuart and early Georgian times a really rather remarkable group of Gothic buildings and designs. The detail is often perfunctory and the organic essence of Gothic – the unfolding of part from part – is completely missed. But in composition there lacks neither invention nor technical skill. The group of London steeples in the Gothic style was mentioned in connexion with the City Churches. St Dunstan's-in-the-East (1698) is a brilliant experiment on the theme of old St Mary-le-Bow and perhaps from Wren's own pencil, the clock-stage being very close to that of Tom Tower. Much later come the towers of St Mary Aldermary (1702), probably Dickinson's work, and St Michael Cornhill (1721), certainly by Hawksmore. The former has an interesting relationship to the base of Tom Tower, while the latter is obviously paraphrased from that of Magdalen College, Oxford. The plainer tower of St Alban's, Wood Street (1682–7, or possibly later), is a fourth member of the group.

On paper, one of the most remarkable Gothic products of the Office was a design for rebuilding St Mary's, Warwick, which was burnt in 1694.[1] The drawings, which seem to be in Dickinson's hand, show a west tower and spire modelled in a most thoughtful and interesting way, while in one version there is a central domical lantern very close in silhouette to Tom Tower. Equally interesting is a project (1722, signed by Dickinson) for a central tower for Westminster Abbey. The twelve-sided drum and dome, from whose apex rises a pinnacled lantern, is a quaint reduction of the giant theme of St Paul's, naïf in detail but, in composition, sensitive and interesting.

It was left for Hawksmore to erect, after Wren's death, the last monuments of this circumscribed and somewhat intellectual school of neo-Gothic. He it was who designed, just before his death, the present west towers of the Abbey. Their dour proportions, emphasized by strong, shelf-like cornices, stamp the design as his, relating it to the twin towers at All Souls, Oxford, and, less obviously, to some of those classical towers by him in which there is so strong an element of Gothic research. It is his All Souls work, however (p. 193), begun in 1715 and continuing till the erection of the 'monastick' cupola on the west gate in 1734, which concludes this whole Gothic episode. Its spirit is exactly the spirit of Wren's Tom Tower, which, incidentally, the cupola echoes. Gothic is used without the least sympathy for its inherent qualities, without the least sentiment for its epoch, but with a boldness and intelligence born of no small measure of appreciation.

The Wren school of Gothic had no influence outside the Office of Works, nor was it ever used by its exponents except where, as in churches and colleges, the style was dictated by circumstance. For a medievalism of a totally different character, a medievalism exploited emotionally, we must look to Sir John Vanbrugh. His house at Greenwich (Plate 140A) was built, in 1717, with the deliberate intention of evoking the associations of an ancient fortress. There is not a scrap of Gothic detail about it and, as originally built, its symmetry was strict. But its steep proportions, narrow, heavy windows, and round towers with pointed roofs are emotionally Gothic. It is the first English 'sham castle'.

Vanbrugh, unlike Wren, had a real feeling for the romantic associations of the English past. He tried to preserve the 'Holbein' Gate at Whitehall and incurred the rage of the Duchess of Marlborough for wishing to retain the ruins of old Woodstock Manor in the park at Blenheim. He had, in fact, an emotional and dramatic appreciation of decaying Gothic which, if shared already by a mind as singular as Pope's,[2] had never yet appeared in an architect. There is no sign of it, even, in Hawksmore, Vanbrugh's close colleague.

Vanbrugh's romantic castle and the few medievalist touches in his great houses and their lodges cannot have been very influential. Nor do they represent any study whatever of English Gothic buildings – they are, in fact, closer to Italian and French stage designs in which Gothic was, for theatric purposes, introduced. But Vanbrugh is symptomatic. By the time he died, the notion of Gothic retrospection for the pleasure of it was alive.

The Gothic of William Kent

It was not the intellectual medievalism of Wren, nor the emotional medievalism of Vanbrugh which was to give the eighteenth century its Gothic language. This, oddly enough, seems to have been the invention of a man whose curiosity about Gothic was infinitely less than Wren's and whose invention was of the fancy rather than of the imagination. But there seems little doubt that it was William Kent (p. 203) who evolved the flimsy decorative equivalents for Gothic which were to persist throughout the eighteenth century and only to disappear under the censure of the Victorian Gothic school itself.

The evidence relative to Kent's Gothic work is rather meagre. There was never much of it and still less survives. One of his first essays must have been in connexion with the rebuilding of part of the Clock Court at Hampton Court. Here he at first proposed a classical building, but Sir Robert Walpole (not usually remembered as a promoter of Gothic) induced him to abandon this and to imitate the Tudor work of the old Palace. The result (seen on the right in Plate 1B) includes a gatehouse with a plaster vault over the entry, a window in three divisions rather curiously grouped under a single arch, and an angular panel bearing the date 1732. At once, in the sharp flimsiness of the design, we recognize the authentic character of Georgian Gothic, here expressed perhaps for the very first time. More clearly still we recognize it in Kent's reconstruction of the Tudor buildings at Esher Lodge, built for Henry Pelham some time between 1729 and 1739 (the gatehouse only survives). Here occur some essential features of the style – large quatre-foil openings and straight Tudor labels over pointed arches; and the quatre-foil is found again in the rough-built 'Temple of the Mill' at Rousham (p. 207). But the most important specimens of Kent's Gothic were the screen to the Courts of Chancery and King's Bench, at the south end of Westminster Hall, 1738–9, and the screen in Gloucester Cathedral, erected 1742. These elucidate Kent's attitude to Gothic very well. Clearly it was an affair of selecting Gothic features which appealed to him as characteristic and decorative and then arranging them conformably to his classically trained taste. In these designs there is just a trace of the influence of the French decorators who influenced his furniture design. The depressed ogee arches, which occur in both, have the lax curvature of scrolls meeting under a console table, and the corbel-table which adorns the cornice in the Westminster design is made up of little pendants which might almost be the points of a French *lambrequin*. More important is the way Kent tended to reduce his Gothic material to familiar classical formulas, articulating architrave, frieze, and cornice when possible or suggesting superimposed orders. This, perhaps, as much as anything made his Gothic acceptable and, moreover, easy to imitate.

Kent's style became immediately popular and already in 1736 'the modern Gothick' was praised for its delicacy and whimsicality, qualities hardly found in the Gothic of Wren and Hawksmore but appropriate to the creations of a decorator such as Kent. By 1742 the style had sufficiently circulated for Batty Langley (p. 221) to think it worth while devoting one of his text-books to it, which he did under the following title: *Gothic Architecture, improved by Rules and Proportions, in many Grand Designs of Columns, Doors, Windows, Chimney-pieces, Arcades, Colonnades, Porticos, Umbrellos, Temples, and Pavillions etc.* The designs do not, as one might expect, plagiarize Kent, and although the spirit of them is Kentian (especially as regards the reduction of Gothic columns to equivalents of the five orders), their detail shows first-hand acquaintance with authentic examples including Westminster Abbey, whose 'order' is engraved, if not accurately at least recognizably. Technically, the designs are quite able, in the sense that the distribution of enrichments and the moulded profiles show a mind not insensitive to the grammar of classical design.

The Gothic of Kent, and of Batty Langley, was, fundamentally, a free variation of classical forms constituting not an imitation but an *equivalent* of Gothic. The Chinese was being used in much the same way. And both the Gothic and the Chinese, in the middle of the eighteenth century, enjoyed a freedom somewhat akin to the Rococo which, from across the Channel, sent occasional eddies of influence across Palladian England.

Gothic buildings, conceived in the Kent spirit, became common in the forties and by 1753 it was even possible to regard the Gothic fashion as outmoded. That date, in fact, marks very well the end of the purely Kentian phase and the beginning of another. It is the date of two interesting Gothic churches. Shobdon, Herefordshire, built for Lord

Bateman, is a pure example of the Gothic style of Kent and, although built several years after his death, must have been designed, if not by him, by somebody[3] in his circle. Hartwell, Bucks. (Plate 141), an octagonal church with a rich plaster vault, built for Sir Henry Lee by the architect Henry Keene (1726–76), is Kentian in parts but advances notably towards archaeological correctness.[4] This same year, 1753, saw the completion of two houses by two famous amateurs of Gothic – Sanderson Miller's Lacock Abbey and the first part of Horace Walpole's Strawberry Hill. It is the intrusion of the amateur into the Gothic story which really marks the beginning of the new phase. The amateur brings a new spirit to the game, new sentiments, new emotions – poetical, literary, nostalgic. And the two amateurs just mentioned need consideration in detail.

The Amateurs: Sanderson Miller and Horace Walpole

Sanderson Miller (1717–80) was a Warwickshire squire with a taste for architecture which he carried so far as to become an amateur architect, providing designs for his friends and his friends' friends. His largest work is the house he built for Lord Lyttelton at Hagley (1751–9), a Palladian building of no particular importance. More interesting are his essays in Gothic, which earned him a certain reputation as a virtuoso. He started on his own estate at Radway, where he built first a picturesque thatched cottage (1744; on Edgehill), then altered his own house, Radway Grange, in the Gothic style and finally erected a sham castle and tower, with drawbridge, on Edgehill. The sham castle idea caught on and he was soon building one at Hagley; then another for Lord Chancellor Hardwicke at Wimpole; and there were others, as well as Gothic summer-houses and other trifles. At Wroxton (for Lord North) he built a church tower and at Hagley Church a new chancel, but of these only the tower, a plain enough object, exists. His best surviving contribution to the Gothic movement is unquestionably the new hall at Lacock Abbey, built in 1753–5 for John Ivory Talbot. It still stands (Plate 140B) and strikes one immediately as a work of the Kent school, with some minor originalities such as the pierced parapet and the 'rose' window. The interior is provided with many niches, filled with Baroque terra-cotta statues by a German sculptor working in London, V. A. Sederbach. The whole thing was done (as the surviving correspondence confirms) as a light-hearted extravaganza. Such was the spirit of all Miller's commissions. With Walpole (who was no friend of Miller, though he was obliged to praise the Radway tower), light-heartedness is tinged with something a little more serious.

Sanderson Miller was, in an approximate sense, an architect. Horace Walpole (1717–97) was not; but of the two he was incomparably the more important promoter of the Gothic style. Fourth son of the great First Minister, Sir Robert, he was born to affluence without responsibility. He was at Eton and King's College and made an extended Grand Tour, in company with Thomas Gray. He entered Parliament as Member for a pocket borough and held a number of valuable sinecures. He never married and, thwarted of an active political career, constructed out of private idleness, out of the pleasures of friendship and dilettantism, a career as assiduous and responsible as any in public life. He constituted himself prime observer of the age. 'I am a dancing senator. Not that I do dance, or do

anything by being a senator, but I go to balls, and to the House of Commons – to look on.'
In the arts, too, Walpole's position was that of observer. He designed nothing, but he
observed everything, knew a great deal, collected a great deal, and was as infinitely
curious about the past as about the present. For architecture, which always interested him,
he had a fine taste, though no special susceptibility. He would have been incapable of
initiating or even of patronizing any great departure in the art. His contribution consists
in one thing only – that he discovered, or re-discovered, a certain kind of literary pleasure –
the pleasure of elaborating the appeal of history by the imitation of historical monuments.
Whether they were imitated with taste did, of course, matter to him; taste, indeed, was
more important than accuracy. But therein he was merely of his age. In practising the
pleasures of evocative imitation he was a pace ahead of it.

The story of Walpole's contribution to architecture is the story of his house – Strawberry Hill, Twickenham. He was thirty when he bought the remainder of the lease of an
ordinary little house overlooking the Thames, as a place of retirement not too far from
London; and it was a year or two before the idea occurred to him of enlarging it in a
spirit of caprice, of making the fabric of the house reflect the studies he was then enjoying –
topography, county history, and the antecedents of his own family.

Naturally, an architect was needed and in 1749 Walpole engaged a safe and sound man,
William Robinson (c. 1720–75), who had lately succeeded John James as Clerk of the
Works at Greenwich. Robinson's name is not often remembered in connexion with
Strawberry Hill, the reason being that he had no flair for Walpole's new approach to
Gothic designing and so was used from first to last simply as the professional executive.
But the fact is that much of Strawberry Hill is by Robinson. His must be the 'carcase', the
general proportions, and much, indeed, of the general exterior appearance (Plate 142A);
and all those things are Gothic of a very ordinary kind for the date and very close to the
style of Kent. In the earlier (eastern) parts of the house, built 1748–54, there is scarcely
anything which Kent might not have done ten years earlier.

The novelties at Strawberry Hill gradually reveal themselves against this ordinary
background. They are novelties of detail and originated in the minds of Walpole and
those few special friends who formed the 'Committee', among whom Richard Bentley
(1708–82) was for a time the most important. Now Bentley was no more an architect
than Walpole. He had, to be sure, a facility in Rococo ornament (his illustrations to Gray's
poems, 1753, derive perhaps from Jean Bérain) and passed easily from this to an innocent
foolery with Gothic patterns. A number of his designs exist, and innocent foolery is all
they are. He designed the north entrance, scarcely more truly Gothic than Robinson. He
designed the staircase, with traceried panels in the balustrade; and he designed the screen
and chimney-piece in the Holbein Chamber. These last works are more strictly Wal-
polean, for here Bentley's Rococo spirit is merged with the spirit of archaeology; the
screen is said to borrow its theme from some gates at Rouen and the chimney-piece is a
fabrication based on Archbishop Warham's tomb at Canterbury.

Besides Bentley, the amateur architects at Strawberry Hill included John Chute of the
Vyne (1701–76). His were the interiors of the Great Parlour and Library (Plate 142B)
added in 1745 and deriving their themes from Dugdale's illustrations of old St Paul's and

from a tomb in Westminster Abbey. While to Thomas Pitt, later Lord Camelford, is due the design of the Gallery (1759–62), with its canopied niches, filled with mirrors, and its ceiling adapted from one of the aisles of Henry VII's chapel. The fireplace here, however, is by Chute.

The 'designs' of all these gentlemen were to the last degree amateurish and their execution at the hands of Mr Robinson in no way disguises the fact. They have indeed a Rococo prettiness but at least half the pleasure of them, to Walpole and to the public which continually sought admission to his famous house, was that they were truly Gothic and that by laying the Middle Ages under tribute they paid the greatest possible tribute to the Middle Ages themselves, an epoch still very generally regarded as one productive of no artistic fruits whatever.

As Strawberry Hill increased in size, extending westwards from the original nucleus, Walpole became more confident in the merits of an irregularly designed building. Already in 1750 he had expressed himself as being 'almost as fond of the Sharawaggi, or Chinese want of symmetry, in buildings, as in grounds or gardens'. But the earlier parts of Strawberry were, externally, still affected by the tradition of symmetry and it was only with the projection of a great circular tower at the south-west corner that asymmetry was frankly admitted. This was begun in 1759 and eventually rose to a battlemented parapet with a corbel course of tiny pointed arches. By this time Robert Adam was the bright new star in architecture and it was he who handled the themes imposed, concocting a ceiling from a window in old St Paul's and a fireplace from the Cosmati work of the Confessor's Chapel (1766–7).

The arrangement of the west end of the house was entirely free. A 'Tribune', containing a Cabinet, with ceiling after the York chapter-house, was built in 1763 and, finally, in 1777, the Beauclerk Tower was inserted between this and the Round Tower. This was the work of James Essex (1722–84) who became Walpole's architect for a few years after the death of Robinson.

The deliberate irregularity of the western part of Strawberry Hill was, architecturally, its most important innovation – an innovation authorized, let us observe, by literary dilettantism rather than by architectural feeling. For here is no study in asymmetrical composition as such, but simply a whimsical pursuit of those fortuitous effects which groups of ancient buildings so often give. Here, in this imitation of the fortuitous, Walpole started something of more far-reaching significance than he can have guessed. He opened the door to the architecture of the Picturesque.

The influence of Strawberry Hill was unquestionably very great, for it soon became one of the most famous houses of its time, and Walpole was obliged to limit parties of sightseers to one each day. Perhaps its chief message to the people of taste who saw it and heard and read about it was that modern Gothic building must seek its authority not merely in the taste of this or that architect but in the monuments of the Middle Ages themselves. Batty Langley, to be sure, had claimed to have recovered the lost rules of Gothic, but the claim and the way it was asserted were both fatuous. Walpole demonstrated for the first time a loyalty to medieval precedent which appeared, on the face of it, to be as fastidious as that of any classical architect to the precedents of Rome.

If the general aspect of Strawberry Hill could have added little to the repertory of Georgian Gothic as it stood already in the 1740s, one feature, the Round Tower, merely attached to an angle of the building and with no subsidiary towers to support it, no second tower to balance it, must have made a wonderfully deep impression. Indeed, there is no feature which so constantly recurs in 'picturesque' architecture up to the end of our period.

The influence of Strawberry Hill must not, however, be taken too easily for granted. It was, as we have seen, certainly *not* the source of Georgian Gothic in general, and Gothic houses or churches of the 1760s, 70s, and 80s are, for the most part, perfectly free of any suggestion of Strawberry influence. Walpole himself, who despised Kent's Gothic, recognized few Gothic houses besides his own as being true specimens of the style. It was not till 1785 that he was able to hail a new house as 'a child of Strawberry' and that house was Lee Priory, Kent, the work of an architect of a much younger generation, James Wyatt. To Wyatt's career we shall come presently, but it is worth noting here the reasons why Walpole found this house, built for his friend Thomas Barrett, so acceptable. One was undoubtedly its deliberate irregularity. According to Hasted,[5] the three fronts of the house (remodelled externally in the nineteenth century) conveyed 'an idea of a small convent never attempted to be demolished, but partly modernized and adapted to the habitation of a gentleman's family'. It had, in fact, that air of natural growth through centuries which Walpole had sought at Strawberry. In addition, there was an almost complete absence of the old Kentian formulas and, instead, very fully detailed features such as an octagon tower and spire, a two-storey porch, and an oriel window. Here Walpole recognized an advance in archaeological correctness which made Strawberry Hill look amateurish. 'Neither Mr Bentley, nor my workmen,' he wrote to Barrett, 'had studied the science, and I was always too desultory and impatient to consider that I should please myself more by allowing time, than by hurrying my plans into execution before they were ripe. My house is therefore but a sketch by beginners, yours is finished by a great master.'

If Lee was an acknowledged 'child of Strawberry', Wyatt's Fonthill and Wyatt's Ashridge can be no less. They are the greatest houses of their kind and belong near the end of the century. So do most of the 'castellated' houses whose prominent round towers are ultimately of Strawberry origin. Walpole's literary diversion bore extravagant fruit half a century after its conception. Meanwhile the Kentian equivalents – so easy to use, so amenable to the pencils of classically trained designers, ran their course. Both Adam and Chambers, when they designed in Gothic, did so in a spirit nearer to Kent than to Walpole, displaying neither curiosity nor reverence with regard to ancient precedent, and insisting all the time on symmetry. It is to the castles of Wyatt and John Nash and the Monk's Parlour of Sir John Soane's Museum that Walpole's ideas ultimately lead us.

We cannot leave the amateurs without mentioning one other name, which is that of Browne Willis (1682–1760), a man thirty-five years older than Walpole, who was helping to revive the Society of Antiquaries when Walpole was born and was perhaps the most serious student of English Gothic antiquities between Dugdale and Grose. Willis was not in any sense an architect, but when the church of Fenny Stratford, Bucks., of which he was patron, was rebuilt in 1724–30, it was rebuilt in a sort of elementary Gothic. The builder was Edward Wing of Aynhoe,[6] and it was he, perhaps, who, eleven years later, as 'Wing of Leicester', built the curious church of Galby, Leicestershire, which has a nave which might be a late relic of the true Gothic vernacular and a tower, partly classical but with pinnacles of egregious emphasis. This architect's son built the more sophisticated Gothic church of Norton-by-Galby, in the same county, in 1770. This little group of Gothic village churches may be extended to include Wicken, Northants., designed in 1758 by a gentleman-architect, Thomas Prowse, who, on the one hand, knew Browne Willis and, on the other, was a personal friend of Sanderson Miller. These examples merely serve to illuminate a by-way of the Gothic movement where the initiative seems to have come, in the first instance, not from the world of dilettantism but from the antiquarian enthusiasm of country clergymen.

NOTES TO CHAPTER 24

1. There are several versions. None was executed and the church was eventually rebuilt by Sir William Wilson in a totally different kind of Gothic. See p. 160.

2. Pope's *Eloisa to Abelard*, which came out in the same year that Vanbrugh built his Greenwich house, contains such lines as these, quoted in K. Clark, *Gothic Revival*, 38:

> These moss-grown domes with spiry turrets crowned,
> Where awful arches make a noon day night,
> And the dim windows shed a solemn light.

3. Marcus Whiffen (*Stuart and Georgian Churches*, 69) suggests Richard Bentley, Walpole's friend (p. 242), on account of Lord Bateman, the owner of Shobden, being a nephew of another friend of Walpole for whom Bentley did design something. If there is any Walpole connexion, I suggest William Robinson (p. 242) as a likelier name. The work seems to me too professional for Bentley, and Robinson, who was in the Works, will have been intimate with the Kent style.

4. Keene was Surveyor to the Dean and Chapter of Westminster from 1746. Another Gothic work of his is Arbury, Warwickshire, which Mr Colvin tells me was begun to be Gothicized as early as 1750. It has a ceiling copied from the vault of Henry VII's Chapel. Keene's classical work includes much of Worcester College, Oxford, the building at the south-west corner of Balliol College, and the Town Hall at High Wycombe.

5. *History of Kent*, 1778–99.

6. His name is given thus on a print of Fenny Stratford Church in the British Museum (King's Maps, VIII, 8).

PART FIVE

NEO-CLASSICISM AND THE PICTURESQUE
⟨1750–1830⟩

CHAPTER 25

NEO-CLASSICISM: ENGLISHMEN ABROAD

'NEO-CLASSICISM' is here used to describe that new spirit which, about the middle of the eighteenth century, altered the balance of the European's attitude to the past and therefore to the present and future. The Neo-classical point of view arrives at the moment that an essentially *historic* view of antiquity is grasped – antiquity, that is, as something fundamentally separate not only from the Dark and Middle Ages but from the revival of antique art and literature at the Renaissance. It is precisely at this moment that validity is conceded to the culture of the Middle Ages (we saw this happening, in the case of Walpole, in the last chapter). Thus, European man, instead of looking back on his past as a single continuous cultural stream, unhappily broken by the medieval collapse of classical values, begins to see it in distinct compartments – the world of antiquity, the medieval world, and the world of the Renaissance. With the springing into relief of these separate entities belonging to the past, three new concepts automatically emerge. First, the concept of art through archaeology, that is, of the enrichment of the present by persistent inquiry into the nature of the past (as opposed to the acceptance of a traditional theory of antiquity). Second, a wider concept of eclecticism, of the power to choose between styles or to combine elements from different styles. Third, by analogy, the concept of a modern style, a style uniquely characteristic of the present. These three concepts – the archaeological, the eclectic, and the modernist – we shall need to bear distinctly in mind through the remaining chapters of this book.

That Neo-classicism constantly overlaps or fades into 'romanticism' is a fact which it is scarcely necessary to underline. Both archaeology (fundamentally, an irrational quest for the golden age of the past, classical or medieval) and modernism (based on an equally irrational idealization of the future) are essentially romantic in their origins. Only eclecticism, with its refusal to surrender to any ideal, is opposed to romanticism and strives to effect an immediate, if temporary, reconciliation of values.

The germs of Neo-classicism are discernible in European architecture long before the critical years of change around 1750. They are discernible in the archaeological-aesthetic inquiries of Colbert's Academy from 1683 onwards and, even more readily, in the English Palladian point of view as illustrated in the works of Burlington. The hall at Holkham and the Egyptian Hall at York both subtend the new outlook and constitute, for a brief time, easily the nearest approach to it anywhere in Europe. But that point of view was blurred in the conservative and consolidating work of architects like Taylor, Paine, and Carr and the main stream of European Neo-classicism takes its origin in France.

Origins of Neo-classicism

Neo-classicism in architecture is, after the English episode, the joint creation of France and Italy, Italy being a more or less passive partner. By 1750, Italian Baroque had reached the reserved grandiloquence of Galilei's façade of St John Lateran[1] (1734) and Fuga's at S. Maria Maggiore (1743). The style added nothing to what Bernini and Borromini had created in the previous century and there was a tendency towards revision and purification – a tendency not inimical to the spirit of Neo-classicism but wholly independent of it.

This late Italian Baroque was of only slight interest to the English or the French. The English had reacted strongly against their own version of Baroque and settled into Palladianism, while the French, confident in their own initiative, cultivated the style of J. Hardouin Mansart, which reaches from the reign of Louis XIV, far into that of his successor. It bridges the years of the Rococo, which, almost limited to interiors and decoration, enjoyed only a brief florescence, to be extinguished soon after the coming of J. A. Gabriel. Gabriel was no great innovator. His work purifies but confirms the French tradition deriving from Lescot, François Mansart, and Perrault; and if his sobriety of manner approximates to the Neo-classic ideal it is due rather to the pull exercised by English architecture towards simplicity and restraint than to any deep reconsideration of classical antiquity.

It is not to Gabriel so much as to J. N. Servandoni (1695–1760) and J. G. Soufflot (1714–80) that the twist towards the new viewpoint is due. Servandoni, born in France, became a pupil of G. P. Pannini, the painter of the Campagna and of Roman ruins. Turning to operatic decoration and thence to architecture, he brought into play a feeling for Rome and her monuments livelier than anything which had been experienced since the Renaissance came to France. In 1733 his design for the façade of S. Sulpice, Paris, was accepted. Its grave Roman colonnades and square silhouette would have seemed less extraordinary in the London of Hawksmore and Vanbrugh than in a Paris whose typical church fronts were fundamentally Vignolesque, and whose salons glittered with the Rococo of Boffrand, Meissonier, and Oppenordt. Servandoni built little else, and although he came to England and designed a gallery in a house at Hammersmith, his stay here left no noticeable trace.

Soufflot, although more original, achieved a less sudden independence of French tradition. He studied in Rome and, in 1750, made a second visit to Italy and drew – of all strange things for that period – the Greek temples at Paestum. In 1757 he designed the great church of Ste-Geneviève, Paris, later to become the Panthéon. There he developed, with wonderful integrity, the theme of the Roman Bath as a domed cruciform church, creating the great monument of the first phase of Neo-classicism in France.

In Soufflot the feeling for a renewed loyalty to the discipline of ancient Rome is strong, and the feeling was immediately reflected in his followers, especially such of them as gained the Grand Prix at the Academy and became the Academy's *pensionnaires* in Rome.

That link between Paris and Rome was to prove of high importance at this juncture, and not only for France. For it was out of the continual exchange between French architectural thought and Roman archaeology that mature Neo-classicism in its international implications emerged.

The outstanding architectural theorist of the early phase of Neo-classicism was a Frenchman – the Abbé Laugier, whose *Essai sur l'architecture* was first published in Paris in 1753. The book contains little that was wholly new to architectural theory, but it does express with force and clarity a rationalist view of classic architecture and of the manner in which it should be adapted to modern use. For Laugier, the hypothetical 'rustic cabin' of primitive man is the beginning of architecture – 'the model upon which all the magnificences of architecture have been imagined'.[2] And in his treatment of the orders and their use he insists on the preservation to the utmost extent of the simple logic of the cabin. Thus, he condemns forthwith all pilasters and pedestals. The order must rise from the pavement and be in the round. Even engaged orders are an unfortunate necessity, for the perfect building consists entirely of free columns. Broken entablatures, entablatures supported on arches and pediments not expressing roofs are all abominations and 'one should never put anything in a building for which one cannot give a solid reason'.

Alongside this strict rationalism, Laugier allows considerable freedom. He does not consider the Vitruvian orders necessarily final, criticizes them in detail, and considers that the door is always open to improvements and the invention of new 'composed orders'. Further, he admits that in many buildings no order is practicable. Here, it is necessary to rely on proportion (an intuitive matter) and on varied geometric shapes in the plan.

Laugier's work, important and influential in itself, is valuable as putting the Neo-classical view into a nutshell. Here, at one blow, all the rich development of architectural language since the Renaissance is discarded, and the architect is urged to seek truth on the one hand in a grasp of first principles as demonstrated in the architecture of the ancient world and on the other by proceeding from these first principles to the design of modern buildings which shall have the same logical limitations as the classical temple. A hard road, but one which some of Laugier's contemporaries – notably Soufflot – and many of his successors were ready to attempt.

There is a passage in Laugier which leads us directly to the archaeological side of the matter. Speaking of the orders, he says that 'architecture has only midling obligations to the Romans, and ... owes all that is precious and solid to the Greeks alone'. This opinion was not, in 1753, by any means generally accepted. Laugier had perhaps taken it from the Comte de Caylus whose great *Recueil d'antiquités* had begun to appear in 1752. De Caylus, on the basis of his researches, stressed the 'plus noble simplicité' of Greece at the expense of Rome, and this seems at once to have received acceptance in France. Within five years the opinion received overwhelming support. In Germany, Winckelmann's *Gedanken über die Nachahmung der griechischen Werke*, recommending the imitation of Greek instead of Roman work, appeared in 1755, in 1758 Goguet roundly asserted that 'the Greeks invented architecture', and in the same year appeared the first graphic architectural evidences in the case, J. D. Le Roy's *Les Ruines des plus beaux monuments de la Grèce*, with its relatively accurate engravings of the buildings on the Acropolis.

In Italy, where a patriotic tradition conceding priority only to the Etruscans had been developed during twenty-five years, the Grecian revolution was wholly unwelcome. The challenge was taken up, not indeed by an archaeologist but by an architect and artist of extraordinary capacity, in the person of Giambattista Piranesi (1720–78).

As the influence of Piranesi is one of the most vital elements in English architectural development from the beginning of Robert Adam's career till the end of Soane's, we must pause here to consider who and what he was. Born near Venice, his first master was the painter, Carlo Zucchi. Going to Rome, however, he came under the influence of Giuseppe Vasi, from whom he learnt to etch. His first publication, the *Prima parte di architettura e prospettive*, appeared in 1743. It consists of free reconstructions of types of Roman buildings, and is stamped with the character of the late Baroque of Piranesi's time. The *Antichità romane*, 1748, consists of views of Roman buildings in their existing condition. Both these books belong to traditional types of publication and were, accordingly, for the use of amateurs and architects. But in 1750 came the *Carceri*, fantastic compositions of meaningless architecture festooned in ropes and chains and cluttered with monstrous tackle of uncertain purpose. This showed the calibre of Piranesi's imagination and his fierce passion for the idiosyncratic and original. The *Trofei di Ottaviano Augusto* of 1753, on the other hand, was a work involving archaeological inquiry and offering new antiquarian discoveries as a contribution to modern architecture. By this date, therefore, Piranesi had shown himself on the one hand an industrious collector of archaeological material and on the other an artist of unpredictable and exotic invention. It was the combination of these two capacities which made him, eventually, so potent an innovator.

It was as a polemical archaeologist that Piranesi next exerted his talents.[3] Two works had come to his notice urging the revolutionary view that the Greeks were to be preferred to the Romans as having brought classical architecture to its zenith. These works were an anonymous pamphlet from England, *The Investigator, a Dialogue on Taste*,[4] in which both the Greek and the Gothic were set above the Roman; and the book by J. D. Le Roy, just mentioned as the first illustrated description of Greek architecture. These books incited Piranesi to produce the work entitled *Della magnificenza ed architettura de' Romani*, a series of magnificent plates, crowded with details of Roman architecture and intended to prove by sheer weight of evidence the overwhelming superiority of Rome over Greece.

The *Della magnificenza* came out in 1761. Three years later, Mariette, the French connoisseur and collector, published a letter against Piranesi in the *Gazette Littéraire*, and this in turn produced, on Piranesi's part, another sheaf of didactic etchings. This time, however, he argued on different ground. Relinquishing the (by then scarcely tenable) theory of priority for the Etruscan and pre-eminence for the Roman, he changed the *rôle* of archaeologist for that of creative artist, criticized not only the Greeks but Vitruvius and staked everything on genius. The result was the *Parere su l'architettura* (1765), a series of compositions as original as the *Carceri* but more strictly architectural, being elevations and sections of incredible buildings made up of archaeological motifs disposed in a complex jig-saw owing something to Michelangelo. In the next four years, Piranesi compromised still further with archaeology, recommending, in the *Diverse maniere d'adornare i cammini*, that the artist should study Greek, Roman, Tuscan, and Egyptian art. His last works were the studies of the Greek temples at Paestum, published by his son.

As artist, architect, archaeologist, pamphleteer, and, above all, as etcher, whose works could be readily acquired and circulated, Piranesi became a factor of immense importance in the whole European scene. In him, archaeology and original genius met, the one fused by the other in works which might be and often were called mad and ridiculous but which had an attraction which proved irresistible.

Piranesi in Rome and the Abbé Laugier in France may be said, at the risk of gross over-simplification, to be the two principal influences in English Neo-classicism. They are, in any case, symbolic: Laugier of the new rationalism and the sense of truthful, economical expression; and Piranesi of the new archaeology, and of the search for inspiration through the exhumation of more and more of the ancient world.

Englishmen Abroad

This widening of the boundaries of knowledge was prosecuted not only, as with Piranesi, by the exhaustive study of the yields of Italian soil, but also by the examination and description of remoter sites in the ancient Roman world. Here Frenchmen and Englishmen, with their fresher curiosity and greater eagerness for travel, took precedence over the Italians. Englishmen, indeed, were the greatest travellers of all, and Robert Wood's *Ruins of Palmyra*, published in 1753, was the first of a series of works which made the English contribution to architectural scholarship of outstanding importance in the second half of the eighteenth century.

Robert Wood (1716–71) was not an architect but a private gentleman who eventually became an under-secretary of State. Nor did the idea of visiting and recording the remote Syrian city originate with him, but with two friends, John Bouverie and James Dawkins (1722–57), the latter the son of a Jamaican merchant of great wealth, who was to finance the expedition. Wood, more experienced in travel than either of his companions, led the expedition, the incentive to which seems to have combined adventurousness with a desire to make a striking addition to existing knowledge of antiquity. The party was in Rome by 1750, when, having recruited an Italian draughtsman, Borra, they proceeded to Syria. Bouverie succumbed to the journey, but the other two, with Borra, were back in England in time to bring out the *Ruins of Palmyra* in 1753. As the result of only three years' work, involving a hazardous journey and a vast amount of field-work under most difficult conditions, the book is a magnificent performance; and it was followed in 1757 by a further volume, *The Ruins of Balbec*, which the party had also found time to survey.

Parallel with this expedition was another of equal consequence. In the dilettante circles of Rome Wood and his friends had met two Englishmen, James Stuart (1713–88) and Nicholas Revett (c. 1721–1804), who had already in 1748, while visiting Naples (and no doubt Paestum), formulated proposals for an expedition to Athens to delineate and describe its monuments. These proposals were warmly approved by Wood and his companions, who included the Earl of Malton and the Earl of Charlemont. Financial support being thus forthcoming, Stuart and Revett sailed for Greece at the beginning of 1751.

Passing through Greece on their way home Wood's party found Stuart and Revett at work. Their book, *The Antiquities of Athens*, was announced in 1751, but it was not until 1755 that Stuart and his companion returned to England, and the first volume of the book only appeared in 1762. The second was delayed for another twenty-eight years. Meanwhile the Frenchman, J. D. Le Roy, had also visited Athens and managed to forestall Stuart and Revett by bringing out his less painstaking *Les Ruines des plus beaux monuments de la Grèce* in 1758.

The initiative of Robert Wood and his friends and of Stuart and Revett[5] was closely followed by another exploit, independent again, though possibly inspired by the interest which Wood's book had created. To Robert Adam we shall need to devote ample space later. Here he enters our story for the first time and does so as an architect-traveller intent, like Wood and Stuart, on making a spectacular addition to existing knowledge as regards the architecture of antiquity. Adam was the second son of William Adam, who we have seen to have been the leading architect in Scotland up to his death in 1748. He left Scotland in 1754, at the age of twenty-six, and went first to France. There he made the acquaintance of one of the finest architectural draughtsmen of the time and a sometime Grand Prix winner, C. L. Clérisseau. Clérisseau accompanied him as far as Nîmes. Adam arrived in Italy in 1755 and in the following year was in Rome. He was travelling in the style of a gentleman doing the Grand Tour and not as a mere professional student, and in 1757 undertook an expedition to record the remains of Diocletian's Palace at Spalato (the modern Split). Clérisseau by this time had rejoined him and he took him and two other draughtsmen and in five weeks collected enough material for the great folio, the *Ruins of the Palace of the Emperor Diocletian at Spalatro, in Dalmatia*. Adam was back in England by the beginning of 1758. The book appeared in 1764.

Adam's visit to Spalato was only incidental to the main purpose of his Italian visit which was, unquestionably, to qualify himself for the leadership of English architecture. The Spalato book was a superb trophy of the visit, but the real advantages which Adam gained abroad were from the first-hand study of antiquity, of the work of the Renaissance masters, and of contemporary archaeology in Italy itself. Thus, he was both student and explorer, at one and the same time collecting material and developing his capacity to use it. No English architect had previously been to Italy with such ample intentions, nor, perhaps, with such an individual and critical point of view. In Adam, the student, the explorer, the architect, and the grand-tourist were united.

After Adam, Nicholas Revett once again set out for the Middle East, this time in a party headed by the Oxonian scholar, Richard Chandler, and sponsored by the Society of Dilettanti.[6] They collected material not only in Greece but in Asia Minor, during the years 1764–6, and in 1769 the Society was able to publish the first part of *Ionian Antiquities*, a work of superb quality which, with the additions made in 1797, supplied English architecture with a fresh vocabulary of profiles and enrichments.

From the 1750s onward the presence of English artists and architects in Rome becomes rapidly more common. Adam, indeed, was not the only considerable architect there in his time. His visit just failed to overlap that of William Chambers, who left Rome in the year that Adam entered Italy; while in the year that Adam returned to

England (1758), two prizes at the Academy of St Luke were carried off by a countryman of his, twenty-four-year-old Robert Mylne, who must have been studying in Rome for several years.

Of these two, Chambers was to play a principal, Mylne a subordinate, *rôle* in English Neo-classicism. Chambers was to be Robert Adam's chief contemporary and rival in England. His career and Adam's, both of which will be discussed in the next chapter, were in many respects remarkably similar. Chambers's broad intentions in Italy must have been almost identical with Adam's. Like Adam, he was travelling as a gentleman rather than a student and, again like Adam, his studies ranged over renaissance as well as antique work, and were strongly inflected by contemporary France. He did not, indeed, collect material of the kind which made the *Ruins of Spalatro* so striking an advertisement of its author, but he had already even more outlandish data to publish; for while Adam was still with his family in Edinburgh, Chambers had been to China as super-cargo on a Swedish merchantman and was able to bring out his *Designs of Chinese Buildings* in 1757. That book was the first by an English author to bring forward authentic evidences of Chinese architecture, superseding the vague *chinoiseries* borrowed from France by such designers as the Halfpennys.

Robert Mylne's visit to Italy was less pretending than those either of Chambers or Adam. Being the son of a Scottish architect of equal eminence with the elder Adam, one may surmise that the two ventures were not unconnected. But he was six years younger than Adam and only twenty when, accompanied by his brother, he started out for Paris and Rome. He was, in fact, a more or less inexperienced student and attempted, so far as we know, no schemes of discovery or archaeological publication. He did, however, achieve the very remarkable feat of winning the principal competition, the *Concorso Clementino*, at the Academy of St Luke. What is equally remarkable is that Mylne's design (still preserved at St Luke's Academy) is neither English Palladian nor Italian Baroque but distinctly French and comparable to the work of Soufflot and his followers in Paris. Moreover, it must have been on this score that it earned the award, for among the competition designs, there is only one other showing the same Neo-classical tendencies and that (by an Italian) was placed second. All the other designs were in Baroque of the Vanvitelli school. For some reason, inscrutable to us, the assessors of 1758 crowned a design by a Scotsman in the new manner of Paris, in preference to the current style of the Italian studios.[7]

Mylne's amazing success in Rome and its consequent repercussions in London advertised the advantages of an Italian visit as a preliminary to successful practice. Old George Dance, the Clerk of Works to the City of London, sent two of his sons, Nathaniel and George, to Rome about the year (1758) that Mylne won his laurels at St Luke's. George, the architect, carried off the prize not, indeed, at St Luke's, but at the younger Academy of Parma. That design (1763) likewise exists and we shall consider it later. By this time, James Wyatt was in Italy, measuring antiquities in Rome and studying architectural painting under Viscentini at Venice. He was followed closely by the Yorkshireman, Thomas Harrison, who made a small stir at the Papal Court in the 1770s; while in 1776 John Soane came on the scene as George III's travelling student.

In the list of *Professori Accademici* of the Academy of St Luke we find the names of Adam, Mylne, Dance, and Harrison. Mylne, Dance, and Soane were members of the Parma Academy, Mylne and Soane of the Academy of Florence, and Mylne of that of Bologna. Thus, from Adam to Soane there is a continuous tradition of participation by young Britons in the current architectural thought of the Italian academies and this was at least as important to English architecture as the advantages gained from the measurement of antique buildings, which, after all, had been pretty well studied and, for the most part, adequately published in the first half of the century. It is customary to consider English architecture of the late eighteenth and early nineteenth centuries as a more or less insular development from the work of Chambers and Adam. But this is far from being the case, and we shall find that after the first excitement of the Adam revolution was over, it was to Franco-Italian Neo-classicism that the more progressive architects turned. The influence of French practice and of French publications was great, but behind this was the actual contact made in Italy with the mixed French and Italian thought of international student circles where the influence of Laugier, of Soufflot and his successors, and of Piranesi merged with that of antiquity in its many aspects, always freshened by new research and empirical restoration.

Adam and Chambers, it is true, dominate English architecture of the third quarter of the century, and in neither of them shall we find more than a streak of the pure influence of Neo-classicism. But it is there; and in Dance, Harrison, and Soane it is separated out, leading to the astonishing Soane manner of the 1790s and beyond to the Greek purism of Wilkins and Smirke and Inwood with which this history ends.

NOTES TO CHAPTER 25

1. The façade of this church has a resemblance to All Saints, Oxford, which would have to be dismissed as coincidence were it not that Galilei is known to have spent seven years in England.

2. Quotations are from the English edition of 1755.

3. In what follows I am very extensively indebted to R. Wittkower's paper on the subject (see Bibliography).

4. Actually by the Scottish painter, Allan Ramsay.

5. The later careers of both Stuart and Revett are of considerable interest, though somewhat detached from the main current of English architecture. Stuart, in 1758, built for Lord Lyttelton at Hagley a small Greek Doric temple, the like of which was scarcely seen again in England till Smirke built his Covent Garden portico exactly fifty years later. The Hagley temple, however, is distinctly an exotic park ornament, somewhat in the category of the Pagoda,

'Cathedral', and 'Alambra' at Kew (see next Chapter, p. 257). From 1763 he was working for Thomas Anson. For him he built 15 St James's Square, whose stone façade is Palladian in composition but has an Athenian order, and, at Shugborough, Staffs., imitations of the Monument of Lysicrates, the Tower of the Winds, and the Arch of Hadrian at Athens, which fall into the same category as the Hagley temple. Belvedere, near Erith, and 22 Portman Square (for Mrs Montagu) are later works. All his works show some Greek detailing but are not particularly advanced in composition. His decorative paintings, at Spencer House (before 1761) and elsewhere, are Roman in style and were mentioned with respect by Adam.

Nicholas Revett built the Greek Ionic west portico of West Wycombe Park soon after 1766, using material gathered on his second voyage. At Standlynch, now Trafalgar, near Salisbury, he built a Greek Doric portico. His most important work, however, is the church at Ayot St Lawrence, Herts., 1778, with a Greek Doric portico linked by columnar screens to flanking lodges.

The careers of Stuart and Revett have been very ably described by Lesley Lawrence (see Bibliography), but I am also indebted here to the articles prepared by Mr Howard Colvin for his forthcoming dictionary.

6. Founded in 1732 as a convivial club with artistic interests derived from the Grand Tour, the Society flourished throughout the eighteenth and early nineteenth centuries and published several important works of classical scholarship, the last of which was Penrose's *Principles of Athenian Architecture*, 1852.

7. I am indebted to the President of the Accademia di S. Luca for permission to inspect the drawings in question and to Signori Tomassetti and Pirotta for their kind assistance.

CHAPTER 26

WILLIAM CHAMBERS AND ROBERT ADAM

FROM about 1760 till about 1790, a period of thirty years, English architecture was dominated by the two men whose names stand at the head of this chapter. William Chambers was born in 1723, Robert Adam in 1728. Adam died in 1792, Chambers in 1796. Both are buried in Westminster Abbey.

The careers of the two men are, in some respects, wonderfully alike. Both came of well-to-do middle-class families, and were able to endow themselves liberally with the advantages of foreign travel and leisured study before starting to build. Both were arrogantly ambitious; neither had to wait for success; and it is probably safe to say that each envisaged himself, from the very beginning, as indisputable primate of English architecture. Either would unquestionably have achieved this position had it not been for the other. In a sense, both achieved it – Chambers as the greatest official architect of his time and the consolidator of English tradition, Adam as an innovator of great power whose influence flashed suddenly into English architecture, penetrated far beyond that of his contemporary but vanished sooner. It is hardly necessary to add that there was a certain rivalry, not to say antagonism, between the two.

These two careers are each so self-consistent that it is a matter of no consequence which we describe first, though Chambers's five-year seniority and slightly earlier commencement in practice gives him at least a nominal priority.

William Chambers

Chambers was born at Gothenburg, Sweden, the son of an English merchant there. As a boy, he was taken to Ripon, perhaps for schooling, but returned to Sweden and joined the Swedish East India Company, sailing as a 'cadet' at about the age of seventeen. During the next nine years he made voyages, first as 'assistant', then as 'supercargo', to Bengal and China, at the same time applying himself to languages, mathematics, and, particularly, to architecture; between voyages he visited England, Scotland, the Low Countries, and part of France.

Quitting the Company's service in 1749, Chambers, then twenty-five, went to Paris and studied architecture for about a year. As he later refers to Jacques François Blondel as 'mon ancien maître', it looks as if he may have joined that master's atelier, which had then been running for some six years and where such future leaders of French architecture as Richard Mique, Charles de Wailly, and M. J. Peyre became and remained close personal friends of Chambers, as did J. D. Le Roy, while he certainly knew the great Soufflot, the leader of the group.

This Parisian introduction to architecture made a deep impression on Chambers and inflected his taste in a particular way so that when, in 1750, he went to Italy, he saw the

Italian scene through eyes already accustomed to the refinements and precision of Soufflot and his circle. He was in Italy for the better part of five years, visiting Paris again during the period, and returning to England in 1755.

He was successful at once. Introduced by the Earl of Bute to the Prince of Wales, he became his architectural tutor and, shortly after, architect to the Princess Dowager. This resulted in his erecting, between 1757 and 1763, a number of ornamental buildings in the gardens at Kew, including the Roman arch, the Pagoda, and some classical temples and alcoves.[1] Simultaneously (1757) he brought out his *Designs of Chinese Buildings*, based on accurate drawings of buildings, furniture, and costumes made by him in China. Two years later, with work in hand for many of the best patrons in Britain, he produced the first edition of his *Treatise on Civil Architecture*.

Chambers's *Treatise* is a manifesto of his taste. It deals with the orders and their use and with decorative adjuncts such as doors and windows, fireplaces and ceilings. There is nothing about planning or construction and this limitation was emphasized when, in the third edition (1791), the title was expanded to *A Treatise on the Decorative Part of Civil Architecture*. In general treatment, Chambers seems to have followed the relevant sections of Ware's *Complete Body* (p. 218), which came out in the year after he arrived in England. His declared object in writing the book, however, was rather more sophisticated. Ware's was simply to collate a 'library' of information, 'supplying the place of all other books'. Chambers, on the other hand, was intent on *abstracting* the best from many sources and condensing it in the light of his own aesthetic judgement. His is a more personal and more cultivated book, written against a wider background of experience. Ware compiled from printed sources alone, Chambers used both printed sources and his own first-hand experience of Italian architecture. That experience extended over much sixteenth- and seventeenth-century architecture, still unfamiliar to the ordinary English architect, including, for example, the work of Sansovino, Peruzzi, Sanmichele, Ammanati, Bernini, and Pietro da Cortona, the Genoese Baroque of Bianco, and the latest Roman Baroque of Salvi. Though he does not say so, Chambers emphasizes by implication that Serlio, Palladio, Vignola, and Scamozzi are not the only Italian architects since Bramante, and that to have produced treatises does not establish them as the only Italians worth the student's attention. Chambers, in other words, broadened the basis of architectural study to take in the Italian schools entire, not indiscriminately but as a source of inspiration parallel to the main body of antiquity.

Chambers's French training proclaims itself in a certain delicacy of selection and in the decorative character of some of the original designs included in the book. He adopts no theoretical standpoint, though the engravings of two forms of the 'rustic cabin' may be a concession to Laugier.[2] Moreover, his English loyalties are firm and Inigo Jones is rated as high as any foreigner. It is at least possible that the circulation of the *Treatise* in France had as much influence there as the French element in the book had on the architecture of England. His book on Kew and his China book were certainly influential on the Continent.

For some fifteen years from 1759 Chambers was actively building town- and country-houses, gateways, stables, and monuments for the nobility. His houses[3] rarely depart far from the Palladian style of plan and composition, though in detail they are more eclectic than anything by Taylor, Paine, or Carr, and considerably more refined. The interiors, especially, are different. The Kent-Inigo Jones style is abandoned and the ceilings and fireplaces have the lyres, sphinxes, garlands, and flowing acanthus of the decorators of Louis XV, all used with the greatest elegance and reserve.

Chambers showed himself most able in small things. The Casina he built for Lord Charlemont at Marino, near Dublin (designed before 1759, as part of a façade for Harewood, but not built till 1769; Plate 143A), is deservedly one of his most famous works – an exemplary combination of strictly classical elements to fit a Greek-cross plan. The staircase at Carrington House, Whitehall (1765; demolished 1886; Plate 143B), with divided flights entering an Ionic loggia on the first floor was another impeccable essay, based on a Genoese Baroque theme. And when we come to his greatest work, Somerset House, we find that, still, Chambers's genius is for the small unit rather than for the comprehensive whole.

Somerset House

Somerset House was begun when Chambers was fifty-two and very willing to give up the tiresome business of house-building for cantankerous and unreliable peers. He had been architect to the King and a Commissioner of the Board of Works since 1760 and had been given the Comptrollership on Flitcroft's death in 1769. The Surveyorship had by this time become a political rather than a professional appointment[4] and was held by a Yorkshire squire, Thomas Worsley, so that Chambers was, in effect, the chief architect of the royal Works. Oddly enough, such was the state of the administration in the 1760s that this did not necessarily oblige or even entitle him to design new government buildings. Indeed, when the Public Offices scheme was projected it was the Secretary to the Board, William Robinson (c. 1720–75), who took the work in hand. Robinson was an indifferent designer,[5] and Chambers pressed Worsley and the Prime Minister (Lord North) to ensure that a scheme of such magnitude and importance should be conducted by one of the senior architects attached to the Board. Robinson conveniently dying in 1775, the task was given to Chambers.

A scheme for uniting certain Government Offices in one great public building had long been debated and at one time it was proposed to use the site of the Savoy. Eventually, however, the Somerset House site was selected and the grand old Palace, a treasury of English architectural genius over three centuries, razed to the ground. Chambers would gladly have saved Inigo Jones's work and some more recent additions, but by the time he was in authority, in 1775, the decision had been made. He was thus presented with the entire Thames-side site on which to plan the greatest English public building since Greenwich.

Faced with such a problem, one would expect Chambers to look back to the last English plans for a strictly comparable site – those, namely, of Inigo Jones for Whitehall. On the contrary, his first proposal was for a great oval courtyard communicating with three narrow rectangular courts, by means of vaulted entries at various points. This scheme,[6] involving so many inconveniences in internal planning, soon disappeared, to be replaced by a rectangular court, flanked by two narrow courts of the same depth.

The first stone of the existing building was laid in 1776; the Strand block (occupying only the central third of the width of the whole site) was completed in 1780 and the central court soon after. That is nearly all that was achieved in Chambers's lifetime. The river-front is his design, but the eastern and western extensions behind it date from 1835 and 1856 and at the latter date the river-front was extended, though in a way which does not much affect the symmetry originally intended.

Somerset House is an extremely thoughtful and sensitive example of that eclecticism which we find in the early phases of the age of Neo-classicism. It is very evidently the work of a man unfitted for, or at least unaccustomed to, monumental design in the grand manner. Like so many English architects since, Chambers made his name and formed his style as a domestic architect and, in middle age, had not the confidence and assurance requisite for complete success in a great public building. Somerset House fails to give a total impression either of magnitude or magnificence, and when we come to analyse it we find that its beauties are precisely those we should expect to find in a great town-house or a nobleman's park.

It is essentially a building to look at in parts, and the parts separate out easily enough. The Strand block (Plate 146A) is a thing by itself, with an unbroken façade to the Strand and another, with short projecting wings, to the central court. The Strand façade, with its attached Corinthian order carried on an arcuated ground-floor, might be set down as a development from Inigo Jones's New Gallery (p. 117) which Chambers had regretfully seen disappear from the site. But there is more to it than that. Chambers had visited Paris in the spring of 1774 to see the buildings which had gone up since his last visit, some twenty years earlier. He will have seen, just approaching completion, J. D. Antoine's Hôtel des Monnaies. This not only has, like Somerset House, a high attic with statues in front of it but also a triple-arched vaulted entry which, along with Le Vau's much earlier specimen at the Louvre, is the obvious prototype of Chambers's entry to Somerset House. In this part of the work, Chambers certainly eclipsed both Le Vau and Antoine–at least from the point of view of sheer technical elaboration. His coupled columns, from which spring sparingly decorated cross-vaults are the same Baroque loggia theme which he used in the Carrington House staircase, but admirably adapted to the function of a vaulted entry in which lateral doorways occur.[7]

The detail of the Strand block is, like the detail throughout the building, selected with fastidious discrimination. Michelangelo and Palladio and, probably, Ammanati have been laid under tribute, while the cartouche above the attic hints that Salvi's Fontana di Trevi (which Chambers had drawn in Rome) is remembered. All this learning does not, it must be confessed, render the composition more telling than if it had been designed in ordinary Palladian terms. It only makes it very characteristically a work of Chambers.

The central court (Plate 146B) has, besides the Strand block on the north, which stands separate, three contiguous sides, each with a Corinthian centre pavilion. The plainer sections of the façades might well be town-houses in a London square; indeed, the door-ways are much like those which Chambers designed for some houses in Berners Street.[8]

The pavilion on the main axis, forming the centre of the river-front, is surmounted by a pediment and dome, the latter having about the scale and consequence of a fair-sized garden pavilion.

The river-front itself (Plate 144) is, in spite of the lack of monumentality which pervades the whole building, extremely dignified. Chambers had the happy idea of breaking up this long line of building into three several blocks, connected by what are, in effect, Palladian bridges; the bridges, with their colonnades à jour, occurring over the water-gates which punctuate the embankment arches into which the Thames used to flow before the Victoria Embankment arrived to 'shelve' the whole structure. These water-gates take the theme of the York Water-Gate, heightening its silhouette by the imposition of a solid attic with a giant Michelangelesque swag,[9] slung under a tablet.

The water-gates are within the compass in which Chambers was a master; so too are the rusticated Doric archways which lead into the side courts. The sculpture throughout the building had the advantage of Cipriani's pencil and was mostly executed by Chambers's artist friends – Carlini, Wilton, and Bacon. While the interior ceilings and fireplaces are among the very finest of Chambers's decorations in the delicate version of Louis XV ornamentalism which he made his own.

Chambers's Social Position

While Chambers was at work on Somerset House, legislation promoted by Edmund Burke had the effect of considerable reorganization within the Office of Works.[10] Worsley had died in 1779, and when his successor Whitshed Keene, another layman, followed him in 1782, the Comptrollership was abolished and Chambers made Surveyor-General. He was the first real architect to hold the office since Wren. This recognition of Chambers was also a recognition of the legitimacy of his profession, whose status Chambers did more than anyone of his time to promote.

Chambers as a social figure was, in fact, of considerable importance to English architecture. His position in relation to the King, first as tutor, then as architect, gave him a special standing and he used this to forward the foundation of the Royal Academy in 1768.[11] He became its first Treasurer at the same time that his friend Reynolds became the first President. In 1770, in return for the gift of a set of drawings of Kew, the King of Sweden conferred on him the order of the Polar Star, a compliment which George III considerably heightened by allowing its recipient to assume the style and title of English knighthood. Thus, although Chambers was not actually the first Englishman to be knighted for his services as a professional architect, he became conspicuously the decorated head of his profession.

And Chambers was, in the strict sense, a professional man, conducting a well-regulated business, charging a regular scale of fees which he was at pains to check against the practice of other architects. Moreover, like Taylor and Paine, he took pupils. With his title, his social standing, his position in the Academy, and, ultimately, as Surveyor-General, he became the type of the successful professional architect, and the model of many subsequent careers.

Many of Chambers's letters survive and they convey the impression of a mind of unusual strength and capacity for detail, fiercely impatient of stupidity and discourtesy, but not ready to lose a friend for a trifle. There is no doubt that Chambers was hostile, for different reasons, both to 'Capability' Brown, the landscape-gardener, and to Robert Adam. Brown displaced him as architect to Lord Clive at Claremont and this, together with a certain contempt for Brown's methods, led Chambers to write his *Dissertation on Oriental Gardening* (1772), a book which combined sharp satire at the expense of Brown with some authentic ideas of Chambers's own and a great deal of nonsense, which was perhaps taken more seriously than its author intended.[12] In any case, it drew from William Mason the *Heroic Epistle to Sir William Chambers*, in which the architect's own missiles were returned to him with some force.

As for Adam, it was a case of a clash of two not wholly dissimilar temperaments, as we shall readily understand after reviewing the career of Sir William's chief contemporary.[13]

Robert Adam

We have already met Robert Adam as one of those travellers who, in the middle part of the century, helped to broaden the architect's view of antiquity by penetrating to unexplored classical sites and publishing the results of his work in full architectural detail. But we must now consider Adam's Italian visit of 1754–8 from another point of view, that of the creative artist which Adam very consciously was both before and during his trip to Italy and Dalmatia. His consciousness of being an artist and potential innovator is conspicuous from the very beginning. Before they set foot in Italy, both he and his younger brother James were sketching freely in a Palladian manner, very close to Kent, stressing, even exaggerating, Kent's staccato quality, combining it with Gibbsian features and with themes from Robert Morris's books. Already in these sketches there are hints of the 'movement' which the Adams were later to place so high in the scale of architectural values. The *staccato* of Kent (i.e. originally, of Burlington) recurs throughout the whole Adam *œuvre*, defying, right up to the end, the smooth, flattening influence of international Neo-classicism.

In the Soane Museum are dozens of sketch-designs made by Robert during his Italian visit (Plate 147A). Some of them are for more or less impossible buildings and some are fantasies of the most exaggerated kind, towers of Babel to which human conditions almost cease to be relevant. The influence of Piranesi, with whom Adam established a firm friendship, is no doubt in part responsible for these things, but that influence can easily be over-stressed. Even in the wildest flights there is more of William Kent than of the Italian etcher. The freedom of these designs, the feeling that the artist is designing 'out of his head', the occasional introduction of Italian Romanesque and Gothic themes, is very remarkable and something entirely new for English architecture. Adam was probably the first English architect consciously to break with the spirit of servitude to antiquity in this arrogant way. He knows he is, or is determined to be, a man of original genius.[14]

The Italian sketches include, besides fantastic designs, compositions of landscape and ruins in the tradition of Pannini and influenced by Clérisseau, but, rather curiously, no measured studies of classical or Renaissance buildings. These Adam seems to have taken in his stride, relying on existing books and bought drawings for exact information about them. He would only apply the methods of the scholar when, as at Spalato, there was a net dividend of fresh material to be won. That he absorbed, in Italy, not only the antique but much of what the Renaissance had to offer, is perfectly clear from his later work, though the evidence is less in his manner of composition than in his details and particularly his treatment of interiors, where he effected that revolution in design for which the name of the Adam brothers will always be famous.

The Adam Style: its Sources

The nature of the Adam style and its sources constitute a rather complex subject, and it will be convenient to try to clear it up in a methodical way before describing any of the executed works. Adam's sources can be reduced, in the main, to four, as follows:

1. Palladianism of the Burlington-Kent school, as exemplified in Holkham and the Horse Guards. What Adam particularly seized here was the variety of silhouette resulting from breaking a façade into towers and flats, the towers rising into high attics (as at the Horse Guards, Plate 122A). This, with a rather Burlingtonian selection of window openings, gave a sense of 'movement', a word which Adam himself explained thus: 'Movement is meant to express, the rise and fall, the advance and recess, with other diversity of form, in the different parts of a building, so as to add greatly to the picturesque of the composition'. Movement in architecture, like the same quality in landscape, involves 'an agreeable and diversified contour, that groups and contrasts like a picture'. With rare exceptions, Adam's compositions, from the earliest sketches to the latest executed works, illustrate this principle and it can almost be said that wherever there is 'movement' there is a recollection of his earliest Palladian enthusiasms. Vanbrugh, whose works Adam intensely admired, calling them 'rough jewels of inestimable value', may have been an influence in support of the 'movement' theory, though it is never apparent in the works.

2. French influence, partly resulting from his stay in Paris on the way to Italy and partly from the use of such books as J. F. de Neufforge's *Recueil élémentaire* and G. P. M. Dumont's *Recueil*. France provided Adam with certain ideas in domestic planning, notably contrasting shapes in a suite of rooms, but more especially with decorative themes which Adam took and used in his own way. His favourite types of iron baluster, for instance, are French and many of his furniture designs are on French models. The French arabesque designers may have been of some use to him, though the most 'Adam-like' French decorators (the brothers Rousseau, for instance) may, equally, owe something to Adam.

3. Archaeological influences from Italy, Dalmatia, Syria, and Greece. This source, to which Adam contributed himself by the publication of the Spalato book, was the one which he most enjoyed and most exhaustively exploited. Spalato, as it happens, provided him with less material than, for instance, Robert Wood's Palmyra and Balbec folios or Le Roy's description of the ruins of Greece. Palmyra is constantly

echoed in ceilings of the 1760s, while Le Roy introduced him to the Ionic order of the Erechtheum, of which Adam versions abound.

As for Italy, we can take the major antique monuments for granted, as one suspects Adam virtually did. What interested him chiefly in classical archaeology was the recapture of the Roman style of *interior* decoration, which he rightly insisted was something wholly different from the marble temple architecture whose survival was so much more conspicuous and which had therefore been adapted, without sufficient thought, to modern interior requirements. Here, his researches were helped by the engravings of Santo Bartoli and these, with the works of Montfaucon and de Caylus, opened up the vista of what contemporary scholars considered to be Etruscan art. Piranesi lent his weight to the propagation of the Etruscan idea and Adam evolved an 'Etruscan style' in which he designed several important rooms.[15]

4. The influence of the Renaissance masters, among whom Adam mentions Michelangelo, Raphael, Giulio Romano, Pirro Ligorio, Giovanni da Udine, Domenichino, Polidoro, Zuccari, Vasari, and Algardi. The interest here was mainly, though not exclusively, in decorative work – *grottesche* and compartments such as we find in the Vatican loggias and the Villa Madama. Adam took the view that in the sixteenth century many more Roman interiors survived than were standing in the eighteenth and that these masters had learnt their style from such originals.

It has been necessary to classify the sources of the Adam style in some detail, not only because that style is inexplicable without doing so but because it is as well, at this point in our story, to emphasize the almost limitless wealth of material which was becoming available to the English architect. In Robert Adam's case we find a great variety of influences fused in a style which is extremely personal. As to this, the preface to the first number of the Adams' published works (1773) makes no pretence at under-statement. 'The novelty and variety of the following designs, will, we flatter ourselves, not only excuse, but justify our conduct in communicating them to the world . . . we have not trod in the path of others, nor derived aid from their labours.' Even if the last sentence is rather too flagrant an exaggeration, there is no question that everything which the Adams touched they made completely their own.

What is the essence of this style? The answer can best be given by considering Adam's attitude towards a single unit of classical design – say, a Corinthian entablature. To an architect of the Palladian school a Corinthian entablature was a more or less inflexible thing – a grammatical construction in the Latin of architecture. To Adam, on the other hand, it was a thing whose qualities could be abstracted and then rendered back with an infinity of variation, the whole reduced or expanded to fit the occasion. 'The proportions of columns depend on their situation.' Even though not a single ratio or a single enrichment remained exactly as Vitruvius or the Renaissance theorists had defined it, the total effect in the new model was still of such an entablature. But in its new form it possessed an intensified character.

The notion of abstracting and rendering back the character of the classical units was made possible by the revelation, for which Piranesi was largely responsible (p. 250), that the Romans had not confined themselves to one or two or a dozen types of any given unit but had, in fact, enjoyed a freedom which, in smaller buildings and interiors, was quite unlimited. In other words, the 'rules' of architectural grammar were seen to be not a question of rules at all but of style, of feeling, of taste. Hence the Adam style – a personal revision and reconstitution of the antique into which many threads from a variety of sources were drawn and interwoven. It is essentially a decorative style – a style of decoration. It tends to smallness of scale, through the sub-division (sometimes excessive) of parts and the sub-enrichment of enrichments. Moreover, it diverges sharply from the Adam conception of exterior design, which never became anything like as free or as felicitous as his management of interiors. It is as an interior architect that Adam is chiefly remembered, and with some justice. Opportunity and temperament both conspired to make him such and it was in the planning and adornment of the most lavish interiors of his time that he fulfilled himself.

The Works of Robert and James Adam

The columnar screen in front of the Admiralty, Whitehall, a French conception, with some few novelties of sculptural detail, was Adam's first important work when he started practice in 1759. But public buildings in the capital were not to be his destiny. Within two years he had his hands full of country domestic work of the most illustrious kind. Oddly enough, this does not mean that he was building houses. Indeed, for the first ten years of his career he hardly built any houses at all, his major undertakings being the completion of houses half-built by others or the transformation of old houses within their existing shells. At Hatchlands, Surrey, and Shardeloes, Bucks., both built by other architects, we find the first Adam interiors. They are still near-Palladian, and unconventional only in their choice of themes for wall and ceiling designs and in an unusual variety of enrichment. By 1761, however, Adam was beginning some of his most considerable works and those in which he rapidly developed his style. These houses include Harewood, Yorks. (for Edwin Lascelles), Croome Court, Worcestershire (for the Earl of Coventry), Compton Verney, Warwickshire (for Lord Willoughby de Broke), Kedleston Hall, Derbyshire (for Sir Nathaniel Curzon, later Lord Scarsdale), Bowood, Wilts. (for Lord Shelburne, later Marquis of Lansdowne), and Osterley Park (for Robert Child). In 1762 he was employed by Sir Hugh Smithson (later 1st Duke of Northumberland of the new creation) to recast the whole interior of Syon House, Middlesex. These, with the slightly later Mersham-le-Hatch, Kent (1762–72; the first completely new house), Lansdowne House, Berkeley Square (1762–5), Newby Hall, Yorks. (c. 1767–85), Luton Hoo, Beds. (1766–1770) and Kenwood (1767–8), now in the County of London, constitute the bulk of the Adams' output in their first period.

Since most of these houses were in progress over many years, so that different rooms are differently dated, it is impossible to trace the architects' development through each in turn. We can, however, take different aspects of the Adams work and illustrate them from the evidence which the houses supply. Thus, as planners, it is Syon which illustrates their manner most clearly, in spite of the fact that they were working within the shell of a

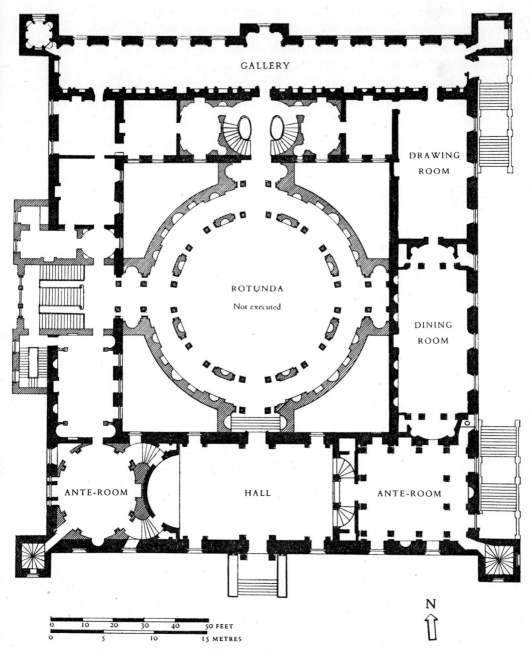

Figure 35. Syon House

Jacobean house. It was a quadrangular house, which the Adams replanned to comprise a progression of state-rooms, continuing round all four sides. The result (Figure 35) is thoroughly Neo-classical, in the sense that it contains a variety of geometrical shapes, contrasting happily with each other and each originating in a classical prototype. Thus the entrance hall, based on the basilica idea, is a rectangle with an apsidal end. In one direction

265

it connects with an oval ante-room, in the other with an ante-room which is a rectangle reduced to a square by a screen of free-standing columns on one side. The dining-room is a long room with apses at the ends, on the chords of which are columns *in antis*, an arrangement which Adam effectively repeated at Kenwood and Newby.

In the Adams original plan for Syon, the centre court was to be occupied by a great domed hall, a 'Pantheon' which was to be the 'general *rendez-vous*' of the house. It was not executed, but the idea recurs in the central 'tribune' at Luton Hoo (Figure 36) and once again at the Edinburgh Register House, built ten years later (1772 onwards).

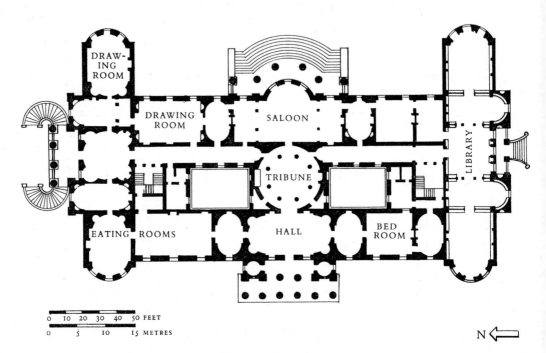

Figure 36. Luton Hoo

A plan as monumental as that of Syon postulates an equally monumental vertical expression. The hall and south ante-room at Syon, together with the hall and saloon at Kedleston and the sculpture-gallery at Newby, illustrate Adam's domestic-monumental style. At Kedleston, where the basic themes were given by the already half-executed plan of Paine, Adam is colder and less himself than at Syon. At Syon, the hall has a Doric order with high attic and flat, beamed ceiling. Adam borrows from the *cinquecento* for the treatment of the attic windows; otherwise he is fairly restrained but shows his temperament clearly in the busy filling of the triglyphs, and the 'spotting' of the walls with paterae, painted medallions, and swags. In the adjoining ante-room (Plate 148), the twelve Ionic columns, whose shafts, of verd antique, were found in Rome, are partly disposed in the manner of the classical triumphal arch – i.e. as support for salient entablatures carrying detached figures. This theme, here introduced for the first time in an English interior, links with the very remarkable exterior use of the same theme at Kedleston.

The south front of Kedleston (Plate 151A) is as near being wholly Adam as the pre-determined plan of James Paine (p. 225) would allow, and it was Adam who introduced, here again, the triumphal arch theme, as the exterior expression of the great domed saloon which is the main apartment of the house. This is a Neo-classic gesture of a kind which we do occasionally find in Adam at this period. It is, in this case, not quite new, for Salvi, in his Fontana di Trevi at Rome (1735), had led the way. But its use in a purely domestic building is original; it might be compared with Reynolds's introduction of the stance and gesture of the Apollo Belvedere in his portrait of Keppel.

A rather similar piece of Neo-classicism is the double portico at Osterley (Plate 151B) which derives partly from the propylaeum of the Temple Enclosure at Palmyra and partly from the Erechtheum. Its integration with the house as an open passage-way is thoroughly Neo-classical in feeling. Neo-classicism with an archaeological twist again occurs at Bowood, where the long 'Diocletian Wing' is so called because it faintly echoes the pattern of the *crypto-porticus* at Spalato; it introduces, moreover, a favourite 'composite' capital of Adam's, based on a pilaster found at Spalato, and consisting of a fluted bell with only one row of acanthus leaves.

The Neo-classical streak in Adam appears fitfully. The extreme reserve of true Neo-classicism was inimical to his theory of 'movement', and it is only in these occasional gestures, where antiquity provided the idea for some dramatic columnar episode, that we recognize Adam's affinity with the new school of thought developing on the Continent.

The Adam style of interior decoration, as we see it in the bulk of the later work, emerges alongside the more monumental style in the country-house installations of the sixties. The Gallery at Syon (1763–4; Plate 149) marks an important stage. It is a very long room, in fact an unusually long Jacobean 'long gallery', on which, obviously, no antique space-conception could be imposed. Adam seems to have accepted the challenge in a spirit of gaiety, producing an unconventional result. He divided the walls into bays, certain of which are again subdivided by tiny, slim pilasters, while in these bays there is a subsidiary order of diminutive Ionic pilasters. Enrichments, necessarily minuscule in scale, cover nearly every surface; there are arabesques and medallions in the panels and arabesque panels in the pilasters, while the dado has the S-fluting of the typical antique sarcophagus. The ceiling is a miniature beam-and-panel arrangement of extreme delicacy, almost Jacobean in spirit. The whole effect is of a delicate interweaving of linear patterns, an embroidery of architecture, skin-deep and as agreeable (it seems) to the touch as to the eye.[16] The room, which Adam described as being 'in a style to afford great variety and amusement', attains that degree of integration of varied thematic material which was to make the later interiors possible.

The period of country-house installations may be said to close with the beginning of a great London venture into which the Adams poured their fortunes as well as their talents. This was the Adelphi (Plate 145). In 1768 the brothers leased the Thames-side site of Durham House and proceeded to invest a huge sum of money in embanking it and raising on the embankment several streets of houses, planned to make a monumental whole. They were disappointed in their expectation of letting the vaults to the Ordnance

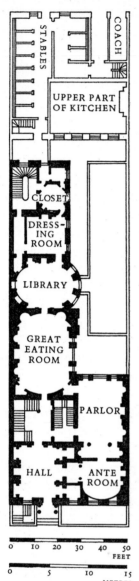

STABLES

COACH

UPPER PART
OF KITCHEN

CLOSET

DRESS-
ING
ROOM

LIBRARY

GREAT
EATING
ROOM

PARLOR

HALL

ANTE
ROOM

0   10   20   30   40   50
FEET

0   5   10   15
METRES

Figure 37. Derby House,
Grosvenor Square

Department, with the result that the speculation proved too much for them, and they only extricated themselves by the expedient of a lottery.

However, the Adelphi was built, most of it between 1768 and 1772. It consisted, mainly, of a great terrace of houses towards the river, a street behind this and two lateral streets whose end houses projected somewhat further towards the river than the line of the terrace, thus making effective terminals for the whole group and giving it a touch of 'movement'. All the houses were brick, with ornaments in stone or a patent terra-cotta. The great terrace, consisting of eleven houses, was composed in what had, by then, become the traditional way – i.e. with the centre and end houses breaking slightly forward and decorated with a full order. At the Adelphi, however, the order consisted of the thinnest pilasters, supporting a shallow frieze and cornice only, and the pilasters had sunk panels with anthemion enrichment. In other words, Adam had brought his new interior style out-of-doors to provide a neat, inexpensive decoration for the London house.[17]

At Portland Place, where the Adams again speculated (from 1773), though on a smaller scale, they again introduced these slim, simple trimmings which instantly became the universal fashion for London terraces and remained so until the advent of John Nash and the Regency.

The Adelphi introduces what may be called the London period of the brothers' career – the period whose chief products were three great houses, two of which still exist. These are No. 20 St James's Square (1772–3; for Sir Watkin Williams-Wynn) and No. 20 Portman Square (1775–7; for the Countess of Home).[18] The vanished house, on the site of the present No. 26 Grosvenor Square, was built in 1773–4 for the Earl of Derby and demolished in 1862. In each of these three houses, in turn, Adam tackled the problem of planning, in the spirit of Syon, on the restricted site and reduced scale necessitated by the dimensions of a plot in a London Square. Kent, in No. 44 Berkeley Square (p. 204), had faced this problem but lavished most of his attention on the staircase alone. Adam's three plans are an advance on this, for he does succeed, by extraordinary ingenuity, in fitting together whole suites of rooms so that they give precisely the sense of progressive contrast which we noted in the plan of Syon. The plan of Derby House (Figure 37) was perhaps the most skilful of all. Here, the hall, ante-room, parlour, great eating-room, and library were all *en suite* and carefully contrasted in shape, character, and proportion. Home House is scarcely less ingenious and here the tower-like domed staircase is (allowing for the inescapable disadvantages of a top-lit stair) most effectively introduced.

The decoration of the rooms in these houses represents the full development of that linear weaving of detail which we noticed in the gallery at Syon (1763). The music room at Home House (Plate 150) may be taken as representing the summit of this development. Here is a pilaster order even slimmer than the one in the Syon gallery and supporting the mere ghost of an entablature, while the cornice next the ceiling is reduced to almost nothing. The enrichments are very restrained and there is none of the 'spottiness' in their application which is found in Adam decoration of the sixties and was due to a failure to integrate the assembled elements into a single formal idea. The ceiling, based on a simple theme of contiguous roundels, is a harmonious echo from the stuccos of Hadrian's villa.

Wynn House, slightly earlier than Home House, has not quite the same perfect fluency and restraint. Of the lost rooms at Derby House, the ground-floor parlour (Plate 152B), covered by a segmental cross-vault, slightly reminiscent of some of the Corneto tombs, must have been especially interesting.

After about 1775, the career of the famous brothers descends rapidly in significance, and we need trouble with few buildings belonging to the last seventeen years of Robert's life. Probably the war with America, resulting in high taxes and scarcity of timber, temporarily reduced the will to build extravagantly and when it was over the Adams had lost something of their prestige. The names of younger men were being advertised, and such expressions as 'gingerbread' and 'sippets of embroidery' (Horace Walpole), 'filigrane toy-work' (Chambers), and 'puerile ornaments' (Peacock, the architect) were heard as epithets for the Adam manner. Nevertheless, there are a few buildings which cannot be overlooked. The extraordinary church at Mistley, Essex (1776; Plate 152A), consisting of a central nave with identical towers, in imitation of a Roman tomb, at east and west ends, is one of them.[19] Then there is the work at Edinburgh. This includes the Register House (1772–92) where Adam realized the conception of a domed hall within a square, which he had introduced in his design for Syon; and the University (1789–92), whose façade (Plate 147B) echoes back in a curious way to the elements of the Doric hall at Syon and back still further to the cloud-capped palace designs of the Italian journey (Plate 147A). In Charlotte Square, Edinburgh (1791), and in Fitzroy Square, London (1790), Adam made his final contribution to street design, building, in both cases, in stone and introducing (if rather artificially) more 'movement' than a flat row of identical houses might be thought capable of.

The eight thousand Adam drawings at the Soane Museum are a monument to the capacity and fertility of invention of the two brothers and mainly, of course, of the leader and chief innovator, Robert. They include many unexecuted designs, some, like those for Lincoln's Inn or the King's College and University buildings at Cambridge, on a great scale. They also include designs for organ- and piano-cases, mirrors, furniture, sedan-chairs, coach-panels, candle-sticks, salt-cellars, and door-furniture. They illustrate, very clearly, Adam's use of colour which was not, as is too often and disastrously thought, a gay 'picking-out' of decorative motifs, but a subtle and gentle modification of the traditional white finish which Adam found too glaring in practice. Even the richest schemes are carefully built up from this principle.

Of Robert Adam as a man we have just enough information to see him as a worldly, society-loving person, much at his ease, witty enough for his company, passionately confident in his own ability, and wholly inattentive to criticism. He wrote little about his art, but the introductions which he and his brother provided for the *Works in Architecture of Robert and James Adam*, which appeared in instalments between 1773 and 1779 (a posthumous volume being added in 1822), contain perceptive and lucid criticism.

Chambers, Adam, and Neo-classicism

To what extent can the two architects who have been dealt with in this chapter be regarded as exponents of Neo-classicism? The answer is different in each case. Whatever is Neo-classical in Chambers is merely a reflexion of the work of Soufflot and his school in France. Although he read Laugier he certainly did not take him to heart; he never dispensed with pilasters and rarely made his orders spring from the ground; nor do his plans ever hint at the geometry of antique *thermae*. If, in the unbroken sky-line and judicious modulations of Somerset House there is a feeling of Neo-classicism, it is simply this French influence ironing out the bolder terms of English Palladianism.

With Adam it is quite different. A more vigorously personal artist than Chambers, he involuntarily took from Neo-classicism whatever fitted in with his feeling for 'movement' and discarded what did not. Thus, in planning he is, sometimes, truly Neo-classical: as, for instance, at Syon, where the (proposed) central 'pantheon', surrounded by suites of rooms of varied shape and proportion, is in the spirit of quite advanced Neo-classical planning. Again, his selection of archaeological themes has sometimes, as we saw at Kedleston and Osterley, that sense of spatial drama which belongs to Neo-classicism, while his ideal of reconstructing a system of Roman interior decoration – the ideal which resulted in the 'Adam style' – is one of which Laugier himself might have approved. On the other hand, nothing could be more remote from Neo-classical standards than Adam's feeling for composition in mass, and his retention of the Kentian towers and flats with occasional arbitrary high attics, ornamental cupolas, and purely decorative pediments. Adam was a law unto himself. When Neo-classicism suggested the varied geometry of antique planning he accepted it; it meant 'movement'. When, on the other hand, it suggested a ruthless identification of exterior composition with the columnar structure of temples, he rejected it (or failed to notice it); it was inimical to 'movement'. And there the matter ends.

NOTES TO CHAPTER 26

1. All the buildings at Kew were engraved in *Plans . . . of the Gardens and Buildings at Kew*, published by Chambers, at the royal expense, in 1763. Not all the buildings are by Chambers. The 'Gothic Cathedral' is acknowledged to be by the Swiss painter John Henry Müntz, while another hand was responsible for the 'Alambra', of which the original drawing, in the Royal Institute of British Architects library, is dated 1750, executed 1756.

2. The first French edition of Laugier, 1753, has a

frontispiece showing a primitive hut in course of erection. The English edition of 1755 has a different design of the same subject.

3. Chambers's classical country-houses include Lord Bessborough's house (now Manresa Jesuit College), Roehampton (c. 1760), Duntish Court (formerly Castle Hill), Dorset (c. 1760), Peper Harow and Duddingstone, both begun 1763, the stables at Harewood, and the gateway at Wilton. His only Gothic house, Milton, he himself described as 'a vast, ugly Gothick house in Dorsetshire'. His only surviving large town-houses are Lord Charlemont's house, Dublin (1763; now a museum), Sir L. Dundas's house at Edinburgh (1770–1; now the Royal Bank of Scotland), and Albany (old Melbourne House, 1771–3), Piccadilly. Carrington House, Whitehall (1765), was destroyed in 1886.

4. All the Surveyors-General after Wren, up to the reorganization of the Office of Works in 1782, were politicians, usually with an amateur interest in architecture. Wren's successor, Benson, was probably the most architecturally active.

5. We met him in the last Chapter (p. 242) as Walpole's executive at Strawberry Hill.

6. Drawings of this are in the Soane Museum.

7. That such doorways should occur in such a place is a piece of thoroughly bad planning, of which no Frenchman would have been guilty!

8. Two fine stone door-cases by Chambers still exist at Nos 20 and 56 Berners Street.

9. Piranesi may be the more immediate inspiration. Chambers had met him in Rome and, with reservations, admired his work. 'Forget not Piranesi,' he wrote to his pupil, Edward Stevens, in 1774, 'he is full of matter, extravagant 'tis true, often absurd, but from his overflowings you may gather much information.'

10. Under 22 Geo. III, cap. 82, all the royal buildings were put under the management of one officer who was to be 'bona fide by profession an architect or builder'.

11. The Academy resulted from the secession from the Incorporated Society of Artists of a number of its original members. Chambers submitted their case to the King, a memorial was presented in November 1768, and the Royal Academy founded on 10 December.

12. Chambers confesses, in a letter (1772) to

Frederick Chapman, the King of Sweden's Master Ship-builder, that he merely fathered his own ideas on the Chinese (Add. 41,133, f. 78). As Chambers was well known to have been to China and to be the authority on Chinese architecture, the hoax was not easily penetrated.

13. Writing to Lord Grantham in 1778, Chambers takes exception to the Adams' 'presumptuous' claim to have introduced a new manner of decoration, eliminating the ponderous units of the previous period. At Melbourne House, he says, he had done as much 'in a manner almost diametrically opposed to theirs'. (Add. 41,134, f. 34.)

14. Genius, and the idea of inspiration, become important about this time. Edward Young's *Conjectures on Original Composition* came out in 1759 and *Ossian* shortly after. See N. Pevsner, *Academies of Art*, 1940, p. 190. The appeal to genius and inspiration is the direct consequence of the new, objective view of Rome which tended to destroy the *legend* of Rome as the final arbiter in aesthetic matters.

15. Surviving 'Etruscan' rooms are at No. 20 Portman Square and Osterley. The essentials of such a room seem to have been mural paintings introducing panels or medallions with 'Etruscan' vase figure-subjects and corresponding colouring.

16. The craftsman's contribution to this and other Adam rooms must not be forgotten, for the interpretation of Adam's drawings for plaster-work by the plasterer, Joseph Rose, is an important factor in the final result. The same may be said of an arabesque painter like M. A. Pergolesi, who worked at Syon.

17. The Adelphi was destroyed in 1937, though a few houses in the side and rear streets survive, notably No. 7 Adam Street, with well-preserved pilasters and pediment.

18. No. 20 St James's Square is now part of the premises of the Distillers Company, who have doubled the frontage to St James's Square. The Adam unit has been most carefully repeated and the six-bay façade is certainly handsome, though now completely foreign to Adam, who would scarcely have treated a long façade in this fashion. No. 20 Portman Square is now the Courtauld Institute, University of London.

19. The body of the church has been destroyed, but the towers survive.

CHAPTER 27

NEO-CLASSICISM: THE SECOND PHASE

AT the beginning of the last chapter it was observed that Chambers and Adam dominated English architecture for thirty years from 1760 – the first three decades of George III's long reign. Although this is true in the sense that at any time during that period the condition of architecture can only be assessed in relation to what those men were doing, the statement must now be considerably modified. First, as to Adam. His actual pre-eminence in English architecture only lasted for a decade or a little more and had he died in 1775 (when he was forty-seven) his status in history would have been very much what it is. Not only had he done all his most important work, but he had achieved that revolution in taste of which he himself was so arrogantly conscious.[1] The effect, from 1770 onwards, of that revolution can hardly be exaggerated. The slim pilasters of Kenwood and the Adelphi, the elongated columns of Lansdowne House, the decorative doorways, fire-places and ceilings in those buildings had all been imitated by known and unknown architects before 1775. In St James's Street, Boodle's (by R. Crunden) plagiarizes the Society of Arts building; Bedford Square and Stratford Place followed hard on Portland Place; while James Pain, a carpenter, refers, in his *Practical Builder* of 1774, to the 'very great revolution' which had taken place in architecture, a revolution which the plates in this and other books steadily promoted.

Chambers had no spectacular success quite like this. His style, so studied and so eclectic, was not infectious. On the other hand, he maintained his position better. When people began to tire of Adam novelties they turned to Chambers for the solid comforts of scholarship and precedent. His *Treatise* became a standard work and, after three editions in his lifetime, was handsomely edited and republished by Gwilt as late as 1825.

In 1775, therefore, it may be said that the Adam revolution was over and that Chambers, settling down to the long labours of Somerset House, was the most respected figure in English architecture, a figure, however, receding somewhat into the background. For by 1775 it is clear that a new generation has entered the field, a generation inclining more to Chambers than to Adam, but aiming at something rather different from either – something more decisively Neo-classical than Chambers, less inconstantly and fancifully so than Adam; in short, at an English interpretation of the Neo-classicism then in its first flowering in France. It is with the architects of this generation that we must now deal.

Most of them were born in the 1740s; but considerably ahead of the main group is Robert Mylne (1734–1811). As we have seen (p. 253), Mylne went to Rome in the same year as Adam and became in 1758 the first British medallist at the Academy of St Luke. His career as an architect does not altogether fulfil this extraordinary promise. He was, indeed, very successful, both as architect and engineer, but his contribution to architectural development was modest. His most famous work was his first – Blackfriars Bridge, which he began in 1760 and successfully completed in 1769; it introduced elliptical arches (a

French innovation) to the Thames and the Roman device of mounting two columns on each breakwater, supporting a projecting portion of entablature and balustrade – a device used time and again up to Rennie's Waterloo Bridge of 1811. In feeling, the design probably owed something to a well-known engraving by Piranesi, to which we shall have occasion to refer again (p. 275). The bridge survived till 1868.

Mylne built several other bridges, many town- and country-houses, and a few public buildings. He was engineer to the New River Company, the Gloucester and Berkeley Canal, and several harbours; and Surveyor to Canterbury and St Paul's Cathedrals. His domestic style shows some Adam influence, but has a quiet distinguished character of its own, with Neo-classic traits such as a liking for lunettes. Wick House, Richmond, Surrey (for Lady St Aubyn, 1775), is an almost perfect work of its kind and a forerunner of the villa-planning of around 1800. His chief public building (apart from Blackfriars Bridge) was the City of London Lying-in Hospital (1770–3; destroyed), a composition aiming, apparently, at Adam's 'movement' and crowned by an exceptionally tall, spired cupola. The east front of Stationers' Hall, London (c. 1800; Plate 153A), is, on the other hand, perfectly simple and, like all Mylne's work, faultless in proportion.

Since Mylne need not detain us we can go on at once to the group of younger architects just mentioned, and it is convenient to consider first those who show a distinct loyalty to Sir William Chambers, being either pupils of his or followers, and forming a distinct school of design.

The School of Chambers

Most important among these people were two young men, Thomas Cooley (1740–84) and James Gandon (1743–1823), who were to find great opportunities in Ireland and to build, in Dublin, a series of public buildings which rank as the finest products of the Chambers school.

Gandon was of French descent. He was in Chambers's office, and at the age of about twenty-six became the newly founded Royal Academy's first Gold Medallist. In the same year (1769) he published, with the nominal collaboration of John Woolfe (an elderly Works official), the first of two excellent volumes in continuation of *Vitruvius Britannicus*. In the second volume, which appeared in 1771, we find a design by Gandon himself for the County Hall at Nottingham.[2] It is a surprising design for its date, stark and heavy with a frontispiece of four Ionic columns carrying an over-simplified entablature of almost Tuscan character. Evidently Gandon had seen something of the most advanced French Neo-classicism, possibly work or designs by E. L. Boullée, Chalgrin, or Brongniart.

Gandon had competed, in 1769, for the new Royal Exchange (now the City Hall) at Dublin and had received the third premium. The first had gone to the other member of the pair under discussion, Thomas Cooley. Cooley had not, it seems, been in Chambers's office. He had, in fact, been working for Robert Mylne on Blackfriars Bridge, a fact which explains a good deal. The Dublin Exchange (Plate 153B), which he completed in 1779, shows the influence of Mylne's Rome design (p. 253) and has rather more of the French Neo-classic spirit than most of Chambers's executed or published works. The combination of giant pilasters and rusticated walling, the latter treated as an in-filling so that the pilasters seem not to be mere architecture in relief, is an interesting departure at which Chambers's works never more than hint. The circular-domed interior with its great composite order penetrated by a subsidiary Ionic is very close in character to one of Chambers's designs for St Marylebone Church, though this latter cannot be earlier than 1770.

Two years after finishing the Royal Exchange, Cooley started a Public Offices building on the north bank of the Liffey; but in 1784, at the age of about 44, he died. In the following year it was decided to absorb this new building into a much larger scheme for new Law Courts and the whole thing was placed in the hands of James Gandon.

Gandon, whom we left a moment ago in London, was now in Dublin as architect to the new Custom House (Plate 155), the commission for which had been secured for him, in an oddly conspiratorial way, by Lord Carlow. Almost 'smuggled' over to Ireland, he began the building amid threats of mob violence in 1781 and completed it ten years later. Built around two courtyards, the Custom House has a finely composed river front owing a little to Chambers and a dome closely following those of Greenwich – borrowings wholly justified in their use, except for an unfortunate loss of scale in the dome, too abruptly mounted on a façade of serene, unfaltering excellence.

When, in 1785, Gandon took over the Public Offices and proceeded to incorporate them into the new Four Courts, he put such failings behind him and produced a composition of real power (Plate 154). The four court-rooms he placed on the diagonal axes of a square block with a circular domed hall in the centre. Above this hall he raised a colonnaded drum, sufficiently reminiscent of St Paul's for one to expect a dome and lantern. But there are none – only a low domical roof, so that the feeling is nearer to that of the palace design in the *Œuvres* of Chambers's friend, M. J. Peyre. That Wren was the main inspiration, however, is confirmed by the main river façade which derives from the lower part of the west front of St Paul's. This façade is linked to the Cooley block and its duplicated counterpart on the east by open-arched screens with triumphal arches in the centre of each.

If both Gandon's Liffey-side buildings[3] are infinitely more powerful than Somerset House, the main reason seems to be that Gandon could open his mind to Wren, whereas Chambers belonged to a generation which still profoundly distrusted his Baroque liberties. Wren's influence appears once again in the felicitous cupola of the King's Inns, Dublin, which Gandon built, from 1795, in partnership with H. A. Baker.

Both Cooley and Gandon contributed other buildings to Dublin and to other Irish towns and left behind them, through their later contemporaries and pupils, a tradition of good classical design which held its ground till far into the nineteenth century. In England, the Chambers school had a more limited success, probably because opportunities here were greater in private than in public architecture, and it was in private houses and speculative work that the Adam fashion proved irresistible. Naturally, the Royal Academy encouraged the style of its Treasurer. The first Professor of Architecture, Thomas Sandby 1721–98), gave a course of lectures closely adhering to the point of view of Chambers's *Treatise*; and his own designs, not numerous, are in the same spirit. His chief executed work was the Hall of the Freemasons' Tavern, Great Queen Street (1775–6; burnt 1883), an interior with Doric pilasters and a rich, coved ceiling pierced by lunettes, the whole evidently proportioned and adorned with reference to the recommendations in Chambers's book. Sandby achieved a vicarious triumph when he exhibited at the Royal Academy in 1781 a magnificent design for a Triumphal Bridge over the Thames. The design was, in reality, an almost literal copy of the bridge in the Piranesi engraving mentioned in connexion with Mylne (p. 273). It was none the less influential for that.

Apart from Chambers and Sandby, the only other architects among the foundation-members of the Academy were John Gwynne, known for his bridges at Shrewsbury and Attingham and a remarkable book on the planning of London, and George Dance II, to whom we shall shortly return. William Tyler makes a third if we consider him as an architect rather than a sculptor, in which capacity he joined the Academy; his only important building, the Ordnance Office at Westminster (1778–9; demolished 1806), suggests that he, like Sandby, conformed to the Chambers school.

Of Chambers's pupils, the most important, apart from Gandon, were John Yenn (c. 1745–1821) and Thomas Hardwick (1752–1829).[4] Yenn, who was the second Royal Academy Gold Medallist, held a variety of offices in the Works, was elected A.R.A. in 1774, R.A. in 1791, and succeeded his master as Treasurer in 1796. His drawings, and such works of his as have not been demolished or forgotten, show him to have followed Chambers conscientiously and without much talent of his own. Thomas Hardwick was, likewise, a terribly uninspired loyalist of the Chambers office, though his works – principally London churches – were many and important. St Mary's, Wanstead (1787–90), and St James's, Hampstead Road (1792), are much alike in their box-like, and rather Gibbs-like, simplicity, relieved in the first case by a Doric porch, in the second by a Doric pilaster order above the entrance, and in both by a little bell-tower over a western pediment. St John's Wood Chapel (1814) is still on the same lines, but with a giant Ionic order which gives it more consequence. Finally, Hardwick was called upon to enlarge another, similar, chapel which he was building for St Marylebone, into a parish church to seat three thousand people. Thus, he was given a task to which his master had devoted much fruitless effort in 1770–7.[5] It cannot have been easy to inflate a half-built chapel into so monumental a work, but Hardwick produced in the present St Marylebone Church (1813–17) a building which has, at least, a certain cold dignity. The breadth of the 'west' (actually north) front, obtained by extending it in both directions into staircase wings, is perhaps a reminiscence of the Chambers design, while the pairs of columns which terminate these wings are one of the most familiar of all Chambers motifs.

Thus, the Chambers tradition, so firmly founded in the *Treatise* of 1759, penetrates at last to the Regency, an elderly, outmoded Roman in the London of the Elgin Marbles and St Pancras Church.

George Dance II

The only original architect Royal Academician who was not subordinate to Chambers in talent or originality of approach was that younger son of the old Clerk of the City Works whom we have already mentioned as having visited Italy on the heels of Adam and Mylne. George Dance (1741–1825), son of the architect of the Mansion House, went to

Italy about 1758. Five years later, at the young and somewhat internationally minded Academy of Parma, Dance obtained, in competition with twenty-eight others, the Gold Medal for a design for a Public Gallery. The design, which survives in the Soane Museum, is more rigorously Neo-classical than Mylne's St Luke's design of 1758. Here, at last, we have the real thing – a serenely balanced composition, a plan conceived entirely in simple geometrical forms, of antique provenance, and elevations expressed in terms of columns and, where columns were inappropriate, of solid rusticated wall. Laugier might, indeed, have criticized the use of full entablatures throughout, irrespective of function, but otherwise the conditions of the Jesuit puritan of architecture are fulfilled.

Returning to England, at the age of about twenty-two or twenty-three, Dance was soon called upon to build, and the small but very remarkable church of All Hallows, London Wall (Plate 156), was erected by him in 1765–7. It is simply a barrel-vaulted compartment with lunettes piercing the vault, and an apse at the east end. But the springings of the vault, between the lunettes, are supported on an attached Ionic order, and this order has *no entablature other than a highly enriched frieze*. This may be supposed a mere whim of Dance's, but it is, on the whole, more likely to be a deliberate application of the rationalism propounded by the Abbé Laugier (p. 249). Soane tells us how as a young man, just conversant with the Palladian grammar, this bold omission had struck him as a lapse of taste and how, later, he came to appreciate its significance. It was, indeed, the first step to his own grammatical freedoms.

The exquisite detail at All Hallows seems to owe something to Adam, more particularly to the ante-room at Syon; and the ceiling introduces 'Etruscan' motifs adapted from Bartoli. It is a marvellous performance for a man of twenty-four and must have been recognized as such by Sir William Chambers; for Dance became, as we have seen, one of the four first Royal Academicians in 1768.

Dance's aged father, the architect of the Mansion House, dying in that year, his son, still only twenty-seven, succeeded him as Clerk of the City Works. Almost immediately, one of the greatest building projects the City had ever undertaken was placed in his hands, and in 1769 he was designing Newgate (Plate 158).

Newgate Prison (destroyed in 1902) was one of the most original English buildings of the eighteenth century – a fact recognized by Durand when he included it among the few English examples in his *Recueil et parallèle des édifices* of 1800. The problem of designing a great prison was, in 1769, a baldly empirical affair. John Howard had not yet given the world his conception of prison life as a matter demanding organization and discipline and Dance's plan, therefore, is of no particular interest. It is his conception of the great blind walls which enclose the prison and of the placing of the governor's house and the two porches – in short, the dramatization of the whole – which make Newgate so remarkable.

It is tempting – perhaps a little too tempting – to associate the giant drama of Newgate at once with Piranesi and especially with the *Carceri* series of fantasies published in 1750. Very likely there is a connexion of mood, but it accounts for nothing in the composition or detail of the building, except possibly the macabre festooning of chains over the doorways. The composition was, in essence, Neo-classical. It had the true Neo-classical reluctance to emphasize the centre, and consisted, broadly, of two great masses with a hollow between them. In this hollow were placed the governor's house and the two entrance lodges, a trinity of subsidiary features, in a different key from the rest. Again, each of the two lateral masses was itself subdivided to emphasize the ends, not the centre, of each. All this corresponds with the feeling of Dance's Parma design, and indeed the plain rusticated walls of Newgate definitely find their inception there.

The handling of the various parts is wonderfully resourceful. The governor's house, with its close-set windows and busy pattern of rustication, may conceivably be a reminiscence of Vanbrugh. With more certainty we can trace the great arched recesses which relieve the principal masses, for they derive partly from Palladio's Palazzo Thiene and partly from Giulio Romano's work at Mantua – the Palazzo del Té and his own house. This is an unexpected derivation, for although both Chambers and Adam recognized Giulio's genius, they thought rather of his association with Raphael and Giovanni da Udine at the Villa Madama than of the Mannerist singularities of his Mantuan buildings. But there can be very little doubt about it; and the way that Dance succeeded in integrating Giulio Romano with Palladio within a Neo-classical totality forcibly illustrates his unusual power of imagination.

It has often been assumed that, after his first church and the great prison, Dance never did anything else of the slightest importance. It is excusable, perhaps, to be disappointed by the monotonous façade and tame emphasis of St Luke's Hospital, Old Street (1782–4; survives, much altered, as a printing works). But there are, or were, other buildings by Dance whose significance is very great. Thus, in 1777, he built the Council Chamber in the Guildhall (destroyed 1906), a square-domed hall lit only by a glazed *oculus* in the centre (Plate 157). Dance gave this dome a highly original character by marking off the divisions between pendentives and dome with *flat curves* instead of a horizontal line, thus bringing the dome down to eight points, much in the shape of an open umbrella. The source of this innovation, which breaks right away from the tradition of dome design, is extremely baffling. It is in the spirit of some of the mid eighteenth-century Italian innovators, such as Vittone in Turin, and it may be that Dance and, after him, Soane, owe more to this source than has hitherto been recognized.

Another highly imaginative design was for Lord Lansdowne's library[6] in Berkeley Square, begun about 1792. Dance here made a long flat-vaulted room open at both ends into semi-domed *exedrae*, rising higher than the roof and lit, therefore, from windows above roof level, not seen in the body of the room. As the room was not completed by Dance, but by Robert Smirke after his death, we cannot judge the effect originally intended, nor have we the exquisite mural decorations he designed, inspired partly, it seems, by Raphaelesque work and partly by Herculaneum. But the room was a most striking conception and here again, as at the Guildhall, one which profoundly affected Soane. His treatment of the Rotunda at the Bank (see later, p. 288) derives from it.

After the turn of the century, when Dance himself had reached his sixtieth year, his style changes considerably. From this period (1803–4) dates Stratton Park, Hants. (Plate 159A), remodelled and reduced in size for Sir Francis Baring. Perhaps as a result of freer communications with the Continent during the short peace of 1801–3, Dance had become acquainted with the post-revolutionary Neo-classicism of Paris, with its austere articulation, its archaeological spirit, and its details based on Pompeian and Egyptian motifs and the constant use of an element like the lid of a Roman sarcophagus – a flat 'pediment' between two lugs or 'acroters'. The main exterior feature of Stratton is a heavy four-column Greek Doric portico, probably the first strictly Greek Doric portico to be applied to an English country-house.[7] The staircase hall has a Greek Ionic order (from the temple on the Ilissus), significantly reminiscent in arrangement of the frontispiece in A. L. Dubut's *Maisons de ville et de campagne* (1803). The rooms have delightful and surprising details very freely adapted from Pompeian, Egyptian, or *cinquecento* decoration.

Very clearly, in this house, we see the beginnings of the so-called 'Greek Revival' of Smirke and Wilkins. Indeed, the façade at Stratton forecasts Robert Smirke's at Covent Garden Theatre (1809), a building in which we know that Dance gave the younger man some assistance. Dance, by then, was building the Greek Ionic portico of the College of Surgeons, in Lincoln's Inn Fields (1806–13), the first strictly Greek portico in London. Smirke, at the Post Office, the College of Physicians, and the British Museum ensured, in due course, that it was not the last.

Thus, Dance, having achieved at least three buildings of profound originality before he was thirty-five, went on to suggest to the succeeding generation the different course they were to follow. As Dance's later work cannot, apart from the College of Surgeons, have come much under public notice (he scarcely exhibited anything at the Royal Academy, except the charming portrait drawings which he did as a hobby), it is probable that his influence was spread largely through Smirke. Smirke, equally with Soane, must be regarded as Dance's artistic legatee. Soane, nearer Dance's age, borrowed as extensively but converted his borrowings and produced a personal style parallel with late Dance, but very different indeed. It was Smirke who spread the Greek Revival manner and eventually solidified it into the cold expressionless thing it became in the eighteen-thirties.[8]

Holland and Wyatt

After George Dance, the most important architects of the group born between 1740 and 1750 are Henry Holland and James Wyatt. Indeed, if one measures importance by contemporary celebrity or extent of opportunity Wyatt certainly and Holland probably are more considerable figures than Dance. Dance, indolent, fastidious, a *dilettante* musician and portraitist, and not particularly ambitious, was more original, more complex, and left a deeper impression on his successors.

Henry Holland (1745–1806) was the son of a substantial builder. At twenty-six he became assistant to 'Capability' Brown, the landscape-gardener, helped him with the architectural side of his practice, and married his daughter. His first important work was Brooks's Club, St James's Street, and through this he came into touch with that inner circle of the Whig aristocracy for whom, and for hardly anyone else, he worked for the rest of his life. Brooks's, built in 1776, shows at once that Holland was not going to be a follower of the Adams. The exterior belongs rather to the Chambers school, of which it is a respectable specimen, apart from the weak relationship of front and side elevations. The charming Subscription Room (now the Sitting Room) on the first floor is, to be sure, indebted to the Adams, but their style is here deliberately and severely simplified.

This introduction to Whig society led, a few years later (1783), to the greatest commission of Holland's career, the reconstruction of Carlton House (Plate 160A) as a town residence for the Prince of Wales. Here, he scored a triumph. In remodelling the old plan (Figure 38) he borrowed from Adam's fine treatment of Luton Hoo. At the centre of the Adam plan (Figure 39) was a circular *tribune*[9] which Holland rendered as an octagon, prefacing it to an extremely grand double stair, sweeping up curved walls and detailed with extreme care. Whig taste was, at that moment, enthusiastically French, and Holland managed to capture much of the grace and elegance of the latest Paris manner in his building. The north front had a great Corinthian portico, deep enough to serve as a *porte cochère*, and in front of this was a screen of coupled Ionic columns, raised on a podium. There is an irresistible parallel here with the Hôtel de Salm, Paris, begun only a year or so before Carlton House by Pierre Rousseau; and although it is very doubtful if Holland can have learnt anything from this unfinished building, the similarity of feeling shows how close he came to the modernity of French Neo-classicism.

The interior of Carlton House, which delighted Walpole by its 'august simplicity', its 'taste and propriety', in short by its restoration of those qualities which the Adams had decorated away, was as much and as little indebted to those architects as the Subscription Room at Brooks's. A Louis XVI element was apparent in much of the decoration and most of the furniture, but we need not suppose that Holland necessarily expressed himself in this style, for, as Miss Stroud has shown, his leading assistant, J. P. T. Trécourt, was a Frenchman, and he also employed a French foreman, French furniture makers, and decorative painters. In fact, so far as one can judge on the internal evidence of this and other works by Holland, he was not a designer of very great personal gifts. He was a good planner, had fine taste and was able to prune and modify the Adam style into something approximating to French Neo-classicism, while at the same time marshalling French designers and craftsmen in such a way as to contribute to a successful whole.

Holland had a persistent fondness for simplified Greek versions of the Ionic order, such as that of the Temple on the Ilissus, and used this order, or something like it, again and again, always on a very small scale. At Carlton House it appeared in the hall and again in the fore-court screen, with the columns coupled. When, in 1787, the Duke of York employed him to add a vestibule and screen wall to his house in Whitehall (Plate 160B; now the Scottish Office), Holland again produced his Ionic order, mounting individual columns against a plain rusticated wall[10] and bringing out a four-column portico of the same order in the centre. Behind the screen wall the circular Doric vestibule, lit from a dome and half filled by a flight of steps leading into the older house beyond, is a charming interpretation of a familiar Adam disposition.

The little Ionic occurs again in Lord Spencer's library at Althorp (1786) and in the Duke of Bedford's sculpture gallery (begun as a conservatory) at Woburn (1787; there is a Temple within, with the pure Ilissus order), while at Brighton, where Holland enlarged an old house into a royal residence (eventually the Pavilion, completely transformed by

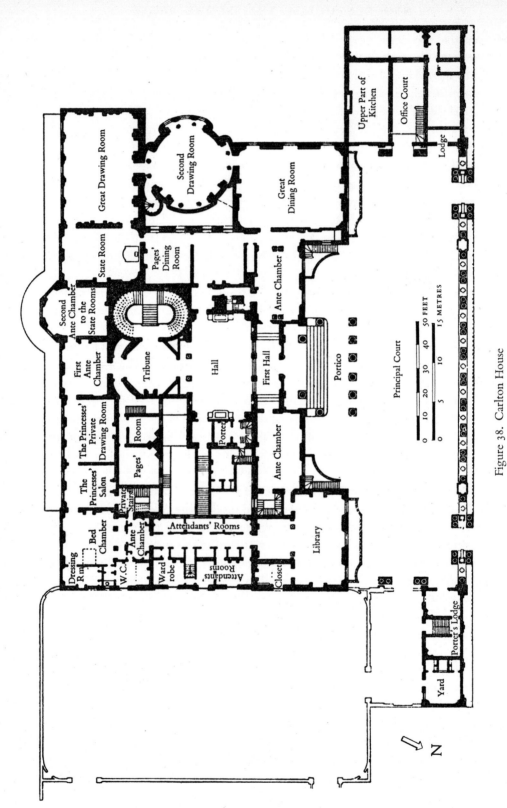

Figure 38. Carlton House

Nash from 1815), he paraded it round the central drawing-room bay, making a feature which again recalls the Hôtel de Salm. The same order still follows us at Southill, Beds. (1795; for Samuel Whitbread), linking the new centre elevation to the remodelled wings. Only in the last (or nearly the last) of his houses, that for Lord Spencer at Wimbledon Park, did Holland exchange his Ionic for a Tuscan, building (1801) a majestic portico in the style of Covent Garden Church, though without a pediment and with Greek caps substituted for the Vitruvian.[11]

Holland's delicate but limited art had no great influence either before or after his death. Soane, who was under him for a short time, is somewhat indebted to him in his early houses and Nash was to adopt the baby Ionic as his own, to introduce it into his houses and trot it all the way round Park Crescent and Park Square.

Compared with Holland, James Wyatt (1747–1813) seems, on first acquaintance, a man of the most brilliant and various attainments. Far from cultivating a narrow personal style, there would seem to have been no style in which he could not perform rather better than anyone else. Saluted as a genius at the beginning of his career and courted perpetually, in spite of an impudent contempt for the elementary obligations of a professional man, Wyatt's success beat all previous reputations. He was the Adams rival when the brothers were at the height of their fame. He overshadowed Chambers and when the latter died in 1796, stepped into his office as Surveyor-General, holding it till his sudden death in a coach accident, in 1813.

But Wyatt's achievement, for all its glitter, does not bear very close inspection. He had technique, taste, and some invention; and a capacity for taking up a style and using it as if it was, and always had been, his own. Under all this, the essential Wyatt is barely discoverable; it is, to all intents and purposes, not there.

Wyatt was the son of a Staffordshire timber-merchant who practised as a builder and, on one occasion at least, as an architect. James went to Italy, apparently under the patronage of certain noblemen connected with an embassy to Venice, in 1762, and remained there for six years, two of which were spent under the Venetian architect-painter-engraver, Antonio Viscentini. He made the acquaintance of at least two English celebrities – Consul Smith, the great collector, and Richard Dalton, George III's librarian.

Partly through Dalton's influence and partly through that of an elder brother, Wyatt succeeded, in 1770, in winning the competition for rebuilding the 'Pantheon', in Oxford Street, as a rendezvous for masquerades. He finished the building in two years and it was an unqualified success. It was burnt down in 1792 and rebuilt, rebuilt again as a theatre, converted into a bazaar, then into a warehouse, and finally demolished in 1937.

The Pantheon, certainly, was a building of uncommon distinction. It had only a narrow, unimportant front to Oxford Street, but the interior of the great room was on the scale of a very large church or theatre (Plate 159B; Figure 39). A curious thing about this room is that the prototype for its general composition was unquestionably the church of Sancta Sophia at Constantinople.[12] Not only did the Pantheon room consist of a great domed space, surrounded by aisles, but the central space opened, in two directions, into apses covered by semi-domes, while, on the other two sides, the openings were filled with two tiers of columns and, above them, a tympanum in the arch.

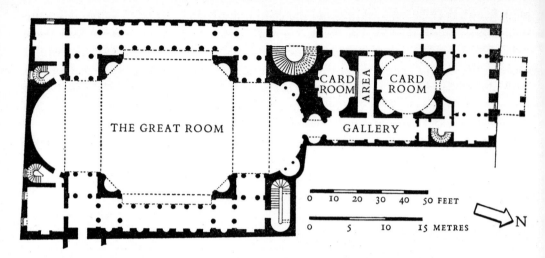

Figure 39. The Pantheon, Oxford Street

The divergencies from this unexpected model are, of course, legion, for the composition was wholly reinterpreted in Neo-classical terms. The hemispherical dome followed closely the Roman Pantheon, while the arches supporting it were reduced to flat segments – the shape introduced by Adam in the great drawing-room at Kenwood. The ornament in general showed some Adam influence; indeed a certain 'composed' capital of the Adams was, according to them, reproduced entire. As for the structure, the whole of the upper part of the building was of carpentry, so that the statical problems shouldered by Wyatt were not quite of the calibre of his Byzantine precursors.

The lucky choice of a recondite theme and the clever handling of it, rocketed Wyatt to fame and a vast number of buildings (Dale lists as many as 131) are associated with his name. Few of them need detain us. His classical houses include Heaton, near Manchester (1772), parts of Heveningham (see p. 224) after Taylor's death in 1788, and Dodington, Glos. (1798–1808). Heaton is in the Adam manner, done at least as well as the Adams were doing it and with greater restraint in the interiors. At Heveningham the interiors are, again, in a purified Adam manner of great beauty. Dodington (Plate 161B), built when the Adam fashion had gone out, combines a Greek-proportioned portico with a staircase and other features derived from Chambers.

That Wyatt was a stylistic weather-cock and turned with the breeze of fashion is not only obvious from his works but is confirmed by a chance confession of his own that 'when he came from Italy he found the public taste corrupted by the Adams, and he was obliged to comply with it'. That was said in 1804 and is thus a rather belated claim to early independence. On the other hand, there is plenty of evidence that while Wyatt played Adam with one hand he had the Chambers pack up the other sleeve. Mausolea by him at Cobham (*c.* 1783) and Brocklesby (1787–95) are based on designs in Chambers's *Treatise*, and the fine Doric Canterbury Gate (1778) and Oriel College library (1788; Plate 161A) at Oxford are soberly classical. When both Adam and Chambers were dead and it was Wyatt's turn, as Surveyor-General, to set any fashion he liked, there was, obviously, nothing he really wanted to say. For the church at Dodington he seems to have raided Soane's House of Lords design, which he had just been instrumental in quashing; while the design he produced for Downing College, Cambridge, after 1800, although original in its reintroduction of pavilions, is flat and poorly proportioned and was, excusably, considered inadequate to the occasion (see p. 305).

Failing any particular ambition in the way of classical developments, Wyatt in his later years fell back upon the special reputation which he had acquired in another direction altogether – as a master of Gothic.

Wyatt's Gothic

It may seem illogical to introduce so important a phase of the Gothic movement as that led by Wyatt into a chapter dealing with Neo-classicism. But we have seen that one of the attributes of Neo-classicism is the recognition of a plurality of valid styles, and it would be impossible, even if it were desirable, to separate the Classical and Gothic movements, except in so far as the latter has origins remote from those of the Neo-classic point of view. In Wyatt, to turn from classic to Gothic involved a change of mood scarcely more signifi-cant than that involved in a switch from the Chambers to the Adam manner, or from Byzantine-Roman to Greek. Wyatt is a typical Neo-classical figure and his stylistic catholicity is part of his Neo-classicism.

His first Gothic house was Lee Priory, near Canterbury, built, as we saw in Chapter 24, for Horace Walpole's friend, Thomas Barrett, in 1782. According to Dale, it is unlikely that Wyatt received a special impetus to the study of Gothic either from Walpole or from Barrett. Barrett chose Gothic simply because his site appealed to him, having some vague suggestions of 'monastic' seclusion. But, as Walpole instantly recognized, Wyatt not only gave Barrett a Gothic house, but almost the very first Gothic house to show a substantial technical mastery of the style. Strawberry Hill had been almost entirely the work of amateurs, carried into execution by an architect and craftsmen with no special experience of Gothic. Lee, on the contrary, was thoroughly professional, as expertly detailed as the most elegant portico or an Etruscan ceiling. Wyatt, of course, knew Strawberry Hill and Strawberry Hill, certainly, was his starting-point. There still exists, at Lee, a 'Strawberry Room' which is palpably imitated from the 'Holbein Room' designed by Chute at Strawberry. But it is imitation with enhanced knowledge of how Gothic really works. The mouldings are real Gothic mouldings and die into each other as Gothic mouldings should. The octagon library at Lee is even more accomplished – a little toy souvenir of the crossing at Ely, with clustered shafts, all carefully articulated and brought up into ribs which meet the rim of a radial-panelled dome.

Such work as this, although far from being really scholarly or exact, does imply con-siderable preparatory study of Gothic monuments and a knowledge greater than anybody, except probably Henry Keene, had then possessed. Keene, from whom Wyatt may con-ceivably have learnt something, was dead and, after Walpole's praise of Lee, Wyatt became, and remained till his death, the undisputed master of the Gothic style. Apart from

Lee, Sheffield Place and West Dean, both in Sussex, Fonthill in Wiltshire, and Ashridge in Hertfordshire, were Wyatt's most important Gothic houses. The first three were irregular in composition, and intended, like Lee (and, indeed, Strawberry), to give the appearance of ancient houses enlarged and altered at various times. The most spectacular of them, and the one with which Wyatt's genius and his failings are most dramatically associated, is Fonthill. This was the house which William Beckford commissioned, in the first instance, as a mere landscape feature, an artificial ruin with sufficient 'intact' accommodation for a day to be spent there without inconvenience. That was in 1795. Five years later a building of a very different kind was being rushed to completion – a vast residence planned on a great irregular cross, from the centre of which there emerged, out of a cluster of turrets and gables, an octagon steeple challenging the spire at Salisbury.

Fonthill was an altogether exceptional house and its plan (Plate 162B) is startling. It is only when one remembers the chaotic but suggestive pattern of the Palace of Westminster as it stood in Wyatt's time, that the source of the design becomes evident. But Fonthill's significance is far less as a work of architecture than as an expression of the personality of William Beckford. Beckford was, if anyone ever was, a Great Romantic. Wyatt was not; nobody was ever further from such a qualification. Wyatt was clever, and Beckford employed him on a conception for which cleverness was not nearly enough. Beckford's architect should have been Ledoux (around whom, as it happens, he fabricated a most curious study in the occult) or, failing him, a brave simple-minded engineer like Telford. His employment of Wyatt was catastrophic. Doubly so. First because, as a design, Fonthill was nothing but an inflation and a piling up of the not very virile kind of Gothic the architect had evolved at Lee and West Dean. And, second, because Wyatt's indolence and the dishonesty of his subordinates resulted in the collapse of the great tower a quarter of a century after it was built.

As a composition, Fonthill was sheer chaos – chaos, however, which grouped dramatically from certain points of view (Plate 162A). Some of the interiors must have been, at the lowest estimate, sensational; especially the central octagon (Plate 163) – the Ely theme again, elongated to a fabulous height; while much of the detail seems to have been an advance, in quality of technique, on anything Wyatt had yet done.[13]

In his last Gothic house, Ashridge, Herts., begun in 1806 for the Earl of Bridgwater, Wyatt retreated from the extravagant irregularity of Fonthill, building, on a symmetrical plan, a house whose main feature is a central hall occupying the entire height of a tower. Here we can still experience something of the grotesque sensationalism which made Fonthill, in its time, the talk of the world.

Wyatt's influence was, in his lifetime, considerable. He showed how to make the Adam manner neater, more economical and crisp than its authors had done. His Gothic proved wildly infectious. Even George Dance, whose 'Gothic' was a peculiar mix of his own – an equivalent rather than an imitation – must have had Fonthill in mind when he built the polygonal hall at Coleorton for Sir George Beaumont in 1802. In 1803, William Porden (c. 1755–1822), who had perhaps been in Wyatt's office, borrowed the silhouette of one of the fronts of Lee Priory and elaborated it, with other borrowings, into Eaton Hall, Cheshire (for Earl Grosvenor; largely remodelled in 1870); and the same architect built

the giddy Wyatt-like staircase at Taymouth Castle. Finally, one cannot ignore the possibility that the plan of Fonthill – four arms spreading from an octagon – gave Charles
Barry the germ of his conception of the Houses of Parliament.

Leverton, Bonomi, Harrison

Among the contemporaries of Wyatt, of Holland, and of Dance there are three who must
be noticed before we pass on to a younger group and a new initiative. Thomas Leverton
(1743–1824) presents us with a teasing problem. The son of an Essex builder, he found a
patron in a London banker but did not, so far as we know, go to Italy. Nor do we ever
find him mentioned, in his lifetime, as an important artist. His epitaph at Waltham Abbey
tells us that he 'rose to honour, wealth, and comfort, by relying humbly on God, acting
with integrity, industry, and true benevolence', qualities which will not necessarily have
assisted him in producing some of the most brilliant small-scale interiors of the seventeen-
seventies and eighties. In a case like this one is tempted to look for a 'ghost', and the
temptation is the greater since it is known that the Italian Joseph Bonomi was at one time
in his office as a 'drawing assistant'. It is true that what we know of Bonomi's work under
his own name does not support this supposition; but perhaps we do not know enough.
The whole subject needs considerably more research and, in the meantime, we can only
recognize Leverton as at least the foster father of such remarkable interiors as those of
Woodhall Park, Herts. (1778; for Paul Benfield, Esq.), and of a number of houses in
Bedford Square,[14] including his own (No. 13) and the very special No. 1 (1780), where
the domed entrance hall (Plate 164), opening to lobbies in two directions, richly decorated
yet almost innocent of cornices, would be 'advanced' even for Dance and forecasts
Soane's work of fifteen years later. The 'Etruscan' hall at Woodhall Park is similarly
domed, but the dome rests on wall-arches of flat parabolic curvature, a Leverton innovation met with elsewhere.

Of Joseph Bonomi (1739–1808), Leverton's suspected 'ghost', we know, as we have
just had reason to recognize, too little. He was born in Rome, trained in the studio of the
aged Marchese Teodoli, came to England in 1767, at the invitation of the Adams, but
remained in touch with Rome for most of his life. He must have gone to Leverton very
soon after his arrival in England. No work under his own name is dated earlier than 1784,
from which year he rapidly became a popular designer of country-houses. One of his first
is Longford Hall, Salop. (for R. Leeke, Esq., 1789–92), an ordinary enough house, with a
dull plan, but singular by reason of the use of an 'architrave cornice' (i.e. an entablature
with the frieze elided) and a big, deep Doric portico, over which the architrave-cornice
looks very uncomfortable. At Eastwell House, Kent (1793–9, for G. Finch Hatton, Esq.),
Bonomi again elided the frieze from his entablature and again built an immense portico,
this time of *five* columns – one in the centre. This deliberate impropriety has the effect of
emphasizing that the portico is to be entered laterally and is, in fact (like Holland's great
portico at Carlton House), a *porte cochère*. The order is Ionic, with a coarse Michelangelesque cap. At another house, Burrells, Warwickshire (1792; for R. Knight, Esq.), Bonomi
built a double portico, again of very great projection, so that carriages could drive in; the

upper stage becomes, of course, grotesquely large for an English balcony. Finally there is Roseneath, Dumbartonshire (1803–6; for the Duke of Argyll; Plate 165A), where we again find a great *porte cochère* portico, with a central column.

There is a marked insensibility about these designs – or is it merely the strangeness of an Italian hand meddling with the English tradition? Bonomi's work has, in any case, an Italianate vigour which tends to disqualify him as the author of Leverton's fragile interiors. The saloon by him in the house Stuart built for Lady Montagu in Portman Square (burnt in 1941) had a segmental ceiling decorated in a flattened *cinquecento* style; while the all-stone church of Great Packington, Warwickshire (1790), has something of the *terribilità* of Piranesi's Paestum engravings. Bonomi was elected an Associate of the Royal Academy in 1789. A rather more historic distinction was conferred on him by Jane Austen who mentioned him by name in *Sense and Sensibility*.

Lastly, in the group of architects born in the forties, there is Thomas Harrison (1744–1829). Here was a man of outstanding ability who built nothing in London and, with his headquarters in Chester, spent his life in designing public works in Midland and northern towns. Born a poor Yorkshireman, Harrison was sent to Rome by Lawrence, Lord Dundas. He spent seven years there and attracted the personal notice of Clement XIV, becoming one of the few English *professori accademici* of St Luke's Academy.[15] Returning home in 1776, he exhibited some of his Roman designs at the Royal Academy. His earliest known works are at Lancaster. They include the bridge over the Lune (1783–8), a noble compeer of Mylne's Blackfriars Bridge; the tower of St John's Church (1784; a *tempietto* in the Chambers manner); and Lancaster Castle. The latter, begun in 1788, was a tremendous scheme, including gaol, county and crown courts, and county offices, which Harrison failed to finish. It is a Gothic building, but on a dramatic Neo-classical plan, with a broad semicircular end which the site sets off most admirably.

Parallel with this, Harrison was building Chester Castle (1793–1820), a building serving the same multiple functions of gaol and court-house, with the additions of armoury and exchequer. Here, however, he worked in the classical style and produced the building by which he is chiefly remembered. Chester Castle (Plate 165B) is planned round a great court, with detached blocks on each of three sides, and a 'propylaeum' on the main axis, facing the portico. All the buildings are long and low in proportion, Greek in detail, with something of the melancholy restraint which one finds in the Grand Prix designs of the period. In the centre of the main block, behind the portico, is the principal court-room, with a grand hemicycle of Ionic columns, again very much in the manner of the Paris school. Indeed, it would be surprising if the engravings by Prieur of the Grand Prix designs were not in Harrison's library. The 'propylaeum', with its two guard-houses, is a delightful essay in columnar arrangement.

Nothing else of Harrison's is so important, or so distinct in its loyalties, as Chester Castle. Many of his lesser works are very tame, and one feels that his isolation in a provincial centre may have prevented him from reaching the standard which his abilities ought to have made attainable. On the other hand, it may be proper to class him with Robert Mylne, as a man primarily of an engineering bent, whose capacities as an artist were sound but limited. His last work, the gigantic 200-ft.-span Grosvenor Bridge over the Dee (executed by Jesse Hartley, C.E., from 1827 to 1832), significantly closes his career where it began – on the engineering plane.

John Soane: his Work before 1800

The architects we have just been considering account for nearly the whole of what is important in English architecture between the moment when Chambers and the Adams had passed the peak of their influence (a moment dateable roughly at 1775) and the onset of the Picturesque movement a few years before 1800. The Picturesque in architecture is the subject of the next chapter, where we shall find that its two leading figures, Humphry Repton and John Nash, come abruptly into the story as middle-aged men with earlier careers of no particular significance. We shall also, in the same connexion, meet John Soane, a man of almost identical age with Repton and Nash, but with a career behind him of altogether outstanding interest and importance. Soane's career, therefore, must be dealt with in two halves. We must look at him first, here and now, as the youngest of the group of Neo-classical architects practising after 1775, reaching his own highly individual Neo-classical conclusions by 1795; and secondly, later on, as the man who succeeded, in his own peculiar way, in identifying the essentials of Neo-classicism with those of the Picturesque.

John Soan (the 'e' was acquired on his marriage) was the son of a small Berkshire builder and was born in 1753. At fifteen he had chosen the profession which, with passionate affection and unabated ambition, he pursued till his death, in his eighty-fourth year, in 1837. He entered the service of George Dance and was with him till 1772, when he transferred to Henry Holland to acquire more constructional knowledge than Dance (who was somewhat weak on the practical side) could give him. Meanwhile, he attended Sandby's lectures at the Royal Academy, won the Silver Medal in 1772 and the Gold Medal in 1776, receiving it at the hands of Sir Joshua Reynolds. Sir William Chambers introduced him to the King, who nominated him Travelling Student for three years. He left England for Italy in 1778 and returned in 1780.

Soane's student period has some importance. The designs he made before and during his Italian visit exhibit once and for all his character and limitations as a classical architect. His Gold Medal design for a Triumphal Bridge (1776) will have been influenced by Sandby's similar project (p. 275) and thus by the Piranesi design from which that derived; but the approaches show close study of a Palace design in Peyre's book. The designs for a senate house and a royal palace, both made in Italy, are likewise indebted to Peyre and other Neo-classical sources. All the designs are technically adept, but all show a peculiar uncertainty of handling which, in due course, we discover to be an ineradicable characteristic of the architect.

In Italy, Soane seems to have followed closely in Dance's steps and interested himself in all that Dance had admired – the *cinquecento* work as well as the Temple of Vesta at Tivoli; and at Parma he presented a revised version (Greek Doric instead of Corinthian) of his Triumphal Bridge to the Academy. Making the acquaintance of the formidable Bishop of Derry (not then yet Earl of Bristol), he produced some designs for him, including a monumental kennel or 'residence for a canine family', of which he composed two versions – one for 'ancient times', the other, less ornate, for 'modern times', thus forecasting the dichotomy which exists all through his own work, between the fully developed columnar manner (from the Triumphal Bridge onwards) and the more diagrammatic style which became so personal and characteristic an attribute.

Golden promises from the Bishop of Derry brought Soane hurrying back from Italy in 1780, only to find that the Earl-Bishop had lost interest in him and that he had to make a beginning in architectural practice with no more princely patronage than that of country gentlemen to whom introductions and his small fame had made him known. There follows a period of ten years during which he built the houses illustrated in his *Plans... of Buildings executed in Several Counties*, 1788, and a few more, given in *Sketches in Architecture*, 1793. These were not his first publications, for a small book of *Designs in Architecture* had appeared while he was in Italy, in 1778. These three books give a clear, but rather distressing, picture of Soane's early development. Uncertainty, lack of confidence, self-conscious originality are everywhere apparent. Here he affects, affectedly, Chambers or Wyatt, here he relies on his experience with Holland, here attempts the naked masculinity of Burlington; he is hesitant in proportion, trifling in detail. The promise of the Triumphal Bridge seems dissipated in an amateurish lack of decision.

Probably the event which had the effect of reclaiming Soane from this agitated bathos of experiment was his appointment, on the recommendation of William Pitt, to the Surveyorship of the Bank of England, on Sir Robert Taylor's death in 1788. It had been a valuable appointment to Taylor and was to prove even more so to Soane. Moreover, by 1792, he was rebuilding the Bank Stock Office in a style which was, far and away, the most original architectural language in Europe at that moment.

The Bank Stock Office (Plate 166A) sets us the curious problem, how to account for Soane's sudden recovery from the uncertainty and affectation of the country-house period and his creation, at one stroke, of a building as truly original as this. The answer, beyond doubt, lies in the influence of George Dance. Many preliminary designs for the Stock Office are in the Soane Museum, and it is clear that at every step but the last Soane consulted either Dance's designs or Dance himself, and probably both. All Hallows, London Wall, and the Lansdowne House library were potent influences. To these was added Taylor's last work at the Bank, the Reduced Annuities Office (p. 224), where the circular side-lit lantern, over pendentives, made its first appearance.

The final result, however, is Soane's very own. There must, at some stage, have been a conscious decision on his part that a building of this kind, where material conditions as regards lighting and fire-protection were of decisive importance, should detach itself from purely classical conceptions and rely on basic, *primitive* considerations of structure and utility, on the analogy of Laugier's primitive hut. Such a decision would sanction the unclassical proportions and formal relationships of the building; it would sanction also the substitution of rudimentary grooved strips and diagrammatic ornaments for pilasters and entablatures which, in the context, would have suffered intolerable distortions.

To the Bank Stock Office Soane added, in 1796, a Rotunda, to replace that by Sir Robert Taylor (p. 223) which was prematurely dilapidated, and here Dance's collaboration is proved up to the hilt by the presence of sketches from his hand among the Soane drawings. Here, again, the ornament consists of diagrammatic grooved patterns instead of the usual ribs and coffers. This mode of ornamentation derives, probably through Dance, from Piranesi's Egyptian designs. Soane used it constantly, sometimes with brilliant, sometimes, alas, with ludicrous effect! For Soane never achieved real confidence and authority, even in his own style. There is always a temperamental factor, expressing itself in a sense of deflation, as if all *mass* had been exhausted from the design. This is partly due to awkward proportions and partly to the various devices, notably these grooves and sinkings which Soane began, at this time, to develop as an ornamental vocabulary. This deflationary tendency belongs peculiarly to Soane and makes his buildings, for all their feeling and invention, slightly subhuman. His architecture never commands; it shrinks into itself and nervously defines the spaces which it encloses.

To the same year as the Bank Stock Office belongs the first house he built for himself in Lincoln's Inn Fields (No. 12), where his curious 'starfish' ceiling, evidently derived from one of the tombs at Corneto (given in Santo Bartoli), occurs for the first time (Plate 166B). Buckingham House, Pall Mall (destroyed), likewise belongs to 1792, and here Soane paraphrased in his new style the staircase of Kent's house (p. 204) in Berkeley Square. Other works of the 1790s are Tyringham, Bucks. (for Wm. Praed, Esq.), with a remarkable conception of hall and 'tribune' which was to be expanded considerably in the later works.

After this group of very extraordinary buildings, executed when he was between thirty-nine and forty-two, and in which the Soane style is fully manifest, Soane's work begins to develop in a way which can only be explained in relation to certain aesthetic currents of the time which we have not yet had occasion to examine. Here, therefore, we leave Soane, for the present, and turn to the theme which takes precedence in all architecture from the end of the century – the Picturesque.

NOTES TO CHAPTER 27

1. He claimed, in the introduction to the first number of the *Works* (1773), to have 'brought about, in this country, a kind of revolution in the whole system of this useful and elegant art'.

2. The building had just been executed, in a modified form. The façade still exists.

3. Both buildings were partly destroyed in the agitations of 1921–2, but both have been rebuilt.

4. Two other Chambers pupils deserve mention. Edward Stevens, who became an Associate of the Royal Academy in 1770, died five years later in Rome at an early age. Willey Reveley travelled extensively and, becoming a convert to the Greek taste, replied to Sir William Chambers's criticisms of Greek work in his supplementary volume to

Stuart & Revett, 1794. His church of All Saints, Southampton (1791–98; destroyed 1940), showed a curious mixture of Greek and Chambersite detail. He died in 1798.

5. One of Chambers's designs, a domed church showing Soufflot's influence, is preserved in the Soane Museum.

6. Drawings in the Dance Collection at the Soane Museum.

7. Revett's portico at Standlynch (p. 254) is, of course, earlier, but it is more in the nature of an elaborated porch.

8. It is impossible to deal fully with other aspects of Dance's extremely interesting career. He must, however, be mentioned as the town-planner who

brought to London the ideas developed by John Wood in Bath. He laid out (1769) the main roads joining the Thames bridges to St George's Circus, Southwark; in 1796 he produced a design for the reconstruction of the Port of London, involving twin bridges (replacing London Bridge) leading to an immense Crescent on the south bank; and he left a brilliant layout (c. 1799) for Lord Camden's estate at Camden Town. He also made plans, partly executed, for the northward development of the City.

Dance's Gothic buildings form another aspect of his work which cannot be fully dealt with. His Gothic is totally unlike that of Kent or, on the other hand, of Wyatt. He made no attempt to imitate the style but tried to evolve an equivalent, appropriate to the Neo-classical point of view. The south front of the Guildhall (1789) is a most curious example of this, and it is seen again in the designs for Coleorton (1802–8) and Ashburnham Place (1813–20). He designed two Gothic churches, St Bartholomew-the-Less, London (c. 1789), and Micheldever, Hants. (1810), both on octagonal plans.

9. The use of this word in England for a ceremonial vestibule probably comes from Buontalenti's octagonal *tribuna* in the Uffizi, Florence.

10. The source of this design is, no doubt, the 'Stoa or Portico', given in Vol. 1 of Stuart & Revett, and also in Leroy. The smallness of scale of this building and of some of the Greek temples given in Stuart probably encouraged the use of small orders which were found convenient for domestic designs.

11. This fine portico, which might well have remained to adorn what is a permanent open space, was wastefully demolished in 1949.

12. This was recognized at least as early as 1804, when the derivation is referred to by Thomas Hope in his letter criticizing Wyatt's design for Downing College. That good plans of Sancta Sophia were available in the eighteenth century is shown by the existence of one among the Adam drawings in the R.I.B.A.

13. Fonthill has entirely disappeared, except for the 'Sanctuary' and 'Oratory' which formed the termination of the north wing. This fragment now stands alone on the otherwise empty site.

14. The general elevations of the four sides of the square are often attributed to Leverton, for the moderately good reason that he was concerned with many individual houses. It is worth noting that the pilaster porticoes on the north and south sides have each a central pilaster, and that this is a peculiarity of the porticoes of some of Bonomi's country-houses.

15. The records at St Luke's Academy, which I have inspected, show that Harrison was premiated in the Concorso Balestra and admitted in 1773. He seems to have failed to win the medal and was obliged to present two petitions to the Pope before his admission. The article in the A.P.S. Dictionary mentions designs done for the Pope, in 1770 and later, and states that the Pope presented him with gold and silver medals and 'ordered his name to be added to the members of the Academy of S. Luke'.

CHAPTER 28

THE PICTURESQUE AND THE
CULT OF STYLES

W E have had occasion, here and there, to touch on the history of landscape-gardening. In particular, we mentioned it in connexion with William Kent, at whose hands the inclinations of such literary minds as those of Temple, Addison, and Pope to oppose the tradition of axial lay-out, were, in some degree, fulfilled. We mentioned it again in connexion with Lancelot ('Capability') Brown, who reduced the new irregular landscaping to a system of his own in which the main elements were clumps, belts, and lakes distributed in an otherwise close-shaven terrain. Finally, we noted that Sir William Chambers, in his mock-serious *Dissertation* on what purported to be Chinese gardening, ridiculed Brown and opened the door to further reconsideration of the subject.

In none of these allusions did the relation of landscape to architecture find much of a place. The style and composition of the house remained unaffected by the changing notions of how its setting should be composed. True, there was the problem of disposing of the service quarters so as not to obtrude them in a landscape so carefully groomed. Brown, for instance, liked to sink them (as at Claremont) under the house; others hid the service wing behind shrubs. And there was always the question of ornamental buildings within the landscape – temples, obelisks, columns, arches, or grottoes. But these, though carefully set relative to the pictorial conception of the scene, were not necessarily modulated to the key of the landscape. The temples at Stourhead, Wilts., and Pains Hill, Surrey,[1] and Chambers's buildings at Kew are essays in classical, Chinese, or Gothic, picturesquely placed but not in themselves picturesque.

It was not till near the end of the eighteenth century and during the last phase of the Georgian art of landscape that architecture itself began to feel the effects of the picturesque idea. It was only then, indeed, that 'picturesque' began to take on a more or less precise meaning; only then that an aesthetic of the picturesque, charging the word with a much weightier significance than it had hitherto possessed, was evolved. 'Picturesque', applied to landscape, had meant, roughly, the kind of landscape which recalled landscape-paintings, especially the paintings of Claude Lorrain, Salvator Rosa, and Gaspar Poussin. It meant, sometimes, something more abstract than that, as when Robert Adam defined his conception of 'movement' in architecture as being calculated 'to add greatly to the *picturesque* of the composition'. But its meaning remained usefully imprecise until the 1790s, when it became the subject of close analysis and heavy argument.

The beginning of the real Picturesque period fixes itself conveniently at 1794–5, when it was inaugurated by the appearance of three books by three authors whose names are inseparably associated with the movement. The first book was *The Landscape, a Didactic Poem*, by Richard Payne Knight (1750–1824), the son of a clergyman with an inherited fortune, and a scholar and aesthetician of great capacity. This poem was an attack on the Brown school of landscaping and it was dedicated to a Welsh squire, a close contemporary and friend of Knight, Uvedale Price (1747–1829). Uvedale Price replied immediately with his *Essay on the Picturesque* (1794), a brilliantly lucid book in which, sharing his friend's contempt for Brown's methods, he raised the standard of the Picturesque, which he attempted to define as a category of aesthetic values supplementary to those two which had been postulated, thirty-eight years before, by Edmund Burke – the Sublime and the Beautiful.

The third book, which appeared in 1795, was by a practising landscape-gardener (the first to adopt the title professionally), Humphry Repton. It was based on the results of six years' practical work and was entitled *Sketches and Hints on Landscape Gardening*. Repton was friendly with both Knight and Price, and although the views of the three men never precisely coincided and, indeed, diverged considerably as time went on, he can be considered, with them, as one of the chief protagonists of the movement.

We cannot here undertake to elucidate the character of the new landscaping movement, except merely to say that it involved a much greater respect for raw nature than Brown's had done. Price's main thesis was that the Picturesque, a quality *per se*, should be studied with constant reference to the landscape masters and preserved and enhanced whenever it was found in practice. Repton's principle was that every estate had certain latent characteristics, which it was the aim of 'improvement' to elucidate and reinforce. He was not quite as confident as Price in the didactic importance of the Old Masters.

Payne Knight stood rather outside such minor differences of application. His intellectual range was a good deal wider than Price's or Repton's and his *Analytical Enquiry into the Principles of Taste*, published in 1805, covers a considerable philosophical field. Further, Knight had held some very definite ideas on the subject of architecture and landscape long before he or Price or Repton had published anything whatever, and these ideas are, for us, of special importance. In 1774, at the age of twenty-four, he had begun to build Downton Castle, near Ludlow; it was more or less finished four years later. Downton Castle (Plate 167A) is an *irregular* castellated building, with a classical interior. Its irregularity of plan is, for the date, astonishing. Strawberry Hill was irregular, chiefly as a result of being extemporized over a period of years and because it was Walpole's whim to make no disguise, but, on the contrary, a virtue of its inconsequence. The major irregularity at Strawberry – the round tower of 1759 – appears to be echoed at Downton, though another source of inspiration was evidently the medieval castle-architecture of Wales. Pevsner sees in Downton an imitation of the irregular masses of building in Claude's landscapes, a view justified by a passage, written much later, in the *Analytical Enquiry*. But whatever its sources, there is no doubt that Downton was the prototype of the 'castellated' style which flourished for nearly half a century from 1790.

If the history of 'picturesque' architecture – including the 'castellated' style and Gothic and Italian equivalents – starts with Downton, its further progress is associated with a remarkable partnership – the partnership between the landscape-gardener, Humphry Repton, and the architect, John Nash.

Repton and Nash

Humphry Repton (1752–1818), son of a Collector of Excise, tells us that he turned to landscape-gardening professionally in 1788, when he was thirty-six. Up to that date his employments had been miscellaneous and none too successful. But once a landscape-gardener he never looked back. Almost at once he found a patron in the Duke of Portland, for whom he 'improved' Welbeck, and by the date of publication of *Sketches and Hints* in 1795 he had advised the owners of at least fifty-seven considerable estates. Two of these were properties of the Hon. Edward Foley and it was probably through the Foleys that he met the man who, for a brief but important space of years, was to be his architectural partner.

This man was John Nash (1752–1835). He was exactly Repton's age and, like Repton, had had a somewhat chaotic early career. The son, it seems, of a Lambeth millwright, he had been employed, as a youth, in the office of Sir Robert Taylor. A legacy from a merchant uncle enabled him to strike out on his own and at thirty he was already building stucco-fronted houses (then rare and novel) in London. A group at the corner of Great Russell Street and Bloomsbury Square survives. But in 1783, he became bankrupt and retired to Wales. Here, the unknown and unsuccessful London builder made a new start, rapidly converting himself into a fashionable architect, designing miniature Newgates for Welsh county towns, and houses for the squirearchy of Wales and Herefordshire.

Nash seems to have joined Repton about 1795, soon after which date he left Wales and returned to London. The partnership lasted till about 1802, when there was a misunder-standing, and architect and landscape-gardener went their several ways. But while it lasted, it was fruitful. While Repton 'improved' estates, Nash rebuilt or altered the houses on them and adorned them with lodges, cottages, dairies, and other trifles. In doing so he adopted a style intended to be *in itself* picturesque. Almost certainly the inspiration came from Downton and its owner; and a house such as Luscombe, Devon (Plate 167B and Figure 40), built for the banker, Charles Hoare (1800), has much the same deliberate irregularity, though within smaller compass. From Payne Knight Nash will certainly have derived the idea of an Italian type of house, of irregular silhouette with a round, conical-roofed tower and deep eaves; for this type, used in small villas such as Cronkhill, Salop. (1802; Plate 169 and Figure 41), and others elsewhere, derives very obviously from the canvases of Claude Lorrain, a source which Payne Knight believed that architects might, with advantage, explore.[2] The house is in the vernacular of the Italian campagna, a style which had no architectural credentials whatever but which, seen through Claude's eyes, had 'picturesque' beauty. In a house such as Cronkhill, Nash gives us the architectural essence of the Picturesque movement.

Before the rupture with Repton, Nash had already found himself (no doubt, as Repton's partner) at the court of the Prince of Wales, for whom he designed a conservatory in 1798. Patronage in this high quarter, cemented apparently by a *mariage de convenance* which was of service to the Prince, was to lead Nash to the fame and fortune of his later years. But up to the time of the Regency he was engaged exclusively as a country-house and ornamental-

293

cottage builder. Though some of his houses, like Rockingham, Co. Roscommon (for Lord Lorton, 1810), were classical, most were 'castellated' or Gothic, like the rambling groups of Caerhays, Cornwall (for John Bettesworth, Esq.), or, at the other end of England, Ravensworth Castle (for Sir Thomas Liddell, Bt) both built in 1808; or, indeed, his own magnificent castle at East Cowes, I.o.W. (1798 onwards; destroyed 1950). While these illustrated the Picturesque idea in a grand way, his cottages and lodges neatly

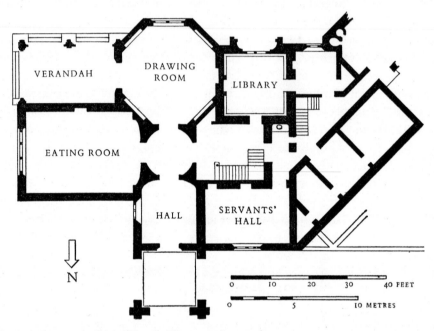

Figure 40. Luscombe

epitomized it. With hips, gables, and dormers, brick, half-timber, and thatch, Nash became as versatile as any Tudor cottage architect of a century later. At Blaise Castle, near Bristol, he built (1811) a whole set of these cottages, assembling in one group designs he had executed elsewhere, and they survive as a most interesting anthology of these little essays.

The rediscovery of the cottage, primarily as a component in an improved Picturesque landscape, but secondarily as an architectural toy with an intrinsic interest of its own, led to a whole series of books of designs for such things being published. In the period 1790 to 1810 they came out at an average rate of more than one a year.

They are very different from the usually rather blockish farm and cottage designs of earlier authors and have three main sources of inspiration – first, the 'primitive hut', that hypothesis so dear to Neo-classical theory; second, the ancient vernacular of the English country-side as painters such as Gainsborough and Morland saw it; third, the Italian vernacular as illustrated in the seventeenth-century classics of landscape-painting. Soane, in his *Plans of Buildings* of 1788, gives a dairy (at Hamels, Herts.) which is a prototypal temple in timber, and there are further examples in his *Sketches* of 1793, including porches made of 'trunks of trees decorated with woodbines and honeysuckles'. Robert Adam had already played with this kind of thing and may indeed have been its originator: Soane probably knew him well enough to have seen his sketches. Trunks of trees come into books by Charles Middleton (1790–3) and J. Plaw (1795 and 1800), but James Malton, in his *Essay on British Cottage Architecture*, 1798, focuses attention on old English cottages which, with country churches, he regards as 'the most pleasing... ornaments of art that can be introduced to embellish rural nature'. Malton's designs are deliberately irregular, for which affectation he was criticized by Richard Elsam in his *Essay on Rural Architecture* of 1803, where the cause of symmetry is upheld. In 1805, Joseph Michael Gandy, a protégé of Soane, published two very curious books in which the 'primitive' idea is pushed to a grotesque extreme, influenced perhaps by some of the post-Revolutionary modernism of France. From the same year there are books by William Atkinson and R. Lugar, the latter much in the Nash-Repton style. The later books, by E. Gyfford, James Randall, W. F. Pocock, T. D. W. Dearn, J. B. Papworth, and C. A. Busby are all more or less derivative and increasingly miscellaneous.

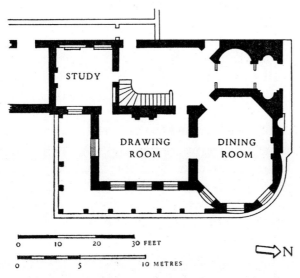

Figure 41. Cronkhill

With this spate of cottage designs came also designs for garden shelters and pavilions, as well as balconies and verandahs – ephemeral paraphernalia which came in quite suddenly in the last years of the eighteenth century and are the product of the Picturesque. The verandah seems to have come from India with the 'nabobs', and Repton probably had a hand in propagating it, combining it with *treillage* from France. The decorated iron window-guards and ornamental balconies, which flourished equally in country-houses and London streets, were a modern Italian inspiration. Indeed, the prototypes of familiar London designs can still be seen on eighteenth-century houses in the Corso in Rome. The

Picturesque, encouraging and encouraged by travel-books with excellent engravings, ranged over the scenery of the world, suggesting themes now from Switzerland, now from Italy, now from Egypt,[3] now from India. India was, for a short period, a source of special interest, for the obvious reason that so many Englishmen, bringing their fortunes thence, desired exotic souvenirs in their surroundings.[4] The monuments of the Indian phase are few indeed but they merit attention.

Indian Styles

The first symptom of the new objective interest in exotic styles which, with the Greek and Gothic 'revivals' is one of the by-products of Neo-classicism, is to be found at Kew. Already, before Sir William Chambers came on the scene, somebody had designed (1750) a Moorish building for Prince Frederick; the Dowager executed it in 1756, calling it the 'Alambra'. In the same park were eventually built, as we have seen, a Turkish mosque, a Chinese pagoda, and a Gothic 'cathedral'. But there was nothing, as yet, remotely reflecting the architecture of India. Indeed, it was not till after the exploration of India by the artist, Thomas Daniell, who went there, with his nephew William, in 1784, that the idea of reproducing the Indian styles in England took shape. And in this adventure one of the main participants was the Picturesque landscape-gardener, Humphry Repton.

The first two Indian buildings in England belong to about the year 1803. The first, probably, by a short head, was Sezincote, Glos. (Plate 168A), built for 'an eminent servant of the East India Company', Sir Charles Cockerell. Cockerell consulted Repton about his grounds and also about the style of his house, showing him illustrations of what he had seen in India. Repton was enthusiastic and, with Daniell's drawings before him, helped to pick out the most appropriate elements for reproduction. The task of building Sezincote was then handed over to the owner's brother, S. P. Cockerell (1754–1827), an able and distinguished architect[5] who had been in Taylor's office along with Nash. The resulting house, though planned in the English way, exhibits the multi-foil arches, the deep bracket-cornice, and the onion dome of the architecture of Islam.

The second building was at Brighton, where William Porden (1755–1822) was employed by the Prince of Wales to build stables for the Royal Pavilion. As Porden had been in Cockerell's office and as the details of the Brighton stables are in character with those of Sezincote, the two projects can hardly be unconnected. The stables (now the 'Dome' concert-hall) consist of a huge domed building, modelled structurally on the Paris Halle au Blé but detailed Saracenically.

While Sezincote and the Prince's stables were finishing, Repton was commanded down to Brighton to advise the Prince on the style to be adopted in his further building projects. Finding the stables already finishing in Indian and with his head full of Sezincote, he unhesitatingly recommended that the Pavilion itself should be remodelled in the newly recognized style and, in fact, himself produced a complete set of designs, with an essay on the principles of Indian architecture. The Prince was enchanted. 'Mr Repton,' said he, 'I consider the whole of this work as perfect, and will have every part of it carried into immediate execution; not a tittle shall be altered.' Nothing of the sort happened. In due course, John Nash came on to the scene and, from 1815, started orientalizing the Pavilion in his own way. Repton's designs, which he had published in 1806, were forgotten.

Nash's Pavilion at Brighton has often been stated to be a brazen plagiarism of Repton's designs. That is not so. Repton had followed Sezincote rather closely, almost reproducing its central 'Taj Mahal' feature. He borrowed also from Porden's stable building, and the design as a whole, every part of which can be traced ultimately to Daniell's views, has very little real character. Nash, on the other hand, extemporized boldly and, while far less fastidious in his handling of oriental detail, he did produce a building which has some real strokes of architectural genius. In any case, the two great rooms (Banqueting and Music Rooms; Plate 168B) which were his first additions (1815–18) to the old building, are not Indian at all. Their interior shape, with flat domes on pendentives or arches and an effective suggestion of a state tent in the convex ceilings of the lateral extensions, is most original, though not, perhaps, unconnected with a tendency which we shall see presently in Soane's work. The detail is a mixture of Gothic and Chinese, while the exterior silhouette is crowned in each case by an inverted funnel, again imitating the falling lines of a tent.

The Indianizing of the Pavilion came later; but here, again, it is not in any oriental illusionism that the charm of the building lies but in some happy strokes of composition which might have been effected in any style. One such stroke is the detachment of the porch as an all-but-free-standing canopy over the arriving or departing Prince. Another is the pierced-stone curtaining of the loggias of the east front, giving an enchanting effect of frailty and brightness. The 'movement' of the whole composition is charming, too, as well as undeniably picturesque. Indeed, in spite of its exact symmetry the Pavilion is an excellent example of Uvedale Price's conception of Picturesque values applied to architecture.

Apart from Sezincote and the Pavilion, with its stables, the Indian style cannot be said to have flourished, for not a single other building of importance is known to have been designed in it.

Nash's Later Work

There would be a strong case for designating John Nash the greatest figure in the whole Picturesque movement. His work embraces every aspect of it, while there is nothing in his enormous *œuvre* (excepting only his Tayloresque early houses) which does not illustrate it. It was he who popularized the irregular castellated house and the picturesque thatched cottage. It was he who first drew architectural inspiration direct from Claude. It was he who built an 'Indian' building which, by virtue solely of picturesqueness of handling, possesses virtues beyond that of contemporaneous novelty. But, above all, it was John Nash who brought the Picturesque to town, who made London parks and even one of London's greatest streets conform to its principles.

The story of Nash's creation of Regent's Park and Regent Street and of all the schemes which developed within and from it is one which cannot be told in detail in a book which does not claim to embrace the history of town-planning. The architectural implications, nevertheless, cannot readily be isolated, so that a compressed sketch of the whole story is unavoidable.

It begins in 1811, with the reversion of Marylebone Park to the Crown. The development of this property (consisting of farms and fields) had been under consideration for many years, but no satisfactory plans had been formed. So in this year, two official architects were instructed to prepare schemes. One of these was John Nash who, since 1806, had been surveyor to the Office of Woods and Forests; the other was Thomas Leverton (see p. 285) of the Office of Land Revenue. Each scheme was to include proposals not only for developing the park as a first-rate residential area, but for forming a new street to provide convenient access to Westminster and St James's.

The two schemes were as different as they could well be. Leverton, seeing the problem with an eighteenth-century eye, conducted the existing criss-cross of Bloomsbury and Marylebone across the fields, arresting it only where a more open sector allowed for the disposition of detached villas. Nash, on the other hand, with mind and eye schooled in the aesthetic of the Picturesque, saw the problem more humanly and set down on paper a truly remarkable conception of what we might to-day call a garden-city – the park landscaped on Reptonian lines, with over fifty villas half hid in groves of trees, and belted by terraces, all of which had full enjoyment of the park; a decorative lake, a pleasure palace for the Prince, a new Marylebone church, and even a National Valhalla.[6]

All this went rather beyond the bare requirements of the Treasury, while for the new street (which Leverton excused himself from studying) Nash made a striking and monumental proposal based on the idea of a Royal Mile leading from Carlton House to the Park. It must have been clear to everybody that this scheme of Nash's was something more than an official document from a government department, that there was something, Somebody, behind it, and that it was the outcome of intentions reaching as far back, perhaps, as Nash's appointment to the Office of Woods in 1806. The scheme bore the unmistakable stamp of Carlton House.

Nash's plan for the Park was accepted, with slight modifications, almost at once, and the first sites were let in 1812. The plan for the street – Regent Street to be – received further study and was ultimately accepted in 1813, when the necessary legislation was obtained. In that year, Nash was already sixty-one years old; yet when he died, twenty-two years later, not only had the whole vast scheme been carried through but it had been expanded to take in St James's Park and the new Buckingham Palace, while Pall Mall East, Trafalgar Square, and West Strand were in train.

Nash's design for Regent's Park was a synthesis of extraordinary brilliance, both on the material and psychological planes. It combined the formal Bath ideas of circus, crescent, and terrace with the informality of Reptonian 'improvement', while at the same time solving problems of access, marketing, supplies (the Regent's Canal was related to the scheme), and services simply and directly. The architectural character seems to have developed slowly. An early panorama preserved in the Ministry of Works, and apparently drawn by a Frenchman,[7] bears no relation to the buildings as executed. Of these, Park Crescent (Plate 170A), the southern half of an intended circus, was the first (from 1812). With its colonnade of coupled Ionic columns, wittily echoing Holland's Carlton House screen which closed (till 1827) the southern end of Regent Street, it remains the simplest and perhaps the best. The later terraces are far more elaborate, but so carelessly designed that much of their effect is squandered. The most interesting is Cumberland Terrace (1827; Plate 171A), designed to be on the axis of the Prince's new palace and therefore of special architectural consequence. It is an immensely long terrace, consisting of three linked blocks and obviously inspired by the river-front of Somerset House. In respect of sheer monumentality it has more breadth and assurance and firmer emphasis than Chambers's work, but like so much of Nash's architecture it is only half thought out and its nobility is sapped by negligent and affected detail. This bad detailing, for which the fact that Nash's designs were carried out by speculative builders is only in part responsible, pervades all his work. His country-houses are nearly always feebly detailed and one gathers that he really had no feeling for the finer points of design. To such an extent was this the case that, when the executant architect of Gloucester Terrace took it into his head to *double* the scale of the cornice mouldings (with an effect which may still be observed), Nash was content with an observation that they had 'come out larger than he expected'.

As Regent's Park proceeded, the Treasury made certain modifications, eliminating the northern terraces and all but a very few of the villas, while the idea of a Summer Palace receded with the years and was extinguished at George IV's death in 1830. The double circus in the inner circle and the National Valhalla were also excised. Thus, the Park to-day is a very pale ghost of the garden-city originally conceived by Nash. But still it has the true character of the Picturesque, in the planting, in the disposition of the terraces to make a continuously pleasing circuit, in the combination of freedom and formality.

If the Park is a masterpiece of the Picturesque, so too was Regent Street as Nash left it. Here, indeed, there developed a most fascinating interplay of Picturesque aesthetics and economic expediency – a double empiricism. The very line of the street was an empirical solution, designed to steer between the Scylla of compensation and the Charybdis of inconvenience. Changing direction at Langham Place and Oxford Circus, and sweeping in a great curve to Piccadilly (Plate 170B), the street resigned all formality except where it approached Carlton House at Waterloo Place, in the two circuses themselves, and in the placing of two or three public buildings. For the rest, it was an extemporization, a pictorial succession of architectural incident, moulded by luck and persuasion to the uncertain pattern presented by the disposal of sites in the speculative market (Plate 171B).

By 1825, Regent Street was nearly finished. Its architect was seventy-three and would gladly have retired to his happy domain at Cowes. But one belated and ill-starred adventure awaited him; he was commanded to build a Palace. Buckingham Palace, created in and round the carcase of old Buckingham House, was the result, and this time the architect's constitutional inability to mature a composition beyond the sketch stage was his undoing. He proposed a most gallant design, as full of movement as Blenheim – and as difficult of successful realization. The King was ageing and impatient, and the work was rushed. In 1828 much of it was complete, but the wings of the forecourt were such a hopeless failure that it was desired to demolish them. A dome, designed for the garden aspect, made an unfortunate appearance in the Mall. The Palace became a laughing-stock and its architect was cross-examined by a Select Committee. On the King's death in 1830, he was dismissed.

By this time, Carlton House had been removed; the two Carlton House Terraces (Plate 172) and the steps between them had been built; St James's Park had been planted; Trafalgar Square had been formed. The deposed architect had achieved for London the first great planning enterprise of its history – and, so it seems to-day, the last.

Considered purely as an architect, Nash always engages but rarely satisfies us. He possessed abounding invention and was attracted by all influences within reach. Roman, Greek, Gothic, Indian, Chinese were within his range, though he understood none really well. He took much from Inigo Jones's Whitehall designs and more from Chambers's Somerset House; he knew, and constantly imitated, the public works of Paris – Gabriel's twin palaces are reflected in Carlton House Terrace and his interiors sometimes pay tribute to Percier. From his English contemporaries he borrowed constantly. Holland's baby Ionic columns played hide and seek all the way up Regent Street to the Park; Soane's manner was borrowed, equally, for the façades of Piccadilly Circus and the billiard-room at East Cowes.

In this universal, hasty, slick eclecticism we recognize, unmistakably, the end of an epoch. When the time has come that everything can be done, quickly and easily, it is time for somebody to think again. Nash died in 1835. In 1836, A. W. Pugin published his *Contrasts*, and architecture had, once more, become difficult.

Soane and the Picturesque

Born within a year of each other and dying, one in 1835, the other in 1837, Nash and Soane are the two great figures in the last phase of English classicism. They were totally unlike each other in almost every respect – in physique, in temperament, and in their approach to architecture. It is no accident that one always thinks of Nash in terms of *exteriors*, Soane in terms of *interiors*. Nash's mind was comprehensive and generalizing; Soane's departmental and particularizing. Nash moved easily in public life, enjoyed the fray; Soane was uneasy in society and afraid of criticism. The two were sometimes rivals and Soane was jealous of the successful and worldly colleague whose architecture he despised.

As artists they were a world apart; yet Soane, scarcely less than Nash, can be shown to be, in his later years, at least a partial product of the Picturesque movement. The great difference between them is that whereas Nash interested himself in all the styles on the market and turned rapidly from one to another, Soane developed, slowly and painfully, one personal style of his own, a style which, however, was sufficiently fluid to take into itself characteristics from many other styles.

We have already seen (p. 288) how, in the Bank Stock Office of 1792, Soane arrived, quite suddenly, at that personal interpretation of Neo-classicism which, thereafter, he proceeded to expand and develop till his retirement in 1833. It is in the development of this style, particularly from about 1806, that a distinctly Picturesque element enters. The Picturesque in Soane has several distinct forms. There is an affectation of primitivism, associated with his cottage designs of 1788–93. There is a feeling for Gothic – not for the reviving of Gothic, but for the distillation of its *effects* in his own style. There is a feeling also for Pompeiana. And, deeper than any of these, there is what he himself liked to call the 'poetry of architecture'. This meant, abstractly, a disposition of planes in such a way that the eye was drawn through one after another instead of being halted by inert consciousness of a wall or a ceiling. It is exactly analogous to some of the landscape effects most valued at the time.

Unlike Nash, Soane did not move in the circle of Picturesque aestheticians which included Payne Knight, Price, and Repton. Their thought came to him through their books and through those intangible channels of influence which operate when an idea is 'in the air'. He read and carefully annotated both Price's *Essay* and Knight's *Analytical Enquiry*. And he read a great deal else; for it was in 1806 that he was elected Professor of Architecture at the Royal Academy, and this appointment incited him to a spell of intellectual

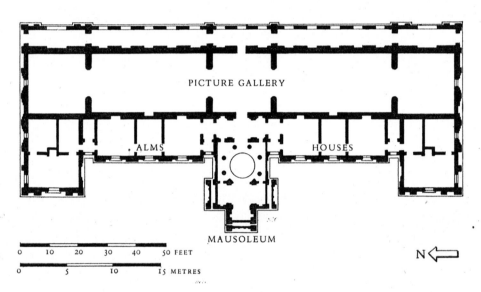

Figure 42. Dulwich College Art Gallery

effort in the preparation of lectures which had considerable repercussions on his architecture. In the early part of his life he was not much of a scholar – the introductions to his books are at once pedantic and puerile. But as Professor he set himself to master the whole range of architectural history as it was then known. This greatly enriched his vocabulary of form and enhanced his appreciation of architects whose works were not necessarily then in vogue. In his work after 1806 we find remote and unexpected recollections.

The Dulwich Art Gallery (Plate 173; Figure 42)[8] is a fascinating example of this. It was built in 1811–14 as the result of a bequest and there was not much money to spend. An important feature was to be the founder's (Sir Francis Bourgeois) mausoleum. Soane conceived the building in that primitivist style which he made so readily adaptable to simple brick construction. But the composition, in which each element is detached from its context by some slight break or recession, is intensely original, and unique at that date. It seems to owe much to Vanbrugh who, as 'the Shakespeare of Architects', is the hero of the English section of the Lectures. Soane, like Adam and Reynolds before him, could not speak too highly of Vanbrugh's compositions. The mausoleum, standing out in front of the main block, is strangely eloquent in a rather Vanbrughian way. Its plan-form, evidently suggested by an antique catacomb, Soane had already used in a similar building at the back of Bourgeois's house in Marylebone (1807). Transferring this to Dulwich, it was necessary to find for it an appropriate exterior expression. Here, it was Robert Adam – another of Soane's heroes – who provided the answer, for the Dulwich mausoleum is, in effect, a primitivist version of Adam's towers at Mistley[9] (p. 269).

Thus, with a great range of sources at his command and a vital personal style which could assimilate what it needed, and discard what it did not, Soane was able to produce building after building of outstanding originality. At Dulwich, Soane's Picturesque allies itself with the Picturesque of Adam and of Vanbrugh and that alliance of names is indicative of Soane's position in English architecture. At his own house, No. 13 Lincoln's Inn Fields (1812), which he was to leave, with all its contents, to become the Soane Museum, the Picturesque element expresses itself in the treatment of the principal rooms, courts, and corridors. In the library (ground-floor front) there are hanging arches, Gothic-inspired, which 'detach' the ceiling from the walls; tall bookcases, inset with strips of mirror, stand beneath and beyond the arches, while above the bookcases, and remoter still, is a deep mirror-frieze which, reflecting the whole ceiling, hints at yet further receding planes. It is impossible to say on which plane the actual wall exists; for all aesthetic purposes it is not there. Similarly, in the adjoining dining-room, an ample window looks out into the Monument Court, furnished with fragments to be seen in relation to the vases and pots ranged on the broad cill inside the room, blurring the division between room and court. Recession was always the aim, its effect intensified, very often, by ingenious top-lighting, which, from being a necessity at the Bank, became, in Soane's other works, an invaluable instrument of effect. Thus in the little domed breakfast room at the Museum (Plate 174), concealed lantern-lights on two sides allow sunshine to slip in between the dome and the wall, so that the wall is brighter than the centre of the room, where, however, its brightness is reflected in tiny convex, circular mirrors.

Along with the Dulwich Gallery and his own house and museum, the most interesting works of Soane's Picturesque period are the stable building (1814–17) at Chelsea Hospital – again, a 'primitivist' conception with receding concentric arches in brick walls, and the later halls at the Bank, in which the thin arch-lines sweep up from the floor with Gothic ease, while the dome and pendentives flow together in a single spherical plane (Plate 175). The last of the halls was completed in 1823, when Soane was seventy. In that year he was heavily engaged with public works at Westminster, including the whole series of Law Courts around Westminster Hall which had been begun in 1820. Here, we find him expanding old ideas in the most intrepid manner. Thus the Court of Chancery (destroyed 1883) was, in essence, an enormously expanded version of the 'tribune' at Tyringham, the lower arch-lines drawn out into a mere camber, the lantern rising from a ceiling whose hanging arches remind us of the dining-room in the Museum. There is no new invention here, only an incredible determination to stretch the old themes as far as they would go, and perhaps even a little further.

Not all of Soane's buildings have the intensity and economy of means of those which have been mentioned, and even these, his best, contain that worrying element of *malaise* mentioned in connexion with his earliest works. He was never completely sure of himself, and never quite happy in his management of proportion, which he believed, following Laugier, to be a purely intuitive affair, incapable of systematization. Again, a determination to fulfil the implications of his style betrayed him sometimes into grotesque mannerisms. The grooved lines which, at Dulwich, do give a wonderful extra tension to the components of the mausoleum lantern, are elsewhere (his own house, for instance) mere affectations, while the sarcophagi and cinerary urns which he piled on the sky-lines of some of his buildings to give them picturesqueness are merely quaint and have, perhaps, done more harm to his reputation than anything else.

Soane is remembered for his personal and unique mode of abstraction from Neo-classicism; but this is only one side of his work, for he never wholly relinquished the fully articulated classicism which he first displayed, so brilliantly, in the Triumphal Bridge of 1776, and in the designs he made in Italy. This latter style, however, crystallized almost at once and changed very little; so little, in fact, that a design for a Palace, done in Rome in 1779, and a design for a Palace for George IV, done after 1821 – forty-two years later – are barely distinguishable as the works of two different periods. Indeed, almost all his academic works, including important parts of the Bank, hark back either to the Triumphal Bridge or to the designs for a senate house and a palace done in Italy. Soane, it would seem, knew intuitively that the last great chapter in the history of classicism since the Renaissance was closed. There was nothing to add. In his personal style he sought new boundaries.

NOTES TO CHAPTER 28

1. The landscape gardens at Stourhead, formed by Henry Hoare between 1741 and 1783, include a Corinthian 'Pantheon' and a Doric 'Temple of Flora'. At Pains Hill, Charles Hamilton began his improvements about 1750, building, among other things, a Doric Temple of Bacchus.

2. 'The best style...for irregular and picturesque houses...is that mixed style, which characterizes the buildings of Claude and the Poussins.' *Analytical Enquiry*, pp. 218–19.

3. Egyptian influence in architecture was curiously slight, considering the part it played in furniture. P. F. Robinson (1776–1858) built the Egyptian Hall, Piccadilly, in 1811–12 (demolished 1904) and Foulston imitated it in a Masonic Hall at Stonehouse. Robinson, a pupil of Henry Holland, was perhaps the most versatile of the style-conjurers of the period, his works including a 'Norman' villa and the 'Swiss Cottage' at St John's Wood.

4. James Malton, in his *Essay on British Cottage Architecture*, 1798, p. 10, has an interesting passage on these innovations: 'The rude ornaments of Indostan supersede those of Greece; and the returned Nabob, heated in his pursuit of wealth, imagines he imports the *chaleur* of the East with its riches; and we behold the stretched awning to form the cool shade, in the moist clime of Britain; the new fashioned windows of Italy, opening to the floor, with lengthened balcony, originally intended to survey the lawns, the vistas, and the groves of *Claude*, in their summer attire, or the canals of Venice; are now to be seen in every confined street of London'.

5. Samuel Pepys Cockerell was a pupil of Sir Robert Taylor at the same time as Nash and became

a very successful architect and surveyor with a large practice. Some of his buildings, from about 1795 onwards, show very marked French influence of an advanced kind. An example is the west tower of St Anne's, Soho (1800; added to an older church, but since 1940 the only portion standing). The upper part somewhat recalls Père Lachaise monuments of the period but can also be regarded as a 'modernization' of the south tower of Saint-Sulpice, with the addition of a strange four-dial clock on the summit. Soane spoke of it with the greatest contempt and nobody seems to have liked it. A house by Cockerell showing French influence of a less debatable kind is Daylesford, Worcs., built for Warren Hastings.

6. I think it very likely that the conception as a whole was inspired by C. N. Ledoux's ideal city, illustrated in his *L'Architecture considerée sous le rapport de l'art, des mœurs, et de la législation*, 1789–1804.

7. Many of the buildings shown are French in manner and there is at least one note written in French. The obvious inference is that the panorama was prepared by Augustus Charles Pugin (1762–1832), who, as a refugee, had attached himself to Nash in his Welsh days and was associated with him for many years.

8. The Gallery was wrecked by a flying bomb in 1944, the mausoleum being almost demolished. The re-erection of the whole has now (1953), however, been completed.

9. Soane's interest in Mistley is confirmed by his borrowing the theme for his church towers at St Peter's, Walworth, and Holy Trinity, Marylebone (1823 and 1825).

CHAPTER 29

GREEK AND GOTHIC:
ARCHITECTURE AFTER WATERLOO

IN 1791 an Architects' Club was founded. Wyatt, Dance, Holland, and S. P. Cockerell started it. Chambers, Robert Adam, and Mylne joined, representing an older generation. The other twelve founder-members included comparatively young men like Soane and Hardwick, while Carr of York, Revett, Sandby, and Gandon came in as honorary (country) members. The Club was extremely exclusive, since no one was to be elected unless a Royal Academician, Associate, or Gold Medallist or a member of one of the principal foreign academies. In 1792 a rather less exclusive Surveyors' Club was inaugurated. This still exists, but what became of the Architects' Club nobody knows. It is the first recorded instance of the professional association of English architects and its foundation marks, therefore, an important stage in the profession's history. There is also much significance in its exclusiveness and in its being imitated by an association denominated the *Surveyors'* Club, in spite of the fact that there was at the time no strict difference between the two professions. The Architects' Club, obviously, constituted an *élite* and the names do, in fact, include nearly every important figure in English Neo-classicism from Adam to Soane.

Soane was the youngest original member of the Club and one of the few still in practice in 1815, by which year it is obvious that the situation out of which the Club issued had completely changed. The French wars had been fought and England herself had changed a good deal. An aristocratic society with bourgeois leanings had become a bourgeois society with aristocratic yearnings, and it was such a society which the next generation of architects grew up to serve. It was in close sympathy with the changing mentality of England that the Neo-classical tradition split itself, in the early 1800s, into two parallel and unopposed movements, since christened the 'Greek Revival' and the 'Gothic Revival'. 'Revival', in this context, is inexact, and in regard to the Greek movement, positively absurd, but the term is now too well established to be disposed of.

The movement called the 'Greek Revival' may conveniently be dated from 1804. This was the year in which Thomas Hope published a diatribe against James Wyatt's design for Downing College, Cambridge, pleading for the substitution of a pure Greek Doric design, or, if that was impracticable, a pure Greek Ionic. Hope's point of view was that of a doctrinaire Neo-classicist (no pilasters; the parts of the entablature to be considered as functional, etc.) who went a step further than his predecessors in preferring absolutely the Greek orders to the Roman.

This attitude was new. Soane who, in his student designs of 1778–80, had been among the first to appreciate the value of Greek Doric,[1] never considered Greek work in general as superior to Roman; and, in fact, used Roman orders and ornaments till the very end.

Oddly enough it was George Dance, Soane's senior by twelve years, whose late works did lead directly to the Greek Revival: the Greek Doric portico he designed for Stratton Park (p. 278) belongs to the year before Hope's pamphlet. But Thomas Hope (*c.* 1770–1831) is the significant newcomer. He was not a professional architect, but a very rich amateur, the son of an English merchant in Amsterdam; he had spent eight years travelling, observing and sketching architecture, and had decided that the preference for all things Greek, which had been increasing steadily since Winckelmann's day, was one which it was now time to enforce in all its rigour. The time was propitious. Between 1806 and 1812 Lord Elgin was assembling the Parthenon sculptures in London and if conventional opinion followed Payne Knight in believing them to be Hadrianic, the younger critics and artists were deeply stirred by them. Long before their purchase by the nation in 1817 they had set a new standard in sculpture, extended, by analogy, to architecture.

Hope himself was a collector on a large scale in his two houses, one at Deepdene, Dorking, the other in Duchess Street, Portland Place. At both these houses he carried out extensive building works, to his own designs, showing in both instances that his conception of Modern Greek was closely linked to the French romantic modernism of the 1790s. His pamphlet on Downing College was his first public advocacy of the Greek style, but it was followed in 1807 by a book of furniture and interior decoration designs, based on Greek themes, for which he made most of the drawings himself. Books on ancient and modern costume followed in 1809 and 1812.

Hope's plea for pure Greek at Downing was completely successful and the design of William Wilkins, in which the Erechtheum Ionic order controls the composition throughout, was substituted for Wyatt's. William Wilkins (1778–1839) was then twenty-six, and the circumstances suggest that he was in close touch with Hope from the beginning of the affair. He was a Cambridge man, the son of an architect who, starting as a plasterer in Norwich, became associated with Repton and designed Donington Park, one of the best Gothic houses of the 1790s. Young Wilkins had been at Caius College, graduated 6th Wrangler in 1800, and gone abroad in the following year as one of West's travelling bachelors. He had worked in Italy, Greece, and Asia Minor, and the main fruits of his research were published as the *Antiquities of Magna Graecia* in 1807.

Downing College (Plate 176A) was built in 1806–11, though the great centre block, containing Chapel and Library, was omitted. The buildings show a rather priggish loyalty to Neo-classical ideals and, with their servile reproduction of Erechtheum detail, are about as *doctrinaire* as they could be. In their extreme reticence of silhouette they probably owe something to the French Grand Prix tradition,[2] but they constitute, for England, the first monument of the Greek Revival proper.

Up to 1810, Wilkins busied himself with buildings as utterly Greek as Downing. They include Haileybury College (1806), which has exactly the restraint and pedantry of the Cambridge building, and Grange Park, Hants. (for Henry Drummond, Esq.), the latter an old house remodelled to include a Theseion portico and other Athenian references. Another opportunity for a Theseion portico was provided by the Literary and Scientific Institution (Kingston Rooms) at Bath (1808–10; destroyed 1933), while in Dublin Wilkins raised a Greek Doric column in Sackville Street as a pedestal for a statue of Lord Nelson.

Meanwhile, another young architect had subscribed his talents to the Revival. Robert Smirke (1781–1867), eldest son of the Academician painter of the same name, was three years younger than Wilkins. Articled to Soane in 1796, he disagreed with him and left the office after only a year, but managed to secure the Royal Academy Gold Medal in 1799. From 1801 to 1805 he was abroad, in Paris, Rome, Naples, Athens, and Sicily. His first great opportunity came in 1808 when Covent Garden Theatre was burnt down and he was entrusted with its rebuilding. It was a testing responsibility for an architect of twenty-seven, but we are assured by Farington that Dance, an old friend of Smirke senior, helped him. This we can readily believe, for the long façade of the theatre, with its four-column Greek Doric portico, its end pavilions and attic, strongly recalls Stratton Park.

Smirke's Covent Garden was completed within a year and survived till its destruction, again by fire, in 1856. It was London's very first Greek Doric building and proved extremely influential. In London it had been imitated, within twenty years, in two orphan schools, a literary institution, and an almshouse; while in the provinces, the Moot Hall at Newcastle (William Stokoe, 1810) and the Trinity Almshouses at Hull (Charles Mountain, 1834; bombed 1941) were typical if crude recollections of it. Smirke had shown how a plain mass of building could be endowed with immense gravity by comparatively simple means, with Doric *antae* at the angles giving just that effect of stability which was so difficult with rustications and more so with pilasters. Smirke demonstrated again the usefulness of the *anta* as a pier when he built the Royal Mint porches in 1809–11.

Both Wilkins and Smirke were immensely successful. Smirke especially, who was cool, businesslike, and an extremely able constructor, climbed rapidly to fortune. He was only thirty-three when, on Wyatt's death, he was appointed, with Nash and Soane, as one of the three architects to the Board of Works, an appointment which led to his designing the public works for which he is chiefly remembered. Wilkins remained in private practice, but churches, colleges, and public buildings came his way so that his powers were by no means starved. Up to about 1815, these two men were not only the leaders of the Greek Revival but pretty well its only practitioners. After that date, the movement spread with the utmost rapidity, visiting every corner of Britain and becoming, in effect, the dominant style of the post-Waterloo period.

Hundreds of houses, churches, institutions, and public offices of the Greek Revival taste survive or are recorded and a study of them underlines forcibly the debt of the whole movement to Robert Smirke. Few young architects after 1815 followed Soane;[3] none, if they valued their reputations, followed Nash. Wilkins was too pedantic and not, at first, sufficiently in the public eye. Smirke, therefore, with his directness of approach and simplicity of detail, was the model for younger architects all over the country.

The Greek Revival after 1815

The great expansion of town life after Waterloo brought with it the need for a variety of new public and semi-public buildings, and it was in these that the Greek Revival found its main opportunities. The movement broadens suddenly out about 1811, the first year of the Regency and the first, likewise, of Nash's Regent's Park adventures. To that year belongs Drury Lane Theatre, where Benjamin Wyatt[4] borrowed Smirke's notion of a monumental theatre front framed by pairs of *antae* – this time, however, without a portico (the present portico is later). In 1811, also, John Rennie began the bridge eventually to be called Waterloo Bridge, coupling gigantic Greek Doric columns on each pier. Meanwhile, the Greek Ionic columns of Dance's College of Surgeons were emerging from scaffolding. In 1812, David Laing (1774–1856), a pupil of Soane, designed the new Custom House,[5] with Greek Ionic porticoes flanking a round-arched centre in the French manner; and Joseph Kay[6] introduced Athenian details into the east side of Mecklenburgh Square, a composition based on Adam's Fitzroy Square but brought up to date.

Among the new types of buildings called for when the war was over was the professional man's club – a type somewhat different from and more institutional than the older political and gambling clubs. Smirke erected the United Services Club (not the present building[7]) in 1816–17; its round-headed windows and panels of enrichment brought in a French way of modelling a façade which was to be much imitated. Wilkins's University Club[8] followed in 1822–6, introducing to London the Erechtheum treatment he had employed at Downing, while in Trafalgar Square the Union Club and the College of Physicians were united by Smirke, in 1824–5, in a single block whose façade (still existing though altered) has a giant Ionic order, with subsidiary orders, derived from the Choragic Monument of Thrasyllus, expressed in the two ranges of windows.[9] This Thrasyllus motif proved extremely useful; great play was made with it in George Smith's old Corn Exchange, Mark Lane (1827; demolished), while Wilkins made it, at St George's Hospital (1827), an excuse for placing a central *anta* between the windows of the wings.

Smirke's career was crowned by two immense London works, the General Post Office of 1824–9 (demolished 1913) and the British Museum, begun in 1823 but not finished till 1847. By the time he started these he had become indissolubly wedded to the giant Ionic theme which Dance had introduced at the College of Surgeons, and few indeed of his buildings are without it. The Post Office (Plate 177A) had three Ionic porticoes on an otherwise plain elevation while at the British Museum a tremendous Ionic colonnade continues without interruption round the whole of the main façade. The British Museum must inevitably be accounted one of the great representative buildings of the period, one of the few which dispenses with petty idiosyncrasies of style and aims at a timeless grandeur. Nobody, however, has ever found it a very interesting building and to say that it lacks imagination is probably an understatement.

Smirke planned the Museum round an oblong open quadrangle,[10] bringing forward two of the sides as wings to form a forecourt, and marking the entrance with a pedimented portico. The order of the portico continues round every part of the building visible from the approach, without any contact with the mass behind it or any relief in the shape of a pier or *anta*. This, in principle, is the plan of the old Parliament House in Dublin (p. 228); but it is also a quite simple evolution from the 'centre and ends' arrangement of Smirke's Post Office. The galleries of the interior are magnificent up to a point, but Smirke's practice of using *antae* alone without either pilasters or columns in the round, gives them a reticence which is rather forbidding. This is particularly so in the King's Library (1825), where the Corinthian columns in the centre bay are scarcely noticed.

William Wilkins's career has not quite the complacent flatness of Smirke's. The two major buildings of his later years, University College, London, and the National Gallery, show a somewhat more original if less practical mind. At University College, built as the London University in 1827–8, only the main block, with its grand portico (Plate 177B), is by Wilkins, the side wings having been altered in execution by others. The portico, raised on a great podium with steps, is tremendously grand but has an arbitrary relation to the wings, while the dome behind it is either too bulky or miserably small, according to one's conception of it as an incidental cupola or a culminating feature. The truth seems to be that when Wilkins broke with the purism of his Downing days he was unable to train himself to manage the freer style of composition which a building such as University College involved. He was not, like Soane, soaked in the English tradition ascending through Wren, Vanbrugh, and Adam; nor, on the other hand, was he sufficiently acquainted with the contemporary French school which C. R. Cockerell, his junior by ten years, was just then making his own.

At the National Gallery, which Wilkins started to build in 1833, the same lack of experience is evident. The building stands on the site of the Royal Mews (p. 206) and something of Kent's 'staccato' seems to have crept into its composition. As at University College, the portico and steps are well handled, but the dome, attended by a short attic to hide an awkward junction, is an absurdity. Of the two kinds of pavilions which punctuate the façade, one is based on Athenian themes, but the other (incorporating the columns from the lately demolished Carlton House portico) is of a type introduced by Chambers. The general result is patchy and inadequate to so commanding a site.

As represented by Smirke and Wilkins, the Greek Revival in England is an unsatisfactory interlude. Smirke's extremely limited vision, and Wilkins's incapacity to handle anything much bigger than a single unit of design, place them in a category well below the masters of the eighteenth century. Scarcely a single building by either has any striking excellence of plan or composition. The aged Nash, careless and inconstant though he may have been, had more command of design; and Soane, squeezing the last drop of novelty out of his old inventions, is invariably more interesting. With Nash and Soane almost in their dotage and Smirke and Wilkins plodding ineffectively behind them, it is not surprising that, in the 1820s, informed sections of the public began to feel that something was wrong with English architecture. This uneasiness, often and sharply expressed in the periodicals, had the effect of increasing the tendency of people of taste to turn to Gothic antiquarianism. It had, also, the more immediate effect of inducing the Opposition in Parliament to ask, in 1828, for a Select Committee on the Expense of Public Buildings. As the evidence given before the Committee amply testifies, it was not only the expense but the quality of the buildings which was exercising the public conscience.

With Smirke and Wilkins, however, the Greek Revival does not end. There was a small group of younger designers who, up to 1830, gave every sign of redeeming the cause by bringing to it great ability and a realization that France had become, once again, the metropolis of European classicism. The careers of these younger men pass beyond the limits of this history, although by 1830 both C. R. Cockerell (1788–1863) and Charles Barry (1795–1860) had made their names. Cockerell's competition design for University College (in the Victoria and Albert Museum) is immeasurably more confident and re-sourceful than Wilkins's, and his churches (to which we shall come later) stand out as the most original classical solutions of their time. Barry, in 1824, built the Royal Institution (now the Art Gallery) at Manchester (Plate 178A), a Greek Ionic building, somewhat immature, but with a sense of spatial values in the projection and recession of a façade which Smirke never approached. At the Travellers' Club (Plate 178B), in 1829, he turned away from Greek Revivalism and led English architecture back to a Renaissance opulence of texture and shadow.

To these names of younger and stronger leaders of the classical movement one might add, with reservations, that of Decimus Burton (1800–81) who, before he was much over thirty, had built the arch and screen at Hyde Park Corner (Plate 179A), and the Athenaeum Club (Plate 179B), externally Roman, but with an Athenian frieze and a splendid staircase and drawing-room with Athenian details. Burton, however, did not really see much beyond the Smirke horizon. His villas and country-houses are pleasant enough examples of the Greek school of around 1830, but to the Victorian continuation he contributed nothing of the slightest importance. More important figures, near Burton's age, were George Basevi (1794–1845), a pupil of Soane, and James Pennethorne (1801–71), Nash's pupil and ward. But in both cases their careers only become important after the close of this history.

The Greek Revival spread fairly consistently throughout England, partly as the result of London architects building in the provinces and partly because a few outstanding provincial men took up the new manner. In the first category, to the examples already quoted may be added Smirke's Shire Hall at Hereford (1817) and his Council House at Bristol (1824–7) and, more important than these, the old Town Hall at Manchester[11] (Plate 180A) by Francis Goodwin (1784–1835), a building which seems to have been an attempt to do for secular architecture what Inwood, at St Pancras (p. 316), had just done for ecclesiastical. Among provincial men who promoted the style in their own districts, perhaps the most important were Foulston of Plymouth and Foster of Liverpool. John Foulston (1772–1842), a pupil of Thomas Hardwick, won a competition in 1811 for the group of buildings in Plymouth comprising the Royal Hotel, Theatre, and Assembly Room. The design, carried out in 1812, echoed the Greek Ionic simplicity of Dance's College of Surgeons, while the interior of the Assembly Room was an up-to-date version, with segmental ceiling and Lysicratean details, of Sandby's Freemasons' Tavern of 1775–6 (p. 274). These buildings,[12] bringing the latest London fashions to the West, proved the foundation of a highly successful career and, after Waterloo, Foulston laid out a whole quarter of Plymouth with its square, terraces, and crescent, and several minor public buildings.

John Foster (c. 1786–1846) was the son of the Surveyor to Liverpool Corporation. He was in Greece with C. R. Cockerell and, returning in 1816, joined the family firm and eventually built (1828 onwards) the Liverpool Custom House (Plate 180B), a vast structure on an H-plan with a hall in the central block, rising to a drum with a low domical roof (compare the Four Courts, Dublin, p. 274). Ionic porticoes and *antae* in the Smirke manner make the building typical of its period. It was gutted in the air-raids of 1941 and has since been demolished. Like Foulston at Plymouth, Foster was concerned with street improvements, Lord Street, the destroyed St George's Crescent, and adjacent streets being laid out and designed by him.

The Greek Revival in Scotland

Scotland's economic recovery during the eighteenth century culminated, in Edinburgh, with the period which saw the building of the New Town – a long period with two distinct phases. It was in 1763 that a bridge was begun over the Nor' Loch, leading to the new site, and this was completed by William Mylne (brother of Robert Mylne) in 1769. The first part of the New Town was being laid out at this time by James Craig. It was a parallelogram of streets, with two squares. Charlotte Square, on the west, was designed, as we have seen (p. 269), by Robert Adam and was in progress when he died in 1792. In the eastern square, the principal building was the Dundas house, by Sir William Chambers.

During the war period of 1793–1815, the New Town stood still, but on the eve of peace the second phase of development began and continued for fifteen years. With the new streets came new public buildings, new churches, and monuments and – since England was now no longer the only outlet for Scottish genius – a school of Edinburgh architects to design them. Of the interesting group among whom the opportunities of the new Edinburgh were distributed, the eldest was Archibald Elliot (1761–1823). It is characteristic that he should have begun his career by seeking his fortune in London, and not surprising, in the circumstances, that his first important work in Edinburgh should have been a direct imitation of John Nash's approach to Regent Street, in front of Carlton House. Waterloo Place, Edinburgh, with its two porticoes flanking the entrance to the street, echoes Waterloo Place, London, important differences, however, being that Elliot used stone, and strictly Greek detail.

Elliot's Waterloo Place leads to a new road cut round the Calton Hill, an eminence which soon became a kind of 'acropolis' for the 'Modern Athens', dotted with monuments to men of valour and intellect and crowned by the beginnings, too soon abandoned, of a National Monument in the shape of the Parthenon. The southern slope of the hill provided a site for what is surely the noblest monument of the Scottish Greek Revival – the Edinburgh High School (Plate 181).

The architect of the High School was Thomas Hamilton (1785–1858), a local man and untravelled. The building was begun in 1825 and is thus close in date to Wilkins's London University to which it bears a (probably coincidental) resemblance. Hamilton, like Wilkins, mounted a temple portico above a grandiose arrangement of steps, to provide a symbolic centre for his design in the treatment of its main feature, the Hall. At Edinburgh, the hall is a Greek Doric temple, far more happily united with the wings than is the Corinthian portico at University College. Hamilton used the contours of the site and the fact that the road frontage is curved, to great advantage, and, with the Propylaea at Athens as his inspiration, produced a composition more picturesque and imaginative than anything of its kind south of the border.[13] The Burns monument near Ayr (1820) and the similar one on the Calton Hill (1830) both underline Hamilton's uncommon sensitiveness in the handling of classical forms. Nor are his later works less distinguished.

The New Town expanded in four distinct areas, each planned in a formal manner, though with due appreciation of the discoveries of the Woods of Bath and of what Nash was doing at Regent's Park. Each lay-out includes a circus, a crescent, or a double crescent, or (as in the case of the Moray estate, laid out by James Gillespie Graham) all three of these features. The architecture is, generally, a dour Grecian, with little imaginative enterprise. The last of the 'new towns' was planned by W. H. Playfair (1789–1857) for the area north of the Calton Hill. It was interrupted by financial difficulties, though not before Playfair had begun Royal Terrace on the north slope of the hill, a symmetrical composition nearly a quarter of a mile long, with three Corinthian and four Ionic porticoes. For sheer sullen gloom this is surpassed by St Bernard's Crescent, laid out by another architect on Sir Henry Raeburn's property across the Water of Leith. Here, inset Greek Doric colonnades give an extraordinary impression that the building is some sort of residential mausoleum.

Playfair became, in due course, the most eminent of the Edinburgh group and left behind him the city's two most conspicuous classical buildings – the Royal Institution (now the Royal Scottish Academy) and the National Gallery, both on the Mound in full view of all Princes Street. Only the former comes within our period, having been begun in 1822 – a Greek Doric quasi-temple, related to Smirke and Wilkins; it was altered, before its final completion in 1836, by the addition of some further columns and much sculpture, providing a welcome relief from the dumbness of the original design.

Exactly contemporary with Playfair was William Burn (1789–1870), whose reputation really belongs to Victorian times. He was a pupil of Smirke, and of the three public buildings he contributed to Edinburgh before 1830, it is enough to say that they all derive their façades directly from Smirke's Covent Garden.

The Greek Revival in Scotland was not for long limited to Edinburgh. In Glasgow, the Royal Exchange, by David Hamilton (1768–1843), shows its influence in 1829–30, though it shows, equally, the influence of Soane's academic manner and, in the rear elevation, his personal mannerisms. The more important Greek buildings of Glasgow belong to the middle and later decades of the century.

The Gothic Revival

A significant fact with which we may introduce the Gothic Revival of the period before 1830 is that nearly all its important monuments were designed by men who have already been mentioned for their contribution to the Greek Revival. In other words, far from there being any distinct school of Gothic men at this period, the style was cultivated as a 'second language' by every architect of repute, and many of none. This, of course, had been the case with Dance, Nash, and Soane, though the latter was both reluctant and unhappy with the style. It was still more the case with Smirke, Wilkins, Cockerell, Barry, Goodwin, Burton, Foster of Liverpool, and the Edinburgh men. All of these practised Gothic extensively. Nearly all of them respected it and took pains to master its details to the extent to which the publications available at the time enabled them to do so. None of them, however, produced Gothic buildings which subsequent generations have seen fit to praise; and, indeed, of all the English schools of architecture, the Gothic of the early nineteenth century is the one which has been most consistently and unequivocally condemned. Why is this? An analogy with literature may help to supply the answer. In those novels of Sir Walter Scott whose scene is set in the Middle Ages (*Ivanhoe*, the first of them, came out in 1820) we are presented with descriptions of events, scenes, and buildings in which the author is at great pains to give an impression of truthfulness to period. To his first readers, he probably did; to us, however, these descriptions give anything but a medieval impression and, indeed, are among the passages which tie the books most securely to the reign of George IV. It is not merely that the descriptions are inaccurate, which of course they are; it is that there is a conscious insistence on detail – heraldic and architectural – which the narrative does not require and which can only please if the reader shares the author's mood of wonder that such things have a historical reality. That mood is fugitive and to-day can be recaptured only by the very innocent or the exceedingly flexible mind.

Exactly the same conscious insistence on detail – not for its quality but for the excitement of displaying a historical trophy – is what we find in the Gothic architecture of the 1820s. Whatever charm this architecture had vanished as soon as a deeper familiarity with medieval architecture prevailed – as soon, that is, as a richly traceried window ceased to be interesting *as such* and was judged by combined standards of archaeological and aesthetic taste. It might be thought that some, at least, of the Gothic architecture of the twenties might be as acceptable to posterity as the novels of Scott. But none is as acceptable, the reason being, surely, that if Scott had left only such novels as *Ivanhoe* and *The Monastery* behind him, novels groaning with the 'properties' of medievalism, he would not to-day rank higher than the architects of, say, Lowther Castle or the gateway of King's College, Cambridge.

This analogy with a literary form is especially appropriate in that the Gothic Revival had essentially literary origins and was fed by a series of books whose character was, at once, antiquarian and topographical rather than technical. The father of this kind of literature was, unquestionably, John Carter (1748–1817), the son of a monumental mason, who made a career for himself as an architectural draughtsman and, in a small way, as an architect.[14] He represents a type which becomes familiar as the century advances – the introverted creature who, in boyhood, has his imagination set on fire by the mystery of time past and over whom the stones of Gothic England cast the spell of self-dedication. Carter drew for the Society of Antiquaries and collected a great store of notes and sketches which eventually led to his publishing a series of books, including the miniature *Views of Ancient Buildings in England* (1786–93) and *Ancient Architecture of England* (1795 and 1807). In the last of these, details of Gothic buildings are more truthfully and sympathetically represented than in any previous books. Carter, moreover, had a mind capable of analysis and nomenclature. He called medieval architecture Pointed Architecture and divided its English manifestations into styles and sub-styles, introducing the expressions First Pointed, Second Pointed, etc., which persisted far into Victorian times. But perhaps his greatest importance lay in his activity as a correspondent to the *Gentleman's Magazine*, where, between 1798 and his death in 1817, he delivered himself of no fewer than two hundred and twelve articles attacking the neglect, destruction, and fake restoration of English cathedrals, churches, and castles. His invective is of the kind later employed with so much force by A. W. Pugin, who must, in this respect, be regarded as Carter's legatee.

Carter was followed by a very different, but no less industrious character, John Britton (1771–1857). This individual started in the wine-trade and after experience as a cellarman, an attorney's clerk, and a hack writer for the theatre, tried his hand in the topographical line with *The Beauties of Wiltshire*. This being successful, it led on to a whole series of *Beauties* which by 1816 had covered England and Wales entire. It was not architecturally of much significance, but while it was in hand Britton started *The Architectural Antiquities of Great Britain* (1804–14) and, when that was complete, *The Cathedral Antiquities of Great Britain* (1814–35), his most important work and one which, as an architectural survey of the British Cathedrals, has still not been superseded. It attains a very fair level of accuracy and some of the engravings, particularly those of Mackenzie and Le Keux, are admirable. Britton published many more works, his last being an autobiography in which we see him as something of a vulgarian with a vast opinion of his achievements and a singular flair for a marketable line in architectural literature. He sailed home to success on the tide which bore along the Waverley Novels.

Different again was Thomas Rickman (1776–1841), a Quaker, who from medicine was drawn irresistibly to the study of Gothic architecture and thence to architectural practice, flourishing as a builder of churches, chiefly in midland industrial towns. His great literary contribution was *An Attempt to Discriminate the Styles of English Architecture*, written apparently in 1812 but printed only in 1817. This was the book which gave us those none too felicitous but now probably immortal phrases – 'Early English', 'Decorated', and 'Perpendicular' – phrases which superseded Carter's First Pointed, Second Pointed, etc. The book proved immensely popular, a seventh edition being printed in 1881. The earlier editions begin, rather curiously, with a brief disquisition on the Greek and Roman orders and the later (and larger) part of the work is thus seen to be an attempt to render 'Dec.' as easily distinguishable from 'Perp.' as Tuscan from Ionic. In this reduction to methodical order of an apparently chaotic subject lay Rickman's popular appeal. By mid-Victorian times most parsons could tell off the parts of their church in correct Rickmanese and the terminology got into all the guide-books.

Finally, there was Augustus Charles Pugin (1762–1832). He was a Frenchman who, coming to this island after the Revolution, was employed as a draughtsman by John Nash while the latter was still practising in Wales. His introduction to Gothic will therefore have been through the medium of the Nash-Repton practice with its almost total ignorance of details other than coarse pinnacles, crude battlements, and the most elementary types of tracery. The stylistic deficiencies of this kind of thing induced Pugin, with Nash's encouragement, to bring out, in 1821–3, two volumes of *Specimens of Gothic Architecture*, containing meticulous measured drawings of Gothic buildings and details. There was an able text by E. J. Willson, but the main thing about the book was the technical accuracy of the plates which demonstrated to the draughtsman exactly how to set up such things as ogee canopies, cusps, and quatrefoils. Carter, in his books, had delineated these things sensitively and accurately. But Pugin gave the exact centres from which the curves were struck.

Carter, Britton, Rickman, and A. C. Pugin are the principal names in the literature of what might well be called the 'Waverley' phase of the Gothic Revival, a phase in which interest in the style moves from the merely Picturesque to a serious sentiment for Gothic as a *national* style and, moreover, a style as complex, as difficult chronologically and technically, as the classical. At the end of our period it remained only for liturgical enthusiasms to be added to the patriotic and the Victorian Gothic Revival had been born.

Naturally, the Gothic buildings of the early nineteenth century did not keep abreast with the rapid advances in scholarship of the literary exegetists. Generally speaking, the Wyatt manner with its falsity of scale and liberal misapplications (tiny 'Henry VII' fan-vaults as drawing-room ceilings and so forth) prevailed till well after 1830. The 'castellated' style, moreover, stemming from Downton and early Nash, held its ground firmly. Smirke's first successes, Lowther Castle (1808–10, for the Earl of Lonsdale) and Eastnor Castle (1815, for Earl Somers; Plate 182A), are in this style. They have some genuine dramatic power, perhaps because, as at Covent Garden, Smirke had the advantage of George Dance's advice; but they neither display, nor needed to display, any great knowledge of Gothic forms. The same could be said of 'castellated' houses by nearly every architect of the time in England and Scotland, while in Ireland the 'castles' of Francis and Richard Johnstone and Richard Morrison merely serve to amplify the evidence. Dozens of these castles appeared in the two decades after Waterloo, and one seeks almost in vain either for scholarship or for originalities more captivating than superficially new arrangements of the round and octagon towers of the Downton school.[15]

For country-houses, an alternative to 'castellated' was 'Tudor Gothic', an easy and manageable style for which Hampton Court and Thornbury Castle provided good models. Thornbury was imitated in Costessey Hall, Norfolk, built in 1825 by a descendant of the Earl of Stafford who built Thornbury. The architect was John Chessel Buckler (1793–1894) and the house could still be described by Eastlake in 1870 as 'one of the most important and successful instances of the Revival in Domestic Architecture'. Anthony Salvin (1799–1881), a pupil of Nash, achieved some early successes in this style before becoming the great castle builder and restorer of Victorian times; and Edward Blore (1787–1879), discovered by Sir Walter Scott, was another youthful champion of 'Tudor Gothic'.

The style was naturally adaptable to collegiate work. Rugby in 1809 and Harrow in 1820 both adopted it. In 1822, King's College, Cambridge, invited designs for the completion of its great court. Of nineteen designs submitted five were Gothic, in deference to the Chapel, the remainder classical, in deference to Gibbs. The Fellows determined on Gothic, and chose the design of William Wilkins. Famous for his Greek researches and his application of the purest Greek detail at Downing, Wilkins was no stranger to Gothic, and had already built 'Tudor' houses in Scotland and Cornwall. His screen and gateway at King's (Plate 182B) are carefully detailed, but they show the same misapprehensions regarding scale as most of the Gothic work of the time, while his design for the south side of the court and a Gothicized version of the Gibbs building (not executed) are, at best, the kind of things which Victorians called 'good for their period'.

It is curious how one automatically adopts Victorian criteria for these Georgian Gothic buildings, and it seems to confirm the suspicion that they have no genius of their own. Their departures from medieval precedent are very rarely felicitous, and there is little energy in their freedom. Immensely popular at the time they were built, they were outmoded within as little as ten or fifteen years and sometimes condemned even by their own creators.

In London, Gothic buildings of the twenties, later thought of as 'good for their period', included the hall of Christ's Hospital, begun in 1825 by John Shaw (1776–1832), and St Katharine's Hospital, Regent's Park (1826), by Ambrose Poynter (1796–1886). The sole reason why these were 'good' was that, in proportion and distribution of openings as well as in detail, they showed a fair appreciation of Tudor or Gothic precedents – a virtue due in both cases almost certainly to the publication of Pugin's *Specimens*.

Greek and Gothic Churches

If it has been possible to deal satisfactorily in outline with both the Greek and Gothic Revivals without once mentioning churches, it is for an important reason. Church-building in England had, by 1800, practically dropped out of the national life. Churches were built from time to time but they were either replacements of old ones become ruinous, or mere 'proprietary chapels' speculating in pew-rents. There was no church-building *movement* of any kind and, hence, no particular interest regarding the architectural possibilities of the contemporary church. It is true that, here and there, an architect faced with the unwonted task of building a new church, might bestir himself to produce something original and, perhaps, fine. The circular church of St Chad, Shrewsbury (p. 211), Bonomi's church at Great Packington (p. 286), and Daniel Hague's church of St Paul, Bristol (1789–93), whose tower paraphrases in Gothic that of London's Royal Exchange, are only three of a number of really interesting churches of the 1790s. But they led nowhere and each initiative faded into the general apathy which hedged the subject of church-building. During the French wars, fewer churches, probably, were built than at any time since the Commonwealth, and it was not till a year or two before Waterloo that a movement did start which brought forth hundreds of new churches of a distinct and characteristic kind.

This movement is always, and rightly, associated with the Act of 1818 providing for the expenditure of one million pounds on the building of churches in London and other parts of the country. The statute, however, was itself a product of a movement which had already gathered momentum and expressed itself in some important London and provincial churches. The first of these was St Marylebone which, as we have seen (p. 275), was begun by Thomas Hardwick as a chapel in 1813 and later enlarged into a great church. This was followed by the new church of St Pancras, proposed in 1816, begun in 1819, and completed in 1822.

St Pancras Church (Plate 183) is one of the great representative buildings of the Greek

Revival though, by a freak of chance, it is the work of an architect who does not figure as an important influence and is, indeed, remembered for this building alone. H. W. Inwood (1794–1843) was the eldest son of William Inwood, a London architect, and it was as his father's partner that he submitted designs for the new church and received, in a limited competition, the first award. That was in June 1818. In 1819, young Inwood was in Greece and the church must have been begun in his absence. The conception of the building as a close imitation of the Erechtheum does not, therefore, follow Inwood's Greek journey but precedes it and will have been inspired by the engravings of Stuart and of Leroy, and the Erechtheum fragments brought back by Lord Elgin.

There is a sort of innocent ingenuity about this building. The exterior composition is that of St Martin's-in-the-Fields, but everything has been translated into Greek, including the steeple, which is put together out of the elements of the Tower of the Winds and the Choragic Monument of Lysicrates.[16] St Pancras only breaks away from the Gibbs model at the east end where the need for two large vestries condones the copying of the Erechtheum tribune which, by an additional stroke of ingenuity, serves to monumentalize the entries to the vaults. The fancy-dress fits like a glove.

Internally, the church is simply a great flat-ceiled hall with galleries and an apse. The details are taken, where applicable, from the Erechtheum and the other famous Athenian monuments, but these do not give the recipe for everything and, where they do not (as in the vestry ceilings or the pulpit), Inwood showed himself singularly resourceful in the adaptation of more recondite archaeological material. The whole building, indeed, in spite of the blatant and much ridiculed copyism, evinces a real sensibility.

Both St Marylebone and St Pancras were the immediate outcome of urban expansion, unprecedented in London's history. In Bath, the same cause produced John Pinch's fine Gothic church of St Mary, Bathwick, while in Liverpool John Foster (p. 310) built two large churches, one classical on the St Martin's model, the other Gothic. These, and a few others like them, were designed, if not dedicated, before the 'Million Act' of 1818. But they were churches built by the rich for the rich and situated in the better-class suburbs. The monuments which line the walls of St Marylebone and St Pancras show where the pew-rents and burial fees came from – 'nabobs' from India, Jamaican merchants, men from the provinces who had carried their ambitions to London and fulfilled them there, lawyers, and government servants. Such churches left untouched the problems of what was soon to be called 'spiritual destitution' in the poorer suburbs, the spread of free-thinking, atheism, and radicalism. Such problems could only be dealt with in two ways – philanthropically or by the State. Philanthropy, which was to provide, in due course, the mainspring of Victorian church-building, was open-handed enough in 1818 to bring into existence the Incorporated Church Building Society. But it was the State, through the Commissioners appointed by the Act of that year, which provided for that wave of church-building so characteristic of the years which immediately followed.

The 'Commissioners' Churches' vary greatly in style and much more so in quality, but are almost always recognizable. There is a peculiar drabness about them, a slackness in the proportions, a lack of vitality, as if their designers had driven themselves to a task for which they had no heart. Several reasons might be given for this, but an obvious and

Y

immediate one is a fatal lack of leadership. The Commissioners had at their disposal the three architects to the Board of Works – Nash, Soane, and Smirke – and each contributed several churches; but not one of them was capable of giving a lead such as Wren had given after the Fire or Hawksmore in 1711. Soane was the only one to put much thought into the problem, and he produced, in 1818 or very soon after, a most curious design for a segmental-vaulted church with thin round-arched arcades, a compromise between Classical and Gothic forms, horribly low and 'creepy' in proportion. His church of St John, Bethnal Green (1824-5; remodelled internally), was on these lines. Holy Trinity, Marylebone Road, and the very similar church in Walworth Grove have a little more dignity; and their towers are interesting as essays on the theme of Adam's towers at Mistley.

Nash's only important church was All Souls, Langham Place (1822-4), but the exceedingly witty treatment of the circular, spired vestibule[17] as a feature in his new street does not make the church itself anything but what it is – an ornate but ordinary galleried hall.

By and large, the architects of the Commissioners' churches worried their heads with two problems only. First, how to get two thousand people into a presentable rectangular box, with galleries, at so much a sitting; and second, how to make a great show at the west end and still keep within the spending limit. The four Greek Revival solutions in Lambeth known as the 'Waterloo Churches',[18] all built between 1822 and 1824, are representative not only of London churches but of many in the larger provincial towns. They have heavy Greek temple porticoes and, above, steeples which are Greek either by quotation or merely by the affectation of an extremely restrained silhouette. These churches are by architects much younger than Nash and Soane, but the initiative they show is not impressive, being limited to the display of something grandiosely Greek or, here and there, some peculiarly ingenious way of making a tower harmonize with a classical portico. Only in the case of one London church of the period do we find evidence of a mind of some calibre at work on the problem and that is C. R. Cockerell's Hanover Chapel, Regent Street (1823-5; demolished 1897). Here, for once, the interior contained a positive idea, and in the interpretation of an atrium covered by a windowed dome we are reminded of Hawksmore's mode of thought. Being on the west side of the street, the church had to be entered in its east wall, from vestibules behind the altar, and the portico was at this end. Instead of one central tower, Cockerell provided two, one on each side of the portico, forecasting the arrangement exploited by Hittorf in his Church of Saint-Vincent-de-Paul in Paris. Both churches probably borrowed the idea from a Grand Prix design of 1809; that Cockerell should do so would be natural, for his leanings towards Paris were already marked.

In London, the earlier Commissioners' churches were almost exclusively classical, and Greek. The first Gothic church to which they contributed was St Luke's, Chelsea, begun by parochial initiative in 1820. It was designed by James Savage (1779-1852), who also designed one of the better Greek churches.[19] Since Eastlake's time, St Luke's has always been regarded as a pioneer, though in fact it probably owes much of its character to a far better church, already mentioned (p. 317), St Mary's, Bathwick, Bath (Plate 184), built in 1814-20 by the local architect, John Pinch (1770-1827). St Luke's is badly proportioned externally, especially as regards the junction of nave and tower, but the interior, completely vaulted in Bath stone, is fairly advanced for its time. No London church before 1830 attempted to rival it, the best things of the time being young Charles Barry's cheap Gothic churches in Islington (1825 onwards) which Sir Gilbert Scott tolerantly described, many years later, as 'really respectable and well-intentioned'. Barry himself, in his later years, would not have said as much.

In the provinces, for reasons which it would not be easy to discover, the church-building movement after Waterloo took on, almost at once, a Gothic character. Pinch's church at Bath and Foster's at Liverpool were, no doubt, locally influential and they were followed by Thomas Rickman's important church of St George, Edgbaston, Birmingham (1819–22; Plate 185B), which was to win the respect of Victorians (in spite of its cast-iron tracery) for being relatively correct in detail. Barry built Gothic churches at Brighton and Manchester in 1822–3 and Francis Goodwin, the architect of Manchester's Greek town hall, built many Gothic churches, all much alike, in many parts of the country. His Holy Trinity, Bordesley (1823; Plate 185A), forms an instructive contrast to Rickman's Edgbaston church. Rickman and Goodwin, in fact, are the representative architects of the Gothic provincial church-building of the period, Goodwin tending to be 'incorrect' and harking back to the Wyatt school and Rickman 'correct' and tending forward to the orthodoxy of *The Ecclesiologist*. Both of them sometimes designed in Greek.

Of two hundred and fourteen churches built by the Commissioners, one hundred and seventy-four were Gothic, but most of these belong to the period after 1830 when the movement ran to cheapness and numbers, and all quality was lost.

Greek and Gothic Villas

The Greek and Gothic movements – or, rather, the Greek-Gothic movement, for it was but one movement with the same mainspring of style-conscious antiquarianism – penetrated into every department of architectural life. We have found it in country-houses as in colleges, in churches as in town halls, in clubs as in almshouses. It penetrated equally into the street-architecture of London and Edinburgh and the other great towns and into that new kind of urban expansion which characterized the post-Waterloo period and whose architectural type is the *villa*.

The use of the word villa to describe an English gentleman's house came in with the Palladians. It was not unnatural to apply it to houses which followed the Italian villa style as closely as Burlington's at Chiswick or Pembroke's at Marble Hill. At that level of usage the word remained for most of the eighteenth century. But after 1790 it began steadily to descend. It met the need for a word to describe the kind of house which, although not a full-size mansion set on a large estate, was yet a house of quality and distinction, inhabited by people of gentle blood or genteel pretensions. Such houses came to be built in greater numbers as a result of the increase in social importance of merchants and professional men and the ever-increasing facilities for investment in other things than land. Where, at the beginning of the century, a successful merchant or lawyer would hasten to exchange the gold at his bankers for real estate, he now invested in the Funds, reserving only a portion of his capital wherewith to buy or build a small but dignified little house, with just enough land to make a setting for it. Very naturally, such houses tended to be within easy distance of the great towns. Round London they flourished.

John Nash built several of these villas in the late nineties. There was one at Dulwich, called 'Casina', for a lawyer, another at Sundridge, near Bromley, for a banker, another at Kingston for a General. They were smallish houses, but very decorative and formal. By 1800, this kind of thing was in the forefront of architectural interest and shared with the Picturesque cottage the attentions of a considerable number of young architects who, in imitation of Soane, desired to place the fruits of their genius (whether executed or not) before the public. The introductions to some of their books (the more important of which were mentioned in Chapter 28) are at pains to make clear the differences between an important *cottage* and a modest *villa*. The differences are less significant than the fact that there was hardly any difference at all. Obviously, a new type of bourgeois house had come into existence which could affect either rusticity (the *cottage orné*) or urbanity (the villa), but which in size and accommodation and even in plan was often the same in one case as the other. Already by 1815, the word 'villa' was being used for this sort of house, whatever its architectural character.

After Waterloo, therefore, we have Grecian villas, Italian villas, and Gothic villas springing up in profusion, often almost next to each other along the highways leading out of the towns, each in its own fairly ample garden. Then, we have the device, introduced early in the century, of clapping two or three small houses together in such a way that they give, collectively, the appearance of one substantial villa. Nash, almost certainly, was at the bottom of this. Long before his Regent's Park days he had designed a village in which the principle of making three cottages look like one villa seems to have been employed.[20] In Regent's Park he used this device in a way which is not appreciated until one realizes that the houses numbered in York Terrace, for instance, comprise not only the two terraces proper (east and west) but several 'villas' which, in turn, are split into two or more separate houses. At the north-east corner of the Park, Nash amused himself with the lay-out of the Park Villages, east and west, where, according to his own statement, he was reverting to the practice introduced by him in his early essay. The houses in the Park Villages, dating from 1824 onwards, are almost all in pairs, each pair giving the external appearance of one villa. The 'villas' are in a quaint variety of styles – Gothic, Tudor, Italian, French, Greek; the latest of them are probably by James Pennethorne, but in general conception they represent the last adventure of John Nash in a field in which he was probably the earliest pioneer.

Disguising two small houses as one 'villa' comes to mean, of course, nothing but the building of semi-detached houses with some unifying feature on the exterior (a pediment, a gable, a false central window, or merely an inscribed panel) to distract the eye from the duality. The semi-detached pair of houses was not, in itself, a novelty. There is an example in Hampstead (22 and 24 Rosslyn Hill) dated 1702; there are plans in the Bodleian[21] of a lay-out for semi-detached pairs in Westminster, of 1719–20; and at Highgate is an even earlier example. But the semi-detached house only began its socially successful career after the introduction, probably by Nash, of the unified 'villa' exterior, giving an aesthetic and social consequence to two houses at the price, as it were, of one. Once this idea was established nothing could stop the word 'villa' descending one step lower and being applied to *each* semi-detached house in a pair.

So the designing of villas during the first three decades of the nineteenth century ranges from the elegant small country-house for a man of fortune down to picturesque pairs of very small houses on a suburban estate. Both these types, and the types between them, occupied architects, especially the younger architects, constantly throughout the period. One whose name is chiefly connected with villas was John Buonarotti Papworth (1775–1847) who, starting in the Chambers school, picked up his later ideas from Nash, Soane, and a wide variety of other sources and became one of the most versatile architects and decorative artists of the period. He contributed views and designs to Ackermann's *Repository of Arts* for nearly twenty years, some of the designs for houses appearing in 1818 as *Designs for Rural Residences*. In London he was much in request for shop-fronts and warehouses, in the country roundabout he built or remodelled many villas, mostly for tradesmen and professional men, and designed villas and terraces for suburban estates (Plate 186A). At Cheltenham he built the Montpellier Pump Room (1825–26; a toy Pantheon) and laid out the Montpellier Estate. Cheltenham reflects excellently the taste of Papworth and his age and while the Montpellier Pump Room was in progress another architect, John B. Forbes, was building the Pittville Pump Room, with its Greek exterior and Soanean interior, at the same time laying out the estate for villa development.

The Pittville estate is one of many such lay-outs associated with spas and seaside resorts and deriving their inspiration mainly from Regent's Park. Decimus Burton's classical villas at Calverley Park, Tunbridge Wells, and the same architect's Gothic villas at St Leonard's, Sussex, are in the same category, while in the suburbs of Bath are groups of villas, both Greek and Gothic, of considerable distinction by local architects. Edward Davis's coupled houses at Entry Hill (Plate 186B) are more than usually self-conscious specimens in the Gothic line, sited with studied irregularity. London, which had led the way in suburban villa-building, showed a terrible falling-off in quality during and after the Regency. A fine lay-out for St John's Wood, in the Bath manner, but consisting entirely of sites for semi-detached houses, dates from as early as 1794, and aerial views of it were exhibited by John Shaw at the Royal Academy in 1803 and 1804. But it was never carried out and the eventual builders of St John's Wood were speculative builders who provided their own designs, which were rarely remarkable. 'The speculative builder', wrote Papworth in 1818, 'has ... superseded the artist, for the architect is there [in London] rarely called upon, unless it be to remedy the errors, or supply some of the deficiencies, as well of art as of practical science.' Hence it is that Bath, Clifton, Cheltenham, Brighton, Worthing, and a dozen other provincial resorts provide better material for the study of the last Georgian phase of villa design than St John's Wood, Clapham, Brixton, or Islington. In London, in 1815, Thomas Cubitt had introduced the conception of a contracting firm equipped to supply all the building trades, with the trade of architect thrown in. Cubitt designs, whether for terraces or villas, are invariably of high quality; but the principle was one which too readily admitted aesthetic irresponsibility, and it was in London that the descent to chaos had already, in 1830, begun.

Architecture in 1830

The story of English architecture comes, in 1830, to a natural halting-place; scarcely, however, a place where one would wish to halt long, for at no moment, perhaps, in the whole period we have traversed was English architecture so feeble, so deficient in genius, so poor in promise. Why was this? The answer lies in the whole drift and texture of English society in the period after the French wars. It lies in the rapid expansion of the class to which, rather than to the state or to the elder aristocracy, architecture had come to look for patronage. Such an expansion had long been on the way, though its consequences were not estimated. Thus, Sir William Chambers, introducing the third edition of his *Treatise* in 1791, had observed that 'even men of inferior rank now aspire to taste in the fine arts' and he had seen in this the hope of a broadening pyramid of emulation which would sustain rather than debase artistic standards. Such optimism proved completely wrong, for the next generation of these 'men of inferior rank' was not only much more numerous but found standards of its own – standards remote from any which Sir William could have approved, standards confused and debilitated by the literary antiquarianism which, in Regency England, marched in step with the sentiment of patriotism on the one hand and the bourgeois adulation of ancestry on the other. A love of antiquarianism is much easier to acquire than an eye for classical proportion, and in the 1820s it was antiquarianism which carried the day.

To this lapse into a sentimental antiquarianism there were many contributory causes. A notable lack of genius among recruits to the profession of architecture, and a corresponding dilution by uneducated newcomers, was one of them. Another was the failure of George IV to be a discriminating as well as an extravagant patron of architecture or to impose, through others, any effective discipline of taste at his own Court. Yet another was the peculiar constitution of the Royal Academy which, far from being a national school of design, was simply a private society whose loyalties inclined to self-interest rather than to national prestige. All these failures, in turn, prove, on examination, to be characteristic and inevitable. The qualitative dilution of patronage rendered architecture an unattractive field for first-rate talents. Few able young men saw anything to inspire them in the villa-building and estate-surveying which constituted the early practices of Soane, S. P. Cockerell, or Hardwick; and even among the pupils of the royally patronized Nash there was no bigger man than Anthony Salvin. In George IV, whose taste surrendered to every kind of whimsical novelty, we find the bourgeois sentimentality of the age epitomized. While the academic defects of the Academy were a true reflexion of that reluctance to incorporate and centralize authority which is so marked a characteristic of English social institutions.

As the history of English architecture passes beyond the boundary set for this book, we notice only two men, C. R. Cockerell and Charles Barry, creatively prolonging the grand tradition of eighteenth-century classicism. Barry's career was soon anchored to that one gigantic work of his – the Houses of Parliament, where his classicism compromises so deftly with the antiquarianism which the age imposed. Cockerell's career was more varied. But it is significant that his achievement cannot be assessed in its English context, where he stands in utter isolation, but only in relation to the new school of classicism in France – the school of Hittorf, Duc, and Labrouste, which established Paris as the home of classicism for the remainder of the century.

From the bathos of 1830, English architecture was to ascend only very slowly and then by a devious route through antiquarianism to an impassioned medievalism, while in its humbler manifestations it not only did not ascend at all but slumped further into the chaos of incompetence, whither the illiterate patronage of the industrial age conducted it. At 1830, we are on the threshold of the period of professional association which, foreshadowed in the Architects' Club described earlier in this chapter, became in the 1830s the means by which the better element in the profession tried to retrieve architecture's lost reputation and to provide for it a status independent of the fluctuations and degradations of patronage by the individual. It was avowedly to counteract contemporary criticism of architecture and to restore its dignity that an Institute of British Architects was founded in 1834, with an Earl as its President and, in due course, a Royal Charter of Incorporation.

But as we leave our subject it is not to the founders of the Royal Institute of British Architects – industrious and worthy men – that we commit its future, but to some who, in 1830, were obscure lads, imprescient of their future: to the poor parson's son, George Gilbert Scott, plodding through a sordid articled pupilage, to that perfervid prodigy, Welby Pugin, turning his father's attic into a model theatre, and to a still lonelier child, devouring the Waverley Novels in a garden at Herne Hill, the garden of his father, the sherry merchant, Mr Ruskin.

NOTES TO CHAPTER 29

1. Thinking of it, however, as essentially primitive, 'ultra-Tuscan' in character. A Greek Doric order executed in this spirit at the same period is that applied by Thomas Johnson (d. 1800) to Warwick Gaol in 1779–82.

2. This applies particularly to the centre block, which was omitted. The design shows an entirely columnar building, the walls being recessed so that the columns are almost completely in the round.

3. There were, however, some notable exceptions. At Plymouth, John Foulston's St Catherine's church and the (destroyed) Cottonian Library were entirely in the Soane manner. Edward Davis of Bath was another who brought the Soane style to the west country. Soane's most useful contribution to the architecture of this period was probably the top-lit interior of the Bank Stock Office type; this was imitated far and wide.

4. Benjamin Dean Wyatt (1775?–1850) was a son and pupil of James Wyatt. Apart from the theatre, his chief works were Lancaster House, St James's, for the Duke of York (begun by Smirke, 1820; Wyatt took over in 1825), and the remodelling of Apsley House (1828) for the Duke of Wellington. Neither is of much importance in general design but both contain interiors in the Louis XV style, which Wyatt seems to have introduced, though whether he designed them himself is uncertain. He designed the Duke of York's column.

5. Completed in 1817, but the centre part failed and had to be demolished in 1825. Smirke rebuilt it as it now stands, with the Ionic order repeated in the centre, and Laing went into retirement. He published a book of his executed designs, including the Custom House, in 1818.

6. Joseph Kay (1775–1847) was a pupil of S. P. Cockerell and son-in-law of William Porden, whom he assisted with Eaton Hall. Street improvements at

Greenwich (Nelson Street, etc., after 1823) and the remarkable semicircular church of St Mary-in-the-Castle, Hastings, are his most important works.

7. Smirke's building was on the site of the present Junior United Services Club, at the corner of Charles II Street.

8. Now the United Universities Club, rebuilt in 1906.

9. The articulation of the jambs and mullions of windows as subordinate piers and *antae* probably derives from French practice. Dubut (1803) uses the device extensively and Dance probably followed Dubut in a design, in the Soane Museum, for a house for Lord Bristol. Dance's influence on Smirke has already been noted.

10. Covered in, 1854–7, to form the present domed reading room, for which Sydney Smirke was the architect.

11. Destroyed; but part of the façade was re-erected in the grounds of Heaton House, near Manchester.

12. The Theatre was destroyed before 1939 and replaced by a cinema; the rest of the buildings were gutted in 1941 and have since been razed.

13. It would be interesting to know if Hamilton could have been acquainted with contemporary Grand Prix designs, particularly that of Blouet, 1821, for a Palais de Justice.

14. As an architect, he assisted the Roman Catholic priest, John Milner, with the chapel he built at Winchester in 1792. It is a Gothic building and perhaps, as Sir Kenneth Clark says, 'the first chapel built in that style from what we may call Gothic Revival motives'. Milner was certainly the first to cultivate the idea that Gothic was essentially a Roman Catholic as opposed to a Protestant style, an idea fully developed in his *History of Winchester* of 1798. Architecturally, the Winchester Chapel is of no greater architectural importance than most of the domestic Gothic of the period.

15. It would be improper to leave this subject without mentioning, in passing, Sir Jeffry Wyatville's remodelling of Windsor Castle for George IV, from 1824 onwards. Wyatville was a nephew of James Wyatt and changed his patronymic as an 'honourable augmentation' when he began work at the Castle; he was knighted four years later. He designed the entrance hall and stables at Longleat (classic, with Soanic influence) and completed his uncle's work at Ashridge, but his architecture never rises to an important level.

16. This monument had already been adapted to a similar, though less ambitious, purpose by James Elmes in his church of St John, Chichester, 1812.

17. Inspired, no doubt, by Archer's church at Deptford (p. 188).

18. It was suggested in 1818 that a sum voted by Parliament for War Memorials should be devoted to church-building, but the churches were, in fact, built out of a separate grant. The term 'Waterloo Churches' is a popular designation with no historic sanction.

19. St James's, Spa Road, Bermondsey, 1827–9. It has a fine barrel-vaulted interior, supported on Ionic colonnades.

20. The whereabouts of this village is a mystery. Two exhibits in the Royal Academy of 1798 are probably related to it and they are referred to by Richard Elsam in his *Rural Architecture* of 1803.

21. Gough Maps 41 G. 4.

APPENDIX I

ARCHITECTURE IN SCOTLAND
1530–1707[1]

ARCHITECTURE in Scotland, nearly up to the Act of Union of 1707, is as distinct from English architecture as the latter is from, say, Danish or Spanish architecture. While there are broad analogies with England and occasional incursions of English influence, Scottish architecture is marked by a strong persistence of native types, a taste in ornament quite different from that of any English school, and a direct, though far from passive, relationship to the domestic architecture of the Loire school in France. For this independence the reasons are clear enough. Feudalism survived far longer in Scotland than in England. The central authority was weaker and the need for the defensible house remained. The Scottish Reformation came a generation later than the English; the Dissolution of the Monasteries was organized less systematically than under Henry VIII. Scotland, moreover, had few external cultural relationships. Although her political relationships during the sixteenth century were often of European importance, her geographical position minimized her capacity to share the culture of the Continent, while from England she was divided by long-standing political hatreds. Scotland, indeed, had fewer opportunities than any European country, except Ireland, for contacts with the main streams of artistic influence flowing from Italy, Germany, and France. The result was a somewhat delayed development and a vigorous tendency to convert old forms to new purposes, to make the utmost of such foreign ideas as did come to hand and sometimes to borrow from early Scottish architecture themes which seemed to fit the contemporary occasion.

In the broad ebb and flow of architectural history, Scotland does, to be sure, present a rough parallel to England. At 1530 (a less convenient starting-point in Scotland than in England) we find our interest directed at once to the building affairs of the Scottish Court. Soon afterwards we enter a somewhat barren stretch of about twenty years during which there is virtually no architectural initiative. Then, round about 1560, we notice, in Scotland as in England, the rapid formation of a new national school under the patronage of a newly risen class – no longer the old nobility, but a class of rich or well-to-do landowners in the country, and a prosperous merchant class in the towns. If we do not find, in Scotland, anything equivalent to the 'prodigy houses' of Elizabethan England, it is because the great Scottish families had neither the cultural horizon nor the convertible wealth of the English; and further, no doubt, because the grand incentive of the English builders was missing – for the Queen of Scots was by religion and upbringing almost a stranger in her own realm and could never, perhaps, even had her reign been prolonged, have been, as Elizabeth was, the inspiration of great feats of architecture. The greater Scottish houses and the lesser are therefore similar both in plan and style; the range of design is narrow.

In the seventeenth century, the analogy with England persists for a time, even after

James VI has become James I, taken his Court to London, and become the master of Inigo Jones. Collegiate and municipal buildings in the Scotland of his reign are comparable with those of England, and Scottish architecture remains full of promise till the Commonwealth. It was at the Restoration of 1660 that the first blows against the Scottish tradition in architecture were dealt. We saw in Chapter 16 how Sir William Bruce imposed the taste of Whitehall on Holyroodhouse. The Scottish School did not long survive this interference, and although, up to the end of the century, great houses were built whose design is in every respect Scottish, the surrender to English fashions was thereafter complete and it becomes necessary to treat Scottish architecture as a provincial extension of the English school.

Architecture at the Scottish Court

James V, declared competent to rule at the age of eleven, died at the age of thirty in 1542 and was succeeded by his infant daughter, Mary, whose effective rule did not begin till 1561 and then lasted but six years when another infant, the future James VI and I, succeeded; his effective rule began in 1583. Thus for the greater part of the century Scotland was governed by a succession of Regents, and there was no settled period of Court life during which the arts might have flourished under royal favour. Nevertheless, there was, as in England, a permanent official establishment for the conduct of the royal works. Corresponding to the English Surveyor of the King's Works there was a Master of Works, who was responsible for the maintenance, rebuilding, or extending of all the royal houses. In 1529 we hear of John Scrimgeour occupying this post, but in 1539 Sir James Hamilton of Finnart became 'maister of work principale'. He was executed for treason in 1540, and in 1543 Master John Hamilton, a cleric, was appointed. MacGibbon and Ross supply no further data until 1579 when we hear of the appointment of Sir Robert Drummond of Carnock, who was succeeded in 1583 by William Schaw (1550–1602). Schaw seems to have been both mason and courtier. From his tomb at Dunfermline we learn that 'he travelled in France and other kingdoms for improvement of his mind, wanted no liberal art or science, was skilled in architecture'. In 1589 he accompanied James VI to Denmark and returned with him and his Danish Queen Anne in the following year, acting as the Queen's Chamberlain. Of his architecture we know nothing except that he conducted works to the value of £1000 at Holyroodhouse in or before 1589–90 and also worked at Stirling and Dunfermline. In spite of his exceptional experience and learning, no marked influences in Scottish architecture between 1583 and 1602 can be associated with him.

Schaw was succeeded, on his death in 1602, by David Conyngham of Robertland, who accompanied his master to England in the following year and, as we saw in Chapter 3, made a brief appearance at Whitehall as Surveyor of Works, between William Spicer and Simon Basil. In 1607, a certain James Murray became Master of the Works for Scotland, but this office must have been suspended before the Restoration, when we find that its responsibilities had devolved on the King's Master Mason.

The Master Masons were, of course, of prime importance, especially when the Master of Works was merely a lay official. In the early part of the sixteenth century it is not clear whether one mason was distinguished above his fellows by elevation to this office, but from the appointment of William Wallace (d. 1631) in 1617 there is a clear succession of office-holders, and it looks as if the dignity of the office increased as that of Master of Works declined. Wallace was succeeded by John Mylne (d. 1657), who surrendered the office to his son of the same name who designed the Tron Church and other important buildings. He died in 1667 and was succeeded by his nephew, Robert Mylne, who, as we saw in Chapter 16, built Holyroodhouse from the designs of Sir William Bruce.

It is the royal masons who are of special importance at the opening of our history, which is to say, towards the end of the reign of James V. James IV seems already to have obtained masons from France and their work is seen in parts of the Palace at Stirling Castle, where there are Renaissance ornaments, and baluster-shafts supporting roughly executed classical figures. But it was left to James V to build in Scotland the first sub-stantial work of the Renaissance – the north courtyard front of Falkland Palace (Plate 187).

The building consists of a façade and very little more, since there is only the width of a corridor between it and the older structure behind. The façade is purely French, of the Loire school; it has buttresses modelled as classical columns[2] attached to piers, raised on pedestals, and surmounted by inverted consoles. In each of the five bays are two typically French portrait medallions. This sudden resort to French classicism in a Scotland still wholly Gothic in its arts, is readily explained. James V married Madeleine, daughter of François I, in 1537; on her death, in the following year, he chose another French bride in Mary of Guise, who long survived him. Both marriages took place in France, where the King must have spent a considerable time. He brought Mary home in 1539 and an inscrip-tion on the building dates its erection between that year and his death in 1542.

The curious thing about this sudden incursion of a purely French style into Scotland is that so little came of it, in spite of the fact that at least three French masons were given Court appointments (two for life) between 1535 and 1539. The only work closely related to Falkland is a set of corbels in Edinburgh Castle. Thirty years were to elapse before signs of Renaissance influence again appeared in Scottish architecture, and then it was of a much less direct and distinguished kind. The explanation lies, no doubt, in the fact that there was practically no royal building after James V's death and, indeed, very little of any consequence in the country as a whole. The pioneer enterprise at Falkland – earlier of its kind than anything in England – was passed by.

The Baronial Castles

The next important phase of Scottish architecture coincides in its beginnings with the arrival from France of Mary, Queen of Scots, in 1561. It has less to do with that event, however, than with those which had immediately preceded it – the crisis of the Protestant revolution and the consequent redistribution of monastic lands. The outcome of the civil war between the Catholic Regent (Mary of Guise) and the Congregation seemed to confirm the régime of Protestantism indefinitely, while across the border Elizabeth had lately ascended her throne with the declared intention of ruling a Protestant England as a

Protestant Queen. It is understandable that a general confidence somewhat like that which was beginning to be felt in Elizabeth's England, should be felt in Scotland too.

In building, this confidence manifested itself in the construction, throughout the country, of stone houses on the estates of the Barons, or lesser nobility; and these houses constitute the peculiar contribution of Scotland to the architecture of Britain. Within the decade 1560–70, an unmistakable national style emerged – the style which the nineteenth century christened, affectionately, 'Scotch Baronial'. It continued to develop, and held its ground for a hundred years, leaving its mark in every part of Scotland from Kirkwall to Kirkcudbright.

Of the indebtedness of the style to French masons from the Loire or Sarthe districts there can be no shadow of doubt,[3] and we have the satisfaction of knowing that life-appointments under the Crown were given to French masons in 1535 and 1557, while there were other appointments of Frenchmen 'during pleasure'. That the style originated among these masons, employed by the Crown, is at least highly probable. Its development, however, was not unrestricted. Conditions in Scotland were very different from those around Tours and Le Mans, and there was a traditional type of Scottish residence which could not at once be displaced. This was the 'peel' or 'fortalice', a fortified type of dwelling which had come into existence about the end of the thirteenth century and consisted of a single tower-like structure, somewhat resembling the donjon of a Norman castle. These tower-dwellings, which had been built throughout the fourteenth and fifteenth centuries and, more sparsely, in the sixteenth, were of the severest kind of architecture, designed as fire-resisting strongholds which could be held in the event of invasion or raids and in which the lord's household and much of his livestock could be protected. Usually of three storeys, they varied little in design and were crowned by a parapet, projecting on corbels, continued into circular bartizans at each corner. Occasionally, a lower building was attached to the tower, giving the plan the form of an L.

This was the only type of stone dwelling (other than the royal palaces and greater castles) known to the Barons of the mid-sixteenth century, and although obsolescent since the coming of artillery, it will have had merits of security and traditional prestige not to be lightly discarded. It was these towers, therefore, which formed the point of departure for the new style. One of the first innovations was the appearance of what MacGibbon and Ross call the Z-plan – a rectangular block, with towers (usually but not always circular) at diagonally opposite corners. An early surviving example, at Colliston, Angus, is dated 1553. This plan seems to be peculiar to Scotland, though the way in which it is handled, here and elsewhere, connects it with French influence. At Colliston there are two features unmistakably French. One is the gabled upper storey of one of the towers, with corbel-courses supporting the oversailing angles and dying into the round; this evidently derives from the practice, common in the Loire district,[4] but not found elsewhere, of bringing an *octagon* tower to a rectangular summit, with a similar use of corbelling. The other French feature is a stair-turret in the angles of this tower with the main block, not reaching the ground, but corbelled out at first-floor level. This, too, is characteristic of the Loire school. Both features constantly recur in Scottish buildings of the sixteenth century.

The gabled round-tower makes its most bizarre and dramatic appearance at Claypotts, near Dundee (Figures 43 and 44), dated 1569–88. Here again we have the Z-plan, with a high-gabled centre-block, two gabled round-towers, and two staircase turrets all within an area no more than sixty feet square, and presenting a picture truly sinister in its ingenious chaos. The Z-plan was used for castles more elaborate and ornate than Claypotts, and to these we shall come presently.

A different departure, in the Scottish architecture of the 1560s, is represented by Grangepans (Figure 45), about seventeen miles from Edinburgh. This house, built by a man later connected with James VI's Court, is a long, rectangular, gabled building, with a tower nearly in the middle of one side and the entrance in the base of the tower. In one angle formed by the tower is a stair-turret, corbelled out between first- and second-floor levels. Every feature here can be paralleled in

Figure 43. Claypotts

Figure 44. Claypotts

such a house as the Manoir de Courtangis, La Ferté-Bernard (Sarthe); and Grangepans is, evidently, a Scottish version of a French manor-house model.

The one striking difference between Grangepans and the Manoir de Courtangis is the absence in the former of the angle-turrets which adorn the sky-line of the latter, but we do not have to look far, at this date, to find these features being used in Scotland. Angle-turrets are to be found at Gardyne Castle, Angus, begun in 1568, the year before Grangepans. This is an early instance, and the whole of each turret, including its conical roof and tiny *lucarne*, is built of dressed stone, a wholly un-French practice and one immediately abandoned (except for a few rare cases) in Scotland. The typical Scottish angle-turret, like its French counterpart, has a slated roof.

The Z-plan at Colliston and Claypotts and the so-called T-plan at Grangepans are types

Figure 45. Grangepans

repeated constantly throughout Scotland. A third type is the L-plan. This seems to derive directly from the peel or fortalice, of which it is really an extended version. It achieves, however, a new architectural character when the wings are equalized, when the angle of the L is filled for part of its height by a stair-turret, and when the whole composition is tied together by a corbel-course. This we find at Balbegno, Kincardineshire, a house finished in 1569, very near the dates of our last two examples. Here, in the upper storey, is some sculpture of Renaissance character, including heads in roundels and a false window with a carved figure looking out across a balustrade – a fancy which recalls the Maison des Échevins at Bourges.

From these buildings of the 1560s which show the Scottish style somewhere near its first crystallization, we can proceed directly to the larger and more celebrated castles of the last part of the century. Of these, Castle Fraser, Aberdeenshire (Plate 188A), is an outstanding example, dated 1576. Its plan is of the Z type, with one round and one square tower, both with stair-turrets in the re-entrant angles. There are corner-turrets to the main block, also to the square tower and these, with the whole upper-works, are tied together by a continuous corbel-course which, rising or falling every few feet, pursues a zig-zag course round the whole building. In the centre of the north side two dormers, and, between them, a fine heraldic panel, break into the steep roof. This crowding of all architectural features near the roof-line is very characteristic of the Scottish castle and very different from the French manors from which its features individually derive.

Another castle on the Z-plan, but somewhat larger and, indeed, palatial in its intentions, is Drochil, Peeblesshire, built by the Regent Morton shortly before his execution in 1581. Morton also built a gateway at Edinburgh Castle (1574) and substantial additions at Aberdour Castle, and the character of the detail in all three buildings is much the same. As Morton will certainly have employed the royal masons, these buildings are an interesting test of the standard of taste among these artificers. There is nothing here approaching the elaboration or technical skill of the Falkland work of 1539–42. Obviously French in origin, the details are modified by the native Gothic with its heavy, but vigorous and not wholly inartistic feeling. There is far less understanding of the classical units than in Elizabethan work of the time, and pediments, in particular, tend to be thought of as equilateral triangular discs. Such disc-pediments were, of course, common in the France of François I, but in Scotland they persist right through the period of Flemish influence and far into the seventeenth century. S-shaped scrolls often cling to their sides, while the finial is frequently the Scottish thistle.

Scottish detail of the 1580s and 1590s, the period immediately before the coming of Flemish influence, is very curious. Not only do Gothic features persist, in a massy and diagrammatic form, but there is something like a revival of Romanesque and Early Gothic, perhaps because it seemed to have an affinity with the antique, about which so little information was available. Billet and cable enrichments are found in Regent Morton's buildings, mentioned above; at Irvine in Ayrshire is a house with a round-headed doorway, with dog-tooth ornament, which might, at first sight, be dated at c. 1200 but is actually close to 1580; while at Edzell, Angus, the wall of the pleasure-garden (c. 1600) has pilasters with dog-tooth caps and vesica-shaped relief panels most happily used to give an effect which is of the Renaissance, though the means are not.

The apparent lack of the books and engravings which circulated so freely in England must be responsible for such a curious feat of originality as the Marquis of Huntly's work at Huntly Castle, Aberdeenshire, restored in 1602–6 with the addition of a fine top-floor gallery with three oriels (formerly with spired roofs) and a richly carved 'frontispiece' and fireplaces. Here is the work of a mason desiring, so it seems, to be Elizabethan, but innocent of the barest elements of architectural book-learning and extemporizing such 'orders' and enrichments as his Gothic hand could devise.

To the ten years on either side of 1600 belong some of the most fantastic and memorable of Scottish buildings, only a few of which, however, can be mentioned here, for their stylistic components are all such as we have discussed. To 1597 belongs Newark Castle, amid the Clyde shipyards, where the L-shaped plan (cf. Balbegno, p. 329) is doubled, giving a symmetrical figure with a carefully balanced façade. Symmetry is also the key-note of Fyvie Castle, Aberdeenshire (Plate 188B), where, in the great four-tower front, the two middle towers are linked by an arch, perhaps in imitation of certain French fortresses in which such a feature had an important function.[5] The towers themselves are round, but corbelled out into the square near the springing of the arch, while their outer angles carry conical-roofed turrets. To this daring combination of familiar themes are added typical dormers and ornaments, so that Fyvie may well be considered the apotheosis of the style. In addition, there is a superb wheel staircase (dated 1603), which MacGibbon and Ross compare with the example at the Château de Chaumont. The builder of Fyvie was Sir Alexander Seton, 1st Earl of Dunfermline, who had been a student both in Rome and in France.

Glamis Castle, Angus, is another building to be reckoned among the high achievements of the Scottish style. Here, the L-plan is most dramatically developed to a height of five storeys, the top storey, balustraded, coming forward between the angle-turrets in each wing. This structure is dated 1606, the year in which Lord Glamis became Earl of Kinghorn; the lower out-buildings, which by no means decrease the whole effect, were added by his successor towards 1620. With Glamis can be compared the slightly later Craigievar Castle, completed by Sir William Forbes in 1626.

These later castles represent the consummation of the Scottish style. The ancient peel is never wholly lost sight of, but fortification has turned gradually into dramatization and features adopted for security and convenience have been developed, both singly and in combination, for effect. The interiors of these buildings are rarely remarkable. At ground level they are often vaulted and the hall occupies the whole of the main block above the vaults. Only rarely is the hall itself vaulted, but there are several cases (including Balbegno) where there is a vault of a pure Gothic kind, suggesting the retrospective tendency already mentioned in connexion with ornament.

French influence is so uniformly predominant in Scotland that where Italian or English influence is found, the effect is particularly striking. Italian influence is almost non-existent, apart from the curious case of Crichton Castle, where a block of building on the north side of the quadrangle is faced with stones dressed in pointed squares, somewhat like the Palazzo dei Diamanti at Ferrara and other north Italian examples. There is a round-arched loggia on the ground-floor and a straight staircase on the usual Italian plan, while the window openings are severely plain rectangles. The builder here was the 5th Earl of Bothwell, who was abroad, perhaps in Italy, before 1581 and whose properties were confiscated in 1592, which is the latest date for his part of Crichton Castle. This is one of the very few cases, either in Scotland or England, of a building with *prima facie* evidence of direct Italian provenance.

English influence is very rare before the Union of the Crowns in 1603 and by no means widespread for many years afterwards. Barnes Castle, Haddingtonshire, built by Sir John Seton, who died in 1594, is possibly the unique case of a Scottish house built on an Elizabethan plan with wings, 'extruded corners' for staircases, and a forecourt with pavilions; here, quite evidently, a 'platt' was obtained from an English surveyor and given to Scottish masons. Long galleries appear here and there, for instance at Earlshall, Fife, with decorative paintings, in 1607, and in 1613 at Pinkie House, Midlothian, built by the same Earl of Dunfermline who was responsible for the rebuilding of Fyvie. Earlshall is otherwise completely Scottish, but Pinkie has, besides the gallery, a wholly English bay-window of three tiers and some Elizabethan ceilings.

These incursions of England's 'new fashion' beyond the border are important only for their singularity. They had no repercussions and Scottish architecture continued, during the reigns of James VI, Charles I, and the Commonwealth, to develop in its own particular way; and when a distinct change of taste occurred, as it did in the second decade of the seventeenth century, it did not bring Scottish architecture any closer to that of the sister kingdom.

William Wallace and the Netherlandish Taste

This change may be dated fairly exactly to the year 1615. Over a doorway in Edinburgh Castle is a cartouche bearing this date, on a panel set in an accomplished specimen of Netherlandish strap-work. We know that William Wallace was paid for work at the Castle towards the end of the year and the cartouche is very probably his. In 1616–18, Wallace stands first in the list of masons at Edinburgh Castle and was paid, in addition, for making moulds for plasterers and carving window-boards. In 1617 he was appointed King's Master Mason.

We must not assume that William Wallace was necessarily the chief agent in the change in style which is seen in so many Scottish buildings after 1615, but he is certainly the representative figure, and the style issues from the official quarter where he was the senior artificer. It would be helpful if we knew something of his early training and whether, like Nicholas Stone, his opposite number in England, he had crossed the Channel. There is no real evidence of this in his work, and it would have been possible for him to acquire his knowledge of Netherlandish ornament by an apprenticeship in England.

In 1617 James VI and I visited Scotland and, finding part of Linlithgow Palace falling into ruin, ordered its reconstruction. The new block (dated 1619 and 1620) is probably Wallace's work. It has the typically Scottish feature of a central tower with a doorway in its base (cf. Grangepans, p. 329) and the windows have the old steep triangular pediments, though their ornamental infilling is Netherlandish. More important as an example of the new taste is Wintoun House, Haddingtonshire, apparently completed by William Wallace for George Seton, Earl of Wintoun, in 1620. Here is a very handsome fireplace with cartouche-work enclosed in a steep pediment. The chimney-stacks at Wintoun are so English as to support the supposition that Wallace had acquired much of his style south of the border.

Wallace's most famous and significant building was begun eight years later. Heriot's Hospital at Edinburgh (Plate 189A; Figure 46) was founded under the will of George Heriot (d. 1624) for the education of fatherless boys. The chief overseer was Dr Walter Balcanquall, Dean of Rochester and later of Durham. He visited Edinburgh in 1627, when he seems to have left a 'paterne' for the building, and this document may very well have determined the general lines of the plan – a hollow square with corner pavilions, and staircase turrets in the inner angles, the main entrance in the centre of one side, the chapel

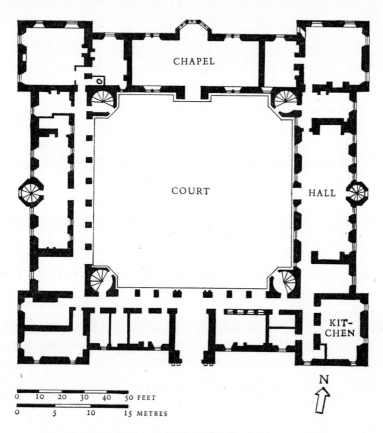

CHAPEL

COURT

HALL

KIT-CHEN

N

0 10 20 30 40 50 FEET

0 5 10 15 METRES

Figure 46. Heriot's Hospital

immediately opposite. This plan plainly derives from a house illustrated by Serlio in his seventh book.

But Wallace is rightly regarded as the real architect of the building and it is the chief exemplar of the style associated with his name. He began it in 1628 and, dying in 1631, left its completion to his assistant, William Aytoun. The works were stopped, for lack of ready money, in 1639, but continued in 1642 and by 1650 the Hospital was nearly finished. Cromwell used it as quarters for his sick and wounded, but in 1659 it was put to its intended use and finally, in 1693, Robert Mylne designed and built the cupola on top of the entrance tower.

Heriot's Hospital represents, in a most interesting way, the application of the Scottish castle style, inflected by Netherlandish and 'Jacobean' taste, to a regular Renaissance plan of the Ancy-le-Franc type – a strange concurrence of influences which has resulted in a building of rather questionable beauty but outstanding historic significance. The four corner towers (one would say 'pavilions' had they not battlements and turrets) are closely related, in their detail, to the castle tradition of Glamis, Fyvie, and Fraser. The chapel, on the other hand, with its central ogee-capped oriel, is a specimen of that belated Scottish Gothic which looks back not merely to the fifteenth but to the fourteenth century. The door and window details are coarse, elaborate 'Jacobean'; but the steep triangular window-heads preserve a Scottish idiosyncrasy going back to the time of James V. The most English features are the octagonal, concave-sided chimney-shafts.

William Wallace died in 1631, but his style (if, indeed, we are correct in supposing him the begetter) long survived him. Already in his lifetime it was caricatured at Caerlaverock (1620) and well imitated in 1628 at Moray House, Edinburgh, the town-house of a Countess of Home. The Master Mason employed here must surely have been the man responsible for the old College buildings in Glasgow, begun about 1632 and completed twenty-six years later, a noble group of buildings, destroyed to make room for a railway-station in 1870. The likeliest name for these works is that of John Mylne, who succeeded Wallace as King's Master Mason and died in 1657. Of his other successor, William Aytoun, we know that he designed Innes House, Morayshire (between 1640 and 1653), a country 'castle' on the L-plan, reconceived in the Wallace style.

But perhaps the most remarkable building emerging from the tradition initiated by Wallace is Drumlanrig Castle, Dumfriesshire (Plate 189B), built on a site commanding the Nith valley by William, 3rd Earl and 1st Duke of Queensberry, between 1675 and 1689. In most respects it is closely modelled on Heriot's Hospital, though the courtyard is oblong instead of square. There are the same turreted pavilion-towers, the same corner stair-turrets, and along one side of the courtyard is a loggia resembling that at Heriot's Hospital. Drumlanrig, however, was built at a time when the rule of classicism was too much in the ascendant to be ignored by an Earl even in Dumfriesshire. Consequently, the centre part of the entrance front is lowered one storey to allow of its conforming with the proportions of an applied Corinthian order. From the centre bay of this front projects a porch, the full height of the order, and surmounted by a cupola finishing in a huge ducal crown, after the manner of the royal crown over the entry at Holyroodhouse. Of the internal arrangements it need only be said that a great hall takes the place, opposite the entrance, occupied by the chapel at Heriot's Hospital. There is a long gallery; and one room is ceiled by a Gothic ribbed vault.[6]

Drumlanrig is the last great gesture of the Scottish castle style. Three years before it was begun, Sir William Bruce had been appointed Surveyor-General for Scotland; by the time it was finished he had rebuilt Holyroodhouse and, at his own Kinross, firmly planted the Inigo Jones tradition in Scotland. The classicism of Drumlanrig has not the slightest kinship with these. It is obstinately Scottish; even though the pediments over the windows take the correct mouldings of their kind, they are still tilted into those steep triangles which had marked the Scottish taste for a hundred years. But if Drumlanrig is the last of the Barons it is also, for Scotland, one of the first of the Senators and as such, presumably, Colen Campbell saw fit to include it in the first volume of *Vitruvius Britannicus*, where, among the works of Jones, of the school of Wren and of the young Palladians it makes a very strange appearance indeed.

Although the style associated with William Wallace and his successors is chiefly evidenced in public works and a few of the greater town- and country-houses, its effect was widespread throughout Scotland. It is found among the town-houses of Edinburgh (Moray House has already been mentioned) and at Stirling there is Argyll's Lodging, a courtyard house, somewhat on the French model, dated 1632. A number of Tolbooths or Town Halls of the seventeenth century survive in various Scottish towns, and the tower of the Glasgow Tolbooth may be classed as in the Wallace manner, in spite of the near-Gothic *corona* which forms its summit. But some of the most interesting examples of the style in its more ornamental aspect are the elaborate fountains, well-houses, and sundials built in the gardens of great houses. At Pinkie, there is an admirable well-house with attached Doric columns and, as a canopy, a Renaissance interpretation of the *corona*, that volatile feature which Scottish masons of the seventeenth century looked back to with such constant affection. The details suggest that it is from the same hand as Moray House and old Glasgow College.

Churches after the Reformation

The history of church-building in Scotland after the Reformation of 1560 makes a curious and instructive contrast to the English story. In England, church-building virtually ceased at the Dissolution, so that we have practically no concrete evidence of the effect of the religious revolution on architectural thought; indeed, we are tempted to think that, where churches were concerned, there was no architectural thought – and that may be very nearly true. In Scotland it is different. The later coming of the Reformation prolonged the working life of Gothic for a generation and, even after the events of 1560-1, church-building proceeded, especially in the counties around Edinburgh. In the first phase of the Reformation, the church-builder's ideal may be expressed in the phrase used in a grant of land to the burgh of Pittenweem, Fife, in 1588, to enable them to build a 'decent, honest, and comely Kirk'. The burgh's interpretation of this phrase has unfortunately been obscured by destructive restoration, except for the tower. This is of considerable interest, for one notices, in the first place, a determined elimination of Gothic detail, in spite of a generally Gothic silhouette; and, in the second place, the use of a conspicuously domestic type of stair-turret – the familiar round tower corbelled into a square at the top.

Also in Fife, and close in date to Pittenweem, is the church on Burntisland, well known for its four-column plan, of unexplained and very puzzling derivation. Built in 1592, the church is rigorously plain.

But such buildings as these do not mark the end of Gothic in Scotland and we see in churches, as we saw in houses, a deliberate revivalism, looking back to the traceried work and vaulting of several centuries earlier, to the spire of Glasgow Cathedral and the *coronas* of Aberdeen and Edinburgh. It is natural to associate such retrospection with the Episcopal element in Scottish religious life, just as we associate much English seventeenth-century Gothic with the outlook of the Laudian revival – but the connexion can only be valid up to a point and remains largely speculative. When the citizens of Glasgow built a new steeple to their Tron church in 1637 they gave it pointed windows, a brooch spire with traceried lucarnes and pinnacles, as festive as the spire of the Cathedral. Edinburgh also possessed a church with this *cognomen*, the whole of which was rebuilt before 1647. The Edinburgh Tron church, the work of John Mylne (son of Wallace's successor), was classical, in the manner of the Wester Kerk at Amsterdam. Clearly, in neither of these comparable cases did style carry any significance. The old Gothic and the modern style subsisted together, were to an extent interchangeable, and could sometimes even be united, as William Wallace himself showed when, at Heriot's Hospital, he gave wheel windows and traceried oriels to the chapel but entered it through a Corinthian frontispiece.

NOTES TO APPENDIX I

1. Throughout this Appendix I am greatly indebted to the two noble works on Scottish architecture by David MacGibbon and Thomas Ross (see Bibliography). Their eight fully illustrated volumes provide nearly all the material that a historian can want. They wrote, however, at a time when architectural history was almost limited to the collection of examples and a rough grouping into periods and types. They made no attempt to discover where or under what conditions the various characteristics of Scottish architecture appeared; nor, so far as I can make out, has any student of the subject done so since. The account of Scottish architecture given here is, therefore, a tentative sketch in which I have tried to select buildings significant for their date as well as their character and to suggest by this means a probable historic pattern for the period. It is a period worthy of far more attention from art-historians than it has hitherto received.

2. This theme occurs in England, thirty years later and in a flattened form, at Kirby Hall (p. 38).

3. The question of French influence on Scottish architecture has, from time to time, been the subject of controversy. R. W. Billings, writing in 1848, loosely attributed the whole character of the Scottish school to France. MacGibbon and Ross, forty years later, took a different view, pointing out that most of the features typical of Scottish houses were found not only in France but in the Low Countries and Germany. Obviously the subject is too complex for generalization, but it certainly seems that the main creative infusion was from France.

4. For instance, at the Château de Candé.

5. The Town Gate at La Ferté-Bernard, Sarthe, a town quoted above in another connexion, is a good example.

6. MacGibbon and Ross state that the name of the Master of the Works at Drumlanrig was Lukup. Failing any further information about this person, one would suspect that the King's Master Mason (at that time Robert Mylne) may have had a hand in the design, particularly having regard to the use of the crown theme over the entry, as at Holyroodhouse, which Mylne built.

ENGLISH ARCHITECTURE IN AMERICA

THE colonization by Englishmen of the eastern seaboard of North America, in the seventeenth century, had the effect of transplanting English architecture to the new world. In the earliest period of colonization, conditions scarcely permitted of buildings being conceived as anything but crude means of shelter and defence, but from the middle of the seventeenth century architectural standards were recognized and cultivated. They were, and long remained, English standards pure and simple. Up to the Revolution of 1775–83 it is not possible to discern any autonomous vitality in American architecture. A remote provincial outcrop of the English school, there was no local leadership of any consequence and a total dependence on contacts with England through the immigration of craftsmen and the circulation of books.

This state of affairs continued till the Revolution. Then a distinctly American point of view began to emerge, owing its expression, in the first instance, to the fact that one of the chief revolutionary leaders, Thomas Jefferson, was an amateur architect of distinction. Largely as a result of his influence America became immediately accessible to the Neo-classical ideas of the end of the eighteenth century, and this tendency continued far into the nineteenth. While this meant that French influence was, even apart from political considerations, eminently acceptable, most of the leading architects were Englishmen by origin, and American architecture up to 1830 can fairly be considered as a branch of the English school – a branch, however, with a rapidly gathering vitality of its own.

The Seventeenth Century: Williamsburg

The first substantial houses built by the colonists were timber-frame structures, frequently on the Tudor model. Such houses had become general in Massachusetts by 1640. All are gabled, boarded externally, with immense chimney-stacks. Brick-building was being practised well before the middle of the century, and in Virginia some remarkable examples survive. They include St Luke's Church, Isle of Wight County (1682), the unique instance of an English Gothic church in America, built entirely of brick, with crow-stepped eastern gable and brick tracery, close in style to English work of an earlier date in Essex. Of brick houses, easily the finest survivor is Bacon's Castle, Surrey County (c. 1670), a house purely Jacobean in plan, with shaped gables and massive end chimney-stacks. Though not large, it must have been among the distinguished houses of its time, and records for us the highest architectural level of the early days.

A landmark in the architectural history of the American colonies comes with the establishment, in 1699, of Williamsburg as the capital of Virginia and the erection of its public buildings. Laid out on a simple but handsome town-plan, the chief buildings were the Capitol, the Governor's House, and William and Mary College. Of these, only the last survives in any real sense and it has been greatly altered and restored. The Capitol, rebuilt during the eighteenth century, was finally burnt by the English in 1781, when the Governor's House was also destroyed. The administration having already moved to Richmond, Williamsburg declined to insignificance. In 1931–3, however, the town was re-created as a permanent historical exhibition, the Capitol and Governor's House, with many other houses, being reconstructed on documentary evidence.

The Williamsburg Capitol, built under an Act of 1699, is a two-storey building on an H-plan, with an open three-arch loggia on the ground-floor of the cross-stroke. The steep hipped roof is surmounted by a tall cupola. It could pass for an English provincial guildhall of twenty or thirty years earlier. Much the same could be said of the Governor's House, a fine double-pile brick mansion with a balustraded platform and cupola. This was begun in 1706 and completed, with its forecourt and service blocks, in 1720. The College of William and Mary (founded 1693) was designed as a quadrangular building and some-what recalls the Restoration blocks of chambers in the Temple.

Determined attempts have been made to link two of these buildings with the name of Wren. For the College there is, indeed, an attribution as early as 1724, which cannot be lightly dismissed; and it would be normal for the Surveyor to provide a plan for a royal collegiate foundation. One would not, however, expect the plan to be very strictly adhered to at such a distance from Scotland Yard. The case of the Governor's House is less promising, depending as it does on a doubtful inference that the plan was obtained in London. If it was obtained from Wren's office in 1705 it would almost certainly reflect the Hawksmorean manner which was then in the ascendant, whereas in fact the house is of a kind which an able mason or carpenter could have built at any time since 1680.

The Governor's House, however (Plate 190A), is of special importance to America, as the first great classical mansion of Virginia – a prototype for many of the houses built on the tobacco plantations as the eighteenth century advanced. Westover, for instance (Plate 190B), in Charles City County, is a house of this type, though with an important alteration in the plan, the entrance hall running through from front to back and containing the stairs at the far end – an arrangement common to most colonial mansions of the period. This house was built soon after 1729, on the site of an earlier house of the same owner, Col. William Byrd. He was one of those Virginians who spared no pains to surround himself with English culture and comfort. The garden iron-work (1711) at Westover would be remarkable even in England, whence it was imported, while mantelpieces and carved stone pots have the same origin. The stone door-case of the house is shown by Waterman to be a close imitation of a plate in Salmon's *Palladio Londinensis*, while the internal joinery and plaster-work are all as English as they can be.

The same intense loyalty to traditional English standards is observable in most American mansions, up to within a few years of the Revolution. Singularities of plan or silhouette are so rare as to make such a house as Stratford, in Westmorland County, Va (1725), outstanding. For its H-plan it may or may not be indebted to the Williamsburg Capitol, but even so, the arrangement in two storeys, of which the upper is the principal, and the grouping of chimneys into two hollow squares, each bound together by arches, make the building wholly exceptional. If it was conceived locally it is a remarkable performance.

One would more willingly believe that it was based on a design originating in the Royal Works circle in London. The chimney treatment especially recalls the Hawksmore-Vanbrugh school.

Builders and Architects

For nearly all the great American houses of the first half of the eighteenth century, the names of architects or builders are missing. The explanation is the obvious one that there were no architects in the modern sense and that, as in most English provincial work of the time, houses were designed by their leading craftsmen who proceeded on the basis of some existing model and the owner's verbal instructions. In so far as architectural scholarship was cultivated at all it was among gentlemen with a turn for that kind of thing. There

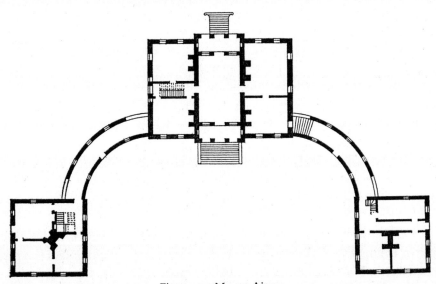

Figure 47. Mount Airey

is the exceptional case of the Scottish painter, John Smibert, who came over with Dean Berkeley and provided the somewhat naively learned design for Faneuil Hall, Boston, in 1742. Waterman has discovered a more regular early 'architect' in Richard Taliaferro (or Toliver, as it is pronounced), a member of a distinguished Virginian family who was certainly concerned in building enterprises and to whom a considerable group of houses, including Westover, may be attributable. More significant is the arrival on the scene of a certain John Ariss, who announces himself in an advertisement in the *Maryland Gazette* of 1751. This tells us that he was then 'lately from Great Britain' and would undertake 'Buildings of all Sorts and Dimensions... either of the Ancient or Modern Order of Gibbs' Architect'. Unfortunately, hardly any buildings can be firmly attributed to Ariss. His mention of Gibbs, however, and other evidence, has led Waterman to associate his name with some of the best Virginian houses of his time, in particular a group of three, all with quadrant connexions to service blocks. The finest of these, Mount Airy, Richmond County (Figure 47), derives one of its elevations very clearly from a plate in Gibbs's

Book of Architecture. It is an excellent house, built of sandstone, with lighter limestone dressings, in about 1755–8, a date by which it may be said that mature English Palladian-ism, with a Gibbsian flavour, had become established in the Colonies.

By the fifties, indeed, America possessed a Palladian master of considerable respect-ability in the person of Peter Harrison (1716–75). He was an Englishman, born in York, who had emigrated to Rhode Island in 1740 and settled in Newport, trading, with his brother Joseph, in wines, rum, molasses, and mahogany. As an architect, he must have been virtually self-taught. Hoppus's Palladio, and Langley's and Gibbs's books will have represented nearly the whole range of his knowledge. Like so many amateurs of the century, however, the very narrowness of his sources and their method-bound character helped to bring out his native capacity for design. His first work, built in 1749–58, was the Redwood Library in Newport, a timber building imitating rusticated stone, prefaced by a handsome tetrastyle Doric portico, with short wings carrying half-pediments, in the manner of a well-known design in Palladio. The rear elevation has three Venetian windows of the kind used by Burlington at Chiswick. The Palladian purity of the whole is most remarkable, anticipating Thomas Jefferson's approach to design by some twenty years.

Harrison's next work was the King's Chapel in Boston, and this brings us to the subject of Colonial churches in general. The seventeenth century had seen the erection of a number of severely plain meeting-houses, barn-like structures, with galleries and tall pulpits. At the beginning of the next century the influence of Wren's London churches came into play. Of this, Christ Church, Boston (1723), which reflects St James's, Picca-dilly, and (for the tower) St Lawrence Jewry, is an important example. It was imitated, almost at once, in Trinity Church, Newport, built in 1725–6 by a carpenter, Richard Munday. Here, however, the pier-system seems closer to St Andrew's, Holborn, though the tower is, again, of the St Lawrence type. An advance on these churches is represented by Christ Church, Philadelphia, designed by the amateur Dr John Kearsley and begun in 1727. It looks as if the influence of Gibbs had arrived in time to determine the character of the nave arcades here, as the piers consist of giant Doric columns, on pedestals, with an isolated entablature unit over each, as at St Martin's-in-the Fields. Christ Church was not finished till 1756 when the west steeple was completed, with ample evidence of reliance on Gibbs.

Harrison's King's Chapel (Plate 191A) was designed in 1749 and completed in 1758, except for the portico, added later. Inevitably, at this date, it pays tribute to Gibbs, but Harrison's quite uncommon sensibility is shown in his choice of coupled, instead of single, Corinthian columns for the piers, thus giving a show of logic to the use of an entablature under arches. From the entablature a cove, which the arches penetrate vault-wise, sweeps up to the flat ceiling, with an effect unparalleled in any English church of the time.

In 1759–63, Harrison built the Synagogue, or Temple Jeshuath Israel, in Newport, externally a plain box on the lines of Gibbs's St Peter, Vere Street, while inside, the cove ceiling is supported by superimposed Ionic and Corinthian columns recalling the White-hall Banqueting House. Inigo Jones was the inspiration, again, for Harrison's Brick

Market (1761–72) at Newport, based on the New Gallery of Somerset House. Finally, Christ Church, Cambridge, Mass. (1760–1), has a charming interior in which the beams from which the cove ceiling springs run across a series of Ionic entablature units. The effect, as Whiffen has pointed out, is rather close to that of St Martin's, Worcester (England), built by a local mason-architect a few years later. The similarity, which must be coincidental, only serves to illustrate how strictly comparable is the best Colonial work to that of provincial work in the mother country. Christ Church might as probably have occurred in Yorkshire as in Massachusetts.

In 1761, Harrison moved to New Haven, becoming in 1768 a Collector of Customs. He was never a professional architect in the strict sense. As a loyalist and a government official he suffered much persecution in his last years, which were also the last of the transplanted Palladianism of which he was the finest exponent.

Harrison stands unequalled for scholarship, precision, and taste in the America of his time. Only rarely does other Palladian work of the mid decades of the century approach his standard. In domestic buildings, one could name a few houses in Charleston, South Carolina, including the important Drayton Hall (c. 1740) and the later Miles Brewton House, the work (c. 1765) of Ezra Waite, a London craftsman. In Annapolis, Maryland, there are some competent houses of the forties. In New York, there is the remarkable Apthorp House (c. 1767) with its end pediments, Ionic pilaster-order, and deeply recessed porch. Also in New York is the Roger Morris (Jumel) House, built about 1765 for an English officer who married an American heiress. The giant portico of this house, if it really is coeval with the main structure, is the first of its kind in America and a surprisingly (if not impossibly) early instance of Adam attenuation crossing the Atlantic. New England has some good houses, but there is nothing near Harrison's standard before the time of McIntyre, whose chief works belong to the eighties and nineties.

Among public buildings – Harrison's own field – there is even less which can be compared with him. The Pennsylvania State House (Independence Hall) at Philadelphia (1729–34) represents the prevailing style for such buildings – a Palladianism totally lacking in scholarship and virtuous only by a combination of chance and instinct. Churches, as we have seen, relied wholly on the Wren-Gibbs tradition, and this held till long after the Revolution. All the churches of New York followed it, up to St John's of 1803–7, and in Providence, Rhode Island, the First Baptist Meeting House, built in 1775 by Joseph Brown, has a Gibbsian interior and a steeple closely following one of the alternatives for St Martin's-in-the- Fields given in Gibbs's book. It is wholly of timber, originally painted to imitate a variety of marbles: a fine work, indeed, but homely compared with Harrison's King's Chapel of twenty-five years earlier.

Thomas Jefferson

Harrison died in 1775, the year in which the Revolutionary war with Britain began. In the events which followed, there emerged into the political life of America a figure who was to prove of equal significance as legislator, economist, educationalist, and architect. This was Thomas Jefferson (1743–1826). Born in Virginia, the son of a surveyor, Jefferson inherited considerable property in Albemarle County. He was educated for the law at William and Mary College and it was in the philosophical circles of Williamsburg that he was first drawn to architectural studies. A man of exceptional intellectual range and vitality with an extraordinary love of precision, he was the first American to consider architecture objectively within the framework of contemporary thought. In a curious way, he placed architecture very much as early eighteenth-century Whig thinkers like Shaftesbury (see p. 197) had placed it. Like them, he considered the architecture of Antiquity as fundamental in character and embodying indisputable 'natural' principles. His whole outlook was strongly coloured by the Lockian tradition of thought: the Declaration of Independence, of which he was the principal author, shows this clearly enough. A free-thinker in religion, he sought fundamentals in Roman and Anglo-Saxon history and in 'natural law'. In architecture, the Roman temple and the Roman villa (as Palladio claimed to have restored it) were the rocks on which he believed that a valid

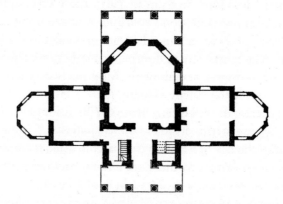

Figure 48. Monticello

theory of architecture could be built. Jefferson might be called a belated Palladian, but only in the sense that he rediscovered for himself the kernel of the English Palladian philosophy – emphatically not in the sense that he identified himself with English tradition, for that could not have been further from his intent. When he visited England in 1786 he found English architecture to be 'in the most wretched style I ever saw', praising only English gardening, Moor Park, and a Doric temple seen at Pains Hill. He found, as we shall see, far more to satisfy his judgement in the Neo-classicism of France – little realizing how much that movement owed to England in its origins.

We first meet Jefferson as an architect when, in 1769, at the age of twenty-six, he started to build himself a house on a high romantic site on his family estate. He later called it Monticello. His first designs are preserved and their sources have been carefully studied by Kimball. Jefferson started, apparently, from a design in Robert Morris's *Select Architecture*, consisting of a square mass with two rectangular extensions. This was gradually modified with reference to Gibbs and then to Leoni's *Palladio*, to which he first had access in 1770. The final design (Plate 191B; Figure 48) shows a centre with superimposed Doric and Ionic porticoes and short low wings, tied in to the centre by the continuation round them of the Doric entablature, above which is an attic. To the house itself was added a great forecourt in the Palladian manner with octagon pavilions at the corners and square pavilions to terminate the advancing wings.

Monticello in its first state[1] showed more real thought than any previous American building, possibly excepting those of Harrison. It was very definitely *thought*, rather than felt. It was as intellectual as Wren's early works and has somewhat the same gaucherie, the gaucherie of a conscious scholar's elegiacs.

With the war of 1775, Jefferson became absorbed in public life. He was elected Governor of Virginia in 1779 and five years later, at the conclusion of the war, was des-patched on a mission to Europe. He was abroad from 1784 to 1789, visiting Paris chiefly, but England in 1786, Southern France and North Italy in 1787, and Amsterdam and Strasbourg in 1788. He visited buildings and bought books. His enthusiasms can be epitomized in two admired buildings: first, the Maison Carrée at Nîmes, the perfect Roman temple; second, the Hôtel de Salm in Paris, the perfect application of Roman forms to a modern programme. Jefferson's conception of the architecture appropriate to a new Republic crystallized rapidly, and it was closer in loyalty to the Maison Carrée than to the Hôtel de Salm. The temple-form dominated. When, therefore, he was asked, in 1785, to send over from Europe a design for the Virginia State Capitol, it was as a great Roman temple that he immediately envisaged it.

The removal of the capital of Virginia from Williamsburg to Richmond and the general plan of the new town had already engaged Jefferson's attention. Now it was a question of determining the character of its chief architectural symbol. He believed that there was 'a favourable opportunity to introduce into the State an example of architecture, in the classic style of antiquity'. He secured the help of Clérisseau, that fount of so much Neo-classical inspiration, but, according to Kimball, nearly everything in the final design was Jefferson's. The design was sent to America and begun forthwith to be executed. The brick-work was up by Jefferson's return in 1789.

The Virginia Capitol (Plate 192A) was perhaps the first case in the world where it was attempted to give an administrative building the external character, undeviatingly, of a classical temple. It is a version, in Ionic, of the Maison Carrée, but with the order con-tinued round the flanks and rear in pilaster form (this modification was perhaps Samuel Dobie's, the architect in charge on the site). Externally, only the necessity for fenestration prevents the temple effect from being absolute. Internally, the pretence is abandoned, and the chief apartment is a room with a dome, invisible from outside. The conception is amateurish and illogical, but the note struck here by Jefferson was to echo through fifty or sixty years of later architecture in America. Nor was it remote from the spirit in which Napoleon, twenty years later, dictated the theme of the building afterwards to become the Madeleine.

In 1789 Jefferson became Secretary of State to the first President of the United States of America, George Washington, and within a year he was deeply immersed in the arrange-ments for the new Federal capital and its chief buildings. Before we come to these, how-ever, we must consider what was happening in other architectural fields.

The Post-Colonial Period

At the close of the Revolutionary war in 1783, the ablest architect of the old craftsman type was probably Samuel McIntyre (1757–1811) of Salem, Mass. A carver by trade, he mastered architectural draughtsmanship and was able, with the help of Batty Langley's books, to design Palladian mansions of good proportion and detail. A number of them survive in Salem. His Salem Court House (1785, demolished 1839), with superimposed orders and a cupola, was one of the most ambitious of its type. A good twenty years behind English standards at the outset of his career, McIntyre's later work shows the influence of the Adam revolution, and in his finest houses, which belong to the nineties, it is very marked. The influence, however, comes in a roundabout way, through the work of a more sophisticated and more travelled architect, Bulfinch of Boston.

Charles Bulfinch (1763–1844) came of a rich and cultivated Boston family, graduated at Harvard and toured Europe in 1785–7, meeting Jefferson in Paris. On his return he practised as an amateur, making designs for his friends and interesting himself in the new public buildings of Boston. In 1787 he submitted a design for a new State House and eventually in 1793–1800 built the structure which still stands, though greatly enlarged, on Beacon Hill. At the time, it was the most prominent public building in the United States and Bulfinch became an acknowledged leader. He built churches, a theatre, town-houses, and the ambitious Franklin Crescent. Financially involved in this latter project, he became bankrupt in 1796 and was obliged to retrieve his fortunes by practising professionally. From 1800, he laid out considerable areas of expanding Boston and was responsible for a long list of private and public buildings before, in 1817, he was called to Washington by President Monroe to supervise the Capitol. He was there till 1830 when he returned to Boston and retired.

Unlike Jefferson, Bulfinch sought no philosophic sanctions for his architecture and was content to form his taste on the best contemporary work of England. His Boston State House goes to Somerset House, London, for its main features, Sir William Chambers's centre pavilion in the river-front being enlarged and elaborated, with the dome inflated to a grand, dominating hemisphere. The grandeur is somewhat amateurish and there are technical flaws, but it is a courageous performance. Bulfinch's later work improved somewhat in technique. It was less the Adam brothers who inspired him than the post-Adam generation of Mylne and James Wyatt, whose style is often reflected in Bulfinch's Boston houses.

When Bulfinch was starting his Boston State House in 1793, the competent architects of America could still almost be numbered on the fingers of one hand. Apart from Bulfinch himself, and McIntyre in Salem, there were only the two McCombs, father and son, in New York, the lately arrived Dubliner, James Hoban, in Philadelphia, and a very few more – not a promising field in which to find a genius equipped to provide the new world's new capital with its major buildings. This task, however, was in the forefront of American architecture from 1790 when the site of the future city of Washington was selected and the Residence Act passed.

It was the Frenchman, Pierre Charles L'Enfant, a volunteer major in the American army, who surveyed the site and made the plan for the new Federal city – a courageous and magniloquent project taking its departure, in many important respects, from the plan of Versailles. To L'Enfant, who was an architect of some ability, as well as an engineer, might have been entrusted the design of the Capitol and other public buildings, but his enthusiasm got the better of him; he became unmanageable and, in 1792, was dismissed. Hence the public competition of 1792–3 which sharply divides two phases of American architecture – on the one hand, the phase in which the half-educated craftsman and the unpractised amateur ruled architecture between them, on the other, the phase in which the trained professional emerged and established an unassailable position.

The first suggestion for a competition for the Federal buildings came from Jefferson in 1791, probably as a result of his observations of French practice in such matters. Advertisements were drafted and approved in 1792 for two competitions – one for the President's House, the other for the Capitol. The President's House competition led directly to the execution of the winning design by the Irishman, James Hoban, a design competently based on Gibbs. The house (eventually to become the White House) was ready for occupation by 1800. The competition for the Capitol was the beginning of a far more complicated story.

Most of the designs for a Capitol received in the summer of 1792 were the work of local (Maryland) builders and carpenters, most of whom also competed for the President's House. Hoban did not compete for the Capitol, but there was a tolerably good Gibbsian design from McIntyre of Salem and a huge Villa Rotonda by the same Dobie who had supervised Jefferson's Richmond Capitol. But far above these, in technical competence, was a design submitted by a Frenchman, Stephen Hallet. Hallet had come to America some six years earlier in connexion with a project for an Academy on French lines in Virginia, and evidently had considerable architectural experience. His design was considered to be the nearest thing to what was required, though far from perfect; and instead of being immediately premiated he was invited to Georgetown (site of the future Washington) to study it further so that it might be 'improved into approbation'. Meanwhile, belatedly, a new candidate made his appearance. This was Dr William Thornton (1759–1828), an English physician from the West Indies who had been an American citizen since 1788 and had designed the Philadelphia Library Company's building in 1789. Thornton had made one design before the competition was announced and this had been approvingly noticed by Washington himself. In April 1793, having seen what Hallet was doing, he produced a new plan and this swept the board. Hallet was remunerated with a premium equal to Thornton's and was employed, injudiciously perhaps, to revise Thornton's design and supervise its execution.

The result was that the first portion of the new Capitol – the north wing, containing the Senate, was built to Thornton's design, persistently modified by Hallet, but decidedly English in character. Thornton also succeeded in imposing the general idea of a rotunda between two wings – an idea to which all his successors were bound. But the association between him and Hallet was not happy. Hallet was dismissed in 1794, and in the following year a new architect was brought in to supervise the work. This was George Hadfield (*c.* 1764–1826). Fresh from Italy and England, where he had been the Royal Academy Gold Medallist for 1784, Hadfield had strong Neo-classical ideas of his own, disliked everything that had been done, and wanted to prescribe a giant order. He was dismissed in 1798, but continued to practice in America, imprinting his taste on several public buildings and notably on the Arlington House near Washington, whose Paestum portico is one of the more spectacular gestures of the American Greek Revival.

The next phase in the history of the Capitol begins with the election of Jefferson as President, the creation by him of the office of Surveyor of the Public Buildings, and the immediate appointment to that office of the most considerable English architect to migrate to the new Republic – Benjamin Henry Latrobe (1764–1820). The completion of the Capitol forms only one incident, though the most imposing, in Latrobe's career, and it will be best to treat it as such.

Benjamin Latrobe

Latrobe was born in a Yorkshire village, where his father was Minister of a Moravian settlement. His mother came of a family with Pennsylvanian antecedents. He was sent to Germany for his education and returned, at the age of twenty-two, with considerable scholastic attainments, and an intense admiration for Frederick the Great. It was only then, apparently, that he turned to architecture, entering the office of S. P. Cockerell and, later (or possibly before), assisting the engineer, John Smeaton, with scouring works in the Fens. He then practised on his own, building a few country-houses.[2] But in 1793 he lost his young wife and in a prolonged period of illness and confusion, terminating in bankruptcy, determined to emigrate. With his good American connexions, his arrival in Virginia in 1796 was not unpropitious and before a year had passed he was being consulted on engineering projects and completing the exterior of the most significant classical building in America, Jefferson's Richmond Capitol.

In 1798–9 he built his first important building, the Bank of Philadelphia (Plate 192B), a milestone, as it turned out, in the history of architecture in America, since it derived not, as one would expect, from recent English precedent, but from the fresh, new American thought of Jefferson. It was a temple building – almost as strictly so as Jefferson's Capitol. It had hexastyle Ionic porticoes at the ends of a cella, and the cella had, at its centre, a square domed hall. Latrobe departed from Jefferson's rather amateurish purism in expressing this domed hall externally, but in detail he was no less classical, turning from Roman to Greek and utilizing (from memory) the order of the Erechtheum. Built all of marble, the building (destroyed during the Civil War) must have been singularly charming. Although Jeffersonian in idea, in handling it is closer to early Soane, the circular lantern over the dome suggesting that Latrobe had made the acquaintance of Soane's Bank Stock Office before he left England.

Latrobe's second building was the pumping station of the Philadelphia Waterworks, of which he was the engineer. This was a low rectangular Greek Doric structure from which emerged a cylindrical tower with a flat dome, which emitted smoke from an opening at its summit. Again, one is reminded of Soane – especially some of the more romantic designs in his *Sketches in Architecture* (1793), which Latrobe may well have seen.

By 1800, Latrobe's outstanding ability was fully recognized and he was busy building houses in Philadelphia and preparing large engineering projects for the Federal Government. Then, in 1803, came the Surveyorship, and the task of completing the Capitol. By this date, the north wing was finished and the south begun. Thornton was still the dominant architect. He had disposed of two uncomplaisant executives – Hallet and Hadfield – but in Latrobe he had to deal with a man of altogether different calibre. Latrobe did not take any more kindly to the Thornton design than his predecessors, but he was induced to accept the inevitable and to build a south wing, reproducing the north. He replanned it internally, however, on different and more imaginative lines. This south wing contained his first House of Representatives, a chamber terminating with circular ends and having twenty-four columns with Lysicratean caps. In the east basement, he built a Soane-like vestibule, in which an 'American order' with maize-leaf capitals was introduced. That was built in 1809. Three years later war with Britain broke out, resulting, in 1814, in the burning of the Capitol and the President's house. Latrobe was invited to take entire charge of the reconstruction, and from 1815 he not only rebuilt the Senate and House of Representatives on a new plan, as semicircular theatres, but designed the Senate Entrance, with its 'Tobacco order', the Senate Rotunda and the great Rotunda between the two wings. Inevitably Thornton criticized and obstructed; in 1817 Latrobe's position with the Commissioners became impossible and he resigned. Not, however, before he had proved himself a Neo-classical master of a higher order than most, if not all, of his generation in Britain.

During the period of his surveyorship, Latrobe was in constant request for all kinds of private and semi-public works – a theatre in Philadelphia, colleges, banks. In Baltimore, he was engaged, from 1804 onwards, in designing and building the Cathedral, preparing, in all, seven or eight designs, including one in Gothic. The church is remarkable as being wholly detached from the Wren-Gibbs tradition. The Paris Panthéon was perhaps in Latrobe's mind when he designed his first scheme in the form of a Latin cross; but the final version is, in essence, a compact aisled rectangle, comparable to Soane's Bank of England halls, with segmental arches and a low, central dome. It is essentially an English classical building, though wholly unlike any church built in England in the period.

From 1817 Latrobe assisted Jefferson with his curious and interesting scheme for the University of Virginia. It was to be a settlement consisting of pavilions, each containing a classroom and a professor's lodging, the pavilions being linked by colonnades in a formal plan, dominated by a great Pantheon. It was Jefferson's last important contribution to American architecture and one which had the effect of initiating the type of American classic house which was to flourish in the thirties and forties.

Much employed as a civil engineer, on canal and drainage schemes, Latrobe was, in 1812, associated with Fulton and others in a steam-boat project. This failed and with it his private fortune disappeared. In 1817 he was bankrupt for the second time, and although his fame and ability would soon have restored him to prosperity he died in 1820 of yellow fever while engaged at New Orleans on a water-supply for that city.

Latrobe left American architecture a wholly different thing from what he had found it on his arrival in 1796. As an artist, he had the imagination to see what was valuable in

Jefferson's approach and to appreciate the connexion between Neo-classic purism and the aspirations of a young republic. As a professional man he brought that all-round competence which characterized the best elements in the English tradition. The direction taken by American architecture after his death was almost entirely due to him. The two leading men of the 1820s were both his pupils. Robert Mills (1781–1855), the first native-born professional architect in America, built Congregational and Unitarian churches and many public buildings in a Greek Revival manner entirely derived from Latrobe, except in so far as it was refreshed by the influence of French Grand Prix designs. Of this latter influence, adumbrating a later phase of American classical architecture, his Washington Monument at Baltimore (1814) and the vast obelisk at Washington (1848–84) are evidence. The second Latrobe pupil was William Strickland (1788–1854). His Second Bank of the United States, Philadelphia (1818–24), follows, in general conception, Latrobe's earlier bank in the same city, though expressed externally as an uncompromised Parthenon. Strickland's chief work, the Tennessee State Capitol at Nashville (1845–59), still adheres to the same type of composition, though it has developed lateral as well as end porticoes and is surmounted by a tower based on the Choragic Monument of Lysicrates.

With Mills and Strickland, the story of American architecture as a province of the English school comes to an end. The real break had, indeed, occurred before their time. It occurred when Latrobe married English Neo-classicism to Jeffersonian Neo-classicism (itself, in a sense, a recapitulation of Burlington's Palladianism) in the Philadelphia Bank of 1798. From that moment, the classical revival in America took on a national form.

NOTES TO APPENDIX II

1. The house was remodelled by Jefferson from 1794 and was completed by him in its present form after 1800.

2. These include Hammerwood and Ashdown Park, both near E. Grinstead, Sussex. Both are advanced in style, with Greek details, taken from Leroy.

BIBLIOGRAPHY

Since James Ferguson's briskly judicial survey in his *History of the Modern Styles of Architecture*, first published in 1862, two general histories of English architecture from the sixteenth to the eighteenth centuries have appeared. Sir Reginald Blomfield's *History of Renaissance Architecture in England, 1500–1800*, was published in 1897. Essentially a literary and critical work, it was dominated by the idea of 'experiment ... mature expression ... decay', Wren being the mature man of the English Renaissance, Adam the decadent. The same feeling for a biological curve informs Sir Thomas Jackson's *Renaissance of Roman Architecture* (Vol. 2, England), which came out in 1921. Neither Blomfield nor Jackson were much concerned with historical method; to them, moreover, the Romantic and Neo-classic movements were merely the nameless aftermath of the Renaissance, the beginnings of an arid epoch of 'archaeology' and 'revivalism'. The present work owes nothing consciously either to Blomfield or Jackson; though since I cannot disclaim a sense of participation in the tradition of architectural writing in which they stand, there may be an unconscious debt which I would gladly acknowledge. A more manifest indebtedness, however, is to the authorities listed hereunder.

GENERAL WORKS

Architectural Publication Society, *Dictionary of Architecture* (edited by Wyatt Papworth). London, 1848–92.

> The biographical articles have been of capital importance to all subsequent writers, including the contributors to the *Dictionary of National Biography*. They have now, however, been largely superseded by the following work.

COLVIN, H. M. *Biographical Dictionary of English Architects, 1660–1840*. London, 1953.

Country Life, published weekly by Country Life Ltd.

> Articles on country-houses and other buildings, mostly by H. Avray Tipping, Christopher Hussey, or Arthur Oswald. Only a few individual articles are quoted below, although nearly every house mentioned in the text of this book has been dealt with in the series, which extends over some forty years. An index of the series is provided with every volume of *Country Life*. See also Tipping, H. A., below.

London County Council and London Survey Committee, *Survey of London*, Vols 1–23; in progress.

> A topographical and architectural work of the first importance, especially for the eighteenth and nineteenth centuries; but much ground has still to be covered.

PEVSNER, N. *The Buildings of England*. London, 1951 *et seq.*

> A valuable survey, by counties, in guide-book form. At the time of going to press, nine volumes have appeared.

Royal Commissions on Historical Monuments (England, Scotland, and Wales), *Reports and Inventories*.

> These fundamental official catalogues of British antiquities have been proceeding since 1910 and the following areas have been covered. *England:* Buckinghamshire, Dorset, Essex, Herefordshire, Hertfordshire, Huntingdonshire, London, Middlesex, City of Cambridge, City of Oxford. *Scotland:* Berwick, Sutherland, Caithness, Wigtown, Kirkcudbright, Dumfries, the Lothians, Outer Hebrides, Skye, etc. *Wales* has been entirely covered. In all but the most recent English volumes (Dorset, Cambridge) and the Welsh series, only monuments prior to 1714 are described.

TIPPING, H. A. *English Homes*. Periods 1–6 (1 or 2 vols each, 9 vols in all; further vols in preparation).

> The material in these books is largely derived from articles in *Country Life* (see above).

WILLIS, R. J., and CLARK, J. W. *Architectural History of the University of Cambridge*. 3 vols. Cambridge, 1886.

Wren Society (ed. A. T. Bolton). 20 vols. 1924–43.

> Relevant not only to Wren but to the whole architectural scene from 1660 to 1715.

CHAPTER I

CLAPHAM, A. W., and GODFREY, W. H. *Some Famous Buildings and their Story*. London, 1913.

> Chap. 1 on the Palace of Nonsuch.

HARVEY, J. *Tudor Architecture*. London, 1951.

HUSSEY, C., on King's College Chapel screen in *Country Life*. 22 May 1926.

KURZ, O. 'An Architectural Design for Henry VIII', *Burl. Mag.*, April 1943.

LAW, E. *History of Hampton Court Palace*. 3 vols. London, 1885–91.

O'NEIL, B. H. St. J. 'Stefan von Haschenperg ... and his Work', *Archaeologia*, XCI, 1945.

O'NEIL, B. H. St. J. *Walmer Castle* (M.o.W. Guide). London, 1949.

BIBLIOGRAPHY

CHAPTER 2

CLARK-MAXWELL, W. G. 'Sir William Sharington's Work at Lacock, Sudeley and Dudley', *Archaeological Journal*, LXX, 1913.

GARNER, T., and STRATTON, A. *The Domestic Architecture of England during the Tudor Period*. 2 vols. London, 1911.

HOPE, W. H. St. J. *Cowdray and Easebourne Priory*. London, 1919.

ROGERS, J. C. *The Manor and Houses of Gorhambury*. St Albans [1934].

SIMPSON, W. D. 'Dudley Castle: the Renaissance Buildings', *Archaeological Journal*, CI, 1944.

CHAPTER 3

BALDWYN-CHILDE, Mrs. 'The Building of Kyre Park, Worcestershire', *The Antiquary*, XXI, 1890.

CLAPHAM, A. W., and GODFREY, W. H. *Some Famous Buildings and their Story*. London, 1913.
Chap. 6 on Beaufort House, Chelsea.

GOTCH, J. A. *Architecture of the Renaissance in England*. London, 1894.

GOTCH, J. A. *Early Renaissance Architecture in England*. London, 1901; 2nd ed., 1914.

SHUTE, J. *The First and Chief Groundes of Architecture*.
Facsimile of the 1st ed. of 1563, with introduction by L. Weaver. London, 1912.

SUMMERSON, J. 'John Thorpe and the Thorpes of Kingscliffe', *Architectural Review*, November 1949.

CHAPTER 4

GOTCH, J. A. As for Chapter 3.

GOTCH, J. A. *The Buildings of Sir Thomas Tresham*. Northampton and London, 1883.

GOTCH, J. A. 'Wollaton and Hardwick Halls', *Archaeological Journal*, LVIII, No. 232.

HOPE, W. H. St. J. *Windsor Castle*. 2 vols. London, 1913.
Chap. 16 on work under Elizabeth.

HUSSEY, C. 'Longleat', *Country Life*. 8, 15, 22, and 29 April 1949.

London Survey Committee, Monograph 11, *Eastbury Manor House, Barking*. 1917.

PEVSNER, N. 'Double Profile' (a study of Wollaton), *Architectural Review*, March 1950.

STALLYBRASS, B. 'Bess of Hardwick's Buildings and Building Accounts', *Archaeologia*, LXIV (1912–1913).

TIPPING, H. A. *The Story of Montacute and its House*. London, 1933.

CHAPTER 5

BOLTON, A. T. *Chilham Castle*. London, 1912.

CLAPHAM, A. W., and GODFREY, W. H. *Some Famous Buildings and their Story*. London, 1913.
Chap. 12 on Northumberland House.

COPE, Sir W. H. *Bramshill; its History and Architecture*. 18–

GODFREY, W. H. 'Brambletye', *Sussex Archaeological Collections*, LXXII.

GOTCH, J. A. As for Chapters 3 and 4.

GOULDING, R. W. *Bolsover Castle*. 5th ed., 1928.

GREGORY, F. W. C. 'Bolsover Castle'. *Thoroton Soc.*, LI, 1947.

ILCHESTER, Earl of. *The Home of the Hollands*. London, 1937.

MARTIN, A. R. *Charlton House, Kent*. London, 1929.

O'NEIL, B. H. St. J. *Audley End, Essex* (M.O.W. Guide). London, 1950.

CHAPTER 6

FOR TOWN-HOUSES

FORREST, H. E. *The Old Houses of Shrewsbury*. Shrewsbury, 1911.

London County Council. *No. 17 Fleet Street*. 1906–7.

PALMER, C. J. *The History and Illustrations of a House ... in Yarmouth*. London, 1838.

PANTIN, W. A. 'The Development of Domestic Architecture in Oxford', *Antiquaries Journal*, XXVII, Nos 3, 4, p. 120.

FOR COUNTRY-HOUSES

AMBLER, L. *Old Halls and Manor Houses of Yorkshire*. London, 1913.

BADDELEY, W. St. C. *A Cotswold Manor* (Painswick). London and Gloucester, 1907.

DAVIE, W. G., and DAWBER, E. G. *Old Cottages and Farmhouses in Kent and Sussex*. London, 1900.

DAVIE, W. G., and DAWBER, E. G. *Old Cottages, Farm Houses, and other Stone Buildings in the Cotswold District*. London, 1905.

DAVIE, W. G., and GREEN, W. C. *Old Cottages and Farmhouses in Surrey*. London, 1908.

FORD, T. F. 'Some Buildings of the 17th Century in the Parish of Halifax', Thoresby Soc., *Miscellanea*, XXVIII.

FORREST, H. E. *The Old Houses of Wenlock*. 3rd ed., Shrewsbury, 1922.

GIBBS, J. A. *A Cotswold Village* (Bibury). London, 1899.

GODFREY, W. H. 'An Elizabethan Builder's Contract', *Sussex Archaeological Collections*, LXV.

GOTCH, J. A. 'The Renaissance in Leicestershire', *Leicestershire Architectural and Archaeological Soc.* 1905.

GOTCH, J. A. *The Old Halls and Manor Houses of Northants*. London, 1936.

GOTCH, J. A. *Squire's Homes and other Old Buildings of Northants*. London, 1939.

MESSENT, C. J. W. *The Old Cottages and Farmhouses of Norfolk*. Norwich, 1928.

OLIVER, B. *Old Homes and Village Buildings of East Anglia*. London, 1912.

PARKINSON, J., and OULD, E. A. *Old Cottages, Farm Houses etc. in Shropshire, Herefordshire and Cheshire*. London, 1904.

CHAPTER 7

GOTCH, J. A. *Inigo Jones*. London, 1928.

HERVEY, M. *Life of Lord Arundel*. London, 1921.

NICOLL, A. *Stuart Masques and the Renaissance Stage*. London, 1937.

SIMPSON, P., and BELL, C. F. 'Designs by Inigo Jones for Masques and Plays at Court', *Walpole Soc.*, XII, 1924.

SMITH, J. SUMNER. 'The Italian Sources of Inigo Jones's Style', *Burl. Mag.*, July 1952.

WITTKOWER, R. 'Puritanissimo Fiero', *Burl. Mag.*, XC, 1948.

CHAPTER 8

CHETTLE, G. H. *The Queen's House, Greenwich* (London Survey Monograph). 1937.

CHETTLE, G. H. 'Marlborough House Chapel', *Country Life*, 5 November 1938.

GOTCH, J. A. As for Chapter 7.

KEITH, W. G. 'The Queen's House, Greenwich', *R.I.B.A. Journal*, 3rd series, XLIV, 1937.

ROWE, C. London University Thesis, *The Theoretical Drawings of Inigo Jones, their Sources, and Scope*. 1947.

> Quoted in Whinney, M., 'Inigo Jones: A Revaluation', *R.I.B.A. Journal*, LIX, June 1952.

WHINNEY, M. 'John Webb's Drawings for Whitehall Palace', *Walpole Soc.*, XXXI, 1946.

WITTKOWER, R. 'Inigo Jones, Architect and Man of Letters', *R.I.B.A. Journal*, LX, Jan. 1953.

CHAPTER 9

BELCHER, J., and MACARTNEY, M. *Later Renaissance Architecture in England*. 2 vols. London, 1897–1901.

BRADFER-LAWRENCE, H. L. 'The Building of Raynham Hall', *Norfolk and Norwich Archaeological Soc.*, XXIII.

CHUTE, C. W. *A History of The Vyne*. Winchester, 1888.

GUNTHER, R. T. *The Architecture of Sir Roger Pratt ... from his Note-books*. Oxford, 1928.

KEITH, W. G. 'Inigo Jones as a Collector', *R.I.B.A. Journal*, 3rd series, XXXIII (1925–6).

TIPPING, H. A. 'Chevening', *Country Life*, 17 and 24 April and 1 May 1920.

WHINNEY, M. 'Some Church Designs by John Webb', *Warburg Institute Journal*, VI, 1943.

WILLIAMSON, H. R. 'Sir Balthazar Gerbier', *Four Stuart Portraits*. London, 1949.

CHAPTER 10

BELL, W. G. *A Short History of the ... Tylers and Bricklayers ... of London*. London, 1938.

COLVIN, H. 'The Architect of Thorpe Hall', *Country Life*, 6 June 1952.

ESDAILE, K. A. 'The Stantons of Holborn', *Archaeological Journal*, XXXV, 149.

GODFREY, W. H. *Swakeleys, Ickenham* (London Survey Committee, Monograph 13). 1933.

HAKEWILL, A. W. *Thorpe Hall*. London, 1852.

HAKEWILL, A. W. *Architecture of the 17th Century*. London [1853].

JUPP, E. B. *Historical Account of the Carpenters' Company*. London, 1848.

KNOOP, D., and JONES, G. P. *The London Mason in the 17th Century*. London, 1935.

NORMAN, P. *Cromwell House, Highgate* (London Survey Committee, Monograph 12). 1926.

SPIERS, W. L. 'The Note-book and Account-book of Nicholas Stone', *Walpole Soc.*, VII, 1919.

WEBB, G. F. 'The Architectural Antecedents of Sir Christopher Wren', *R.I.B.A. Journal*, XL, May 1933.

CHAPTER 11

FOR CHURCHES

ADDLESHAW, G. W. O., and ETCHELLS, F. *The Architectural Setting of Anglican Worship*. London, 1948.

JACKSON, T. G. *St Mary the Virgin, Oxford*. Oxford, 1897.

WHIFFEN, M. *Stuart and Georgian Churches outside London*. London, 1947–8.

FOR UNIVERSITY BUILDINGS

JACKSON, T. G. *Wadham College, Oxford*. Oxford, 1893.

WILLIS and CLARK. See under General Works.

FOR SCHOOLS

FISHER, G. W. *Annals of Shrewsbury School*. London, 1899.

RIVINGTON, S. *History of Tonbridge School*. London, 1910.

SNELL, F. J. *Blundell's*. London, 1928.

THORNTON, P. M. *Harrow School and its Surroundings*. London, 1885.

CHAPTER 12

ELMES, J. *Memoirs of Sir Christopher Wren*. London, 1823.

GUNTHER, R. T. *Early Science in Oxford*. 14 vols. Oxford, 1920–45.

Royal Institute of British Architects. *Sir Christopher Wren (Bicentenary Memorial Volume)*. London, 1923.

SUMMERSON, J. *Sir Christopher Wren*. London, 1953.

WEBB, G. *Wren*. London, 1937.

WEBB, G. 'Baroque Art', *Proc. of Brit. Acad.*, XXXIII, 1947.

WREN, C. *Parentalia*. 1750.
> The portion dealing with Sir Christopher Wren was republished in London, 1903, as *Life and Works of Sir Christopher Wren. From the Parentalia* (ed. E. J. Enthoven).

Wren Society, *passim*.

CHAPTER 13

BIRCH, G. H. *London Churches of the 17th and 18th Centuries*. London, 1896.

BRETT-JAMES, N. *The Growth of Stuart London*. London, 1935.

'City Companies, Halls of the.' Series of articles in the *Builder*, March 1916, etc.

COBB, G. *The Old Churches of London*. London, 1941–2. Introduction by G. Webb.

GODFREY, W. H. *The Church of St Bride, Fleet Street*. (London Survey Committee, Monograph 15.)

GODWIN, G. *The Churches of London*. 2 vols. London, 1838–9.

NIVEN, W. *London City Churches Destroyed since A.D. 1800*. London, 1887.

REDDAWAY, T. F. *The Rebuilding of London*. London, 1940.

SUMMERSON, J. 'Drawings for the London City Churches', *R.I.B.A. Journal*, LIX, February 1952.

Wren Society, *passim*.

FOR COMPARISON WITH NETHERLANDS BUILDINGS

OZINGA, M. D. *De Protestantsche Kerkenbouw in Nederland*. Amsterdam, 1929.

PLANTENGA, J. H. *L'Architecture religieuse du Brabant*. La Haye, 1926.

CHAPTER 14

The Building Accounts of St Paul's Cathedral have been printed by the Wren Society, Vols 13 to 16. The Society has also published most of the drawings known prior to 1951, as well as engravings, and some modern drawings and photographs. The drawings discovered in 1951, which will probably be published by the Society, were briefly dealt with by J. Summerson in *The Times*, 11 October 1951.

HAMILTON, S. B. 'The Place of Sir Christopher Wren in the History of Structural Engineering', *Newcomen Soc. Transactions*, XIV, 1933–4.

POOLE, R. *Edward Peirce, the Sculptor, Walpole Soc.* XI, 1922–3.

TIPPING, H. A. *Grinling Gibbons and the Woodwork of his Age*. London, 1914.

CHAPTER 15

DEAN, C. G. T. *The Royal Hospital, Chelsea*. London, 1950.

LAW, E. As for Chapter 1.

Wren Society, *passim*.

CHAPTER 16

ANDRADE, E. N. da C. 'Robert Hooke' (Wilkins Lecture), *Proceedings of the Royal Society*, A. CCI, 1950.

CARÖE, W. D. *Tom Tower*. Oxford, 1923.

CLOVIN, H. M. 'Roger North and Sir Christopher Wren', *Architectural Review*, October 1951.

GREEN, T. F. *Morden College, Blackheath*. London Survey Committee, Monograph 10, 1916.

HOOKE, R. *The Diary of Robert Hooke, 1672–1680*. Ed. H. W. Robinson and W. Adams.

HOPE, W. H. St. J. *Windsor Castle*. 2 vols. 1913.
Chap. 18 on work under the later Stuarts.

OZINGA, M. D. *Daniel Marot*. Amsterdam, 1938.

ROBINSON, H. W. 'Robert Hook, Surveyor and Architect', *Notes and Records of the Royal Society*, 1947.

SMALL, T., and WOODBRIDGE, C. *Houses of the Wren and Early Georgian Periods*. London, 1928.

WEBB, G. 'Henry Bell of King's Lynn' in *Burl. Mag.*, XLVII (1925, ii).

Wren Society, *passim*.

CHAPTER 17

COLVIN, H. 'The Bastards of Blandford', *Archaeological Journal*, CIV, 1948.

GOODHART-RENDEL, H. S. *Nicholas Hawksmoor*. London, 1924.

GREEN, D. *Blenheim Palace*. London, 1951.

HISCOCK, W. G. 'William Townesend, Mason and Architect of Oxford', *Architectural Review*, October 1945.

THOMPSON, Francis. *A History of Chatsworth*. London, 1949.

WEBB, G. *The Complete Works of Sir John Vanbrugh*. IV (the letters, ed. with introduction by G. W.), 1928.

WEBB, G. 'Letters and Drawings of Nicholas Hawksmoor', *Walpole Society*, XIX, 1931.

WHIFFEN, M. *Thomas Archer*. London, 1950.

WHISTLER, L. *Sir John Vanbrugh, Architect and Dramatist*. London, 1938.

WHISTLER, L. *The Imagination of Sir John Vanbrugh*. London, 1953.

CHAPTER 19

BIRCH, G. H. As for Chapter 13.

COLVIN, H. M. 'Fifty New Churches', *Architectural Review*, March 1950.

LANG, S., 'Cambridge and Oxford Reformed', *Architectural Review*, April 1948.

WALKER, B. *St Philip's Church, Birmingham, and its Groom-Porter Architect*. Birmingham, 1935.

WHIFFEN, M. As for Chapters 11 and 17.

CHAPTER 20

JOURDAIN, M. *The Work of William Kent*. London, 1948.

KIMBALL, F. 'Burlington Architectus', *R.I.B.A. Journal*, XXXIV, 15 October 1927.

KIMBALL, F. 'William Kent's Designs for the Houses of Parliament', *R.I.B.A. Journal*, XXXIX, 6 August and 10 September 1932.

WITTKOWER, R. 'Pseudo-Palladian Elements in English Neo-Classical Architecture', *Journal of the Warburg Inst.*, VI, 1943.

WITTKOWER, R. 'Lord Burlington and William Kent', *Archaeological Journal*, CII, 1945.

WITTKOWER, R. *The Earl of Burlington and William Kent*, York Georgian Society, Occasional Papers, No. 5, 1948.

WITTKOWER, R. 'Un libro di schizzi di Filippo Juvarra a Chatsworth', *Bollettino Soc. Piemontese d' Archeologia e di Belle Arti*, 1949.

CHAPTER 21

ESDAILE, K. A. *St Martin-in-the-Fields, New and Old*. London, 1944.

LANG, S. 'By Hawksmore out of Gibbs' (the Radcliffe Library), *Architectural Review*, April 1949.

MCMASTER, J. *St Martin-in-the-Fields*. London, 1916.

WHIFFEN, M. 'The Progeny of St Martin's-in-the Fields', *Architectural Review*, July 1946.

CHAPTER 22

CRAIG, M. *Dublin, 1660–1860*. London, 1952.

CURRAN, C. P. *The Rotunda Hospital* [Dublin]. Dublin, 1945.

CURRAN, C. P. 'The Architecture of the Bank of Ireland' in F. G. Hall, *The Bank of Ireland, 1783–1946*. Dublin and Oxford, 1949.

DENING, C. F. W. *The 18th Century Architecture of Bristol*. Bristol, 1923.

Georgian Society of Dublin, *Records of 18th Century Domestic Architecture and Decoration in Ireland*. 5 vols. Dublin, 1909–13.

GREEN, M. A. *The 18th Century Architecture of Bath.* Bath, 1904.

ISON, W. *The Georgian Buildings of Bath.* London, 1948.

ISON, W. *The Georgian Buildings of Bristol.* London, 1951.

PERKS, S. *History of the Mansion House.* London, 1922.

POWERSCOURT, Viscount. *A Description and History of Powerscourt.* 1903.

SADLER, T. U., and DICKINSON, P. L. *Georgian Mansions in Ireland.* Dublin, 1915.

STROUD, D. *Capability Brown.* London, 1950.

WEARING, S. J. *Georgian Norwich: its Builders.* Norwich, 1926.

CHAPTER 23

CRAIG, M. As for Chapter 22.

ISON, W. As for Chapter 22.

RASMUSSEN, S. E. *London: the Unique City.* London, 1937; 2nd ed., 1948.

RICHARDSON, A. E., and GILL, C. L. *London Houses from 1660 to 1820.* London, 1911.

SUMMERSON, J. *Georgian London.* London, 1945.

SUMMERSON, J. 'John Wood and the English Town-Planning Tradition', *Heavenly Mansions.* London, 1949.

CHAPTER 24

CHATWIN, P. 'The Rebuilding of St. Mary's, Warwick', *Birmingham Arch. Soc. Trans*, LXV, 1943–4.

CLARK, K. *The Gothic Revival.* London, 1928; 2nd ed., 1950.

COLVIN, H. M. 'Gothick Survival and Gothick Revival', *Architectural Review*, 1948, 91.

DICKINS, L., and STANTON, M. *An Eighteenth Century Correspondence* (letters to Sanderson Miller). London, 1910.

JOURDAIN, M. As for Chapter 20.

LEWIS, W. S., on Strawberry Hill in *Metropolitan Museum Studies.* v. New York, 1934–6.
> Some of the original drawings reproduced here are given, with notes on Mr Lewis's paper, in *Architectural Review*, December 1945.

WHIFFEN, M. As for Chapter 11.

CHAPTER 25

LAWRENCE, L., 'Stuart and Revett: their literary and architectural Careers', *Journal of the Warburg Inst.*, II, No. 2, 1938.

WITTKOWER, R., 'Piranesi's "Parere su l' architettura"', *Journal of the Warburg Inst.*, II, No. 2, 1938.

CHAPTER 26

BOLTON, A. T. *Robert and James Adam.* 2 vols. London, 1922.

HARDWICK, T. *Life of Sir William Chambers*, prefixed to J. Gwilt's edition of Chambers's *Treatise.* London, 1825.

LEES-MILNE, J. *The Age of Adam.* London, 1947.

MARTIENSSEN, H. M. *Sir William Chambers* (London University thesis, 1949).

SWARBRICK, J. *Robert Adam and his Brothers.* London, 1915.

CHAPTER 27

BOLTON, A. T. *The Works of Sir John Soane.* London, 1924.

BOLTON, A. T. *The Portrait of Sir John Soane.* London, 1927.

CURRAN, C. P. 'Cooley, Gandon and the Four Courts', *Journal of the Royal Soc. of Antiquaries of Ireland*, LXXIX, 20, 1949.

DALE, A. *James Wyatt, Architect.* London, 1936.

GANDON, J. (ed. Mulvany). *The Life of James Gandon.* Dublin, 1846.

HAUTECŒUR, L. 'L'Académie de Parme et ses concours', *Gazette des Beaux-Arts*, 4th Period, IV (1910).

LAPAUZE, H. *Histoire de l'Académie de France à Rome.* 2 vols. Paris, 1924.

LEWIS, Lesley. 'The Architects of the Chapel of Greenwich Hospital'. *Art Bulletin* (U.S.A.), XXXIV, 1947.

LOUKOMSKI, G. *Charles Cameron.* London, 1943.

MISSIRINI, M. *Memorie per servire alla storia della Romana Accademia di S. Luca.* Rome, 1823.

MYLNE, R. S. *The Master Masons to the Crown of Scotland.* Edinburgh, 1893.
> Chap. 13 on Robert Mylne.

PEVSNER, N., and LANG, S. 'Apollo or Baboon' (the Greek Doric order), *Architectural Review*, 1948, 271.

PRICE, J. E. *A Descriptive Account of the Guildhall.* London, 1886.

SANDBY, W. *Thomas and Paul Sandby.* London, 1902.

STEELE, H. R., and YERBURY, F. R. *The Old Bank of England.* London, 1930.

STROUD, D. *Henry Holland.* London, 1950.

SUMMERSON, J. *Sir John Soane.* London, 1952.

CHAPTER 28

HUSSEY, C. *The Picturesque.* London, 1924.

PEVSNER, N. 'Richard Payne Knight', *Art Bulletin* (U.S.A.), xxxi, No. 4, 1949.

ROBERTS, H. D. *A History of the Royal Pavilion, Brighton.* London, 1939.

SMITH, H. C. *Buckingham Palace.* London, 1931. With architectural section by C. Hussey.

SOANE, Sir J. *Lectures* (ed. A. T. Bolton). London, 1929.

SUMMERSON, J. As for Chapter 27.

SUMMERSON, J. *John Nash, Architect to George IV.* London, 1935.

SUMMERSON, J. 'The Vision of J. M. Gandy', *Heavenly Mansions.* London, 1949.

CHAPTER 29

BARRY, A. *The Life and Works of Sir C. Barry.* London, 1867.

BOLTON, A. T. As for Chapter 27.

DALE, A. *Fashionable Brighton, 1820–1860.* London, 1947.

DALE, A. *The History and Architecture of Brighton.* Brighton, 1950.

PAPWORTH, W. *John B. Papworth* (privately printed). London, 1879.

RICHARDSON, A. E. *Monumental Classic Architecture in Great Britain and Ireland.* London, 1914.

SUMMERSON, J. *Georgian London, John Nash,* and *Sir John Soane,* as above.

WALKLEY, G. *William Wilkins*; R.I.B.A. Silver Medal Essay, 1947, in R.I.B.A. Library.

WHIFFEN, M. *The Architecture of Sir Charles Barry in Manchester* (Royal Manchester Institution). Manchester, 1950.

APPENDIX I

MACGIBBON, D., and ROSS, T. *Castellated and Domestic Architecture of Scotland.* 5 vols. Edinburgh, 1887–92.

MACGIBBON, D., and ROSS, T. *The Ecclesiastical Architecture of Scotland.* 3 vols. Edinburgh, 1896–7.

MYLNE, R. S. *The Master Masons to the Crown of Scotland.* Edinburgh, 1893.

APPENDIX II

BRIDENBAUGH, C. *Peter Harrison, First American Architect.* Chapel Hill, U.S.A., 1949.

BRIGGS, M. S. *The Homes of the Pilgrim Fathers in England and America.* London, 1932.

GALLAGHER, H. M. P. *Robert Mills, Architect of the Washington Monument.* New York, 1935.

Georgian Period, The (a collection of papers). 2 vols. 1899 and 1901.

GILCHRIST, A. A. *William Strickland, Architect and Engineer.* Philadelphia, 1950.

HAMLIN, T. *Greek Revival Architecture in America.* London and New York, 1944.

HITCHCOCK, H. R. *Rhode Island Architecture.* Providence, U.S.A., 1939.

JOHNSTON, F. B., and WATERMAN, T. T. *The Early Architecture of North Carolina.* Chapel Hill, U.S.A., 1941 and 1947.

KELLY, J. F. *The Early Domestic Architecture of Connecticut.* New Haven, U.S.A., 1924.

KIMBALL, F. *Thomas Jefferson, Architect.* Boston, 1916.

KIMBALL, F. *Domestic Architecture of the American Colonies and of the Early Republic.* New York, 1922.

KIMBALL, F. 'Jefferson and the Public Buildings of Virginia', *Huntington Library Quarterly,* xii, 2 and 3, 1949.

KIMBALL, F. 'The Bank of Pennsylvania', *Architectural Record,* Aug. 1918.

KIMBALL, F. 'The Bank of the United States', *Architectural Record,* Dec. 1925.

MORRISON, H. *Early American Architecture.* New York, 1952.

WATERMAN, T. T., and BARROWS, J. A. *Domestic Colonial Architecture of Tidewater, Virginia.* New York and London, 1932.

WATERMAN, T. T. *The Mansions of Virginia.* Chapel Hill, U.S.A., 1946.

WATERMAN, T. T. *The Dwellings of Colonial America.* Chapel Hill, U.S.A., 1950.

(A) Chelsea Old Church. Capital, dated 1528, in the
Sir Thomas More Chapel

(B) Hampton Court Palace. The Hall, 1531–6 (Right: gatehouse by William Kent, 1732)

Hampton Court Palace. The Hall, 1531–6

King's College Chapel, Cambridge. The Screen, 1533–5 (*Copyright Country Life*)

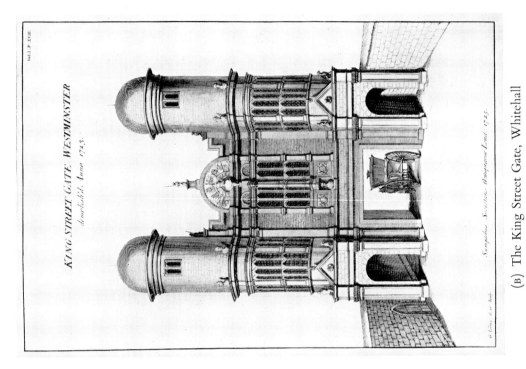

(B) The King Street Gate, Whitehall

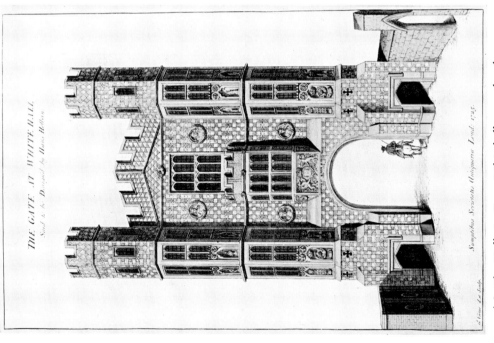

(A) The Holbein Gate, Whitehall, completed 1532

Nonsuch Palace, Surrey, begun 1538

(A) Nonsuch Palace. Design for the decoration of a Throne Room or Presence Chamber

(B) Nonsuch Palace. Fireplace, now at Reigate Priory

6

(A) Titchfield Place, Hants, 1537–40. Thomas Bartewe, mason

(B) Barrington Court, Somerset, probably before 1530

7

Hengrave Hall, Suffolk. The Gatehouse and Oriel, dated 1538.
(The house was begun about 1525)

(A) Lacock Abbey, Wilts. Sharington's Tower, between 1540 and 1549
(19th-century work on left)

(B) Lacock Abbey, Wilts. Carved Stone Table
in Sharington's Tower

9

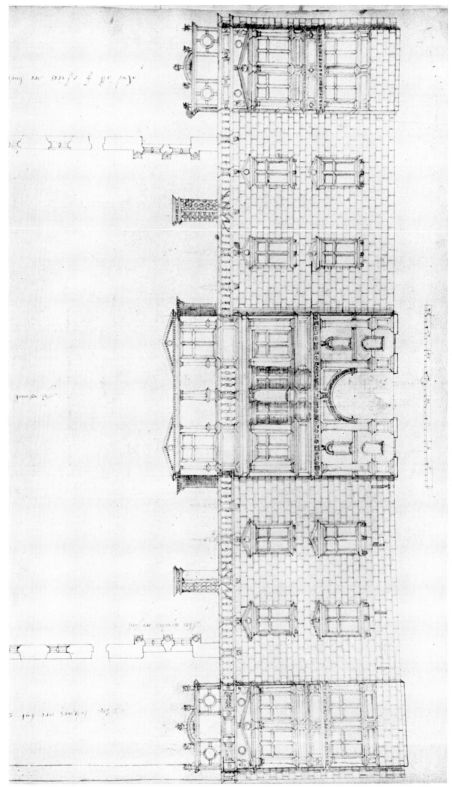

Somerset House, London, 1547–52 (demolished about 1777). John Thorpe's drawing of the Strand front

Somerset House, London. The Courtyard before 1777

11

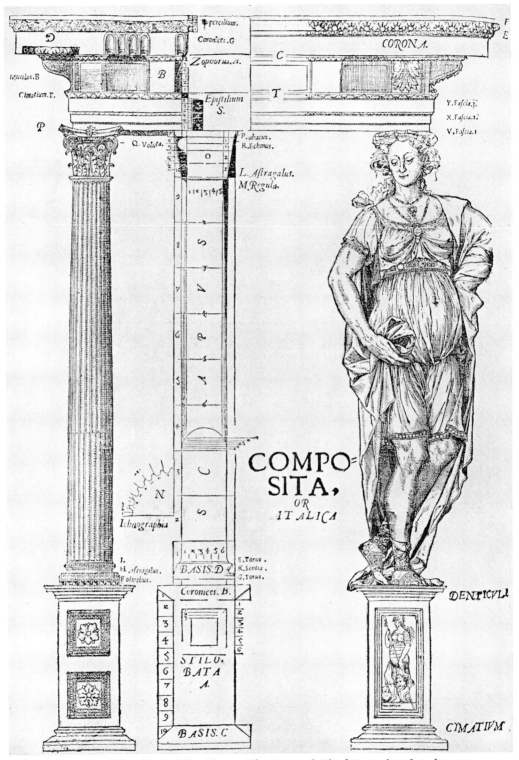

The Composite Order. From John Shute, *The First and Chief Groundes of Architecture*, 1563

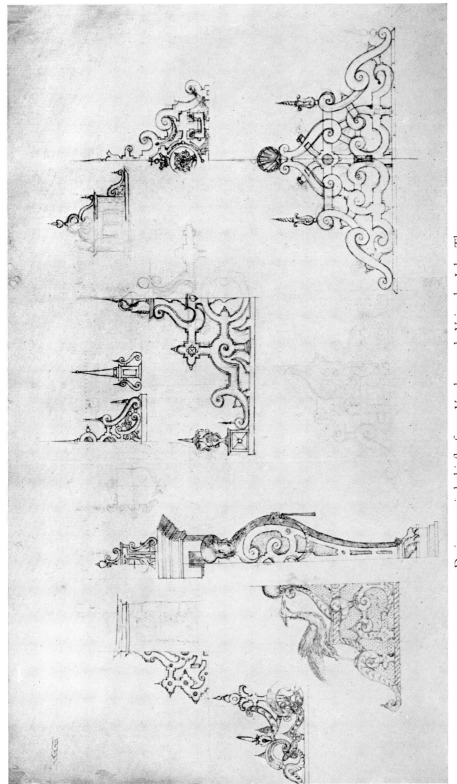

Designs copied chiefly from Vredeman de Vries, by John Thorpe

Longleat, Wilts., 1567–75, but incorporating work done from 1553 onwards

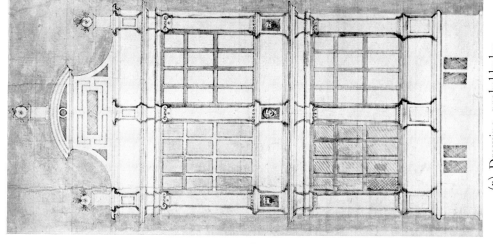

(B) Drawing, probably by Robert Smythson, related to Longleat

(A) Longleat, Wilts. Typical Bay

Wollaton Hall, Notts., by Robert Smythson, 1580–8

(A) Worksop Manor, Notts., before 1590. Probably by Robert Smythson

(B) Screen for Worksop Manor. Drawing by Robert Smythson

17

Hardwick Hall, Derbyshire, 1590–7. The Long Gallery

(A) Barlborough Hall, Derbyshire, dated 1583

(B) Hardwick Hall, Derbyshire, 1590–7. Probably by Robert Smythson

(B) Burghley House, Northants. The Courtyard, 1577–85

(A) Kirby Hall, Northants. The Porch, dated 1572

(A) Kirby Hall, Northants., 1570–5. The Courtyard, looking North

(B) Burghley House, Northants. Entrance Front, 1577 onwards

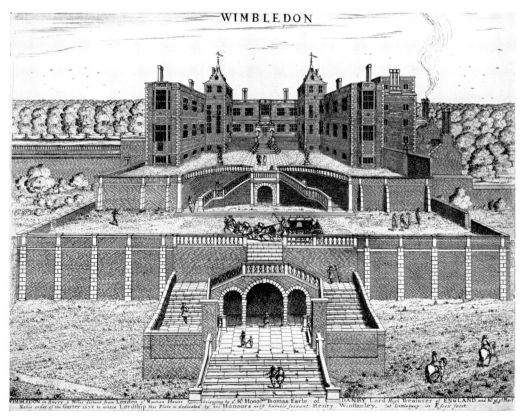

(A) Wimbledon House, Surrey, begun 1588

(B) Montacute House, Somerset, finished *c.* 1599

22

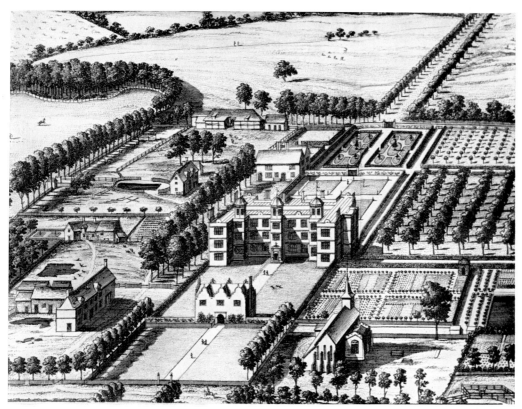

(A) Doddington Hall, Lincs., c. 1595

(B) Condover Hall, Salop, 1598. Walter Hancock, mason

23

(A) Lyveden New Bield, Northants., begun 1594

(B) Plan for a house, based on the initials I T. By John Thorpe

Audley End, Essex. By Bernard Johnson, 1603–16

Bramshill, Hants, 1605–12

Charlton House, Greenwich, 1607

27

(A) Hatfield House, Herts. South Front, dated 1611

(B) Hatfield House, Herts. Entrance Front

Hatfield House, Herts. The Staircase

(A) Holland House, Kensington, *c.* 1606–7

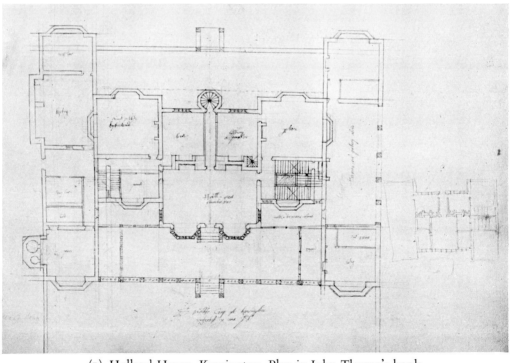

(B) Holland House, Kensington. Plan in John Thorpe's book

Bolsover Castle, Derbyshire, 1612 onwards

31

(A) Sherar's Mansion, Shrewsbury, before 1573

(B) Stanley Palace, Chester, dated 1591

Sir Paul Pindar's House, formerly in Bishopsgate; probably *c.* 1624.
Now in the Victoria and Albert Museum

'My Lady Cooke's House', Holborn, drawn by John Smythson, 1619

34

(A) Middle House, Mayfield, Sussex, dated 1575

(B) East Riddlesden Hall, Yorks., c. 1640

(A) Eastbury Manor House, Essex, 1572–3 (*Copyright Country Life*)

(B) Yeoman's House, Broughton, Northants.

36

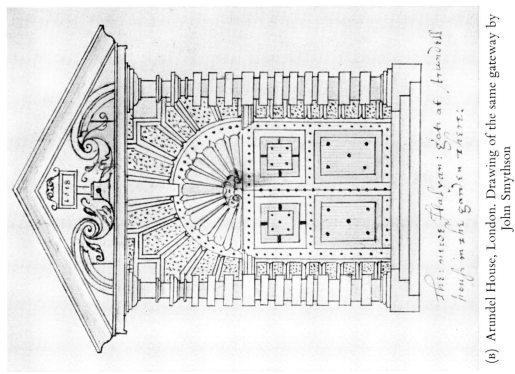

(B) Arundel House, London. Drawing of the same gateway by
John Smythson

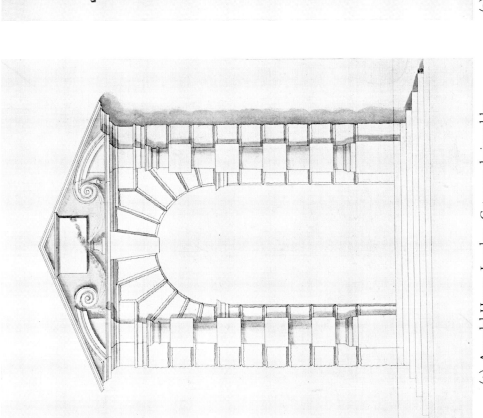

(A) Arundel House, London. Gateway designed by
Inigo Jones, *c.* 1618

Inigo Jones. Design for *Oberon*, a masque produced in 1611

(A) Inigo Jones. The Queen's House, Greenwich, 1616–35. The South Front

(B) Inigo Jones. The Queen's House, Greenwich, 1616–35. The North Front

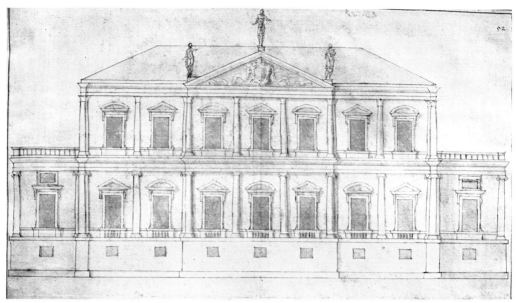

(A) Inigo Jones. Preliminary sketch for the Banqueting House, Whitehall

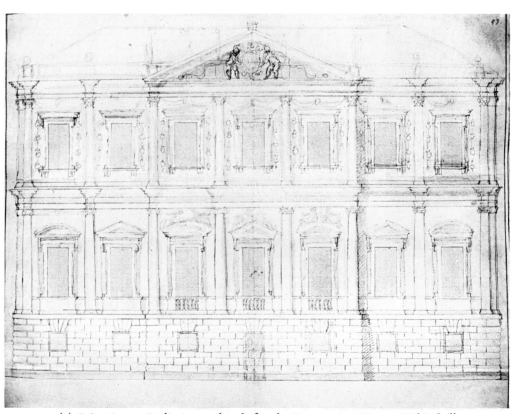

(B) Inigo Jones. Preliminary sketch for the Banqueting House, Whitehall

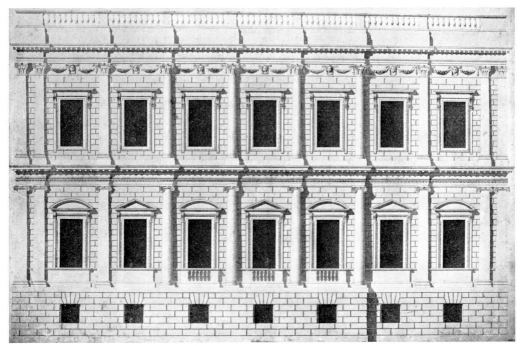

(A) Inigo Jones. The Banqueting House, as executed, 1619–22

(B) Inigo Jones. The Banqueting House, Whitehall, 1619–22

(A) Inigo Jones. Capital of the upper order of the
Banqueting House, now in the Soane Museum, London

(B) Inigo Jones. The Queen's Chapel, St James's Palace
(now Marlborough House Chapel), 1623–7

Inigo Jones. The Queen's Chapel, St James's Palace
(now Marlborough House Chapel), 1623–7

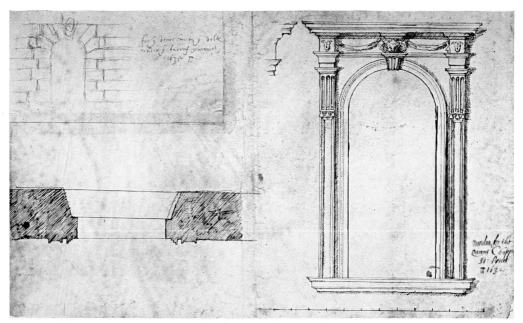

(A) Inigo Jones. Drawing for the Queen's Chapel, Somerset House, 1630–5

(B) Inigo Jones. Screen in the Chapel, Somerset House, 1630–5

Inigo Jones. West front of old St Paul's Cathedral, begun 1633 (burnt 1666)

45

(A) Inigo Jones and Isaac de Caux. Covent Garden Piazza, begun 1630

(B) Chevening, Kent

46

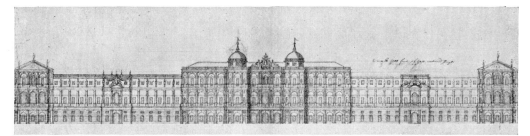

(A) Inigo Jones. Design for Palace of Whitehall, *c.* 1638. River Front

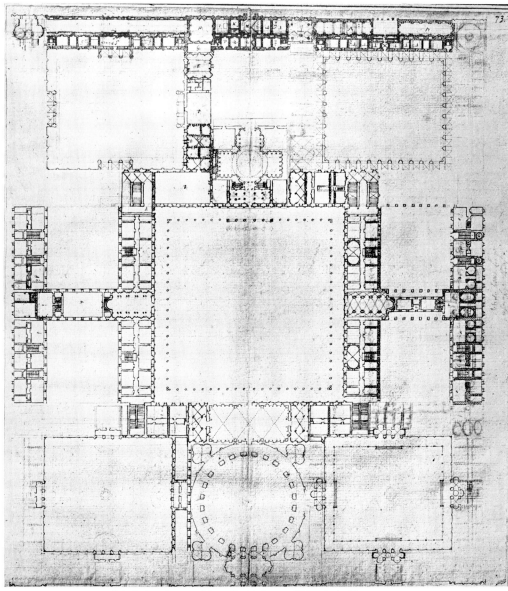

(B) Inigo Jones. Plan for Palace of Whitehall, *c.* 1638

47

(A) Inigo Jones. Wilton House, Wilts., after 1647

(B) Castle Ashby, Northants., showing the centre block of *c.* 1635

Inigo Jones. Wilton House. The Double Cube Room, *c.* 1649 (*Copyright Country Life*)

(A) Balthazar Gerbier. The York Water Gate, Victoria Embankment Gardens, 1626–7

(B) Balthazar Gerbier. Design for gateway at Hampstead Marshall, Berks., c. 1660

(A) Roger Pratt. Coleshill, Warwicks., *c.*1650 onwards (burnt down 1952) (*Copyright Country Life*)

(B) Roger Pratt. Coleshill, Warwicks. The staircase hall (*Copyright Country Life*)

Roger Pratt. Clarendon House, Piccadilly, 1664–7 (demolished 1683)

Belton House, Lincs. William Stanton, mason, *c.* 1689

(A) Leathersellers' Hall, London, 1623 and later

(B) The Dutch House, Kew Gardens, 1631

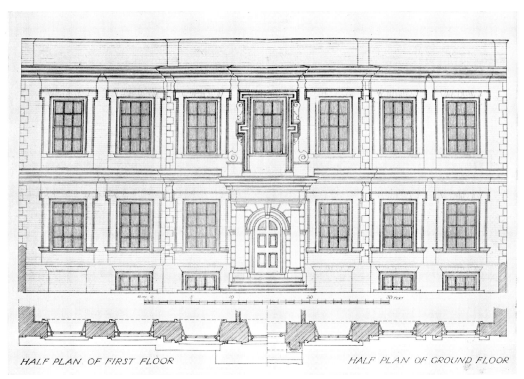

(A) Cromwell House, Highgate, 1637–8

(B) Raynham, Norfolk, c. 1635

55

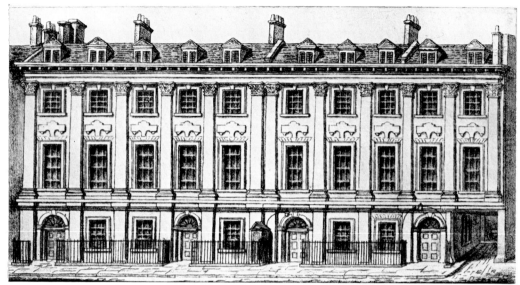

(A) Houses in Great Queen Street, London, 1637 or later

(B) Lindsey House, Lincoln's Inn Fields, 1640

Lees Court, Kent, begun *c.* 1640 (*Copyright Country Life*)

(A) Thorpe Hall, Northants., 1653–6

(B) Thorpe Hall, Northants. Interior detail

(A) Nottingham Castle, 1674–9. Samuel Marsh, mason

(B) The Citadel Gateway, Plymouth, dated 1670.
Probably by Sir Bernard de Gomme

(B) The Font Cover, Durham Cathedral

(A) St John's Church, Leeds, 1632–3

(B) Gonville and Caius College, Cambridge.
The Gate of Honour (restored), 1572–3

(A) Gonville and Caius College, Cambridge.
The Gate of Virtue; after 1565

61

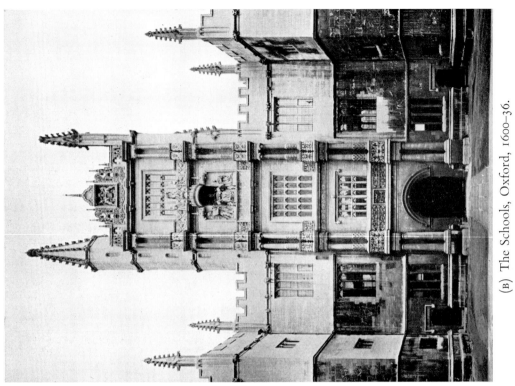

(B) The Schools, Oxford, 1600–36.

(A) St Mary the Virgin, Oxford. South Porch, 1637

St John's College, Oxford. Canterbury Quadrangle, 1632–6

(A) Burton Latimer School, Northants., dated 1622

(B) Shrewsbury School, 1627–30

64

Abbot's Hospital, Guildford, begun 1619 (*Judges*)

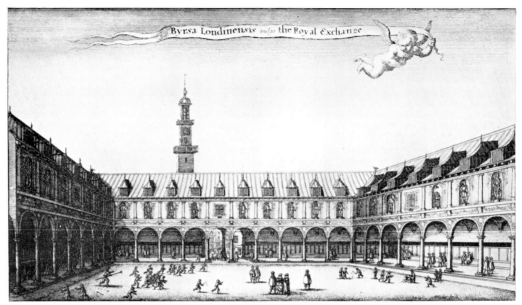

(A) The Royal Exchange, 1566–71 (burnt 1666)

(B) Middle Temple Hall, London, 1562–70

Hugh May. Eltham Lodge, Kent, c. 1664

67

(A) The New Gallery, Somerset House, London, 1661–2 (demolished c. 1776).
The design attributed to Inigo Jones

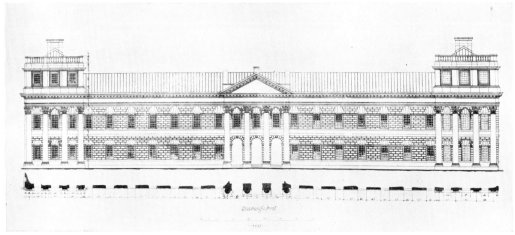

(B) John Webb. The King Charles Building, Greenwich Hospital, 1665

(A) Sir Christopher Wren. The Sheldonian Theatre, Oxford, 1662–3. From the South

(B) Sir Christopher Wren. The Sheldonian Theatre, Oxford, 1662–3. From the North

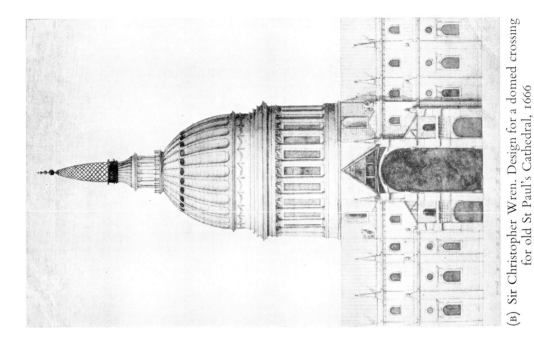

(B) Sir Christopher Wren. Design for a domed crossing for old St Paul's Cathedral, 1666

(A) Sir Christopher Wren. Pembroke College Chapel, Cambridge, 1663

(A) The Royal Exchange, as rebuilt after the fire by Edward Jerman
and completed 1671 (burnt down 1838)

(B) The Custom House, London, as rebuilt after the fire by Sir Christopher Wren,
1669 (burnt down 1718)

(A) Brewers' Hall, London, screen and panelling, *c.* 1670 (destroyed by bombing, 1941)

(B) Entrance to Haberdashers' Hall, London,
as rebuilt after the fire by Edward Jerman
(burnt 1864)

(A) Sir Christopher Wren. St Mary-le-Bow, Cheapside, London, 1670–7 (gutted 1941)

(B) Sir Christopher Wren. St Bride, Fleet Street,
London, 1670–84 (gutted 1941)

(A) Sir Christopher Wren. St Lawrence Jewry, London, 1670–86 (gutted 1941)

(B) Sir Christopher Wren. St Lawrence Jewry, London. Interior looking East

74

Sir Christopher Wren. St Stephen Walbrook, London, 1672–87

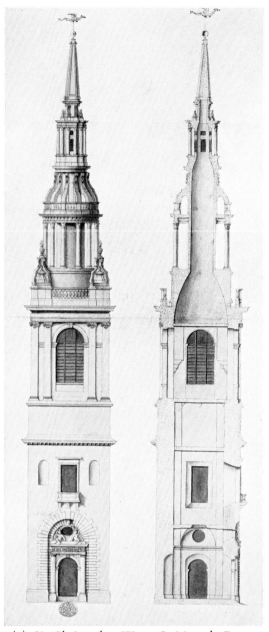

(A) Sir Christopher Wren. St Mary-le-Bow,
Cheapside, London,
1670–7

(B) Sir Christopher Wren. St Bride,
Fleet Street, London, 1670–84.
Spire, 1702

(A) Sir Christopher Wren.
St Magnus the Martyr.
Steeple, 1705

(B) Sir Christopher Wren. St Vedast,
Foster Lane, London.
Steeple, 1697

(B) Sir Christopher Wren. St Antholin, Watling Street, 1678–91 (demolished 1875)

(A) Sir Christopher Wren. St James's, Piccadilly, 1680–4 (burnt 1941; restored 1952)

(A) Sir Christopher Wren. St Paul's. The Great Model, 1673

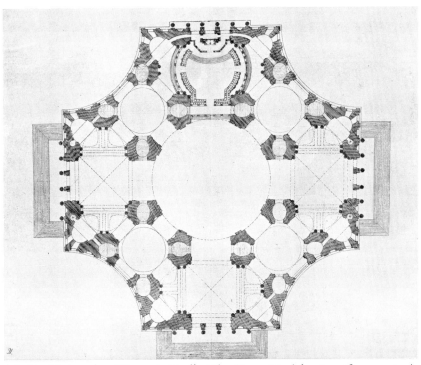

(B) Sir Christopher Wren. St Paul's. The Great Model, 1673 (first version)

(A) Sir Christopher Wren. St Paul's. The Warrant Design, 1675

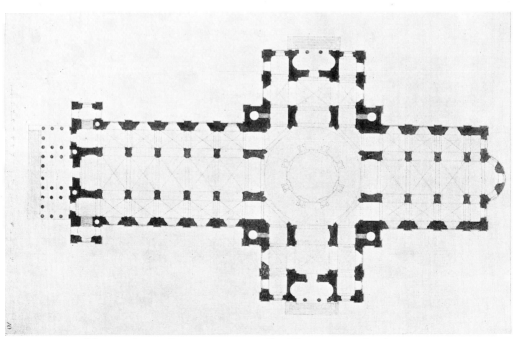

(B) Sir Christopher Wren. St Paul's. The Warrant Design, 1675

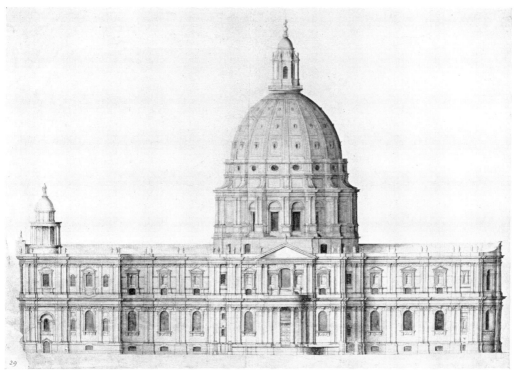

(A) Sir Christopher Wren. St Paul's. South elevation, as designed in 1675

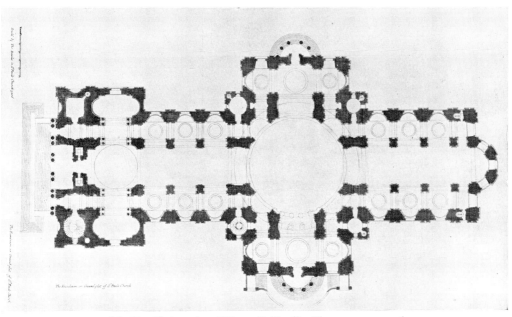

(B) Sir Christopher Wren. St Paul's. Plan, as executed

Sir Christopher Wren. St Paul's from the North-west

Sir Christopher Wren. St Paul's. Detail of West Front

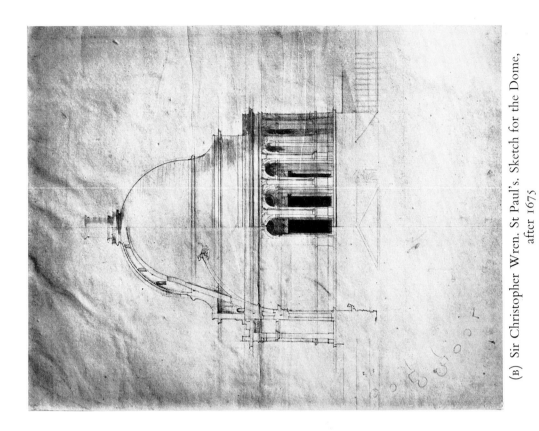

(B) Sir Christopher Wren. St Paul's. Sketch for the Dome, after 1675

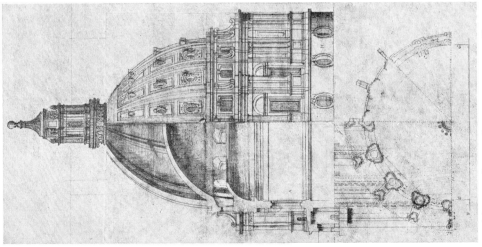

(A) Sir Christopher Wren. St Paul's. Dome design of 1675

84

Sir Christopher Wren. St Paul's. South Transept and South-west Tower

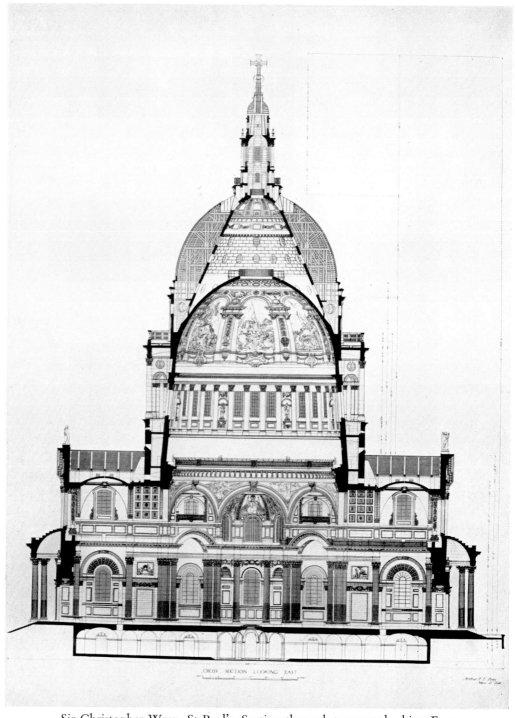

Sir Christopher Wren. St Paul's. Section through transepts looking East
(by courtesy of Arthur F. E. Poley)

(A) Sir Christopher Wren. St Paul's. Pendentives and diagonal arch of Dome

(B) Sir Christopher Wren. St Paul's. Choir Stalls

87

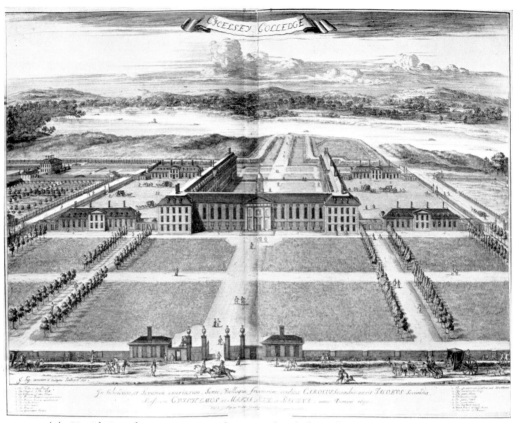

(A) Sir Christopher Wren. Royal Hospital, Chelsea, from the North, 1682–9

(B) Sir Christopher Wren. Royal Hospital, Chelsea. Courtyard, 1682–9

88

Sir Christopher Wren. Royal Hospital, Chelsea. The Portico

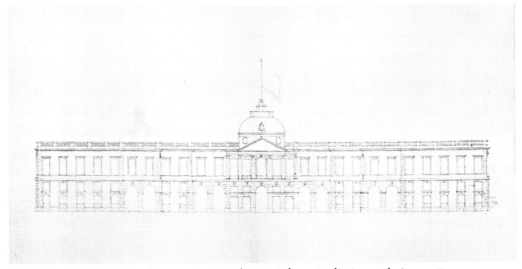

(A) Sir Christopher Wren. Winchester Palace. Preliminary design, 1682–3

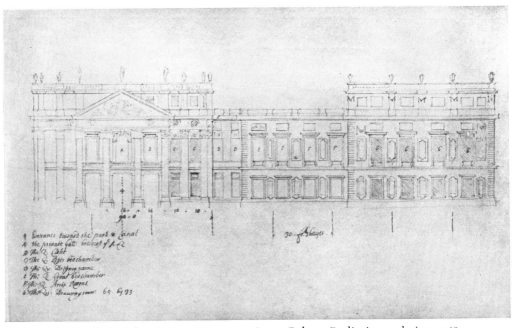

(B) Sir Christopher Wren. Hampton Court Palace. Preliminary design, 1689

Sir Christopher Wren. Hampton Court Palace, from the Park

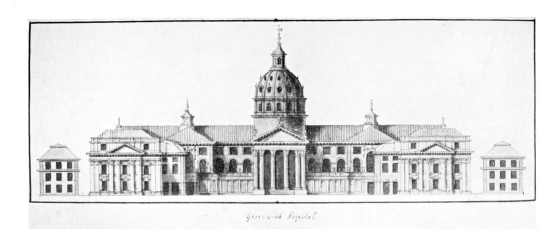

(A) Sir Christopher Wren. Greenwich Hospital. Elevation of 1694 Design

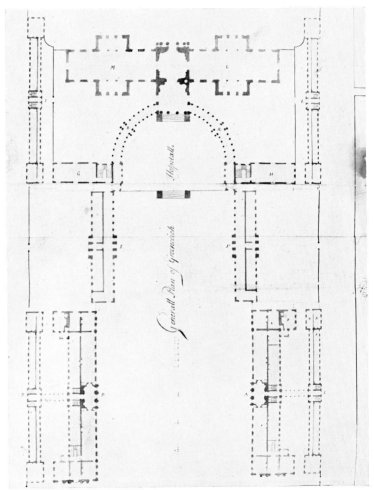

(B) Sir Christopher Wren Greenwich Hospital.
Plan of 1694 Design

Sir Christopher Wren. Greenwich Hospital. The Hall, 1698–1707

93

(A) Sir Christopher Wren. Trinity College Library, Cambridge, 1676–84

FACIES SPECULÆ SEPTEN:

(B) Sir Christopher Wren. Greenwich Observatory, 1675

Sir Christopher Wren. Tom Tower, Christ Church College, Oxford, 1681–2

Robert Hooke. Bethlem Hospital, London, 1674–6 (demolished 1814)

The Elevation of Thoresby hall in the County of Nottingham the Seat of the Rt Honble the Marquiss of Dorchester to whom this plate is most humbly Inscribed.

Elevation de la Maison de Thoresby dans la Comté de Nottingham.

I.a Campbell Delin.

William Talman. Thoresby, Notts., ? 1671 (burnt down 1745)

97

(A) William Winde. Buckingham House, London, 1703–5 (destroyed 1825)

(B) Henry Bell. Custom House, King's Lynn, Norfolk, 1683

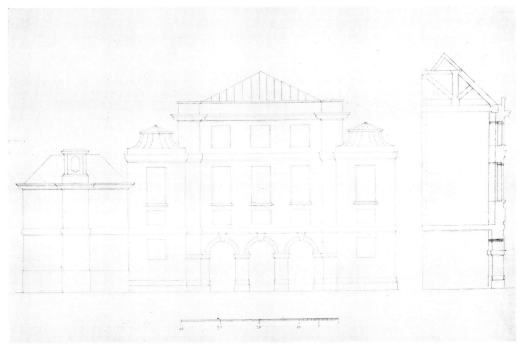

(A) Sir Christopher Wren and Nicholas Hawksmore. Sir John Moore's Writing School, Christ's Hospital, London, 1692–3 (destroyed 1902)

(B) Sir John Vanbrugh. Goose-pie House, Whitehall, 1699 (wings, 18th c.; all destroyed 1906)

(A) Project for a New Palace of Whitehall, c.1699

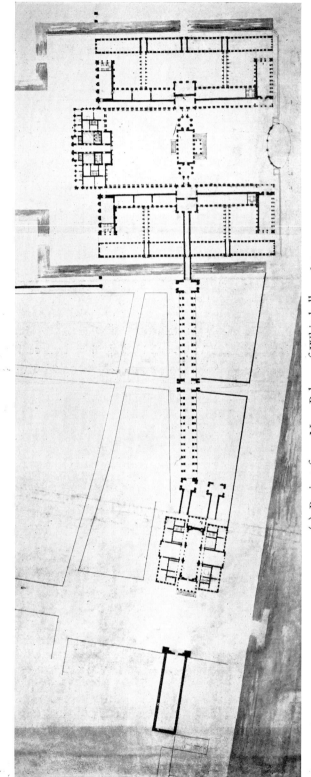

(B) Project for a New Palace of Whitehall, c.1699

(A) Sir John Vanbrugh. Castle Howard, Yorks., 1699–1712

(B) Sir John Vanbrugh. Blenheim Palace, Oxon., 1705–24

Sir John Vanbrugh. Castle Howard, Yorks., 1699–1712

Sir John Vanbrugh. Blenheim Palace, Oxon., 1705–24

Sir John Vanbrugh. Castle Howard. The Entrance Hall

(A) Sir John Vanbrugh. Grimsthorpe, Lincs., begun 1722

(B) Sir John Vanbrugh. Seaton Delaval, Northumberland, 1720–9

105

Nicholas Hawksmore. Castle Howard. The Mausoleum, begun 1729

Sir Christopher Wren. Greenwich Hospital. East Dome and Colonnade, after 1716

The Orangery at Kensington Palace, begun 1704

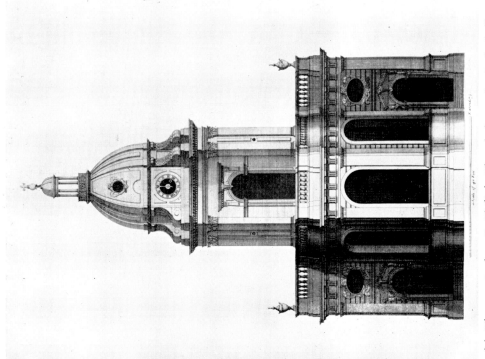

(B) Thomas Archer. St Philip's Church (now the Cathedral),
Birmingham, 1709–15

(A) Henry Aldrich. All Saints, Oxford, 1707–10

(B) Nicholas Hawksmore. St George-in-the-East, London, 1715–23 (gutted 1941)

(A) Nicholas Hawksmore. Christ Church, Spitalfields, London, 1723–9

(B) Nicholas Hawksmore. St George-in-the-East, London, 1715–23 (gutted 1941)

(A) Nicholas Hawksmore. Christ Church, Spitalfields, London, 1723–9

III

Nicholas Hawksmore. St Anne, Limehouse, 1712–24

(B) Nicholas Hawksmore. St George, Bloomsbury, 1720–30

(A) Nicholas Hawksmore. St Mary Woolnoth, London, 1716–27

113

(A) Thomas Archer. St Paul, Deptford, 1712–30

(B) James Gibbs. St Mary-le-Strand, 1714–17 (compare Plate 146A)

(A) Henry Aldrich. Peckwater Quadrangle, Christ Church College, Oxford, 1705–6

(B) Design for University Buildings at Cambridge, 1721

(A) Nicholas Hawksmore. The Queen's College, Oxford, South Quadrangle, 1709–34

(B) Nicholas Hawksmore. All Souls College, Oxford, completed 1734

116

(A) Colen Campbell. Wanstead House, Essex, 1715–20 (demolished 1822)

(B) Colen Campbell. Mereworth, Kent, 1723

117

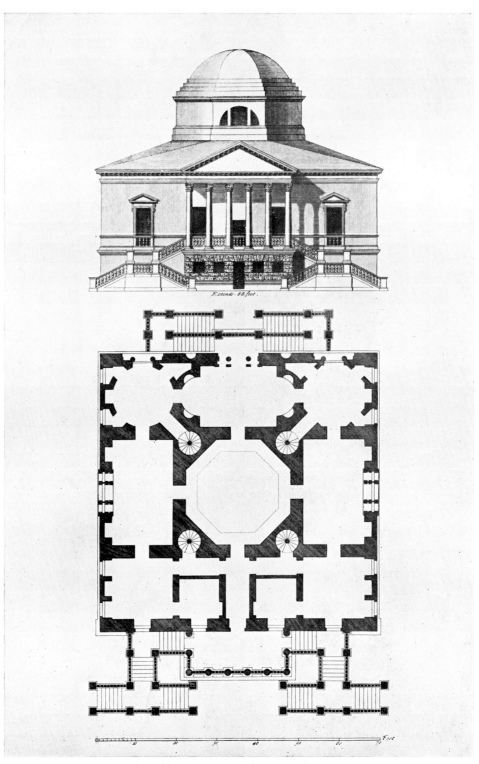

Lord Burlington. Chiswick House, begun 1725

(A) Lord Burlington. Assembly Room, York, 1730

(B) Lord Burlington. Assembly Room, York, 1730

William Kent. Holkham Hall, Norfolk, begun 1734

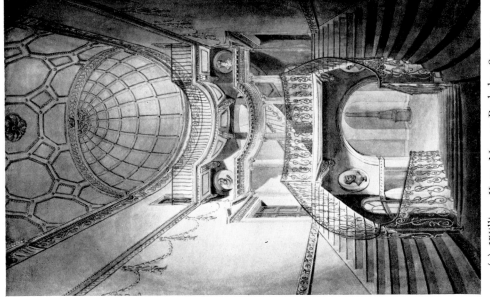

(B) William Kent. No. 44 Berkeley Square.
The Staircase, 1742–4

(A) William Kent. Holkham Hall.
The Staircase

(A) William Kent. The Horse Guards, London. Executed by J. Vardy, 1751–8

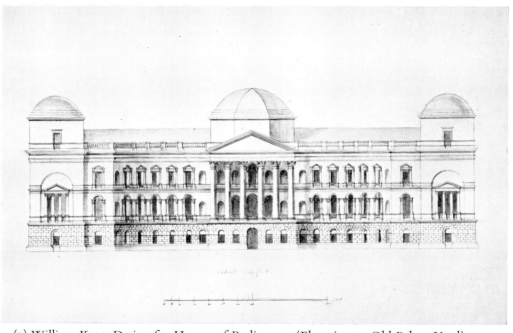

(B) William Kent. Design for Houses of Parliament (Elevation to Old Palace Yard), 1739

122

(A) James Gibbs. Sudbrook Lodge, Petersham, *c.* 1718

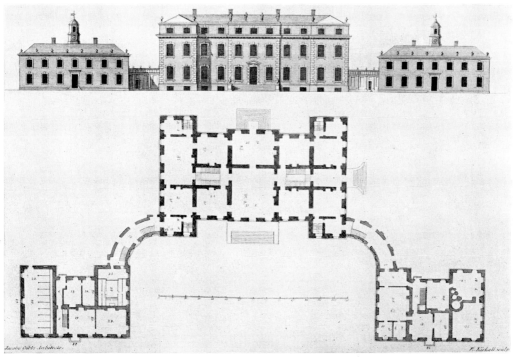

(B) James Gibbs. Ditchley, Oxon., 1720–2

123

(A) James Gibbs. Design for St Martin-in-the-Fields, London, *c*.1721

(B) James Gibbs. St Martin-in-the-Fields, London, 1721–6

James Gibbs. St Martin-in-the-Fields, London, 1721–6

(A) James Gibbs. Fellows' Building, King's College, Cambridge, 1724 (*Copyright Country Life*)

(B) Lord Pembroke and Roger Morris. Palladian Bridge, Wilton, Wilts., 1736

126

James Gibbs. The Radcliffe Camera, Oxford, 1739–49

Isaac Ware. Wrotham Park, Middlesex, 1754 (*Copyright Country Life*)

(A) John Vardy, after General Gray. Spencer House, London, 1756–65

(B) The Bank of England. The centre block by George Sampson, 1732–4,
the wings by Sir Robert Taylor, 1766–83

Sir Robert Taylor. Asgill House, Richmond, Surrey

James Paine. Wardour Castle, Wilts., 1770–6 (Copyright *Country Life*)

(A) William Adam. Hopetoun House, Linlithgowshire

(B) William Adam. Royal Infirmary, Edinburgh, 1738

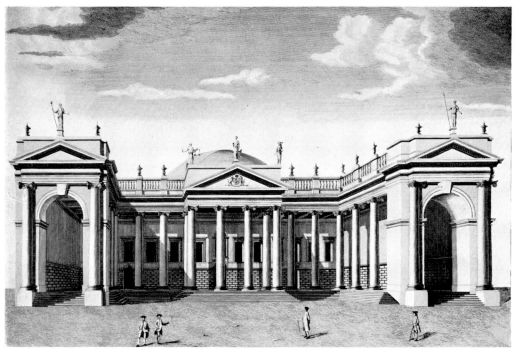

(A) The Parliament House (now Bank of Ireland), Dublin, 1728–39

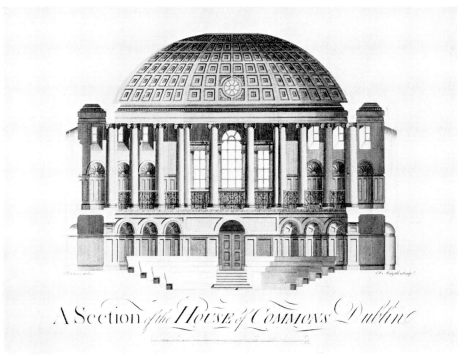

A Section of the House of Commons Dublin

(B) The House of Commons in the old Parliament House, Dublin, 1728–39

(B) Schomberg House, Pall Mall, c. 1698

(A) Carlisle House, Soho, London, c. 1670 (bombed 1941)

Giacomo Leoni. Queensberry House, Burlington Gardens, London, 1721
(balcony and other alterations, 1792)

Grosvenor Square, London, showing (*left*) houses by Edward Shepherd, *c.* 1727 (demolished)

John Wood I. Queen Square, Bath, North Side, 1729 onwards

John Wood I. The Circus, Bath, begun 1754

(A) John Wood II. Royal Crescent, Bath, 1767–75

(B) John Carr. The Crescent, Buxton, Derbyshire, 1779–81

(A) Sir John Vanbrugh. Vanbrugh Castle, Greenwich, 1717 (*Copyright Country Life*)

(B) Sanderson Miller. Lacock Abbey, Wilts., The Hall, 1753–5

Henry Keene. Hartwell Church, Bucks., 1753 (derelict in 1952)

(A) Strawberry Hill, Twickenham, from the South, 1748 onwards (*Copyright Country Life*)

(B) Strawberry Hill, Twickenham. The Library. Designed by John Chute, 1754
(*Copyright Country Life*)

(A) Sir William Chambers. Casino at Marino, Clontarf, built in 1769, but designed ten years earlier

(B) Sir William Chambers. Staircase, Carrington House, Whitehall, 1765 (demolished 1886)

Sir William Chambers. Somerset House, London. River Front, 1776–86, the wings completed 1835 and 1856

Robert Adam. The Adelphi, 1768–72

145

(A) The Strand, London, with Somerset House, by Sir William Chambers, on the right and
St Mary-le-Strand, by James Gibbs (compare Plate 114B), in the middle distance

(B) Sir William Chambers. Somerset House. Courtyard looking South

(A) Robert Adam. Sketch for a Palace, *c.* 1758

(B) Robert Adam. Edinburgh University, 1789–92

Robert Adam. Syon House, Middlesex. The Hall, 1762–3
(*Copyright Country Life*)

Robert Adam. Syon House, Middlesex. The Gallery, 1763–4
(*Copyright Country Life*)

Robert Adam. No. 20 Portman Square, London. The Music Room, 1772–3
(*Copyright Country Life*)

(A) Robert Adam. Kedleston Hall, Derbyshire. South Front, *c.* 1761 (*Copyright Country Life*)

(B) Robert Adam. Osterley Park, Middlesex, begun 1761 (*Copyright Country Life*)

(A) Robert Adam. Mistley Church, 1776 (only the towers survive)

(B) Robert Adam. No. 26 Grosvenor Square, London.
The Parlour, 1773–4 (demolished 1862)

(A) Robert Mylne. Stationers' Hall, London. East Façade, *c.* 1800

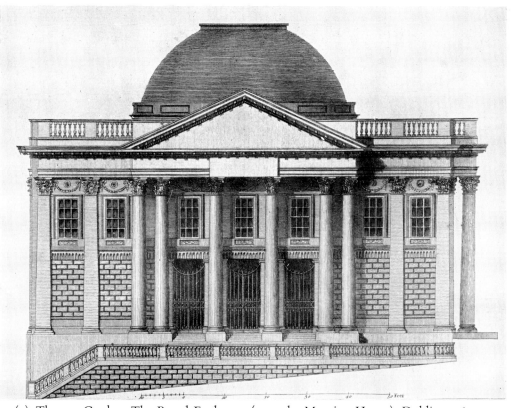

(B) Thomas Cooley. The Royal Exchange (now the Mansion House), Dublin, 1769–79

153

James Gandon. The Four Courts, Dublin, 1776–96 (*Judges*)

James Gandon. The Custom House, Dublin, 1781–91 (*Judges*)

George Dance II. All Hallows, London Wall, 1765–7

George Dance II. The Council Chamber, Guildhall, London, 1777 (demolished 1906)

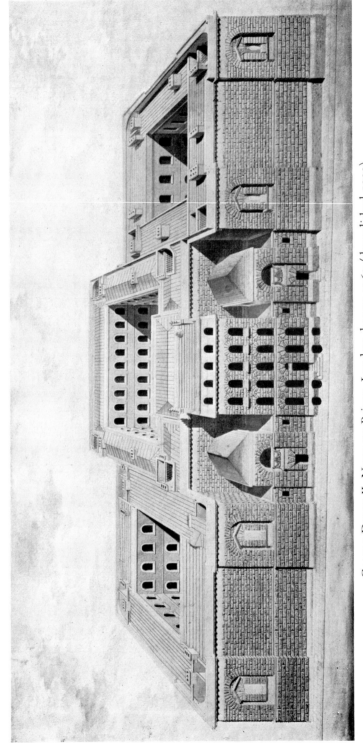

George Dance II. Newgate Prison, London, begun 1769 (demolished 1902)

(A) George Dance II. Stratton Park, Hants, 1803–4

(B) James Wyatt. The Pantheon, Oxford Street, London, 1770–2
(burnt down 1792; finally demolished 1937)

(A) Henry Holland. Carlton House, London, 1783–95 (demolished 1826)

(B) Henry Holland. Dover House, Whitehall, 1787

(A) James Wyatt. Oriel College, Oxford. The Library, 1788

(B) James Wyatt. Dodington House, Glos., 1798–1808

(A) James Wyatt. Fonthill Abbey, Wilts. South West View, 1795–1807

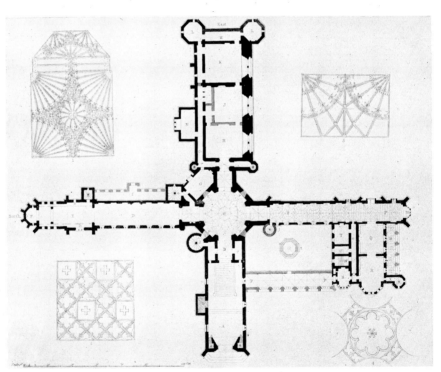

(B) Fonthill Abbey; the plan

Fonthill Abbey. The Octagon

163

Thomas Leverton. No. 1 Bedford Square. Entrance Hall, 1780 (*Copyright Country Life*)

(A) Joseph Bonomi. Roseneath, Dumbartonshire, 1803–6

(B) Thomas Harrison. Chester Castle, 1793–1820

(A) Sir John Soane. Bank of England. Bank Stock Office, 1792–3 (demolished 1927)

(B) Sir John Soane. No. 12 Lincoln's Inn Fields. The Library, 1792

166

(A) Richard Payne Knight. Downton Castle, Salop, 1774–8 (*Copyright Country Life*)

(B) John Nash. Luscombe, Devonshire, 1800

(A) S. P. Cockerell. Sezincote, Glos., 1803 (*Copyright Country Life*)

(B) John Nash. Royal Pavilion, Brighton. Banqueting Room, 1815–18

John Nash. Cronkhill, Salop, 1802

(A) John Nash. Park Crescent, Regent's Park, London, begun 1812

(B) The County Fire Office and the Quadrant, London. By John Nash, 1819–20,
with Robert Abraham as architect of the Fire Office (all demolished)

(A) John Nash. Cumberland Terrace, Regent's Park, London, 1827

(B) John Nash. Regent Street, London, looking South (demolished)

John Nash. Carlton House Terrace, London, begun 1827

Sir John Soane. Dulwich College Art Gallery. The Mausoleum, 1811–14

Sir John Soane. No. 13 Lincoln's Inn Fields (the Soane Museum):
the Breakfast Parlour, 1812

Sir John Soane. The Bank of England: Old Dividend Office, 1818–23
(demolished 1927)

(A) William Wilkins. Downing College, Cambridge, 1806–11. The Master's House
(*Copyright Country Life*)

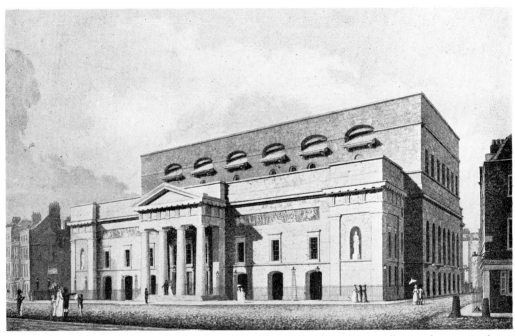

(B) Sir Robert Smirke. Covent Garden Theatre, London, 1808–9 (burnt down 1856)

(A) Sir Robert Smirke. General Post Office, London, 1824–9 (demolished 1913)

(B) William Wilkins. The London University (now University College), 1827–8

(A) Sir Charles Barry. The Royal Institution (now the Art Gallery), Manchester, 1824–35

(B) Sir Charles Barry. The Travellers' Club, London (garden front), 1829

(A) Decimus Burton. Arch and Screen at Hyde Park Corner, 1825

(B) Decimus Burton. The Athenaeum, London, 1829–30 (before addition of the attic);
Travellers' Club adjoining on right

(A) Francis Goodwin. The old Town Hall, Manchester, 1822–4 (demolished 1912)

(B) John Foster. The Custom House, Liverpool, begun 1828 (destroyed by bombing 1941)

Thomas Hamilton. The High School, Edinburgh, begun 1825

(A) Sir Robert Smirke. Eastnor Castle, Herefordshire, *c.* 1808–15

(B) William Wilkins. Screen of King's College, Cambridge, 1822–4 (*Copyright Country Life*)

W. and H. W. Inwood. St Pancras Church, London, 1818–22

John Pinch. St Mary's, Bathwick, Bath, 1814–20

184

(B) John Rickman. St George, Edgbaston, Birmingham, 1819–22

(A) Francis Goodwin. Holy Trinity, Bordesley, Birmingham, 1823

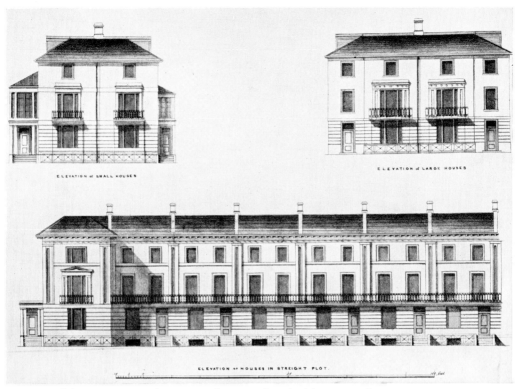

(A) J. B. Papworth. Design for semi-detached houses and a terrace, 1829

(B) Edward Davis. Houses, Entry Hill, Bath, 1828

Falkland Palace, Fife. North Façade of Courtyard, 1539–42 (*Copyright Country Life*)

(A) Castle Fraser, Aberdeenshire, dated 1576

(B) Fyvie Castle, Aberdeenshire, about 1600–3 (*Copyright Country Life*)

188

(A) Heriot's Hospital, Edinburgh, begun 1628

(B) Drumlanrig Castle, Dumfriesshire, 1675–89 (*Copyright Country Life*)

(A) Williamsburg, Virginia, U.S.A. The Governor's House, 1705 (as rebuilt, 1932)

(B) Westover, Virginia, U.S.A., *c.* 1730

(A) Peter Harrison. King's Chapel, Boston, U.S.A., 1749–58

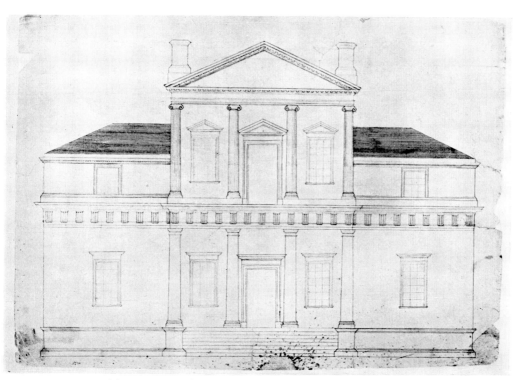

(B) Thomas Jefferson. Monticello. First Design, *c.* 1770
(*Clara Amory Coolidge College, Massachusetts Historical Society*)

191

(A) Thomas Jefferson. Virginia State Capitol, Richmond, Virginia, U.S.A., 1785–96

(B) Benjamin Latrobe. The Bank of Philadelphia, Philadelphia, U.S.A., 1798–9 (demolished)

INDEX

Where several page references are given under a single entry, that in **heavy type** is the principal. Entries in *italics* refer to plates. References to notes give the number of the note concerned after the number of the page on which it appears, thus: 62[7]. Buildings in towns are generally indexed under the name of the town in which they are situate; but buildings and streets in London, Paris, and Rome are indexed directly under their names; thus, Kilmainham Hospital will be found under the main heading 'Dublin', but St George's Hospital (London) in its alphabetical place under S.